Wissenschaftliche Untersuchungen
zum Neuen Testament · 2. Reihe

Herausgegeben von
Martin Hengel und Otfried Hofius

98

Jon Laansma

'I Will Give You Rest'

The Rest Motif in the New Testament with Special Reference to Mt 11 and Heb 3-4

WIPF & STOCK · Eugene, Oregon

Wipf and Stock Publishers
199 W 8th Ave, Suite 3
Eugene, OR 97401

I Will Give You Rest
By Laansma, Jon C.
Copyright©1997 Mohr Siebeck
ISBN 13: 978-1-4982-7921-5
Publication date 11/13/2015
Previously published by Mohr Siebeck, 1997

For Lisa

Foreword

This study was originally written under the supervision of I. Howard Marshall and Paul Ellingworth, and submitted to the University of Aberdeen in January of 1995. Several stylistic changes have since been made in hopes of achieving greater clarity. No attempt was made to update the discussion though there was time to interact slightly more with Ben Witherington's *Jesus the Sage*, which had come into my hands only a few weeks before the submission of the dissertation. I contemplated changing the title of the study to *The* Rest *of the Story*, but finally admitted that too many readers would be unacquainted with a certain American radio commentator.

I would like to express my appreciation to the editors of this series for their interest in my work and for their patience as I prepared the manuscript for the press. Thanks are due to Bantam Doubleday Dell publishers for permission to quote a lengthy passage from B. Layton, *The Gnostic Scriptures* (1987). Dan Treier and Mark Bowald generously donated their time in preparing the indices. Technical support was provided by Greg Gaertner, Steven Albrecht and Philip Barker.

My warmest greetings go out to those with whom we shared life in Scotland during the memorable years of life there, especially Jan and Soo Min van Regteren, Andrew and Libby Lau, and Roger and Eunice Connon.

My loving thanks go to my wife, Lisa Jayne, for her continuing support and patience while I worked yet more on this seemingly interminable project. Hopefully we will be seeing this one move out of the house once and for all. And well it should, as I doubt Kiersten Elise, though a newcomer herself, would have tolerated its presence for long.

Soli Deo gloria

Jon Laansma
Chicago, Illinois
August, 1997

Contents

Foreword VII

Chapter One
Matthew 11,28-30 and Hebrews 3-4 in Modern Discussion

1. Introduction 1
2. History of interpretation 2
   2.1. Mt 11,28-30 2
   2.2. Heb 3-4 10
3. Prospectus 14

Chapter Two
The Rest Motif in the Hebrew OT

1. Introduction 17
2. Part one 18
   2.1. Introduction 18
   2.2. The Deuteronomistic rest 20
       2.2.1. Preliminary considerations 20
       2.2.2. Deut 12,9f. and related passages 23
           2.2.2.1. Deut 12,9f. 23
           2.2.2.2. 2Sam 7 25
           2.2.2.3. 1Kgs 5 27
           2.2.2.4. 1Kgs 8 27
           2.2.2.5. Josh 21, Josh 23, Deut 25 29
           2.2.2.6. Deut 28 31
           2.2.2.7. Ex 33 32
       2.2.3. Summary 33
   2.3. Chronicles -- Israel's מנוחה 34
       2.3.1. Overview 34
       2.3.2. David and Solomon 35
       2.3.3. Kings after Solomon 36
       2.3.4. Summary 38

Contents

- 2.4. Chronicles and Ps 132 -- YHWH's מנוחה 38
  - 2.4.1. Overview 38
  - 2.4.2. Ps 132 39
  - 2.4.3. 2Chr 6 40
  - 2.4.4. Summary 40
- 2.5. Ps 95 -- "My מנוחה" 41
- 2.6. Isaiah 46
  - 2.6.1. Overview 46
  - 2.6.2. Isa 11 47
  - 2.6.3. Isa 14 49
  - 2.6.4. Isa 28 49
  - 2.6.5. Isa 63 50
  - 2.6.6. Isa 66 51
  - 2.6.7. Isa 32 52
  - 2.6.8. Summary 52
- 2.7. Jeremiah 53
  - 2.7.1. Overview 53
  - 2.7.2. Jer 31 54
  - 2.7.3. Jer 50 54
  - 2.7.4. Jer 6 55
  - 2.7.5. Summary 56
- 2.8. Lamentations 56
  - 2.8.1. Lam 1 56
  - 2.8.2. Lam 5 57
  - 2.8.3. Summary 57
- 2.9. Micah 57
- 2.10. Summary and conclusions of part one 58
  - 2.10.1. Presence and prominence of the rest tradition 58
  - 2.10.2. An eschatological rest 58
  - 2.10.3. The land 59
  - 2.10.4. The temple 59
  - 2.10.5. The Davidic dynasty 59
  - 2.10.6. Weariness, distress, etc. 60
  - 2.10.7. Additional related motifs 60
3. Part two 61
  - 3.1. Introduction 61
  - 3.2. The rest motif and the Sabbath 61
    - 3.2.1. Introduction 61
    - 3.2.2. The significance of the Sabbath rest 62
    - 3.2.3. Conclusions 65
  - 3.3. An eschatological Sabbath? 65
  - 3.4. מנוחה and the Sabbath 67
    - 3.4.1. The land 67
    - 3.4.2. The temple 68
    - 3.4.3. The kingship 69

3.4.4. The divine *otiositas* 70
3.4.5. Summary and conclusions 73
3.5. Summary and conclusions of part two 75
4. Summary and conclusions 75

Chapter Three
The Rest Motif in the LXX

1. Introduction 77
2. The rest tradition 78
   2.1. Introduction 78
   2.2. The MT rest tradition in the LXX 79
      2.2.1. Comparison 79
      2.2.2. Evaluation 80
   2.3. Passages unique to the LXX 81
      2.3.1. Deut 5,33 82
      2.3.2. Isa 25,10 82
      2.3.3. Isa 32,17 82
      2.3.4. Ezek 34,14.15 83
      2.3.5. Jdt 9,8 83
      2.3.6. Sir 24,7-11 84
      2.3.7. Sir 36,18 (15) 85
      2.3.8. Sir 47,13 85
      2.3.9. Additional LXX passages 86
         2.3.9.1. Isa 14,1.30 86
         2.3.9.2. Isa 57,20 87
         2.3.9.3. Micah 4,4 87
      2.3.10. Summary 88
   2.4. Summary and conclusions 88
3. The Sabbath 89
   3.1. Comparison 89
   3.2. Evaluation 90
4. Further developments in the wisdom literature 91
   4.1. Introduction 91
   4.2. Rest as the result of wise behavior 91
   4.3. The nature of wisdom's rest 92
   4.4. Wisdom's offer of rest 93
   4.5. Summary 94
5. A technical meaning of κατάπαυσις? 94
   5.1. Introduction 94
   5.2. Summary of the MT terminology 95
   5.3. Ἀνάπαυσις and κατάπαυσις 96
   5.4. Summary and conclusions 99
6. Summary and conclusions 100

Chapter Four
The Rest Motif in Other Jewish and Christian Literature

1. Introduction 102
2. OT Pseudepigrapha 103
   2.1. Introduction 103
   2.2. Post-mortem and eschatological rest 104
   2.3. The idea of a future resting "place" 106
      2.3.1. The hope of rest in the future world 107
      2.3.2. Entrance into eternal rest upon death 109
      2.3.3. Entrance into an intermediate rest upon death 110
   2.4. Summary 111
3. Qumran 111
4. Philo of Alexandria 113
   4.1. Introduction and overview 113
   4.2. The debate between G. Theißen and O. Hofius 115
      4.2.1. G. Theißen 115
      4.2.2. O. Hofius 117
   4.3. Summary and conclusions 121
5. Rabbinic literature 122
   5.1. The hope of "rest" 122
      5.1.1. The "world which is wholly Sabbath and rest" 122
      5.1.2. Other aspects of "rest" as an object of hope 123
   5.2. Ps 95 in rabbinic exegesis 124
      5.2.1. The historical understanding of Ps 95,11 124
      5.2.2. The eschatological understanding of Ps 95,11 127
   5.3. Summary 128
6. Post-apostolic 129
   6.1. Introduction 129
   6.2. Odes of Solomon 129
   6.3. Ignatius 133
   6.4. Barnabas 134
   6.5. 2 Clement and the Gospel of the Hebrews 138
   6.6. Epistula Apostolorum 141
   6.7. Clement of Alexandria 142
   6.8. Summary 144
7. Gnostic 145
   7.1. Introduction 145
   7.2. Rest and gnostic mythology 146
   7.3. The metaphysical background of the gnostic rest 149
   7.4. Excursus: Gnosticism and the New Testament 150
   7.5. Summary 151
8. Summary and conclusions 152

Appendix: Rest in Gnostic Mythology 154

Chapter Five
Mt 11,28-30 and Matthew's Wisdom Christology

1. Introduction 159
2. The Wisdom myth 163
3. Matthew's Wisdom Christology? 167
   3.1. Mt 11,19 (Q 7,35) 167
   3.2. Mt 11,25-27 (Q 10,21-22) 171
       3.2.1. Mt 11,25f. 172
       3.2.2. Mt 11,27 174
   3.3. Mt 23,34-36 (Q 11,49-51) 180
   3.4. Mt 23,37-39 (Q 13,34-35) 183
   3.5. Summary 185
4. Mt 11,28-30 and Wisdom 186
   4.1. Introduction 186
   4.2. Matthean redaction of the Logion in 11,28-30 187
   4.3. Comparison of Mt 11,28-30 and Sir 51 195
       4.3.1. Mt 11,28-30 is not an allusion to Sir 51 196
       4.3.2. Two questions 200
       4.3.3. The "paradox" of yoke and rest 203
       4.3.4. Once again, Matthean redaction 205
   4.4. Conclusions 206
5. Conclusions 207

Chapter Six
The Meek King and God's Promise of Rest

1. Introduction 209
2. Explaining Matthew's redaction: the Servant 209
3. Explaining Matthew's redaction: the Son of David 211
   3.1. Introduction 211
   3.2. Matthew's Son of David Christology 213
   3.3. Two verbal pointers to Mt 21 218
   3.4. Conceptual parallels 222
   3.5. The OT rest tradition 223
4. Other indications that the OT rest tradition underlies 224
   4.1. The rest tradition in Matthew's sources 224
   4.2. Verbal similarities to Ex 33,14 and Jer 6,16 in 11,28f. 227
   4.3. The idea of an eschatological Sabbath in Matthew 229
   4.4. Something greater than the temple 231
   4.5. Summary 232
5. The wisdom of the Son of David 233
6. Jesus the sage 235

7. The promise of rest 238
    7.1. The weary and heavy laden 239
    7.2. The easy yoke 244
    7.3. Rest 246
8. Conclusions 250

Chapter Seven
A Promise Remains

1. Introduction 252
    1.1. Overview 252
    1.2. Key terms 253
2. Exegetical questions 259
    2.1. General questions 259
        2.1.1. Background? 259
        2.1.2. Context? 264
        2.1.3. Typology? 274
        2.1.4. Definition of terms 276
            2.1.4.1. What is a σαββατισμός? 276
            2.1.4.2. Κατάπαυσις: place and/or state? 277
        2.1.5. Exposition of 4,1-11 283
            2.1.5.1. Introduction 283
            2.1.5.2. Exposition of 4,1-11 285
            2.1.5.3. Working assumptions 301
                2.1.5.3.1. As the Holy Spirit says 301
                2.1.5.3.2. A promise remains 301
                2.1.5.3.3. Not without us 302
                2.1.5.3.4. Heir of all things 303
            2.1.5.4. Summary 304
        2.1.6. Present and/or future? 305
        2.1.7. "Wandering" and/or waiting? 310
    2.2. The temple and the Sabbath 314
        2.2.1. The heavenly temple? 314
        2.2.2. A Christian Sabbath? 316
    2.3. Questions arising from a dualistic interpretation 317
        2.3.1. Rest in God? 317
        2.3.2. Speculation on the number 7? 320
        2.3.3. Is God's rest a state of inactivity? 321
        2.3.4. Does rest = stability? 325
        2.3.5. A purely heavenly rest? 327
            2.3.5.1. General response 327
            2.3.5.2. Two specific sub-points 332
                2.3.5.2.1. Anthropological dualism 332
                2.3.5.2.2. Joseph and Aseneth 333

    2.4. Summary 334
3. Proposals on the background of the κατάπαυσις 335
    3.1. Isa 66,1 in Acts 7 335
    3.2. Philonic and gnostic (dualistic) 338
        3.2.1. Review of the case 338
        3.2.2. Evaluation 340
        3.2.3. Conclusion 341
    3.3. Jewish Apocalyptic 342
        3.3.1. Review of the case 342
        3.3.2. Evaluation 343
        3.3.3. Conclusion 346
    3.4. Independent Hellenistic Jewish Christian 347
        3.4.1. General indications of independence..........................347
        3.4.2. The use of Gen 2,2 349
        3.4.3. *Auctor*: A unique expression of the rest motif............354
    3.5. Conclusions on background 356
4. Conclusions 357

Chapter Eight

Conclusion 359

Abbreviations 367
Bibliography 368
Ancient Writings Index 417
Names and Subject Index 454

Chapter One

Matthew 11,28-30 and Hebrews 3-4 in Modern Discussion

1. Introduction

According to their Scriptures, in the course of history God promised salvation to his chosen people. This meant liberty from the yoke of Egyptian slavery and the end to the nomadic existence begun when God's summons reached Abraham in Ur. Ultimately it meant a *place*, and a *sine qua non* would be *secure dwelling* in this place. Not only was this security itself a fulfilment of God's covenantal promises to his people and thus a sign of his continuing faithfulness and care, but it also vouchsafed the conditions under which *their* covenantal obligations would be realized by and among them. At the heart of this gift of *rest* was the presence of YHWH among them and chief among the obligations entailed in this gift was the requirement to recognize the place which YHWH would choose, the resting place of the ark of the covenant where YHWH's name would dwell in their midst. Under the pressure of historical circumstances, the OT had already begun to transfer these ideas and hopes to the ultimate future.

Parallel to this soteriological theme, though nowhere directly connected to it, was another which also used the idea of rest to set in relief YHWH's redemptive activity on behalf of his people: the Sabbath. This regular festival was a reminder of the nation's exodus from forced labor and of the covenant established thereby; this rest was to be faithfully extended by the community to *all* of its members, especially to those bearing the yoke of forced labor among the settled tribes. It was a rest which stayed the impulse to claim the land as one's own, which reminded of God's gracious provision in salvation, protection, and sustenance, which symbolized and even realized in a special way the covenant, and which paved the way for a season specially devoted to the worship of YHWH. God himself celebrated the Sabbath at creation, and Israel's celebration was seen to take its lead from that Sabbath as well.

Perhaps not surprisingly the *Auctor ad Hebraeos*, henceforth *Auctor*,[1] drew upon key passages from both of these OT themes to epitomize the hope which his Christian readers were in danger of forfeiting. Unless that New Covenant community rallied itself, unless it came to grips with its situation "at the end of the ages" and the peril of refusing to listen to the Son, the goal of the whole history of salvation would be closed to it. And this generation would not be the first to meet with such a fate.

This same theme, the biblical theme of *rest*, will occupy our attention too; more exactly, we will consider the rest motif in Mt 11,28-30 and Heb 3-4. These are both important passages in their own right, and they are generally recognized to be the chief NT usages of the rest motif. It will be our contention that Matthew, no less than *Auctor*, was drawing on both of the above mentioned OT themes in an expression of the fulfilment of God's salvation promises. As we shall see, however, this has not usually been recognized, since the predominant interpretation of this Logion[2] has associated it with a different stream of Jewish thought and with a particular strand of Matthew's Christology.

Yet the importance of these two passages and the issues which require attention in them will be better appreciated if we first consider how they have fared in modern interpretation.

2. History of interpretation

2.1. Mt 11,28-30

Mt 11,28-30 is a poignant promise of rest to the weary, but it has been the view of scholarship over the last century or so that this Logion is only ostensibly concerned with soteriology. Its real concern is with Christology.[3] But how did this understanding come about, and has it put Mt 11,28-30 in its proper light?

The earlier period of modern scholarship in relation to Mt 11,28-30 has been adequately and clearly reviewed in a well known article by H.D. Betz,[4]

---

[1] For stylistic relief the masculine pronoun will also be used; this seems justified in view of the masculine participle in Heb 11,32. Beyond that no theory of authorship of Hebrews will be argued or assumed.

[2] Used in this way (uppercase L), "Logion" will always refer to Mt 11,28-30 or its earlier versions.

[3] Cf. Stanton 1992a, 364-366, for a review of earlier liturgical uses of Mt 11,28-30; in that context the stress was on soteriology.

[4] Betz, 11-20; a more concise survey, dependent on Betz, is given in Stanton 1992a, 366-368. Cf. also Luz, 2:222-224.

but for convenience's sake a summary of his article will be given here with a few of the more recent treatments added.

Writing in 1863 D.F. Strauss appears to have been the first to point up the similarity of Mt 11,25-30 to Sir 51,1-27,[5] though he stressed the differences in tone and content between the two passages. He only cited them side by side and wondered whether an identification of Jesus with Wisdom[6] might not be a step on the path toward a Logos Christology.[7] In 1913 E. Norden advanced beyond Strauss in the comparison of these two passages. Differences between the passages told against direct dependence and suggested that they represent variations on a particular type of schema drawn from Oriental theosophical mysticism: (1) A prayer of thanksgiving (Mt 11,25f.; Sir 51,1-12). (2) The revelation of Wisdom (Mt 11,27; Sir 51,13-22). (3) An invitation to the ignorant (Mt 11,28-30; Sir 51,23-30). Thus Mt 11,28-30 belonged with vv. 25-27, and together they made up a hymn; moreover, the whole passage was drawn from Q[8] and was not authentic teaching of Jesus.[9] Norden's three-part schema fell victim to criticism, and differing religious historical explanations were adduced for vv. 25-30, but the belief that vv. 25-30 formed a unit in Q was generally maintained by subsequent scholars.[10]

In particular, Arvedson, who saw himself continuing on along the lines of Norden, undertook an extended and detailed study of 11,25-30. Taking in a broad sweep of religious historical parallels he concluded that this passage was part of a mystery ceremony in the early church; it was a

...liturgy, originally intended for a celebration of the mysteries, the center of which was the enthronement of Christ. Verses 25-27 form the hymn which Jesus begins to sing as he enters into the Father's presence -- not only as a mystagogue in the name of the

---

[5] Infra, 196, for the texts.

[6] The figure of personified Wisdom will be formally introduced below, 163ff. When the upper case is used, "Wisdom," the reference is always to personified Wisdom and to literature or traditions associated with her. When used in reference to Christology (Wisdom Christology), it always refers to a full identification of Jesus and Wisdom, as opposed to speculation which related the two figures more loosely (wisdom Christology).

[7] D.F. Strauss, 92f. The point that Strauss was the first to note the parallel in Sir 51 is based on Betz' research (Betz, 11); I know of no earlier study observing this parallel.

[8] The document, Q, will be accepted as a working hypothesis in the present study.

[9] Norden, 277-308. Parallels to this schema were found in Sir 24; OdesSol 33; and in the *CorpHerm*.

[10] Cf. the summary in Betz, 13-16; Stanton 1992a, 367. Note especially: Bousset, 83ff.; J. Weiss 1914, 120-129; 1907, 320-325; E. Meyer, 280ff.; Rist, 63-67; Dibelius, 245, 279ff. Dibelius, 282, states that in 11,25-30 "is proclaimed the typical saving Gospel of Gnosis. The form of the Redeemer in this gospel, however, is of divine nature and cosmic form -- a mythological being."

mystics but also in his own name. The hymn is at the same time a self-introduction, which introduces the invitation to the mystery.[11]

In terms of the invitation (vv. 28-30), which he considered to be in form a religious propaganda discourse, Arvedson maximized the parallels with Sirach and tended to read gnostic mythology[12] into the saying with the result that 11,28-30 was read along very mystical and even gnostic lines.[13]

The judgment of Bultmann, however, became a turning point on the question of whether 11,25-30 formed a pre-Matthean unity. He argued that only vv. 25-27 derived from Q;[14] vv. 28-30 he saw as a separate wisdom saying placed in the mouth of Jesus.[15] The view that vv. 28-30 do not derive from Q has subsequently been widely accepted on the following grounds:[16] (1) Luke's omission of Mt 11,28-30 is very difficult to explain.[17] (2) *GosThom* 90 is evidence that the Logion of Mt 11,28-30 circulated independently of 11,25-27. (3) The discovery of 11Q Ps[a] has shown that Sir 51 was not originally a unit, thus breaking the three-part parallel which Norden had stressed with Mt 11,25-30.[18] With the collapse of the pre-Matthean unity of the Logion much of the highly speculative substance of the earlier interpretations such as those of Norden and Arvedson also fell to the ground.[19]

In brief, from Strauss to Bultmann, two primary convictions endured and they continue to shape interpretations of this Logion. First, it is widely believed that there is a deliberately fashioned and meaningful relationship

---

[11] Arvedson, 108 (this is Arvedson's own summary, and is italicized in the original); this translation of the German is from Betz, 16.

[12] On the gnostic use of the rest motif as well as the larger issue of Gnosticism, see below, 145ff., 154ff. More generally, certain terms, esp. apocalyptic, dualistic, gnostic, and Hellenistic, are often used in scholarship, but are in need of definition. Yet since these terms are more important for our treatment of Heb 3-4 than for Mt 11, they will be discussed at the beginning of Ch. Seven.

[13] Arvedson, 93ff., 158-231 (esp. 228-231).

[14] Certainly earlier scholars had entertained this; cf. Zahn, 442.

[15] Bultmann 1972, 159f., 412f.

[16] Cf. Betz, 17-21; Suggs, 79-81; Kloppenborg 1978, 134; Stanton 1992a, 367f.; Deutsch 1987, 48f. It is often observed that vv. 28-30 differ in form from vv. 25-27.

[17] In Luke's parallel (Lk 10,21-24) his macarism (cf. Mt 13,16f.) seems to fit with the saying; furthermore, we might think that Luke would have reworked rather than omitted vv. 28-30.

[18] 11QPs[a] 21,11-17; 22,1 contains an independent version of Sir 51,13-19.30, which shows that this portion was originally a separate composition subsequently inserted into Sirach; cf. J.A. Sanders 1965, 79-85; Deutsch 1982.

[19] Betz, 17; Suggs, 77-83 (with further criticism of Arvedson on pp. 100f.); Stanton 1992a, 367f. For a more recent case that the thought structure of Sir 51 was constitutive for the whole of Mt 11,25-30, cf. Luck.

between Mt 11,28-30 and Sir 51,23ff.,[20] and second, Mt 11,28-30 is believed *not* to have been derived from Q,[21] and thus is thought to have been located if not composed by Matthew.

Yet another of Strauss' suggestions has also proved resilient, that of positing a relationship between Mt 11,28-30 and Sir 51 on the one hand, and the later Logos Christology on the other. The metaphor of a "trajectory" seems to be the most fitting to express this, though it is not usually invoked. This way of viewing Mt 11,28-30 in terms of the history of Christology manifests itself in different ways, depending on the particular interests of the study in question.

In his study of the Logion, Betz had no particular interest in the later Logos Christology, yet his suggestion as to the history of the Logion is clearly fashioned according to the paradigm of a trajectory.[22] Betz was impressed by certain arguments suggesting that the gnostic citations of Mt 11,28-30 (esp. *GosThom* 90 and *Pistis Sophia* 95) were not dependent on Matthew's Gospel.[23] On this basis he drew the conclusion that with *GosThom* 90, *Pistis Sophia* 95, and Mt 11,28-30 we are probably dealing with a series of pre-Matthean wisdom sayings which were originally independent of each other. Reading back from the gnostic setting he suggested that at some point prior to Matthew these independent sayings were all subjected to a "gnosticizing" transformation and then were finally

---

[20] Fridrichsen has noted a parallel in *Arrian's Discourses of Epictetus* IV,8,28: συνενλθετε πάντες οἱ ποδαγρῶντες, οἱ κεφαλαλγοῦντες, οἱ πυρέσσοντες, οἱ χωλοί, οἱ τυφλοί, καὶ ἴδετέ με ἀπὸ παντὸς πάθους ὑγιᾶ ("Come together, all you who are suffering from gout, headaches, and fever, the halt, and the blind, and see how sound I am, and free from every disorder"). Yet that there is a meaningful *Formgeschichte* connection between this passage and Mt 11,28-30 remains to be demonstrated; Gnilka, 1:440 n. 51; cf. Witherington, 135. Other parallels from *CorpHerm*, OdesSol 9, and Philo are increasingly distant and irrelevant; rightly Bultmann 1972,159; Gundry, 220; *contra* Dibelius, 279-285. Betz, 16 n. 44, notes the Pseudo-Justinian *Oratio ad Graecos* 5. Cf. also W.D. Davies 1962, 119-144.

[21] Cf. Betz, 18; Stanton 1992a, 368. Some recent exceptions to this general view include Lührmann, 60f., 67, 99; Koester 1980, 244-250; and with strong reservations, Crossan, 192f., 257; cf. also Grundmann 1978, 182f. Davies-Allison, 2:237f., agree that 11,28-30 would not have been in Q, though it might have been in a very late version of Q accessible to Matthew and not Luke (Q^{mt}). Witherington waffles a bit on this question. First, 205, he assigns the Logion to M, as part of his argument for the multiple attestation of a Wisdom Christology. Only a little later, 214 (cf. 235), he argues that it was included in Q. It should be noted that the present argument does not turn on whether or not Q contained Mt 11,28-30. If Q did contain these verses, either in Matthew's location or somewhere else, we are still dealing with a pre-Matthean saying the form of which can only be tentatively determined through careful examination.

[22] Betz, 20, writes that "we can observe the logion at three different points on its way from wisdom literature to Gnosticism: in wisdom thought itself, in Matthew, and in gnostic thought." Cf. Christ, 103f.

[23] Infra, 189f. for texts and discussion.

taken up into their present contexts.[24] Betz believed that "in pre-Matthean Christian tradition...Jesus has taken the place of hypostasized wisdom," though he admitted that we can know nothing sure about the earlier context.[25] When he turned to interpret the Logion in Matthew's Gospel he stressed the connection with vv. 25-27 which depict Jesus as the "Revealer" and which "have a tendency toward Gnosticism,"[26] though otherwise he almost entirely ignored the question of Sir 51 and a Wisdom Christology.

Entering the discussion three years after the publication of Betz' article, M.J. Suggs had as his primary concern to put Matthew's Wisdom Christology on the map once and for all.[27] Suggs was fundamentally influenced by J.M. Robinson's argument that the literary *Gattung* of Q and *GosThom* was that of sayings of the wise (λόγοι σοφῶν), and that the theology expressed in Q would ultimately empty into the pool of Gnosticism.[28] While Suggs was cautious about reading gnostic elements back into the gospel tradition, he agreed that the collection of Q was amenable to gnostic interpretation.[29] Yet Suggs argued that previous scholarship had too closely identified Jesus and Wisdom in Q's theology. It was his contention that in Q as "in the gnosticising speculations of Jewish wisdom and apocalyptic literature...the ultimate source of revelation is Sophia";[30] Jesus remains an envoy of Wisdom, albeit the last and greatest

---

[24] Betz, 19f.

[25] Betz, 22.

[26] Betz, 22.

[27] Suggs, 2. In the same year (1970) both D.W. Smith and F. Christ published their studies of the Wisdom Christology of the Synoptics. Christ's study has not proved as influential as Suggs, probably due to Christ's failure to allow for much if any development in the traditions so far as a Wisdom Christology is concerned; cf. Hamerton-Kelly 1971, 239f. Smith independently arrived at conclusions on Q and Matthew not too dissimilar to Suggs'.

[28] Suggs, 6-11; cf. esp. J.M. Robinson 1971, 84-130; 1962. According to Robinson, "the personified Wisdom of OT wisdom literature developed into the gnostic redeemer myth, especially as it identified Jesus with that redeemer, and thus understood Jesus as bringer of the secret redemptive *gnosis* or *logoi*" (1971, 120); Robinson was thus concerned to "make intelligible the development from Q to the Gospel of Thomas, as an aspect of the general development from Jewish wisdom to Hellenistic Gnosticism, from God's Sophia to the gnostic redeemer" (1971, 129 n. 95). Put differently, "the tendency at work in the *Gattung logoi sophon* [i.e., Q and *GosThom*, as the chief representatives] was coordinated to the trajectory from the hypostasized Sophia to the gnostic redeemer" (1971, 130). Robinson's own appraisal of Suggs' work was positive (1971, 129), leading Robinson to the conclusion that "prior to the elimination of the *Gattung* of Sayings Collections completely from emergent orthodoxy, one can sense a development [i.e., the identification of Jesus and Wisdom] whose more radical correlative and ultimate outcome can be seen only in Gnosticism." Cf. also J.M. Robinson's later article, 1975, esp. 14f. For an important recent criticism of this view of Q, see Witherington, 211-221.

[29] Suggs, 9-13.

[30] Suggs, 28.

envoy.³¹ It was Matthew's self-appointed task to correct this tendency by a series of deliberate and systematically executed modifications of several Q sayings (Mt 11,19; 11,25-30; 23,34-36; 23,37-39 = Q 7,35; 10,21f.; 11,49-51; 13,34f.); the end result is that Matthew identifies Jesus and Wisdom.³² In regard to 11,25-27 it is precisely Matthew's addition of vv. 28-30 which converts the whole pericope (11,25-30) into a full Wisdom Christology, "a development," added Suggs, "which was required before the gnosticising tendencies of [Matthew's] opponents could issue in the developed Gnosticism of the second century."³³

If one is to judge by scholarly acceptance, Suggs' proposal has been anything but a "cul-de-sac."³⁴ Most have been inclined to agree with his conclusions. Jesus remains an envoy of Wisdom in Q;³⁵ it is Matthew who is credited with the identification of Jesus and Wisdom,³⁶ and thus Matthew clearly has a keen interest in this aspect of Christology. This situation has all but locked 11,28-30 into its supposed Christological function of representing Jesus as speaking *in persona sapientiae*. Thus C. Deutsch, writing some years after Suggs, was able to conduct a search almost entirely in various intertestamental *wisdom* texts for the background to the individual elements of Mt 11,25-30.³⁷ Having done so she concluded, not surprisingly,

---

[31] Suggs, 19, 28, 96.
[32] Suggs, 60f., 97, 106-108; 130.
[33] Suggs, 96. At this point Suggs cites Grant, 153, on Mt 11,28-30: "There is a Wisdom-Christology in this passage which points to the Gnostic speculations about Wisdom."
[34] In spite of the judgment of Goulder 1971, 569.
[35] E.g. S. Schulz, *passim*; Hamerton-Kelly 1973, 36; Stanton 1973, 36-38; Edwards, 59; Kloppenborg 1978, 146f.; Hengel 1979, 159-160; Burnett, 50, 52 (but see p. 53 in Burnett); M. de Jonge 1988, 194-199; Dunn 1989, 204-206; Piper, 162-173 (esp. 169-173); Luz, 2:209; Gnilka, 1:425. Independently of Suggs: Lührmann, 99; D.W. Smith, 119-122. For others cf. Piper, 263 n. 60; Kloppenborg 1978, 131 n. 16.

Taking the view that Jesus and Wisdom *are* identified in Q are, among others (both before and after Suggs), Arvedson, esp. 209-211; Christ, 74f., 153f.; Wilckens 1971, 515f.; Beardslee, 236; Fiorenza, 17; J.M. Robinson 1975, 9f.; Deutsch 1987, 103, 111; 1990, 36f.; Jacobson (with hesitance), 141, 230; Witherington, 221-236. For others in favor of a Wisdom Christology in Q, cf. Deutsch 1987, 172 n. 198; Kloppenborg 1978, 131, esp. n. 16; Piper, 263 n. 59. A recent survey of the discussion of Q's wisdom Christology may be found in Meadors, 33-37.

[36] E.g. Dunn 1989, 197-206; Hamerton-Kelly 1973, 67-83; Hengel 1979, 160f.; Burnett, 33-50; Stanton 1973, 36-38; M. de Jonge 1988, 195; Schweizer, 446f.; cf. Piper, 168. Independently of Suggs: D.W. Smith, 85-101, 119-122; Stendahl, 27, 142.

Though J.M. Robinson 1975, 9f., argues for an identification of Jesus and Wisdom in the last stages of the Q tradition (Mt 11,27), he is in agreement with the case that Matthew carries "forward the Q trajectory more than does Luke"; likewise, Deutsch 1987, 111; Fiorenza, 17; Witherington, 228f., 349-368. In other words, the gap is not great between their position and that of Suggs with regard to Matthew's interests.

[37] Similarly, F. Christ, though he was not influenced by Suggs' study which appeared in the same year.

that the only true parallel to Mt 11,28-30 is Sir 51,23ff. (cf. Sir 6,28),[38] and also, not surprisingly, that Jesus is speaking as Wisdom.

Another example of this general approach to Mt 11,28-30 comes with the study of J.D.G. Dunn, *Christology in the Making*. Dunn's particular interest was in the Christological question of *pre-existence*,[39] and according to Dunn there was no concept of the pre-existence of Christ prior to the application of Wisdom categories to him. His analysis of Q and Matthew largely followed the trail blazed by Suggs.[40] In Q Jesus' sayings spoke of Wisdom and presented Jesus' teaching in the form of Jewish wisdom, but Jesus was not identified with Wisdom. Dunn summarizes:

Throughout the earliest stages of the Synoptic tradition prior to Matthew, but including Luke, Jesus is presented *not as Wisdom, but as the messenger of Wisdom, as the eschatological envoy of (God in his) wisdom*. And the implication is that Jesus thought of himself (if at all) in the same terms. Only Matthew moves beyond this to embrace an explicit Wisdom Christology (Jesus = Wisdom) -- and he does this by careful but obviously deliberate redaction of his Q source. In short, the Synoptic tradition strongly suggests that there was a time when there was no Wisdom christology; but we also know of a later stage when Wisdom christology could be taken for granted (in the hymns of Colossians and Hebrews and in John). Matthew shows us one of the transition points.[41]

Once again, Mt 11,28-30 is significant with reference to Sir 51 on the one hand,[42] and the Logos Christology of John on the other. Specifically, Mt 11,28-30 is to be understood within the framework of Matthew's very developed Wisdom Christology.

It is not to be thought that the foregoing studies and others beside are in agreement on the extent of the "trajectory," and specifically on whether any heed should be paid to the gnostic use (or "tendency") of the Logion. What is evident, however, is that for some time now Mt 11,28-30 has been fixed on a line which extends from OT and intertestamental wisdom thought to John's Logos Christology, if not to second century Gnosticism.[43] *In Mt 11,28-30 a modified version of a Wisdom saying (Sir 51,23ff.) and a developed interest in Wisdom speculation (i.e. Matthew's) appear to intersect.* This convergence has proved compelling, but the fact that the Logion is independently evidenced in the gnostic *GosThom* 90, the supposedly closest parallel to Q, seems to clinch the matter. Yet as

---

[38] Deutsch 1987, 118, 130.
[39] Likewise, Hamerton-Kelly 1973, 22-102 (esp. 68-70). Dunn's interest in pre-existence was part of his larger interest in the incarnation.
[40] Dunn 1989, 197-206.
[41] Dunn 1989, 210f.; italics in original.
[42] Dunn 1989, 200f.
[43] Cf. also Schweizer, 274.

suggestive as all this is and in spite of the repeated affirmations, the Wisdom Christology of Mt 11,28-30 has remained only an intriguing possibility.[44]

At this point, however, the reader may have begun to wonder whether the foregoing survey has not departed from consideration of our theme, "rest." In fact this appearance of disinterest in the rest motif is an accurate representation of the discussion of the Logion. Certainly the idea of ἀνάπαυσις has been addressed in arguments for a Wisdom Christology,[45] but in a decidedly subordinate manner as the discussion has been overwhelmingly biased toward Christological interests. Thus the chief interest of scholars in examining the rest motif has been to establish that Jesus speaks as Wisdom,[46] with only a secondary interest (if any) in the rest motif as a soteriological symbol.[47] Indeed, the whole Wisdom interpretation has tended to deflect interest away from the explicit promise of rest,[48] and toward the encoded Wisdom Christology.

By itself this relative disinterest in the rest motif is not necessarily a fatal flaw of the Wisdom interpretation, but it does highlight a certain awkwardness in that approach to the Logion. When we turn to consider Mt 11 directly it will be necessary to engage with this line of enquiry, but for now we will continue with our overview of scholarship on the NT passages.

---

[44] For alternative approaches to the Logion, cf. Haering; Hoskyns, 76-78; Curnock; T.W. Manson, 477-479; Bauer 1961; Hunter; Cerfaux, 153-159; M.D. Johnson, 60f.; Maher; Stanton 1982, 3-8 (repr. in Stanton 1992a, 364-377; cf. 340-342); Bacchiocchi 1984, 288-316; Allison; De Conick; Charette.

[45] Cf. esp. the major studies: Arvedson, 201-208, 222-228 (the result of Arvedson's study is a thoroughly mystical and gnostic idea); Christ, 103-107, 117-119; Deutsch 1987, 116f., 120, 123f., 128, 135-137.

[46] This is clear from most treatments of this Logion, where the chief function of the rest motif appears to be as a pointer to Christology, i.e., to Wisdom. Thus, Christ's conclusion on the significance of the rest motif is that "Im Kontext des Heilandsrufs weist also die Ruhe klar auf Jesus als die Weisheit" (Christ, 107).

[47] Deutsch's attempt to find how "the Jewish sources parallel and so elucidate the content of the rest promised to those who come to Jesus" is uncompelling because it first shifts into a focus on the dynamic involved in the "paradox" of yoke and rest (which is apparent without the aid of any parallels), and then addresses this dynamic in terms of Matthean theology which has little if anything to do with Wisdom (1987, 136f.). In the end her answer is that the "rest" is to be equated with Jesus' "presence." In that case, it appears that Ex 33,14 is the clearer parallel. Note also Witherington's remark, following his treatment of the Logion (p. 207): "There are still some enigmatic aspects of this saying," including, "what sort of rest did he offer?" Thus the chief feature of the saying remains simply "enigmatic" in the light of the Wisdom approach. For the remainder such attempts only show how little the rest motif in Mt 11,28-30 owes to Sirach. Probably in recognition of this, Christ, 105, remarks that Jesus appears in this saying as both Wisdom *and* messiah.

[48] Both Suggs, 100, and Deutsch 1987, 46, believe that the *yoke* image dominates Mt 11,28-30, but this is simply an attempt to place the equation Jesus' yoke = Wisdom's yoke = Torah front and center.

2.2. Heb 3-4

Auctor's treatment of our theme in Heb 3-4 tells us that Gen 2,2 was always embedded in the warning of Ψ 94,7-11 [95,7-11]. This by itself has appeared unconvincing to most moderns, though they might indulge *Auctor*, given the exegetical conventions of his day. Yet his manner of pursuing the midrash on these OT passages has proved difficult to follow, leaving us with the impression that the original readers knew more than we do. The quest for this background knowledge is thus commissioned.

In an essentially pastoral work which is remarkable for the circumstances under which it was composed no less than for the major studies it has provoked,[49] E. Käsemann set the agenda for subsequent discussions of the κατάπαυσις-idea by making Heb 3-4 a departure point for his thesis (1939)[50] that,

> ...all the utterances in Hebrews culminate in the description of Christ's high priestly office, but take their basis, which supports and purposefully articulates the individual parts, from the motif of the wandering people of God.[51]

The motif of the "wandering/travelling[52] people of God" is in turn grounded in the heavenly journey of the gnostic *Urmensch*.[53] It was not Käsemann's thesis that Hebrews is a gnostic document, but rather that *Auctor* -- like any good communicator -- packaged his message in thought forms familiar to his readers, though the gap between his message and the gnostic one was great.[54]

As for the κατάπαυσις, it is to be understood as the *spatially conceived* goal of the Christian journey, portrayed here against the backdrop of the wilderness generation. Such a hope of a heavenly resting *place* combined with speculation about the seventh day and pictured as the goal of a spiritual journey struck Käsemann as singularly foreign to the OT -- from which it

---

[49] See the "Preface to the Second German Edition," Käsemann, 15f.; Thurén, 23 n. 70. Although earlier scholars (e.g., Windisch; cf. Hofius, 5) had related Hebrews to Gnosticism, Käsemann's work remains the real starting point for our discussion. A good survey of the discussion from Käsemann to Hofius is given in Hofius, 5-16. More recently, see Feld, 42-48.

[50] Here I am following the date given by Feld, 42f., who points out that the date usually cited, 1938, is erroneous.

[51] Käsemann, 240; this passage is italicized in the original.

[52] With few exceptions, we will opt for "travel" or "journey" over "wander" for the intended idea; see below, 310.

[53] Käsemann, 87ff.

[54] "The myth is drawn upon to make clear the Christ kerygma in a Hellenistic environment, but only within strict limits, without its being allowed to define or overrun this proclamation" (Käsemann, 167). See further the sharply put qualifications in Käsemann, esp. 174-182; also 86, 95f., 150-152.

was ostensibly drawn -- and yet strangely reminiscent of certain ideas in Philo.

> The enigmatic idea of "rest" in Hebrews has found its historical origin in the [Philonic] notion of the aeons, according to which the highest aeon, the realm of the divine Spirit, the Sabbath, and the ἀνάπαυσις are identical. In the single instance we need not decide how many Alexandrian theories may be assumed as known to Hebrews. At any rate, there, too, the κατάπαυσις is construed spatially, thus as aeon-like, as a heavenly sphere, and is linked to Sabbath speculation. ἀνάπαυσις and κατάπαυσις alternate.[55]

Nonetheless, in view of the differences between Philo and Hebrews Käsemann broadened his search to take in gnostic literature, and believed that here above all one would find the closest religious historical parallel to Hebrews' hope of the κατάπαυσις. Both Philo and Hebrews, Käsemann surmised, were independently drawing on gnostic patterns of thought.

Käsemann's basic thesis has its adherents to this day. G. Theißen, in his *Untersuchungen zum Hebräerbrief* (1969) argued that two strands of thought about ἀνάπαυσις are to be found in Philo, one being a more "gnostic" conception which Philo ultimately rejected in favor of a more "Jewish" understanding.[56] Theißen believed that the "gnostic" strand embedded in Philo's writings was the closest parallel to Heb 3-4. Among others,[57] J.W. Thompson (1982),[58] H. Braun (1984),[59] and E. Gräßer (1990)[60] have also taken up variations on Käsemann's thesis.[61]

A frontal assault on this line of argument, especially as expressed by Käsemann, was made with the publication in 1970 of O. Hofius' 1968 dissertation, *Katapausis. Die Vorstellung vom endzeitlichen Ruheort im Hebräerbrief*.[62] Since Theißen had criticized Hofius' work in the intervening year, especially regarding Philo's thought, Hofius included a

---

[55] Käsemann, 73.
[56] Theißen 1969, 124ff. These labels are Theißen's.
[57] Cf. Hofius, 6-16. Our present concern will be confined in the main to scholars who have taken this line since Hofius wrote.
[58] J.W. Thompson, 81-102. Thompson also groups Philo and Gnosticism together as the closest parallels to Heb 3-4, though his interests are with Philo more than with Gnosticism.
[59] Braun, 90-93.
[60] Gräßer, 1:210f. Gräßer has been arguing this for some time; cf. 1965, 105-115; Hofius, 10, 14.
[61] Yeo, 2-33, rejects this line of interpretation, but after comparing the κατάπαυσις-idea of Heb 3-4 with Yin-Yang philosophy Yeo ends up positing an interpretation which sounds very Philonic and even gnostic. Spicq, 2:95-104, also highlights the parallels with Philo.
[62] This is not to overlook R. Williamson 1970, 539-557, who at about the same time as Hofius argued against a Philonic understanding of the κατάπαυσις in Heb 3-4. He makes many important observations which will be useful to us, but what was for him one point among very many was Hofius' whole concern.

response to Theißen's arguments in the published version. We will take up the latter debate on Philo later;[63] for now we shall review Hofius' case against Käsemann.

Hofius' response to Käsemann was threefold. First, against Käsemann's assumption that the idea of a resting *place* (i.e. the local idea) is paralleled only in gnostic thought, Hofius argued that this is the very meaning of מנוחה/κατάπαυσις in Ps 95/Ψ 94, both in the OT and in subsequent Jewish (apocalyptic) interpretation; i.e., the psalm was understood to say, "they shall not enter my resting *place*." Since one is thus confronted by *two* religious historical candidates for the background of the local κατάπαυσις in Heb 3-4 -- contrary to what Käsemann had led us to believe -- Hofius compared the merits of the respective candidates, and the Jewish apocalyptic conception emerged as the closer parallel. A subsidiary argument of this section of Hofius' dissertation is an argument that מנוחה/κατάπαυσις in Ps 95,11/Ψ 94,11 is best understood as a reference to the temple,[64] God's resting place. It is arguable that this is how the rabbis took it, and the use of "entering in" language elsewhere in Hebrews lends itself to this suggestion.

Second, whereas Käsemann had assumed that the word σαββατισμός in Heb 4,9 was essentially synonymous with κατάπαυσις and thus had as its referent a heavenly expanse, the seventh "aeon" or Hebdomas, Hofius argued that for *Auctor* the σαββατισμός was in fact descriptive of the event to take place *in* the κατάπαυσις, namely, a Sabbath *celebration*. Such a notion was anticipated in widespread Jewish hopes concerning the "world-to-come" as "a day which is wholly Sabbath and rest" and thus indicates no indebtedness to Gnosticism.

Finally, Hofius argued that the theme of Heb 3-4 is not that of the *travelling* people of God, but rather that of the *waiting* people of God. Thus, instead of a mythologically conceived journey through the cosmos as in Gnosticism, one should envisage a people waiting expectantly for the world which is now hidden in heaven to appear, an event which is on the verge of occurring.

Ultimately, then, the κατάπαυσις in Heb 3-4 has as its referent the Most Holy Place, God's resting place in the heavenly temple into which Jesus has already entered as the forerunner of believers, and in which they will engage in an eternal, joyous Sabbath celebration around the throne of God. Like the

---

[63] Infra, 115ff.

[64] In fact it is the wilderness tabernacle, the tent, with which Hebrews is concerned throughout; neither the word ἱερόν nor ναός occurs in Hebrews. This is probably due to a primary interest in the Pentateuch as the basis for tabernacle/temple worship. Yet since the concern of Hebrews encompasses the temple and may reflect contemporary temple practice (cf. Horbury, 50-52; but see Ellingworth, 454), we will habitually refer to the *temple* in our discussion. The idea of the heavenly sanctuary would stem from stock Jewish ideas of the heavenly *temple*.

"fathers" in Num 14 who were waiting on the banks of the Jordan to cross over into Canaan, so also now the believers are poised, ready and waiting to enter into God's κατάπαυσις. Whether they will make that entrance depends on whether they listen to God's voice "today."

Although Hofius' study has been very influential,[65] we have already noted a family of studies continuing into the present that trace their lineage rather to Käsemann while feuding with Hofius, and there have of course been mediating positions.[66] In addition, several shorter studies or parts of studies have participated along the way in the discussion from one perspective or another. Thus studies on the use of the OT[67] and specifically the issue of typology,[68] as well as the issues of eschatology,[69] the warning passages in Hebrews,[70] and the Sabbath[71] have shown an interest in this passage.[72] It is unnecessary at this point to trace the paths of these various studies, though some of their insights will be of assistance to us.

In sum, the debate between Käsemann et al. and Hofius et al. has controlled the discussion of the κατάπαυσις-idea in Heb 3-4. In most cases the participants in the discussion have been concerned with the larger question of the religious historical background of Hebrews as a whole; the interpretation of the κατάπαυσις follows on from or, as the case may be, supports the answer to this general question. Since, however, these schools have tended to polarize the options and have not brought us closer to a resolution, a fresh look at the evidence is necessary.

---

[65] Commenting on this and other contributions of Hofius, Feld, 45, states, "Die Arbeiten von Hofius können in ihrer Bedeutung kaum überschätzt werden: für die Erforschung des religionsgeschichtlichen Hintergrundes des Hebr sind sie die erste entscheidende Wendemarke seit dem Erscheinen der Untersuchung von Käsemann." Neither Lane nor Ellingworth devotes a separate excursus to this theme, though their lengthy discussions of this passage lean in the main toward Hofius' conclusions. Cf. also, e.g., Zimmermann, 129-145; Woschitz, 622-624. Many of the studies in the following notes have also been influenced by Hofius.

[66] The studies in the previous note could probably be cited here as well; cf. also Lombard (Lombard is more sympathetic with Theißen than Hofius); Darnell, 308; also the excurses in Attridge, 126-128; and Weiss, 268-273. See also Michel, 184-186, who had somewhat earlier argued for a primarily apocalyptic interpretation.

[67] Cf. Lane, 1:cxii-cxxiv.

[68] Esp. Attridge 1980; cf. Goppelt, 161-178, esp. 171f.

[69] Riehm, 798-808 (cf. also 809-819); Barrett; Laub, 246-253; Toussaint; Sharp, 292-294; Rissi, 127f., cf. 13-21; Scholer, 201-207.

[70] Mugridge; Oberholtzer 1988. Oberholtzer mentions his own dissertation (1984) as well as that of Dunham.

[71] E.g., Bacchiocchi 1977, 63-69; Rordorf, 89f., 98-100, 111f.; Lincoln 1982, 205-214.

[72] Other helpful treatments of our passage/topic in Hebrews include A.D. Martin; Hutton; Schierse, 112-115; Losada; Graham; W.C. Kaiser 1985, 168-172 (expanded repr. of 1973); Bénétreau, 1:180-187; Lindars 1991b, 47-50. See also: Attridge 1988, 96-100; Rose 1989a, 63f.; Peterson 1992, 224f.; Isaacs, 78-88; P. Walker, 50-52; Desilva, 452-454.

3. Prospectus

Aside from the common use of the rest motif, Mt 11,28-30 and Heb 3-4 might appear to be strange bedfellows. It is with good reason, however, that we consider them together. Mt 11 and Heb 3-4 stand out as the NT passages wherein the rest motif is expressed thematically. Recognition of this fact is evident in the scholarly precedent of citing either one or both of these passages when making reference to the rest motif in the NT, and also the tendency to link these passages in one way or another. As will already have become evident, one of these links has been the belief that both Mt 11,28-30 and Heb 3,7-4,11 are best understood in terms of the development of Gnosticism, and that their use of the rest motif in particular should be associated with this line of development. Another link has been the belief, however vaguely articulated, that the two passages express in similar fashion the idea of an eschatological rest, which is united to the idea of an eschatological Sabbath.[73]

Both of these links will be given serious consideration in this study. Our conclusion will be that the former -- the shared link with developing Gnosticism -- is to be rejected. The latter suggestion is more promising, however, and we will seek to sharpen it. Our own suggestion -- which will only become clear as we advance through the discussion -- will be that both Mt 11 and Heb 3-4 envisage a fulfilment in Christ of specific OT themes of rest, and that this involves a similar employment of Christological ideas. It will thus emerge that our interpretations of these two passages are mutually confirmatory.

In particular, we shall contend that the dominant interpretation of Mt 11,28-30 -- i.e., the Wisdom interpretation[74] -- has missed Matthew's interests in the OT. Even when interpreters have recognized his use of the OT themes, the nature and depth of his interest has not been rightly appreciated. It has of course not been possible to miss *Auctor*'s interest in the OT, an interest which is at least formal if not substantive. Yet the κατάπαυσις-idea of the passage has been taken up into the struggle of competing religious historical assessments of Hebrews, and the character of the κατάπαυσις has thus been pulled in the direction of one or the other world of thought, usually with a distorting effect.[75]

---

[73] It is not uncommon to find these two passages discussed together in treatments of the Sabbath in the NT.

[74] For the sake of convenience, we will refer to Suggs' general approach as the "W/wisdom interpretation."

[75] Again, for the sake of brevity, we will use shorthand expressions such as "apocalyptic interpretation" (e.g., Hofius) or "dualistic/gnostic interpretation" (e.g., Gräßer). Certain ambiguous terms, namely, apocalyptic, dualistic, gnostic, and

It is not our purpose to harmonize these two passages nor to establish a definite link between them. Rather, we shall begin by conducting a wide ranging survey of the use of the rest motif in the OT as well as other Jewish and Christian literature (Chs. Two-Four). Using this large canvas as a backdrop we will examine with some care both Mt 11,28-30 (Chs. Five-Six) and Heb 3-4 (Ch. Seven). In the course of the examination of Hebrews we will also take into view other NT passages which use the rest motif. In keeping with the peculiar features and exegetical issues of Mt 11 and Heb 3-4 respectively, we will discuss them separately and only return in the final chapter to a closer comparison and contrast of them.

As for the ordering of the following chapters, two points of clarification may be offered. (1) In spite of the fact that we will be concerned with the use of the OT on the part of two first century authors who wrote in Greek, and both of whom made use of the Greek OT, it is proper to begin our investigation with the MT rather than the LXX.[76] Firstly, we shall take the position that Matthew knew both Hebrew and Greek, and that he knew the OT in both Hebrew and Greek. Thus, the Hebrew OT is a potentially direct influence on Matthew's thinking. Secondly, a translation -- in this case the LXX -- is best understood in relation to that which it translates -- the Hebrew OT. Although we will devote considerably more space to the treatment of our theme in the MT, we will make clear the shape of the relevant traditions in the LXX. Here we are interested not only in how the OT ideas come to expression in the Greek version, nor merely in the use of particular Greek words, but also in the evidence of the continuing and living development of that which is manifested in the older writings. Thirdly, even if the Hebrew OT is not a direct influence on the author of Hebrews, it stands as a broad influence on many of the writers whose thinking came to expression in the literature we will survey in Ch. Four, and thus as a potentially indirect influence (beyond the LXX) on *Auctor*. Fourthly, it would be foolish not to take advantage of the OT scholarship which has already treated our theme with all its expertise, and of course this specialist discussion has focused almost entirely on the Hebrew text. The insights gleaned from this scholarship can only the better prepare us to work with the LXX (see the second point, above). Therefore, we shall begin with the Hebrew OT.

(2) The ordering of the treatments of Mt 11 and Heb 3-4 is largely immaterial, since we are dealing with each within its own frame of reference. It is necessary to devote an entire chapter to the examination of

---

Hellenistic, will be discussed at the beginning of Ch. Seven, since they have been crucial to the discussion of Hebrews.

[76] For clarification on the issues of the MT text, the LXX, the question of the canon in the first century, and Matthew's and *Auctor*'s use of the OT, see below, 17 n. 1, 77 n. 1, 162f., 258.

Matthew's interest in a Wisdom Christology, even though our conclusions on the matter are largely negative. This chapter (Five) is closer in conception to the background material, and once we have dealt with it the way is prepared for the two chapters (Six-Seven) that treat the rest motif positively. For this reason, and in order to avoid allowing Hebrews to overshadow Matthew, it seemed proper to advance from the more subtle (Matthew) to the more highly developed (Hebrews), and to take up other NT usages of the rest motif in connection with the latter, before drawing our separate findings together and taking the discussion a step further in the final chapter.

The following editions of the biblical text will be utilized: for the NT, NA^{27}; for the OT, BHS; for the LXX, *Septuaginta* (Göttingen). Except for our main texts (Mt 11,28-30 and Heb 3,7-4,11) and unless indicated otherwise, quotations from the English translation (ET) are from the New International Version (NIV) or the New Revised Standard Version (NRSV). Editions/translations of other primary sources are noted in the body of this study (see also the bibliography), usually with the first quotation of that source.

In the following, where reference is being made directly to the text of the LXX we will give the LXX's chapter and verse numbers first, along with the LXX's title (abbreviated)[77] where it differs from the English; in these cases, the ET and/or MT reference will be supplied in brackets where necessary.[78] For the remainder we have used the ET titles and references first, with alternative (MT/LXX) numbering in brackets;[79] in these cases, the context will make clear whether we are including or excluding the LXX. References to Q will follow the conventional system of using Luke's references prefixed with "Q." Thus Q 7,35 = Mt 11,19//Lk 7,35.

---

[77] 1-2Sam = 1-2Kgdms; 1-2Kgs = 3-4Kgdms; 1-2Chr = 1-2Par; Ps = Ψ. When it is not sufficiently clear from the context that we are referring directly to the LXX we will try to give some indication (e.g., by prefixing the reference with 'LXX') that it is the LXX which is in view.

[78] E.g., Ψ 94,11 [95,11]; LXX Jer 38,31 [31,31].

[79] We will prefix the bracketed reference with MT and/or LXX; e.g., 1Chr 6,31 [MT/LXX 6,16].

Chapter Two

The Rest Motif in the Hebrew OT

1. Introduction

Since the importance of our theme in the Hebrew Scriptures is often overlooked, it will be our task in this chapter and the next to examine carefully the way in which the rest motif is exploited soteriologically in Israel's sacred writings.[1]

Our study will be confined to two specific soteriological usages of the rest motif. Part One of the present chapter will be limited to the examination of a particular and fairly well-defined tradition. The use of נוח (Hi/1) and מנוחה in the Deuteronomistic history has been the subject of several brief studies, and will be the starting point of this one. Additionally, we will take in Chronicles, the psalms, and the prophets. Part Two will be a study of the rest motif in relation to the Sabbath. The following chapter will take up the LXX.

In view of the length and the involved nature of the following survey it may be helpful to state clearly our purposes and interests. These interrelated points apply to both this chapter and the next:

---

[1] The questions of the OT "canon" in I A.D. and the relative weight of individual books are still open, with some arguing that the canon was essentially "closed" as in our MT, and others arguing that it remained somewhat "fluid" during this period. The issues are reviewed and principal studies/scholars represented in *HJP²*, 2:314-321; Beckwith; Ellis, 3-50; J.A. Sanders 1992; Grabbe, 2:537-545. Ellingworth, 37-42, discusses this question in connection with the OT in Hebrews. This important issue, does not, however, affect the argument of this study. Thus, when we come to assess whether Matthew was alluding to Sirach, our focus will be on the strength of the parallel and Matthew's development of the Logion, and *not* on the weight of "canonical" vs. "non-canonical" parallels. In general, we will avoid the use of terms such as "canon," "non-canonical," and "apocryphal."

Recent scholarship has also stressed the fluidity of the Hebrew text of the OT in the first century, even the presence of different texts (Cross-Talmon; Mulder; cf. Stanton 1992a, 350f.). For the purposes of the present chapter we will rely on the text of BHS. When we come to consider Matthew (Hebrews does not depend directly on the Hebrew OT; see the following note) we will attempt to take account of the possibility of alternative readings in Matthew's Hebrew text.

(1) As has already been stated, it is necessary to appreciate the prominence and importance of the rest motif as a soteriological symbol in writings that were of primary importance to the NT authors.² This is not merely a matter of word counting, but of considering the manner in which the motif is exploited in specific traditions. By working carefully with the OT as well as the other Jewish and Christian literature, my desire is to provide a fairly full perspective and to make possible a sense of proportion.

(2) We want to perceive some of the specific contours of these OT traditions as well as the clustering of associated motifs, e.g. the temple and Davidic dynasty, the exodus and the land. This will enhance our ability to spot interest in these OT traditions on the part of the NT writers. It will also enable us to

(3) gain an understanding of how the two traditions (מנוחה and Sabbath) were already related in the OT period and literature. This is of special interest in view of the linkage of Ps 95 and Gen 2 in Heb 3-4; a linkage which is echoed to some extent in Mt 11,28-30.

(4) Some attention will be given to linguistic questions which bear on the interpretation of the word κατάπαυσις in Heb 3-4, but also on the general translation of these traditions into Greek. Our ability to do this is limited to the extent that we appreciate the whole tradition to which Ps 95 belongs.

(5) When we come to examine Mt 11 and Heb 3-4 we will be making reference to a number of the passages out of these two OT traditions. This chapter and the next will provide the opportunity to examine those OT passages individually within their own frames of reference.

Hopefully these points will provide some specific guides for working through the following material.

2. Part one

2.1. Introduction

A study of the rest motif could, if desired, take in a very broad range of words and passages.³ Our interests are more limited. In the Deuteronomistic (Dtr) history -- Deuteronomy, Joshua, Judges, 1-2

---

[2] Although we will take the position that Matthew knew the Hebrew OT (infra, 162f.), we will work on the assumption that the author of Hebrews knew only the Greek OT (infra, 258). The statement made in the text applies equally to this chapter and the next. See also the previous note.

[3] Note the inclusive list of words in Sun, 142.

Samuel, 1-2 Kings -- there is a usage of the rest motif which is sufficiently distinctive to merit separate discussion, and which performs definite functions within the narrative and theological framework of the history (§ 2.2). It is because this particular use of the rest motif is said to span several revisions of the Dtr history and is also used in other OT literature, that we will use the word "tradition." For simplicity's sake it is referred to as the "Deuteronomistic (Dtr) rest," "rest tradition," "נוח and/or מנוחה tradition," etc.

The tradition in question has a *terminological* core in the verb נוח (Hi/1) and its cognate noun מנוחה. *Conceptually*, the tradition has as its core the idea that YHWH gives his people Israel "rest" from travelling and from warfare in the land of promise. A correlate of this is that the land of Palestine can itself be called their "resting place"; indeed, the tradition concerns a situation which is inextricably bound up with the land. Yet within the Dtr history there is a particular strand which is from the start (cf. Deut 12,9-10) associated with the centralization of the cult, so that it is when YHWH gives his people rest that they will be obliged to take their offerings to the "place" he will choose. This theme recedes somewhat (though not entirely!) in Joshua, before coming to the center in 2Sam 7, 1Kgs 5, and, finally, 1Kgs 8, the last being Solomon's dedication of the temple. Elsewhere (e.g., 2Chr 6,41; Ps 132,8.14) this association with the temple is strengthened yet further by the designation of the temple as YHWH's מנוחה, his "resting place," though it does not seem that this precise usage explicitly surfaces in the Dtr history. Because this joining of themes -- rest and temple -- comes to a head with David and Solomon there is a strong connection formed with the Davidic dynasty, this too being quietly anticipated in Deut 12. After Solomon's dedication of the temple in 1Kgs 8 the rest tradition does not recur in the Dtr history.

This theme of the Davidic dynasty seems to maintain its link with the rest motif in several usages of the tradition outside the Dtr history, not least in Chronicles (§ 2.3) where it becomes attached even more strongly to Solomon, a "man of rest," than to David. Although, in contrast to the Dtr history it occurs with kings subsequent to Solomon they are all of the Davidic dynasty. Moreover, as already mentioned, the idea of "YHWH's resting place" -- the temple -- becomes prominent, especially in a quote from Ps 132 in 2Chr 6 during the dedication of the temple (§ 2.4). Ps 95 stands squarely in this tradition, yet it is unique in its manner of expression; we will devote a separate discussion to it (§ 2.5).

In the prophetic books of Isaiah (§ 2.6), Jeremiah (§ 2.7), Lamentations (§ 2.8), and Micah (§ 2.9) many of the above ideas continue to appear, but additional elements become prominent. The "rest" becomes a powerful symbol of God's judgment as well as his gracious gift; it is an element of the eschatological hope; it gravitates more than in the aforementioned literature toward the broader concept of שלום; it is more closely associated with social justice and even becomes descriptive of the responsibility the Israelites were to fulfil with each other.

In brief, "rest" is a pronounced OT *Heilsgut* which has been taken up into definite traditions and given emphatic expression. As such it deserves careful consideration.

2.2. The Deuteronomistic rest[4]

2.2.1. *Preliminary considerations*

Such is the tradition in broad outline, and for a closer look we may begin with the Dtr history. The first steps are to remove any doubt as to the distinctiveness of the tradition by considering further its linguistic features, and to define the specific group of passages which will occupy us.

The rest tradition passages have a common denominator in vocabulary and form. Note the following: נוח (Hi/1): Deut 3,20; Deut 12,10; Deut 25,19; Josh 1,13.15; Josh 21,44; Josh 22,4; Josh 23,1; 2Sam 7,1.11; 1Kgs 5,4 [MT 5,18]. מנוחה (Nf): Deut 12,9; 1Kgs 8,56.[5] To these could be added the use of מנוח (Nm) and רגע (Hi; intransitive) in Deut 28,65, as well as שקט (Qal) in Josh 11,23; Josh 14,15; Judg 3,11.30; Judg 5,31; Judg 8,28; Judg 18,7.27; 2Kgs 11,20.[6]

First of all, in terms of meaning, נוח (Hi/1) is used *uniformly* throughout this body of literature -- with the sense of, "grant rest from military engagement/travelling" --, although outside the Dtr history it often takes different meanings.[7]

Moreover, a formal pattern of usage can be recognized. W. Kaiser, looking at the OT generally, offers a concise statement:

Whenever the *hiphil* stem of this root [נוח] is followed by the preposition *l*ᵉ plus a person or group, it usually assumes technical status. The resulting form in some twenty instances is

---

[4] See esp. von Rad 1966b; Frankowski; Braulik 1968; 1988; Hulst 1970; W. C. Kaiser 1973 (later expanded and reprinted in W.C. Kaiser 1985, 153-175); W. Schulz, 111-162, 165-170; Roth.

[5] Regarding Judg 20,43, cf. Preuß, 304. 2Sam 14,17, apart from the use of מנוחה, would appear to have little to do with the tradition in question. The use of מנוחה in Ruth 1,9 and מנוח in 3,1 may be noted here, though they are not part of the Dtr history, and the usage there does not seem to be theologically related to the tradition here being investigated; the idea is that of a "home."

[6] Braulik 1988, 228f., adds Judg 2,14; 8,34; 1Sam 12,11; and 1Kgs 4,25 [MT 5,5] where the נוח form is not used, but associated ideas are present.

[7] Cf., e.g., Ex 17,11 (Moses "rests" or "lowers" his arms); Isa 30,32; Ezek 37,1; 40,2; 44,30 ("cause to rest/settle on"); Ezek 5,13; 16,42; 21,17 [MT 21,22]; 24,13 ("cause to cease/to be pacified").

henîah l^e. This rest is a place granted by the Lord (Ex. 33:14; Deut. 3:20; Josh. 1,13, 15; 22,4; 2 Chron. 14:5), a peace and security from all enemies (Deut. 12:10; 25:19; Josh. 21:44; 23:1; 2 Sam. 7:1, 11; 1 Kings 5:18 [5:4]; 1 Chron. 22:9, 18; 23:25; 2 Chron. 14:6; 15:15; 20:30; 32:22 -- probable reading?) or the cessation of sorrow and labor in the future (Isa. 14:3; 28:12).[8]

From the perspective of form at least, the rest motif has received a distinctive stamp in this tradition, thus enabling us to separate it out for discussion.

This is not to say, however, that all the usages of the formula fit one mold. There is tension between some usages, e.g. between 1Kgs 5,3f. [MT 5,17f.] and 2Sam 7,1.11,[9] and there are differing ways of grouping passages, including those based on assessments of redactional activity.[10] We will spare ourselves the attempt to unravel these problems, since there is no evidence that the NT writers with whom we are primarily concerned occupied themselves with such questions. Rather we will set to one side two groups of passages from the list given above and then concentrate on the remainder.

(1) First we may set aside the passages in Joshua and Judges (cf. 2Kgs 11,20) which use שקט (Qal).[11] These passages are not entirely unrelated to the נוח formula; the Chronicler clearly saw them as related.[12] Moreover, Neh 9,28 uses נוח (Qal) to recall these "שקט periods." Just the same, it is to be noted that in the Dtr history the two usages -- נוח (Hi/1) and שקט -- are

---

[8] W. Kaiser 1985, 157; he notes further that "the other *hiphil* usages of this root use other prepositions, for example *b^e* in Ezekiel 5:13; 16:42; 21:22; 24:13, or are followed by such accusatives as 'his hand' in Exodus 17,11; or 'my spirit' in Zechariah 6:8. Also when the *hiphil* form is followed by an accusative of a thing with a place name, the meaning is 'to deposit,' 'lay or set down' or 'let lie'" (1985, 157 n. 8). On the formula, see further Roth, 6-7, and Braulik 1988, 229. In addition to labelling it a "formula," Roth also calls this a "*coined idiom*," the horizon of which is "coextensive with that of the literary work; the coined idiom profiles and defines the literary work." Braulik provides an excellent presentation wherein he plots the several variables of the formula on a chart. Veijola, 72ff., also refers to this as a "Ruheformel."

[9] For such "tensions" in the Dtr use of the idea, cf. Von Rad 1966b, 97; Braulik 1968, 76; W.C. Kaiser 1985, 156; Roth, 5.

[10] For the latter, see esp. Roth; Braulik 1988; W. Schulz, 111-162, 165-170. The discussion of the literary development of the Dtr history, with all its subtleties and in-house disputes, is daunting for non-specialists; cf. S.L. McKenzie. Though we will not enter directly into this aspect of the rest tradition we will listen carefully to Roth and the others who have.

[11] With the exception of Judg 18,7.27 (cf. 1Chr 4,40; also Jer 30,10; 46,27) and 2Kgs 11,20 (cf. 2Chr 23,21; Brueggemann 1971, 325), these usages of שקט (Qal) are also labelled a "formula"; cf. Boling-Wright, 316. This formula occurs nowhere else in the Dtr history; related usages are all in the Chronicler's work (noted in the text); not utilizing this same form but similar are the following: Isa 14,7; Zech 1,11; Ps 76,8 [MT 76,9].

[12] Cf. 2Chr 14,1 [MT 13,23]; 14,5f. [MT 14,4f.] and 2Chr 20,30. Note also Isa 14,3.7.

never *directly* linked and the latter passages do possess a distinctive flavor.[13] We will draw them in a little later,[14] but we cannot afford them a separate discussion.

(2) Second, there are several among the remaining passages which more or less group together and which do not directly attach to the temple traditions we will be tracing in Deut 12 and the related passages. For W. Roth, Deut 3,20; Josh 1,13.15; 21,43-45; and 22,4 all "refer to the complete and final occupation of the land of promise on *both* sides of the Jordan. It stresses it as divine gift, more exactly, as the divinely granted state of rest in which Israel enjoys the gift of the land."[15] In each of these passages the same event is in view: the responsibility of the trans-Jordan tribes to fight alongside their brothers until all of the tribes have been granted rest from their enemies. The accent is on the idea that YHWH gives Israel rest *from* her enemies ("'rest from' the struggles of the conquest of the land of promise"[16]), with no further word as to the goal of that gift or Israel's responsibility in it.

Josh 21,44 sits least easily in Roth's presentation. In defence of Roth's view it may be noted that the rest formula in 21,44 is immediately followed by Joshua's address to the 2 1/2 tribes in 22,1ff. G. Braulik, however, correctly observes that 21,43-45 is somewhat complex, and defies a simple categorization; he distinguishes it sharply from the others in this group.[17] Along with 1Kgs 8,56 it contains a strong reference back to Deut 12,[18] and unlike Deut 3,20; Josh 1,13.15; and 22,4 it locates the achievement of rest chronologically after the settlement. Otherwise Braulik also stresses the association with the 2 1/2 tribes in this group of passages.[19]

---

[13] This is stressed by W.C. Kaiser 1985, 157; cf. Carlson, 100; R. Braun 1976, 584 n. 9; *et al*. Nonetheless, it is possible to distinguish them too sharply; cf. Woudstra, 199 n. 19.

[14] Infra, 30, 36f.

[15] Roth, 13f. This close association of "rest" and land is anticipated in Gen 49,15, which we will not otherwise discuss in this study; on this verse see Preuß, 304: "Bereits im alten Issachar-Spruch Gen 49,15 sind Ruhe und Wohnen im Land (hier: Freiheit zur Niederlassung) miteinander verbunden..., was sich dann at.lich als ein wesentlicher Zug der Gabe der Ruhe für den Menschen durchhält." Interestingly, the rest idea is closely connected here with a willing submission to forced labor.

[16] Roth, 13. Braulik 1988, 226, notes that the additional qualifiers, such as "from all your enemies," are missing from this group (Braulik does not include Josh 21,44 here) and that this may suggest that these passages focus more on the idea of rest from travelling.

[17] Braulik 1988, 227. Braulik groups 21,44 with Deut 12,10; 25,19; Josh 23,1 (see below; also, without the formula, Judg 2,14; 8,34; 1Sam 12,11; 1Kgs 4,25 [MT 5,5]); all of these have to with threats from *without*, as opposed to those in Deut 3,20 etc. which concern enemies *within* the land; cf. Braulik 1988, 230.

[18] Braulik 1988, 221f.

[19] Braulik 1988, 225f.

This leaves for our examination Deut 12,10; 25,17-19; Josh 23,1 (cf. 21,44); 2Sam 7,1.11;[20] 1Kgs 5,3-5 [MT 5,17-19]; as well as מנוחה in Deut 12,9 and 1Kgs 8,56. For Roth, the distinguishing mark for all of these usages is that of "rest *for*." In these passages,

...a periodization of Israel's history is presupposed and the notion that the (for a time only partial) possession of the land, the establishment of David's dynasty and the erection of the temple can happen only on the basis of divine initiative. The LORD grants rest from time to time so as to give to Israel the opportunity to respond -- it is "rest *for*."[21]

The passages we have excluded deserve the glance we have given them since they reinforce the importance of the rest motif and are clearly related to those we will be examining. My intention is not to create a false impression by artificially isolating one group; rather, the distinctive characters of the three groups (i.e., the two aforementioned and the following) are, I think, fairly apparent and the aforementioned passages do not dilute the features we will be stressing below.

2.2.2. *Deut 12,9f. and related passages*

2.2.2.1. *Deut 12,9f.*

We begin with Deut 12, not only because it is first in the list but also because it would appear to be of programmatic significance,[22] a fact which will become apparent as we move on to 2Sam 7, etc.

The use of מנוחה in v. 9 is parallel to the idea of the "inheritance" and is thus rightly understood as a local conception which refers to Palestine. The connection with the centralization of the cult, i.e. the temple, cannot be missed.[23] It is when the Israelites receive the resting place and are given

---

[20] Cf. Veijola, 71-74, who judges 2Sam 7,1.11 to be secondary in that context; also Preuß, 301.

[21] Roth, 14.

[22] So von Rad 1966a, 92; also, 1966b, 96. For an exegetical demonstration of Deut 12,9f.'s programmatic role, see especially Braulik 1988, 221, 228, and elsewhere in the same article. Braulik differs in several particulars from von Rad with respect to evaluation of the redaction, and this affects the manner in which the text is understood to be programmatic.

[23] Stressing this relationship, though not identifying the מנוחה as the temple, are e.g. Roth, 10f; Carlson, 97f; Mayes, 226; McCarter, 204. On the other hand, Braulik's attempt to argue that מנוחה in 12,9 refers directly to the temple fails (1988, 220ff.). The two nouns, "resting place" and "inheritance" are objects of the same verb (בוא), and the verb נתן simply accentuates a dimension of the *Heilsgut* assumed in the use of נוח (Hi/1): it is a gracious gift of YHWH, sovereignly bestowed. The use of these two nouns demanded some such verb (cf. 1Chr 22,9). It is questionable that 1Kgs 8,56 refers directly to the temple either, and is in any case textually far removed from Deut 12,9. Even if Deut 12,9f. evidence more than one editorial hand, the verb in v. 10 is bound to control our

rest round about from their enemies that they will bring their sacrifices to the place God will choose as a dwelling for his name.

Closely connected with the land, the "rest" is thus "an altogether tangible peace";[24]

> Da ist es das ganz konkret zu nehmende glückliche Leben im 'guten Lande', eine Verheißungsgabe an das jetzt noch von Feinden geplagte, müde gewanderte Volk...Gottes 'Name' selbst wird inmitten seines auserwählten Volkes im Heiligtum wohnen, sein Volk aber wird in Freude vor ihm leben.[25]

The element of covenant faithfulness is to be found here as well, as Israel is exhorted to take her offerings only to that place which YHWH chooses and to banish foreign practices from the land.[26] The gift of the מנוחה itself is not explicitly made conditional here, but the larger context of Deuteronomy suggests it is (28,65), and it is appropriate to stress that if the gift is very "earthy" yet it transcends the merely natural and profane;[27] it is no less a "spiritual" notion (having to do with the relationship of God and humanity) for being "concrete."[28] A semantic dichotomy which pits "material" against "spiritual" is not a particularly helpful one. Insofar as the land and life in the land are described in terms of the rest motif, the recipient's attention is being directed to YHWH as the giver of rest, the one who grants and safeguards the land and life in it. The element of responsibility, where this enters in, only makes explicit what is elsewhere implicit, and emphasizes this further and along specific lines.

We have just noted the close nexus of the מנוחה and the temple in this passage, and it is this distinctive juxtaposition of ideas which leads us directly to the related contexts of 2Sam 7; 1Kgs 5; and 1Kgs 8, the last of these rounding out the account of the temple. Josh 23,1 and Deut 25,19 which Roth groups with these, are less obviously related; Roth sees the connection in the general idea of "rest *for*." But the temple would seem to

---

understanding of the noun in v. 9. Hofius, 37-39, also comes too close to identifying the מנוחה and the temple in 12,9, though he admits that the identification is not explicit as in Ps 132.

[24] Von Rad 1966b, 95; von Rad also warns against spiritualizing any of this. About the land itself in Deuteronomy, he asserts that it is "undeniably the most important factor in the state of redemption to which Israel has been brought, and on this basis the nation is to expect an additional gift from Yahweh -- 'rest from all enemies round about.'" For further on the land in this connection, see von Rad 1966a, 79ff.; Kaiser, 1973, 141f.; 1985, 158ff. Note the almost paradisiacal descriptions of the land in Deut 11,10-12.

[25] Braulik 1968, 75.

[26] Cf. Braulik 1968, 75f. Stolz 1976a, 45f., sees in this use of the rest motif "ein umfassendes Heilsverhältnis zwischen Gott und Mensch." Cf. also von Rad 1966b, 96f.

[27] Correctly, Braulik 1968, 76.

[28] Cf. von Rad 1966b, 95, where he states that "we must not spiritualise any of this." Yet his point is well taken; this certainly should not be etherealized.

be too prominent in Deut 12; 2Sam 7; 1Kgs 5; and 1Kgs 8 to merit such a generalized categorization.

Yet it is appropriate to issue a caveat. Despite the seemingly careful use of this formula by the biblical authors, they were apparently not concerned with a completely systematized presentation. The נוח formula, as such, expresses the gracious and sovereign provision of YHWH for his people: peaceful dwelling in the land, freedom from military engagement, freedom *for* covenant obedience, i.e., for full life. That this is a period of inactivity is excluded in every case; in one case (Deut 25) it even means freedom from military engagement *for the purpose of military engagement*! Clearly some of the usages are intended to be taken together, but none of them is necessarily exclusive.

2.2.2.2. 2Sam 7

These remarks will be borne out further as we return to our discussion of the Dtr passages. Turning to 2Sam 7,1ff.[29] we are immediately struck not only by the clear connection with Deut 12, but also by the formal similarities with Josh 23. In both 2Sam 7 and Josh 23 the account begins by looking back over a considerable stretch of time, notes that YHWH had given rest, and records (as a result) the leader making an announcement. Yet in 2Sam 7 the notion of the centralization of the cult comes to the fore as the place which YHWH will choose where his Name will dwell.[30]

D. McCarthy has subjected 2Sam 7 to an examination based on the thesis that it, along with Josh 1,11-15; Josh 12; Josh 23; Judg 2,11-23; 1Sam 12; and 2Kgs 17,7-23, "sets in relief a carefully worked out over-all structure in the deuteronomic history as a whole."[31] As evidence for this he notes firstly that David is referred to as "my servant David" (v. 5);

...the only other occurrence of this precise phrase, "my servant N.," in the whole of the deuteronomic work is "my servant Moses" in the words of Yahweh to Joshua when he takes over the leadership of Israel. Not even Joshua himself merits the title; besides Moses only David does. This calls attention to David's importance -- he merits comparison with

---

[29] Deut 25; Josh 21; and Josh 23 will be passed over until after 1Kgs 8.
[30] Cf. Deut 12,5.11.14; 2Sam 7,13.
[31] McCarthy, 131. Hertzberg, 284, comments in connection with the rest saying of 2Sam 7,1 that "Chapter 7 is the climax of the whole Davidic tradition." For further on the place of 2Sam 7 in the Dtr history, as well as the literary history of this chapter, cf. McCarter, 217-231, and Anderson 1989, 112ff. Carlson, 97-106, argues that "compositional patterns derived from the cultus have inspired the incorporation of 2 Sam. 7 into this context, and influenced the structure and form of the unit" (106); cf. Kraus 1989, 476ff.

Moses -- and the important new thing, the institution of the Davidic monarchy, which begins with him.[32]

Alongside this connection with the foregoing Dtr history is another: the rest motif serves as a link between 2Sam 7 and the preceding literature by binding the ancient hopes of rest in the land to David and his dynasty, further by echoing the manner in which Deut 31,1-6 (Joshua's commissioning) links the people's destiny with their leader, and finally by presenting David and his line "as the true successors of the judges who will bring on the lasting rest from Israel's enemies which the earlier leaders were unable to achieve."[33] In terms of what follows, 2Sam 7 is related structurally to 1Kgs 8 -- where Solomon's reign comes to a climax[34] --, and 2Kgs 17.

This grant of rest not only reminds us of Deut 12 and the cult center, a house for YHWH, but the context joins the notion inseparably to the Davidic dynasty, David's house (v. 11). The epoch of David's reign becomes an important realization of the rest promise,[35] even if the condition of covenant faithfulness lingers (v. 14).[36] David's offer to build YHWH a house is mildly rebuked; rather YHWH declares that he took David from his humble post of shepherding, made him ruler, gave him victory, and will now make his name great. For his oppressed people he provides a place[37] and he will give David ("you") rest from enemies (v. 11).[38] Further, YHWH proposes to build David a house and to raise up his son to reign securely, for YHWH will establish his throne forever. YHWH declares that this son will build a house for his Name.

---

[32] McCarthy, 132.

[33] McCarthy, 133; cf. McCarter, 217-220; Carlson, 100f.

[34] McCarthy, 134: "...the account of Solomon's reign is so structured as to come to a climax in I Kings 8, that is, in the completion of the temple, at once the fulfilment and the guarantee of the promise."

[35] The rest under Joshua is ignored to say the least (vv. 10f.). This can be contrasted with 1Kgs 5,3f. [MT 5,17f.], where it is at least noted that YHWH put David's enemies under his feet. Yet even 2Sam 7 points us ahead: v. 11.

[36] Cf. Anderson 1989, 121.

[37] The "place" of v. 10 has been identified with the temple; for literature and discussion see McCarter, 202f. Yet it is probably better taken as a reference to the land, as in Murray, 298-320; cf. also Anderson 1989, 121.

[38] The suggested emendation of v. 11 (McCarter, 191, 193) so that it refers to Israel (vs. David) is without textual evidence (Anderson 1989, 112 n. 11b) and is unnecessary, "remembering the king's role as a 'corporate personality'" (Carlson, 108). Braulik 1988, 224f., probably over-stresses the restriction of the promise to David here (and to Solomon in 1Kgs 5 and 8) and thus too sharply distinguishes 2Sam 7; 1Kgs 5; 8; and Deut 12 from the other passages. We will see below that Josh 21-23 may also hint at a connection with the ideas of centralization and the kingship.

V. 11 should probably be taken as a promise referring to the future.[39] Thus, immediately after the declaration of David's rest in v. 1, the text points us yet again to the future. R.A. Carlson refers to the "rest" of v. 1 as "temporary," and comments that this passage "deprives David of his commission to build the temple, charging him instead with the completion of the 'Wars of Yahweh'. This mighty enterprise is sufficient to hinder him, once and for all, from building a temple, cf. 1 Kings 5:17."[40] Thus he manages to harmonize 2Sam 7,1.11 and 1Kgs 5,3f. [MT 5,17f.]. Support for such a harmonization, however, is meager. It may be best to let the tension stand.

2.2.2.3. 1Kgs 5

1Kgs 5,4 [MT 5,18] includes the rest formula in Solomon's letter to Hiram, king of Tyre. Here it is said that David was unable to build the temple because he was busy with warfare, "until YHWH put them under his feet." Now, however, YHWH has given Solomon rest on every side; there is no adversary or impending disaster.[41] Therefore Solomon intends -- in accordance with the word given to David in 2Sam 7,12-13 -- to build a temple for the Name of YHWH. With the qualification in v. 3 [MT 17b] the rest granted David (2Sam 7) is nearly ignored, and the formula is joined rather to Solomon his son; similar to that under David (and Deut 12), however, the rest formula is associated with the temple.

2.2.2.4. 1Kgs 8

We have already noted that 1Kgs 8 is structurally and conceptually related to 2Sam 7, and that Solomon's reign comes to a climax here. The Ark is brought to the temple, the cloud of YHWH's glory prohibits the priests from performing their service, Solomon declares that YHWH's promise to his father David has been fulfilled and then utters a lengthy prayer of dedication which would have clear relevance to a readership now in exile. Following this Solomon turns to bless the people before offering sacrifices (for the first time the actual event of Deut 12 is fulfilled!),[42] celebrating with the people and finally dismissing them with joy. The

---

[39] As with McCarter, 191, 204; Carlson, 107, 116f.; *contra* Hertzberg, 285; Anderson 1989, 120.
[40] Carlson, 120, cf. 119.
[41] Note the use of שלום in 1Kgs 4,24f. [MT 5,4f.]. Braulik 1988, 225, stresses that this verse has to do with threats to Solomon personally (as king) rather than national enemies.
[42] J. Gray, 214, calls this "the culmination of the desert wandering and conquest of Palestine in the *Heilsgeschichte*."

statement of rest (v. 56) -- here not a formula but instead using the noun, מנוחה -- comes at the beginning of the blessing of the people.

Clearly this statement should be linked with those discussed above. In addition to the structural relationship of 1Kgs 8 and 2Sam 7, one can observe that v. 56 is reminiscent of Josh 21,43-45; 22,4; 23,14, with their stress on the fulfilment of YHWH's promise,[43] not one of YHWH's words failing. Moreover, vv. 57ff. are reminiscent of Josh 23,2bff. with the stress on covenant fidelity.

At the same time the saying is markedly different. The נוח formula is dispensed with in favor of נתן מנוחה (he gave rest) "to his people Israel, in accordance with all that he promised." The phraseology recalls Deut 12,9: "You have not yet reached the resting place [המנוחה] and the inheritance which YHWH your God is giving [נתן] you." For this reason it is possible to understand the referent here, as there, to be, "the land"[44] or, less probably, the temple.[45]

However, without questioning the strong ties to both the land and the temple in 1Kgs 8 it may be observed that neither is drawn into connection with the מנוחה in the blessing (8,56-61). Moreover, the absence of the definite article with מנוחה sets this usage off from Deut 12,9, where both the article and the parallel idea of "inheritance" make the reference to the land unmistakable. It is true that Gen 49,15 and Num 10,33 do use the anarthrous מנוחה in reference to a locale, and in Ruth 1,9 the noun is also used without the article, possibly with the meaning of resting place. Thus the noun could refer to a locale in 1Kgs 8,56 as well. Still, in the absence of any other qualifier מנוחה in v. 56 lacks the focus which is found in Deut 12,9; Micah 2,10; Isa 28,12 ("*the* resting place"), or Isa 11,10; 66,1; Ps 95,11; Ps 132,8.14 ("*his/your/my* resting place"). It is primarily in view of these usages, all of which are within the rest tradition, that I think it less likely that מנוחה in 1Kgs 8 is a local idea and that there is a direct reference to the land or the temple.[46]

Thus, while maintaining clear ties with the land, the Davidic dynasty, and the temple, the motif is here subtly distanced from them; its relevance to a people in exile, who have lost all three of these things, is apparent. W. Roth is to some extent justified in declaring that here the מנוחה is loosed from a specific time and place. This text

> ...equates with "rest" Israel's certainty that its God is day by day, day and night accessible and sees to it that justice is done to his people among the nations, that is, his people in exile. The earlier grants of rest verbforms!) [sic] made manifest the divine initiative which

---

[43] Cf. Würthwein, 101; McCarter, 204.
[44] E.g., Darnell, 328f.; *HALAT*, 568.
[45] Cf. Braulik 1988, 223 (cf. 230).
[46] Cf. Stolz 1976a, 46 (Preuß?, 305); BDB, 630; Hofius, 171 n. 253.

ultimately established "the rest for the people of Israel" -- a situation in which, wherever it may be, the LORD is graciously turned to his people, and they wholly toward him. Israel's rest has become a relational term!⁴⁷

Suffering under the oppressive conditions of exile, yet the people in some sense possess YHWH's מנוחה so long as their hearts are fully committed and they continue in faithfulness, even as YHWH has been faithful to his promises. After this occurrence, this tradition does not occur again in the Dtr history. "Denn alle weitere Geschichte könnte und müßte ja ein Leben gehorsamer Treue zu Jahwe aus diesem Heilszustand heraus sein."⁴⁸

One important qualification to this interpretation is in order: if 1Kgs 8 evidences some aspect of realization that would have relevance to a people in exile it would nonetheless likely have remained a hope that had to do with the every day circumstances of God's people (political, social, etc.), and could not have been loosed from Israel's attachment to a her own place and temple. All of the passages we have so far surveyed have had a "relational" dimension of significance, and in 1Kgs 8 מנוחה is not *merely* a "relational term."⁴⁹

2.2.2.5. Josh 21, Josh 23, Deut 25

If we look back over the foregoing references, taking as our starting point Deut 12,9-10 and ending with 1Kgs 8,56, a line of development is perceptible.⁵⁰ The move from Deut 12 -- where נוח and מנוחה are associated with the cult center -- to 2Sam 7 -- where the rest formula maintains the identification with temple but accumulates the Davidic dynasty --, is a clear and direct one. From there the tradition advances to Solomon (1Kgs 5) -- still associated with the temple and the Davidic dynasty --almost at the expense of 2Sam 7,1. Finally it moves on to the context of 1Kgs 8,56 -- the first real fulfilment of the event envisioned in Deut 12, i.e., the actual bringing of sacrifices to the centralized place of worship --, where the

---

⁴⁷ Roth, 12; cf. also Braulik 1968, 76, where he emphasizes that, over against Deut 12, 1Kgs 8,56 has "der Zustand des Heils" in view.
⁴⁸ Braulik 1988, 223f.
⁴⁹ Würthwein, 101, remarks, "Es ist bemerkenswert, daß nach der Krise des Exils dtr Kreise zu solchen Aussagen finden. Zwar muß die Erfüllung, weil es sich um Geschichtsdeutung handelt, in die Vergangenheit verlegt werden; aber die Aussagen sind Ausdruck dtr Zukunftshoffnung."
⁵⁰ Von Rad 1966b, 99f., warns against imposing the concept of development -- in the sense that "each succeeding link in the chain supersedes and exhausts the force of its predecessor" -- on the data (including Chronicles and Ps 95). He opts instead for the metaphorical description of a "chain of witness in which both the overall plan and the particular mode of expression are governed pre-eminently by the insight of each living witness." The view taken here is consistent with this paradigm.

promised rest, now *finally* realized, seems to be launched on its way beyond the loss of land, monarchy, and temple. If Deut 12 is programmatic, then 2Sam 7 is pivotal, and 1Kgs 8 is climactic. In view of the high profile given the Davidic dynasty and the temple in this tradition we might return to Josh 21; 23; and Deut 25 to see if they also evidence a connection with these ideas.

In Josh 23,1 the rest from enemies comes "a long time afterward" and Joshua is characterized as very old (23,1; cf. 13,1). In spite of the statement concerning rest "from all their enemies all around" the same idea of 13,1 -- that there are large areas of land yet to be taken -- is present (23,4-5).[51] If one assumes that already with Deuteronomy-Judges the complex of rest and temple had been connected with the kingship,[52] and recalling the explicit contrast of David's epoch with that of the judges (2Sam 7,10f.; *includes Joshua*), one might suppose that Josh 23 serves as a midpoint on the way to David with the accent on YHWH's faithfulness to his promise (23,14f.) and Israel's responsibility to walk in faithfulness.

It is also possible that there is an indirect link with the idea of a centralized cult in the employment of both the שקפ and the נוח formulas in Joshua.[53] Thus after the use of the שקפ formula in Josh 11,23 there is the lengthy treatment of the distribution of the land (chs. 12-17), and then the account of the meeting of the people at Shiloh -- after the country had been "subdued" (18,1) -- to set up the Tent of Meeting (18,1),[54] "which *qua* the dwelling place of the Ark, represents the idea of centralization."[55] Moreover,

The Deuteronomic passage Josh. 21:43-45, with its *hēniah* [נוח] element in v. 44, precedes the description in chapter 22 (v. 4) of the 'decentralizing' erection of an altar across the Jordan. Here the 'tabernacle'...of Yahweh serves as the *bāchar* [בחר; "chosen"] thematic component which prohibits all sacrificial cults elsewhere, vv. 19ff. The settling of the

---

[51] Note that also in 2Sam 7, whatever the actual chronology involved, the narrative has no trouble moving from 7,1 on to v. 11 and the accounts of David's wars and struggles in chs. 8ff. This observation about the use of the rest formula would seem to mitigate the force of the "contradiction" between 2Sam 7,1.11 and 1Kgs 5,4 [MT 5,18] which Roth, 7, stresses.

[52] Carlson, 101, suggests that there is a probable connection between Deut 12,8, and Judg 17,6; 21,25 (cf. 18,1; 19,1) -- "in those days there was no king in Israel; every man did what was right in his own eyes" -- with the implication being that the period of the Judges was "a time of only intermittent rest, due to political and religious tensions." Cf. also McCarter, 217f.

[53] Noted by Carlson, 100; R. Braun 1976, 584 (cf. n. 9 in Braun). One may also note that the "inheritance" motif figures in both Deut 12 and Josh 11,23 (cf. Josh 14,9.13).

[54] Infra, 32f.

[55] Carlson, 100; R. Braun 1986, 224.

controversy leads to the introduction of the complete *hēniaḥ* phrase in 23:1 as an ingress to Joshua's exhortation and the renewal of the Covenant in chapters 23-24.[56]

Finally, it is arguable that Deut 25,19 is also related to the Davidic dynasty and to centralization, even if at a distance. It is interesting, to begin with, that in the account of Saul's defeat of the Amalekites (1Sam 15,2ff.), which looks back to Deut 25,17-19, the rest formula does not occur; in fact it never occurs in direct connection with the Amalekites anywhere after Deut 25. On the other hand, R.A. Carlson argues that because of its association with the promise in Deut 25,19, David's defeat of the Amalekites in 1Sam 30 (cf. 2Sam 8,12) gave the "rest" achieved under David a "deeper ideological importance" than was present with Joshua; this paved the way for the erection of a permanent "house of cedar" as a replacement for the tabernacle, "which could still be connected with the 'rest' of Joshua's day."[57] Considering the function of the passage within Deuteronomy, it appears that Deut 25,17-19 and Deut 12,9-10 are "designed to frame the Deuteronomic law corpus"; "the emphasis on the centrality of worship is balanced by the insistence to keep apart from foreign nations, especially Amalek who actively opposed Israel on its way to Canaan."[58]

It is possible, then, that the connection with the temple and with the kingship was not absent in the use of our tradition in Josh 21; Josh 23; and Deut 25.

2.2.2.6. *Deut 28*

Before leaving the Dtr corpus, we may address two additional "rest" passages, beginning with Deut 28,65. We have said that the נוח tradition is used in the Dtr history primarily in the sense of "rest from travelling" or "from warfare." It is true, however, that the broader ideas of weariness and oppression have been present in a couple of contexts. For instance, in 2Sam 7,10-11 the rest granted to the people is contrasted with the *oppression* they suffered at the hands of the wicked. Again, Deut 25,17ff. recalls how the Amalekites took advantage of the Israelites when they were *weary and worn out* in the desert.[59] It is when YHWH gives Israel rest that

---

[56] Carlson, 100-101.

[57] Carlson, 101.

[58] Roth, 11 (cf. n. 16 in Roth). Braulik 1988, 221f., also notes that the rest formula in Deut 12,9f. and Deut 25,19 serves as a "Rahmenelement des dtn Gesetzeskorpus, seiner Kult- und Sozialordung."

[59] On the motifs of weariness and rest, see esp. Brueggemann 1972, 19ff., esp. 22 (on Deut 25,19) and 30 (on Deut 28,65). Brueggemann argues that the linking of these motifs is pervasive in the OT and of theological significance for royal theology; he also points to the relevance of this to Mt 11,28-30 (37f.).

she is to blot out the Amalekites. So also in Deut 28,65 the situation of disobedient Israel will be one of weariness, anxiety, and despair in exile. Using different vocabulary but clearly intended as a reversal of fortune (to Deut 3,20; 12,9f.), it is said that the Israelites will find no "repose" (רגע [Hi; intransitive]), no "resting place" (מנוח [Nm]) for their feet.

2.2.2.7. Ex 33

Lastly, is Ex 33,14.[60] This brief statement conforms to the נוח form, but is otherwise distanced from the other occurrences. The larger context of ch. 33 deals in general with the problem of the continuing presence of God[61] with his people. Thus in 33,1, following the sin of the Golden Calf in ch. 32, YHWH commands Moses to depart from Mt. Horeb (Sinai), but announces that he will not accompany the people. They respond by a show of repentance. Vv. 7-11 suddenly shift to speak of the "Tent of Meeting," though it is not entirely clear how all of the details given are relevant to the immediate context. As M. Noth emphasizes, the Tent was a place of periodic visitations (v. 9) in contrast to the Ark which was associated with YHWH's presence in a more constant fashion (cf. Num 10,35).[62] V. 11 (cf. vv. 12-13.17ff.) emphasizes the intimacy of Moses' communion with YHWH.

Vv. 12-17[63] then contain dialogue between Moses and YHWH in which Moses speaks rather forcefully. Moses wants to know whom YHWH will send with the people, and he also wants to receive further revelation ("teach me your ways so that I may know you and find favor"). To these requests YHWH responds, "My presence[64] will go with you, and I will give you rest [נוח]." Not satisfied, Moses persists, expressing reluctance to depart without YHWH's presence, and reminding YHWH that only his

---

[60] Considered Dtr by Preuß, 301.

[61] Barr 1960, 35, calls Ex 33 "the most sophisticated and delicate discussion of the seeing of God in the OT. Practically all the presentations, if we may so call them, of the deity are here used in one passage."

[62] Noth 1962, 255f.

[63] According to Noth 1962, 256, Ex 33,12-17 is "a subsequent literary addition to ch. 32 about whose period and derivation nothing definite can now be said." On the other hand, vv. 7-11 are a "pre-Priestly, pre-deuteronomistic tradition," for which vv. 1-6 ("Deuteronomic") were composed as an introduction.

[64] Regarding the reference to YHWH's פנים (face), von Rad,1:285, expresses uncertainty; he suggests that it may have "served as the aetiology of a cultic mask," while acknowledging the alternative of reading it simply as "I" (285 n. 9; cf. 2Sam 17,11). Eichrodt, 2:38, sees this occurrence as "another *form of self-manifestation of the transcendent God*, by means of which his presence is at the same time made tolerable to men and guaranteed to them" (italics in original); he goes on to suggest that the Ark may be in mind. Noth 1962, relates it to the cult.

presence distinguishes his people from others. YHWH responds favorably to Moses' request, "because you found favor in my eyes and I know you by name." Moses still persists by requesting to see YHWH's glory, to which request YHWH again acquiesces, specifying the location, limits, and *gracious* nature of this revelation.

The promise of rest in v. 14 is ambiguous. It has been considered to be nothing more than a simple assurance,[65] while some see in it a reference to the land.[66] Isa 63,14, which may have Ex 33,14 in mind, makes the "Spirit of YHWH" the subject; there it is certainly the land which is in view. In view of Ex 33,16 it would seem that YHWH's presence is related to very concrete concerns regarding potential enemies. These considerations along with the use of the נוח formula suggest a more concrete idea, at least the assurance of safe passage and sustenance if not a direct reference to entrance into and conquest of the land.

What this passage expresses in seminal form is the connection between YHWH's *presence* and *rest*. This basic connection is portrayed on a grand scale in the rest tradition as a whole, which joins inseparably YHWH's rest and Israel's.

2.2.3. Summary

The נוח formula provided the biblical writers with a powerful statement of YHWH's continuing faithfulness, and a summary of his good gifts to them; it was also associated with Israel's faithfulness. Among the passages we considered, Deut 12,9f. was judged to possess programmatic importance, as it announces YHWH's promise of rest to his people and associates this promise with the centralization of the cult. This coupling of themes is picked up in 2Sam 7,1.11. There God gives David rest from his enemies, paving the way for David's expression of a desire to build a "house" for the Ark. YHWH promises instead to build David a "house," to give him rest from his enemies, and to raise up a son for him who will be the one to build a "house" for YHWH. This is developed further when Solomon claims to have been given rest, thus enabling him to undertake the building of the temple (1Kgs 5,4 [MT 5,18]). Finally, with the dedication of the temple in 1Kgs 8, and with the first reports of sacrifices being brought to the central place of worship, Solomon gives a prayer of thanks to YHWH for having given his people "rest" (מנוחה). Ironically, this climactic passage seems most suited to give hope to those Jews who had now lost land, temple, and dynasty. Following 1Kgs 8 the formula does

---

[65] E.g. Noth 1962, 257; Roth, 13 n. 21.
[66] E.g. Stolz 1976a, 46; Preuß, 301,302; W.C. Kaiser 1985, 157; Hofius, 36; von Rad, 1:224 n. 82, 288.

not recur in the Dtr history. Having established the importance of the temple and the kingship for the aforementioned passages we returned to Deut 25,19 and Josh 23,1 (also Josh 21,44) and found that these ideas seemed to have a part in them as well.

It should be clear from our discussion that the נוח tradition does not play a minor role in the Dtr history. It has both conceptual and structural functions within this body of literature. Structurally it forms one of the elements that mark out 2Sam 7 as a key passage for the entire history, picking up the previous promises of rest and anticipating a climactic point in 1Kgs 8. Conceptually it is not only bound up with the land, the temple, and the Davidic kingship, but it serves to express the sum of the blessings YHWH has bestowed on his people (1Kgs 8,56). Ex 33,14 highlights its fundamental connection to YHWH's presence with his people.

2.3. Chronicles -- Israel's מנוחה

2.3.1. Overview

The following passages require consideration: נוח (Hi/1)[67]: 1Chr 22,9.18; 1Chr 23,25; 2Chr 14,6.7 [MT 14,5.6]; 2Chr 15,15; 2Chr 20,30 (possibly, 2Chr 32,22); מנוחה: 1Chr 22,9; 1Chr 28,2 (cf. also נוח, 2Chr 6,41).[68] To these can be added the use of מנוח (Nm) in 1Chr 6,31 [MT 6,16]; שקט (Nm) in 1Chr 22,9; and שקט (Qal)[69] in 1Chr 4,40; 2Chr 14,1 [MT 13,23]; 2Chr 14,5.6 [MT 14,4.5]; 2Chr 20,30; 2Chr 23,21.

While the Chronicler is clearly dependent on the Dtr literature for the use of this motif, he introduces several innovations according to his own concerns. To begin with, when the events of 2Sam 7 are recorded in 1Chr 17 *both* references to rest from enemies are missing. In 1Chr 17,1 it is simply deleted, and in 17,10 it is replaced with "I will subdue all your enemies." Then, when we come to Solomon, we find our motif being applied to him in ways which go beyond the Dtr account. Again, we find the motif being applied to kings *after* Solomon, something which has no parallel in the Dtr corpus. Moreover, the נוח formula is juxtaposed with the שקט formula familiar from Joshua and Judges in a couple of these contexts. Lastly, the notion of *YHWH's* (or the Ark's) rest finds its way into the Chronicler's use of the מנוחה/נוח terminology.

---

[67] As with נוח in the Dtr history, this form (Hi/1) of נוח occurs only in this formula throughout the Chronicler's work. On the reading of 2Chr 32,22, cf. *HALAT*, 642; BDB, 628.

[68] Regarding 1Chr 2,52 and 8,2, see Preuß, 304.

[69] Cf. also 2Chr 23,21 (2Kgs 11,20) and 1Chr 4,40 (Judg 18,7.27; also Jer 30,10; 46,27).

2.3.2. David and Solomon

We begin with the use of the motif in the accounts of David and Solomon. The deletion of the נוח formula from 1Chr 17 is in accord with its absence from the alleged earlier layer of 2Sam 7.[70] Yet it is also in accord with larger redactional interests which become evident in the Chronicler's work.

There are in fact two passages (1Chr 22,18; 23,25) where the נוח formula is applied to David's reign, and one passage (1Chr 6,31 [MT 6,16]: מנוחה) which speaks of the Ark coming to rest during David's reign. Moreover, in 1Chr 28,2 David speaks of his desire to build a house of מנוחה for the Ark of the Covenant and as a footstool for God, a desire which was to be denied him by God. However, both 1Chr 22,18 and 23,25 have been judged to be secondary additions to the text.[71] Whether this is correct or not their presence does not necessarily contradict the assignment of rest to Solomon, nor do they lessen the emphasis the Chronicler places on Solomon's rest.

If we examine how the motif is used in connection with Solomon, it becomes clear that not only is its association with Solomon magnified relative to the Dtr history, but it is closely bound up with the erection of the temple during his reign.[72] Thus in 1Chr 22,7ff., based on 1Kgs 5,3-4 [MT 5,17-18] (otherwise omitted from its parallel in 2Chr 2), David explains to Solomon that he was unable to build the temple because YHWH disqualified him on the basis of his blood stained reign (1Chr 22,8).[73] Clearly in reference to 2Sam 7 the account of 1Chr 22 goes on to say that YHWH had spoken to David of his son, Solomon, who will be a man of מנוחה (in contrast to David, 1Chr 28,3, who is a "man of wars"),[74] to whom YHWH will give rest (נוח [Hi/1]) from his enemies on every side. His son's name will be Solomon[75] and YHWH will give (נתן, cf. 1Kgs 8,56; Deut

---

[70] Cf. Veijola, 71-74; Preuß, 301.

[71] So Mosis, 95 n. 43, 96 n. 45.

[72] Cf. R. Braun 1976, 581-590, on the Chronicler's special interest in Solomon.

[73] The idea in 1Kgs 5 is actually closer to the notion that David was simply preoccupied with warfare and thus unable to engage in such a building program. According to Noth 1987, 171 n. 13, for the Chronicler the blood which David spilled violated his cultic purity, thus leading to his rejection as temple builder.

[74] Solomon is a "man of rest" because YHWH gives Israel rest during his reign (Preuß, 305). The concern of the Chronicler is not with the moral or cultic merits of Solomon; see below. Von Rad 1966b, 97f., interprets the phrase, "man of מנוחה" in 1Chr 22,9, also in reference to *YHWH's rest* in the temple. In view of the manner in which these two ideas -- YHWH's provision of rest and his own rest -- coalesce in Chronicles it may not be possible to sharply separate them.

[75] Cf. 2Sam 12,24-25. It appears that in 1Chr 22 Solomon's name is being connected with the word שלום. Solomon's name was not mentioned in Nathan's oracle, either in

12,9) to Israel שלום and שקט during his days. Solomon is to be the one who will build a house for YHWH's name. He will be YHWH's son, and YHWH his father, and YHWH will establish his throne over Israel forever. David then goes on to express his desire that YHWH might give Solomon discretion and understanding, and to charge Solomon with his need of covenant fidelity so that YHWH might give him success.[76]

By way of clarification, R. Mosis argues that the use of the rest motif in relation to Solomon is part of a larger effort by the Chronicler to portray *epochs* in Israel's history, more than it is a concern with the personal merits and demerits of Solomon vis-à-vis David.[77] David's epoch -- during which the Ark dwells in a tent and YHWH's presence with his people is accordingly "vorläufige" (tentative) -- is a period of wars, while Solomon's epoch -- during which the temple is built and YHWH comes to his final resting place with his people -- is a period of rest. "Rest round about" is thus neither a "political assumption" for the erection of the temple nor its result, nor a virtue or achievement of Solomon, but rather a *Heilsgut*, which, together with the temple is bestowed along with the final and complete presence of YHWH with Israel.[78] Once again, we see displayed on a large scale the basic connection encapsulated in Ex 33,14 between God's presence and "rest".

2.3.3. Kings after Solomon

As already noted, another of the innovations in the use of the rest tradition on the part of the Chronicler is in the ascription of rest to kings following Solomon (Asa -- 2Chr 14,1 [MT 13,23]; 14,5ff. [MT 14,4ff.]; 15,15; Jehoshaphat -- 2Chr 20,30; cf. also 2Chr 32,22). One difference between these kings and Solomon, is that the later episodes are circumscribed temporally; only Solomon's reign as a whole is characterized as one of rest.[79] It may also be observed that in both 2Chr 13-14 (cf. 2Chr 15,15) and 20,30 the נוח formula is used in conjunction with the שקט formula encountered in Joshua and Judges.[80] Doubtless we are to see here an approach influenced by the Chronicler's concern with

---

2Sam 7 or 1Chr 17, but it is inserted here and explained in terms of the rest motif and in connection with the temple; cf. R. Braun 1976, 585f.

[76] Dillard 1987, 4, suggests a further function of the rest motif in relation to Solomon: it contributes to the parallels drawn between Solomon and Joshua as the successors who took the people into the rest.

[77] Mosis, 94-101.

[78] Mosis, 101.

[79] Cf. Mosis, 100.

[80] Cf. 2Chr 14,1 [MT 13,23]; 14,5f. [MT 14,4f.]; 20,30; supra, 21f.

"immediate retribution."⁸¹ It is beyond the scope of this study to map out this theological approach in the Chronicler's work, but it can be noted that the שקט formula functions within a somewhat similar framework in the book of Judges.⁸² The fact that שקט formula is now being joined with the נוח formula in passages shaped by the Chronicler according to his theology of "immediate retribution" is probably deliberate.⁸³ Thus we see once again the way in which the נוח formula can be used in a variety of ways by different or even the same author/s. In this case, the relationship of the rest motif to covenant fidelity and "seeking YHWH"⁸⁴ comes into sharp focus. It can also be noted once again how distant inactivity is from the idea of rest as used in these passages (esp. 2Chr 13-14). "Rest" is rather a time for productivity and constructive activity.

Yet just as rest came as a "gift" from YHWH to Solomon, so also with the subsequent kings in the successful military campaigns of 2Chr 10-36. As P. Welten observes, in each case a miraculous element is prominent. Though Judah possesses a formidable force it is scarcely needed for the actual war; it is YHWH who steps in to deliver her.⁸⁵ The result for Judah is that her victories remove the enemy threat quite literally "round about" ("nach allen vier Himmelsrichtungen"), an observation which sheds further light on the application of the formula to kings following Solomon.

Damit sind in umfassendem Sinn die möglichen Bedrohungen von Juda zur Zeit des Chronisten erfaßt. Ergebnis dieser Kriegszüge ist, daß, durch Gott gewirkt, der König erstarkt..., daß sich Ruhe ausbreitet..., daß also für den König und damit für Juda Ruhe

---

⁸¹ Cf. Dillard 1984; further, 1980; 1987, 76-81; also R. Braun 1986, xxxvii-xxxix; Noth 1987, 98f. Braun comments that "retribution is the major, if not the sole, yardstick used in writing the history of the post-Solomonic kings" (1986, xxxvii). Similarly, Dillard 1987, 79f., mentions that this theological perspective "is concentrated mainly in [the Chronicler's] account of the divided kingdoms...; it is less prominent in the record of the united kingdoms, largely due to the author's idealizing of that period..."

⁸² Note in Judges the cycles of disobedience-judgment, repentance-mercy; cf. Welten, 49f., 15ff., 97, 201f.

⁸³ R. Braun 1986, xxxix, observes that the idea of "prosperity" is "found in 2 Chronicles without parallel in the writer's *Vorlage* for each of the kings to whom he is most favorably disposed (Solomon, 2 Chr 7:11; Asa, 14:5; Jehoshaphat, 2 Chr 20:20; Uzziah, 2 Chr 26:5; and Hezekiah, 2 Chr 31:21; 32:30). Such a selection can hardly be accidental." If we accept his suggestion that נוח should be read in 2Chr 32,22 (1986, 225; also Dillard 1987, 254), then in three of these four post-Solomonic kings there is also the occurrence of the נוח formula. In relation to Hezekiah, it is possible that the occurrence of the נוח formula further establishes the parallel drawn between him and David and Solomon (Dillard 1987, 254). One may wonder if the prominence of the temple *throughout* 1-2 Chronicles paved the way for the application of the נוח formula to later kings.

⁸⁴ Cf. 2Chr 14,2-7 [MT 14,1-6]; 15,15; 20,4.30; 31,21; 32,22; and Welten, 50.

⁸⁵ Cf. 2Chr 13,15; 14,12 [MT 14,11]; 20,22; 26,7; and Welten, 201f.

eintritt. In der Summe der vier Kriegszüge heißt das, daß Juda ringsum diese Ruhe geschenkt bekommt.[86]

2.3.4. Summary

What is important for us is to see is not only how the rest tradition is bound up with the Davidic dynasty and temple traditions, but how it is a very important component in the Chronicler's theologically motivated reworking of the Dtr history.

The shift of emphasis toward Solomon, *the chosen temple builder*, is evident both from the absence of the formula in 1Chr 17 (par. 2Sam 7) and its amplification in 1Chr 22; this is not, however, to completely marginalize the references to David's rest. The formula is applied to subsequent Davidides (no others), but in a qualified manner with respect to the idea of "immediate retribution," and apparently with a view to portraying the idea of rest *round about*.

2.4. Chronicles and Ps 132 -- YHWH's מנוחה

2.4.1. Overview

The idea of YHWH's rest among his people occurs in 1Chr 28,2 (מנוחה) and 2Chr 6,41 (נוח).[87] Terminologically the notion of the temple as YHWH's resting place is an addition of the Chronicler to the Dtr presentation, but there is some precedent for it.

We have already seen how the promise of rest is bound up with the temple in the Dtr history. Already in Num 10,33ff. the ideas of a resting place (מנוחה) for the travelling people and the coming-to-rest of the Ark of the Covenant (נוח [Qal]) are closely related.[88] Moreover, Ps 132, which Solomon quotes in 2Chr 6,41, may well be earlier than Josiah's reign;[89] it is generally agreed that this psalm has the events of 2Sam 6-7 in view. Within Chronicles the two ideas are closely related in 1Chr 23,25.

It seems clear in Num 10 and 2Sam 7 that the notion of the temple as YHWH's resting place does not envisage a coming to rest following *vertical*

---

[86] Welten, 201.

[87] Cf. the use of מנוח in 1Chr 6,31 [MT 6,16], in reference to the Ark; the Ark is also in view in 1Chr 28,2 and 2Chr 6,41

[88] Cf. Carlson, 102; Carlson (103) relates Num 10,35f. to the events of 2Sam 6, and sees this chapter as a prelude to the נוח formula of 2Sam 7,1 and David's desire to build a temple.

[89] L.C. Allen 1983, 208; cf. Dahood 1970, 241f. Regarding the relationship of Ps 132,8 to Num 10,33ff., Allen (202) suggests that there "the ark set out explicitly in order to seek a [מנוחה] for the Israelites: as there, setting out and resting may be associated here [Ps 132]."

movement -- such as the Spirit resting (נוח [Qal]) on the elders (Num 11,25f.) or on Elisha (2Kgs 2,15) -- so much as a coming to rest following *horizontal* movement. YHWH has been travelling with his people; he gives rest to them and then finds his resting place in their midst, thus establishing and confirming his presence among them and placing a seal on their presence in the land.

2.4.2. Ps 132

Ps 132, a Psalm of Ascent, is generally associated with 2Sam 6-7, possibly as a liturgical re-enactment of those events.[90] Thus David's desire in the psalm to find a "place" for YHWH (v. 5) recalls 2Sam 6,17, where they set the Ark in its "place" in the tent David had pitched for it in Jerusalem. The echo of Num 10,33ff. in the psalm (v. 8)[91] is also contained in 2Sam 6.[92] Vv. 11-12 remind us of YHWH's promise to David in 2Sam 7 (cf. Ps 89).

The uses of מנוחה in vv. 8 and 14 both seem to have in view first of all the end of the Ark's "travels," a conclusion further evidenced by the echo of Num 10 and the association with 2Sam 6-7. Whether or not we should translate מנוחה as "throne" in v. 14, the מנוחה and YHWH's enthronement are closely related there.[93]

Moreover, within the psalm David's throne and that of YHWH are connected. V. 10 expresses the desire that YHWH not reject his anointed one and vv. 11f. reiterate the promise of YHWH spoken to David (2Sam 7; Ps 89); if David's sons are faithful to the covenant and obey the statutes which YHWH teaches them, David's dynasty will remain secure. The basis for this is in vv. 13ff.: YHWH has chosen Zion as his dwelling. There YHWH's throne is established, and it is his מנוחה forever; YHWH himself

---

[90] Kraus 1989, 472ff., gives a lengthy discussion of Ps 132's form and setting. See also L.C. Allen 1983, 199ff.

[91] Kraus 1989, 480f., comments, "The cultic call in v. 8 probably represents not only a reflective allusion to the ark saying in Num. 10:35f., but the incorporation of the old war call into the cultic ceremonial."

[92] Carlson, 103, states, "2 Sam. 6:2 is seen through the association verse 1 Sam. 4:4, as corresponding to Num. 10:36, the words spoken when the Ark was exhorted to return to its place of 'rest'...Thus the idea of 'rest' in 7:1b is once more seen to be connected with the Ark."

[93] On the translation of מנוחה as "throne," cf. M. Metzger, 157; Cross, 94; cited favorably by Kraus 1989, 482. Dahood suggests that the use of "resting place" in Ps 132,8 is meant to imply that this is a "temporary dwelling, until the temple is built" (Dahood 1970, 245). This does not follow, however, from the use of the term מנוחה and v. 14 tells against it; cf. Kraus 1989, 481.

will care for the poor, clothe the priests with salvation, bring joy to the saints, and establish David's throne securely.⁹⁴

2.4.3. 2Chr 6

Solomon's citation of Ps 132,1.8-10⁹⁵ at the end of his long temple dedication prayer in 2Chr 6 serves to mark the fulfilment of David's desire expressed in 1Chr 28,2; from 1Chr 28,2 the reference is clearly back to 1Chr 22,6ff. In both 1Chr 22 and 28 David speaks of his disqualification as the temple builder on the grounds that he has spilled much blood and is a "man of wars." Solomon, a man of מנוחה, David's son and YHWH's chosen one, will be the one to build the temple. This joining of the erection of YHWH's house of מנוחה to the epoch during which YHWH grants שלום and שקט to his people may suggest that YHWH's "rest" entails not only his permanent residence among the people, but also the *effect* of his presence. This suggestion is made more probable by the consideration that 2Chr 6,41 seems to replace 1Kgs 8,56 in the Chronicler's source (note also 2Chr 6,41b).⁹⁶ It may also be, as G. Braulik comments regarding Ps 132, that, "der (schon 2 Sm 6 und 7 vorausgesetzte) Gedanke an den untragbaren Zustand der Wanderschaft der Bundeslade wurde hier theologisch transparent für eine endzeitliche Erwartung. Jahwe bestimmt für immer den Sion zu seiner Ruhestatt. Dies enthält aber zugleich die Zusicherung des Segens, der dem ganzen Volk gilt."⁹⁷

2.4.4. Summary

The statements about YHWH's rest and the designation of the temple itself as his מנוחה are additions of the Chronicler to his Dtr sources, but the idea itself had antecedents. From the start YHWH's rest is closely connected to with Israel's. YHWH gives his people rest and then himself (i.e., the Ark) comes to rest in their midst. There is a very close connection between YHWH's מנוחה in the temple and his throne, and indeed the two might be equated. Although YHWH's rest does not precede the

---

⁹⁴ Cf. Kraus 1989, 482.

⁹⁵ Ackroyd, 113, suggests that in view of the disagreements between 2Chr 6,41f. and Ps 132, "it is better to suppose that the Chronicler here makes use of a text which has not otherwise survived than to suppose that he has gathered odd fragments together." This is a possible, but not a necessary conclusion; see Meyers, 38; and Dillard 1987, 51. L.C. Allen 1983, 203, follows W. Rudolph 1955, 215, in suggesting that the substitution of נוח for מנוחה in 2Chr 6,41 is due to the influence of Num 10,36.

⁹⁶ Cf. Mosis, 100. 2Chr 6,41 is referred to by von Rad 1966b, 98, as a "stabilization of the nation's relationship to God" (cf. 1Chr 23,25).

⁹⁷ Braulik 1968, 77.

giving of rest to Israel (it is the other way round), it is the case that his coming to rest lends security to David's throne, and seems to radiate "rest" (שלום, care for the poor, etc.) to the nation. There may even be a hint of an eschatological hope.⁹⁸

2.5. Ps 95 -- "My מנוחה"⁹⁹

Ps 95, whose importance for our discussion owes as much to its use by the book of Hebrews as to its unique formulation of the rest tradition, deserves careful consideration here.¹⁰⁰ Structurally it divides in two, vv. 1-7a, and vv. 7b-11. The first half of Ps 95 issues a repeated invitation (vv. 1.2 and 6) to come before YHWH. V. 2 stresses the idea of YHWH's presence (his "face"), which is what was called into question in the events of Massah/Meribah recalled in v. 8.¹⁰¹ YHWH is characterized here as both creator (vv. 4-6) and Israel's Shepherd (v. 7a). Along with Pss 50 and 81 it has been associated with the autumn festival of Booths; ancient Jewish tradition associates this psalm with the Sabbath.¹⁰²

The word מנוחה is contained in the oath of v. 11: "they shall not enter my מנוחה." If we mentally review the passages we have already considered it will become apparent that Ps 95's use of the rest tradition is "expressed most unusually."¹⁰³ The clause (they shall not enter [the] מנוחה) is most reminiscent of Deut 12,9f.,¹⁰⁴ i.e. the land as Israel's resting place. The phrase (my מנוחה), however, is most reminiscent of Ps 132,14 where it

---

⁹⁸ Cf. Sir 36,18 [15]; Jdt 9,8; *SifreDeut* § 1; GenR 56,2.

⁹⁹ Pss 23 (מנוחה, v. 2) and 116 (מנוח, v. 7) will not receive separate treatment here; they do not appear to belong within the rest tradition (*contra* Darnell, 335ff.; W.C. Kaiser 1985, 158).

¹⁰⁰ G.H. Davies, 183-187, gives an excellent, if concise, survey of interpretation of Ps 95 up to the time of his article (1973); also Hofius, 33ff.; more recently, Tate, 496ff. The dating of the psalm is predictably debated. Early Greek period: Briggs-Briggs, 2:293. Exilic or early post-exilic: Tate and Gunkel. Late pre-exilic: Jörg Jeremias, 18f. Pre-monarchical: A.R. Johnson, 18f. Dahood 1968, 353, comments simply that "from the text itself there are few clues as to the date of its composition." It seems to make little difference in interpretation if we accept a late pre-exilic or early post-exilic date.

¹⁰¹ Cf. esp. Ex 17,1-7 and Num 20,1-13; also Deut 6,16; 9,22; 33,8; Ps 81,7 [MT 81,8]. G.H. Davies, 194, comments, "The oracular warning is saying not only, 'Do not be rebellious as your fathers were about the waters of Meribah', but it is also saying 'Do not question the presence of God here today, as your fathers questioned it at Massah'." Cf. also Tate, 502.

¹⁰² Cf. Oesterley 1959, 420; Weinfeld, 511.

¹⁰³ Jörg Jeremias, 112.

¹⁰⁴ Compare אם־ יבאון אל־ מנוחתי (Ps 95,11) with אל־ המנוה עתה עד־ באתם לא (Deut 12,9). For the oath see Num 20,12; alternatively, 14,21-23.30.

refers to the temple, YHWH's resting place.[105] This ambiguity, which is amplified by the abrupt ending of the psalm, has led to a range of interpretations.[106]

In the present investigation special notice is due O. Hofius' interpretation because of its impact on his understanding of Heb 3-4. Taking a hint from the ambiguity of v. 11, Hofius proposes that the psalm envisages a *typological* application of the oath to the worshippers using Ps 95. In other words, just as God barred the "fathers" from entrance into the *land* (= מנוחה), so now the worshippers will be barred from entering the *temple* (= God's מנוחה) unless they listen to God's voice.[107] Hofius is almost certainly justified to insist on a local understanding of מנוחה here,[108] but his further point that the noun refers directly to the temple is less convincing. There are two primary arguments which Hofius uses to establish this, but both of them are of questionable worth.

First, Hofius cites lexical evidence to the effect that the noun מנוחה is used in three distinct ways in the OT: with respect to the land; with respect to the temple; and with respect to both the land and the temple.[109] Hofius then argues that Ps 95 belongs in the third category as a special usage, and thus that the noun can refer to both the land and the temple in the typological fashion just mentioned. These three categories of usage are, however, somewhat artificially distinguished in Hofius' presentation. It is artificial, firstly, to consider the noun apart from the verb נוח in the tradition. Moreover, in view of our survey of the Dtr history, Chronicles and Ps 132 it is apparent that both the land and the temple are in view in *all* of the usages we considered, not just a few special ones. On the other hand, there is no one usage (including Deut 12,10) where the noun מנוחה refers simultaneously to the land *qua* Israel's resting place and the temple building *qua* YHWH's resting place. In other words, while rest in the land and the temple are fundamentally related throughout the tradition, there is no established use of the noun with such a dual referent (land and temple building). This does not mean that Ps 95 cannot be exceptional -- I think it is -- but it would be just that and not part of an established, special usage.

---

[105] Cf. also Isa 66,1. The phrase "your rest" occurs in Ps 132,8 and 2Chr 6,41 in reference to YHWH's rest in the temple. "Your rest (מנוח)" also occurs in Ps 116,7 in reference to one's own soul. The phrase, "his מנוחה" occurs in Isa 11,10 (cf. Zech 9,1), in reference to the "Root of Jesse."

[106] E.g., Preuß, 304, rejects the idea that this is "JHWHs Ruhe" and prefers to read here merely the "Wohnen im Land." Stolz 1976a, 45, groups this text with Deut 12,9, and sees in both "ein umfassendes Heilsverhältnis zwischen Gott und Mensch beinhaltet." Further examples in G.H. Davies, and below.

[107] Hofius, 40-41. "Der Einzug der Väter in das Land Kanaan ist Typos des Einzuges der gottesdienstlichen Gemeinde in das Heiligtum auf dem Zion" (Hofius, 40).

[108] Hofius, 35-41.

[109] Hofius, 37-40. The third usage is found in Deut 12,9ff.; 1Chr 23,25; and 2Chr 6,41.

Second, Hofius is heavily dependent on theories of a liturgical use of Ps 95 in temple worship.[110] Thus it is that as the worshippers are singing the psalm they are approaching the door of the temple. At the door they are stopped, however, and given the warning of Ps 95,7b-11. In this light the possible typological application is plausible; the worshippers will be denied actual entrance into the temple, YHWH's (my) מנוחה, just as the "fathers" were denied access into the land. The verbal echo of Ps 132 is reinforced by the actual events of the liturgy.

In response, it is not possible to sort out here whether or not Ps 95 would ever have been used in a liturgy, and, if so, whether it would have been used in just this way. Suffice it to say that not all are convinced.[111] Yet even among those who subscribe to a liturgical setting for the psalm, few adopt such a "typological" interpretation which refers directly to the temple.[112] For instance, A. Weiser understands מנוחה simply as "peace."[113] H.-J. Kraus identifies the מנוחה firstly as the land, but then also as "a salvific blessing that is not material but personal, and that has its root and center in God himself."[114] In any event, it is very difficult to see what relevance this liturgical setting would have for the interpretation of Heb 3-4 unless we have evidence that Ps 95 was being used this way in the first century A.D. Yet here the remarks of E. Gerstenberger are apropos:

All in all, we have to read the Psalter as a whole in light of Jewish community organization in Persian and Hellenistic times to understand its significance at this latest stage of liturgical use. The psalms, then, were read and prayed in local assemblies and, at least primarily, not in the temple community of Jerusalem. Zion for the most part seems far away... Worship without traditional sacrifice is all-important and must be defended against those who doubt its justification... In short, at this latest stage the Psalter is not exactly a hymnbook of the second temple but more precisely a hymnbook of the many synagogal communities that lived with their hearts turned toward the Holy City but ritually independent of her.[115]

---

[110] Cf., e.g., Gunkel, 417; Weiser, 625; Dahood 1968, 353; A.R. Johnson, 18; Kraus 1986, 91, 76f., 84ff.; 1989, 245f.; Jörg Jeremias, 108f.; see further G.H. Davies, 181-187, 188ff.

[111] Tate, 498, is somewhat sceptical of the "rather colorful descriptions of the worship event reflected" in this psalm; "we are on safer ground to work on the basis that liturgical occasions provided the compositional shape of the psalm rather than to assume that it is part of an actual liturgy and recited while the liturgical actions were happening."

[112] For support Hofius cites only Herkenne, 317. G.H. Davies, 195, also follows a typological logic, but instead of entrance into the temple the worshippers are denied "the favor of the blessing of God revealed in some cultic act of revelation or epiphany, such as the carrying forth or unveiling of the ark."

[113] Weiser, 627.

[114] Kraus 1989, 248.

[115] Gerstenberger, 28.

The imprecise formulation of v. 11 is not going to permit of a final solution, however precise the "original" meaning might have been. Yet taking our lead from the other rest tradition passages we should probably understand this מנוחה also as a mundane and tangible good rather than "a wholly personal entering into one's God."[116] We might note as a parallel Ps 81, which has been judged to be the closest to Ps 95.[117] Here also it is said that obedience will be rewarded, and though the rest tradition is not invoked it is conceptually present. Thus, after recounting the testing at Meribah, Israel's lapse into idolatry, and God's judgment on her, YHWH declares:

Oh that my people would listen to me,
that Israel would walk in my ways!
Then I would quickly subdue their enemies,
and turn my hand against their foes.
Those who hate the LORD would cringe before him,
and their doom would last forever.
I would feed you with the finest of the wheat,
and with the honey from the rock I would satisfy you.
(Ps 81,13-16 [MT 81,14-17])

Allowing for the adjustment necessary to apply the oath of 95,11 to a people already in the land, might not the same general idea expressed in Ps 81,13-16 be present in Ps 95,7-11? Indeed, placing ourselves in the shoes of a people in exile, the notion of a *re*-entrance into the land is entirely possible. Later on, under the influence of apocalyptic, it would be applied to entrance into the world-to-come generally.[118]

Moreover, there is a better way of construing the oath of Ps 95,11 which also takes account of its similarity to both Deut 12 and Ps 132 yet without separating them in a "typological" interpretation. It is to recognize that just as the whole land shared in the holiness of YHWH by virtue of his presence in the temple,[119] and just as the land could be called both Israel's and YHWH's land,[120] so there is a sense in which the land is Israel's resting place by virtue of the fact that it is YHWH's resting place;[121] conversely,

---

[116] I.e., *contra* Kraus 1989, 248; von Rad 1966b, 99.

[117] Weiser, 625, states that Ps 95 "is most closely related to Psalm 81." Likewise, Tate, 498, observes that the "compositional pattern is very similar to Ps 81."

[118] Infra, 127f.

[119] Cf. *Kel* 1,6-9. Hofius, 43, 172 n. 263, properly stresses that it is first of all the temple itself which is thought of as YHWH's resting place, though Zion and all of Israel are ultimately in view as well.

[120] Cf. von Rad 1966a, 79-93.

[121] Cf., e.g., Preuß, 306; Briggs-Briggs, 2:296; Jörg Jeremias, 112; further references in Hofius, 172 n. 266. A.R. Johnson, 21 n. 1, 68f., prefers to view the land as YHWH's resting place, or "home," and only secondarily as the resting place, or "home," of Israel.

YHWH's rest in the temple appears to mediate "rest" to the people throughout the land as we noted above in connection with Ps 132 and 2Chr 6. A fitting paradigm for understanding Ps 95,11 might then be found in Ex 15,17:[122]

> You brought them in and planted them on the mountain of your own possession, the place, O LORD, that you made your abode, the sanctuary, O LORD, that your hands have established.

Entrance into the land and into Zion telescope into a single image.[123]

In sum, it is difficult to disprove completely Hofius' typological interpretation which, as far as the psalm's application is concerned, restricts the referent of the noun מנוחה to the temple building. Nonetheless, it is based on questionable lexical evidence, and on a hypothetical reconstruction of the psalm's liturgical setting which is of dubious relevance. The alternative suggestion that the ideas of the land as Israel's resting place and YHWH's resting place have to some extent coalesced under the influence of the tradition's general interest in both themes is more credible. In this fashion the oath sums up the covenantal blessings promised to God's people -- blessings of a secure life in the land -- which were bound up with God's presence among them. A more precise understanding would conceivably emerge under the influence of given liturgical settings and would be as varied as the historical circumstances of those settings.

Was the psalmist -- as one ancient interpreter argues (Heb 3,6ff.) -- deliberately appointing "another day" when the offer of rest was being made anew, an offer of rest which he distinguished from the rest realized in Joshua's day? It may not be finally possible or necessary to answer this question. Nonetheless, in using the perpetually contemporaneous directive -- "*Today* if you hear his voice..." -- , long after the occupation of the land, there is certainly a forward looking orientation, and it is not unreasonable to suspect that the psalmist would have appreciated the suggestiveness of this. There are certainly other instances of the rest tradition being projected into the future.[124]

---

[122] Jörg Jeremias, 112. Cf. also A.R. Johnson, 21 n. 1, 68f.; Briggs-Briggs, 2:296.

[123] Even Ps 132,14, while it doubtless intends the temple in the narrower sense, nonetheless calls "Zion" (v. 13) YHWH's resting place, and his blessings go out from there to all the land.

[124] Cf. Isa 11,10; 14,3; 32,18; etc.; see below. W.C. Kaiser 1985, 163f., suggests that Ps 95 should be read with Ps 96 as anticipating an eschatological "millennium," but this is probably reading too much modern theology into the text. The grouping of the psalms which Kaiser assumes -- Pss 93-100 -- has been questioned; cf. Tate, 504ff., who surveys the discussion and groups Pss 93 and 96-100 together.

2.6. Isaiah

2.6.1. Overview

We have now seen the importance of the rest tradition in the Dtr history and in Chronicles; we have also observed that it found significant expression in Israel's worship. Not surprisingly, then, we find it present among the prophets as well. A sense of the presence of the rest motif in Isaiah can be gained from a glance at the following passages:[125] מנוחה: 11,10; 28,12; 32,18; 66,1; נוח (Hi/1): 14,3; 28,12; 63,14; נוח (Qal): 14,7; 23,12; 57,2;[126] נחת (Nf): 30,15; שקט (Hi): 7,4; 30,15; 32,17; 57,20;[127] שקט (Qal): 14,7 מרגעה (Nn): 28,12; שאנן (adj): 32,18; 33,20.

Two observations can be made. (1) Not all of these passages belong to the rest tradition. For instance, in some passages rest-terminology is used to depict a peaceful situation,[128] and in others it is used ironically to portray a scene of judgment.[129] Conversely, the picturesque language of the prophet means that there are passages which do not employ rest-vocabulary but which are conceptually close, e.g. 2,1-4. Our own survey will be confined to those passages which actually use rest-terminology.

(2) In Isaiah the promise of rest is semantically close to שלום, "peace."[130] Several times in Isaiah שלום is descriptive of the expected final state, a

---

[125] This list is not exhaustive. For the other occurrences of this terminology (other words could doubtless be added to the list), one may also note the following: נוח (Hi/1): 30,32; נוח (Hi/2): 14,1; 28,2; 46,7; 65,15; שקט (Qal): 18,4; 62,1; רגע (Hi): 51,4; שאנן (adj): 32,9.11 (where the meaning is closer to "complacency"; cf. also 37,29). The use of דמי (Nm) in 38,10; 62,6.7 may be semantically related, but the usages are not obviously relevant; the command to give YHWH no דמי (quiet) until he establishes Jerusalem is probably not theologically related to the idea of "YHWH's rest" discussed above. Isa 14,1 has the sense of "settling" or "placing and leaving" Israel in the land; it would be tempting to read theological significance into the text (cf. 14,3.7) but this would not be justified. It is notable that the LXX inserts a large amount of rest vocabulary into 13,20-14,6. The use of שקט in 62,1 (contra 18,4) pictures YHWH as refusing to remain "quiet" until Zion's "righteousness shines out like the dawn"; again, this is probably not to be connected with "YHWH's rest." On YHWH's rest, in the sense of his inactivity (18,4), cf. Keller, 91-94.

[126] In 57,2 used as a euphemism for death. It may be that we should include here 11,2 -- "the Spirit of YHWH will rest on" the shoot from Jesse (cf. 11,10) --, and 25,10 -- "the hand of YHWH will rest on this mountain," bringing to it peace and prosperity. Semantically related to 11,2 and 25,10 but less relevant are Isa 7,2.19.

[127] Isa 7,4; 30,15; and 32,17 all depict trustful attitudes; cf. also נחת in 30,15. This motif of restful or peaceful trust is used elsewhere with different vocabulary; cf. 26,3: "You keep in שלום the one whose mind is steadfast because he trusts (בטח) in you."

[128] E.g. Isa 65,10 in reference to the "resting place" (רבץ) of herds of sheep

[129] E.g., 34,14, where the repose --רגע [Hi] and מנוח -- of wild animals symbolizes the destruction of Israel's enemy, Edom; similarly: 35,7 -- רבץ.

[130] The word שלום occurs 29x In Isaiah: 12x in chs. 1-39; 9x in chs. 40-55; 8x in chs. 56-66. They are: 9,6.7 [MT 9,5.6]; 26,3 (2x = "perfect peace").12; 27,5 (2x); 32,17.18;

return to paradisiacal conditions;[131] this is the case even where the word is not used, as in, e.g., 2,2ff and 11,1ff. In 9,6f. [MT 9,5f.] the "child" will be known as the "prince of שלום," and the increase of his government and שלום will have no end. This same figure is clearly recalled in 11,1ff. as the "root of Jesse," on whom the Spirit of wisdom and understanding rests (נוח); his reign ushers in justice for the oppressed, judgment for the wicked, and an earthly state of affairs reminiscent of Gen 1-2; his מנוחה will be glory (v. 10). Although this semantic overlap of מנוחה with שלום was also present in the Dtr history[132] and Chronicles,[133] it is pronounced in Isaiah.

The relevant passages in the above list are 11,10; 14,3 (cf. v. 7); 28,12; 63,14; 66,1; and 32,18. These fall into those sections of Isaiah which scholarship has designated as Proto- (chs. 1-39) and Trito-Isaiah (chs. 56-66), yet since the first century A.D. reader would have read the book as a unity, we will discuss them together.[134]

2.6.2. Isa 11

Assessments of the authorship and literary structure of Isa 11 vary.[135] 11,1ff., with its reference to a "stump" may take up the Divine Forester

---

33,7; 38,17; 39,8; 41,3; 45,7; 48,18.22; 52,7; 53,5; 54,10.13; 55,12; 57,2.19 (2x).21; 59,8 (2x); 60,17; 66,12. For the idea see von Rad 1964; Youngblood; Durham; cf. de Vaux, 1:254. The closeness of "rest" and "peace" in Isaiah can be seen in 57,2.19-20; 32,17f.

[131] Cf. 9,7 [MT 9,6]; 32,17f.; 52,7; 54,13; 55,12; 60,17; 66,12.

[132] Note 1Kgs 5,4 [MT 5,18] which was anticipated by the use of שלום in 4,24b-25 [MT 5,4b-5]. Though the word שלום does not occur in Deut 28,65 (negatively); 2Sam 7,10f.; or 1Kgs 8,56, it might be understood. The Holiness Code already spoke of שלום in the land in a fashion which encompassed the Dtr rest theology (Lev 26,6). שלום is often presented as the counterpart of war, as in, e.g., Ex 3,8 and Ps 120,7, but Beck-Brown, 777, may be correct in observing that "שלום is the opposite not so much of war as of any disturbance in the communal well-being of the nation, a disturbance which, of course, may in certain circumstances make it necessary to go to war"; cf. also, Carr, 931.

[133] Most notably in 1Chr 22,9, where מנוחה, נוח, שקט, and שלום are explicitly juxtaposed; there is little doubt that here the notion of "rest" is very inclusive (cf. also: 2Chr 14,1-7 [MT 13,23-14,6]; cf. 2Chr 15,5-6). Rest or peace is envisaged not only as a political or military matter, but as a condition which permeates society.

[134] I am not aware of a study which considers the rest motif in these passages with reference to the usual divisions of Isaiah (Keller considers the idea of "restful trust" in Proto-Isaiah). It may be noted, however, that four of the six passages considered below fall into Proto-Isaiah (11,10; 14,3; 28,12; 32,18). The two in Trito-Isaiah (63,14 and 66,1) are somewhat distinct.

[135] E.g. O. Kaiser 1972, 152ff., judges 10,33-11,9 to date back to Isaiah, while vv. 10ff. are a post-exilic addition. Clements 1980, 122, however, calls 11,1-9 post-exilic as well. Both Kaiser and Clement discuss v. 10 with vv. 11ff., while Watts 1985, 167ff., includes v. 10 with vv. 1-9, and G.B. Gray, 222ff., discusses vv. 9-16 separately from vv. 1-8.

imagery of 10,33-34. A severely reduced Davidic dynasty will yet produce a shoot upon which the Spirit of YHWH will rest, granting to this king the traits necessary for a successful reign: wisdom and understanding, counsel and power, knowledge and fear of YHWH. The emphasis is thus placed on the role of YHWH in bringing about the state of affairs here depicted.

This king will judge the "poor" (helpless ones) with righteousness and will give decisions with justice for the "afflicted ones."[136] The effect of this king's reign is peace (cf. 2,1-4) which permeates even the animal world.[137] Since the "land" (here parallel with "my holy mountain") will have become full of the knowledge of YHWH "they" will neither harm or destroy in it.

"In that day" (v. 10; cf. v. 11) the "Root of Jesse" will stand as a "banner" (or signal)[138] for the people, and the nations will rally to him. V. 12 then pictures the Israelites being re-gathered out of exile as a sort of New Exodus (v. 16). The מנוחה of the Root of Jesse, or the "Banner," will be glory (v. 10b). H. Wildberger comments on this that the מנוחה will be the "Einbruchstelle göttlicher himmlischer Herrlichkeit auf Erden... Von dort strahlt sie aber aus in die weite Völkerwelt."[139]

Isa 11 "presumes the connection of the king to the two-hundred-year-old dynasty and its ideals including divine choice, promise, and sustenance (2 Sam 7). It equally presumes God's (and therefore, the king's) priorities of justice for the poor and helpless."[140] On the other hand, "the tendency of the Vision is to lead readers to see God's purposes which can be fulfilled in ways other than political and military authority and power."[141] Maintaining its ties with the Davidic dynasty and with the dwelling place of YHWH (Mt. Zion, v. 9), the מנוחה has become a thoroughly eschatological hope, most likely with reference to the whole earth.[142] Within this context it is clear that the מנוחה refers not only to an end of travelling or relief from warfare, but to the total condition of the society under this king.[143]

---

[136] Cf. esp. O. Kaiser 1972, 159; Watts 1985, 172.

[137] O. Kaiser 1972, 161, says of the Davidide, that "he is to bring righteousness into the world. Where righteousness truly prevails, the whole world is brought into the condition intended for it by God." Clements 1980, adds, "The person of the king in the ancient Near East was, as v. 2 affirms, more than an official functionary. Through him the divine power and blessing were made available to his people and affected the entire order of life."

[138] G.B. Gray, 225, comments, "That a root should stand as a signal, or banner, is an extraordinary combination of figures."

[139] Wildberger, 1:459.

[140] Watts 1985, 173.

[141] Watts 1985, 175.

[142] Watts 1985, 173. Alternatively the referent might be Jerusalem (Preuß, 305; also G.B. Gray, 225) or the land (Clements 1980, 126; Darnell, 330).

[143] As in Ps 132, M. Metzger, 157, suggests that מנוחה should be translated here as "throne." "Die Bezeichnung [מנוחה] für den Thron wäre hier gewählt, um Ausdruck zu bringen, daß die Herrschaft des künftigen Königs den Völkern [מנוחה] (=Friede) bringt."

2.6.3. Isa 14

Following a prophecy against Babylon in ch. 13, the נוח formula occurs in Isa 14,3,[144] again as an eschatological expectation. To emphasize Babylon's devastation it is said (13,20f.) that no shepherd will cause his flocks to lie down (רבץ [Hi]; cf. Ps 23,2), but instead desert creatures will repose (רבץ [Qal]; cf. Isa 14,30) there. Yet YHWH will have compassion on Israel; he will choose her again and "settle" (נוח [Hi/2]) her on her land again. Aliens will join Israel and she will make captives of her captors (cf. 11,14). "In the day" that YHWH gives them "relief" (v. 3) from their suffering, turmoil,[145] and "hard labor,"[146] they will take up a taunt against Babylon: YHWH has brought the oppressor to an end, leaving "all the land" to be "quiet" (שקט [Qal]) and at rest (נוח [Qal]; cf. 23,12); singing breaks out even among the trees of Lebanon because no woodsman comes to cut them down (cf. 10,34).

2.6.4. Isa 28

Although in Isa 28,12 the use of נוח (Hi/1; imperative), מנוחה, and מרגעה might be associated with the attitude of quiet trust espoused by the use of שקט in Isa 7,4; 30,15; and 32,17,[147] or with the concern of Isaiah with social

---

Whether or not "throne" is the appropriate translation, Metzger is correct in seeing מנוחה as descriptive not only of a locale, but of the effect of the king's reign for the subjects.

[144] Recognized as such by W.C. Kaiser 1985, 157; Preuß, 302; Stolz 1976a, 46; Wildberger, 2:538; O. Kaiser 1974, 26. Here נוח [Hi/1] is an infinitive construct with היה; cf. Deut 25,19. G.B. Gray, 247, compares this usage with that of Ex 23,12; Deut 5,14; and Job 3,17 (all using the Qal form), and contrasts this verse with the use of the Hiphil in Deut. 3,20, etc. Watts 1985, 204 (cf. 185), however, observes that 13,22b-14,7 "is the key element in the chiastic structure of chaps. 13-14...As such it draws together the themes of the entire section. Oppression has ceased because Yahweh himself has broken the power of rulers. *All the land is at rest* because of Yahweh's intervention" (Watts' emphasis). Such a deliberate use of the motif in v. 7 following on the use of the נוח formula in v. 3, and using the two words most closely associated with our tradition, is not likely accidental. Gray's point nonetheless highlights a similarity with the Sabbath rest, which also commemorated release from bondage.

[145] G.B. Gray, 247, explains "turmoil" (רגז) here as "strong mental agitation proceeding from various causes, here the disquiet of a slave who lives in fear of 'the voice of the taskmaster.'" Compare this with the use of רגז (adj) in Deut 28,65, and רגז in 2Sam 7,10.

[146] Watts 1985, 203: "'labor' means the slave labor imposed by an oppressive government or conqueror. The parallel in Israel's tradition is that of slavery in Egypt. Chap. 40 will pick up that theme again." O. Kaiser 1974, 26, points to the parallel phrase in Ex 1,14 and 6,9 (cf. also Deut 26,6).

[147] So Clements 1980, 228. Cf. also נחת in 30,15; בטח in 26,3.

justice,¹⁴⁸ it is likely that also here we have the use of the Dtr נוח tradition.¹⁴⁹ All the other uses of מנוחה in Isaiah have clear local components of meaning (11,10; 32,18; 66,1), and נוח is no where used in Isaiah (in any form) as an attitude; in any case, it is unclear how restful trust could be bestowed on the weary by the leaders.

The reference to the "weary" (עיף; cf. Deut 25,18f.) in this context no doubt extends beyond the image of weariness from "travelling," to the more general notion of the "poor" in the land. It is correct to see an element of social justice here, but it is unnecessary to oppose this to the idea of the rest (place) which YHWH gives. Rather, this expression, although it assumes that YHWH is the giver of the מנוחה, teaches that YHWH intended for his people to bring the מנוחה to realization with one another in the land.¹⁵⁰ Having failed in this and having refused to "listen," the people forfeit their מנוחה (cf. Mic 2,10, below).

2.6.5. Isa 63

Isa 63,14 is part of a context (esp. vv. 11ff.) recalling the exodus under Moses. The נוח (Hi/1)¹⁵¹ formula of v. 14 is reminiscent of Ex 33,14, though now YHWH's Spirit is the subject.¹⁵² The context is one wherein God's presence among his people and his saving deeds are recalled in view of the fact that Israel's rebellion has made YHWH their enemy. The plea is

---

¹⁴⁸ Stolz 1976a, 46, states in regard to Isa 28,12 and Jer 6,16 that "diese Aussage hat nichts mit dem erwähnten dtr. Gedanken zu tun, sondern entspringt prophetischem Interesse an socialer Gerechtigkeit."

¹⁴⁹ E.g. Preuß, 305; W.C. Kaiser 1985, 157. Both Darnell, 330f., and Watts 1985, 364, argue that this verse is closest in conception to Deut 12 and Ps 95 (Watts also refers to Ex 33,14). Wildberger, 3:1060f., associates this usage with the Isaianic temple theology (1280): "Hat Jahwe dort seinen dauernden Wohnsitz gefunden, dann bedeutet das, daß auch sein Volk zur Ruhe kommen soll"; in "Jerusalem unter Jahwes Schutz sichere Geborgenheit zu finden wäre." O. Kaiser 1974, 246, sees *both* the idea of Deut 12 (in the use of מנוחה) and that of "trust" (in the use of נוח); this is possible in view of the importance of 7,4; 8,17; 26,3; 30,15; 32,18 for the theology of proto-Isaiah (Keller, 81-97). The saying in 28,12 probably refers all the way back to "Yahweh's original offer to Israel of *rest* in Canaan" (Watts 1985, 364; his emphasis).

¹⁵⁰ Cf. Isa 40,28-31 where it is YHWH who gives strength to the weary; also 50,4, where the servant "sustains" the weary by an instructed tongue. In 28,12, however, the agents of rest are the people. It is along these lines that Jenni, 19, connects the מנוחה idea of Deut 12 to the social dimension of the Sabbath institution (cf. also de Vaux, 2:481). The Sabbath was thus intended to be a full realization of the מנוחה which YHWH granted the people; the slaves were to enjoy what all Israel enjoyed on her release from Egypt; infra 63, 68. In favor of such a connection is the usage in 14,7 where the 'rest' is rest from "hard labor."

¹⁵¹ On the text cf. Westermann, 390; Watts 1987, 327 n. 14a; *contra* J.L. McKenzie, 189.

¹⁵² Cf. "angel of his presence/face," v. 9; Holy Spirit, v. 10; Spirit, v. 11.

then made that YHWH would treat Israel with compassion again, and that he would not allow Israel to become hard in heart and wander away. We should probably take נוח in v. 14 as a reference to the entrance into and conquest of the land,[153] as the successful culmination of YHWH's saving acts in that former period. Though this verse is retrospective, the implication is that YHWH will again act in this way in the future.

2.6.6. Isa 66

It is reasonably clear that Isa 66,1 has in view the tradition of YHWH's rest in the temple ("my מנוחה"), though here it is not a man-made temple, but the temple made by and for YHWH himself: creation. Though this passage has been interpreted as a blanket condemnation of the whole temple idea,[154] we should probably opt for something less drastic.[155]

C. Westermann emphasizes that the form and content of vv. 1f. are similar to that of certain psalms[156] as well as 1Kgs 8,27 and 2Sam 7,5f., and he concludes that "these passages are sufficient to show that Isa. 66.1-2 are not entirely solitary in the Old Testament."[157] Further, this perspective rules out "any idea that the verses represent polemic against the building of a particular temple, whether that of the Samaritans or of some other schismatics. Instead, they are as general as the normal language used in the Psalms."[158] Rather, we should see an effort to shift the post-exilic community's faith away from a sacred building to YHWH himself.[159] It is in the humble reception of YHWH's word (Isa 66,2b) that YHWH's presence is to be sought and found (cf. Ps 113,5ff.; Isa 57,15). Ps 51,15f. may stem from a similar outlook, though it has different concerns: "For you have no delight in sacrifice; if I were to give a burnt offering, you would not be pleased. The sacrifice acceptable to God is a broken spirit; a broken and contrite heart, O God, you will not despise." Passages like 1Sam 15,22 and Hos 6,6 should probably be cited in this connection.

While this occurrence of מנוחה is closely bound to the temple idea, and while its positive meaning is left only implicit, it is clear that YHWH's מנוחה here takes in Mt. Zion at least, if not the whole land, and even the whole earth. This runs parallel to the idea of 11,9.10, where the מנוחה of the Root

---

[153] So Whybray, 259; Young, 3:486; Watts 1987, 333; Stolz 1976a, 46.
[154] E.g. de Vaux, 2:330; M. Metzger, 153f.
[155] Cf. Whybray, 280; Levenson, 296; similarly, Watts 1987, 353.
[156] E.g., Pss 50 and 113,5f.; 11,4; 51,16f.; 103,19; 132,7.
[157] Westermann, 413; cf. Watts 1987, 355.
[158] Westermann, 412. Vv. 3ff. depict people who *both* offer sacrifices and commit murder; it is an abuse of the cult which is in view, rather than a radical and absolute rejection of it.
[159] Cf. Watts 1987, 352.

of Jesse is situated on Zion while the condition of rest and peace extends to the whole earth. It is interesting, then, that both of these references to a מנוחה (Isa 11 and 66) follow hard on a vision of profound and universal harmony; indeed the phrase, "they will neither harm nor destroy on all my holy mountain," occurs word for word in both passages immediately prior to the announcement of a מנוחה. This observation lends itself to the suggestion that also in Isa 66 the מנוחה pertains not only to the "resting" of YHWH, but to the "rest" which issues from his presence.[160]

We may also note briefly that here as in 11,4 the rest motif is closely joined to the "humble"[161] and "afflicted"[162] in spirit. It is the one who "trembles" at YHWH's word (cf. v. 5) whom YHWH esteems and helps. We have noted that the demand for covenant faithfulness occurs in tandem with the rest motif throughout its usages, becoming especially sharp in Ps 95 and Isa 28,12. The addition of this passage is its depiction of the character of those who listen.

2.6.7. Isa 32

With these passages in mind we may conclude that Isaiah[163] was familiar with and using the Dtr rest tradition. Although 32,18 applies the מנוחה idea specifically to private dwellings (cf. Ruth 1,9; 3,1), it may be that this passage too should be included in our survey.[164] Here it occurs as an object of hope, where the gift of resting places is associated with a call to the proud and complacent to humble themselves in the face of impending doom. Over against the images of destruction stands the eschatological outpouring of the Spirit (v. 15), bringing in its train a state of justice and righteousness in the land.[165]

2.6.8. Summary

In its use of the rest tradition, Isaiah creatively adapts it to new situations and to an eschatological and cosmic outlook. It is still possible, however, to discern the distinctive presence of the נוח tradition.

---

[160] Cf. M. Metzger, 157f. Note the reference to שלום in 66,12f.

[161] עני/ענו; "poor," "lowly"; 14,3 and 28,12 are not distant in thought.

[162] נכה occurs elsewhere only in 2Sam 4,4 and 9,3, both times in the sense of "crippled."

[163] Cf. 11,10; 14,3.7; 28,12.

[164] Wildberger, 3:1061, 1280, associates Isa 32,18 with 28,12 and 11,10. Cf. further, Hofius, 45; Darnell, 331f.

[165] Brueggemann 1972, 22, remarks that, "the movement from...weary land to resting place, is through the establishment of royal order (vs. 1) which will be characterized by righteousness and justice (vss. 2, 16, 17)."

Isa 11 presents a sweeping vision of eschatological שלום for Israel (cf. Isa 32,18). The passage foresees victory over the enemy, the expulsion of the oppressor, justice for the needy, care for the poor, Edenic conditions of peace among beasts and people, and the propagation of knowledge throughout the earth, all stemming from the reign of the one anointed with the Spirit of wisdom and understanding. All of this is encapsulated in the statement that the Root of Jesse's מנוחה (located on Mt. Zion) will be glory.

It is also said that the "peoples" will rally to him, signalling a New Exodus, led this time by a Davidide. This motif of a second exodus comes into sharper relief with Isa 14,3 where the language is reminiscent of the release from Egyptian bondage. In so depicting the expected "rest," the motifs of bondage, suffering, and turmoil come to the fore. It is no longer simply "rest from travelling" or "from warfare" which is envisioned.

Isa 28 introduces a new element when it suggests that YHWH's bestowal of rest on his people brought the responsibility for them to give rest to the "weary" among them. A concern for social justice is thus apparent, and the land as their מנוחה, their "resting place," is made contingent on the maintenance of justice for the weak and listening to YHWH.

As in 11,10, the מנוחה of Isa 66,1 -- creation as YHWH's temple -- is associated with conditions of profound, Edenic peace. Moreover, it is associated with people who are "humble" and "afflicted" in spirit, with people who "tremble" at YHWH's word.

2.7. Jeremiah

2.7.1. Overview

מנוחה: 45,3; 51,59; שקט (Qal): 30,10; 46,27; 48,11; שקט (Hi): 49,23; רבץ (Nm): 50,6; רגע (Hi): 31,2; 50,34; מרגוע (Nn): 6,16; שאן (Qal): 30,10; 46,27; 48,11; שלה (Qal): 12,1; שלו (adj): 49,31.[166]

Among these the rest tradition is evident only in 31,2; 50,34;[167] and 6,16, none of which use נוח (Hi/1)[168] or מנוחה.[169] If the Dtr rest tradition is present it is being conveyed through different terminology (רגע [Hi]; מרגוע).

---

[166] שלום occurs 31 times: 4,10; 6,14 (3x); 8,11 (3x); 8,15; 9,8 [MT 9,7]; 12,5.12; 13,19; 14,13.19; 15,5; 16,5; 20,10; 23,17; 25,37; 28,9; 29,7 (3x).11; 30,5; 33,6.9; 34,5; 38,4.22; 43,12.

[167] Kronholm, 348, translates 31,2 and 50,34 as "ruhig machen." W. Rudolph 1953, 36, renders, "Ruhe schaffen; R. hb., bekommen." רגע (Hi, trans.; cf. the use of the Hi/intrans. in Deut 28,65) and נוח (Hi/1) would seem to be very close in conception.

[168] This form is not used anywhere in the book. There are three occurrences of נוח, all Hi/2: 14,9; 27,11; 43,6.

[169] In 45,3 Baruch complains that he is worn out and "finds" (מצא; cf. 6,16: "you will find rest for your souls"; cf. also Lam 1,3; Ruth 1,9) no מנוחה; cf. Brueggemann 1972, 21.

2.7.2. Jer 31

31,2 refers back to the desert journey,[170] although the suggestion is that Israel can expect the same in the future.[171] The verse echoes the נוח/מנוחה tradition, and seems to have both Ex 33,14[172] and Deut 28,65[173] in mind. As in Isaiah we have a reference to a "New Exodus,"[174] and an early use of the rest motif.[175] The passage answers the question, "How and why had Israel come to be, and how could its renewed existence as a national community become a reality once again?"[176] Thus the way is prepared for the announcement of a New Covenant later in the chapter (vv. 31ff.).

When YHWH will restore Israel to the land their forefathers possessed (30,3), break off the "yoke" of foreign powers (30,8), raise up David their king (30,9), give them quiet (שקט) and security (שאן; 30,10), rebuild the city and palace (30,18), punish those who oppress them (30,20), be their God (30,22), "give them rest" (רגע) in the "desert," so that farmers can work the ground and the watchman can again call the people to "go up to Zion, to YHWH our God" (31,6.23)[177] who will refresh the "weary of soul" (עיפה נפש) and satisfy the faint (31,25),[178] we find ourselves surrounded by the same constellation of ideas we have previously encountered.

2.7.3. Jer 50

Jer 50,34 is part of a section which pronounces judgments to fall on Babylon. As in 31,11, YHWH is portrayed as Israel's "redeemer," who

---

This does not appear to be a use of the rest tradition. In 51,59 מנוחה is descriptive of a military position ("officer of the מנוחה").

[170] Cf. Carroll, 587, who gives the literal rendering as, "going to find him rest Israel"; also Holladay, 2:152, 180; *contra* NIV. J.A. Thompson, 566, suggests that the sense is that "Israel escaped from Egypt, and was searching for the land promised to her forefathers (cf. Exod. 33:14; Deut. 28:65)."

[171] Cf. W. Rudolph 1968, 193f.; Carroll, 590, comments that in vv. 2-3, "past and future have become as one."

[172] W. Rudolph 1968, 193, notes that the clause, "find favor" (Jer 31,2) occurs 5 times in Ex 33,1.12-17. Bright, 280, comments that "Although the language is not the same, one sees reminiscences of Exod xxxiii 14; Deut xxviii 65."

[173] Note the use of רגע in Deut 28,65. Cf. Carroll, 587, and J.A. Thompson, 566.

[174] Considered a precursor of the Isaianic New Exodus by Bright, 280; cf. J.A. Thompson, 566.

[175] Jer 31,2 is generally considered to be authentic, and is associated with Josiah's reign; cf. the lengthy discussion of Holladay, 2:155ff., esp. 158; also Bright, 284; but see Carroll, 588.

[176] Clements 1988, 185.

[177] Nicholson, 60, comments that the "point of the passage is that...Zion [will be] acknowledged as the focal point of Israel."

[178] Cf. Brueggemann 1972, 23.

will bring "rest" to the land of the "oppressed" (50,33),[179] even as he brings "unrest" to Babylon.

2.7.4. Jer 6

In view of the use of רגע (Hi) in these two passages it is reasonable to expect that we have the same idea being expressed with מרגוע in 6,16. Both the phraseology and the context are reminiscent of Isa 28,12.[180] Although it is common to understand מרגוע here in purely psychological terms,[181] it is more likely that the promise of rest takes in "all den Gefahren überhaupt, die sie bedrängen können."[182] Rudolph, while he distinguishes this usage from "den Vollsinn, den Jesus Mt 11,29 diesem Jeremiawort beilegt," yet sees here a vision of "nationale Sicherheit und Wohlfahrt."[183] By way of analogy, and ignoring other distortions in application, one can note the implications of the verse when A. Solzhenitsyn applies it to present day Russian society as an exhortation to return to pre-Bolshevik values and policies.[184] This verse envisions a very real change brought about in the total circumstances of society by the intervening activity of YHWH.

The degenerate and untrustworthy priests and prophets are invited along with the people to stand at the point of decision, to return to the "ancient paths"[185] and walk in the "way to good"[186] where they will find[187] מרגוע for themselves; they are unwilling, however, to listen (cf. 6,10.16.17) to the prophet's words and thus stand under the threat of destruction by the enemy. Their hope based on the practice of the cult is misplaced (v. 20), perverted as it is by their wickedness (v. 13).[188] Social ills such as violence,

---

[179] Duhm, 365, and W. Rudolph 1968, 305, suggest that this rest extends to the whole earth, and compare this usage with Isa 14,7.

[180] Cf. מרגעה in Isa 28,12; Althann, 242f., compares Jer 6,16 to both Isa 28,12 and Ps 95,11.

[181] As, e.g., McKane, 149, who interprets it as "a quietness of mind."

[182] Wildberger, 3:1061; similarly, Keller, 88f. W. Rudolph 1953, 22, associates this word with the Hiphil form, and translates it, "Ruhe(platz)"; for the local idea cf. J.A. Thompson, 261; W. White, 833.

[183] W. Rudolph 1968, 47; similarly, Holladay, 1:221 ("it is close to the current phrase 'national security,' the ability to live without constant tension and uneasiness before the threat from disaster abroad.").

[184] Solzhenitsyn, 54.

[185] Probably the Mosaic Law as embodied in Deuteronomy, as suggested by Holladay, 1:221; also J.A. Thompson, 261. Craigie-Kelley-Drinkard, 106, prefer the more general "way of life and faith walked in by their ancestors, which was the way of the covenant."

[186] As against, "good way"; cf. Holladay, 1:221.

[187] מצא; cf. Jer 45,3; Lam 1,3; Ruth 1,9; Sir 6,28.

[188] Holladay, 1:226, comments, "This tradition of tension with the cult would find its culmination in the astonishing words of Trito-Isaiah (Isa 66:1-4) and its New Testament seal in Jesus (Mark 11:15-18) and his interpreters (Heb 9:11-10:18)."

destruction, and greed, cloaked by seriously misleading prophecies of שלום have led to the forfeiture of the מרגוע.

2.7.5. Summary

In Jeremiah, the verb רגע (Hi) in 31,2 and 50,34, as well as the noun מרגוע in 6,16 bear the marks of the rest tradition. As in Isaiah the tradition is caught up into pronouncements of judgment (loss of rest) as well as eschatological expectations (New Exodus). Along with the motifs of the land, the temple, and the Davidic kingship, the context of 31,2 anticipates national security, judgment for the oppressor, and refreshment for the "weary" and "faint." The tradition appears almost in passing in 6,16,[189] and this may lead us to miss what is worth noting: the מרגוע effectively encapsulates the essence of Israel's desire, viz, secure dwelling in the land, freedom from threat and harassment, freedom for covenant life.

2.8. Lamentations

2.8.1. Lam 1

Two passages, Lam 1,3 (מנוח) and 5,5 (נוח [Ho/1]), are of relevance. In his study of the background of the theology of Lamentations, B. Albrektson has pointed to two traditions stemming out of ancient Israel's faith: on the one hand the cult traditions of Jerusalem, especially relating to Zion, and on the other hand the "fundamental ideas which characterize the theology of the Deuteronomist."[190] In the former, the leading themes "are the election of David and of his house, and the idea of Zion and its temple as the abode of God";[191] bound up with this tradition is the belief that Jerusalem is invincible.[192] Under the weight of historical reality -- the loss of the city and the destruction of the temple -- this faith is pressed to the breaking point. The solution to this problem comes from the other tradition, that of divine retribution as expressed, above all, in Deut 28. Among several specific instances of clear allusions to Deut 28, Albrektson includes Lam 1,3 (cf. Deut 28,65).[193] After "affliction" and "hard labor" Israel has gone into exile and finds (מצא) no מנוח; YHWH's yoke of discipline is on Zion's neck, for she has been handed over to those she

---

[189] In view of Isa 28,12, is this to be taken as a variation on a well known expression?
[190] Albrektson, 238.
[191] Albrektson, 219.
[192] Cf. M. Metzger, 152, on the function of the Mountain of God idea in Lam 5,18.
[193] Albrektson, 231; he observes that the noun מנוח occurs only five times in the whole Old Testament apart from Deut 28,65 and Lam 1,3. On Deut 28,65, see above, 31f. Both Kraus 1960, 27, and H. Groß, 12, associate Lam 1,3 with Deut 12,9.

cannot resist, and her strength is sapped (v. 14). As Hillers points out, the reference to rest here "is of considerable weight: 'rest' in the Promised Land was an important part of Israel's conception of what belonged to her as God's people, and its removal was a sign that his favor had departed."[194]

2.8.2. Lam 5

The imagery of a "yoke" is probably also to be found in 5,5,[195] as is that of "weariness." The complaint is made in v. 2 that their "inheritance" has been turned over to strangers, and here in v. 5 that they have no rest. Once again, "'We have no rest' means not only 'we are very weary,' but 'one sign of our status as God's people has been removed.'"[196] Both here (5,18) and in 1,4ff. the loss of the temple and its festivals is mourned.

2.8.3. Summary

The idea of "finding" (מצא) rest (מנוח) encountered in Jer 6,16 recurs here (Lam 1,3), only this time as a statement of Israel's tragic existence in exile; immediately on its heels the loss of the temple festivals is also mourned (1,4). The loss of the resting place is associated with "affliction and hard labor," a homeless, wandering existence, and constant vulnerability to the enemy's threat. The claim that she has lost her מנוח becomes here a powerful symbol of YHWH's rejection of Israel. Likewise, in 5,5 Israel is weary and has no "rest," meaning that her "inheritance" has been turned over to strangers (5,2), the crown has fallen from her head (5,16), and Mt. Zion lies desolate (5,18).

2.9. Micah[197]

The noun מנוחה occurs once in Micah, and in a context which appears to be relevant. The powerful among the people are seizing the "inheritance" (2,2) from the powerless. These oppressors cling to those who prophesy prosperity in the form of their dissipated lifestyle (2,11), while the prophets make a pretentious show of indignant scorn for those who foretell destruction (vv. 6f. cf. Jer 6,14). Women are driven from their homes and YHWH's blessing is taken from their children (v. 9). Because of their

---

[194] Hillers, 19.
[195] So Kraus 1960, 88; Groß, 39.
[196] Hillers, 104. Brueggemann 1972, 22, comments that, "Weariness is being enslaved to a false lord; rest means being in the service of the only true Lord (cf. Lev 25:42)."
[197] On מנוחה in Zech 9,1, see Darnell, 335; Preuß, 305; this passage does not appear to be relevant to the present investigation and will be passed over here. Cf. also נוח (Hi/1) in Zech 6,8; שקט (Qal) in 1,11; שלו (adj) in 7,7.

unlawful and cruel eviction of the weak from their inheritance, YHWH evicts them: "Get up! Go! For this is no מנוחה" (v. 10).[198] The land is defiled[199] and ruin awaits them. This use of מנוחה should also be taken as a reference to the tradition of Deut 12,9.10. The statement that this is no מנוחה permits of a dual understanding. It is no מנוחה, firstly, because it is ridden with injustice and oppression (cf. Isa 28,12).[200] It is so, secondly, because the land is as good as lost to them; as in Lam 1,3 and 5,5, the loss of the מנוחה holds serious implications for their status as YHWH's people.

2.10. Summary and conclusions of part one

Having already provided an overview at the beginning and summaries along the way, it will now be helpful, in the briefest manner, to group the insights gained from our survey under several headings.

2.10.1. Presence and prominence of the rest tradition

There can be little doubt of the presence of the נוח tradition in the Dtr history, but it has also been seen that this tradition plays a very prominent role, both structurally and thematically, in this literature. When the Chronicler undertook a rewriting of the history he did not merely copy the references to this tradition but carefully used them in order to advance his own theological interests. Pss 95 and 132 testify to the fact that the tradition was a living component of Israel's liturgy, and the prophets kept it before the people as a memory of what YHWH had done in the past, as a warning of what they stood to lose in the present, and as an ultimate hope for the nation, indeed the whole earth.

2.10.2. An eschatological rest

With passages such as Isa 11,10; 14,3; and 32,18, "rest" becomes an important expression of Israel's hopes. Other passages, such as Jer 31,2,

---

[198] So Smith-Ward-Bewer, 62; L.C. Allen 1976, 298; and R.L. Smith, 27. Alternatively, Wolff 1982, 54, and W. Rudolph 1975, 61, place this statement on the lips of the oppressors. Mays, 71f., argues that the earliest version had the first half of the verse on the lips of the oppressors, reading, "'Arise and depart, for this is no home (for you)'"; cf. Ruth 1,9; 3,1; Isa 32,18. Later, because of the impact of the Babylonian crisis (Mays, 25) and under the influence of the Dtr rest tradition the verse received its present form, which is "a summons to people under judgment to depart."

[199] In addition to the מנוחה tradition, L.C. Allen 1976, 298, points to the land tradition of Lev 18,24-28, wherein the Canaanites are expelled from the land because they defiled it with their rites.

[200] Cf. Darnell, 334f.

cloak such future expectations in recollections of YHWH's past deliverance, but the effect is the same. In most of these passages it is the exodus which has formed the larger framework for the pattern of YHWH's dealings, although in the future exodus it appears to be a Davidide who will become the rallying point of the peoples (Isa 11).

2.10.3. The land

The association of the "rest" with the land is so evident as to need little comment here. The land itself, i.e. Palestine, is Israel's מנוחה (*resting place*), even if there are points in the prophetic vision when the boundaries of YHWH's final act seemingly embrace the whole earth. Israel does not seem to have ever been tempted to translate this particular hope of "rest" into a purely psychological or "spiritual" experience, nor into an "other worldly" one (though see Isa 66,22). This must qualify the eschatological hopes of a future מנוחה.

2.10.4. The temple

The temple quickly came to the fore in our discussion as we took up the group of passages in the Dtr history which are associated with Deut 12,9f. The erection of the temple becomes possible only when YHWH gives his nation rest, and in both the Dtr history and in Chronicles this is seen to find its ultimate realization under Solomon. This connection with the temple was evident in several of the prophetic passages as well.

Looking at Ps 95,11 it was determined that a simple identification of "my rest" with the temple is untenable. In view of the ambiguity of the expression and usage elsewhere it is possible that the whole land with Zion at its center was being construed as at once Israel's and YHWH's מנוחה. The covenantal blessings of the land as a מנוחה -- blessings bound up with God's presence among them -- are in view. As in Ps 95 these blessings depend on Israel's willingness to *listen* in Isa 28; 66; and Jer 6.

Isa 66,1 is not so much a rejection of the temple idea as it is a declaration that YHWH has built his own temple in creation. He esteems the humble and those who tremble at his word. In some passages (Isa 66,1; Ps 132; Isa 11) YHWH's מנוחה may allude to his throne. In a passage like Isa 11 this throne has its earthly location on Mt. Zion in the temple, from where the effect of his reign, his "rest," radiates out to the whole earth.

2.10.5. The Davidic dynasty

In both the Dtr history and Chronicles the ultimate achievement of the "rest" occurs under David and Solomon. In Chronicles Solomon is himself called a "man of מנוחה." Ps 132 brings David's and YHWH's throne into relationship with each other, and Isa 11,10 declares that, as a result of having been anointed with the Spirit of wisdom and counsel, the Root of Jesse's מנוחה will be glory.

2.10.6. Weariness, distress, etc.

Mt 11,28-30 is a promise of rest to the "weary and heavy laden." Although it is commonly noted that the use of נוח (Hi/1) signifies rest from a journey, rest from war, or both, it is also true that the motifs of weariness, oppression, affliction, distress, and the like play a part in the OT tradition. This feature may be seen from the side of what rest meant positively, what loss of rest implied, and also the social responsibility which YHWH's gift of rest entailed.

Thus in Deut 25,18-19 it was said that when the Israelites were in the desert, when they were "weary" (עיף) and "worn out" (יגע) the Amalekites cut off the stragglers; when, however, YHWH gives them rest they are to take action against the Amalekites. Likewise in 2Sam 7,10-11 YHWH promises rest from the wicked ones who "trouble" (רגז) and "oppress" (ענה) them. In Isa 11, where the Root of Jesse's מנוחה (place of rest) is glory, it is said that he will judge the "needy ones" with righteousness, and the "poor ones" ("humble" ענו) with justice (v. 4); his reign ushers in edenic conditions. Isa 14 states that YHWH will give the Israelites rest from their "suffering" and "turmoil" (רגז), and "hard labor" (העבדה הקשה; cf. Ex 1,14; 6,9; Deut 26,6). Following the recollection of the earlier (exodus) rest in Jer 31,2, there comes the promise of v. 25, that YHWH will "refresh the weary (עיף) of soul" and "satisfy the faint." Cf. also Isa 32,7.17-18.

In Deut 28,65 the loss of rest is depicted as life with an anxious (רגז) mind, longing eyes, and a despairing heart. Likewise, the loss of rest is depicted in Lam 1,3 as a distressing existence which follows "affliction" (עני) and "harsh labor," and again in 5,5 as being weary (יגע). Cf. Jer 45,3.

In the prophets an additional element of the 'rest' surfaces which was not made explicit elsewhere: YHWH's grant of rest created a responsibility for Israel to "give rest to the weary" (עיף; Isa 28,12). The failure of the leaders to heed this call meant loss of the resting place. The same idea surfaces in Micah 2,10, where the oppression and exploitation of the powerless so disgusts YHWH that he exclaims, "Get up! Go! This is not your resting place, because it is defiled, it is ruined beyond remedy."

2.10.7. Additional related motifs

Other motifs which figure significantly in this tradition would include YHWH's presence (Ex 33,14; Ps 95; Isa 63), Israel's responsibility to listen to YHWH (implied in several passages, but made pressing in Ps 95; Isa 28,12; Jer 6,16) and the exodus (e.g. Ex 33,14; Deut 3,20 and related passages; Deut 12,9f.; Isa 14,3; Isa 63,14; Jer 31,2).

3. Part two

3.1. Introduction

The Sabbath is of interest to our investigation not only because it represents an important use of the rest motif in the OT, but because Heb 3-4 connects the κατάπαυσις of Ψ 94,11 [95,11] with God's seventh day rest of Gen 2, and summarizes the Christian hope as a σαββατισμός. Mt 11,28-30, moreover, is immediately followed by the two Matthean Sabbath pericopae, a phenomenon which seems neither accidental nor incidental.

It is not necessary to include a discussion of the Sabbath institution as such -- its origin, development, and observance -- nor to engage specific passages exegetically.[201] Instead, we will target three specific areas. First, we will consider the significance of the rest motif in the Sabbath institution. Second, because of the eschatological outlook of Heb 3-4 and Mt 11 we will ask whether and how we may speak of an eschatological Sabbath in the OT. Finally, because of the joining of the מנוחה and Sabbath traditions in Hebrews and Matthew, we will ask how these uses of the rest motif are related in the OT.

3.2. The rest motif and the Sabbath

3.2.1. Introduction

When both versions of the decalogue, along with Ex 23,12 and 31,17, give the rest motif such prominence in the Sabbath, "to affirm that the Sabbath is a day of rest, i.e., a day without the performance of work, is carrying coals to Newcastle."[202] It is true that the verb שבת means "cease" or "stop," without necessarily implying "rest" or "refreshment,"[203] yet in more than one Sabbath passage the latter ideas are plainly implied by the

---

[201] In general see Andreasen 1972 (cf. 1974b) and G. Robinson, 1975. For discussion related specifically to the decalogue cf. Hossfeld, 33-53, 247-252; Crüsemann, 53-58. Though the matter is still a subject of debate, a concise summary of the Sabbath's development in the OT is given by Biggs, 12-23.

[202] Andreasen 1972, 122.

[203] This is insisted upon by G. Robinson 1975, 180-185.

verb,[204] and in some cases the idea of "rest" is explicit.[205] It does not matter for our purposes whether or not this association of rest with the Sabbath stems all the way back to the earliest Sabbath celebrations,[206] but only that ultimately the Sabbath was assumed to be a day without work, a day on which even the slave and ox could rest, just as God himself had been refreshed (נפש) on the seventh day.[207]

3.2.2. The significance of the Sabbath rest[208]

Apart from the implications for "keeping covenant," the work prohibition, at least early on, was "understood simply in terms of the seven day schedule, and probably as a means to achieve rest and restoration, both in a physical and in a mythical way."[209] This function of rest as an opportunity for rejuvenation is applicable to the land's rest as well.

---

[204] Stolz 1976b, 864, though he groups these verses under the general meaning of "aufhören," yet states that in connection with the Sabbath, שבת in Ex 16,30; 23,12; and 34,21, designates "das zu diesen Zeiten gehörige Ruhen und Feiern" of men, beasts, land, and God. *HALAT*, 1308, gives "ruhen, feiern" as a separate meaning (from "aufhören") and lists under it Gen 2,2f.; Ex 16,30; 23,12; 31,17; 34,21; Lev 36,34f.; and 2Chr 36,21. Andreasen 1974b, 465 n. 68, states that with the use of שבת, Ex 31,17 "clearly intends along with Ex 20 11 that Yahweh rested, for he was refreshed (*npsh*)." Even G. Robinson is willing to admit (1975, 185; cf. 184, 173f.) that the use of שבת in Ex 23,12 and 34,21 (in their present forms) may "secondarily mean 'rest from labour'."

[205] נוח is used in Ex 20,11; 23,12; and Deut 5,14 properly for "rest"; cf. *HALAT*, 642; Coppes, 562; Preuß, 300; Stolz 1976a, 44; the arguments against this (Berry; G. Robinson 1975, 176-180; 1980) are forced and linguistically dubious. Though Robinson is keen to downplay the idea of rest in relation to נוח, he acknowledges (1975, 180) that "perhaps" in its use in Ex 23,12 (with נפש) the "rest idea is dominant." Elsewhere (1975, 270) he states that the "rest-motif becomes central in Ex 20:11 (וינח) and in Ex 31:17b (וינפש)." On נפש see, Waltke, 587ff.; *HALAT*, 672; Wolff 1974, 139f.; 1972, 70.

[206] Cf. esp. G. Robinson 1975, 220, 312f., 314-377, and *passim*. He argues that the Sabbath was not originally a day of cessation from work and rest, but that prior to the exile it was a monthly cultic festival, associated with the new moon. It was only after the exile that Sabbath became associated with an already existing seventh day institution involving the cessation of work, and was henceforth a weekly "day of rest." Andreasen 1972, 264, on the other hand, reaches the very different conclusion that the Sabbath "appears in the earliest strata of the Old Testament as the seventh day on which work is prohibited."

[207] On "work" in the OT, cf. Ebach and Dumbrell who allow that work was not an entirely negative idea in the OT. P.D. Miller 1985, 87, portrays work as a "necessary evil," but does recognize that it can be given a favorable coloring when "understood in the wholeness of God's intention." Crüsemann, 57, on the other hand, attributes to work an almost exclusively negative valuation.

[208] Against the idea of the Sabbath rest as speculation on *time*, see G. Robinson 1975, 202-207; *contra* Heschel, 15; de Vaux, 2:480; Tsevat, 457, *et al*.

[209] Andreasen 1972, 138. By "mythical," Andreasen 1972, 135, is referring to those theories which suggest that "the real 'reason' for the seventh day and the sabbatical year (Ex. 23:10-11) is a mythical and cultic understanding of land and people, namely, that these are not at Israel's free disposal, but must after having been used be allowed to return

In this connection the Sabbath was extended with special emphasis to the slaves and beasts who might otherwise have been ignored (Ex 20,10f.; 23,12; Deut 5,14f.). In so doing, and in connecting this with the redemptive act of YHWH on behalf of the whole nation (Deut 5,15), the Sabbath shows a strong humanitarian interest, albeit one with a theological basis and orientation.[210] It is not merely that the servants and slaves were included in the communal day of rest, but that on "sabbaths all the Israelites stand equal before God."[211] "On this day 'the servant would walk side by side with his master,' the rich would not become richer, and the poor would not become poorer."[212]

More than one exegete of the Sabbath texts has noted that the act of YHWH which released Israel as a nation from bondage and brought her into her מנוחה is hereby fulfilled in the Sabbath, where special stress is laid on the rest of the slaves. Thus, "das Ruhen am Sabbat, so wie Dt es versteht, enthält einen Hinweis auf und dient als Zeichen für die $m^e nuh\bar{a}$, die Ruhe, die ja bekanntlich im Dt ein Heilsgut ist."[213] Admittedly the נו tradition is concerned with a "rest" from travelling, warfare, and foreign oppression, a "rest" which paves the way for constructive and productive activity, while the Sabbath is a "rest" from just such common labor. Yet in a few passages the מנוחה/נוח rest, like the Sabbath, is related to social justice in domestic affairs (Isa 11,10; 28,12; Micah 2,10) and the parallel with release from bondage is a real one (2Sam 7,10-11; Isa 14,3; Jer 31,2; Lam 1,3; 5,5).

Insofar as the land was also to enjoy a rest, the Israelites were reminded that the land belonged to YHWH, that he remained sovereign over it and them, and that they were absolutely dependent on him.[214] This lesson may be said to have been present in the weekly Sabbath as well, as the Israelites were compelled to stay their hands from working the ground, teaching them that "'Yahweh is the proper and the only owner of the land.'"[215] In using this day for participation in the cult they would be reminded further that "one does not live by bread alone, but by every word that comes from the mouth of the LORD."

---

to their original state, by means of a rest, so that restoration of spent powers can be accomplished." In spite of what Andreasen says here, elsewhere (1972, 218) he seems to hesitate at pressing the presence of the "mythical" element, suggesting that it "is found only on the fringes of the Old Testament traditions, if it is there at all" (1972, 266).

[210] Cf. Hulst 1966, 155.
[211] G. Robinson 1975, 414.
[212] Andreasen 1974a, 293.
[213] Hulst 1966, 156; likewise, G. Robinson 1975, 418; Jenni, 19; Bacchiocchi 1986, 162f.; Renner, 21f.; de Vaux, 2:481; P.D. Miller 1985, 88.
[214] G. Robinson 1975, 129, 170; Andreasen 1972, 217ff.; Tsevat, 453f.; Wolff 1972, 68.
[215] G. Robinson 1975, 170.

As for *God's Sabbath rest*, it is not likely that Gen 2,2f. (cf. Ex 20,11; 31,17) functions as a Sabbath etiology in view of the fact that it is in no way explicitly exploited toward that end in that context.[216] Still, if the Sabbath of the creation account is not an etiology, "it has a cosmic outlook, related as it is to the creation of the world."[217]

> Gen. 2:1-3 is more closely related to the creation than to the Sabbath, although it certainly has implications for the Sabbath institution as well as for the creation account, e.g., it is universal, was created at the beginning, and so it is fundamental to Israel. But its main function is to provide a particular conclusion to the creation account. The creator, having completed his work, is at rest...The whole creation is thus also at rest on the seventh day, a day characterized by completion, sanctity, and blessing.[218]

A little further on we will consider the ancient idea of the divine *otiositas* in relation to God's Sabbath following creation. In contrast to such notions, YHWH's rest is not a withdrawal from active involvement in the affairs of the world.[219] It may be, however, that God's Sabbath rest of Gen 2 is the Hebrew response to or version of the *otiositas* of the myth. As N.-E. Andreasen observes, in other Near Eastern creation accounts, "for whatever reason, the creative deity rested at the conclusion of his creative work, immediately after the creation of man... There is, therefore," continues Andreasen, "very likely a relationship between the creation Sabbath and the *otiositas*, but it is a broken relationship, for the author of Gen. 1:1-4 understood the *otiositas* simply as a Sabbath, the first Sabbath."[220]

G. Robinson has gone somewhat further than this in his discussion of the primordial Sabbath. Noting that in the Babylonian version of the divine *otiositas* Marduk came to rest in his temple, Robinson opines that in Ex 20,11 God enters his מנוחה, his *temple* (Ps 132,13f.; 2Chr 6,41f.) following the work of creation.[221] However, such a suggestion goes far beyond the evidence (see further below).

Finally, though the divine and human Sabbaths are closely related (Ex 20,11; 31,17), there is no indication that men and women participate in

---

[216] Andreasen 1972, 65 n. 1, 184f., 244 n. 2. By way of contrast, note the "one flesh" word of Gen 2,24. Wallace, 243, however, sees such an etiology in Ex 31,12-17, which in turn must influence the reading of Gen 1-2.

[217] Andreasen 1972, 245, 195.

[218] Andreasen 1972, 224f.

[219] Andreasen 1972, 185: "That the creator should rest [i.e., enter into a divine *otiositas*] after making the world and mankind, but before making his people Israel, is to the Old Testament and to P a preposterous idea." Likewise, Renner, 19, argues that the verbs "bless" and "sanctify" "categorically exclude a passive worklessness or idleness (*otiositas*) on his part."

[220] Andreasen 1972, 185f.

[221] G. Robinson 1975, 348.

God's Sabbath, either now or in the future.[222] Whatever the immediate implications of God's Sabbath rest for his creation and for humankind, it was not, in the OT, something in which people participated.[223]

3.2.3. Conclusions

The Sabbath rest is the rest of laborers for the purpose of refreshment.[224] In the application of the Sabbath law a humanitarian concern becomes prominent as slaves and beasts are singled out for special notice; the point is that *all* Israel is to enjoy the Sabbath. In this vein, there is often noted a point of contact with the מנוחה tradition of rest in the land. Further, both in terms of the "rest" of the land and that of the people, the suggestion is strong that the land belongs to YHWH, and that he is sovereign over it and the people.

God's "rest" (שבת) in Gen 2,2f. probably does not function as an etiology for the human Sabbath. It does, however, likely serve as a response to the divine *otiositas* motif of other creation accounts, characterizing YHWH's rest as a Sabbath rest. This rest of God is nowhere presented as a reality or an experience in which Israel participates or will participate (but see the following section).

3.3. An eschatological Sabbath?

The simple and short answer to this question is, "no." The OT does not express, in so many words, the expectation that the world-to-come will be "a day which is wholly Sabbath and rest [מנוחה] for eternity,"[225] or that a σαββατισμός remains for the people of God.

But that answer may be too simple and short. The OT knows of an age which will see the unsullied celebration of the Sabbath continuing unbroken (Isa 66,23), when "all flesh" will come to worship before YHWH.[226] Also

---

[222] Renner, 19.

[223] In this sense, at least, von Rad's claim, 1966b, 101, seems well grounded, to wit, that God's Sabbath rest following creation "has no immediate bearing whatever upon human life." But see the very different view expressed by von Rad in his commentary on Genesis: "that God has 'blessed,' 'sanctified'..., this rest, means that P does not consider it as something for God alone but as a concern of the world, almost as a third something that exists between God and the world" (1972a, 62f.). Note also the repeated references to "my Sabbaths"; e.g. Ezek 20,12; 13,16.20f.24.

[224] Andreasen 1974a, 290 n. 32, says of the "mythical" understanding of the Sabbath rest that it "is very interesting, but it does not, it seems to me, come to the surface in the Old Testament literature."

[225] *Tam* 7,4; infra, 122ff.

[226] Interestingly, this vision of the eschatological Sabbaths falls in the same context as one of the only two usages of "my resting place" (v. 1; cf. Ps 132,14) outside of Ps 95,11.

in Isaiah the hope is extended to foreigners that if they will observe Sabbath they will be included in the celebration on Mt. Zion (56,1-7).[227] Again, although the Sabbath of Gen 2 cannot be said to be an "eschatological Sabbath in embryo..., it may have some typological overtones. Moreover, it has a cosmic outlook, related as it is to the creation of the world."[228]

There is also something in the belief that when the later rabbis spoke of the future world as a Sabbath day they were probably taking their lead from the OT.

> The reiterated, even if only implied, Biblical parallels between the Sabbath of Genesis -- Adam's life in the Garden of Eden before his expulsion -- and the end of days could not have been lost on the Rabbis of the Midrash. Consciously or unconsciously these parallels -- the latter time as the return of Edenic conditions -- must have registered on the Rabbinic mind.[229]

In this vein one might note the characterization of the eschatological age as a time of material abundance,[230] of peace between man and beast,[231] of a light more refulgent than the sun,[232] and as a time when human infirmities will vanish,[233] all of which seem to refer back to "Edenic conditions typified especially by the Sabbath."[234] Moreover, it has been argued that Dan 9 preserves a form of "chronomessianism,"[235] which anticipated the coming of the messiah by means of a sabbatical structuring of epochs. Further, Isa 61 describes the Anointed Servant's ministry in terms of the Year of Jubilee.[236] Indeed, following 400 pages of detailed treatment of all the OT Sabbath contexts, Robinson summaries:

> Thus, sabbath grows into a symbol signifying man's salvation and freedom, freedom from bondage, both external (oppression and slavery in Egypt) and internal (sin of estrangement from God and fellowmen); freedom from anxieties as to what to eat (cf. Ex. 16:27ff.; Lev. 25:6., 20f.) and where to live (Is. 56:2-7). Sabbath thus acquires an eschatological

---

[227] Cf. G. Robinson 1975, 415ff.

[228] Andreasen 1972, 225. For understanding Gen 2,2f. as the "ultimate rest for the people of God," cf. Dressler, 29.

[229] Friedman, 444.

[230] E.g. Amos 9,13f.; Joel 3,18 [MT 4,18]; Isa 6,7; 30,23; Jer 31,12.

[231] E.g. Hos 2,18 [MT 2,20]; Isa 11,6; 65,25.

[232] E.g. Isa 30,26; Zech 14,6f.

[233] E.g. Isa 35,5f.; 30,26; Jer 30,17; 33,6.

[234] Bacchiocchi 1986, 162; for discussion of these themes and passages along with later Jewish literature see Bacchiocchi, 1986 and Friedman.

[235] Wacholder 1975, 201-209; cf. Bacchiocchi 1986, 172-174.

[236] Cf. Lev 25,10. The Year of Jubilee was never called a Sabbath, but it was calculated by means of sabbaths of years (Lev 25,8) and inaugurated on the Day of Atonement, a Sabbath (Lev 25,9; 16,31; 23,32). See Sloan, 12-18; Bacchiocchi 1986, 174f. G. Robinson 1975, 418f., takes Lev 25,10 as referring to the "Messianic age to come."

meaning. By abstaining from his work every seventh day man stands before God in absolute freedom, rejoicing in his salvation (cf. Is. 58:13f.), thus looking forward to the realisation of this joy of God's salvation and freedom for all people at all times.[237]

Without pursuing the matter further we may judge that such observations as these are not without foundation. The Sabbath does serve as a sort of capstone to both creation and the exodus, and Israel's future hopes were expressed largely in images taken from these events. Moreover, the description of the future age in terms of מנוחה and שלום would naturally lend itself to sabbatical conceptions. Without reading later notions back into the OT, maybe we may say that the characterization of the "hereafter" as a day which is "wholly Sabbath" finds some justification in the OT, even its starting point, although it is a formulation which is lacking there.

3.4. מנוחה and the Sabbath

Heb 3-4 interprets the oath of Ps 95,11 with reference to the record of God's Sabbath in Gen 2,2. From a modern perspective this is often judged to be forced and artificial. The conception of Gen 2 and that of the מנוחה tradition, it is said, "have absolutely nothing whatever in common."[238] This impression is not entirely justified, however, as there is more than one way in which the Sabbath institution and the promise of a מנוחה overlap and possibly relate to each other *in the OT*. If we do not restrict ourselves to God's own Sabbath but consider the Sabbath more broadly, it emerges that the Sabbath is very significantly tied to basic components of the מנוחה tradition: the land (e.g. Deut 12,9f.), the temple (e.g. Ps 132), and the kingship (e.g. 2Sam 7), all of which are central to the on-going life of Israel. If we focus directly on God's own Sabbath there is some evidence of contact as well.

3.4.1. *The land*

We have already noted that both the seventh day and seventh year Sabbaths were marks of YHWH's ownership of and sovereignty over the land. Arguing that the basic concern of the earliest command to stop work every seventh day was that of "other gods," Robinson makes the point that the seventh year was a "confessional act" (*Bekenntnisakt*) wherein Israel acknowledged "that Yahweh was the sole owner of the arable land and the author of its prosperity. For a [sic] early religious community, which was

---

[237] G. Robinson 1975, 420; similarly, Wolff 1972, 75; 1974, 141f.
[238] Von Rad 1966b, 101.

dependent on the produce of the land, this *šᵉmiṭṭā* truth has to be reminded [sic] more often than once in seven years. Not once in seven years, but once in seven days."²³⁹

Not only was the Sabbath a reminder of YHWH's ownership of the land, but it was celebrated as a reminder of the redemption out of bondage in Egypt (Deut 5,15). This does not concern itself directly with the land as a gift, but it does presuppose the idea of land possession; those who continue to be landless (the slaves) are not to be treated as such on this day. Moreover, on the Year of Jubilee their land, the inheritance of such dispossessed Jews, is to be returned to them (Lev 25,8-55).

Related to the latter point, we have already noted that the Sabbath rest can be construed as itself a realization of the מנוחה. Just as Israel had been brought out of bondage into her resting place, so those in bondage within her boarders were to be given rest on the seventh day. E. Jenni sees the מנוחה as constituting the "Bindeglied zwischen Sabbatfeier und Heilsgeschichte"; the "Heilsgut" of rest, "das durch die Heilsgeschichte verwirklicht wird, spiegelt nun der Sabbat, an dem das ganze Volk in Erinnerung an das Heilsgeschehen ruht.²⁴⁰ Likewise Robinson claims that the Sabbath is "the symbol of *mᵉnûḥā*, the ideal living condition in the *naḥᵃlā*, in the promised land."²⁴¹

Finally, "during the period of the O.T. the Israelites thought of the seventh-day-rest sabbath *only in relation to the promised land*, particularly in the context of the city of Jerusalem...The sabbath rest of the people is identical with the sabbath rest of the land. The person who faithfully observes the sabbath gets a portion in the land of Yahweh."²⁴²

3.4.2. The temple

Speaking of the exilic community, Andreasen writes that "we learn that the Sabbath was understood to be closely associated with the now lost temple, and we may presume, therefore, that the exiles considered an appropriate Sabbath celebration to be a temple celebration."²⁴³ This close nexus of Sabbath and temple is visible in several passages,²⁴⁴ and many priestly laws assume the celebration of the Sabbath in the temple.²⁴⁵ Robinson goes so far as to state that "almost all the sabbath-references in

---

²³⁹ G. Robinson 1975, 200, cf. 129, 170, and *passim*; Andreasen 1972, 217ff.
²⁴⁰ Jenni, 19.
²⁴¹ G. Robinson 1975, 418.
²⁴² G. Robinson 1975, 297, 299 (Robinson's emphasis); cf. Andreasen 1972, 242.
²⁴³ Andreasen 1972, 241 (cf. n. 2 in Andreasen).
²⁴⁴ E.g. 2Kgs 11,4-12; 16,17f.; Isa 1,10-14; and Lam 2,6; cf. G. Robinson 1975, 77-109, 56-63, 284ff.; aside from Lam 2 these are all considered pre-exilic by Robinson.
²⁴⁵ E.g. Lev 23,3; Num 28,9-10; Ezek 22,8.26; 23,38; 45,17; 46,4-5.

the O.T. attest sabbath's close relation to the cult around a local sanctuary or around the temple at Jerusalem."²⁴⁶

Robinson has also argued that the reference to a "Sabbath structure" (מיסך השבת) in 2Kgs 16,18 is probably related to the root שׂ/סךְ (*sk*) which is used elsewhere only in Ps 76,2 [MT 76,3]; Lam 2,6; Amos 9,11; and possibly Ps 27,5. His conclusion is that "the *sk* was some sort of a structure in the Jerusalem temple, which stood in close connection with the Davidic kingship." He continues, the

> ...*sk* seems to have become so identified with the Davidic kingship and the Judean kingdom, that *for the people of Judah the destruction of the sk meant the end of the Davidic kingship and the cessation of the observance of the sabbath (Lam. 2:6) and the restoration of the sk meant the restoration of the Davidic kingship (Am. 9:11) and the sabbath.*²⁴⁷

Along somewhat different lines, and in reference to the tabernacle, H.N. Wallace writes,

> The structuring of the narrative in Exodus 25-40 binds the sabbath observance closely with the construction of the sanctuary. Both are...tightly connected with the question of the presence of Yahweh with his people. Thus, in the thought of the P writer, the sabbath is a significant element in the celebration of the presence of Yahweh with his people. Just as the tabernacle was built along lines specified by divine decree, so too in the sequence is the human sabbath institution modelled on the divine pattern (Ex 20:8-11; 31:17). The sabbath shares in the task of proclaiming the self-revelation of Yahweh. It is also tied to the notion of the presence of Yahweh. Since the tabernacle, which is patterned on the divine plan, reveals the presence and shares in the role of heavenly temple to proclaim the sovereignty of the deity, so the sabbath shares in the proclamation of the sovereignty of Yahweh.²⁴⁸

Likewise, M. Weinfeld argues that Gen. 1:1-2:3 (the creation of the world) and Ex. 39:1-40:33 (the completion of the tabernacle) "are typologically identical. Both describe the satisfactory completion of the enterprise commanded by God, its inspection and approval, the blessing and the sanctification which are connected with it."²⁴⁹

3.4.3. The kingship

The remarks of Robinson concerning the *sk* apply here as well, since they reveal a basic connection between the Sabbath and kingship. This connection is evident in 2Kgs 11,4-12, where several items in the story would seem to suggest that the ruling king (or queen) regularly visited the

---

[246] G. Robinson 1975, 293.
[247] G. Robinson 1975, 107, 108 (Robinson's emphasis).
[248] Wallace, 246f.
[249] Weinfeld, 503. Weinfeld is able to show that this correspondence extends down to the manner of expression used in the two accounts.

temple on Sabbaths, and that the Sabbath was a preferred day for coronations in Judah.[250] Moreover, in addition to the *sk* (or, "Sabbath structure") mentioned above, 2Kgs 16,18 refers to a "king's entrance" to the temple, which would have symbolized the sovereignty of the king. The removal of this gate along with the *sk*, as in 2Kgs 16, would therefore symbolize the loss of this king's sovereignty.[251] The *sk*, probably a small tent located near the king's entrance, would have served as a place for the king as he led the people in worship or addressed them on the Sabbath.[252] This close relationship between the king, the temple, and the Sabbath is apparent in Lam 2,6, where the writer associates the cessation of Sabbath with the termination of the kingship and the laying waste of the *sk*.[253]

3.4.4. The divine otiositas

These broad areas of overlap between Israel's Sabbath rest and the מנוחה already alert us to the possibility of a definite relationship. This possibility is enhanced when we consider the ancient idea of the divine *otiositas*, to which we have referred more than once.

"It is a feature common to numerous myths of creation that the creative Being, once his work is complete, no longer leads any but an idle existence, characterized by an attitude of indifference towards men and worldly concerns generally."[254] Thus R. Pettazzoni summarizes the concept of the divine *otiositas*, which is elsewhere described as the "inactivity and rest of the creator god following the struggle or excessive effort involved in creating the world or ordering the chaos into a created cosmos, or following some other disruptive event."[255] This may be made clearer with a few examples.

---

[250] G. Robinson 1975, 92-95.
[251] G. Robinson 1975, 102ff.
[252] G. Robinson 1975, 108.
[253] A further development of this is noted by Robinson in Ezekiel. In the new order YHWH alone is king; thus YHWH takes the place of the king, making his entrance in the king's gate ("the gate facing east"; Ezek 43,4; cf. 20,33). As a result the Sabbath comes to be designated as "my Sabbaths" (Ezek 20,12; 13,16.20f.24 and *passim*) and the eastern gate is shut (44,1-3) except for the Sabbath (46,1-2a) when the "prince" alone may enter through it. "*Sabbath henceforth symbolizes the royal sovereignty of Yahweh*, his victory over the gods, over the astral powers, over the moon, the sun and the hosts of heaven, and his reign over them all (Isa. 24:23)" (G. Robinson 1975, 341, cf. 301f., 332ff.; his emphasis).
[254] Pettazzoni, 32. Cf. Andreasen 1972, 174ff.; Wallace, 237-241; Weinfeld, 501ff.
[255] Andreasen 1972, 174 n. 1.

In the Babylonian creation epic, the *Enūma eliš*,[256] Apsu and Tiamat, the primeval waters, were denied rest by the surging of the lower gods. Apsu cried out,

Their ways are very loathsome unto me.
By day I find no relief, nor repose by night.
I will destroy, I will wreck their ways,
That quiet may be restored. Let us have rest!"[257]

One of the gods, Ea, however, defeated Apsu, and as a result had "profound peace and rested."[258] Subsequently a battle took place between Tiamat and Ea's son, Marduk. When Marduk gained victory over Taimat he created and organized the world, creating man to be "charged with the service of the gods that they may be at ease!"[259] The other gods are so pleased that they pay homage to him by building him a "shrine":

The Anunnaki opened their mouths
And said to Marduk, their lord:
"Now, O lord, thou who hast caused our deliverance,
What shall be our homage to thee?
Let us build a shrine whose name shall be called
'Lo, a chamber for our nightly rest'; let us repose in it!
Let us build a throne, a recess for his abode!
On the day that we arrive we shall repose in it."[260]

Another example comes from the old Egyptian creation account, "The Theology of Memphis."[261] Here creation is accomplished by the divine word of Ptah, and when he has finished with creating it is said, "And so Ptah was satisfied [or, "rested"], after he had made everything, as well as all the divine order."[262]

Pettazzoni suggests that the presence of the *otiositas* motif in the various creation accounts can be explained as "a kind of elimination of the Creator in face [sic] of other deities who in the end push him into the background,"

---

[256] Dated to the first part of the second millennium B.C. (*ANET*, 60).
[257] *ANET*, 61.
[258] *ANET*, 61.
[259] *ANET*, 68. The notion that man is created to "carry the yoke" of the gods, thus giving the gods rest, is found also in the creation account of the Atra--Hasis flood story; cf. Lambert-Millard, 45, 59f., 73, and discussion in Andreasen 1972, 176f.; Wallace, 238.
[260] *ANET*, 68.
[261] Andreasen remarks that "the god Ptah may have been known in Syro-Palestine as early as the middle of the second millennium B.C." (1972, 178 n. 3).
[262] *ANET*, 5 (cf. n. 19 in *ANET*). Another Egyptian example of a primordial temple, though without the rest motif, is in the "Instruction for King Merikare"; cf. Beyerlin, 44, 46; *ANET*, 417; for discussion and comparison to Gen 1-2, cf. Doukhan, 120ff.

or, alternatively, as belonging "to the essential nature of the creative Beings," and as being "in a way the complement of their creative activity":

> The world once made and the cosmos established, the Creator's work is as good as done. Any further intervention on his part would be not only superfluous but possibly dangerous, since any change in the cosmos might allow it to fall back into chaos. Once the world is made, the existential function of the Creator could be nothing but prolonging its duration and ensuring its unaltered and unalterable stability. The *otiositas* of the creative Being,...is the most favorable condition and the one naturally best suited to maintain the *status quo*.[263]

As pointed out by Andreasen, however, it may not be an either/or, as both of these explanations fit the accounts to some degree.[264] He observes further that if the gods rest in order to ensure the stability of creation, then it is also the case that the stability (or chaos) of the world affects the ability of the gods to repose.[265]

Our reason for reviewing these well known passages is to make evident that when these myths climax in the building of a temple in which the gods "rest" or "repose" following victory over their enemies, there is a startling parallel to the idea of YHWH's מנוחה in the temple following the defeat of Israel's enemies. According to Andreasen it is OT passages such as 2Chr 6 and Ps 132 which provide the closest biblical parallels to the myth since here "we have the ark or throne of Yahweh identified as the place of his rest; and we learn that when Yahweh is at rest in Zion, national and political security is established..."[266]

On the other hand, we have already had occasion to note examples of ways in which these myths are used to explain Gen 1-2. Our present purpose does not allow us to enter into these separate discussions, but we may note that when the traditions of both YHWH's מנוחה in the temple and his Sabbath rest following creation seem to exhibit definite links with the very same Near Eastern mythological traditions, the temptation is strong to merge the two OT traditions into one and to claim that YHWH's rest following creation (as in Ex 20,11) is none other than his מנוחה in the temple (Ps 132).[267] This position must be located at the pole opposite from the one which says that these traditions had "absolutely nothing whatever in common."

---

[263] Pettazzoni, 32f.
[264] Andreasen 1972, 179f.
[265] Andreasen 1972, 182.
[266] Andreasen 1972, 182f., also 185f. Carlson, 98, also asserts that the events depicted and motifs employed in 2Sam 5-7 which lead up to David's desire to build a house for the Ark correspond "exactly to the ideas connected with the building of a temple...in the ancient Near East generally." The achievement of rest from the enemies round about "demands to be made manifest in the building of a temple..."
[267] G. Robinson 1975, 348.

Support for some such joining of the two traditions may be found in the possibility that the priestly circles -- who were, so it is believed, responsible for the accounts of Gen 2,2f.; Ex 20,11; and Ex 31,17 -- were acquainted with the tradition of the divine *otiositas* as it found expression in YHWH's מנוחה in the temple.[268] Further, both Wallace and Weinfeld have argued against the backdrop of the divine *otiositas* motif that the Sabbath and the tabernacle are brought into the closest possible connection in Ex 39-40, and that this correspondence includes the patterns of the two narratives, Ex 39-40 and Gen 1-2.[269] Along similar lines, J. Levenson points out how significantly the number seven crops up in the account of the completion of the temple in 1Kgs 6 and 8. It is likely, he concludes, "that the construction of the Temple is presented here as a parallel to the construction of the world in seven days."[270]

Continuing with Weinfeld's line of argument, he points out that just as Marduk's victory over his enemies is followed by the creation of the world, Marduk's enthronement, and the erection of a temple, so in Ex 15 -- the "Song of the Sea" -- we find that, immediately following the account of YHWH's victory over his enemies in the sea, there is a reference to YHWH's "holy dwelling," his "sanctuary," on the mountain of his inheritance (vv. 13.17), and that YHWH "will reign forever and ever" (v. 18).[271] This means that on the one hand, the temple and creation link up in Ex 39-40, and, on the other hand, the temple and YHWH's victory/enthronement link up in Ex 15. These three components (temple, creation, enthronement), then, are found to converge in Ps. 93, which, along with other psalms, likely formed a part of Sabbath temple liturgy.[272]

It is possible, then, that there was an assumed relationship between YHWH's מנוחה in the temple and his Sabbath rest following creation by association with well-known mythology.

3.4.5. Summary and conclusions

The land, temple, and kingship are all basic features of Israel's life, and it may be less than remarkable that both the Sabbath and the מנוחה are

---

[268] Andreasen 1972, 185.
[269] Wallace, 235-250; Weinfeld, 501-512.
[270] Levenson, 289. J. Robinson, 111, adds the following comment to 1Kgs 8,56: "At the creation God was said to have rested when the work had been completed satisfactorily, and here, since God has fulfilled all his promises, Israel has now reached the same state of rest." Levenson, 295f., also notes that Isa 66,1-2 amounts to a designation of creation itself as God's temple.
[271] Weinfeld, 507; cf. Cross, 121-144.
[272] Weinfeld, 508ff. Levenson, 291f., notes the conjoining of Sabbath, temple, and enthronement in Isa 56,1-7 (cf. also his discussion of Isa 61,1-2; 293f.).

related to these three things. The point, however, is that we are confronted with two, very important and prominent usages of the rest motif in the OT, and they *both* bear important links to these features of Israel's existence. When it is appreciated that both the Sabbath and the מנוחה were in their own way a symbol of God's redemption out of Egypt, the distance between the two traditions does not seem so great. When we look through the lens of the ancient, mythological idea of the divine *otiositas* at both God's rest in the temple and his rest on the seventh day a common ancestry appears possible.

Yet it may also have been evident that the way in which these two traditions related to the land, the temple, and kingship differed substantially. The land is where YHWH gives Israel "rest" (נוח) from travelling and from her enemies, and can itself be called her "resting place" (מנוחה), just as the temple (or Zion) can be called YHWH's "resting place." None of this can be said of the Sabbath in relation to the land or the temple; it is only with some effort that the "appeasement" of YHWH's anger following the defeat of his foes (as in the myth) can be wrung out of נוח in Ex 20,11.[273] Likewise, it is kings David and Solomon whose reigns enjoy a divinely bestowed rest (נוח) from enemies, paving the way for the erection of the temple; in the future it is the Root of Jesse whose מנוחה will be glory. This is somewhat different than the connection between the *Sabbath* and kingship which has to do by and large with the king's part in Sabbath celebrations in the temple.

Regarding the divine *otiositas* we are forced to recognize substantial arguments for tracing both YHWH's מנוחה in the temple and his Sabbath rest following creation back to a common conceptual starting point. Indeed, the parallels are intriguing, and an explanation which relates the two is almost demanded.[274] Nonetheless, the stubborn fact remains that at no point does the idea of a Sabbath rest, or the Sabbath institution generally, bear a direct connection with the מנוחה in any of the passages examined earlier in this chapter, and the temple or tabernacle is never characterized as YHWH's "resting place" (מנוחה) in direct connection with the Sabbath. A text where these two traditions come together in a promising way is Isa 66 where, in v. 1, creation as YHWH's temple -- one of the only two usages of "my resting place" outside of Ps 95,11 (cf. Ps 132,14)[275] -- is found in the same

---

[273] Redaction critically, this verb's presence in Ex 20,11 has been explained by Hulst 1966, 162, as resulting from this verse's dependence on Deut 5 where it is used of man's rest; likewise Hossfeld, 52.

[274] For differing explanations, cf. G. Robinson 1975, 348; Weinfeld, 510, 512; Wallace, 241-243, 248-250; Levenson, 288.

[275] Also, Isa 66,1 is the only other κατάπαυσις text quoted from the LXX by the NT (Acts 7,49), in a speech in which more than one NT scholar has found parallels to Hebrews.

context as one of the clearest expressions of eschatological Sabbaths (plural; v. 23); yet even here there is no direct connection drawn between the two. It seems that an inner connection between these traditions -- Sabbath and מנוחה -- was probably observed by some in ancient Israel, but we should not ignore the fact that the two traditions never do what some modern scholars want to force them to do: they do not explicitly mix the one with the other, YHWH's rest in the temple with his rest following creation. It is enough to recognize the connection in Israel's traditions, and to observe that this connection is probably not merely apparent.[276]

3.5. Summary and conclusions of part two

In brief, Part Two has sought (1) to establish the presence and significance of the rest motif in connection with the Sabbath, (2) to determine the sense in which we may speak of an eschatological Sabbath in the OT, and, finally, (3) to ask how the Sabbath and the מנוחה traditions relate to each other. The conclusions to (1) and (3) have already been given.[277] As to (2), though the Sabbath has a place in OT eschatological expectations it is as a recurring festival rather than as a symbolic description of the eschatological age itself. Nonetheless many of the elements of the latter (and later) idea may be found in the OT when the eschatological age is described in terms which are consistent with Sabbath theology.

4. Summary and conclusions

Part One focused on the tradition of Israel's rest in the land and YHWH's rest in the temple, most commonly associated with the verb נוח and the noun מנוחה. The study anchored itself in the Dtr history, but included also Chronicles, Psalms, Isaiah, Jeremiah, Lamentations, and Micah. In almost none of the many relevant contexts does the tradition occur incidentally; it appears to have been a weighty concept which was invoked in each case for a good reason. *The rest tradition is a very prominent OT redemptive category* (§ 2.10.1) which was incorporated into Israel's eschatological hopes (§ 2.10.2). In order to facilitate an answer to the question of whether and how the OT influenced the NT passages we isolated several motifs which cluster about the promise of rest, especially

---

[276] Wenham, 65, 87, finds that some of the language in the Genesis creation narrative, e.g., 2,10-14, resonates with ideas of the tabernacle and temple.
[277] Supra, 65, 73-75.

the land (§ 2.10.3), the temple (§ 2.10.4), the Davidic kingship (§ 2.10.5), and weariness (§ 2.10.6).

Part Two of this chapter shifted its attention to the Sabbath, as another major OT area wherein the rest motif is connected with redemption. First we considered the role of the rest motif in the Sabbath (§ 3.2). It was found that precisely where the Sabbath is associated with redemption from bondage it comes closest to the promise of rest (מנוחה) in the land. In the case of the Sabbath rest, it is a humanitarian concern for the physical relief of the enslaved laborer and beast of burden. As for God's Sabbath rest, it may bear implications for Israel's Sabbath, but it was probably addressed more directly to the subject of creation -- as a response to the myth -- than to the Sabbath institution as such.

There are shadows of what may be called an "eschatological Sabbath," though these never hardened into expectations of a "day which is wholly Sabbath." At best, the Sabbath was associated with Israel's future hopes as a token of on-going and purified covenant life, free of hostile and profane interference (§ 3.3). Finally, the relationship of the Sabbath to the מנוחה was explored. The significant areas of overlap, along with the common ties to the mythological divine *otiositas* motif, make theories of some sort of relationship between the two traditions credible. Yet the many differences and their almost complete textual independence caution against freely reading elements of the one tradition into the other (§ 3.4).

Chapter Three

The Rest Motif in the LXX

1. Introduction

The previous chapter has prepared the way for a discussion of the use of the rest motif in the LXX.[1] This is of great importance for our study, since

---

[1] It is necessary to make five points. (1) The *Vorlage* of the LXX is now usually distinguished from the MT (Mulder, 98f., 103f.; cf. above, 17 n. 1). With this caveat in mind we might nevertheless *compare* the two to get a general picture. In most of the relevant passages it is sufficiently clear that the MT was identical to the LXX's *Vorlage*. (2) It is doubtful that there was only one Greek translation of the OT in circulation in the first century A.D., and also that the texts were fixed. In spite of which we shall follow accepted scholarly convention by using the abbreviation (the) "LXX" in reference to the Greek translation used by a NT author. We will need to take account of this complexity when considering the use of the LXX by Matthew and *Auctor* (see the following footnote). In general, however, we have assumed the theory behind the Göttingen editions of the LXX -- to wit, that "a single set of original translations of the Hebrew scriptures into Greek was effected in several stages, and in locations not known for sure; ...[that] the last parts were completed by the first part of the 1st century B.C.E." (Peters, 1094; cf. Jellicoe 1968; 1974; *HJP*[2], 3/1:474-493; Tov) -- and have accordingly relied on those editions. This provides us with a LXX text for the purposes of the present chapter, and a firm starting point for consideration of the use of the LXX in the NT. In this vein, see the recent remarks of Barr 1994. (3) Sirach, in particular, is a difficult case: "great prudence is needed when speaking of the text of Ben Sira" (Gilbert, 292). On the whole matter see Gilbert, 290-292; Skehan-Di Lella, 51-62; *HJP*[2], 3/1:202-205. In simplified form the history of the texts can be outlined as follows: the Hebrew original was penned in Jerusalem by Ben Sira in 190 B.C. (Hebrew I), and this work was translated into Greek in Egypt by his grandson in 132 B.C. (Greek I); from 50 B.C. until about A.D. 150 the Hebrew text underwent changes, including a few additions (Hebrew II), and sometime between A.D. 150 and 200 a second Greek translation was made on the basis of Hebrew II (Greek II). Accordingly, in theory, at least, a first century writer like Matthew could have known Hebrew I, and/or Greek I, and/or some form of Hebrew II. Our researches will be based primarily on the Göttingen LXX edition of Ziegler, with reference to the work of Skehan-Di Lella and Skehan on the Hebrew of Sir 51. (4) On the question of "canon," see above, 17 n. 1. For the purposes of the present chapter we will consider works generally included in modern editions of the LXX. (5) When we refer to Matthew's or *Auctor*'s "LXX," we are not implying that their collection of OT books or their OT text (or texts) was necessarily the same as that of the modern editions.

the author of Hebrews knew the OT only in Greek and since the LXX was used by the author of Matthew.[2] It is necessary, therefore, to ascertain how the rest tradition fared in the Greek version (§ 2), e.g., in terms of noteworthy developments or omissions. Since different words are used in Mt 11 (ἀναπαύω, ἀνάπαυσις) and Heb 3-4 (καταπαύω, κατάπαυσις), we need to ask to what extent these terms are representative of the tradition. Generally speaking, unless the text of the LXX gives us reason to modify the conclusions we have already reached regarding the contours and content of the rest tradition in the OT, our approach will be to assume what we have already covered, and the same will be the case for the Sabbath (§ 3).

We will add to these two sections a treatment of the rest motif in wisdom literature (§ 4). Alongside the rest tradition and the Sabbath, this is one of the most significant usages of the rest motif in the LXX, and it is somewhat distinctive relative to the other two usages.[3] This usage has become very important in discussions of Mt 11,28-30, and we will also have reason to note it in connection with Philo and Gnosticism. While this usage finds expression in Job, Proverbs, and Ecclesiastes, it is more highly developed in later works, especially Sirach.

Finally, since one aspect of the debate in Heb 3-4 has centered on the meaning and use of the word κατάπαυσις in the LXX it will be necessary to subject this word to an examination (§ 5).

2. The rest tradition

2.1. Introduction

We will first confine ourselves to the passages we have already considered in the MT, making some general observations about them (§ 2.2), and then look individually at relevant passages which are unique to the LXX relative to the MT (§ 2.3).

---

[2] On Matthew's use of the OT, see below, 162f.; on *Auctor*'s use of it, see below, 258. See also the previous note.

[3] This "distinctiveness" should not be exaggerated. It consists in that the direct links to the land, the temple, and the kingship which are found in the rest tradition and the Sabbath are not found in this "wisdom usage." Wisdom's rest is concerned with everyday life and with wisdom itself; it does not exhibit the strong link with the history of salvation. Yet these different usages of the rest motif are not completely unrelated, as will ultimately emerge from our own investigation.

2.2. The MT rest tradition in the LXX

2.2.1. Comparison[4]

The following chart combines Deut 3,20; Josh 1,13.15; and 22,4[5] with the rest tradition passages already considered.[6]

	καταπαύω	κατάπαυσις[7]	ἀναπαύω[8]	ἀνάπαυσις[9]	ἀνάπαυμα
נוח Hi/1	Ex 33,14; Deut 3,20; 12,10; 25,19; Josh 1,13.15; 21,44; 22,4; 23,1; 1Par 23,25; 2Par 14,5.6; 15,15; 20,30; 32,22[10]		2Kgdms 7,11; 3Kgdms 5,18; 1Par 22,9; 22,18; Isa 14,3[11]		
נוח Ho/1			Lam 5,5		
נוח Qal		2Par 6,41			
מנוחה		Deut 12,9; 3Kgdms 8,56; Ψ 94,11; Ψ 131,14; Isa 66,1	Isa 32,18	1Par 22,9; 28,2; Ψ 131,8; Isa 11,10; Micah 2,10	Isa 28,12
מנוח		1Par 6,16		Lam 1,3	
שקט	Josh 11,23[12]				
רגע Hi				Deut 28,65	

---

[4] See above, 77 n. 1.
[5] Supra, 22f.
[6] Cf. also the following: Ἡσυχάζω (שקט Qal) in Judg 3,11.30; 5,31; 8,28; and 2Par 13,23 [14,1]; ἡσυχία (שקט) in 1Par 22,9; εἰρηνεύω (שקט Qal) in 2Par 14,4.5 [14,5.6]; and 20,30. Ἡσυχάζω (שקט Qal) in Judg 18,7.27; Jer 26,27 [46,27]; and Zech 1,11 (cf. ἡσυχία [שקט Qal] in 1Par 4,40; and the phrase, ἡσυχάζοντας ἐν ἡσυχία [שקט Qal] in Ezek 38,11) as well as 4Kgdms 11,20 and 2Par 23,21. Cf. ἡσυχάζω (שקט Qal) in Ψ 75,9 [76,8].
[7] Cf. also κατάπαυσις (MT: נוח Qal) in Num 10,35 [10,36], and καταπαῦσαι αὐτὸν κατάπαυσιν (MT: מנוחה) in Judg 20,43.
[8] Cf. also ἀναπαύω (MT: נוח Qal) in Neh 9,28; and Esth 9,16.17.18.22. The same (MT: נוח Hi/1) in Zech 6,8; also (MT: שאן) in Jer 31,11 [48,11].
[9] Cf. also ἀνάπαυσις (MT: מנוחה) in Gen 49,15; Num 10,33; Ruth 1,9; Ψ 22,2 [23,2]; Jer 51,33 [45,3]. The same (MT: מנוה) in Gen 8,9; Ruth 3,1; Ψ 114,7 [116,7]; Isa 34,14; and (MT: נוח Qal) in Isa 23,12.
[10] On the Hebrew of 2Chr 32,22, cf. HALAT, 642; BDB, 628; R. Braun 1986, 225; Dillard 1987, 254.
[11] Cf. the use of ἀναπαύω (נוח Qal) in Isa 14,7.
[12] Josh 11,23 was not considered among the rest tradition passages but it can be included here in view of the Greek version.

It can be noted that a few of the usages of rest terminology in relevant MT passages are without an equivalent in the LXX.[13] Deut 28,65 refers to a מנוח for their feet; the LXX reads στάσις τῷ ἴχνει τοῦ ποδός σου, possibly because of the use of ἀναπαύω in the previous clause. 2Kgdms 7,1 (נוח Hi/1) has κατεκληρονόμησεν, "he gave an inheritance," possibly to harmonize the chapter with 1Kgs/3Kgdms 5 where it said that David could not build the temple because of his wars, but that now Solomon can because God has given him rest (note the future ἀναπαύσω in 2Kgdms 7,11).[14] In Isa 28,12 there is no Greek equivalent for נוח Hi/1 (although ἀνάπαυμα occurs there [MT: מנוחה]). Isa 63,14 (נוח Hi/1) has ὡδήγησεν, "he guided."[15] None of the three passages in Jeremiah contains a reference to rest in the LXX: 6,16 uses ἁγνισμόν ("purification") (MT: מרגוע),[16] and 38,2 reads μὴ ὀλέσητε ("do not slay") (MT 31,2: רגע Hi), while MT 50,34 רגע Hi has no equivalent in the LXX 27,34.

2.2.2. Evaluation

There is little change in the substance of the rest tradition in the LXX with respect to the passages already considered. The fact that Isa 63,14 and the three passages in Jeremiah must be struck from our list as regards the LXX makes little difference to the tradition as a whole in that version.[17] In the main, the features and related motifs remain constant.

All of the relevant passages which are translated with rest vocabulary use either the ἀναπαυ- or καταπαυ- stem.[18] Limiting ourselves to the above chart, the verb καταπαύω is used 16 times while ἀναπαύω occurs 8 times. There is thus a disproportionate use of the verb καταπαύω, since overall in the LXX the two verbs occur with about equal frequency (καταπαύω: 76x; ἀναπαύω: 78x).[19] The same discrepancy could be noted with the nouns:

---

[13] As in the foregoing chart, any of these might be due to a differing *Vorlage*. In addition to those listed in the text, cf. Josh 14,15 (שקט Qal) which uses κοπάζω, "cease or come to an end" (because the same idea was already expressed in 11,23?). Cf. also 2Kgdms 14,17; Jer 28,59 [51,59]; and Zech 9,1, all of which use the word מנוחה in the MT (none of these passages were considered to be relevant in the foregoing discussion).

[14] BHS notes the LXX as a variant at 2Sam 7,1; cf. 1Chr 17.

[15] On the text of the MT, see Westermann, 390; Watts 1987, 327 n. 14a.

[16] Note that the related noun, מרגעה, in the MT of Isa 28,12 also has no equivalent in the LXX: σύντριμμα (calamity; ruin).

[17] The other instances where we noted the absence of the idea of "rest" in the Greek do contain related terms in the same verse or immediate LXX context (Deut 28,65; 2Kgdms 7,1 [cf. v. 11]; Isa 28,12).

[18] The שקט passages in the MT generally use ἡσυχ- in the LXX.

[19] Cf. Hatch-Redpath. Here and in the following sentence the word-count statistics are only meant to be taken generally, since no consideration has been given to variants with the exception of κατάπαυσις.

κατάπαυσις (LXX: 11x)[20] is used 7 times, while ἀνάπαυσις (LXX: over 50x) is used 6 times; though κατάπαυσις is far less common in the LXX it occurs with equal frequency in the rest tradition. Perhaps the note of "cessation" (from travels and troubles) in καταπαυ- was generally favored over that of rest in the sense of "relief" or "repose," yet a glance at *usage* of both of the nouns and verbs does not betray a consistent principle of distinction.[21] Although καταπαυ- might be the more representative term, it would appear that the tradition could be represented just as well with ἀναπαυ-.

2.3. Passages unique to the LXX

The passages just surveyed were limited to those which we recognized as belonging to the rest tradition in the MT. Now we may note that there are several passages unique to the LXX which could be added to this list. Since the following have not yet been treated we may do so here.[22]

---

[20] Cf. Ex 35,2; Num 10,35 [10,36]; Deut 12,9; 3Kgdms 8,56; 1Par 6,16 [6,31]; 2Par 6,41; Ψ 94,11 [95,11]; Ψ 131,14 [132,14]; Isa 66,1; Jdt 9,8; and 2Mac 15,1; as a variant in Ex 34,21 B (2x); Lev 25,28 A B*; and Judg 20,43 A.

[21] Compare, e.g., 2Kgdms 7,11; 3Kgdms 5,18 [5,4], with Deut 12,10; Josh 23,1; see further below, 88f., 96ff. The favoring of καταπαυ- is not made clearer by the following considerations. Καταπαύω in the sense of, "give rest to," or, "cause to rest," is largely confined to the LXX (Bauernfeind 1965, 627; Bauer-Aland, 845, find parallels for the meaning, "zur Ruhe bringen," in TestJob 14,5 and Josephus, *Ant* 3,14); LSJM, 904, does not even list these meanings. On the other hand, ἀναπαύω can mean "make to cease," "give rest (from travelling)," "relieve (from something)," etc. (cf. LSJM, 115; Bauernfeind 1964, 350). While the noun, κατάπαυσις, is used generally in classical Greek in the active sense ("resting"; "being set in a state of rest"; cf. Hofius, 168 n. 212; the single known exception is Theophrastus, *Vent* 18 which uses the passive sense; cf. LSJM, 904; Bauernfeind 1965, 628), it occurs in the LXX only in the passive sense, "rest." In texts which are dependent on the LXX the passive is also used (Hofius, 29-33). Ἀνάπαυσις, however, occurs frequently with the sense of, "repose," "relax," or "rest (from something)" (LSJM, 115). Thus, with both the verb καταπαύω and the noun κατάπαυσις it appears that a word has been used in a unique way in the LXX, when an equally common (in the case of the noun, a much more common) and apparently serviceable word was available and sometimes used. Bauernfeind 1965, 627, suggests that καταπαύω, which otherwise stands for a "painful invasion of my sphere" (e.g., "to cause to cease"; "to prevent"; "to restrain"; "to kill") is used in the LXX with the more positive meaning -- "to bring someone to the point where he ceases to suffer something" -- because of the OT view that "the way of man, if it is to be purposive, is characterized by a superior encroachment, by a pitiless οὐκ ἐπιθυμήσεις." This seems somewhat fanciful.

[22] In addition to those mentioned here, cf. the variant in Lev 25,28 A B*, where κατάπαυσις is used of a person's inheritance. Cf. also Deut 33,12.

2.3.1. Deut 5,33

The Israelites have just heard the voice of the Lord out of the midst of the fire on the mountain, and have asked Moses to approach the mountain on their behalf so as to mediate the Lord's words to them; they will listen to God's words and do them. Hearing this request from the people the Lord expresses his longing that they would remain ever this faithful to him. Calling Moses to himself he announces that he will tell Moses the commands which Moses is to teach to the people. They are exhorted to obey the commands of the Lord in order that καταπαύσῃ σε[23] καὶ εὖ σοι ᾖ καὶ μακροημερεύσητε ἐπὶ τῆς γῆς, ἧς κληρονομήσετε ("that he may give you rest, and that it may be well with you and you may prolong your days on the land, which you will inherit").

2.3.2. Isa 25,10

The prophet declares that he will glorify God (25,1: Κύριε ὁ θεός μου, δοξάσω σε, ὑμνήσω τὸ ὄνομά σου) because God has destroyed the works of the ungodly. The poor people will bless God (25,3: εὐλογήσει σε ὁ λαὸς ὁ πτωχός) for he has been a helper to every lowly city (πόλει ταπεινῇ). The Lord will prepare a feast for his people on "this mount" and in that day they will exalt in the salvation of their God. Further, ἀνάπαυσιν δώσει[24] ὁ θεὸς ἐπὶ τὸ ὄρος τοῦτο (v. 10: "God will give rest on this mountain"), while he brings Moab low so that the feet of the meek and lowly (πόδες πραέων καὶ ταπεινῶν) trample those who were previously exalted (26,6). In this passage, then, Mt. Zion is not first of all God's resting place, but the place where God gives rest to Israel. The configuration of "blessing," rest, and "meek and lowly," reminds of Mt 11,25-30.

2.3.3. Isa 32,17

Our survey of the MT noted the use of the word מנוחה in Isa 32,18 and judged that it fell within the pale of the rest tradition. The idea of the rest tradition seems more pronounced in the Greek version when v. 17 uses the word ἀνάπαυσις[25] ("righteousness will ensure rest"), and v. 18 reads: καὶ ἀναπαύσονται μετὰ πλούτου[26] ("and they will rest with wealth").

---

[23] MT: תחיון, "you may live."
[24] MT: תנוח יד־יהוה, "the hand of YHWH will rest" on this mountain.
[25] MT: שקט Hi.
[26] MT: ובמנוחת שאננות ("and in undisturbed places of rest").

2.3.4. Ezek 34,14.15

The Lord speaks against the shepherds of Israel for failing to care for the flock of Israel. The weak (34,4: τὸ ἠσθενηκὸς), the sick, the bruised, the strays, and the lost have not been cared for, while the strong have been wearied with labor (v. 4: τὸ ἰσχυρὸν κατειργάσασθε μόχθῳ). Because his people have been scattered over the earth and none have sought them out, the Lord is against the shepherds and he declares that he himself will seek his sheep and visit them (v. 11: ἐπισκέψομαι αὐτα). He will bring his people back to their own land and care for them there. He will feed them in a good pasture, on a high mountain (v. 14: ἐν τῷ ὄρει τῷ ὑψηλῷ) they will lie down and "rest" there (v. 14: ἀναπαύσονται; no equivalent in MT). The Lord declares (v. 15): ἐγὼ βοσκήσω τὰ πρόβατά μου καὶ ἐγὼ ἀναπαύσω αὐτά,[27] καὶ γνώσονται ὅτι ἐγώ εἰμι κύριος ("I will feed my sheep and I will give them rest, and they will know that I am the Lord"). The Lord will seek the lost (v. 16: τὸ ἀπολωλὸς ζητήσω) while he judges between the strong and weak sheep. He will raise up one shepherd over them: his servant David (v. 23: τὸν δοῦλόν μου Δαυιδ; cf. 2Kgdms 7,5), who will be their shepherd and a prince before the Lord. The Lord will make a covenant of peace with David, banishing the wild beasts from the land, settling his people around "my mountain", blessing the land, breaking the yoke of those who had enslaved them, and guarding them from the nations which would despoil them.[28] If v. 15 was not influenced by the rest tradition (esp. 2Sam/2Kgdms 7), then it could be mistaken for one which was.

2.3.5. Jdt 9,8

Judith prays to the Lord to deliver Israel from the Assyrians, ἐβουλεύσαντο γὰρ βεβηλῶσαι τὰ ἅγιά σου, μιᾶναι τὸ σκήνωμα τῆς καταπαύσεως τοῦ ὀνόματος τῆς δόξης σου, καταβαλεῖν σιδήρῳ κέρας θυσιαστηρίου σου ("for they have purposed to profane thy sanctuary, and to defile the tabernacle where thy glorious name resteth, and to cast down with the sword the horn of thine altar"; cf. 8,21.24).[29] Part of the impetus for this prayer was probably the fact that God had said that Zion would be his resting

---

[27] MT: "I will tend my sheep and cause them to lie down [ארביצם]."
[28] Cf. Lev 26,1-13.
[29] ET *APOT*, 1:258. Moore, 189, and Hofius, 49, understand this construction to be a genitive of apposition and κατάπαυσις to be a locale; thus, "...the tabernacle, the resting place of your glorious name." The construction and choice is very similar to 1Par 28,2: οἶκον ἀναπαύσεως τῆς κιβωτοῦ διαθήκης κυρίου. Hofius, 49, takes ἀνάπαυσις in the latter text as a state of rest ("house of rest"), and we might do the same here; similarly, Enslin-Zeitlin, 125; RV; RSV; NRSV.

place *forever* (Ψ 131,14 [132,14]). It is also likely that the rest tradition was invoked as a reminder of the "rest from enemies" bound up with the temple in both the Deuteronomist's and Chronicler's accounts, as well as the protection implied in the context of Ps 132.

2.3.6. Sir 24,7-11

Personified Wisdom glories in her exalted status in creation (24,1ff.), and recounts how she sought a resting place (v. 7: ἀνάπαυσιν ἐζήτησα)[30] and an inheritance among all the nations. Then the Creator of everything, and specifically the Creator of Wisdom, caused her tabernacle to rest (v. 8: ὁ κτίσας με κατέπαυσεν τὴν σκηνήν μου) in Jacob, and her inheritance in Israel. Created before the beginning of world, Wisdom will never fail. She served before the Lord in the tabernacle and was thus established in Zion. In the beloved city the Lord gave her rest (v. 11: με κατέπαυσεν) and in Jerusalem was her authority, having taken root among an honorable people.[31] Thus, in this passage, the exalted status of Wisdom, the identification of personified wisdom with the Law,[32] and the election of Israel (on Israel's merits) coalesce, and this with the aid of the rest tradition. This usage of the rest motif evidently stems from the OT temple traditions of Ps 132,8.14 -- although here God's rest is supplanted by the rest of wisdom *qua* Law[33] -- but it is exploited primarily to press home how Israel possesses wisdom (Wisdom) in her Law, and thus also to highlight Israel's own praiseworthy and privileged status.[34]

---

[30] Skehan-Di Lella, 333, compare this use of ἀνάπαυσις to the dove's futile search for a resting place (ἀνάπαυσις) in Gen 8,9. Yet ἀνάπαυσις is also used in Ψ 131,8 [132,8] (cf. 1Par 28,2) and this latter connection corresponds more closely to the use of καταπαύω in vv. 8 and 11 in Sir 24; Smend 1906a, 217, comments that ἀνάπαυσις here "= מנוחה im Sinne von Jes. 11,10"; likewise, *APOT*, 1:397.

[31] This "particularistic" idea that Wisdom found a place among Israel is paralleled in AZ 2b and Midrash *Pesiqta* 186a. By way of contrast is 1En 42,1f.: "Wisdom could not find a place in which she could dwell; but a place was found (for her) in the heavens. Then Wisdom went out to dwell with the children of the people, but she found no dwelling place. (So) Wisdom returned to her place and she settled permanently among the angels" (*OTP*, 1:33).

[32] On wisdom = Law in Sirach, cf. 24,23; also 19,20; 1,25-27 and 6,32-37. Cf. also Deut 4,6; 33,4; Helderman 1984, 57; infra, 165.

[33] Though Wisdom has an exalted, even pre-existent status, and is linked closely to the tabernacle, she remains a creation of God (vv. 8-9) and thus separate from him. This is shown further in that God gives rest to Wisdom in the same way that he gave rest to Israel.

[34] Against reading an *Isis-Aretologie* behind Sir 24,3-7 (cf. von Rad 1972b, 160 n. 17), cf. Helderman 1984, 57.

2.3.7. Sir 36,18 (15)[35]

The context of this usage is a prayer that God will come to the rescue of his people and to humble the Seleucid overlords. Following a plea that God would repeat the saving acts of the exodus and re-gather the "tribes of Jacob" (cf. Isa 11,11f.; 49,6; Jer 38,3.8 [31,3.8]; etc.) "that they may inherit the land as in days of old," it is asked that he will be merciful to his holy city, to Ιερουσαλημ τόπον [B* πόλιν] καταπαύματός σου (v. 18: "Jerusalem, the place of your rest").[36] Here, along with ideas such as "inheritance," "firstborn," and "holy city," the reference to the "place of rest" is intended to stir God to restore Israel's fortunes to that which she once enjoyed. As in Jdt 9,8 the influence of Ps 132,14 is evident; Jerusalem is God's resting place *forever*. As in the rest tradition, the land and the temple are considered together.

2.3.8. Sir 47,13

While praising the "famous men" (44,1ff.) of Israel's history, Sirach comes to Solomon who dwelt in a peaceful time[37] for ὁ θεὸς κατέπαυσεν κυκλόθεν,[38] ἵνα στήσῃ οἶκον ἐπ' ὀνόματι αὐτοῦ καὶ ἑτοιμάσῃ ἁγίασμα εἰς τὸν αἰῶνα (v. 13: "And God gave him rest on every side, that he might build a house for his name and prepare a sanctuary to stand for ever").[39] Though it is said of David that he "destroyed the enemies on every

---

[35] Verse numbers in Sirach correspond to those of Ziegler 1980b.
[36] ET mine. Hofius, 175 n. 299, translates Sir 36,18, "dem Ort deiner Ruhestätte." The Hebrew is, "Jerusalem, the foundation for your throne" (ירושלם מכון שבתיך; cf. Vattioni, 189; Skehan-Di Lella, 413, 422f.; cf. Eberharter, 122). The idea of a resting place in connection with the idea of a "throne" is present elsewhere (cf. מנוחה in 1Chr 28,2; Ps 132, 8.14; Isa 66,1; M. Metzger, 157; Cross, 94), but this is not the likely meaning of κατάπαυμα here. The phrase τόπον καταπαύματός σου is easily understood as a semantic unit, "your resting place" (cf. Isa 66,1; thus LSJM, 904; Hensel-Brown, 255; Oesterley 1912, 231; RV; RSV; NRSV margin; APOT, 1:441, note on v. 13), roughly equivalent to the idea of God's throne in the Heb. Moreover, it has been suggested (APOT, 1:441) that κατάπαυμα was used here "on account of the assonance between שבת (ישב) and שבת," an observation which, if accurate, would probably favor understanding this as a *state*.
[37] Heb: שלמה מלך בימי שלוה. The word play is pronounced; cf. 1Chr 22.
[38] Heb: הניח לו מסביב.
[39] ET RSV; cf. Vattioni, 257. This passage bears many parallels to 1Kgs/3Kgdms 5, on which cf. Skehan-Di Lella, 527; one may also note parallels with 1Chr/1Par 22. The word play on Solomon and "peace" in the Hebrew is of course lost in the Greek translation. According to Barthélemy-Rickenbacher, 255f., נוח occurs elsewhere in Sir 5,6; 6,3; 12,3; 32,21; 34,3.4 (2x).21; 38,7 39,28.32; 40,5; 44,8.23; and 46,19; מנוחה occurs in 6,28. Smend 1906a, 217 assumes נוח in 24,8.11, and suggests (509) that the noun מנוחה belonged to the original reading of 51,27; in fact, it was probably missing from the latter; cf. Skehan-Di Lella, 576, 579.

side" (47,7) there is no peace or rest assigned to his epoch, making the contrast with Solomon strong; the accomplishment of rest is logically connected to Solomon's erection of the temple. Nonetheless, although the achievement of rest under Solomon and the erection of the temple in v. 13 are sandwiched between references to Solomon's wisdom (vv. 12 and 14-17), his success is credited to David's merits (v. 12), probably due to Solomon's later failure (vv. 18ff.). This ascription of Solomon's rest to David's merits was likely brought about under the influence of 1Kgs/3Kgdms 11,11-13.32-33, though such an idea is not linked directly with the rest tradition in either the Deuteronomist's or the Chronicler's accounts.[40] As with Chronicles, this passage thus suggests a reflective utilization of the rest tradition.

2.3.9. Additional LXX passages

It is clear enough that the above passages give expression to the rest tradition. There are a few additional passages in the LXX where this tradition seems to be expressed, though the evidence is admittedly more ambiguous.[41]

2.3.9.1. Isa 14,1.30

We have already counted 14,3.7 among the rest tradition passages in the MT, but the LXX deserves further consideration. Upon the death of Ahaz the Philistines are told (14,28ff.) not to rejoice because the yoke that smote them has been broken, for from the seed of the serpent will come the young of asps, and their young will come forth flying serpents. The "poor" will be fed by "him" (apparently the Lord: v. 32 LXX, and v. 30b MT) and πτωχοὶ ἄνδρες ἐπ᾽ εἰρήνης ἀναπαύσονται (v. 30: "poor men will rest in peace").[42] The Lord has founded Zion and by him σωθήσονται οἱ ταπεινοὶ τοῦ λαοῦ (v. 32: "the lowly of the people will be saved").

The use of ἀναπαύω here recalls the earlier context of Isa 14. In fact, from 13,20 through 14,7 the word ἀναπαύω occurs 8 times (twice as "cease": 14,4). When Babylon is judged by God no shepherd will "rest" there (13,20; MT: ירבצו); rather wild beasts will "rest" there (13,21; MT: ורבצו) and monsters (σειρῆνες) will "rest" there (13,21; MT: ושכנו). The

---

[40] Ψ 131,10 [132,10] does base an appeal for the "anointed one" on the oath given to David.

[41] We can pass over the usages of ἡσυχάζω in 1Mac 1,3 and ἡσυχία in 1Mac 9,58 which are reminiscent of Judg 18,7.27; Zech 1,11; *et al.*; likewise, ἡσυχάζω in 1Mac 7,50; 9,57; 11,38.52; and 14,4 falls in with Judg 3,11.30; 5,31; and 8,28. Cf. also ἄνεσις in 1 Esdras 4,62 and ἡσυχία in 2Mac 12,2.

[42] MT: "the needy will lie down [ירבצו] in safety."

Lord will have mercy on Jacob and choose Israel and the Israelites will "rest" (14,1; MT: נוח Hi/2, "cause to settle") on their land. In that day the Lord will give Israel "rest" (14,3; MT: נוח Hi/1) from her sorrow and vexation and hard servitude, and when he has broken the yoke of sinners he will "rest" (14,7; MT: נוח Qal, "all the lands will rest").

The sense of 14,1 clearly follows from the preceding usages of 13,20f., and is close to the MT, "settle on." Even so, the semantic components of "relief" and "relaxation" may be more pronounced here than is the case in the MT. It is not clear if 14,30 is closer to the idea of 14,1 (repose) or 14,3 ("rest from servitude"), even if the Hebrew favors the former. It is likely that this usage is not so precise as to be consistent with one or the other, but rather that a general picture of peace which issues from salvation is in view.

2.3.9.2. Isa 57,20

The MT of Isa 57,20 states that the wicked are like the tossing waves which are unable to be "still" (שקט Hi); there is no שלום for the wicked. The LXX of the same passage reads ἀναπαύσασθαι οὐ δυνήσονται ("they will not be able to rest"), in contrast to the εἰρήνην ἐπ' εἰρήνην which is promised to Israel. Earlier (v. 13) it was said that those who cleave to the Lord will possess the land and inherit his holy mountain. The Lord is pictured (v. 15) as the Lord Most High ἐν ἁγίοις ἀναπαυόμενος ("resting in the holies") who gives patience to the faint hearted and life to the broken hearted (cf. Isa 66,1f.). The kinship with Isa 66,1f., the conceptual overlap which the promised "rest" has with "peace" (cf. Isa 32,17f.), and the use of ἀναπαύω all lead to detecting influence from the rest tradition.

2.3.9.3. Micah 4,4

In the last days the mountain of the Lord will be exalted among the hills and the peoples will hasten to it to receive instruction. The result will be universal justice and profound international peace. Moreover, ἀναπαύσεται ἕκαστος ὑποκάτω ἀμπέλου αὐτοῦ καὶ ἕκαστος ὑποκάτω συκῆς αὐτοῦ (v. 4: "each will rest under his vine and under his fig"),[43] and there will be none to make them fear. One recalls 1Kgs 4,24f. [MT 5,4f.] (cf. 1Kgs 5,4 [MT 5,18]); note also Micah 2,10. At the very least we have here a vision of eschatological rest and peace, which could easily be read alongside passages such as Isa 11,10; 14,30; and. 32,17f.[44]

---

[43] MT: וישבו, "and they will sit" under their vine etc.

[44] Isa 65,10, where ἀνάπαυσις signifies a resting place of Israel's herds, also suggests such an eschatological vision.

2.3.10. Summary

The LXX has pushed outward the bounds of the rest tradition yet further, while maintaining the features we have already delineated. One notes in these latter passages the association with the land (Deut 5,33; Isa 14,1.30; 25,10; 57,20; Ezek 34,14ff.; Micah 4,4; Sir 47,13), the temple (Isa 25,10; 57,15; Ezek 34,26; Micah 4,1ff.; Jdt 9,8; Sir 24,7-11; 36,18 [15]; 47,13), and the Davidic kingship (Ezek 34,23; Sir 47,13), as well as the continued association with motifs found in Mt 11,28-30 such as lowliness, weariness, and the like (Isa 14,30.32; 25,3; 26,6; Ezek 34,4.16). The hope of an eschatological rest is also advanced in these passages (Isa 14,1.30; 25,10; 32,17; 57,20; Ezek 34,14f.; Micah 4,4).[45]

At the same time there are features which are somewhat novel. For instance, it can be noted that in Deut 5,33 a promise of rest for Israel (καταπαύω) is in close contextual proximity to the idea of the Sabbath rest (ἀναπαύω).[46] In Isa 25,10 (cf. Ezek 34) the idea that God will *give* rest to Israel "on this mountain" binds Israel's own experience of rest more closely to the temple and Mt. Zion; this usage is in that respect reminiscent of Isa 11,10, but otherwise makes explicit an idea hinted at in passages such as Ψ 131,14f. [132,14f.]. Sirach tailors the rest tradition to his own perspective and concerns. It would appear that the tradition continued to be a living, important component of Israel's faith and hope.

2.4. Summary and conclusions

For the sake of simplicity, where necessary we will term the passages with an equivalent in the MT as Grp. A;[47] the passages that are unique to the LXX will be termed Grp. B.[48]

As regards terminology, καταπαύω and κατάπαυσις are in some respects the more representative terms, but ἀναπαύω and ἀνάπαυσις are also serviceable. Although a few of the MT usages find no corresponding translation in the LXX, yet the LXX actually includes a larger total number of relevant passages. There is probably no one reason for this increase.[49]

---

[45] Sir 24,7-11 and 47,13 look back, but Jdt 9,8 and Sir 36,18 pick up on the belief that Jerusalem is God's resting place "forever." There is nothing overtly eschatological about Deut 5,33, but inasmuch as it is an addition to that passage we might hear an exhortation to obedience with a view to God's future action.

[46] Infra, 90f.

[47] Supra, 79ff.

[48] Supra, 81ff.

[49] When Isa 14 and 32 already contained references to the rest tradition in the MT, we may assume that the LXX version is an enhancement of its *Vorlage*. Isa 57,20 may have

For instance, Sir 24,7-11 mixes temple and Wisdom traditions. Again, most of the Grp. B passages have an eschatological orientation, suggesting that "rest" was a living component of Israel's future hopes. Sir 47,13, like 2Bar 61, recalls the time of David and Solomon as a time of wisdom and rest, the subduing of the enemy, and building of the temple. Interestingly, Jdt 9,8 and Sir 36,18 incorporate the idea of Jerusalem as God's resting place (Ps 132) into prayers for deliverance; this may be a traditional prayer.

From the vantage point of the Grp. B passages we may make some additional observations about the translation of the tradition.

(1) With the exception of Deut 5,33, the καταπαυ-group tends to be used with a connection to the temple in Grp. B. This does not mean that passages in Grp. B using ἀναπαυ- are unrelated to the temple (e.g., Sir 24,7; Isa 25,10; 57,15), and this rule does not apply to Grp. A generally (cf. e.g. Deut 3,20 etc.). It suggests, however, that several passages in Grp. B were strongly influenced by the specific strain of Grp. A passages which we found to have a direct link with the temple traditions (Deut 12 etc.).

(2) Aside from Sir 24,7 the relevant passages in Jdt and Sir all use καταπαυ-. This confirms this stem as the representative one, and also the continuing close connection with the temple traditions.

(3) In Grp. B (except Sir 24,7), the historical and retrospective passages tend to use καταπαυ-,[50] and those that look forward tend to use ἀναπαυ-.[51] This agrees with the Grp. A passages in respect of those which look forward,[52] but not in respect of historical or retrospective passages. Passages which are in some respects both historical/retrospective and oriented to the future are Deut 5,33 (by virtue of being an addition); Sir 36,18 (cf. Jdt 9,8 and Ψ 131,14 [132,14]; and Ψ 94,11 [95,11].

Otherwise the rest tradition remains as we came to know it in the MT.

3. The Sabbath

3.1. Comparison[53]

Once again, the terms which convey the idea of rest in connection with the Sabbath are ἀναπαύω, ἀνάπαυσις, καταπαύω, and κατάπαυσις, as follows:

---

been influenced by 66,1f.; Ezek 34 by 2Sam 7; Micah 4,4 by 1Kgs 4,24f. [MT 5,4f.] (cf. 1Kgs 5,4 [MT/LXX 5,18] and Micah 2,10).
[50] Deut 5,33; Jdt 9,8; Sir 24,7-11; 36,18; 47,13.
[51] Isa 14; 25,10; 32,17; 57,20; Ezek 34,14f.; Micah 4,4.
[52] Isa 11,10; 14,3; 32,18.
[53] Supra, 77 n. 1.

	ἀναπαύω[54]	ἀνάπαυσις	καταπαύω	κατάπαυσις
שבת Qal	Lev 25,2	Ex 23,12	Gen 2,2.3; Ex 34,21 (2x)	
שבתון		Ex 16,23; 31,15; 35,2;[55] Lev 16,31;[56] 23,3; 23,24; 23,39 (2x); 25,4.5		
נוח Qal	Ex 23,12; Deut 5,14		Ex 20,11	
נפש Ni[57]			Ex 31,17	
no Heb				Ex 35,2; 2Mac 15,1

3.2. Evaluation

If there was any hesitation at affirming the importance of the rest motif for the Sabbath in the Hebrew OT,[58] then there can be none with the LXX.

Regarding the relationship of the Sabbath to the rest tradition, the *terminological* overlap has been significantly enhanced, even if this "enhancement" cannot be assumed to be intentional.[59] In this vein one might highlight the fact that Deut 5,14 (ἀναπαύω) is the Sabbath passage wherein numerous scholars have sensed a theological and conceptual tie to the rest tradition.[60] The Sabbath rest (esp. for the slaves) becomes the fullest realization of the מנוחה rest for the whole nation. Interestingly, it is precisely in this context that the LXX -- against the MT -- contains a promise of rest in the land (v. 33; καταπαύω). In fact Deut 5,32f. with its promise of rest bears ties back to both the prologue of the decalogue and the Sabbath command itself in the idea of the exodus from Egypt and entry into Palestine[61] and the repeated exhortations to "keep" the commands of God.[62] Moreover, there are several ties between this passage in Deuteronomy and Ψ 94 [95]. There is a "contemporization" of the covenant -- it is not with "your fathers" but with you who are here "today"[63] --, repeated references to "hearing" God's "voice" (5,23.24.25.26), the desire expressed by God that such a "heart" of

---

[54] Also Ex 23,12 B* (נפש).
[55] Ex 35,2 A: ἀναπαύω.
[56] Σάββατα σαββάτων ἀνάπαυσις (שבת שבתון).
[57] In LXX Ex 23,12: ἀναψύχω.
[58] Supra, 61f.
[59] For the whole relationship of the traditions, see above, 67ff.
[60] Supra, 63, 68.
[61] Compare Deut 5,6.15.33.
[62] Compare Deut 5,1.12.15.32.
[63] Cf. Deut 5,3: οὐχὶ **τοῖς πατράσιν ὑμῶν** διέθετο κύριος τὴν διαθήκην ταύτην, ἀλλ' ἢ πρὸς ὑμᾶς, ὑμεῖς ὧδε πάντες ζῶντες **σήμερον**.

obedience would remain in the Israelites (5,29), that they would not turn to the right or left according to the "way" (5,32f.), and a recollection of the "testing" in the wilderness.[64]

The LXX thus offers additional grounds for merging the rest tradition with the Sabbath though it does not actually connect them,[65] nor does it advance the idea of an eschatological Sabbath any further. Beyond these observations, the remarks already made about the Sabbath in Ch. Two will suffice.

4. Further developments in the wisdom literature

4.1. Introduction

This section will be confined in the main to the classic works of Job, Prov, Eccl, and Sir. WisSol probably dates somewhat later than the others (ca. A.D. 37-41) and the strong influence of Middle Platonic ideas brings its idea of rest closer to that which we will see in Philo than to that which we find in the other four wisdom books.[66] Its usages will be noted here, but they should not be permitted to skew the general idea gained from the other, earlier works.

The following summary is based on the LXX. The Hebrew will not supply a precise semantic equivalent for the word "rest" in each case, but this does not affect the general picture given here.

4.2. Rest as the result of wise behavior

Among the sages the idea is not uncommon that wise behavior or a wise lifestyle will result in rest or quietness. Thus Prov 29,17 holds forth the hope that if children are disciplined they will bring rest (ἀναπαύω) to the parents.[67] In Sir 22,13, if one avoids a senseless person she or he will find rest (ἀνάπαυσις). Or, negatively, in Sir 28,16, "those who pay heed to slander will not find rest" (ἀνάπαυσις).[68]

---

[64] Cf. Deut 6,16-19.

[65] It is to be admitted that Deut 5,33 only evidences contiguity of the Dtr rest and Sabbath traditions broadly conceived. There is no mention of people sharing in God's rest.

[66] The date and background of WisSol are discussed in Winston, 3-96. Other proposed dates range from II B.C. to mid-I A.D.; cf. HJP^2, 3/1:568-579.

[67] Cf. Jub 25,19; 36,15.

[68] In different forms the same general idea is found when ἀναπαύω, ἀνάπαυσις, ἡσυχάζω, and ἡσυχία are employed in the LXX at Job 11,19; Prov 26,20; Sir 3,6; 18,16; 20,21; 36,29 (26); and 38,14. Cf. also TGad 7,3; TAsh 6,3.

4.3. The nature of wisdom's rest

Already in these examples, the mundane nature of this "rest" as a life of serenity, tranquillity and sometimes -- though not always -- of prosperity is evident (Prov 8,18f.21). Sir 51,27f., at least, is very direct about the material benefits of wisdom when it joins the "rest" found in wisdom with the acquisition of silver and gold.[69]

This characterization of wisdom's rest as one of this-worldly serenity and tranquillity is brought into sharper focus by the oft encountered contrast between "rest" and the suffering, pain, and toil of life.[70] For instance, the rest or quiet gained through wisdom is further defined as a life which does not dread disaster (Prov 1,33). Elsewhere (Sir 40,1-6) the present life can be characterized as one of hard work, perplexities, anxiety, fear of death, anger, envy, trouble, and unrest ($\sigma\acute{\alpha}\lambda o\varsigma$), so that even during sleep ($\dot{\epsilon}\nu$ $\kappa\alpha\iota\rho\hat{\omega}$ $\dot{\alpha}\nu\alpha\pi\alpha\acute{\upsilon}\sigma\epsilon\omega\varsigma$) one is beset with troubles and he gets little or no rest ($\dot{o}\lambda\acute{\iota}\gamma o\nu$ $\dot{\omega}\varsigma$ $o\dot{\upsilon}\delta\grave{\epsilon}\nu$ $\dot{\epsilon}\nu$ $\dot{\alpha}\nu\alpha\pi\alpha\acute{\upsilon}\sigma\epsilon\iota$). For his part, Job mourns that $o\ddot{\upsilon}\tau\epsilon$ $\epsilon\dot{\iota}\rho\acute{\eta}\nu\epsilon\upsilon\sigma\alpha$ $o\ddot{\upsilon}\tau\epsilon$ $\dot{\eta}\sigma\acute{\upsilon}\chi\alpha\sigma\alpha$ $o\ddot{\upsilon}\tau\epsilon$ $\dot{\alpha}\nu\epsilon\pi\alpha\upsilon\sigma\acute{\alpha}\mu\eta\nu$, $\mathring{\eta}\lambda\theta\epsilon\nu$ $\delta\acute{\epsilon}$ $\mu o\iota$ $\dot{o}\rho\gamma\acute{\eta}$.[71]

By way of contrast with later writers such as Philo and the Gnostics,[72] it may be noted that in wisdom's focus on the "unrest" of life there is no metaphysical contrast drawn with a transcendent sphere of stability and immovability.[73] It is the nature of *life*, more than it is the nature of *being* which is characterized in undesirable terms.

Although it is not contingent on a life of wisdom, the "rest" of death can become the ultimate restful escape from life, for "eternal rest" ($\dot{\alpha}\nu\acute{\alpha}\pi\alpha\upsilon\sigma\iota\varsigma$ $\alpha\dot{\iota}\hat{\omega}\nu o\varsigma$[74]) is better than a miserable life of, e.g., chronic sickness (Sir 30,17).[75] Yet there is no developed idea of an other-worldly existence

---

[69] Skehan-Di Lella, 579, comment on 51,27-28 that, "the point of both bicola is that wisdom pays off even in the practical realm, and not only in the religious"; cf. Sir 6,18-31 (cf. v. 28). Further: Job 3,26 (negatively); 14,6; Eccl 4,6; Sir 11,19; and 40,5.6 (negatively).

[70] Cf. Helderman 1984, 56-58.

[71] Job 3,26; cf. also Job 2,9; 3,13.17.23; 10,20; 11,19; and 14,6; also Eccl 4,6; 6,5.

[72] Infra, 113ff., 145ff.

[73] WisSol is an exception to this, on which see below.

[74] Text as in Ziegler, 267.

[75] Cf. also Job 3,13.17.23; Eccl 6,5. There is, however, hardly a uniform use of the rest motif in relation to death. In Job 21,13, Job laments over the fact that the wicked *both* live the good life *and* rest in Hades. Prov 21,16, rather than presenting rest as the *result* of wisdom, presents the "rest" of the grave as the result of having *forsaken* wisdom (righteousness); Sir 22,11 implies that the "rest" of death is better than life for the fool. It is to be noted that in Job, Prov, and Eccl there is no distinction between the destiny of the wicked and the righteous in regard to death's rest. Sir 22,11 probably implies the same; the metaphor is incidental in Sir 38,23 and 39,11. For Sir 47,23 see 1Kgs 11,43. In assessing these and similar passages, Hofius, 69 (esp. nn. 416-418 in Hofius), rightly

evident in this use of the rest motif and it is for the most part viewed from the perspective of those who might be struggling with the pain of life. Descriptions of afterlife existence as "rest" in such passages of this genre are as shadowy as Sheol itself.[76] An exception to this is WisSol 4,7 which does assign rest to the destiny of the righteous man specifically, and reflects a belief in immortality as a gift from God.[77] If a person dies at a young age he will still be at rest (Δίκαιος δὲ ἐὰν φθάσῃ τελευτῆσαι, ἐν ἀναπαύσει ἔσται), for it is the amount of wisdom rather than the number of years which will earn the honored titles of "gray hair" and "old age."

The rest to be found in wisdom (excluding WisSol) can thus be characterized as essentially mundane. It is the *good life* which is the result of wise and virtuous behavior and which is contrasted with the suffering, labor, and turmoil of life. To those suffering acutely or to those simply overwhelmed with life's evils even death can hold forth the hope of rest, though the latter idea is neither necessarily contingent upon being wise nor is it developed into a clear hope of the afterlife.

4.4. Wisdom's offer of rest

From the observation that wise behavior effects "rest" it is only a short step to the idea that wisdom as a category -- personified Wisdom[78] -- brings rest. This is apparent in Prov 1,33 when Wisdom promises that those who listen to her will be secure and rest without fear of evil (ἡσυχάσει ἀφόβως ἀπὸ παντὸς κακοῦ).[79] The two passages in Sirach -- where accepting Wisdom's yoke will lead to rest (6,25ff. and 51,26f.) -- belong here also.[80]

---

stresses that a distinction must be made between the grave as the rest(place) of the body, and hades or heaven as the rest(place) of the soul following death.

[76] Skehan-Di Lella, 86, make the general observation that the Greek version of Sirach has brought into the text notions of retribution during the afterlife which were not there in the Hebrew. I do not, however, perceive *in Sirach's use of the rest motif* an attempt to delve into theoretical depictions of a reality to be experienced in the afterlife.

[77] On the hereafter in WisSol cf. Nickelsburg 1992b, 686f.; on WisSol 4,7, see Winston, 137 (cf. 126f.).

[78] On personified Wisdom, see below, 163ff.

[79] Cf. also WisSol 8,16 and Winston, 195f. Winston finds the closest parallels to WisSol 8,16 in writers such as Aristobulus, Philo, Plato, and the Gnostics; see also Sir 6,28; 36,29 (26).

[80] About Sir 51,27 it should be noted that the Hebrew (Hebrew I) lacked the reference to "rest"; cf. Skehan, 398; Skehan-Di Lella, 576, 579; *pace* Smend 1906a, 509, who conjectured that the original of 51,27 used מנוחה, as in Sir 6,28. It is arguable, then, that if Mt 11,28-30 is dependent on Sir 51, it is dependent on the Greek text of Sirach. See, however, the general remarks above, 77 n. 1.

4.5. Summary

The result of living wisely -- equivalent to living righteously, to acquiring wisdom, to studying Torah[81] -- is "rest" in the shape of this-worldly tranquillity and possibly prosperity. This is the hope held forth in Sir 6,28 and 51,27 to the bearer of Wisdom's yoke. Death is frequently characterized as "rest" or "quiet," but it is not a clearly formulated hope, nor is it an experience confined to the wise.

Metaphysical ideas of rest are not found here, but rather a philosophically unsophisticated, human longing for relief from life's troubles. Gnostic and Philonic ideas of rest should not be read into these usages.[82] Rather, the expression of "rest" found in this wisdom literature contributed to that of Philo and the Gnostics.[83]

5. A technical meaning of κατάπαυσις?

5.1. Introduction

This is probably the most fitting place to take up the question of definition with respect to the noun κατάπαυσις. In his treatment of this noun in the LXX, Hofius came to the conclusion that it carries a local component of meaning -- "resting *place*" -- in seven texts: Deut 12,9; 1Par 6,16 [6,31]; 2Par 6,41; Ψ 94,11 [95,11]; Ψ 131,14 [132,14]; Isa 66,1; and Jdt 9,8. He suggested, moreover, that in "allen 7 Stellen bezeichnet das Wort den Tempel in Jerusalem," while other "Gesichtspunkten von 'Ruhestätten'" utilize ἀνάπαυσις. From this he deduced that "der lokale κατάπαυσις-Begriff in der Septuaginta bereits so etwas wie ein theologischer *Terminus technicus* sein dürfte,"[84] i.e., a technical term for the temple. In the context of Hofius' overall argument, this point reinforces the belief that κατάπαυσις in Heb 3-4 refers to the Most Holy Place of the heavenly temple. Conversely, others have insisted that ἀνάπαυσις and κατάπαυσις are largely synonymous, and that the latter noun generally refers to a state,

---

[81] On Wisdom and Law in Sirach, cf. 24,23; also 19,20; 1,25-27 and 6,32-37. Cf. also Deut 4,6. It is a mistake to identify Wisdom and Law in Sirach; rather, Wisdom is embodied in the Law, but is not exhausted thereby (Witherington, 86, 94).

[82] Cf. Helderman 1984, 79 n. 102: "man solle das gnostische Verständnis von ἀνάπαυσις nicht in das Ruheverständnis Ben Siras zurück projizieren."

[83] Cf. Helderman 1984, 56-58. Regarding Philo, Williams 1981, 826f., comments that his "portrayal of the stability in which the wise man participates" is an "example of the cross-fertilization of Jewish wisdom tradition" with the Platonic theme of participating in the *stability of the Transcendent*; see below, 113ff., 142-144, 145ff.

[84] Hofius, 49f.; my emphasis.

"rest."[85] The questions for us to consider are therefore whether, where, and how κατάπαυσις is to be taken locally, the extent to which κατάπαυσις overlaps with ἀνάπαυσις in terms of meaning (synonymity), and how the term κατάπαυσις is used in relation to the temple.

We have already made some observations about the use of the stems ἀναπαυ- and καταπαυ- in the LXX,[86] and further on we will make some observations specifically about the terminology used in Philo and gnostic sources.[87] At present we will briefly review the use of relevant vocabulary in the MT, then look at the usages of the two nouns, ἀνάπαυσις and κατάπαυσις, before drawing the conclusions for Ψ 94 [95]. In addition to the literature already surveyed we will include at this point the evidence from Joseph and Aseneth.[88]

5.2. Summary of the MT terminology

In our survey of the MT we considered four nouns: מרגוע, מנח, מנוחה, and מרגעה, but since neither of the latter two find an equivalent in the LXX we will set them aside here.

The noun מנח occurs altogether 7 times (Gen 8,9; Deut 28,65; Isa 34,14; Ruth 3,1; Lam 1,3; 1Chr 6,31 [MT 6,16]; and Ps 116,7), and in all but 1Chr 6,31 [MT 6,16] and Ps 116,7 it is fairly clear that the idea is a local one.[89]

The noun מנוחה occurs 21 times: Gen 49,15; Num 10,33; Deut 12,9; Judg 20,43; 2Sam 14,17; 1Kgs 8,56; Isa 11,10; 28,12; 32,18; 66,1; Jer 45,3; 51,59; Micah 2,10; Zech 9,1; Ps 23,2; 95,11; 132,8.14; Ruth 1,9; 1Chr 22,9; and 28,2. Once again, the local idea is prominent. It is the resting *place* of Issachar (Gen 49,15), the Israelites in the wilderness (Num 10,33), Israel in the land (Deut 12,9; Isa 28,12; Micah 2,10; = Palestine; Isa 32,18 = homes), the Root of Jesse (Isa 11,10), God in the temple in Jerusalem (Ps 132,8.14),[90]

---

[85] E.g. Attridge, 127 n. 55.
[86] Supra, 80f., 88f.
[87] Infra, 113, 145f.
[88] The noun κατάπαυσις does not occur in the Pseudepigrapha outside of JosAsen; cf. Hofius, 29f.
[89] Although Preuß, 306, and Hofius, 49, consider מנח in 1Chr 6,31 [MT 6,16] to be a local idea, the preposition מן suggests a temporal aspect and gives it the force of an infinitive, "from the coming to rest of the ark" (so BDB, 629; R. Braun 1986, 89; cf. NIV; RSV; NRSV; NEB; KJV; Moffatt). *HALAT*, 568 (cf. Holladay 1971, 201), and Becker, 35, manage to preserve a local idea by translating it as, "nachdem die Lade eine bleibende Stätte gefunden hatte," although in his comment Becker renders it, "Nachdem die Lade unter David zur Ruhe gekommen ist..." A "coming to rest" is probably the most natural way of understanding the construction, even if the local element is somehow preserved.
[90] Cf. נוח Qal in 2Chr 6,41 (par. Ps 132,8).

and Ruth in her home (Ruth 1,9). Ps 95,11 must be included among these.[91] It may be noted that of those 12 contexts using מנוחה which seem to be most clearly within the rest tradition (Deut 12,9; 1Kgs 8,56; Isa 11,10; 28,12; 32,18; 66,1; Micah 2,10; Ps 95,11; 132,8.14; 1Chr 22,9; and 28,2), only 1Kgs 8,56; Isa 66,1; 1Chr 22,9; and 1Chr 28,2 do not carry the local component of meaning, though 1Chr 28,2 and Isa 66,1 are clearly descriptive of locales.[92]

Beyond the question of whether or not a local component of meaning is present in the use of the word in given contexts, we may note where the noun מנוחה is used in relation to a temple. This is clearest in Ps 132,8.14 (cf. נוח Qal in 2Chr 6,41), where the noun refers unmistakably to the "temple." In 1Chr 28,2 the temple is a "house of מנוחה," so that מנוחה does not *mean* resting place, but it is part of a phrase which does refer to the temple; likewise Isa 66,1. The noun does not refer to the temple in Deut 12,9 or 1Kgs 8,56, but it is closely associated with the temple there.[93]

5.3. Ἀνάπαυσις and κατάπαυσις[94]

The following charts illustrate (1) usages of ἀνάπαυσις and κατάπαυσις as regards a local idea (excluding Ψ 94,11 [95,11]), (2) usages of these terms that reflect synonymity, and (3) the usage of κατάπαυσις in relation to the temple.

(1) We should exclude 1Par 6,16 [6,31]; Isa 66,1; and Jdt 9,8 from the instances of κατάπαυσις that Hofius defined locally,[95] and include in the list

---

[91] Supra, 41ff.

[92] According to *HALAT*, 568, in addition to those listed here, the local meaning is present in 1Kgs 8,56; Ps 23,2; Isa 66,1; Jer 51,59; Zech 9,1; and 1Chr 28,2; it is a psychological rest in Judg 20,43; 2Sam 14,17; Jer 45,3; and 1Chr 22,9; likewise BDB, 629f., except that it sees a local meaning in 2Sam 14,17 and a state of rest in Ps 23,2; Isa 28,12; 1Kgs 8,56; and Ruth 1,9. Regarding Isa 66,1 and 1Chr 28,2, it is not clear just how these authorities would actually translate these "local" usages, e.g., whether they would paraphrase Isa 66,1 with Hofius, 173 n. 270, "Wo ist denn ein Ort, wo meine Ruhestätte sein könnte?" or whether מקום would assimilate the local idea of מנוחה, "place (מקום) of rest (מנוחה)" (= resting place; NRSV; NIV). If the latter, the resulting idea does not appear to be far removed from the claim that מנוחה in Isa 66,1 and 1Chr 28,2 means simply "rest." Hofius, 171 n. 253, excludes from the local usages Judg 20,43; 1Kgs 8,56; Isa 28,12; Jer 45,3; 1Chr 22,9; and 28,2, though it is not clear how the usage in Isa 66,1 is local while that in 1Chr 28,2 is not. It is proper to stress, however, that the temple is not a place *characterized* by rest (relaxation; relief), but it is a *resting place* of the Ark.

[93] The same might be said of Isa 11,10 (local) and 1Chr 22,9 (non-local), both of which are contextually associated with the temple.

[94] Supra, 79f. (including references in the notes), 81ff., 88f.

[95] Supra, 94f. On Jdt 9,8, see above, 83f. Isa 66,1 uses the phrase, τόπος τῆς καταπαύσεώς μου, which would make a local component of meaning in κατάπαυσις redundant (likewise, Attridge, 127 n. 55; Bauernfeind 1965, 628; LSJM, 904; Bauer-

of local meanings JosAsen 8,9 (καὶ εἰσελθάτω εἰς τὴν κατάπαυσίν σου).[96] Yet ἀνάπαυσις in JosAsen 15,7 and κατάπαυσις in 22,13 should, like Isa 66,1, be construed as a state.[97] Non-local usages of κατάπαυσις considered local by Hofius are underlined.[98]

	local	non-local
ἀνάπαυσις	Gen 8,9; 49,15; Num 10,33; Ruth 1,9; 3,1; Ψ 131,8; Isa 11,10; 17,2; 37,28; 65,10;[99] Micah 2,10; Sir 24,7	1Par 28,2; Isa 25,10; Jer 51,33 [45,3]; Lam 1,3 and _passim_[100]
κατάπαυσις	Deut 12,9; 4Kgdms 6,41; Ψ 131,14; JosAsen 8,9[101]	Ex 35,2; Num 10,35; 3Kgdms 8,56; 1Par 6,16 [6,31]; Isa 66,1; Jdt 9,8; 2Mac 15,1; JosAsen 22,13[102]

(2) Without suggesting that the nouns are simply synonymous,[103] yet a glance at the passages in the above chart will bring to light a large degree of

---

Aland, 845; _contra_ Hofius, 49, who takes the construction as epexegetic). In 1Par 6,16 [6,31] the prepositional phrase with κατάπαυσις (ἐν οἴκῳ κυρίου ἐν τῇ καταπαύσει τῆς κιβωτοῦ) should be taken temporally as in the MT (supra, 95), and in the closest parallel phrase, Num 10,35 [10,36] (ἐν τῇ καταπαύσει [of the ark]); thus, "in the house of the Lord, _when_ the ark came to rest." Hofius, 49, takes 1Par 6,16 [6,31] as local, in spite of its similarity to Num 10,35 [10,36] which he takes as a state of rest (32).

[96] It would be begging the question to appeal to the evident dependence on Ψ 94,11 [95,11]; the local idea is clear, however, from JosAsen 15,7 (τόπον αὐτοῖς ἀναπαύσεως ἡτοίμασεν ἐν τοῖς οὐρανοῖς) and 22,13 (τὸν τόπον τῆς καταπαύσεως αὐτῆς ἐν τοῖς ὑψίστοις), assuming that the same reality is in view in each instance. Cf. also Burchard (in _OTP_, 2:213 n. f2).

[97] For the texts see the previous note. The word τόπος would presumably assimilate the local idea in these statements. For Hofius' interpretation of Isa 66,1 and JosAsen 22,13, see Hofius, 49f.; in both cases he takes the construction as epexegetic. Attridge, 127 n. 57, judges Hofius' exegesis of JosAsen 22,13 to be "forced." On the text of JosAsen 15,7, cf. Burchard, 61, 66, 67.

[98] This chart is meant to facilitate comparison, and is not intended to be exhaustive. For further evidence see the lexicons.

[99] Possibly also Isa 23,12 and 34,14.

[100] See further above, 90; also ἀνάπαυμα in Isa 28,12.

[101] Cf. also Lev 25,28 A B*.

[102] Cf. κατάπαυμα in Sir 36,18 (15).

[103] Attridge, 127 n, 55, and others point to Ex 35,2 (ἓξ ἡμέρας ποιήσεις ἔργα, τῇ δὲ ἡμέρᾳ τῇ ἑβδόμῃ κατάπαυσις, ἅγιον, σάββατα, ἀνάπαυσις κυρίῳ) as evidence of the closeness of the terms. Yet in this passage there is a perceptible distinction in usage, with κατάπαυσις signifying primarily "cessation," and ἀνάπαυσις signifying primarily "rest." Note also Sir 38,23 which uses a play on words: ἐν ἀναπαύσει νεκροῦ κατάπαυσον τὸ μνημόσυνον αὐτοῦ καὶ παρακλήθητι ἐν αὐτῷ ἐν ἐξόδῳ πνεύματος αὐτοῦ; this play on words is taken over from the Hebrew (cf. Skehan-Di Lella, 440). But Ex 35,2 can be compared with 23,12; see the chart below. For further on the distinction of these terms, see below, 113, 145f.

overlap. Considering usage, we may note several examples in which the terms appear to be interchangeable:[104]

ἀνάπαυσις	κατάπαυσις
the land as a resting place: ἡ ἀνάπαυσις (Micah 2,10)	τὴν κατάπαυσιν (Deut 12,9)
the temple as a resting place: ἀνάστηθι...εἰς τὴν ἀνάπαυσίν σου (Ψ 131,8) ἀνάστηθι...εἰς τὴν ἀνάπαυσίν σου (Ψ 131,8) οἶκον ἀναπαύσεως (1Par 28,2)	Αὕτη ἡ κατάπαυσίς μου (Ψ 131,14) ἀνάστηθι...εἰς τὴν κατάπαυσίν σου (2Par 6,41) τόπος τῆς καταπαύσεως (Isa 66,1)
the Sabbath: ἓξ ἡμέρας ποιήσεις τὰ ἔργα σου, τῇ δὲ ἡμέρᾳ τῇ ἑβδόμῃ ἀνάπαυσις (Ex 23,12)	ἓξ ἡμέρας ποιήσεις ἔργα, τῇ δὲ ἡμέρᾳ τῇ ἑβδόμῃ κατάπαυσις (Ex 35,2)
further: ἀνάπαυσις in Num 10,33 τόπον...ἀναπαύσεως (JosAsen 15,7)	κατάπαυσις in Num 10,35 τὸν τόπον τῆς καταπαύσεως (JosAsen 22,13)

(3) Finally, leaving out Ψ 94 [95], the total number of occurrences of κατάπαυσις in the LXX break down as follows with relation to the temple:

1. κατάπαυσις -- not belonging to rest tradition	Ex 35,2; 2Mac 15,1
2. κατάπαυσις -- related to the temple	2Par 6,41; Ψ 131,14; Isa 66,1; Jdt 9,8[105]
3. κατάπαυσις -- coming-to-rest of the Ark	Num 10,35;[106] 1Par 6,16
4. κατάπαυσις -- indirectly related to the temple	Deut 12,9; 3Kgdms 8,56
5. ἀνάπαυσις -- related to the temple	1Par 28,2; Ψ 131,8; less clearly in Isa 11,10

Only two of these ten occurrences of κατάπαυσις do not belong to the rest tradition (row 1). Of the other eight, six are directly concerned with the temple or the coming-to-rest of the Ark (rows 2-3). This leaves only two occurrences of κατάπαυσις besides Ψ 94,11 [95,11], and both of these are bound up with the temple in their contexts (row 4). Nonetheless, these last two do not refer directly to the temple, and there are instances where the noun ἀνάπαυσις is directly related to the temple (row 5).

---

[104] Note also Sir 24,7-11; this passage begins by saying that Wisdom sought an ἀνάπαυσις among the nations, a desire which was fulfilled when God gave her rest (καταπαύω) in Jerusalem (vv. 8 and 11).

[105] Note also κατάπαυμα in Sir 36,18 (15).

[106] We did not give this passage separate consideration, but it is very much a part of the rest tradition.

5.4. Summary and conclusions

We may return to Hofius' claim that *in its local usage*[107] κατάπαυσις *is a technical term for the temple* in the LXX. It is doubtful, to begin with, that in Isa 66,1 and Jdt 9,8 κατάπαυσις means "resting place,"[108] and it is most likely that it does not in 1Par 6,16 [6,31] either. Thus, leaving aside Ψ 94,11 [95,11] there are not six local usages but only three on which to base the claim of a technical usage. Of these three, Hofius includes Deut 12,9 as a κατάπαυσις text which has the notion of the temple embedded in it.[109] Certainly the temple is present in the LXX context of Deut 12, as also in the MT, but it is unconvincing to use this text as evidence that wherever κατάπαυσις occurs in the LXX as a local idea (resting place) it "bezeichnet...den Tempel in Jerusalem."

Again, if κατάπαυσις was just such a technical term, it is strange that ἀνάπαυσις would have been used as an exact parallel of κατάπαυσις in the very same context and for the same Hebrew word (Ψ 131,8.14 [132,8.14]), and that ἀνάπαυσις was chosen in 1Par 28,2. Hofius finds it significant that ἀνάπαυσις is used in Chronicles when the Hebrew, in his judgment, signifies "rest" (*qua* state; 1Par 22,9 and 28,2), while κατάπαυσις is used where the Hebrew contains the "local" idea (1Par 6,16 [MT 6,16; ET 6,31] and 2Par 6,41),[110] yet it appears rather arbitrary to argue that מנוחה is not a local idea in 1Chr 28,2 while arguing that it is in Isa 66,1,[111] and מנוח in 1Chr 6,31 [MT 6,16] is probably better construed primarily as a state of rest ("coming to rest"), and only secondarily as a locale.[112] While JosAsen 8,9 is evidence of a local understanding of Ψ 94,11 [95,11], it is also evidence that the referent of κατάπαυσις in the psalm was not always understood to be the temple.[113]

What remains is Hofius' observation that when κατάπαυσις is used locally it is only for the temple, and not for "other" resting places; in the latter cases it is ἀνάπαυσις which is used. Yet (1) Deut 12,9 is dubious as a

---

[107] For Hofius: Deut 12,9; 1Par 6,16 [6,31]; 2Par 6,41; Ψ 94,11 [95,11]; Ψ 131,14 [132,14]; Isa 66,1; and Jdt 9,8.

[108] Cf. also κατάπαυμα in Sir 36,18 (15). This point about the meaning of κατάπαυσις in Isa 66,1, etc. must be stressed against the claim of a "technical" meaning of the local usage Otherwise it can be readily admitted that the idea of, e.g., τόπος τῆς καταπαύσεως, is self-evidently that of a "place of rest," i.e. a local idea.

[109] Hofius, 49; cf. Preuß, 306.

[110] Hofius, 49.

[111] *HALAT*, 568, and BDB, 629, list 1Chr 28,2 as a local usage of מנוחה (cf. NIV: "a house as a place of rest") alongside Isa 66,1, while Hofius, 171 n. 253, distinguishes them.

[112] Supra, 95.

[113] Hofius himself, 50, points this out: "JA mit der κατάπαυσις den Gedanken an das Land Kanaan bzw. an Jerusalem mit dem Tempel nicht mehr verbindet."

reference to the temple;[114] (2) a local component of meaning is questionable in more than one of the κατάπαυσις-passages cited by Hofius; (3) ἀνάπαυσις is by far the more common noun to begin with, so that it is not surprising it picks up the "other" resting places; and (4) ἀνάπαυσις is used identically for the temple.

In the end, possibly the most significant observation to be made is that a relatively uncommon noun, κατάπαυσις, is used with relative frequency within the "rest tradition" generally, and it is used very frequently in connection with the temple. This in itself would very likely highlight the word κατάπαυσις,[115] giving it a special significance not by virtue of *meaning* but by virtue of *association*. It is very difficult and probably misleading, however, to consider it a "technical term" for the temple in its local usage.

Returning to the questions regarding κατάπαυσις in Ψ 94,11 [95,11] -- whether it is a place or a state, and whether it refers to the temple -- , these questions cannot be solved on the basis of a so-called technical usage. The best indication continues to be the phrase, εἰς τὴν κατάπαυσίν μου, in view of its similarity to the phrases in Deut 12,9 (εἰς τὴν κατάπαυσιν); 2Par 6,41 (εἰς τὴν κατάπαυσίν σου); Ψ 131,8 [132,8] (εἰς τὴν ἀνάπαυσίν σου); and Ψ 131,14 [132,14] (ἡ κατάπαυσίς μου), all of these being local usages. For the remainder, the interpretation of this psalm in the LXX is essentially the same as that already given.[116] It is no more likely in the LXX than it was in the MT that with the use of κατάπαυσις a direct reference is being made to the temple building, although it *is* less likely that the referent would fail to include any trace of temple theology.

6. Summary and conclusions[117]

The rest tradition is represented in the LXX with the words, ἀναπαύω, ἀνάπαυσις, ἀνάπαυμα, καταπαύω, and κατάπαυσις Of these the latter two stand out, though ἀναπαύω and ἀνάπαυσις are used often and in the same manner. In broad outline, the tradition remains much as we found it in

---

[114] Note also κατάπαυσις in Lev 25,28 A B*: καὶ ἀπελεύσεται εἰς τὴν κατάσχεσιν [κατάπαυσιν] αὐτοῦ. Hofius, 32, 169 n. 220, considers this usage to be of a state of rest, but it would seem rather to be a "resting place" (cf. Ellingworth, 235), thus, "and he shall return to his possession [resting place]." Here the local usage of κατάπαυσις unquestionably refers to the land as such.

[115] Similarly with καταπαύω.

[116] Supra, 41ff.

[117] For conclusions on the use of the rest motif in the wisdom literature, see above, § 4.5.

the MT. The several passages unique to the LXX suggest that this was a *living* tradition.

The words ἀναπαύω, ἀνάπαυσις, καταπαύω, and κατάπαυσις are also used to give expression to Sabbath rest. The frequency with which this motif surfaces in connection with the Sabbath is increased in the LXX, at the same time that greater terminological overlap is evident with the rest tradition. In addition, one LXX text, Deut 5,14 (cf. v. 33), might manifest a contextual link of the two traditions which is more than coincidental.

The noun κατάπαυσις is not in its local usages a technical term for the temple. The interpretation of Ψ 94 [95] can not, therefore, be decided on the basis of a specialized usage. It is true, however, that this noun is used in such a way throughout the LXX that a reader of the Greek would doubtless have a tendency to associate it closely with the temple, and almost certainly do this in the context of Ψ 94 [95] for the reasons already given in the treatment of the MT.

Chapter Four

The Rest Motif in Other Jewish and Christian Literature

1. Introduction

The rest motif is ubiquitous. We have already experienced the proof of this in the Old Testament, but a vast sea of Jewish and Christian literature must yet be navigated before we can pull up on the shore of Mt 11 and Heb 3-4.

Rest, such a common experience and longed after good, lends itself to an almost limitless variety of figurative applications. A sense of this might have been gained if the wider sampling of examples noted at the beginning of §§ 2.6 and 2.7 in Ch. Two (Isaiah and Jeremiah) were given a look.[1] Yet we isolated and followed carefully particular usages of the motif -- the rest tradition and the Sabbath -- as two of the most outstanding and characteristic strands in the OT, and also as the strands most evidently taken up by the NT writers. In addition to these two we considered the use of the motif in wisdom literature.

What will follow will not be an attempt to systematically trace these same two traditions through the Jewish and Christian literature, but rather to detect the shapes of our motif which are most characteristic of the several domains of thought. This literature has an intrinsic importance as a potentially indirect or even direct influence on the thought of the NT. Indeed, the usages of the rest motif in Philo, Gnosticism, the Pseudepigrapha, and rabbinic literature have each been adduced as the key to Heb 3-4. Thus our concern, as it was also in the foregoing chapters, is to explore both the explicit usages of the rest motif and also the concepts and ideas associated with them, so that we may understand the NT material against the background of the current use of the words and the ideas which may have shaped the thinking of its various authors. The discussion extends to documents which post-date the NT[2] since in the opinion of some scholars

---

[1] Supra, 46, 53.
[2] As a rule, dates have been given with the first significant citation of the works to which reference is made (occasionally, but not always repeated). Since some date is

some or any of them may reflect concept/thought/word-usage that was already current in the first century and that may have influenced the NT. By conducting a broad survey and examining particular features and passages, our hope is to present a wide view of the variety of ways the motif was used and developed, and to make possible a degree of comparison and contrast between the various usages.

2. OT Pseudepigrapha

2.1. Introduction

In his study of the rest motif, Hofius included a helpful annotated list of many of the relevant passages from the OT Pseudepigrapha.[3] Hofius' interest, however, was limited to those passages which he found to contain the local idea, "resting *place*." We can therefore take a more general look by way of a preface (§ 2.2) to a summary of his findings (§ 2.3).

Before beginning a brief word may be said regarding the association of the Sabbath with chronologies of world history, an association which does not figure in Mt 11 or Heb 3-4. Beginning most clearly with Dan 9,24-27, one finds speculation that world history would correspond to the hebdomadal or sabbatical schema.[4] Other works, such as Jubilees, reckon world history according to the principle of Sabbath/Jubilee cycles.[5] The cosmic scope of the Genesis creation account -- with the help of Ps 90,4 -- lent itself to the belief that the world's history would see six millennia ("world-week") followed by a world-Sabbath.[6] Though such speculation

---

needed, in most cases I have followed dates given in *OTP*, *NTApocr*[2], and other such standard works of general use, without, however, intending to gloss over the fact that disagreement exists. Of course some works are more strongly debated than others, not least of all T12P, which is variously assessed as an early Jewish work (II B.C.) interpolated by Christians or alternatively as a Christian work drawing on Jewish sources. In the few brief passages of that work to which we will refer it will be evident that we have assumed the former view while attempting to take account of possible interpolations where they are relevant. Whether and how the alternative view would affect our limited concerns remains to be demonstrated. The entire body of rabbinic and gnostic literature is assumed to post-date the NT; see the relevant sections.

[3] Hofius, 59-74. Cf. also Frankowski, 225-230.

[4] Cf. Wacholder 1975, 202-209; Bacchiocchi 1986, 173f. On the concept of predetermined epochs of history in apocalyptic beginning with Daniel, see Hengel 1974, 1:180-196.

[5] Jub 1,26.29; 2,17ff.; 50,1-5; outside Jubilees (II B.C.) cf. e.g. 1En 91,11ff.; 93,1ff.; TLevi 16-18; 11Q Melch; *Sanh* 97a.b. Cf. Wacholder 1985; Bacchiocchi 1986, 175f.; Buchanan 1978, 3-6.

[6] The use of Ps 90,4 in this manner is first evidenced in Jub 4,30; cf. Lohmann, 231. Cf. *Sanh* 97a; *RH* 31a; *SER* 2; TAb 7,16f. (shorter recension) (I-II A.D.); Ps-Philo 28,6ff.

clearly relates to general expectations of an eschatological Sabbath rest, the *chronological* aspect *per se* is not invoked in the NT and thus will not form a separate part of the following discussion.[7] The chronological element is encountered, however, in other strands of literature, including that of post-apostolic Christian writers.[8]

2.2. Post-mortem and eschatological rest

In the Pseudepigrapha the hope of a post-mortem "rest," already noted in the previous chapter in connection with wisdom thought, becomes considerably more defined. In fact, the general conceptions of the afterlife and final destinies become increasingly developed and nuanced in this literature, and the rest motif simply expands and develops with them.[9] It would be natural, then, that as the idea of a resurrection sharpens, and as rewards and punishments are attached to post-mortem existence and life in the future world, rest would not only become associated with the final state but would be an experience of the *blessed* ones.[10] As an example we may cite TDan 5,10-13 (II B.C.):[11]

Therefore when you turn back to the Lord, you will receive mercy, and he will lead you into his holy place, proclaiming peace to you. And there shall arise for you from the tribe

---

(late-I A.D.) For variations on this schema, see Volz, 35, 62, 71f.; *HJP*², 2:523f., 537f.; Str-B, 4/2:969, 976, 989-994; Lohse, 7:19f. See below, 135.

[7] Though there is no reason to deny NT authors knowledge of "chronomessianism" or the "world-week," I doubt that it is an active ingredient in 2Pet 3,8ff.; Rev 20; Lk 4,18ff.; or elsewhere.

[8] E.g. *Barn* 15, discussed below, 134ff.; cf. 2En 33,1f., which is probably a Christian addition.

[9] This development was not even and consistent; note that as late as III A.D. Sheol is simply "the place of rest, which God determines for men, that they may rest there from the evil things which they saw in their life" (SyrMen II,470ff.; cf. I,34ff.; II,104.126-130.371-376), apparently without distinction of the wicked and righteous. Fairly nondescript usages of the metaphor are in TZeb 10,4; 2En 70,3; Ps-Philo 20,5; 2Bar 85,9. Stone 1989, 144f., notes inconsistency within a single work (4 Ezra).

[10] OT influence may have come from Isa 57,2, which stands in contrast to 57,20f. (cf. Frankowski, 229), though this is not a contrast in *post-mortem* experiences. Cf. also Ψ 65,11f. [66,11f.], a "Psalm of resurrection." On the resurrection in the OT, cf. esp. Isa 26,19f.; Dan 12,2; Nickelsburg 1972, 17-23.

[11] WisSol 4,7 has already been noted as an example of rest as a reward for the righteous. The following may serve as further examples (1En dates from II B.C.-I A.D.), "The righteous ones will have rest from the oppression of sinners" (1En 53,7); The righteous will "eat and rest and rise with the Son of Man forever and ever" (1En 62,14); Those who have experienced pain will hear a "voice of rest" from heaven" (1En 96,3). Cf. also SibOr 2,308 (early I-II A.D.); 2En 42,3 (late I A.D.); 2Bar 85,12 (early II A.D.); ApEl 2,53 (I-IV A.D.); GkApEzra 1,12 (II-IX A.D.).

of Judah and (the tribe of) Levi the Lord's salvation.[12] He will make war against Beliar [= Belial]; he will grant the vengeance of victory as our goal. And he shall take from Beliar the captives, the souls of the saints; and he shall turn the hearts of the disobedient ones to the Lord, and grant eternal peace to those who call upon him. And the saints shall refresh themselves [ἀναπαύω] in Eden; the righteous shall rejoice in the New Jerusalem, which shall be eternally for the glorification of God...The Holy One of Israel will rule over them in humility and poverty, and he who trusts in him shall reign in truth in the heavens.[13]

Likewise, as the locales of the righteous and wicked dead/resurrected are separated it would be natural for the post-mortem and/or eschatological locale of the *righteous* to become known as the resting place.[14]

We also recognized a trend, already begun in the OT, to apply the divinely bestowed מנוחה of the "rest tradition" to the present circumstances of Israel or to project it into the future, usually after the model of the rest which God had given Israel in the past. This use of the מנוחה tradition continues into the Pseudepigrapha,[15] reshaped by the developing eschatological outlook. For example, in a passage heavily influenced by Isa 11, God's Servant, the Anointed One will call all nations and deal with them according to their past dealings with Israel (2Bar 72,2-6).

And it will happen that after he has brought down everything which is in the world, and has sat down in eternal peace on the throne of the kingdom, then joy will be revealed and rest will appear. And then health will descend in dew, and illness will vanish, and fear and tribulation and lamentation will pass away from among men, and joy will encompass the earth...And the wild beasts will come from the wood and serve men, and the asps and dragons will come out of their holes to subject themselves to a child. And women will no longer have pain when they bear, nor will they be tormented when they yield the fruits of their womb. (2Bar 73,1-2.6-7)[16]

It is not unlikely that Isa 11,10 is behind this usage of the rest motif. Elsewhere it is said that if Israel will divest herself of hardness of heart then there will be no posterity for Amalek (cf. Deut 25,19), and "the whole earth shall be at rest from trouble, and everything under heaven shall be free from

---

[12] For an overview of the Davidic messiah in T12P, cf. M. Strauss, 60-64. An earlier version probably foresaw two future figures, one from Judah and one from Levi.

[13] On the question of part or all of this passage being a Christian interpolation, cf. Hofius, 184 n. 385; H.C. Kee (in *OTP*, 1:810) marks only the clause, "living among human beings," in v. 13 (not quoted here) as being Christian; Grundmann 1972, 20 n. 60, considers the references to humility to be Christian.

[14] This contrast in destinies is pronounced in 4Ezra 7,36ff. (late I A.D.); cf. TAb 9,8 [Rec B] (I-II A.D.). But see 1En 38,2-39,4 (cf. 45,3). 1En 38f. is closer to the idea of a "coming to rest," while in 4Ezra 7 the accent is on rest or *relief* as a reward.

[15] Note to begin with 2Bar 61,3; Ps-Philo 25,1; 33,6; 48,4; 55,10.

[16] Early II A.D. This epoch of peace belongs to this world (עולם הזה); cf. Hofius, 66; Str-B, 4/2:965f. Cf. also TLevi 18,1ff., which does not explicitly use the rest motif, but which is dependent on Isa 11.

war.'"[17] In 4Ezra 10,24 Ezra extends encouragement with the words, "'shake off your great sadness and lay aside your many sorrows, so that the Mighty One may be merciful to you again, and the Most High may give you rest, a relief from your troubles.'"[18] Again, it is apparent that Ψ 94,11 [95,11] underlies the use of κατάπαυσις in JosAsen 8,11 and 22,9.[19] Other passages could doubtless be added, but these are enough to indicate that the rest tradition was still being projected into the future, and was absorbed into speculation about the afterlife and the future world.[20]

Another notion which will emerge most clearly in the rabbinic literature is that of an eschatological *Sabbath rest*. The clearest statement in the Pseudepigrapha comes in LAE 51,2 (late I A.D.), where mourning is prohibited for more than six days, "because the seventh day is a sign of the resurrection, the rest of the coming age, and on the seventh day the LORD rested from all his works.'"[21] In this connection it is possible that the association of rest with a restored Eden or Paradise is reminiscent of the Sabbath rest.[22] We may also confront such an idea in 2En 65,9, which describes the "great age" as one without weariness, affliction, worry, want, debilitation, night, or darkness.[23]

In short, the same ideas present in the OT are being encountered here, though they have been reshaped by developing conceptions of the hereafter and eschatology.

2.3. The idea of a future resting "place"

With this overview in mind it will be helpful to summarize Hofius' discussion of the idea of a post-mortem and future resting *place* for the blessed.[24] In this, special attention will be paid to the passages in 4Ezra (ca.

---

[17] TLevi 6,4 (II D.C.).

[18] The immediate context is one of the destruction of Zion and the temple.

[19] Infra, 109f. O.S. Wintermute (in *OTP*, 1:744, 749) finds Ps 95,11 behind ApEl (I-IV A.D.) 2,53 and 4,27, which go "back to the early Jewish stratum within the text"; on ApEl 4,27 see also Hofius, 66f.

[20] TDan 5,12, quoted above, probably indicates such a dependence, for the rest in Eden is parallel to rejoicing in the New Jerusalem, and follows on a description of military conquest. Note also TGad 7,3 (parallel to "inheritance"); SibOr 3,311-318 (mid-II B.C.); Ps-Philo 49,6. Jub 23,29 probably assumes 1Kgs 5,4 [MT 5,18].

[21] Cf. ApMos 43,3 (ApMos is the Gk text of LAE which dates from I-IV A.D.).

[22] E.g., 4Ezra 7,36ff.; 2En 42,3 (God himself rests in Paradise; cf. 8,3; 9,1); cf. Hofius, 68, 74.

[23] Cf. Lincoln 1982, 199. Note also the relevance of the "world-week" which was summarized above, 103f.

[24] Hofius, 59-74.

A.D. 90)²⁵ since Hofius alleges that in this work we have the closest of parallels to Heb 3-4.

2.3.1. The hope of rest in the future world

In this category are included texts which express the belief that at the end of this world or at the beginning of the coming world there will be a resurrection and judgment. The righteous will then enter into eternal blessedness.

The classic expression of the eschatological resting place is 4Ezra 7.²⁶ In v. 26 the groundwork is laid for the idea when it says that along with the revelation of "my servant the Messiah" (v. 28), "the city which now is not seen shall appear, and the land which now is hidden shall be disclosed." While we might often read of the renewal of the earthly Jerusalem, here we encounter the notion of a *pre-existent* reality, a place, which in the end will step into the light.²⁷ Following the death of the messiah there is a period of primeval silence. Then comes the resurrection, judgment, and recompense:

Then the pit of torment shall appear, and opposite it shall be the place of rest; and the furnace of Hell shall be disclosed, and opposite it the Paradise of delight... 'Look on this side and on that; here are delight and rest, and there are fire and torments.' (4Ezra 7,36.38)²⁸

Further on God rebukes Ezra for comparing himself to the unrighteous (8,47), but adds,

...even in this respect you will be praiseworthy before the Most High, because you humble yourself, as is becoming for you, and have not deemed yourself to be among the righteous in order to receive the greatest glory...[But] it is for you that Paradise is opened, the tree of life is planted, the age to come is prepared, plenty is provided, a city is built, rest is appointed, goodness is established and wisdom perfected beforehand. (8,48-52)

In both of these passages we are given a vision of a place of rest which exists already and which is appointed for the future life of the righteous. It is

---

²⁵ On the date and other introductory matters of 4Ezra, see Stone 1990, 1-47.

²⁶ Stone 1990, 204, comments that 4Ezra 7,26-44 is "a presentation of the whole of the eschatological scheme" of the book.

²⁷ Hofius, 182 n. 368; Stone 1990, 213f., 68f., 286f. There appear to have been differing views expressed in the Jewish literature as to whether the heavenly city/temple existed merely in the mind of God or as an entity in heaven; Hurst, 30-32. According to Rowland, 56, the key passage 2Bar 4,2-4 does not refer to an entity existing in heaven.

²⁸ Stone 1990, 221, cites Isa 14,7 and Ps 95,11 as OT precursors of this passage.

essentially identified with Paradise and the "city," *viz* the heavenly Jerusalem with its temple.[29]

The character of the rest itself is defined vis-à-vis *torment*.[30] This is evident not only in 7,36.38, but also in the description of the *intermediate* resting place of the blessed, which we may quote at length here though its content applies to a later section:[31]

> Now this is the order of those who have kept the ways of the Most High, when they shall be separated from their mortal body. During the time that they lived in it, they laboriously served the Most High, and withstood danger every hour, that they might keep the Law of the Lawgiver perfectly. Therefore this is the teaching concerning them: First of all, they shall see with great joy the glory of him who receives them, for they shall have rest in seven orders. The first order, because they have striven with great effort to overcome the evil thought which was formed with them, that it might not lead them astray from life into death. The second order, because they see the perplexity in which the souls of the ungodly wander, and the punishment that waits them. The third order, they see the witness which he who formed them bears concerning them, that while they were alive they kept the Law which was given them in trust. The fourth order, they understand the rest which they now enjoy, being gathered into their chambers and guarded by angels in profound quiet, and the glory which awaits them in the last days. The fifth order, they rejoice that they have now escaped what is mortal, and shall inherit what is to come; and besides they see the straits and toil from which they have been delivered, and the spacious liberty[32] which they are to receive and enjoy in immortality. The sixth order, when it is shown to them how their face is to shine like the sun, and how they are to be made like the light of the stars, being incorruptible from then on.[33] The seventh order, which is greater than all that have been mentioned, because they shall rejoice with boldness, and shall be confident without confusion, and shall be glad without fear, for they shall hasten to behold the face of him whom they served in life and from whom they are to receive their reward when glorified.[34]

If it is borne in mind that the intermediate resting place is a proleptic experience of the final state, then it may be said that this locale into which the disobedient may not "enter" (7,123; cf. v. 121) is a place -- *qua* resting place -- where the righteous will enjoy relief from the suffering of life, where they will dwell quietly without fear, and which is in contrast to the torment of the wicked. This place is also called Paradise and is associated with the heavenly Jerusalem.

---

[29] On the relationship of the "city," "messianic kingdom," and "resting place/Paradise" in 4Ez, see Stone 1990, 287, 286 n. 45, and 335f.

[30] I.e., not vis-à-vis the temple as God's resting place; cf. Hofius, 96.

[31] Below, § 2.3.3.

[32] Similarly, TIsaac 2,13.15 (II A.D.), also in reference to the intermediate resting place.

[33] On the association of refulgent light with the eschatological Sabbath rest, see Friedman, 446; Bacchiocchi 1986, 158-162; Ginzberg, 5:8 n. 19. On this verse see Stone 1990, 97f.

[34] 4Ezra 7,88-98; cf. 7,75.85.

Outside of 4Ezra the idea of an eschatological resting place is not uncommon. 1En 39,4f. refers to the resting places of the holy ones which are beneath the wings of the Lord of the Spirits (v. 7).[35] This locale is set over against the resting place of those who denied the name of the Lord (38,2). TDan 5,7-13[36] is another example of this conception, as are many of the rabbinic passages which will be discussed later.[37] In contrast to, e.g., 4Ezra and TDan, the rabbinic expectation is of a renewal of the earthly Jerusalem rather than the manifestation of a pre-existent city.

2.3.2. Entrance into eternal rest upon death

Some Jewish writers embraced Greek thinking about the immortality of the soul, with the resulting belief that upon death the soul enters immediately into eternal blessedness. In such contexts the rest motif is shaped accordingly.

JosAsen 8,9 (I B.C.-I A.D.), which assumes such an idea of immortality, adapts Ψ 94,11 [95,11] to a prayer of Joseph that Aseneth will be enabled by God to "enter" God's resting place (καὶ εἰσελθάτω εἰς τὴν κατάπαυσίν σου) which he has prepared for his chosen ones, and that she might live in his eternal life forever.[38] Similarly, in 22,13 Levi, the brother of Joseph, is able to see Aseneth's "place of rest in the highest [τὸν τόπον τῆς καταπαύσεως αὐτῆς ἐν τοῖς ὑψίστοις], and her walls like adamantine eternal walls, and her foundation upon a rock of the seventh heaven."[39] Elsewhere, Aseneth's name is "City of Refuge, because...under your wings many people trusting in the Lord God will be sheltered, and behind your walls will be guarded those who attach themselves to the Most High God in the name of Repentance" (15,7). The image of personified Repentance is then developed further. Among other things, she is a daughter of the Most High, gentle and meek (15,7f.). "And she herself is guardian of all virgins, and loves you [Aseneth] very much, and is beseeching the Most High for you at all times and for all who repent she prepared a place of rest in the heavens [τόπον αὐτοῖς ἀναπαύσεως ἡτοίμασεν ἐν τοῖς οὐρανοῖς]"

---

[35] Cf. 62,14; Mt 23,37.
[36] Supra, 104f.
[37] Infra, 122ff. Hofius also discusses the following in this connection: Ps-Philo 19 (not explicit; cf. 28,10; 49,6); 2Bar 73,1; 85,11; and ApEl 4,27.
[38] On JosAsen in general, cf. Collins 1983, 211-218. Burchard's translation of JosAsen in *OTP*, 2:177-247, includes a very helpful introduction and a substantial commentary on the text; cf. also Nickelsburg 1992a, 590. The dependence of JosAsen 8,9 on Ψ 94,11 [95,11] is argued by Hofius, 30; cf. Burchard (in *OTP*, 2:213 n. f2).
[39] This usage may be dependent on Isa 66,1; cf. Hofius, 30.

(15,7).[40] This early work is important evidence of an (individual) eschatological reading of Ψ 94,11 [95,11].[41]

2 Enoch also assumes that the souls of the righteous enter into eternal blessedness upon death.[42] It describes Paradise, the place where God himself rests (8,3), as the place prepared for the righteous as an eternal inheritance (9,1). Later, this same place is referred to as the "paradise of Eden, where rest is prepared for the righteous" (42,3).[43]

2.3.3. Entrance into an intermediate rest upon death

This third category includes passages in which the souls of the righteous enter into an intermediate place of rest upon death while their bodies lie in the grave. Although temporary, this is a foretaste of the final state which follows the resurrection of their bodies.[44] Thus here also we have indirect testimony to the idea of an eschatological resting place.

4Ezra 7,88-98[45] is a good example of this usage. In contrast to the spirits of the godless which "wander about in torments, ever grieving and sad, in seven ways" (7,80), the spirits of the righteous are gathered into their chambers (7,95) which are located in Sheol (4,41); here they enjoy rest. On the day of the renewal "the chambers shall give up the souls which have been committed to them" (7,32) and then the place of rest will be revealed which is opposite the place of torment (7,36ff.).

In Ps-Philo (I A.D.) the intermediate resting places of the blessed are not in Sheol but in heaven. In an ecstatic vision Kenaz is able to see images of just ones dwelling in heaven for 7000 years -- the duration of the world (28,6ff.). He characterizes their existence as one of "repose" (28,20). After that length of time will be the resurrection and judgment, and then there will be another heaven and earth (3,10).[46] Likewise, in 4Bar 5,32 (I-II A.D.)[47] Abimelech cries out, "'I will bless you, O God of heaven and of the earth, the rest [ἀνάπαυσις] of the souls of the righteous in every place.'" This

---

[40] On the text of 15,7 cf. Burchard, 61, 66, 67.

[41] Hofius, 50.

[42] Hofius, 68.

[43] Further examples of this usage include ApSedr 16,3 (II-IV A.D.); SyrMen II,470ff.

[44] Our concern is with the soul's experience of rest (vs. the repose of the corpse); cf. Hofius, 69 (esp. nn. 416-418, 441).

[45] Supra, 108.

[46] Similarly, TAb (I-II A.D.): the souls of the righteous are taken into heaven while their bodies remain in the earth until the 7000 years are fulfilled, and then will come the resurrection (7,16); the intermediate place of the righteous is characterized by rest (9,8).

[47] Allison 1988, 483f., cites this passage in connection with Mt 11,25-30.

appellation is unique, but Hofius may be right that this is best understood as an example of the giver with the name of the gift.[48]

2.4. Summary

Although some of the literature surveyed in this section extends well beyond the first century A.D., discussing it here has enabled us to observe important developments in the use of the motif.

The section on the post-mortem and eschatological rest (§ 2.2) showed that many passages are indebted to the traditions which we already encountered in the OT, *viz* the rest tradition and the Sabbath. Yet in the Pseudepigrapha, conceptions of the resurrection, immortality, and eternal life are much more developed than in the OT. Within the resulting eschatological frameworks the OT traditions about rest receive a new shape or, better, new shapes, while continuing to draw on OT precedents.

These new shapes of the rest motif are amply evidenced in the differing expectations of an eschatological resting *place* (§ 2.3). Whether expressed as a locale in which the righteous will dwell following the resurrection and the renewal of the earth or the appearance of the heavenly Paradise, or as the locale into which the soul enters once and for all upon death, or as the intermediate dwelling place which anticipates the final dwelling, there is a strong and widespread expectation of an eschatological enjoyment of rest in a resting place.

Two works which received special attention were 4 Ezra and Joseph and Aseneth; the importance of these works will be highlighted when we turn our attention to Heb 3-4.

3. Qumran

There are a few places where the OT rest tradition is taken up in the Scrolls, which we will simply mention since they testify to an eschatological application of the rest tradition. The Florilegium from cave 4 provides the following midrash on 2Sam 7,11:

And concerning His words to David, *And I [will give] you [rest] from all your enemies...*, this means that He will give them rest from all the children of Satan who cause them to stumble so that they may be destroyed [by their errors,] just as they came with a [devilish] plan to cause the [sons] of light to stumble and to devise against them a wicked

---

[48] Hofius, 73. That this usage is to be identified with the heavenly or eschatological Jerusalem (cf. 4Bar 5,34f.) is unclear. Other passages discussed by Hofius in relation to the intermediate resting place include TIsaac 2,13.15; TJac 2,26; 5,6; GkApEzra 1,12; *Ket* 104a; *Shab* 152b (cf. also Hofius, 186 n. 417).

plot, that [they might become subject] to Satan in their [wicked] straying. (4Q174 1 = 4QFlor 1)[49]

The immediately preceding context interprets 2Sam 7,10 as a reference to the "House which [He will build for them in the] last days...[Its glory shall endure] forever; it shall appear above it perpetually." The following context interprets the promises of a house and a seed for David (2Sam 7,12-14) -- "I will be his father and he will be my son" -- as a reference to the "Branch of David who shall arise with the Interpreter of the Law [to rule] in Zion [at the end] of time."

2Sam 7 is also alluded to in 4Q504 4 which tells how the Lord established his covenant with David that he might be a shepherd over God's people, "and there was neither adversary nor misfortune, but peace and blessing." The same context refers to the "dwelling place...a resting-place in Jerus[alem the city which] Thou hast [chosen] from all the earth that Thy [Name] might remain there for ever" (cf. Ps 132). 11QT 29 also describes the temple as

...the house on which I [shall cause] my name to rest...I will dwell with them for ever an ever and will sanctify my [sa]nctuary by my glory. I will cause my glory to rest on it until the day of creation on which I shall create my sanctuary [sic], establishing if for myself for all the time according to the covenant which I have made with Jacob in Bethel.

One of the "Pseudo-Danielic" writings reads,

He shall be called son of God, and they shall designate him son of the Most High. Like the appearance of comets, so shall be their kingdom. For (brief) years they shall reign over the earth and shall trample on all; one people shall trample on another and one province on another until the people of God shall rise and all shall rest from the sword. (4Q246 2)[50]

It is interesting that just as in 4QFlor 1 the sonship motif is joined to an eschatological use of the rest tradition.

Finally, we may note a couple of examples which do not use the rest motif but which move in a realm of ideas not far removed from Mt 11,28-30. In the Thanksgiving Hymns the Teacher mourns, "[I have no word] for my disciples to revive the spirit of those who stumble and to speak words of support to the weary" (1QH 8). Similarly in the same collection it is said

---

[49] All trans. of the Scrolls are from Vermes 1987, unless otherwise indicated; cf. on this passage esp. Brooke, 194-197. A summary of the Davidic messianic hopes at Qumran may be found in M. Strauss, 50-60 (cf. 55f., on 4Q174).

[50] For discussion and literature on this text, cf. Collins 1993. Cf. also Eisenman-Wise, 68-71. Collins argues for a (Davidic) messianic understanding of the son of God here. In addition to the passages noted here, a fragment of a prayer blesses "the God who has given us rest" (4Q504 3 ii).

that God opened the "fountain" of the Servant "that to the humble he might bring glad tidings of Thy great mercy, [proclaiming salvation] from out of the fountain [of holiness to the contrite] of spirit, and everlasting joy to those who mourn" (1QH 18).[51]

4. Philo of Alexandria[52]

4.1. Introduction and overview

The noun κατάπαυσις does not occur in Philo's writings; καταπαύω occurs infrequently, and does not itself spark speculation on "rest." In *LegAll* I,5f.16.18 (on Gen 2,2f.) Philo stresses that καταπαύω is intended transitively, "cause to cease," in order to make the point that God does not leave off making things, but rather "causes to cease that which, though actually not in operation, is apparently making," while he himself begins the "shaping of others more divine";[53] Philo explains his meaning by the use of the word παύω, "cease," or, "cause to cease." Accordingly the semantic components of "relief" and "relaxation" were apparently not present in καταπαύω for Philo in contrast to the LXX and Heb 3-4.[54] Ἀνάπαυσις, ἀνάπαυλα, and ἀναπαύω are, however, used frequently in Philo's speculation about "rest,"[55] along with several other terms:[56] e.g. ἠρεμία (quiet), στάσις (standing still; stationariness), ἀκίνητος (unmoved; motionless), ἄτρεπτος (unchangeable), ἵδρυσις (founding; foundation), and εἰρήνη (peace). These terms already indicate the metaphysical context of Philo's conception which will emerge in the following discussion.

The OT מנוחה tradition is barely visible in Philo's writings,[57] but the idea of rest surfaces often in connection with the Sabbath and the number seven.[58]

---

[51] Cf. Deutsch 1987, 120f., for similar imagery in the Scrolls.
[52] See Käsemann, 70-72; Theißen 1969, 124-129; Hofius, 248-257; R. Williamson 1970, 544-548; J.W. Thompson, 84-87; Williams 1977, esp. 179-188; Helderman 1984, 58-60; Deutsch 1987, 123-125.
[53] The translations from *LegAll* I in this paragraph have been altered to read "cease" instead of "rest" (LCL) since this is clearly the meaning. Otherwise, all trans. of Philo are from LCL.
[54] Cf. also *LegAll* III,169; *Post* 183; cf. further below, 145f.
[55] These are not used, however, alongside καταπαύω, even when the latter is in the source to which Philo alludes with ἀναπαυ- (e.g. *Fuga* 173; *Cher* 87); cf. R. Williamson 1970, 544.
[56] Cf. J.W. Thompson, 84, 86; Hofius, 250, 256.
[57] Whether it is to be felt in the following passages is moot: *Abr* 28 (cf. *Gig* 51); *Fuga* 174; *Abr* 27.30; *SpecLeg* II,44; *Somn* I,174; *Post* 183. Note also *SpecLeg* I,69 (*Fuga* 50f.; cf. Mack 1973, 119 n. 11). Most of these are blended with wisdom's rest and thoughts about the Sabbath. Philo also depicts the eschatological age in terms

For Philo the Sabbath is a day of physical rest from work in the usual sense,[59] and with a pronounced humanitarian interest.[60] More importantly, it is a day to be used for the pursuit of wisdom and ethical self-examination.[61] The Sabbath has a cosmic significance.[62] Philo considers the seventh day, "called also in the records the birthday of the whole world, to be of equal value to eternity" (*SpecLeg* I,170); he sees its "marvellous beauty stamped upon heaven and the whole world and enshrined in nature itself" (*VitaMos* II,209).[63] While eschatology is not a dominant force in Philo's thinking, it is not entirely absent.[64] Disregard or violation of the Sabbath/sabbatical rest -- particularly in its humanitarian emphasis (*Praem* 153ff.) -- will lead ultimately to the realization of the law's curses. For the land, however, there will be relief. As she sees

...her market places void of turmoil and war and wrongdoing, but full of tranquillity and peace and justice, she will renew her youth and bloom and take her rest calm and serene during the festal seasons of the sacred Seven...Then like a fond mother she will pity the sons and daughters whom she has lost... (*Praem* 157f.)[65]

Such expectations are fashioned largely after Lev 26,34f.43 (cf. 2Chr 36,21), although Isa 66,23 with its portrayal of on-going cycles of Sabbath celebrations may also have been an influence.

---

reminiscent of Isa 11,6-9 (cf. Wolfson, 2:409f.; R. Williamson 1989, 19f.) and Lev 26,6, as an end of "primary war" and as a reign of a peace which permeates even the animal kingdom (*Praem* 85-93).

[58] "Peace and Seven are identical according to the Legislator: for on the seventh day creation puts away its seeming activity and takes rest" (*Fuga* 173; cf. *Abr* 28) In *Migr* 28ff. the land = Wisdom which, when entered, brings "rest" from studying, toiling, and practicing, since the principle of the year of "release" is operative; as explained by Philo, the sabbatical year stands for the reception of gifts for which one does not labor (cf. *Fuga* 170ff.; *QuaesGen* III,39). *Migr* 28ff. seems to blend freely the Sabbath rest, the מנוחה tradition, and wisdom's rest.

[59] *VitaMos* II,21f.219f.; *SpecLeg* II,60.64. Sabbatical rest for the land: *Dec* 162f.; *SpecLeg* II,39.89.96f.; *Praem* 153.157.

[60] *Dec* 164; *SpecLeg* II,89ff.; *Praem* 154ff.

[61] *VitaMos* II,211f.; *Dec* 96ff.; *SpecLeg* II,60ff.; *Gaium* 156. Cf. Wolfson, 2:265f. Theißen 1969, 125, rightly stresses that this pursuit of wisdom and virtue is not identical with the Sabbath "rest" itself, but is rather modelled after God's own contemplation of his work; cf. esp. *Dec* 97f.; *contra* Barrett, 371.

[62] Cf. Borgen, 270f.

[63] Cf. also *SpecLeg* II,156f.; *QuodDeus* 11.

[64] On the future in Philo (apart from the question of messianism), cf. Wolfson, 2:395-426 (esp. 407ff.); *HJP*[2], 507-509; and R. Williamson 1989, 18-27.

[65] R. Williamson 1989, 23, explains this as "a period of sabbath rest...in which a renewal of the land and its people will take place." Colson *et al.*, 458, point out that the vision of peace here stems primarily from associations of peace with the number seven (*Fuga* 173).

The idea of rest is exploited in other connections as well (e.g. the names Noah and Nahor; Deut 5,31), but for our purposes we may isolate some specific features with the aid of previous discussions.

4.2. The debate between G. Theißen and O. Hofius

In 1969, G. Theißen addressed the matter of the rest motif in Philo of Alexandria, and undertook to demonstrate the derivation of the κατάπαυσις idea in Heb 3-4 from ideas expressed in that source. The unpublished Göttingen dissertation of O. Hofius (*Katapausis. Die Vorstellung vom endzeitlichen Ruheort im Hebräerbrief*, 1968) had been a foil for Theißen's analysis. The following year, Hofius published his dissertation, to which he appended a response to Theißen's remarks. A chronicle of their debate will take us some distance toward understanding the rest motif in Philo.

4.2.1. G. Theißen

In his study of the rest motif in Philo, Theißen argues that there is more than one strand of thought visible.[66] One of these, which Theißen terms "gnostic,"[67] Philo (allegedly) picks up from elsewhere and develops, but ultimately rejects in favor of an idea which is more "Jewish."

The "gnostic" strand is present in *QuodDeus*. 10ff.:

Indeed of the nature of the soul beloved of God no clearer evidence can we have than that psalm of Hannah which contains the words "the barren hath borne seven, but she that had many children languished" (1 Sam. ii. 5). And yet it is the mother of one child -- Samuel -- who is speaking. How then can she say that she has borne seven? It can only be that in full accordance with the truth of things, she holds the One to be the same as the Seven, not only in the lore of numbers, but also in the harmony of the universe and in the thoughts of the virtuous soul. For Samuel who is appointed to God alone and holds no company with any other has his being ordered in accordance with the One and the Monad, the truly existent. But this condition of his implies the Seven, that is a soul which rests in God [ἀναπαυομένης ἐν θεῷ] and toils no more at any mortal task [θνητῶν ἔργων], and has thus left behind the Six, which God has assigned to those who could not win the first place, but must needs limit their claim to the second.[68]

Several ideas converge in this passage. The concept of "resting in God" conveys the idea of communion with God, the *Einheit* and true Being, a very mystical goal which is not attained by all.

---

[66] Theißen 1969, 124-129.
[67] Theißen 1969, 127. The label, "gnostic," is used by Theißen on the basis of "phänomenologischer Kategorien (Gnosis = Rückkehr zum Ursprung vor jeder Schöpfung)" (127 n. 8). He refers here to the analysis of the gnostic idea which was carried out by Vielhauer. See further below, 145ff.
[68] Also for Käsemann, 70ff., this passage evidenced early gnostic ideas.

This thought of "resting in God" is closely associated with an interpretation of the creation account in which humankind's cessation of work is parallel to God's on the seventh day of creation; in that context, then, God's "rest" is a *cessation* of work.[69] It is noted in this regard that the works from which people abstain are valued negatively ($\theta\nu\eta\tau\hat{\omega}\nu$ $\H{\epsilon}\rho\gamma\omega\nu$), which suggests that the parallelism is not complete, or that Philo is hinting at a negative valuation of creation.[70]

Secondly, according to Theißen Philo assumes in the above cited passage the idea that the sixth and seventh numbers correspond to two stages in human life: the natural birth from the earth, and re-birth. Commenting elsewhere on Ex 24,16, where the cloud covers the mountain for six days and Moses is called up on the seventh, Philo again draws on Gen 2, and observes that, "The even number, six, He apportioned both to the creation of the world and to the election of the contemplative nation..." Moses' call on the seventh day, however, is a second birth ($\delta\epsilon\upsilon\tau\acute{\epsilon}\rho\alpha$ $\gamma\acute{\epsilon}\nu\epsilon\sigma\iota\varsigma$) which comes about

in accordance with the ever-virginal nature of the hebdomad. For he is called on the seventh day, in this (respect) differing from the earth-born first moulded man, for the latter came into being from the earth and with a body, while the former came from the ether and without a body. (*QuaesEx* II,46)

Theißen comments, "Das Ziel ist die Verwandlung aus Gewordenem ins Ungewordene, die anima (oder: spiritus) mutata a genita ad ingenitam...Der mystische Einschlag ist unverkennbar."[71]

Thirdly, Philo utilizes Pythagorean speculation about the number seven which equates this number with the *Einheit*, since seven is like

---

[69] Theißen apparently construes God's rest here as complete inactivity; at least he contrasts *QuodDeus* 10ff. with *Cher* 87ff. (below) on this score.

[70] Thus Theißen 1969, 126. He does not choose between these two options, although a negative view of creation would obviously take the idea closer to gnostic thought. Hofius, 251, however, is probably correct in reading these works as the "sins" of *QuodDeus* 7ff. from which the wise are cleansed before drawing near to God; cf. also *LegAll* III,77; I,16-18.

[71] Theißen 1969, 126. LCL renders, "...being changed from a productive to an unproductive form..." In his study of God and man in Philo's thought generally, Runia 1990, XII, 48-75, esp. 69f., states that *QuaesEx* II,46 depicts the "highest form of divinization," though he wonders if "we can still speak of the divinization of *man*" (italics in original). *QuaesEx* II,46, however, is called by Runia (along with *QuaesEx* II,29.40) "remarkable," "difficult," and less "typical" of Philo's thought; it may be wondered, then, if *QuaesEx* II,46 is the best text by which to shed light on *QuodDeus* 10ff. In the context of *QuodDeus*, Philo will return shortly to the "perfect man" who "seeks for quietude [$\H{\eta}\rho\epsilon\mu\acute{\iota}\alpha\varsigma$]" (*QuodDeus* 23), but here in such a manner that the human "quietude" is a qualified parallel of God's (cf. *QuaesGen* IV,1).

the chief of all things: for that which neither begets nor is begotten remains motionless; for creation takes place in movement, since there is movement both in that which begets and in that which is begotten...There is only one thing that neither causes motion nor experiences it, the original Ruler and Sovereign. (*Op* 100)[72]

In this sense, the rest of God is not his experience following creation, but his *eternal* essence, his attribute. Theißen observes, then, that according to *QuodDeus*. 10ff. salvation consists in a share in this rest of God, i.e. in his essence.[73]

Now according to Theißen, Philo elsewhere takes a position which is opposed to the above speculation on two points: first in rejecting the idea that humans rest in God, and second in denying that the essence of God is rest (*qua* cessation of work). The evidence for this comes from *Cher* 87ff.:

And therefore Moses often in his laws calls the sabbath, which means 'rest' [ἀνάπαυσις], God's sabbath..., not man's...For in all truth there is but one thing in the universe which rests, that is God. But Moses does not give the name of rest to mere inactivity [ἀπραξίαν]. The cause of all things is by its very nature active; it never ceases to work all that is best and most beautiful. God's rest is rather a working with absolute ease, without toil and without suffering... rest belongs in the fullest sense to God and to Him alone.

This position, which appears to differ from *QuodDeus* 10ff., employs Jewish concerns about the transcendence of the Creator to *ward off* overly ambitious longings for an unmediated vision of God and a share in his rest (so Theißen). It also assumes Jewish beliefs about the continuing role of God in creation, resulting in an interpretation of God's "rest" as a "sublimeres Schaffen...*Gottes Wesen ist nicht Ruhe, sondern Schaffen*." Thus rest belongs solely to God, and his rest is a "mühelose Tätigkeit" rather than a cessation of work.[74] In Philo's (alleged) tacit polemic, Theißen perceives evidence for the aforementioned "gnostic" thought.

4.2.2. O. Hofius

Hofius has responded to this analysis of Philo by attempting to refute Theißen on two fronts: first, by showing that the above two strands of

---

[72] Philo had a predecessor for his Sabbath speculation in the Jewish philosopher Aristobulus (ca. 181-145 B.C.); a summary of the latter's thought on the Sabbath and the number seven is given by Borgen, 276f.; cf. Hengel 1974, 1:163-169.

[73] Theißen 1969, 126f. It this last point which Theißen finds particularly "gnostic" in character. Again, cf. Runia 1990, XII,48-75, on the subject of God and man and the *limits* of speaking of man as a god in Philo.

[74] Theißen 1969, 127 (italics mine). According to *LegAll* I,5ff.16-18, the seventh day of creation does not signal the cessation of creation, but the beginning of God's creation of immaterial things; cf. Käsemann, 71f.

thought (*QuodDeus* 10ff. and *Cher* 87ff.) are not divergent but consistent with each other when the passages are rightly interpreted; and, second, by demonstrating that the so-called "gnostic" strand is not gnostic in any case.[75]

The two strands of thought are consistent with each other in the two respects by which Theißen had differentiated them: *contra* Theißen, Philo portrays God's essence as *both* rest *and* activity (rather than one or the other);[76] moreover, the claim that Philo denies humans a share in God's rest is unfounded.

For Philo God's *Wesen* is both "rest" and "activity." These are not antithetical but rather complementary, being mutually interpretive. When Philo depicts God's essence ($\phi\acute{u}\sigma\epsilon\omega\varsigma$) as "rest" ($\mathring{\eta}\rho\epsilon\mu\acute{\iota}\alpha\varsigma$; *Post* 28f.) God is thereby contrasted with creation, which is "subject to movement" (*Post* 23).[77] Philo's indebtedness to Platonic metaphysics is evident in this,[78] and it is thus a matter of the important doctrine of the *Deus immutabilis*.[79] On the other hand, passages where Philo stresses that God never ceases to be active[80] are polemicizing against the attempt to depict God's essence as $\dot{\alpha}\pi\rho\alpha\xi\acute{\iota}\alpha$, "inactivity," in other words against the doctrine of a *Deus otiosus*. Philo may not express both elements of the equation with equal emphasis in each instance, but these latter passages are not denying God's rest (cf. *Cher* 87 with 90). God's activity differs from creation's movement precisely in that "God turns not and changes not"; his activity is, unlike creation's movement, without toil ($\kappa\alpha\kappa o\pi\acute{\alpha}\theta\epsilon\iota\alpha$). Philo is thus arguing that God's rest and his activity are not antithetical but that they interpenetrate.

---

[75] Hofius, 248-255.

[76] The alternatives for Theißen are actually "rest *qua* inactivity" and "rest *qua* sublime activity": "Auch für ihn [*Auctor*] ist die Ruhe Gottes kein sublimes Schaffen, sondern wirklich Ende des Wirkens" (1969, 127).

[77] *Post* 23 (quoted at length below) reads, "...that which is unwaveringly stable is God, and that which is subject to movement is creation..." Likewise 28, "...the Existent Being who moves and turns all else is himself exempt from movement and turning."

[78] Cf. Williams 1977, 5, 145-191; 1985, 42f.; Helderman 1984, 60; J.W. Thompson, 86f. In view of the metaphysical context given the rest motif, it is justified to state that in Philo "the association of rest with the spiritual, heavenly realm becomes dominant" (Attridge, 127) and that it is to that extent a symbol for transcendence (J.W. Thompson, 85). Yet the process by which Käsemann, 71-73, *identifies* the $\dot{\alpha}\nu\acute{\alpha}\pi\alpha\nu\sigma\iota\varsigma$ with the heavenly realm, or "aeon," making the $\dot{\alpha}\nu\acute{\alpha}\pi\alpha\nu\sigma\iota\varsigma$ a locale, the transcendent realm itself, seems to me rather circuitous, and according less helpful for understanding Hebrews. "Rest" is an attribute, a characteristic, or a state in Philo, but it does not seem to be primarily a *place* to which one goes.

[79] *Op* 100, which Theißen cited (above) in connection with *QuodDeus* 10ff. should be understood from this perspective. Further passages noted by Hofius in this connection: *Conf* 30f.; *Gig* 49; *Somn* II,223ff.228.

[80] E.g. *Aet* 84; *LegAll* I,5f.16-18; *Op* 7; *Provid* I,6.

Chapter Four: Jewish and Christian Literature

Gott ist vielmehr gerade als der Ruhende zugleich der Schaffende und gerade als der Schaffende zugleich der Ruhende. In beidem ist er in gleicher Weise ewig: sowohl in seinem Ruhen (deshalb die transitive Fassung von κατέπαυσεν Gen 2,3 in all. I 6. 16!) wie auch in seinem Schaffen (aet. 84; prov. I 6).[81]

Not only are both of these -- God's rest and his activity -- elements of Philo's own thought, but also the idea that *humans share in God's rest* is Philo's own conviction, rather than something he picks up and then rejects. *QuodDeus* 10ff.[82] is by no means solitary; the idea is too common to think that Philo rejects it. There are a number of passages where the wise or righteous person seeks after and attains rest. In regard to the rest associated with Noah (Gen 5,29) Philo observes that "it is in the nature of justice in the first place to create rest in the place of toil... [The] crowning purport of righteousness is to give us full rest" (*QuodDet* 121f.).[83] The friend of God (Noah) can himself be designated as rest (ἀνάπαυσις; *Abr* 27; *LegAll* III,77). Moreover, it is said outside of *QuodDeus* 10ff. that humans share in God's rest, for which *Post* 23ff. may serve as an example:

Proximity to a stable object produces a desire to be like it and a longing for quiescence [ἠρεμίας]. Now that which is unwaveringly stable is God, and that which is subject to movement is creation. He therefore that draws nigh to God longs for stability, but he that forsakes Him, inasmuch as he approaches the unresting creation is, as we might expect, carried about. It is for this reason that it is written in the Curses "He shall not cause thee to rest [ἀναπαύσει], and there shall be no standing [στάσις] for the soul of thy feet," and a little later "thy life shall be hanging before thy eyes"[84]... He makes the worthy man sharer of His own Nature [φύσεως], which is repose [ἠρεμίας]...calm [ἠρεμίαν] in a good man, restlessness in a foolish one...[85]

---

[81] Hofius, 251.
[82] Supra, 115.
[83] Note in addition the following: *LegAll* III,77; *QuaesGen* I,87; *Somn* I,174; II,229; also *LegAll* III,114ff.128ff.; *QuodDeus* 23ff.; *Mut* 239f.; *Praem* 116.121; cf. also Helderman 1984, 59. Although in these passages "rest" is a good to be sought after and attained, Philo can also use this motif in a more negative manner: "...it is well that things evil should be in a state of stillness [ἡσυχία]; motion on the other hand is the proper condition for the good" (*Congr* 45.48; cf. also *Sobr* 34ff.44ff., and *passim*); cf. Plato's *Tim* 19B. This latter usage of Philo is based on the association of "rest" and light (φωτὸς ἀνάπαυσις) which Philo reads out of the name Nahor (*Congr* 45); cf. R. Williamson 1970, 545-546.
[84] Deut 28,65f.
[85] Cf. also: *Gig* 49; *Conf* 30f.; *Somn* II,223ff.; *Fuga* 166ff.; *Dec* 86.142.143ff.; *LegAll* III,160; *SpecLeg* IV,79ff., and discussion in Hofius, 252f.; several of these are associated with Deut 5,31. A particularly helpful discussion of "standing" before the Transcendent and participating in its stability and rest -- a discussion which takes in a broader context than Philo -- is given in Williams 1985, 14-15, 74-85, and *passim* (in connection with Philo, cf. esp. 25-27, 43, 74-76, 84, 204-205); also 1977, 179-188; 1981, 824-826.

The point remains, however, that *Cher* 87ff.[86] stresses that God's rest is his own. It should not be missed, however, that in this context Philo has a very specific concern to speak out against the godless bearing which presumes to seize God's own possessions for oneself (*Cher* 77).[87] God alone, Philo insists, can really claim possession of *anything*, including the feasts (83ff.). *This* concern gives rise to Philo's discussion of God's own (Sabbath) rest, what is it and is not, and how it belongs to God alone.[88] Yet in none of this is Philo renouncing the idea that humans share in God's rest. Indeed, immediately before the passage Theißen cites (87ff.), Philo states expressly that God "*Himself has imparted of His own to all particular beings from that fountain of beauty -- Himself.*"[89] Contra Theißen, *Cher* 87ff. and *QuodDeus* 10ff. are shaped by different concerns, not distinct traditions.

If it is the case, therefore, that Philo does not reject the conception of "resting in God" which he expounds in *QuodDeus* 10ff., is this idea nonetheless "gnostic" in character? Hofius demonstrates that the answer must be, "No."[90] "God" and "Rest" are not for Philo (as for gnostic thought) identical and thus interchangeable. The interplay of the divine "rest" and divine "activity" is very uncharacteristic of Gnosticism. The rest of God is not portrayed as the original home of the wise who are coming to rest, which makes it inappropriate to suggest that Philo's idea is that of a "Rückkehr zum Ursprung vor jeder Schöpfung"[91] as in Gnosticism. The ethical alignment of Philo's conception is very different than the gnostic conception. The restlessness of the fool does not, for Philo, stem back to a pre-existent fall out of the divine rest into the domain of the demonic world, but rather to the fool's disobedience and godlessness (*Dec* 86; *Post* 22ff.).[92] On the other hand, the rest in God is granted only to those who strive after perfection, on whose volition the issue is dependent. Those who do come to rest do not, however, become God (*Somn* II,238ff.),[93] and the danger remains

---

[86] Supra, 117.

[87] In the same vein, cf. *Congr* 130; *Sacr* 54.

[88] In addition to stating that only God truly rests, Philo elsewhere sets limits on the rest of people: *Somn* II,230ff.; *QuaesGen* IV,1.

[89] *Cher* 86; italics added. This joining of ideas -- that all things belong to God alone in the true sense, but that he grants a share to humans -- recurs in *Cher* 108ff.; cf. *QuodDeus* 23 with *QuodDeus* 10ff. Borgen, 271, remarks, "Basically feasts and joy belong to God alone, for God alone is entirely blessed, exempt from all evil. But from this joy of God the joy of man flows, as a mixed stream."

[90] Hofius, 254f. What follows is a summary of Hofius' points. Cf. below, 145ff., for further on the gnostic conception.

[91] Theißen 1969, 127 n. 8.

[92] Cf. also *QuaesGen* I,42.

[93] Cf. also *QuaesGen* IV,1.

that they might drift away and lose the rest of the soul (*Somn* II,233). Thus Philo's thought cannot be labelled "gnostic."[94]

4.3. Summary and conclusions

As may be seen from the foregoing analysis, Philo's use of the rest motif is difficult to reduce to a simple presentation. In general, however, it may be said that it is used often and significantly in conjunction with the Sabbath and the number seven. Here it is an attribute of God, and is by extension characteristic of the transcendent realm which is metaphysically closest to God. It is related to the immutability of God, his stability and unmovability, but is construed in such a fashion as to assume God's continuing activity; in this sense, "rest" is uniquely a property of God. Yet insofar as humans stand in proximity to God and that transcendent realm -- i.e., they receive the Logos/Wisdom and live virtuously -- they also participate in that reality, and thus in God's stability or "rest." Often this "rest" is portrayed in terms of the peace and tranquillity which one experiences in everyday life, but there seem to be very mystical elements as well. On the whole, the experience of rest would appear to be realized and individualized.

It is more difficult to speak of a development of the OT with regard to Philo than it was in relation to the Pseudepigrapha. Now the notion of rest appears to have been completely redefined and to have assumed as its conceptual center ideas taken over *en bloc* from Platonic philosophy. Rather than a change of course the train has been moved to another set of tracks.

It must be said that the scattered location of the relevant passages and the extent to which differing developments of the rest idea are blended in given instances make it unlikely that we can speak of sharply defined, distinct usages of the motif. Philo's concerns vary from passage to passage, and appreciation of these differing interests makes Theißen's attempt to set one usage sharply against the other appear forced. There is probably more consistency between the usages which Theißen distinguishes than he allows, and whatever tension is left is no more than could be expected from a prolific writer of such ranging interests. We can allow for a diversity of influences on Philo's thought and also for the possibility that a given statement approximates to a given gnostic conception, but in Philo as in the NT and elsewhere we should not be overly eager to discover hardened traditions behind what may be *ad hoc* formulations. There is, in any event, a

---

[94] In his extensive examination of ἀνάπαυσις in *GosTruth*, Helderman agrees with Hofius as to the chasm separating the Philonic and gnostic conceptions of rest (1984, 60 n. 122; likewise J.W. Thompson, 86f.). For the relationship of Philo to Gnosticism generally as well as Philo's use of the rest motif to that of Gnosticism, cf. Helderman 1984, 20f., 60, 69, and *passim*; Williams 1977, 188-191.

difference in *emphasis* between *QuodDeus* 10ff. and *Cher* 87ff., which may have been due in part to the alternative attractions of more "Jewish" (OT) or more Platonic conceptions, and this difference in emphasis might have allowed for diverging developments among students of Philo. Yet leaving aside the question of defining Gnosticism, it would be premature to say the least to equate Philo's developments of the rest motif with what we observe in the classic gnostic expressions.

5. Rabbinic literature

5.1. The hope of "rest"

5.1.1. The "world which is wholly Sabbath and rest"[95]

The earliest expression of the idea that the future world, the עולם הבא, would be characterized by Sabbath rest, מנוחה, is *Tam* 7,4:

On the Sabbath day they did sing, *A Psalm, A song for the Sabbath day* (Ps 92) -- A psalm, a song for the world that is to come, for the day which is wholly Sabbath rest for eternity.[96]

In *PRE* 18 God creates 7 worlds; the first 6 belong to this age, the עולם הזה, and the 7th is the new world, the עולם הבא, which is already existent and will appear at the end.[97] *ARN* 1 depicts that day as one

...which will be all Sabbath, when there will be neither eating nor drinking nor worldly affairs, but the righteous will sit with crowns on their heads enjoying the brilliance of the Divine Presence, as it is stated, *And they beheld God, and did eat and drink* [Exod 24,11], like the ministering angels.[98]

---

[95] Cf. Hofius, 111-113; also Str-B, 3:687; 4/2:839f.; Volz, 384f. On rabbinic speculation about the "world-week" and the "world-Sabbath," see above, 103f.

[96] All trans. of the Mishnah are from Neusner 1988b, unless indicated otherwise; italics in original. The same idea is to be found in *RH* 31a; *MekShabbata* 1; *CantR* 4,4 § 6; *MidrPss* 92 § 2; *ARN* 1; *PRE* 18; 19; *SER* 2; and *FrgTg* to Ex 20,11.

[97] The idea of the "world which is wholly Sabbath" was not originally associated with the "world-week" and "world-Sabbath," but was only secondarily associated with it; cf. Hofius, 208f. nn. 733, 738, 739; Volz, 384f.; Str-B, 3:844 n. 1 (in spite of 4/2:821, 839f., 991); see above, 103f. Thus, *PRE* 18; *MidrPss* 92 § 2; and *ARN* 1 should not be understood along the lines of the "world-week," *contra* Lohse, 7:20 n. 155; Gräßer, 1:219 n. 149.

[98] All trans. of *ARN* from Cohen 1965, unless indicated otherwise; italics in original.

Though an expression such as, "the day which is wholly Sabbath rest for eternity," is restricted to the rabbinic literature, there is no apparent reason to deny that a first century tradition is preserved.[99]

5.1.2. Other aspects of "rest" as an object of hope

The present celebration of the Sabbath was also an anticipation of the eschatological Sabbath.[100] For instance, *MidrPss* 92 § 5:

A Psalm, a song. For the Sabbath day -- that is, for the day when even the demons rest from their mischief in the world, for the day when God's people abide in peace, as is said *And my people shall abide in a peaceable habitation, and in secure dwellings, and in quiet resting-places* (Isa. 32:18). Or: For the day when men refrain from armed conflict.[101]

Here a vision of eschatological rest (מנוחה) is seen to be realized in the celebration of the Sabbath. Likewise, *GenR* 17,5 states that "the incomplete form of the next world is the Sabbath."[102] Some Sabbath halakah were thus formed after the model of the world-to-come as a day "which is wholly Sabbath,"[103] and the future world came to be depicted in terms of Sabbath ideas, *viz* material abundance, universal peace and harmony, refulgent light, delight, the absence of infirmities, and liberation.[104]

Further on we will take note of the way in which Ps 95,11 was construed eschatologically. Likewise the use of מנוחה in Ps 132 was taken up into speculation about the future world. In *SifreDeut* § 1, R. Yose ben Dormasqit (ca. 130) assumes that since מנוחה always means Jerusalem (Ps 132,14),[105] its occurrence in Zech 9,1 -- "Damascus will be his resting place"[106] -- must mean that in the future Jerusalem will expand like an inverted pyramid (Ezek 41,7) so that her base remains on her "mound" (Jer 30,18) while her walls extend as far as Damascus.[107] Thus the returning exiles will be able to settle

---

[99] Cf. above, 65ff., 103-106.

[100] Cf. *GenR* 17,5; 44,17; *Ber* 57b; *MekShabbata* 1; and Hofius, 209 n. 742; Volz, 384; Friedman, 443-452; Bacchiocchi 1986, 156, 158f., 161ff., and *passim*.

[101] All trans. of *MidrPss* from Braude 1959, unless indicated otherwise; italics in original. As *MidrPss* 92 § 5 shows, the idea of an ultimate Sabbath rest encompassed the idea of rest from war.

[102] All translations of Midrash Rabbah from Freedman-Simon, unless indicated otherwise.

[103] E.g. *Shab* 6,4 ; cf. Friedman, 447-450; Bacchiocchi 1986, 156, 158f., and *passim*.

[104] On which see Friedman, 444-450; Bacchiocchi 1986, 155-162, 165ff.

[105] In *CantR* 7,5 § 3 it is assumed that מנוחה always refers to the temple.

[106] The MT has, ודמשק מנחתו; NRSV and NIV renders the verse: "The word of the LORD is against the land of Hadrach and will rest upon Damascus."

[107] Likewise *CantR* 7,5 § 3; *PRK* 20. The metaphor is actually that of a fig: Israel will expand "like a fig that is narrow below and broadens upward..." According to earlier

therein (Isa 2,2f.). Another midrash (*GenR* 56,2) also unites Zech 9 (v. 9) to Ps 132,14:

Said R. Isaac,[108] "Will this place [the Temple mount] ever be distant from its owner [God]? Never, for Scripture says, 'This is my resting place forever; here I will dwell, for I have desired it' (Ps. 132:14). It will be when the one comes concerning whom it is written, 'Lowly and riding upon an ass' (Zech. 1:9 [sic])."[109]

Finally here, there are passages where at death the soul enters immediately into rest; this is a temporary condition anticipating the resurrection of the body at the end, but it is nonetheless a foretaste of the final state.[110]

5.2. Ps 95 in rabbinic exegesis

The use of Ps 95 in rabbinic exegesis deserves special consideration. First we will take note of the midrash on the psalm itself (§ 5.2.1), and then consider the way in which the psalm was used in eschatological speculation (§ 5.2.2).

5.2.1. The historical understanding of Ps 95,11

MidrPss 95 § 3[111] says,

Wherefore I swore in My wrath that they should not enter into My rest (Ps. 95:11) -- that is, into the Land of Israel, of which it is said *For ye are not as yet come to the rest and to the inheritance* (Deut. 12:9); and also *Zion...is My rest for ever* (Ps. 132:13-14).

The double application of the *gezerah shawah*[112] has directed our attention to the use of the same word in Deut 12 (מנוחה), and the use of the same form (מנוחתי, "my rest") in Ps 132. Clearly, whether read in terms of Deut 12 or Ps

---

belief, Damascus was "to be the seat of the eschatological Sanctuary ...and the place of the Messiah's coming," and this tradition was later reconciled with beliefs about Jerusalem in passages such as *SifreDeut* § 1; so Vermes 1961, 43-49; cited in Hammer, 392.

[108] Ca. A.D. 300.

[109] Trans. from Neusner 1985; the last reference should read Zech 9,9. For further citations of Zech 9,9 in the rabbinic literature, see Str-B, 1:842-844; Michel 1967, 284f.; also Duling 1978, 408.

[110] E.g. *Ket* 104a; *Shab* 152b; cf. Hofius, 60, 69, 73, 186 n. 417; Volz, 257ff.; Str-B, 4/2:1130ff.; Jeremias 1964, 147f.

[111] Strack-Stemberger, 350f., review the dating of *MidrPss* 1-118 and state that "one must undoubtedly assume an extended period of development; this renders...accurate statements impossible. Most of the material certainly dates back to the Talmudic period."

[112] On this rule cf. Strack-Stemberger, 21. Closely related to the *gezerah shawah* was the *heqqesh*, which was a less strictly regulated topical analogy.

132, מנוחה is here being understood in a local sense as the whole land of Israel or more specifically Zion. According to Hofius, "für מנוחה an allen drei Stellen [i.e., Ps 95,11; Deut 12,9; Ps 132,13f.] die *gleiche* Bedeutung angenommen wird."[113] In other words, Ps 132 is seen to determine the midrash, as Hofius makes even clearer:

> Dieses Land ist G o t t e s "Ruhestätte", weil auch er selbst dort wohnt, und zwar auf dem Zion... Der Midrasch versteht also unter der "Ruhestätte" Ps 95,11b im weiteren Sinne das Land Kanaan, im engeren Sinne Jerusalem mit dem Tempel, der zwar nicht expressis verbis erwähnt wird, an den jedoch ganz ohne Frage gedacht ist... *Strenggenommen ist das Allerheiligste als der Ort, an dem die Schekhina Gottes ruht, Jahwes "Ruhestätte"*. Weil jedoch auch die Stadt Jerusalem und das ganze Land Israel Anteil an der Heiligkeit dieses Ortes haben, können auch sie als Jahwes "Ruhestätte" bezeichnet werden.[114]

The citation of Ps 132 in connection with Ps 95,11 proves conclusively that at least some rabbis took מנוחה in the latter as a direct reference to the temple, but it may be that Hofius has exaggerated this one-sidedly.[115] Our own examination of Ps 95 in the OT came to the conclusion that the dual perspective of entrance into the *land* as the resting place from travelling and enemy threat (Deut 12,9f.) and as the resting place of YHWH by virtue of his special presence there (Ps 132)[116] had telescoped into a single image, not unlike Ex 15,17.[117] It may be that something of this is expressed in this midrash as well.

It is also possible, however, that the citation of both Deut 12 and Ps 132 represents two distinct interpretations. For instance, in *SifreDeut* § 1, R. Yose ben Dormasqit (ca. 90-130) insists in connection with Zech 9,9 that מנוחה "always means Jerusalem, as it is said, 'This is my resting-place forever'" (Ps 132,14),[118] while in *SifreDeut* § 2, R. Yehudah (ca. 130-160) states in reference to Num 10,33 that מנוחה "refers only to the land of Israel,"

---

[113] Hofius, 42; italics added.
[114] Hofius, 43; italics added.
[115] The Targum to Ps 95,11 also renders אם יעלון לנייח בית מקדשי, but as Hofius, 47, notes this is late evidence.
[116] Cf. *Kel* 1,6-9. Yet there are also passages where the resting place is spatially restricted; e.g. *MidrPss* 132 § 3; *MekPisha* 1 (1,3,2 according to Neusner's numbering); *SifreDeut* § 1; *CantR* 7,5 § 3; *PRK* 20. These passages suggest that the resting place refers only to the temple or to what falls within the walls of Zion.
[117] In *ExodR* 30,8 Ps 132,14 is applied to Zion in such a manner that it may figuratively include all Israel: "Israel likewise was in Zion, where God dwelt in their midst, as it says, *This is My resting place for ever* [Ps 132,14]; when they sinned, He thrust them away..."
[118] All trans. of *SifreDeut* are from Hammer, unless indicated otherwise; italics in original. It should be noted that in *SifreDeut* § 1, R. Yose is opposed by R. Yehudah who tends to understand מנוחה differently; see the next note.

for which he cites Deut 12,9.[119] There was also a debate over Deut 12,9 -- "you have not yet come to the resting place [מנוחה] and to the inheritance" -- in relation to the question of sacrificing at the altars (high places) prior to the erection of the temple. The order of the words in Deut 12,9 -- מנוחה and inheritance -- was thus important. Was the reference (1) to Shiloh (מנוחה) as the resting place following the conquest and then to Jerusalem (inheritance) as the location of the temple, or (2) the other way around (taking מנוחה with Ps 132), or did *both* terms refer (3) to Jerusalem or (4) to Shiloh?[120] Finally here, *MidrPss* 5 § 1 says in relation to Deut 12,9,

The Temple is also called an *inheritance*, for it is said *Ye are not as yet come to the rest, and to the inheritance (naḥalah) which the Lord your God giveth you* (Deut 12:9)...Thus[121] when Moses said to the children of Israel: *Ye are not as yet come to the rest and to the inheritance* (Deut 12:9), by *rest* he meant 'the Land of Israel,' and by *inheritance* he meant "the Tabernacle of Jacob."[122]

What these various passages suggest is that the rabbis were aware of different ways of taking מנוחה, and that more than once the two nouns of Deut 12,9 were taken to refer to distinct events or entities. Against this backdrop one can take the reference to both Deut 12 and Ps 132 in *MidrPss* 95 § 3 as a reference to two distinct ways of understanding the מנוחה; note that with the citation of Deut 12 it is expressly stated that the reference is to the *land*. Alternatively, it could even be that a chronological perspective is employed, tracing the path of the Israelites from the entrance and conquest to the erection of the temple.

The tersely worded midrash of *MidrPss* 95 § 3 does not admit of a final answer. What it shows, however, is that at least some rabbis took מנוחה there as a direct reference to the temple, and probably that most would have felt the relevance of the temple traditions. Yet there were probably also some

---

[119] In the debate mentioned immediately below (see the next note), R. Yehudah represents the first position; i.e., he took מנוחה as a reference to Shiloh because the Israelites rested there from the conquest.

[120] For the debate and the rabbis see *MidrPss* 132 § 2; *SifreDeut* § 66; *Zeb* 14,6.8; *Zeb* 119a.b; *t.Zeb* 13,20; cf. also *TgOnq* and *TgPs-Jon* to Deut 12. This debate appears to go back to early II A.D.

[121] The intervening argument draws a connection between the temple and a waterbrook (*naḥal*) with the help of Num 24,5f. The word play is thus between "waterbrook" (*naḥal*) and "inheritance" (*naḥalah*).

[122] Such an arrangement underlies the discussion of *Zeb* 119a.b. It says there, "On the view that *'rest'* alludes to Shiloh, it is well: hence it is written, *'to the rest and to the inheritance'*." I.e., "it is well" because Israel arrived at Shiloh (rest) chronologically prior to arriving at Jerusalem (inheritance). "But on the view that *'rest'* alludes to Jerusalem while *'inheritance'* alludes to Shiloh, [Moses] should say, 'to the inheritance and to the rest'? -- This is what he said: Not only have ye not reached the *'rest'* [Jerusalem]; you have not even reached the *'inheritance'* [Shiloh]." In both cases a chronological and geographical progression is assumed.

who took מנוחה in Ps 95,11 as a reference to the "rest" in the land (the resting *place*) following Israel's travels and wars rather than as an extension of YHWH's rest in the Most Holy Place.

5.2.2. *The eschatological understanding of Ps 95,11*

In addition to its treatment in *MidrPss* 95 § 3, Ps 95,11 is taken up into a discussion regarding the destiny of the wilderness generation in the future world. The speakers in the various recensions of the debate differ, but the upshot for our purposes remains constant. Already around A.D. 100 the oath of Ps 95,11 is being interpreted in the context of debates about the age to come.[123]

In one recension of the discussion[124] R. Aqiba († 135) invokes Num 14,35 and the oath of Ps 95,11 to establish that the wilderness generation will have no share in the עולם הבא, while R. Eliezer ben Hyrcanus (ca. 90) quotes Ps 50,5 to demonstrate that it will; he explains away the oath of Ps 95,11 simply by saying that God took the oath *in his wrath* and later repented of it. In another recension it is R. Eliezer who takes the stricter view.[125] He uses Num 14,35 and Ps 95,11 to prove that the wilderness generation will neither share in the resurrection nor be brought to judgment, while R. Yehoshua ben Ḥananyah (ca. 90) counters by citing Ps 50,5 and applying the oath of Ps 95,11 only to the spies and the wicked of that generation.[126]

Though Hofius suggests that in all these passages מנוחה refers specifically to Jerusalem with the temple,[127] it is considerably more likely that it refers to the world-to-come generally. As can be seen in *Sanh* 10,1-4 the framework of the debate is provided by a discussion of the ultimate destiny of respective groups in relation to the עולם הבא:

"The generation of the wilderness has no portion in the world to come and will not stand in judgment, for it is written, *In this wilderness they shall be consumed and there they*

---

[123] JosAsen 8,9 also interprets Ψ 94,11 [95,11] eschatologically, although it is an individual eschatology.
[124] *t.Sanh* 13,10; *Sanh* 110b; *p.Sanh* 10,29c,5. The discussion regarding those who have no share in the world-to-come is also found in *Sanh* 10,1-4, though without a reference to the oath of Ps 95,11. In it R. Aqiba cites only Num 14,35 and R. Eliezer cites only Ps 50,5.
[125] *ARN* 36.
[126] In addition to these passages the lenient view is taken by R. Yehoshua and the stricter by Raba († 352) in *Ḥag* 10a; *p.Ḥag* 1,76c,48ff.; the lenient view is also taken in *NumR* 14,19, and by R. Tachlipha (ca. 270) in *LevR* 32,2; *EcclR* 10,20 § 1. In *Sanh* 99a R. Eliezer interprets Ps 95,10, Deut 8,3, and Ps 90,15 to mean that the days of the messiah will be 40 years according to the 40 years Israel was afflicted in the wilderness. Hofius, 44f., opines that this latter passage belongs with *t.Sanh* 13,10 (= *ARN* 36) because it implies an eschatological reading of Ps 95,11.
[127] Hofius, 45.

shall die (Num. 14:35)," the words of R. Aqiba. R. Eliezer says, "Concerning them it says, *Gather my saints together to me, those that have made a covenant with me by sacrifice* (Ps. 50:5)."

Both Num 14 and Ps 50 are cited but not Ps 95. When Ps 95,11 is brought into that framework[128] the debate focuses on the oath without any attempt to further define the "resting place."[129] This reticence might serve to caution us against speculating beyond equating the מנוחה with the עולם הבא.[130]

These midrashim provide early evidence for the fact that Ps 95,11 was interpreted *eschatologically* in connection with Num 14 as a reference to the future resting *place*.

5.3. Summary

In a variety of ways the rabbinic literature testifies to an expectation that the world-to-come, the עולם הבא, would be characterized by rest. This is most pronounced in connection with the idea that the future age would be a "day which is wholly Sabbath and rest forever." That hope, expressed in various midrashim, was concretely augmented by Sabbath customs which emerged from this expectation, as well as by the weekly recitation of the Ps 92. It was also suggested by the belief that upon death the soul entered into an intermediate place of rest, awaiting the resurrection.

Certain discussions of Ps 132 show that the Jerusalem of the age to come was thought of as YHWH's מנוחה which would expand as far as Damascus so that the returning exiles could settle therein. A later midrash (*GenR* 56,2) joined Ps 132 to Zech 9,9 with the result that the return of the exiles to Jerusalem, YHWH's resting place, was associated with the coming of the one who is lowly and riding on an ass. Ps 95,11 -- which *MidrPss* 95 relates to both Deut 12 and Ps 132 -- was also taken up into speculation about the world-to-come. It was debated whether the wilderness generation, which had been barred from entering the land, would nonetheless be permitted to enter the world-to-come. Whether it is the land or the future world, the *place* into which people might or might not enter is termed the מנוחה.

---

[128] *ARN* 36; *t.Sanh* 13,10; *Sanh* 110b; *p.Sanh* 10,29c,5; etc.

[129] Cf. also *NumR* 14,19. *Ḥag* 10a gives R. Yehoshua's interpretation of Ps 95,11 without invoking the idea of rest. *LevR* 32,2 and *EcclR* 10,20 § 1 do focus attention on the word מנוחה, although these midrashim are later and relate Ps 95 to Eccl 10,20 and Deut 1,34 instead of Num 14 and Ps 50. *LevR* 32 anticipates "another מנוחה," which is variously identified as the eschatological Jerusalem (Hofius, 46), eternal life (Str-B, 3:687), and the second temple (Cohen, in Freedman-Simon, 8:282 n. 1). It is probably the עולם הבא generally, which certainly includes the renewed Jerusalem.

[130] Hofius, 45, concedes that this interpretation is possible. It should be considered all the more likely when we recall how "rest" is generally associated with the hereafter and the future world in the Pseudepigrapha.

Interestingly, *MidrPss* 92 § 5 combines the Sabbath rest with an eschatological use of the rest tradition (Isa 32,18).[131] This is not surprising since, as we saw already in the OT, the Sabbath and the rest tradition overlapped in several significant ways.

6. Post-apostolic

6.1. Introduction

The development of Christian theology from the late first through the second century A.D. was a complex process, with considerable "cross-fertilization" of diverse traditions taking place. A discussion of the rest motif in the post-apostolic church must therefore attempt to take in not only the "Apostolic Fathers," but the NT Apocrypha and gnostic literature as well.

By the second century A.D. Christian Gnosticism and other post-apostolic developments were chronologically parallel. Although we adopt as a working hypothesis the view that there is no firm evidence for pre-Christian Gnosticism, we must not prejudge which *post-apostolic* developments -- including those in gnostic literature -- were more faithful to the apostolic traditions relative to specific elements of doctrine or sayings of Jesus.

We shall find that there is a "gnostic use" of the rest motif which is evidenced in more than one source.[132] This gnostic usage is highly developed and distinctive, owing more to Greek metaphysics and Gnosticism's mythological outlook than to notions derived from either the OT or the NT. On this score it stands apart from the NT, and apart from most of the literature to be surveyed here until Clement of Alexandria. It is for this reason that discussion of it will be deferred to § 7, though its influence cannot be ignored in our consideration of the following literature.

6.2. Odes of Solomon

The Odist declares, "where [the Beloved's] rest is, there also am I" (3,5); "...from above [the Lord] gave me immortal rest; and I became like the land which blossoms and rejoices in its fruit" (11,12); "I was justified by his kindness, and his rest is for ever and ever" (25,12); "...his harp is in my hand, and the odes of his rest shall not be silent" (26,3); "I trusted,

---

[131] Cf. also *Shab* 6,4.
[132] Doubtless some will prefer to speak of gnostic *usages*, just as it is preferable to speak of gnostic myths (vs. "a" gnostic myth). Yet the common features are more important for our purposes.

consequently I was at rest" (28,3); "His Word came toward me, that which gave me the fruit of my labors; And gave me rest by the grace of the Lord" (37,4); "And [the Truth] went with me and caused me to rest and did not allow me to err" (38,4). Beside these there are several other relevant passages.[133]

From the start, the frequency of references to the rest motif is striking; it has even been wondered if 26,3 gives the title of the whole collection, "The Odes of His Rest."[134] On the one hand, this frequency contrasts with the other NT and post-apostolic literature being surveyed here, and on the other it reminds -- on a purely statistical basis -- of gnostic writings, an impression which is reinforced by the relationship of rest and knowledge[135] as well as the heavy emphasis on the present experience.[136] If we were to assume that not only this use of the rest motif but the Odes generally were gnostic, then these passages would be properly taken up in our discussion of Gnosticism.[137] Nevertheless these observations do not conclusively establish that we have here a gnostic expression of the rest idea. Moreover, that this motif finds expression in a dualistic framework and is depicted as "immortal" (11,12) would be amenable to Gnosticism, but not necessarily gnostic in origin.[138] Maybe Koester is right to think that gnostic terms and images had "affected the language of early Christian piety in Syria,"[139] without demanding that the Odes themselves be gnostic. Alternatively, in view of the inconclusive nature of the evidence for the "gnostic" character of the rest motif and the more general case that the Odes as a whole are *not* gnostic, that they are very early (ca. A.D. 100), and that they stem from the

---

[133] Cf. Odes 6,11; 20,8; 26,12f.; 30,2f.7; 35,6; and 36,1. Ode 16,12 quotes Gen 2,2. These references are taken from Charlesworth 1973, 20.

[134] Cf. Charlesworth 1973, 105; he cautions against pushing this hypothesis too far.

[135] Hofius, 83f.; cf. Harris-Mingana, 354f.; Ode 26,12f.

[136] Infra, 141f.

[137] Infra, 145ff. K. Rudolph 1984, 29, considers the Odes gnostic. W. Bauer, in *NTApocr*[1], 2:809f., calls OdesSol a "Gnostic hymn-book," but adds that "here 'Gnostic' must be understood in a broad sense." In their studies of the rest motif, the Odes are assumed to be gnostic by Hofius, 83f. and Vielhauer, 281-299. Helderman 1984, 21, 88, leaves the question of the "gnostic" character of the Odes open.

[138] Cf. WisSol 4,7; 8,16f.; supra, 91ff. On the dualism of the Odes, cf. Charlesworth 1972b, 107-136.

[139] Koester 1982, 2:218. Though he finds several elements of gnostic thought scattered throughout the Odes, Koester states that "it is still an open question whether the Odes of Solomon should...be called a gnostic hymnbook." *HJP*[2], 3/2:787, contends that one must take "the term 'Gnostic' in such an attenuated sense that its application to the Odes becomes hardly meaningful."

same "religious environment" as John's Gospel,[140] we should at least consider other possible explanations to see where they might lead.

Accounting for the manifest fondness for the motif in the community which produced and used the Odes is bound to involve considerable speculation, especially in view of the absence of rest-terminology in the closest known Christian relative, John's Gospel. Yet we have already seen that this motif was used widely in the OT, the Pseudepigrapha, and elsewhere, so a variety of influences can be assumed.[141] In particular, Gen 2,2 (Ode 16,12) and JosAsen have been nominated,[142] though neither of these seem very promising as a key to the general interest; indeed, that there is a single explanation which accounts for all the passages is unlikely. Some of the passages recall the OT idea of *restful trust*.[143] One influence may well have been the sort of this-worldly rest encountered in the *wisdom literature*.[144] This source would suit both the realized aspect and the connection with knowledge. The special interest in *water*, which the Odes share with John, is interesting.[145] "Water" and "refreshment" have a very natural relationship, and this is made explicit more than once in the Odes.[146]

---

[140] Charlesworth 1992, 114, is convinced along with others (see *art. cit.*) that the Odes "must not be labelled 'gnostic.'" For the relationship of the Odes to John, cf. Charlesworth-Culpepper.

[141] Bernard, 11, mentions E. Abbott's suggestion that the ascription of the Odes to Solomon had something to do with the description of Solomon as a "man of rest" (1Chr 22,9). Harris-Mingana, 389, imagine that this description of Solomon underlies Ode 37 (cf. 37,4); they then take Ode 37 as a reference to Solomon's prayer of dedication in 2Chr 6.

[142] Cf. Charlesworth 1973, 20. He notes Odes 4,8; 8,18; 23,2f., as references to the "elect"; cf. JosAsen 8,9 (supra, 109f.).

[143] Odes 28,3; 30,2f.7; 35,6; 36,1. In the OT cf. Isa 7,4; 30,15; 32,17; Ψ 114,7 [116,7].

[144] Supra, 91ff.

[145] For details see, Charlesworth-Culpepper, 312f. This is one of many points where John and the Odes both evidence parallels with Qumran; for parallels from the latter, cf. Deutsch 1987, 120f.

[146] Cf. 30,1-7; 26,12f.; 11,6f.12. In addition to the natural connection between water and refreshment (cf. LXX Jer 38,25 [31,25]), it has been suggested that the baptismal waters were regarded as "waters of rest," as in Ψ 22,2 [23,2] (ἐπὶ ὕδατος ἀναπαύσεως; מנחה); cf. Bernard, 32; Charlesworth 1973, 20. In this connection we might note a passage from John's Gospel which is in some respects already close to Mt 11,28-30, viz Jn 7,37f.: "Let anyone who is thirsty come to me, and let the one who believes in me drink. As the scripture has said, 'Out of [his] heart shall flow rivers of living water'"; cf. Charlesworth-Culpepper, 302, 304f., 308, 313; they comment that the connection between "rest" and "water" is implicit in Jn 7. When we come to discuss Mt 11,28-30 we will be keen to stress the relationship to Matthew's Son of David Christology. From that perspective, maybe it is significant that in Jn 7 Jesus' invitation gives way immediately to debate about his Davidic descent and is preceded by the accusation that he has a demon. Moreover, the controversy in Jn 7 surrounds the Sabbath healing of Jn 5,1-15, a passage which has Jesus making a pronouncement which reminds one of Mt 12 (5,17; cf. below, 323f.). In Mt 11,28-30 the saying is modified in line with Zech 9,9; here in Jn 7 it is

In a different vein, another of the several parallels between the Odes and John is the following:

I love the Beloved and I myself love him,
and where his rest is, there also am I. (Ode 3,5)

In my Father's house there are many dwelling places [μοναὶ πολλαί]. If it where not so, would I have told you that I go to prepare a place for you [πορεύομαι ἑτοιμάσαι τόπον ὑμῖν]? And if I go and prepare a place for you, I will come again and take you to myself, so that where I am, there you may be also. (Jn 14,2f.)[147]

With this parallel in mind we can note another, possibly related passage in the Odes, as well as one from 2 Enoch:

And from above he gave me immortal rest;
and I became like the land which blossoms and rejoices in its fruits...
Indeed, there is much room in your Paradise.
And there is nothing in it which is barren,
but everything is filled with fruit. (Ode 11,12.23)

Many shelters have been prepared for people, good ones for the good, but bad ones for the bad, many, without number. Happy is he who enters into the blessed houses; for in the bad ones there is no rest, nor returning. (2En 61,2f. [J])

Ode 11,23 in particular has been cited as a parallel to Jn 14,2f., but in view of Ode 3,5, maybe it is significant that Ode 11 also includes a reference to rest. Interestingly, then, the word μονή in Jn 14,2 is sometimes construed as a "resting place."[148] Behind both the Odes and John there may be the well-known, apocalyptic idea of a heavenly and eschatological resting place. If this is not forced, then it may be wondered if there is not to be found here a *New Testament* parallel for the idea of a "resting place" which is "prepared"[149] in heaven for the elect, such as we will find in Hebrews. Alternatively, we might at least have evidence for the idea among early

---

probable that Zech 9-14 is in the background (cf. Brown, 1:322f. 326). Rather than thinking of a single saying which has been modified, it would be more likely that if anything John has substituted a similar saying, more suited to his context.

[147] Cf. Charlesworth-Culpepper, 301; also Jn 17,24; *EpApost* 19 Cop., where it is combined with sabbatical imagery (*ARN* 1; cf. *Ber* 17a).

[148] Brown, 2:618f. Brown also compares Jn 14,2 to 1En 39,4, "dwelling places of the holy ones and their resting places"; cf. 1En 45,3. Likewise, Hofius, 184 n. 376; Schnackenburg 1982, 3:60.

[149] In Jn 14, the "preparation" may be less of the "place" and more of the believers; cf. Brown, 2:627. Alternatively, it is the cross and resurrection which "prepares" the place; Carson 1991, 489.

Christian worshippers in Syria. If so, then the realized eschatology stands in stark contrast to Heb 3-4.[150] One can then compare Heb 4,10ff. to Ode 37,3f.

His Word came toward me,
that which gave me the fruit of my labors;
And gave me rest by the grace of the Lord.[151]

If we allow for the difference between a mystical hymn and a theological homily, and also for the distinctive exegetical concerns of the writer of Hebrews, then the gap may not appear so great.[152]

In sum, as to the form or shape of the rest motif, it is no more or less gnostic than are the Odes generally. There are several possible sources of the idea, and its prominence may be due to nothing more than the idiosyncratic interests of the composer/community, if not to the unique interests of mystical hymns of piety. Still, the Odes are problematic, for if they were an established component of early worship then the absence of a comparable use of the rest motif elsewhere in non-gnostic Christianity is remarkable. There are some possible avenues for further investigation, but the evidence is ambiguous and in view of the unsettled state of scholarship on the Odes we will not pursue them further at this point.

6.3. Ignatius

Under the probable influence of passages such as 1Cor 16,18 ($\dot{\alpha}\nu\alpha\pi\alpha\acute{u}\omega$), Phlm 7.20 ($\dot{\alpha}\nu\alpha\pi\alpha\acute{u}\omega$), and 2Tim 1,16 ($\dot{\alpha}\nu\alpha\psi\acute{u}\chi\omega$) the idea of being given psychological and/or physical rest by other Christians is frequently encountered here.[153] As in 2Tim 1, the additional idea is present in *IgnEph* 2,1 ($\dot{\alpha}\nu\alpha\psi\acute{u}\chi\omega$) and *IgnSmyrn* 9,2 (the implied verb is $\dot{\alpha}\nu\alpha\pi\alpha\acute{u}\omega$) that the Lord will reward the givers of rest by giving them rest or refreshment. In both cases the timing of the grant of rest is difficult to ascertain; in either

---

[150] Cf. Odes 3,5; 11,12; 36,1; on the eschatology of the Odes (relative to John and Qumran), cf. Charlesworth 1972b, 120, 126f., 130f., 133.

[151] Cf. also Rev 14,13; Mt 11,28-30. Charlesworth, in *OTP*, 2:758, suggests further that Ode 25,12 is a parallel to Heb 4: "And I was justified by his kindness, and his rest is for ever and ever." The Coptic reads, "your rest." Note that Gen 2,2 is quoted in 16,12, though without any soteriological elaboration. Harris-Mingana, 124f., compare Ode 28,3 and Heb 4,3 as a possible case of dependence one way or the other.

[152] Cf. the remarks of Charlesworth 1972b, 122f., on drawing parallels; also Charlesworth-Culpepper, 313.

[153] Cf. the phrase, ὅτι κατὰ πάντα με ἀνέπαυσαν σαρκί τε καὶ πνεύματι, in *IgnTrall* 12,1, and the use of this idea elsewhere in Ignatius' writings: *IgnEph* 2,1; *IgnMagn* 15,1; *IgnRom* 10,2; *IgnSmyrn* 9,2; 10,1; 12,1; also with ἀναψύχω in *IgnTrall* 12,2. ἀναπαύω is also used in the sense of physical or psychological relief in *ShepHerm Sim* 9,5 (3x).

case it could be immediate, though with a view toward an eschatological fulfilment.[154]

6.4. Barnabas

In *Barn* 15, Gen 2,2 is interpreted eschatologically as part of an effort to discredit the Jewish celebration of the weekly Sabbath. The six days of creation should be understood with the help of Ψ 89,4 [90,4] as six thousand years, at the end of which God will "make an end" (συντελέσει) of everything.[155] The καταπαύων of the seventh day -- *contra* the weekly Jewish rest -- is explained as follows. The Son will come to destroy the time of the wicked, to bring judgment on the godless, and to change the heavenly bodies. "Then he will truly rest (τότε καλῶς καταπαύσεται) on the seventh day." At this point Barnabas buttresses his argument further by pointing out that no one can truly sanctify the seventh day *now* because of sin (cf. Ex 20,8).[156] But, "certainly *then* one properly resting sanctifies it (ἴδε ὅτι ἄρα τότε καλῶς καταπαυόμενοι ἁγιάσομεν αὐτήν)."[157] That is, only at the consummation, "when there is no more sin, but things have been made new by the Lord," and when we have been made holy by the Lord, will we be able to keep the Sabbath holy. Finally, Isa 1,13 is called in to demonstrate God's rejection of the Jewish Sabbath; it offsets God's καταπαύων of all things (καταπαύσας τὰ πάντα) and the beginning of the eighth day (the ὀγδόας), i.e. the "beginning of another world." This reference to the eschatological eighth day then culminates in a reference to the weekly eighth day which the Christians celebrate, on which Jesus arose, was made manifest, and ascended to heaven. Having discredited the Jewish weekly Sabbath on the basis of its eschatological fulfilment, he unapologetically advocates the Christian weekly eighth day on the basis of its eschatological significance.

---

[154] Cf. Lightfoot 1885, 2/2:315. A similar idea is encountered in *ShepHerm Sim* 9,1 (cf. *Sim* 9,27) where the vision of sheep " resting" (ἀναπαύω) under a tree symbolizes bishops and hospitable ones who give shelter to the destitute and widows, and who are (or: will be) in turn given shelter by the Lord.

[155] Though the author, henceforth "Barnabas," follows the MT in his quote of Gen 2,2, which associates both συντελέω and καταπαύω with the seventh day (*Barn* 15,3), his commentary is closer to the LXX, which associates συντελέω with the sixth day; thus Barnabas asks what Gen 2,2 means when it says, συνετέλεσεν ἐν ἓξ ἡμέραις. Cf. R.A. Kraft, 127f. For the use of Ps 90,4, see 2Pet 3,8. Quotes from the Apostolic Fathers will be taken from LCL, unless indicated otherwise.

[156] Bauckham 1982b, 264, observes that the association of holy living with true Sabbath-keeping is found elsewhere in the second century A.D., "though with reference to Christian life in the present and rarely related to the eschatological rest."

[157] Trans. from ANCL 1:128; italics mine.

The basic problem with the passage is that vv. 3-7 speak of 6000 years followed by an unending seventh day which is equated with the new creation, but then vv. 8f. go on to speak of an *eighth* day which seems to at once place a temporal limit on the seventh day and supplant the latter in its connection with the new world. If we treat them as two schemata, then vv. 3-7 are closer to the Jewish parallels which identify the "world which is wholly Sabbath and rest" with the world-to-come,[158] and vv. 8f. are closer to those passages which construe the world-Sabbath as one wherein the world lies fallow or in silence *before* the beginning of the world-to-come.[159] These two schemata can be represented as follows, although it is not being suggested that this chart represents Barnabas' thinking:

this world		world-to-come
days 1-6		day 7 (Sabbath)
days 1-6	day 7 (Sabbath)	(eighth day)

What is sure is that Barnabas does associate both the seventh and eighth days with the new world,[160] and thus with eternity; note the absence of any temporal qualifier for the seventh day in vv. 5-7. Yet in order to advance beyond this initial impression we shall make a series of observations about or pertaining to the passage:

---

[158] E.g. *Tam* 7,4; cf. Hofius, 111-113; supra, 103f., 122f.

[159] E.g. *Sanh* 97a; *RH* 31a; *SER* 2; cf. 4Ez 7,27-31; Hofius, 114f. Thus the Sabbath period belonged to העולם הזה (this present world; days 1-7), rather than to העולם הבא; cf. Str-B 4/2:989-994; *HJP*², 2:523f., 537f.; cf. also TAb 7,16f. (shorter recension); Ps-Philo 28,6ff.; also 2En 33,1-2 though it is probably a Christian interpolation. The "eighth" day is the day of the resurrection in JosAsen 11,1f.; 15,5; cf. Lohmann, 235. The Gnostics also had their doctrine of eight heavenly spheres -- seven corresponding to the seven planets and the eighth to the fixed stars which close them off, the Hebdomad and Ogdoad respectively (cf. Philo, *Dec* 102-104; Daniélou 1956, 255f.). Among the Valentinians the worthy psychics found rest together with the pneumatics in the "place of the Middle," *viz* the Ogdoad, until the end, when the pneumatics graduated to the "bridal chamber" of the Pleroma; cf. K. Rudolph 1984, 67ff., 186. This gnostic cosmology derived in part from astrological and Pythagorean conceptions; cf. Daniélou 1956, 258ff.; Bacchiocchi 1977, 286f. Barnabas, however, is concerned with chronology rather than with heavenly journeys. By way of contrast, the gnostic idea of the Hebdomad and Ogdoad is clearly visible in Clement of Alexandria (infra, 142ff.); cf. also *EpApost* 18 (Bauckham 1982b, 274; but see Hofius, 190 n. 449 Ad b). As to the origin of the designation -- "eighth day" or "Ogdoad" -- which occurs for the first time in Christian literature in 2En 33 and *Barn* 15, cf. the conjectures of Rordorf, 275-285; Bacchiocchi 1977, 278-302; Beckwith-Stott, 117-122; and Bauckham 1982b, 273f. R.A. Kraft, 129, notes the Christian use of "Ogdoad" in SibOr 7,140, which A. Kurfess considers gnostic and late II A.D. (in *NTApocr*¹, 2:707f.; U. Treu [in *NTApocr*², 2:654] does not assign a date), but J.J. Collins questions the gnostic label and leaves the date to anytime during II-III A.D. (in *OTP*, 1:408f.).

[160] Cf. Bauckham 1982b, 291 n. 77.

(1) The passage is not in the first instance a systematic presentation of eschatology. Its essential concern is rather to show what the true and false Sabbaths are as Barnabas will also do with the temple (*Barn* 16), and it may be that in some respects the passage is united only in this overall attempt to discredit the Jewish festival.

(2) While there is a perceptible train of thought running from v. 3 through to v. 9 which is based on Gen 2,2, there is a special concern with Ψ 89,4 [90,4] in vv. 3-5, with Ex 20,8 in vv. 6-7, and Isa 1,18 in vv. 8-9. Barnabas is making more or less distinct points depending on the passage by which he expands on Gen 2,2; the last passage is augmented by the reference to the "eighth day."

(3) Barnabas uses καταπαύω actively in vv. 3.5a.8, and in the middle voice in vv. 5b.7. In the two middle voice usages the verb is intransitive, "rest," while it is probably transitive in the active usages.[161] In v. 5 it is used both transitively and intransitively; thus God's eschatological Sabbath is *both* a "bringing to an end" and a "true rest." The human "resting" in v. 7 is associated with the ultimate Sabbath celebration and the new world which together follow on the dissolution of all things.

(4) Barnabas does not attach rest (καταπαύω) directly with the eighth day in either its eschatological (v. 8) or historical (v. 9) senses. The aorist participle in v. 8 is transitive and probably refers back to the transitive usage in v. 5a. The language of v. 8 suggests that the "bringing to an end" is prior to the eighth day but organically related to it

(5) The "future" Sabbath which is implied by the τὰ νῦν σάββατα in v. 8 is probably associated with this "bringing to an end" *and* the "beginning" of the eighth day.

(6) R.J. Bauckham has shown that by the time of *Barnabas*, the Lord's Day ("eighth day") had already been established as a Christian day of worship, but the idea of "rest" was not associated with it until later; i.e., it was not yet a "Christian Sabbath."[162] This not only satisfactorily accounts for the presence of the eighth day in Barnabas' eschatological schema, but explains why Barnabas does not associate "rest" with the eighth day.

The seventh and eighth days have probably joined in Barnabas' eschatological schema at least in part under the pressure of the Christian day of worship; Barnabas is determined to invoke the latter for polemical reasons

---

[161] Bauckham 1982b, 262, comments that, God's "eschatological rest is...interpreted not as inactivity but as bringing an end to this world (καταπαύσας τὰ πάντα) and bringing into existence the new world"; cf. Hermans, 863-864. This transitive sense is less convincing, however, with 15,5b.7.

[162] On the meaning, origin, and development of the "Lord's day" in relation to the Jewish Sabbath, cf. Bauckham 1982a, 221-250 (esp. 240); 1982b, 251-298 (esp. 263, 269-275, 280ff.). Other helpful treatments of the rise of Sunday as the Christian Sabbath are provided by Rordorf; Bacchiocchi 1977; and Beckwith-Stott.

and he thus forges a link.[163] Bauckham therefore suggests that, "he uses both 'Sabbath' and 'eighth day' as interchangeable terms for the one new world that will follow the Parousia."[164] To say that they are "interchangeable" may go too far, however. It is probably closer to the mark to say that Barnabas' interest in the eschatological seventh day ends as soon as it has been shown to discredit the weekly Sabbath; otherwise the seventh day merges directly into the eighth day as the beginning of the latter.[165] There is, in any case, a degree of consistency between v. 8 and vv. 5-7. The transitive use of καταπαύω in v. 5a anticipates v. 8 (καταπαύσας τὰ πάντα) and the implied "future Sabbath" of v. 8 is associated with the *beginning* of the eighth day; the Sabbath (seventh day) in v. 8 is not so much a limited period as the inauguration of the new world.[166] It is also to be recalled that Barnabas has not mentioned the "true rest" with the eighth day in v. 8, though strictly speaking it takes place during that period (according to vv. 5b.7); this might evidence a certain separation of the "Sabbath" and "eighth day" in his thinking. At the risk of imposing more consistency on the passage than is there the following diagram is offered:

---

[163] Cf. Chester, 275; Bauckham 1982b, 262-264. Another possible influence is the one already noted, i.e., Jewish speculation which located the world-to-come *after* the world-Sabbath; cf. Hofius, 114f.

[164] Bauckham 1982b, 263 (esp. n. 77; italics added); cf. 273. Bauckham calls this a "confusing combination of two systems of eschatological arithmetic," but it is nonetheless "a way of combining the Christian sense of Sunday worship as anticipating the life of the world to come with the inherited Jewish idea of an eschatological Sabbath." For others advocating a similar interpretation, cf. Rordorf, 94 n. 1; Rordorf himself argues that Barnabas was a Chiliast (93-94).

[165] Similarly, Chester, 275. It does not seem necessary to treat vv. 8f. as a secondary addition to vv. 3-7; *pace* Hofius, 113-115; Windisch 1920, 384. Hofius tends to ignore the possible influence of Christian traditions touching the Lord's day; moreover, we must allow for some degree of imprecision in expression.

[166] The "future" Sabbath in v. 8 is connected with the new world rather than "this world"; *pace* Hofius, 114f.

The passage is a blend of Jewish traditions, Christian customs, and creative exegesis, all exploited polemically. Barnabas is not advocating the idea of a "millennium" and he is not a "Chiliast."[167] He is rather associating the Sabbath and its "rest" with the new age/world which God will make after this one -- associated with *both* the seventh and eighth days -- and which has no time limit attached to it. In so doing he attempts to show the meaninglessness of the Jewish Sabbath and the way in which Christians will enjoy the true fulfilment of that command of the decalogue.

This passage in *Barnabas* is naturally reminiscent of Heb 3-4 in that Gen 2,2 is interpreted along eschatological lines and in such a way that it is *this* Sabbath in which believers will ultimately share. Beyond that, however, the passage contains more points of dissimilarity with Heb 3-4 than points of similarity. The over-riding intent to discredit the Jewish Sabbath, the invocation of the one-day-equals-one-thousand-years schema, the use of the word καταπαύω in connection with the judging work of the Son, the focus on rightly sanctifying the Sabbath, and God's rejection of the seventh day in favor of the eighth are all missing in Hebrews 3-4; on the other hand, Ψ 94,11 [95,11] and the whole rest tradition, as well as the idea of "entering" God's κατάπαυσις, are missing in *Barn* 15. If *Barn* 15 has received any impetus from Heb 3-4, it has been only in the most general of senses.

6.5. 2 Clement and the Gospel of the Hebrews[168]

In *2Clem* 5,5 the "homilist" reminds suffering believers that their sojourn in "this world" is short, ἡ δὲ ἐπαγγελία τοῦ Χριστοῦ μεγάλη καὶ θαυμαστή ἐστιν, καὶ ἀνάπαυσις τῆς μελλούσης βασιλείας καὶ ζωῆς αἰωνίου ("but the promise of Christ is great and marvellous, even the rest of the kingdom that shall be and of eternal life").[169] The readers are exhorted further to "bid farewell to the one" world and "to hold companionship with the other" (6,5), ποιοῦντες γὰρ τὸ θέλημα τοῦ Χριστοῦ εὑρήσομεν

---

[167] Cf. also Lohmann, 232f. On chiliasm in the Fathers; cf. Daniélou 1964, 377-404; Bauckham 1982b, 254 (esp. nn. 29-34); Ford, 833f. Early examples include Papias (Eusebius, *HistEccl* 3,39,11ff.) and the gnostic Cerinthus (ca. A.D. 100; Eusebius, *HistEccl* 3,28,2); possibly *AscenIs* 4,15. The association of the messianic period with a world-Sabbath does not appear in the Jewish literature; Str-B, 4/2:989; Volz, 76; Hofius, 210 n. 754; Lincoln 1982, 217 n. 4; *contra* Rordorf, 50. In post-apostolic Christian literature the traditions of the world-week and the millennial reign of Christ were first united by Irenaeus; cf. Lohmann, 233 n. 83.

[168] It would not be significantly helpful to examine separately and in detail the "chain saying" found in the *GosHeb* par.; it is included here in a subsidiary fashion. *1Clem* 57,7 and 59,3 use our motif in OT quotations (Prov 1,23-33; Isa 57,15), and in both cases the rest motif is incidental. Cf. also Isa 66,1 in *Barn* 16,2.

[169] Trans. Lightfoot 1890, 2:308, cf. 220. Note the sequence of wolves-rest (*2Clem* 5,2-5) in the *EpApost* 44 Cop.

ἀνάπαυσιν (6,7; "For, if we do the will of Christ, we shall find rest"); "but if otherwise, then nothing shall deliver us from eternal punishment, if we should disobey his commandments."[170] The repetition of the hope of rest indicates that it is of some importance in this context.

The association of the future rest with a contrast between this world and the world-to-come (*2Clem* 5,1.5.6; 6,3-7) reminds of *Barn* 15. The use of the phrase εὑρήσομεν ἀνάπαυσιν, its association with the "promise of Christ" and obedience to his will, along with the warning of eternal destruction (αἰωνίου κολάσεως), which is found in the NT only in Mt 25,45f., might suggest a free adaptation of the Logion, Mt 11,28-30.[171]

We note also the complex wonder-rest-kingdom (θαυμαστή-ἀνάπαυσις-βασιλείας) in *2Clem* 5,5 which corresponds to a "chain saying" ascribed by Clement of Alexandria to the Egyptian Jewish *GosHeb*, "He that marvels (ὁ θαυμάσας) shall reign (βασιλεύσει), and he that has reigned shall rest (ἀναπαήσεται)."[172] This is a saying which, in turn, finds a parallel -- if not a precedent[173] -- in POx 654 (= *GosThom* 2[174]), "Jesus says, Let him not cease who is seeking...has found, and when he has found...has been amazed he will reign and find rest."[175] In fact, the linkage of "resting" and "reigning" is

---

[170] Trans. Lightfoot 1890, 2:309.

[171] Cf. Bartlet *et al.*, 130; they comment that it is "hard to escape the impression" that *2Clem* is using Matthew at this point. Grant-Graham, 116, also take this as an allusion to Mt 11,28-30.

[172] The saying is in ClemAlex, *Strom* 2,9,45, and is given in a fuller form in *Strom* 5,14,96. The *GosHeb* probably dates from the first half of II A.D.; cf. *NTApocr*², 1:172-176; Koester 1982, 2:223f. Grenfell-Hunt, 5, opine that *2Clem* 5,5 is a "probable reference" to this saying of *GosHeb*; cf. also H.G.E. White, 7f. Koester 1982, 2:233-236, argues for an Egyptian origin of *2Clem*.

[173] Koester 1982, 224, allows that the complex of seeking, finding, marvelling, ruling and resting could "have circulated in the free traditions of Jesus' sayings" and thus found entrance into *GosHeb*, but he is more convinced that *GosHeb* took the saying from *GosThom* which he thinks may have migrated to Egypt at an early date. It is not possible to determine the answer to this here, and even if the saying was taken over by *GosHeb* from *GosThom* it is not clear what the saying would have suggested in *GosHeb*. By any of these channels -- free traditions, *GosThom*, or *GosHeb* -- this sort of saying might have come to the writer of *2Clem*.

[174] On the gnostic use of the rest motif in *GosThom*, cf. Vielhauer, 292-299 (esp. 297f.). Marcovich, 58, points out that "wondering" as a first stage in Gnosis follows "the Platonic-Aristotelian pattern of τὸ θαυμάζειν ἀρχὴ φιλοσοφίας"; cf. Gärtner, 261. On the subject of seeking and rest in the *GosThom*, cf. Gärtner, 258-267. Dibelius, 284 n. 2, notes similar "chain" sayings in *CorpHerm* 4,2; 13,20; 9,10; cf. Helderman 1984, 53f. For the texts of the numerous parallels (ClemAlex; POx 654; Hermetic; NT Apocrypha; etc.) see Marcovich, 56f.; Stroker, 116-119. On the whole question see *NTApocr*², 1:175 ; esp. Koester 1980, 238-244.

[175] The Gk text of POx 654 lines 5-9 has been restored with the aid of the quotes in ClemAlex; cf. Grenfell-Hunt, 4f.; H.G.E. White, 5-8; Fitzmyer 1971, 371-373. Fitzmyer 1971, 371 (based on H.G.E. White, 5) gives the Gk as follows: [λέγει Ἰη(σοῦ)ς·] μὴ παυσάσθω ὁ ζη[τῶν τοῦ ζητεῖν ἕως ἂν] εὕρῃ, καὶ ὅταν εὕρῃ, [θαμβηθήσεται καὶ

common.[176] The history of this saying need not detain us,[177] but this constellation of motifs in sayings reminiscent of Mt 11,28-30 (i.e. 2Clem 5,5; 6,7) is interesting; it is worth noticing traces of this in the NT.[178]

(1) The same pattern of motifs is visible in 2Thes 1,5ff., along with the idea of "eternal destruction." Believers are being made worthy of the kingdom of God (βασιλείας τοῦ θεοῦ) for which they are suffering. God's justice will ensure that the troublers will be afflicted while the believers will be given "relief" (ἄνεσιν). Their enemies will receive "eternal destruction" (ὄλεθρον αἰώνιον) when the Lord comes "to be glorified by his saints and to be marvelled at (θαυμασθῆναι) on that day among all who have believed."

(2) The goal alternates as "rest" (ἀναπαύω) and as "reigning" (βασιλεύω) for 1000 years in two of the seven beatitudes of the Apocalypse

---

θαμ]βηθεὶς βασιλεύσῃ κα[ὶ βασιλεύσας ἀναπα]ήσεται; the translation given in the text is from *NTApocr²*, 1:117. The text of the Coptic *GosThom* 2 -- which replaces the climax of "rest" with that of "reigning" -- is discussed in detail by Marcovich, 56-58; Fitzmyer, *loc. cit.*; and Helderman 1984, 313-317.

[176] For this pairing in Philo, Gnosticism, non-gnostic Christianity, and wisdom thought, cf. Marcovich, 56f.; Bammel, 90 n. 13; Helderman 1978, 41; 1984, 313f.; Bauckham 1982b, 252f.; it is highly improbable that there is one single explanation for this association of ideas. In Sir 6,26-31 those who seek wisdom find rest and wisdom will be worn like a crown. In WisSol 4,7 the "rest" of the righteous is parallel to the description of the afterlife in ch. 3; there the righteous enjoy peace (v. 3) and hold sway over nations (v. 8); cf. 6,20. TDan 5,12f. juxtapose the resting and reigning of the saints in the New Jerusalem. TSim 6,4-7 contains all three motifs, rest, reign, marvel: a global "rest from trouble" and "freedom from war" issues in human "mastery over the evil spirits" (cf. TLevi 18,9.12); Simeon will arise and praise God for his "marvels." Note also 4QFlor 1; 4Q246 2. The idea of seeking and finding YHWH is common in the OT; cf. Amos 5,4; Hos 5,6; Isa 55,6ff.; Jer 29,13ff.; Deut 4,29-30. We have already surveyed the OT use of the "rest tradition," which joined rest closely to the *reigns* of David and his descendants, and have also noted that in the Chronicler's work "seeking" and "finding" YHWH is united to the enjoyment of rest by Davidic kings (2Chr 14,2-7 [MT/LXX 14,1-6]; 15,15; 20,4.30; 31,21; 32,22). A joining of "rest" to OT "royal theology" is also noted by Brueggemann 1968, 156-181; 1971, 317-332; and 1972, 19-38. Cf. also the baptism pericope which Jerome mentions; *NTApocr²*, 1:148f., 177; Bauckham 1982b, 252f., esp. nn. 7 and 9.

[177] See the literature in the previous notes. Not all are of the view that the saying arose solely within the compass of Gnosticism; see Bammel; Grenfell-Hunt, 5; Bauckham 1982b, 253. Note Mt 7,7f. (par. Lk 11,9f.); for "wondering," cf. Mk 10,24; 14,33; Acts 3,10; and Swete, 491; also Mt 13,44 and H.G.E. White, 6; Fitzmyer 1971, 373. The linking of seeking, finding, and rest is found in Jewish wisdom thought; cf. Prov 1,28-33 (*1Clem* 57,3-7) and Helderman 1984, 56f.

[178] 2Thes 1 and Rev 14 are both discussed below, 297f.; Acts 3 is also taken up later; infra, 307ff. In addition to the NT passages below, note that in both Acts 7 (Isa 66,1) and Heb 3-4, God's κατάπαυσις is associated with his *throne*.

(Rev 14,13; 20,6).[179] Interestingly, there is already a degree of similarity between 2Thes 1,7 and Rev 14,13.[180]

(3) This interchangeability is visible in Acts also. The restoration ($\dot{\alpha}\pi o \kappa \alpha \theta i \sigma \tau \eta \mu \iota$) of the $\beta \alpha \sigma \iota \lambda \epsilon i \alpha$ connects with $\kappa \alpha \iota \rho o i$ $\dot{\alpha} \nu \alpha \psi \dot{\upsilon} \xi \epsilon \omega \varsigma$ at the restoration ($\dot{\alpha}\pi o \kappa \alpha \tau \dot{\alpha} \sigma \tau \alpha \sigma \iota \varsigma$)[181] of all things in Acts 1,6 and 3,20f.[182]

(4) Anticipating our findings in Mt 11,28-30, the yoke image in the Matthean context probably involves royal imagery related to Jesus' status as the Son of David. He promises rest not to those who will reign, but to those who will submit to his rule and learn from him.[183] There is no apparent relationship to the "chain saying,"[184] and only a remote resemblance with the reign-rest complex visible in the other NT passages.

Viewed through the lens of the reign-rest complex, *2Clem* 5-6; 2Thes 1; Rev 14; and Acts 3 may give indications of a shared apocalyptic tradition (cf. TDan 5,12f.) otherwise common in Gnosticism. The form of the chain saying in *GosHeb* par. probably stems from "the sapiential theme of seeking after wisdom, revelation, and salvation,"[185] but the linkage of motifs may stem in part from apocalyptic circles.[186] Mt 11,28-30 has no necessary relationship with these circles, but the eschatological context of Mt 11-12 and the royal connotations of the Logion there may indicate that Matthew associated the Logion with such apocalyptic ideas.

6.6. Epistula Apostolorum

It is common for non-Gnostic writers to assign rest to the future kingdom, in contrast to the Gnostics who stressed the present realization of rest.[187]

---

[179] Cf. Marcovich, 56. The other beatitudes are Rev 1,3; 16,15; 19,9; 22,7.14. Note that *EpApost* 44 Cop. appears to conflate ideas from *2Clem* 5 and Rev 14,10f., suggesting a use of traditional conceptions.

[180] Infra, 298f.

[181] The doctrine of the *Apocatastasis* or "Return" (the restoration of the Pleroma) was to become an established feature of gnostic eschatology; cf. K. Rudolph 1984, 196-199, who attributes it to both Jewish-Christian and Stoic thought. In gnostic writings it is sometimes joined directly with the expectation of rest, as here in Acts; cf. *TreatRes* 44; Hofius, 87.

[182] 2Bar 73,1ff., in a vision drawing on Isa 11, predicts, "And it will happen that after he has brought down everything which is in the world, and has sat down in eternal peace on the throne of the kingdom, then joy will be revealed and rest will appear..."; cf. TLevi 18 which also draws on Isa 11.

[183] Likewise, *2Clem* 5-6; Acts 3; 2Thes 1.

[184] Somewhat optimistically, Koester 1980, 246, leaves open the possibility of contact.

[185] Koester 1980, 238-244.

[186] Wisdom and apocalyptic interpenetrate; cf. Helderman 1984, 335 n. 207; Stone 1984.

[187] Bauckham 1982b, 254 nn. 28-33; later non-gnostic examples of this rule include Justin (*DialTrypho* 80,5; 121,3) and Irenaeus (*Haer* 4,16,1; 5,28,3; 5,30,4; 5,33,2).

These viewpoints meet in the Egyptian Jewish *Epistula Apostolorum,* which originated around mid-II A.D.[188] This work, which makes use of gnostic motifs, is anti-gnostic in orientation.[189] The believers' "rest," which is associated with the kingdom,[190] seems to be presently available in heaven (12 Cop).[191] Although believers look forward to enjoying it up there in the future (19; 22; 26; 28),[192] they already enjoy it now in some sense (28). More than one passage is distinctly reminiscent of *2Clem* 5-6:

...to those...who have done my commandment I will grant rest in life in the kingdom of my heavenly Father.[193]

This work testifies to the extent of cross fertilization which was occurring at this period, especially in Egyptian Jewish Christianity.

6.7. Clement of Alexandria[194]

Clement, who has a marked fondness for the rest motif, stands squarely in the tradition of the earlier Alexandrians Aristobulus[195] and Philo in placing the notion of ἀνάπαυσις within the Platonic metaphysical framework, sharing also their interest in Pythagorean speculation. Moreover, Clement

---

Bauckham notes the "catholic" *EpApost* as an exception in its stress on the present. Justin (*DialTrypho* 8,2) and possibly Ignatius (*IgnEph* 2,1; *IgnSmyrn* 9,2; supra, 133f.) could be cited as well; probably also the OdesSol. Cf. also Rordorf, 96, 108ff.

[188] *NTApocr*², 1:251; cf. Koester 1982, 2:236-238.

[189] The frequent appearance of the rest motif in *EpApost*, its location in the heavenly world, and the stress on present enjoyment are marks of contact with Gnosticism (Bauckham 1982b, 254f.; Rordorf, 96), but Hofius, 190 n. 449 Ad b, justifiably argues that the gnostic components of *EpApost* should not be over-stressed; the sayings about rest in particular "stehen ganz in jüdisch-apokalyptischer Tradition." Cf. also Helderman 1984, 80 nn. 108 and 112. Compare *EpApost* 19 with *ARN* 1 (*Ber* 17a).

[190] Cf. 12 Cop.; 26; 28 Cop. As in *2Clem*; Acts 3; and 2Thes 1, it is participation in the kingdom rather than "reigning" which is view.

[191] Also *EpApost* 27, which implies that heaven is the resting place of the departed souls; *pace* Bauckham 1982b, 289 n. 34.

[192] Implied in 44 Cop?

[193] 26 Eth. (the Cop. is much the same); note how 2Clem 5,5 and 6,7 are blended; cf. also 12 Cop.; 28 Cop.; 44 Cop. and *2Clem* 5; Rev 14,10f.

[194] Between the Fathers and the earliest Apologists, the noun κατάπαυσις occurs only twice, both times in dependence on Isa 66,1; cf. *Barn* 16,2; Athenagorus, *Suppl* 9,2; Hofius, 29. Ἀνάπαυσις and ἀναπαύω occur in the Apologists only in Justin's *DialTrypho*, which can be passed over here; cf. Helderman 1984, 61f. On the rest idea in ClemAlex, see J.W. Thompson, 87f.; Bauckham 1982b, 275-277; Helderman 1984, 62; Schneider, 416f. For the other writers of the period, including Irenaeus, Origen, Tertullian, and Augustine, cf. Helderman 1984, 62-69; Schneider; Bauckham 1982b, 277-287. This later evidence is of less assistance to our investigation than it is to the development of the "Christian Sabbath" or the gnostic use of the motif.

[195] Eusebius, *PraepEvang* 13,12,9-16; cf. *OTP*, 2:841f.

stands very near gnostic concerns and the gnostic search for the perfect rest in the Father, a rest which "can be attained to some extent on the earth by means of ἀπάθεια and contemplation, but finds its complete realization at the end of the *Himmelsreise*";[196] "for him the primary reference of the concept of Sabbath and eighth day was to the Gnostic's ascent through the seven heavens to the ogdoad."[197] These elements are evident in the following passages:[198]

The highest expression of *gnosis* is rest (ἀνάπαυσις). (*Paed* 1,6,29)

Gnosis therefore leads man easily towards what is kindred with the soul, divine and holy, and by means of its own light enables him to go through the various mystical levels until it delivers him to the supreme place of repose (τῆς ἀναπαύσεως τόπον): it supposes that he whose heart is pure must contemplate God 'face to face' in a way which is in keeping with science and comprehension. (*Strom* 7,9,57)

The soul after becoming completely spiritual and reaching what is kindred with it remains in the spiritual assembly, in the rest (τὴν ἀνάπαυσιν) of God. (*Strom* 7,11,68)

Such, according to David, "rest (καταπαύσουσιν) in the holy hill of God,"[199] in the church far on high, in which are gathered the philosophers of God...who do not remain in the seventh seat, the place of rest (ἐν ἑβδομάδι ἀναπαύσεως), but are promoted...to the heritage of beneficence which is the eighth grade (εἰς ὀγδοαδικῆς); devoting themselves to the pure vision of insatiable contemplation. (*Strom* 6,14,108)

In a difficult passage regarding the Sabbath command of the decalogue, Clement writes that humans ultimately share in God's nature, which is rest:

And the fourth word is that which intimates that the world was created by God, and that He gave us the seventh day as rest (ἀνάπαυσιν), on account of the trouble that there is in life. For God is incapable of weariness, and suffering, and want. But we who bear flesh need rest. The seventh day, therefore, is proclaimed a rest -- abstraction from ills -- preparing for the Primal Day [i.e., Christ], our true rest...By following Him, therefore, through our whole life, we become impassible; and this is to rest. (*Strom* 6,16,137f.)[200]

---

[196] Lilla, 187 (Lilla's statement is actually made about the Platonic ideal of ὁμοίωσις θεῷ, which is closely associated with the enjoyment of ἀνάπαυσις); cf. Helderman 1984, 62. J.W. Thompson, 87f., does not give sufficient attention to the gnostic aspects of Clement's thought.
[197] Bauckham 1982b, 275.
[198] The first three texts which follow are all citations and translations of Lilla, 187; italics in original; Greek added. The fourth is cited by Bauckham 1982b, 276; trans. from ANCL 12:366f.; Greek added.
[199] Ψ 14,1 [15,1], reads, τίς **κατασκηνώσει** ἐν τῷ ὄρει τῷ ἁγίῳ σου.
[200] Trans. ANCL 12:386. J.W. Thompson, 87f., comments on this passage, "To rest is to share God's being, for Clement concludes from God's resting on the Sabbath that God is 'unwearied and impassible' (ἄκμητος καὶ ἀπαθής)." For further on the association of ἀπαθής and ὁμοίωσις θεῷ in ClemAlex and its parallels in Neoplatonism, cf. Lilla, 106-112. On this passage, cf. also Bauckham 1982b, 276f.

Thus, for Clement, Platonic metaphysics and Pythagorean speculation have been in part mediated through Alexandrian theologians such as Philo, in part directly inherited, and then refracted through more than one strand of Christianity, including Gnosticism. As a result Clement has associated "rest" with the transcendent spiritual spheres of the Hebdomad and Ogdoad and set it in contrast to the troubles of fleshly life. The ultimate goal of Christian piety is "rest" in God (τέλος δέ ἐστιν θεοσεβείας ἡ ἀίδιος ἀνάπαυσις ἐν τῷ θεῷ).[201] "This topic of the *Himmelsreise* of the gnostic soul, of its deification, and of its ἀνάπαυσις...represents a very close link between Clement and Gnosticism."[202]

6.8. Summary

This literature shows such a variety of ways in which the rest motif was exploited that there can be no thought of one established form for the idea. Much as we found in the OT Pseudepigrapha and elsewhere, the rest motif tends to be shaped by the given outlook of the writer and the concerns of the immediate literary context.

The Odes and *2 Clement* (with *GosHeb*) may give us windows to the first century, specifically, to the possibility that "rest" enjoyed popularity in some worship settings more than the NT literature would suggest; that there may have been current in some circles both the idea of a resting place prepared for the elect in heaven and that of a rest from works; also that the stylized pairing of "resting" and "reigning" may underlie more than one expression of the motif in the NT. *Barn* 15 is of interest primarily as a use of Jewish traditions which is at once reminiscent of and very distinct from Heb 3-4. They share an eschatological interpretation of Gen 2,2 against the backdrop of Jewish traditions of an eschatological Sabbath,[203] but they diverge in their exegesis and in their main interests.

The presence of Gnosticism could be felt at more than one point. It is not certain that the heavy use of the rest motif in the Odes should be credited to gnostic influence, but the Odes point to the sort of mystical piety which would have fed into and which was exploited by Gnostics. The "chain saying" we noted in the *GosHeb* (cf. *GosThom* 2 par.) was certainly popular in gnostic circles; whether comparison of it and *2Clem* 5-6 highlights a gnostic influence on *2Clem*, or whether *2Clem* is simply making use of a natural grouping of ideas also taken up into the "chain saying," we did not

---

[201] *Paed* 1,13,102.
[202] Lilla, 229.
[203] Further on (infra, 335ff.) we will observe that Isa 66,1 very likely lurked in the background of Heb 3-4; in that connection it might be significant that Barnabas moves from Gen 2 to Isa 66,1 in *Barn* 16.

determine. Yet when we come to *EpApost* the gnostic imprint is unavoidable; even if the shape of the motif remains within traditional Jewish forms, its use there is plainly due to gnostic influence. Clement of Alexandria represents a wholesale adoption of Platonic thought categories and Philonic and Alexandrian speculation, as well as considerable assimilation of distinctly gnostic ideas.[204] The result is that Clement stands as much apart from the other literature here as Philo does from most of the OT Pseudepigrapha; once again, the substance of the rest idea is indebted primarily to Greek metaphysics.

7. Gnostic

7.1. Introduction

The rest motif is highly characteristic of gnostic literature, and the way in which it is used suggests that it was a basic soteriological category for the Gnostics. Of all the areas of literature covered in this chapter, it is this one which has received the most scholarly attention.[205] It is just this specialist treatment, however, which makes this material difficult to summarize. Moreover, the gnostic literature itself is foreign and strange to the non-specialist. In spite of these obstacles we can attempt to make a few general observations about the use of the rest motif in Gnosticism.

With respect to terminology, we need only to observe that the word κατάπαυσις is virtually absent from gnostic literature, ἀνάπαυσις being far and away the more common word used in connection with the idea of rest.[206] This is probably due to the semantic divergence of these two words which is

---

[204] There is also the possibility that the "eighth day" in *Barn* 15 owes something to Gnosticism, but this is not at all clear.

[205] Käsemann, 73-75; Vielhauer, 281-299; Hofius, 75-90; Ménard, 71-88; J.W. Thompson, 88-91. Full size treatments are in Helderman 1984; Williams 1977; 1985; these two scholars approach the material with different concerns and an integrated study would be helpful. Studies of particular features include Gärtner, 258-267 ("Seeking and Rest"); Bammel, 88-90; Helderman 1978; and Williams 1981, 819-829. Regarding the far-reaching significance of the rest motif as a *Heilsgut* in Gnosticism, cf. Helderman 1984, 12-15. As to tributaries to the gnostic idea, cf. J.W. Thompson, 90; Helderman 1984, 47-84 (cf. 69-71), 338, and *passim*. For a copious list of references see Vielhauer, Hofius, and esp. Helderman and Williams; also Foerster, vol. 2, index, *s.v.*

[206] Hofius, 31f., found κατάπαυσις in gnostic literature only two times (Hippolytus, *Ref* VI 32,8 and VIII 14,1), and these two are dependent on Heb 3-4 or the LXX. Helderman 1984, 321, noted the highest occurrence of ἀνάπαυσις in *GosPhil* and *ParaphShem* ; he lists (1984, 49f.) the following synonyms for ἀνάπαυσις: ἡσυχία; ἠρεμία; γαλήνη; εἰρηνη; χαρά; and ἀνάψυξις. Further on the Coptic terminology and its Gk translation is in Helderman 1984, 16f. (cf. n. 137 in Helderman); 227f.; 319f.

more pronounced outside of the LXX; convention made ἀνάπαυσις the more appropriate term for "rest."[207]

7.2. Rest and gnostic mythology

The frequent occurrence of the motif as well as its significance can be seen in the closing passage from the Valentinian *Gospel of Truth*:

So when it pleased him that his uttered name should be his son, and when he who had emanated from the depth gave him his name he spoke of his secrets, knowing that the father is without evil. Precisely for this reason he produced him -- so that he might speak concerning the place from which he had emanated and his **realm of repose**, and that he might glorify the fullness, the greatness of his name, and the father's sweetness.

All, individually, will speak concerning the place from which they have emanated and the lot according to which they have received their **establishment in the state of rest**. They will hasten to return and to receive from that place in which they (once) **stood at rest**, tasting of it and being nourished and growing.

And his own **realm of repose** is his fullness. Thus all the father's emanations are fullnesses; and he is the root of all his emanations, within that (place) where he caused all to sprout and gave them their destinies. So each is manifest in order that from their own thought <...> For they send their thought to where their root is, their root which carries them up above all the heights to the father.

They cling to his head, which is **repose** for them. And they hold themselves close to him so that, as it were, they receive from his face something like kisses, although they do not give this impression. For they have neither surpassed themselves nor fallen short of the glory of the father. And they do not think of him as trivial or bitter or wrathful; rather, that he is without evil, imperturbable, sweet, acquainted with all ways before they have come into being. And he does not need to be instructed. Such are they who have possessions from above, from the immeasurable greatness, straining toward the solitary and perfect, he who is mother to them. And they will not descend into Hades, nor do they have envy or groaning; nor is death within them. Rather, they **repose** in that being who gives unto himself **repose**, and in the vicinity of truth they are neither weary nor entangled.

But it is precisely they who are the truth. And it is in them that the father dwells, and in the father that they are, being perfect, undivided in what is truly good, and imparting no defect to anything, but rather imparting **repose** and being fresh in spirit. And it is to their

---

[207] The intransitive use of κατάπαυσις is confined to the LXX (where the intransitive sense is used exclusively) and to passages quoting from or dependent on the LXX, with the exception of Theophrastus, *Vent* 18; cf. Hofius, 30-31. Outside these usages, Helderman 1984, 48f., stresses the semantic divergence of ἀνάπαυσις and κατάπαυσις: where the former has as its chief meaning, "rest," the latter is used (outside the LXX) with the senses of "stopping," "putting down," or "deposing"; this same general distinction holds for the verbal forms as well (cf. LSJM, 115 and 904). MM, 36f., contends that "the essential idea" of ἀνάπαυσις/ἀναπαύω is "that of a respite, or *temporary* rest as a preparation for future toil" (italics in original), and notes that this idea contrasts with the use of κατάπαυσις in Heb 4, "the Sabbath followed by no weekday," but Helderman 1984, 72 n. 20, rightly questions this. It is more likely that the semantic component of "temporariness" is dependent on usage rather than the meaning of ἀνάπαυσις.

root that they will listen, being occupied with the things in which one might find one's root and not damage one's soul.
This is the place of the blessed. This is their place. As for the others, then, let them know in their own places that it is not right for me to say more, for I have been in the **place of repose**. No, it is there that I shall dwell, continually occupied with the father of the entirety and the true siblings, upon whom the father's love is poured out and in whose midst there is no lack of him; who truly and obviously dwell in true and eternal life, and speak of the light that is perfect and full of the father's seed, and which is in his heart and in the fullness. In this his spirit rejoices, and it glorifies what it dwelt in. For he is good, and his children are perfect and worthy of his name. Truly, it is children of this kind that the father loves. (*GosTruth* 40,23-43,24)[208]

This lengthy citation illustrates not only how common the rest motif is but to some extent how thoroughly it has been adapted to gnostic mythology. This was already evident from Hofius' examination of the motif, which concluded that "alle wesentlichen Gedanken der gnostischen Theologie, Kosmogonie, Anthropogonie, Anthropologie, Soteriologie und Eschatologie unter Verwendung der 'Ruhe'-Terminologie zum Ausdruck gebracht werden können."[209] Jan Helderman's extensive study has since shown the unified nature of the gnostic conception, and his schema has been summarized in an appendix at the end of this chapter with a brief explanation of Helderman's method. What follows here is largely dependent on the work of Hofius.

Rest is descriptive of the divine *Urgrund*; it characterizes the original state of the Pleroma, and is a name of God himself. As such it is the original home of the Gnostic, prior to the "fall." As a result of the fall the world and indeed the individual person is characterized by "unrest."[210] The following passage describes existence in the material world from which one emerges upon the reception of gnosis. It is as one awakening from a bad dream:

When the light shines on the terror which that person had experienced, he knows that it is nothing. Thus they were ignorant of the Father, he being the one whom they did not see. Since it was terror and disturbance and instability and doubt and division, there were

---

[208] This trans. of *GosTruth* is from Layton, 263f.; emphasis mine. Further quotations from the Nag Hammadi tractates will be from *NHL*, unless indicated otherwise as here. For a detailed treatment of this passage (*GosTruth* 40,23-43,24) concerning the use of the rest motif, see Helderman 1984, 220-227.

[209] Hofius, 75.

[210] Williams 1977, 118, says in regard to "instability" (which is closely related to "rest" in the gnostic sources), "Instability in [gnostic] documents is very often located in the passions: e.g., grief, fear, perplexity (Iren. Adv. haer. 1.4.1); envy, malice, wrath, violence, desire (TriTrac 85,7-9); desire, wrath (ApocryJn BG 40,20-41,1); anger envy, fear, desire (ApocryJn BG 65,12-16). Such passions are the cardinal manifestations of confusion, ceaseless unrest, and disorder." These are, however, merely symptoms of the more fundamental problem of a striving after the truth through "discursive wisdom" rather than through "praise." "Stability is a matter of no longer stalking and frantically circling round and round the Truth, but rather it is a matter of 'being the Truth itself' (GTr 42,21-25)" (1977, 121).

many illusions at work by means of these, and (there were) empty fictions, as if they were sunk in sleep and found themselves in disturbing dreams. Either (there is) a place to which they were fleeing, or without strength they come (from) having chased after others, or they are involved in striking blows, or they are receiving blows themselves, or they have fallen from high places, or they take off into the air though they do not even have wings. Again, sometimes (it is as if) people were murdering them, though there is no one even pursuing them, or they themselves are murdering their neighbors, for they have been stained with their blood. When those who are going through all these things wake up, they see nothing, they who were in the midst of all these disturbances, for they are nothing. Such is the way of those who have cast ignorance aside from them like sleep, not esteeming it as anything, nor do they esteem its works as solid things either, but they leave them behind like a dream in the night. (*GosTruth* 28,29-30,4)

The divine Logos therefore comes to reveal to the fallen Pneumatics their original resting place, from which they emerged in the fall and which they have since forgotten. The Revealer can himself be described as "rest" since he is a "fellow-traveller in this land of error" and "a haven for you in this turbulent sea" and "a rest for your souls" (*ActsThom* 37). The soteriological fruit of gnosis is rest: "Having knowledge...he receives rest" (*GosTruth* 22,9.12). Very often this experience of rest is depicted as a present possession.

Upon death the imprisoned light particle, the divine seed, is freed from the body and returns (the "ascent of the soul") into the kingdom of light, the repose of the father: "While we are in this world it is fitting for us to acquire the resurrection, so that when we strip off the flesh we may be found in rest and not walk in the middle [i.e., death]" (*GosPhil* 66,16-20).[211] Of the rational soul it is said, "She found her rising. She came to rest in him who is at rest. She reclined in the bridal chamber...She received rest from her labors, while the light that shines forth upon her does not sink" (*AuthTeach* 35,8ff.). In the course of the ascent the powers of the material world seek to hinder the rising soul, but the enlightened soul, now free of the bonds of material elements, "rises past the four powers, overpowering them with her gnosis, and attains eternal, silent rest."[212] In the Valentinian conception the "psychic person" ascends to the realm of the demiurge, the Hebdomad, but then may move from there to the "place of the middle," the Ogdoad. The "pneumatic person," however, ascends upon death to the Ogdoad, and from there at the end of the world into the "bridal chamber" of the Pleroma.[213] At the end of history when all of the "estranged particles of light" have been

---

[211] Cited in K. Rudolph 1984, 191; cf. the general discussion of individual and universal gnostic eschatology therein, 171ff., esp. relating to the "resurrection" and the ascent of the soul.

[212] K. King in *NHL*, 523.

[213] K. Rudolph 1984, 186; Vielhauer, 286; Vielhauer, 288, observes that this two tiered resting place (Ogdoad and Pleroma) is not evidenced in *GosTruth*.

restored to the Pleroma then the original condition of absolute rest and silence will return.[214]

7.3. The metaphysical background of the gnostic rest

The present concern is less to explicate in detail the nature of the metaphysical background of the gnostic idea of rest than it is to simply emphasize the fact of that background. Already Käsemann had pointed out that the Philonic -- and thus, in the framework of his presentation, also the gnostic -- idea of rest "is embedded in cosmic and metaphysical speculations."[215] This aspect of the gnostic conception was also stressed by Thompson:

> If we are to account for the importance of ἀνάπαυσις in Gnosticism, we must observe the consistent metaphysic which the term presupposes in the Gnostic literature. Ἀνάπαυσις is the characteristic only of the highest aeon and of the highest deity. The material world is characterized by unrest, movement, and passions...Thus rest consists in leaving the unstable creation for the heavenly world...The highest aeon is regularly described as being ἀσάλευτος, ἀκίνητος, and as possessing στάσις.[216]

The extent to which this is true has been demonstrated by M. Williams, who has shown that not only "rest," but closely related expressions such as "to stand at rest," and "to make firm/be made firm" are used throughout gnostic literature "for both the stability of the Transcendent as well as the stability which is the goal of the Gnostic."[217] Moreover,

> A comparison of the "standing" language in several Gnostic texts with the same language in Plotinus reveals that in both cases this term is used in the same technical sense to describe the stability of the Transcendent and the "standing at rest" of the individual as he withdraws in contemplation of the Transcendent...[The] model of the Gnostic who becomes "established," or "immovable," or "stands at rest" is directly parallel to the "standing at rest" of the sophos in Philo and Plotinus, and...all of these presuppose the same Platonic tradition of the stability of the noetic and of the mind (νοῦς) which behold it.[218]

This is not the place to summarize the body of evidence which Williams has marshalled for these claims.[219] For us it is sufficient to note that the *idea of rest* in the gnostic literature -- to whatever extent it may utilize biblical language and imagery -- is drawn fundamentally from Greek philosophy.

---

[214] K. Rudolph 1984, 196; cf. Hofius, 90.
[215] Käsemann, 71.
[216] J.W. Thompson, 90.
[217] Williams 1977, 4.
[218] Williams 1977, 5.
[219] On the stability of the Transcendent in the Platonic tradition, cf. esp. Williams 1977, 145-167.

7.4. Excursus: Gnosticism and the New Testament

The problem of defining Gnosticism, or the "gnostic viewpoint," is a long standing one. Already the decision as to definition begins to answer the questions as to age and origins. It is therefore with the awareness that it is formulated by someone who argues strongly for first century gnostic constructions that we cite K. Rudolph's summary of gnostic thought:

> Impelled by an anticosmic dualism, which also dominated its anthropology, early Gnostic thought, as far as we can tell, concentrated on the liberation of the hidden, divine core of man (the *pneuma*, the 'self'); despite all that happened in the world and history this core remained secretly united with the original above the heavens, of which it was a copy (it is 'speculation about the self'). This involves belief in the original fall of this (secret) core and its eventual rescue ('ascent of the soul'); this belief is made possible by the 'knowledge' of this complex of ideas, 'knowledge' which is a response to the redeeming 'call' of the Gnostic prophet or revealer (revelatory texts with daring exegetical methods are one of the main types of Gnostic writings). The usual response to these concepts is ascetic or encratite behaviour, but the Gnostics could also dispense with the customary moral and (Jewish) legal teachings. The 'kinship of the souls' ...provided the ideological basis of their communal life; their community centred on the redeemed or 'spiritual' people (pneumatics), while the rest were either unredeemed or still on the way to 'liberation'; thus two sets of moral standards were involved...[220]

As to the age of the gnostic religion relative to the NT, when the extant *literature* of Gnosticism all post-dates NT Christianity one may suspect that Gnosticism -- as we now know it -- is an essentially post-NT phenomenon. This impression is strongly reinforced when *polemic* against (known forms of) Gnosticism -- whether that polemic is Greek, Jewish ("two powers"), or Christian[221] -- also post-dates the first century. The view that the gnostic ideas and systems in the extant documents existed before or along with emerging Christianity and influenced NT theology, especially touching the "redeemer myth," must overcome a virtual conspiracy of silence. Attempts to read the later presentations back into the first century have not produced unanimity, and have been seriously questioned by some.[222]

Admittedly, it is *a priori* unlikely that Gnosticism emerged full-formed in the second century A.D. without any first century precedents, and this extends to systems as much as to individual elements and general "outlook."[223] The more difficult question is its first

---

[220] K. Rudolph 1983, 31.

[221] The Jewish evidence, as analyzed by Segal, 262, "is that opposition to Christian exegesis preceded opposition to extreme gnostic exegesis." By the "Christian" polemic, I have in mind the clearly anti-gnostic rhetoric of late II A.D. and beyond (Irenaeus, etc.).

[222] Yamauchi, along with his own arguments and conclusions provides a good overview of the scholarly debate up to 1983. See also Pétrement, though a Christian origin of Gnosticism is disputed by many.

[223] Cf. K. Rudolph 1983, 21-37, esp. 31f. Rudolph is probably right that "it will be hard to argue for a 'qualitative' leap from a mere Gnostic atmosphere to a 'Gnosticistic' construction" (32) between I and II A.D., although this does not imply agreement with his arrangement and assessment of the NT "evidence" (1983, 31f.; cf. 1984, 299-306). Rudolph 1983, 26, refuses to distinguish between "Gnosis and Gnosticism." For such a distinction, see Wilson 1968, 140-145.

century (and earlier?) forms, and here there is an acute problem of how confident we can be. A period of germination and initial (pre-literary) development followed by a delayed reaction on the part of established groups is not an unreasonable hypothesis.[224] In the stage of its pre-history, however, one may wonder how fragmented, how significant, and how widespread a "movement" it was.[225] When the gnostic movement did emerge in writing, much of it was already very Jewish and Christian in character, albeit in a unique way. It is not easy, nor possible here, to work back to who owes what to whom nor to sort out the question of Jewish and/or non-Jewish origins, which elements might be independent but parallel religious historical developments, the earlier shape of isolated elements, and how fast or slow specific developments might have occurred. Commenting on Gnosticism in the NT, E. Ferguson remarks,

> There is enough to show that many of the materials with which the great Gnostic teachers of the second century worked were around in the first century. It is less clear that these ideas were present in the same combinations, in as developed a form, or within the same framework. The New Testament errorists appear to combine Jewish, pagan, and Christian elements; but these ingredients provide an almost infinite variety of potential combinations.[226]

The present study concurs with this cautious approach to the data without precluding the possibility that something like the later gnostic myths may have existed before II A.D.[227] *No contact with Gnosticism will be assumed with the NT use of the rest motif unless there are clear signs of such contact, signs deriving from the use of (not merely the presence of) the rest motif itself.*[228]

7.5. Summary

The use of the rest motif in gnostic literature has been decisively shaped by gnostic mythology. The usages of the motif are widely diverse but taken together they appear to revolve around the *Weg-Gedanke* which is essential to gnostic soteriology. Accordingly the usages can be plotted on a fairly detailed schema (cf. the Appendix). The extensive use of this motif in the gnostic literature manifests a far-reaching debt to Platonic metaphysical categories.

---

[224] Yet one may stress the contrast with the paradigm of emerging Christianity, which was not nearly so quiet for so long and which provoked an earlier response from Judaism, though seemingly less provocative.

[225] Theories of first century Christian debt to "a gnostic myth" assume a very significant degree of influence from a group which was evidently writing nothing of consequence and against whom we do not possess unambiguous examples of polemic.

[226] Ferguson, 249.

[227] The extreme scepticism of some about our ability to recover Jesus' own teaching is puzzling alongside the unflagging optimism that we can reconstruct a reliable picture of first century Gnosticism.

[228] Obviously, if a NT document, or at least the immediate context is itself "gnostic" then this would be sufficient to establish a "gnostic" use of the rest motif. I am assuming, however, that there is no such "gnostic" context in Mt 11 or Heb 3-4.

8. Summary and conclusions

Rather than detail the specific findings of the foregoing investigation relative to the individual domains of literature, a task already carried out in the summaries and one which will be pursued further in connection with the exegesis of Mt 11 and Heb 3-4, we will confine ourselves here to some general observations about the development of the motif in these writings.

"Rest" is a very common soteriological symbol in Jewish and Christian literature. On the one hand, we cannot fail to notice the pliability of the motif, the sheer variety of ways in which it is molded to the given interests, concerns, and eschatological outlooks. In spite of the elementary nature of the observation, we must say that while certain ideas are repeated -- e.g., the idea of heavenly and future resting places -- there appear to be no set guidelines in what can be done with the motif. Thus there is no basis for insisting that the NT passages we are about to consider must conform to this or that precedent, for if there is any common denominator in the other Jewish and Christian literature it is in the individualized use of the motif within the framework of a given outlook.

At the same time, in the idea of the eschatological Sabbath and in the various expectations of an other-worldly rest or resting place, the hope of rest has received definite shapes. Very often it is as an adaptation of OT ideas, but, in accordance with much larger trends, the hope of rest or of entrance into a resting place is increasingly projected into the ultimate future, possibly even into another (upper or future) world, and often into post-mortem existence. The expectation of an eschatological *Sabbath* is often encountered, albeit in different forms. The future age can itself be called a "day which is wholly Sabbath and rest" and the weekly Sabbath itself becomes a symbol of the coming age. The OT rest tradition is also projected into the future, and Ps 95 itself is applied to speculation about the עולם הבא. More than once the Sabbath and rest tradition converge in these hopes.[229] *These sorts of hopes are being repeatedly expressed during the time of the NT.*

Insofar as one can speak of the large-scale trends in eschatological speculation as a natural extension of the OT and as a property of the Judaisms represented in the main by the Pseudepigrapha and rabbinic literature, we can say that in most cases the rest motif is of a piece with this development. This generalization is set in relief by Philo, Wisdom of Solomon, the Gnostics, and Clement of Alexandria, in whom there is scarcely a residue of the OT with respect to the substance of the rest idea. The decisive factor here has become Greek philosophy, especially Platonic

---

[229] Supra, 122f., 128f. Also TDan 5,10-13?

metaphysics with the basic division between the transcendent, immutable world of stability and the material world of change and movement. "Rest" belongs to God by virtue of his nature and being, and it belongs to the transcendent world around God by virtue of its metaphysical character. Formally, it is the classical association of rest and wisdom which is taken up in these expressions: seeking wisdom, gnosis, brings rest. This is construed as a drawing near to God so as to share in his nature, which is rest.[230] The transformation of the basic wisdom expression into the Platonic form is subtle with WisSol, but it is expressed without reserve by Philo, and with Gnosticism it undergoes a further metamorphosis as it is shaped by the expressions of gnostic mythology; with Clement of Alexandria the tributaries of wisdom, Christianity, Philonism, and Gnosticism have become a wide river.

If we are going to isolate a use of the rest motif which is common to such literature (i.e., Philo, Gnosticism, etc.), it should be with reference to this sort of philosophical and metaphysical bent as characterizing the essence of the usage, and not merely the assignment of rest or the resting place to an upper world. The latter, as a general development in Jewish cosmology and eschatology, is too widespread and varied to be of much use in the attempt to make precise religious historical determinations *of the use of the rest motif* in a given NT writing. For instance, the κατάπαυσις-idea of Hebrews may conform to a "dualism" which locates salvation in the heavenly world and which foresees an ultimate removal of that which can be "shaken." In some respects this is reminiscent of JosAsen, which also makes use of Ψ 94,11 [95,11]. Yet this does not necessarily lead to the conclusion that the κατάπαυσις-idea in Hebrews is defined with reference to the immutability of God or *metaphysical* differences between heaven and creation, and it is not by itself an adequate basis for the hypothesis of indebtedness to Philonic or (proto) gnostic ἀνάπαυσις speculation. There may be potential indications of such dependence, and these might not be altogether misleading, but such dependence is not a necessary corollary of Hebrews' "dualism."[231]

---

[230] As Williams 1981, 827, remarks, "In Jewish wisdom literature, the prototype of the later Gnostic who is rescued from...errors and is restored to stability through reception of gnosis is the wise man who takes on wisdom's yoke and finds rest"; supra, 91ff.

[231] On the use of terms such as "dualism" in connection with Hebrews, see below, 253ff. In this paragraph we have used the term dualism in a broad and inclusive sense.

Appendix to Chapter Four

Rest in Gnostic Mythology

Jan Helderman provides the following schema in order to organize the many and multifarious uses of the rest motif in gnostic literature.[1] In order to supplement our brief discussion in Ch. Four we will summarize his schema here, along with a sampling of the textual evidence. The purpose of including this here is not only to provide an overview, but also to demonstrate the extent to which gnostic mythology has shaped the rest motif. One can justifiably speak of a "gnostic use" of the rest motif. Though an attempt has been made to cite the clearer examples in what follows, it is likely that the appropriateness of a few of the passages will be questioned. The gnostic manner of expression makes this unavoidable, and the reader is referred to the literature in the notes for a fuller exegesis of the passages cited along with further evidence.

Anapausis in the Pleroma

A. Anapausis as a name of the Father

...through the mercies of the Father the aeons may know him and cease laboring in search of the Father, resting there in him, knowing that this[2] is the rest. (*GosTruth* 24,14-20)

Ich preise Dich, o Ruhe... [ἀνάπαυσις][3]

He[4] received mingling with the Rest[5]... (*TriTrac* 90,20-21)[6]

---

[1] Vielhauer initiated the approach of schematicizing the gnostic idea of rest, and was followed in this by later discussions, most notably Hofius'. These earlier schemata are summarized by Helderman 1984, 22f. What follows is my own translation of Helderman's headings, 1984, 318f. Unless noted otherwise, the gnostic passages quoted or cited in the text are all from among those given direct attention by Helderman.

[2] "This" is "the Father"; cf. Hofius, 191 n. 459; Helderman 1984, 107.

[3] *Unbekanntes altgnostisches Werk* 22; quoted by Hofius, 76 (on this gnostic work see K. Rudolph 1984, 27f.); cf. Hofius, 76 for further examples.

[4] I.e., the Logos.

[5] I.e., the "Father"; cf. Helderman 1984, 286, who explains this statement with reference to *TriTrac* 72,14-16; 128,15-19; 91,3-5; and 122,23f.

[6] Cf. *GosTruth* 42,21-23, Helderman 1984, 223-225.

B. Anapausis as an attribute of the Father

...his gladness is in harmony with it, his glory has exalted it, his image has revealed it, his repose has received it into itself... (*GosTruth* 23,25-30)

They[7] possess his[8] head, which is rest for them... (*GosTruth* 41,28f.)[9]

C. Anapausis as a designation of the existence (*Dasein*) of the Father

And the will is what the Father rests in and is pleased with. (*GosTruth* 37,19-21)

...being himself unreachable and unwearied by that which he gives, since he is wealthy in the gifts which he bestows and at rest in the favors which he grants. (*TriTrac* 53,16-20)

D. Anapausis and the emanation of the Aeons or the Pneumatics

He [i.e. the Father] is good. He knows his plantings, because it is he who planted them in his paradise. Now his paradise is his place of rest. (*GosTruth* 36,35-39)

Who therefore, will be able to utter a name for him, the great name, except him alone to whom the name belongs, and the sons of the name in whom rested the name of the Father, (who) in turn themselves rested in his name? (*GosTruth* 38,25-32; cf. *TriTrac* 71,20-21)[10]

E. Anapausis and the stability (*Befestigung*) of the Aeons in the Pleroma

Each one of those [i.e. Aeons] who give glory has his place and his exaltation and his dwelling and his rest, which consists of the glory which he brings forth. (*TriTrac* 70,14-19)

The Logos added even more to their [i.e. the Aeons] mutual assistance and to the hope of the promise, since they have joy and abundant rest and undefiled pleasures. (*TriTrac* 92,4-9; cf. *GosTruth* 24,16-20)[11]

F. Anapausis and the restoration of Sophia or the Pneumatics into the Pleroma or the bridal chamber

About the place each one came from he [i.e. the Son] will speak, and to the region where he received his establishment he will hasten to return again and to take from that place -- the place where he stood -- receiving a taste from that place and receiving nourishment, receiving growth. And his[12] own resting-place is the pleroma. Therefore, all the emanations of the Father are pleromas... (*GosTruth* 41,3-16; cf. 43,1-3)

---

[7] I.e. the "emanations of the Father."

[8] I.e. the "Father's."

[9] Note also *TriTrac* 55,13-19; *Allogenes* 65.

[10] *TriTrac* 71,20-21 is translated in Helderman 1984, 285, "(der Äonen), indem sie Ort des ruhigen...Weges zu Ihm sind." The rest motif is not visible in the translation of *NHL*.

[11] Cf. the discussion of *GosTruth* 24,16-20 in, Helderman 1984, 98-107.

[12] I.e., the Pneumatic's; cf. Helderman 1984, 206, 216; cf. *TriTrac* 70,15ff.

And [they came to know] themselves, [(as to)who they are], or rather, where they are [now], and what is the [place in] which they will rest from their senselessness, [arriving] at knowledge. (*TestimTruth* 35,25-36,3)

From this time on will I [i.e. the ascending soul] attain to the rest of the time, of the season, of the aeon, in silence. (*GosMary* 17,4-7)

Anapausis in the between-world/the Ogdoad

G. Anapausis as a designation of the provisional salvation of the Pneumatic in the Ogdoad

While we are in this world it is fitting for us to acquire the resurrection, so that when we strip off the flesh we may be found in rest and not walk in the middle. For many go astray on the way. (*GosPhil* 66,16-21)[13]

H. Anapausis as a designation of the final, eschatological salvation of the Demiurge and the Psychic in the Ogdoad

For thus they were honored in every place by him, being pure, from the countenance of the one who appointed them, and they were established: paradises and kingdoms and rests and promises and multitudes of servants of his will, and though they are lords of dominions, they are set beneath the one who is lord, the one who appointed them. (*TriTrac* 102,16-26)[14]

Anapausis on earth

I[a]. Anapausis as a designation of the present salvation of the Pneumatic

Having knowledge, he does the will of the one who called him, he wishes to be pleasing to him, he receives rest. (*GosTruth* 22,9-12)

Feed those who are hungry and give repose to those who are weary... (*GosTruth* 33,3-5)[15]

And they [i.e. the Pneumatics] do not go down to Hades nor have they envy nor groaning nor death within them, but they rest in him who is at rest, not striving nor being twisted around the truth. But they themselves are the truth; and the Father is within them and

---

[13] Catagory G, although clearly evidenced in *ExcTheod* 63,1, was found by Helderman only in *GosPhil* 66,16-21, and here it is ambiguous; cf. 1984, 292 and 341. *ExcTheod* 63,1 reads, "Die Ruhe der Pneumatiker findet statt, ...in der Ogdoas" (1984, 87).

[14] Cf. the discussion in Helderman 1984, 289-291. Further examples: *TriTrac* 121,25-28; 131,20-21; 132,12-14 (1984, 291f.).

[15] In connection with *GosTruth* 33,3-5, Helderman 1984, 112-114, takes up the topic of "stability," which is essential to the gnostic idea of rest (cf. 1984, 69, 230, 338). J.W. Thompson, 90, comments, "The highest aeon is regularly described as being $\dot{\alpha}\sigma\dot{\alpha}\lambda\epsilon\nu\tau\sigma\varsigma$, $\dot{\alpha}\kappa\dot{\iota}\nu\eta\tau\sigma\varsigma$, and as possessing $\sigma\tau\dot{\alpha}\sigma\iota\varsigma$." He attributes this feature of gnostic thought -- which runs parallel to ideas already seen in Philo -- to Middle Platonism. On this cf. esp. Williams 1981 and 1985.

they are in the Father, being perfect, being undivided in the truly good one, being in no way deficient in anything, but they are set at rest, refreshed in the Spirit. (*GosTruth* 42,17-33)

[...My] Redeemer, redeem me, for [I am] yours; the one who has come forth from you. You are [my] mind; bring me forth! You are my treasure house; open for me! You [are] my fullness; take me to you! You are (my) repose; give me [the] perfect thing that cannot be grasped! (*PrPaul* A,3-10)[16]

I[b]. Anapausis as the experience of the unity (*Einigkeit*) of the Pneumatics with one another (Homonoia)

The children of the bridal chamber have [just one] name: rest... (*GosPhil* 72,22-23)

If you become one of those who belong above, it is those who belong above who will rest upon you. If you become horse or ass or bull or dog or sheep or another of the animals which are outside or below, then neither human being nor spirit nor thought nor light will be able to love you. Neither those who belong above nor those who belong within will be able to rest in you, and you have no part in them. (*GosPhil* 79,3-13)

I[c]. Anapausis in reference to the approved (*bewärten*) Psychic

He [i.e. the Demiurge] established a rest for those who obey him, but for those who disobey him, he also established punishments. (*TriTrac* 101,25-28)

A shorter version of the above schema was initially constructed by Helderman solely on the basis of evidence available prior to the discovery of the Nag Hammadi tractates. This first version of the schema was expanded in accordance with the usages which Helderman examined in the Valentinian *GosTruth*, and then brought to its final form with passages taken from the Nag Hammadi collection generally.[17] Although categories G-H were evidenced in the first draft of the schema (cf. *ExcTheod* 63,1; 65,2; and Iren, *Haer* I,7,1.5) they were *not* found to be represented in *GosTruth*, probably due to this book's stress on realized eschatology.[18] These categories were, however, evidenced in other gnostic documents.[19] Catagory I was expanded from I[a], which was visible in *GosTruth*, to I[b-c], in accordance with the evidence from the other writings.[20] Thus, aside from categories G-H and I[b-c], all these categories are utilized in the *one* gnostic document, *GosTruth*, and

---

[16] Cf. *ApJas* 3,24-34, and the discussion in Helderman 1978, 34-43; 1984, 283.

[17] For these developments in the schema, cf. Helderman 1984, 86f., 91f., 318f., and esp. 339.

[18] Helderman 1984, 91, 229.

[19] Helderman 1984, 319f. An example of category G was found only in *GosPhil* 66,16-21.

[20] Helderman 1984, 321.

all the categories are confirmed when a broader cross section of literature is taken in. This is taken by Helderman as strong evidence for the unified nature of this schema, and thus the gnostic idea of rest (at least in its Valentinian forms).

This unity is further demonstrated in that the entire complex is shown to revolve around the way-thought (*Weg-Gedanke*) which is essential to gnostic soteriology; thus one may speak of an "ascent to rest" (*Weg-hinauf-zur-Ruhe*).[21] "Aus der Unruhe der Welt gelangen die Gnostiker zur Ruhe der jenseitigen pleromatischen Welt des reinen Pneumas, woher sie stammten."[22] The "ascent" (*Weg-hinauf*), which assumes the "descent" or the "downward-development ("*Abwärtsentwicklung*"; the emanation of the Aeons, fall of Sophia, emergence of the pneumatic spark), is divided into distinct stretches (*Wegstrecken*). The "rest" which is appropriate to each such "stretch" has its own nuance according to its proximity to the goal: the "rest" in the Ogdoad is of another sort than that in the bridal chamber, etc. The levels are aligned according to the degree to which one draws near to the Father. The "ascent" leads from the earth, through the *Zwischenwelt*, the Ogdoad, up into the Pleroma and thus finally to the Father, who always possessed, possesses, and will possess rest (or: was, is, and will be "rest").[23]

So haben denn die unerschütterlichen, feststehenden Pneumatiker schliesslich den Weg zur Ruhe zurückgelegt und die Ruhe im von Ewigkeit her ruhenden, unerschütterlichen, feststehenden Vater erreicht, sind in den Ort der Ruhe eingetreten: diese wahrhaft letze, endgültige *statio* des Weges zur *Ruhe*, ohne Mühe, in tiefer Stille.[24]

---

[21] Helderman 1984, 14f.; 22-27; 85-87. Previous discussions of the gnostic rest-idea had stressed the *absence* of any unified conception (1984, 22f.).

[22] Helderman 1984, 344.

[23] Helderman 1984, 85f. In *GosTruth* there is a strong tendency to stress the anticipatory enjoyment of this salvific rest in the Father already in this life; in other words, there is a pronounced "realized eschatology," though not at the expense of a future realization (1984, 229f.; 339).

[24] Helderman 1984, 231 (italics in original); cf. 339. See the review of Helderman 1984 by Klijn.

Chapter Five

Mt 11,28-30 and Matthew's Wisdom Christology

1. Introduction

With the foregoing survey of the OT and other Jewish and Christian literature, much of the ground has been prepared for a consideration of the rest motif in Mt 11,28-30. There remains, however, some ground to clear.

In Mt 11,28-30 the rest motif is contained in a saying which is considered by most scholars to be an allusion to Sir 51 and a component of Matthew's Wisdom Christology.[1] Matthew's alleged Wisdom Christology is admittedly not visible to the naked eye, but if we arrange the wisdom parallels in a certain way, lay Matthew's translucent text over them, *and*[2] view the whole through the filters of source, form, and redaction criticism, then Jesus Sophia's figure materializes before us with astonishing clarity; it is to Suggs' lasting credit to have demonstrated this clearly. Though the obvious importance of the ἀνάπαυσις-idea to both Sirach and Mt 11,28-30 has attracted some attention, this element of the Logion has usually been treated in a subordinate fashion; the primary interest has been in the Wisdom Christology. It is the "yoke" image which moves to the fore, as it is seen to symbolize the Law in the shape of Wisdom.

It is evident that if Matthew did have a special interest in a Wisdom Christology then it is probable that he would have associated 11,28-30 with it.[3] Including 11,28-30, three of Matthew's five alleged Wisdom Christology passages fall in ch. 11 (vv. 19.25-27.28-30; cf. 23,34-36.37-39)

---

[1] This became apparent in the review of the history of interpretation; supra, 2ff.

[2] This "and" is necessary; a knowledge of the wisdom parallels does not itself bring to light Matthew's special interest in Wisdom. This necessary application of redaction criticism is one important distinction between Matthew's interest in Wisdom and his interest in Moses, whom he also nowhere compares *directly* to Jesus; another difference is in that Matthew's Wisdom Christology is said to be an innovation, whereas the comparison with Moses would probably be traditional.

[3] See, however, Stanton 1992a, 366ff.; 1973, 36-38; Piper, 163; Gundry, 213, 220; Carson 277f., 484. All these affirm Matthew's general interest in a Wisdom Christology while rejecting it in their interpretation of 11,28-30.

and vv. 28-30 are directly appended by Matthew to one of the others; indeed, the Logion itself is a favorite child of this modern day exegetical tradition. In this light, the argument is compelling for many that Matthew's *primary* interest in including 11,28-30 was in drawing a parallel with the Wisdom sayings of Sirach.

Nevertheless, this way of approaching 11,28-30 has located the Logion in a conceptual framework which is of doubtful value to Matthew's purposes[4] and which tends to lead us away from the more likely Matthean interest. Yet before turning to examine Matthew's Gospel on this point we can use the perspective already gained from the overview of Jewish and Christian literature (Ch. Four) to correct one general misperception. We have noted that the interest in Matthew's Wisdom Christology is often fuelled by a more general interest in the development from wisdom thought to Gnosticism;[5] Mt 11,28-30 is sometimes used as a convenient example of this development as it resembles a wisdom saying (Sir 51) and is taken up into gnostic writings (esp. *GosThom* 90).

For example, H.D. Betz, in his important treatment of this saying, considers the wisdom parallel of Sir 51, the gnostic parallels (esp. *GosThom* 90; *Pistis Sophia* 95), and the "chain saying" of *GosHeb*, and having determined that *GosThom* and *Pistis Sophia* were not dependent on Matthew, he concludes that,

> ...we begin to suspect that in all cases we are dealing with wisdom sayings, originally independent, which were gnosticized and then were taken up in different variants into the Gospel of Matthew, the Gospel of Thomas, and the Pistis Sophia...[We] can observe the logion at three different points on its way from wisdom literature to Gnosticism: in wisdom thought itself, in Matthew, and in gnostic thought.[6]

From this observation about religious historical parallels he draws a conclusion as to methodology: "methodologically it is advisable first to seek out and set the relatively clear terminal points in the history of interpretation, in order to sense the meaning of the passage within Matthew's theology."[7]

Later on in this chapter[8] we will examine in some detail the relation of Mt 11,28-30 to Sirach, and also the value of the gnostic parallels for

---

[4] There does not seem to be a void if we remove Matthew's Wisdom Christology. E.g., Davies-Allison, 2:295, comment that "we have not found Matthew's Wisdom Christology to be of great aid in coming to terms with his gospel or his theology"; similarly, Stanton 1992a, 44. The most France, 306, can say is that this theme "fits in...with a whole way of thinking about Jesus which emerges in other ways throughout the gospel." Yet is not this to say that it says nothing distinctive at all?
[5] Supra, 5ff.
[6] Betz, 20.
[7] Betz, 20.
[8] Infra, 186ff.

Chapter Five: Matthew's Wisdom Christology 161

determination of Matthean redaction. It is the prior question of Betz' overall methodology which interests us here. He places a lost group of "originally independent" wisdom sayings on an equal footing and then posits a monolithic "gnosticizing" process to which they were all subjected *before* any of them appeared in writing, including Mt 11,28-30. From here he suggests that we will only understand Mt 11,28-30 if we reckon with the Logion's interpretation in its extra-Matthean contexts, including the gnostic writings.

It is difficult, however, to accept Betz' methodology as stated. To begin with, one would need an extremely broad definition of Gnosticism to say that the Logion in *Matthew's* context is "gnostic" in any meaningful sense, even if a connection is being drawn between Jesus and personified Wisdom.[9] Moreover, by Betz' own reckoning, Mt 11 draws on a source which is *independent* of the gnostic writers' sources. If there is nothing gnostic about the saying in Mt 11, which is certainly the case, then what evidence is there that the saying had been "gnosticized" (whatever that means) in Matthew's source before he took it up?

The "chain saying" in *GosHeb* is at best a distant relative of Mt 11,28-30 which has either long since mutated, or which was only secondarily influenced by our Logion.[10] Neither of these options is a necessary explanation, considering the wide usage of the rest motif. The various versions of the "chain saying" do not evidence a group of independent wisdom sayings which can be assumed to underlie our Logion.[11]

We are forced to ask, further, what we know about the history of unknown, "originally independent" wisdom sayings upon which *GosThom*, for instance, drew and *not* Matthew. Gnostic writers or editors would have taken up the Logion (= Mt 11,28-30) as a word of the "Savior" and as an expression of a favorite motif: "rest."[12] Their willingness to re-contextualize and re-shape non-gnostic sayings makes it impossible to know if any "gnosticizing" process had already taken place in their source. Recognition of the sheer ubiquity of the rest motif in Jewish and Christian writings has made obsolete any suggestion that the motif itself as a

---

[9] Against any gnostic ideas in Mt 11,28-30, cf. Christ, 100-119.

[10] Stroker, 116-119, gives an extended list of parallels to this "chain saying," none of which show any debt to the Logion of Mt 11,28-30. That the chain saying (*GosThom* 2; POx 654) may have been somehow *associated* with Mt 11,28-30 may be evidenced in the positioning of *GosThom* 90 in relation to logia 92 and 94.

[11] Koester 1971, 183 n. 84, also associates the saying in the *GosHeb* with Mt 11,28-30, though he is rightly cautious about connecting them (1980, 246); likewise Vielhauer and Strecker, in *NTApocr*², 1:175.

[12] The gnostic writers exploit the saying for the sake of the rest motif, and not with any sense that the saying depends on Sir 6 or 51; i.e., not with any sense that it expresses a Wisdom Christology.

soteriological symbol is inherently "gnostic."[13] Thus we cannot even know if *GosThom*'s source had been previously "gnosticized."

I do not see, therefore, that Betz' counsel on methodology is good since it pretends to know more than we do about the meaning of the pre-Matthean form of 11,28-30 and since it encourages an anachronistic interpretation of the gnostic parallels such as *GosThom* 90. To speak of a "gnosticizing" process is misleading inasmuch as it implies an inexorable development from Sir 51 to *GosThom* 90, in which development Mt 11,28-30 somehow participates *by design*.[14] Without excluding in principle the possibility that the later gnostic parallels are consistent developments in the use of the Logion, their potential usefulness for determining the significance of the Logion in its earlier usage, especially in Matthew, has been unduly exaggerated.

Therefore, leaving behind any suggestion that Mt 11,28-30 *must* be interpreted with regard to Sir 51 and the later gnostic parallels, it remains for us to examine in detail first, the extent and nature of Matthew's interest in a Wisdom Christology generally, and second, the relationship of 11,28-30 to Sir 51. As will be seen, both of these have also been exaggerated, and evidence that Matthew had quite different interests in including Mt 11,28-30 has too often been ignored. The task of this chapter will be then to clear the way for a better understanding of Matthew's concerns by breaking the spell which Sirach has held over our Logion. The approach will be to review the Wisdom myth (§ 2), to examine the main passages outside of 11,28-30 for Matthew's Wisdom Christology (§ 3), and finally to examine 11,28-30, especially in terms of a comparison with Sirach (§ 4). In the next chapter we will advance to a more promising interpretation of Matthew's use of this invitation and promise.

One further methodological note pertaining to our work with Matthew is in order. It is has been convincingly argued that Matthew knew Greek and

---

[13] According to Vielhauer, 281, "rest" as a *Heilsgut* is "fast völlig fremd" to the NT; it is "ein spezifisch gnostischer Begriff." In support of this he cites the work of Haenchen 1961, 73f.; Käsemann, 68-75, and Dibelius, 280, who labels "rest" in Mt 11,28-30 a "totally unevangelical idea." This assessment of the rest motif presumably underlies the judgment of Vielhauer and Strecker (in *NTApocr*², 1:175) that Mt 11,28-30 is a "foreign body in the synoptic tradition," and Bultmann's remark (1964, 367) that the "eschatological ἀνάπαυσις" is "found in Gnosticism but not in the NT." If all that is meant by such claims is that in the NT rest "is not a technical term directly connected with the state of salvation, as it is in Scriptures Gnostic in origin or influenced by Gnosticism" (Gärtner, 265), then the claim can be accepted; there is a real qualitative and quantitative difference here. But the aforementioned claims appear to go far beyond this sober judgment.

[14] Rightly, Luck, 50 n. 50; Albright-Mann, 146.

Hebrew and that he "knew the OT both in Greek and Hebrew."[15] This is the assumption on which we will work, and if it should be rejected or disproved, our work will need to be modified in some minor points.[16] On our assumption it is reasonable to cite parallels from either the MT or the LXX or from both of those as potential influences on Matthew's thinking.[17]

2. The Wisdom myth[18]

Already we have had several occasions to make reference to personified Wisdom, but since she will become a central actress in the following discussion it will be well to reacquaint the reader with her briefly. This aim is best accomplished through a brief presentation so as not to lose ourselves in information, and the present needs render anything more unnecessary.[19]

---

[15] Davies-Allison, 1:33, who provide an extensive list of evidence in chart form (1:34-57); likewise, Gundry 1967, 147-150, 174-178, and *passim*; Goulder 1974, 123-127; Prabhu, 63-106; Moo, 178-182, 189-210, 352-356, 367f.; Stanton 1992a, 346-363 (Stanton poses the question directly, "Was the LXX Matthew's Bible?" but answers more guardedly: "not necessarily"); cf. Stendahl, 97-127, 138-142, 150f. (Stendahl's argument applies more directly to an alleged "school of St. Matthew" from which Matthew drew). The issue is of course debated, with others contending that Matthew knew only the LXX (e.g., Bacon, 477; Clark, 168-171; Strecker 1962, 24-85). We will not be able to deal with this complex issue here, as it cannot be settled apart from a detailed examination of a number of passages such as Prabhu undertakes for Matthew's infancy narrative, Moo for the passion narrative, and Gundry for the entire Gospel.

[16] E.g., cf. Jer 6,16, infra, 227f., where the parallel to the Logion depends on the Hebrew. Yet since the rest tradition is just as prominent in the LXX as in the MT I expect that the general case I will be making will also be strong on the assumption that Matthew knew only the LXX.

[17] See also our remarks above, 17 n. 1, 77 n. 1, and below, 210 n. 3.

[18] By the Wisdom "myth" I will be referring more loosely to the broader spectrum of features and actions typically associated with Wisdom in discussions of her, although here our presentation will be more illustrative than inclusive. In the interests of explaining second century Gnosticism, the Wisdom "myth" has often been used more narrowly of a story line which Lang, 141, summarizes as follows: "Wisdom is of heavenly origin. One day she descended from heaven to earth, desiring to dwell among humans. She was rejected, however, and in resignation returned to her celestial abode." In this sense the "myth" lies more behind than in our present Wisdom texts; Sir 24, which suggests that Wisdom found a home in Israel, is thus a reworking of the "myth." Lang himself, 141-144, asserts that in the latter sense the Wisdom myth is "an invention and construction of modern scholarship" which has not "stood the test of recent criticism"; likewise, D.W. Smith, 13f. Cf. further Fiorenza, 22-33, and the literature in the following note.

[19] For discussions of Wisdom which touch the present concerns one should now begin with Witherington. There are several briefer summaries carried out with a view to Matthew's Christology, including Suggs; Deutsch 1987; 1990, 17-31; Burnett, 94-98; Dunn 1989, 168-176; and J.M. Robinson 1975, 1-8. A fairly comprehensive listing of

Anyone acquainted with the OT will quickly recall the passages where wisdom is spoken of in very vivid and personal terms; she is, for instance, portrayed as a woman calling out on the street corner, or it is said that her "place" cannot be found by people though they tunnel to the foundations of mountains or sail over seas in search of her.[20] When one conducts a closer reading and comparison of these and similar passages the picture of Wisdom begins to gain in texture and outline, even if enough vagueness remains to sustain lively debate over specific, albeit at times important, features and patterns.

To begin with, Wisdom is conceived of as having been present with God at creation -- she is in some sense pre-existent -- and as having had a mediatorial role in that act.[21] In these terms one thinks of NT passages such as the "hymns" of Colossians and Hebrews, where Jesus is depicted in similar fashion.[22] It is not merely that there is a common way of talking about pre-existence and creation which comes to expression independently in the cases of Wisdom and Jesus, but that the description of Jesus appears to be indebted to that of Wisdom.

In these NT hymns there is, of course, a common substance and method. The substance is primarily that of pre-existence and creation, and the method is not so much to identify Jesus and Wisdom (i.e., to *say* that Jesus is Wisdom, or to call him Wisdom) as to depict him in terms elsewhere used unmistakably of her. It is when we come to the Logos Christology of John that we find an explicit identification made, and also a somewhat more involved story line. Here it is not merely pre-existence and creation, but a coming, an incarnation, and rejection.[23] These latter traits are more typical of the features of the Wisdom myth which are accentuated for the purposes of setting in relief Matthew's Wisdom Christology, though Matthew's

---

relevant Wisdom texts is set out in tables by Christ, 156-163. Further discussion and bibliography may be found in Wilckens 1972, 507-515; R. Meyer, 821f.; Mack 1970; 1973; Ringgren; Camp; von Rad 1972b, 144ff.; Hengel 1974, 1:153-175; Bultmann 1967; Conzelmann, 230-243; Gese.

[20] In general on Wisdom cf. Job 28; Prov 1; 8; 9. Cf. among others also WisSol 6,12-11,1; Sir 6; 24; 51; 1Bar 3,9-4,4. 1En 37-71 (the Similitudes) are usually discussed as well; esp. 1En 42.

[21] Cf. Job 28,25f.; Prov 3,19f.; 8,23-31; Sir 24,3-6; Philo, *Det* 54; *Fuga* 109; *Virt* 62.

[22] For parallels to Colossians 1,15-20, cf. e.g. Prov 8,22.25.27-30; WisSol 7,26; Sir 1,4; 24,9; 43,26; in Philo, *LegAll* I,43; *QuaesGen* IV,97; *QuaesEx* II,118; *Ebr* 30f.; *Heres* 188; 199; *Fuga* 112; in Aristobulus (Eusebius, *PraepEvang* 13,12). For parallels to Heb 1,3f., in addition to several of the foregoing (esp. WisSol 7,26), cf. Philo, *Plant* 8f.; 18; *Heres* 36; *Mut* 256; *Somn* I,241. For a general discussion of the NT hymns from this viewpoint, see Witherington, 249-294.

[23] Cf. e.g. WisSol 9,9; Aristobulus (Eusebius, *PraepEvang* 13,12,10); 1En 42,2; Sir 24,8.

Chapter Five: Matthew's Wisdom Christology

apparent method comes closer to the pictorial comparisons of Colossians and Hebrews than to the direct identification of John.[24]

Thus in the wisdom literature Wisdom is portrayed as calling out to people to heed her, to acquire wisdom.[25] She utters stern warnings, even prophetic oracles of doom,[26] against those who do not heed her call. If anyone does not heed her, she warns, she will withdraw from them and they will not be able to find her though they search for her.[27] The basis of this principle in everyday experience is plain enough, whatever the mythological precedents.

Wisdom is increasingly taken up into the history and institutions of Israel. Thus she is seen to have been at work not only in creation, but in the great redemptive events of Israel's history. She appears as personally involved with the chief figures of Israel's past, watching over them for their good.[28] She finds concrete expression in the Law.[29] In an important chapter of Sirach (ch. 24), many of these traits converge, as Wisdom's role in creation gives way to Wisdom's search for a resting place ($ἀνάπαυσις/κατάπαυσις$) among the nations. Picturing Wisdom as the ark which housed the tablets of the covenant (cf. 24,23),[30] and calling upon the OT temple traditions (2Sam 6-7; 1Chr 6,31; 28; 2Chr 6; Ps 132), it is said that God gave Wisdom rest ($καταπαύω$) among an honored people, among Israel. This accounts for the blessings which Israel has enjoyed, even as wisdom is generally associated with the good life.

One feature of the myth, important for discussions of Matthew's Wisdom speculation but somewhat more vague in the wisdom traditions, is the notion

---

[24] Cf. Jacobson, 228.

[25] Prov 1; 8,1ff.; 9,1-6; WisSol 6,13.16; Sir 24,1ff.19-22.

[26] Prov 1,20-33; Suggs, 16-20. Cf. also Sir 24,33; WisSol 7,27, where the sage's teaching is like prophecy.

[27] Variously expressed in Prov 1,24.28; 1Bar 3,12; 4,12 (cf. 4,1); 1En 93,8. Most important for the withdrawal motif is 1En 42; cf. also 4Ezra 5,9f. Sir 24,8ff., where Wisdom finds a home in Israel (likewise 1Bar 3,15-4,4), stands in sharp contrast to 1En 42.

[28] Cf. Sir. 24,8ff.; WisSol 10,1-11,8.

[29] Esp. Sir 24,23; cf. also WisSol 6,4.9; 9,9; Sir 24,7-11; 51,26 (cf. Deut 30,11-14); 1Bar 3,9; 3,36-4,4; 1En 42; 2Bar 38,4; 51,3f.7; TLevi 13. Cf. Gese, 35f. Witherington, 86, 92-99, corrects the common mistake of identifying Wisdom and the Law in Sirach. Rather, for Sirach, Wisdom remained more general than the Law, which was a particular embodiment of Wisdom.

[30] As always the language is extremely fluid; in the midst of this comparison to the ark, it is said that Wisdom is ministering before God, thus comparing her to the priesthood; in the same chapter of Sirach she is the Spirit (covering creation like a mist; cf. also Isa 11,2; WisSol 1,6-7; 7,22; 9,17; 1En 49,3), a flourishing plant, fruit, spices and incense, honey, water, the Law, a river, and prophecy. This rich mixture of metaphors makes it very easy, too easy, to select traits like beads and to string them into various patterns for the purposes of demonstrating this or that Christological parallel.

that Wisdom sends out her call through human envoys who are rejected, even as she is rejected.[31] A key proof text in this regard is WisSol 7,27f.:

> ...in every generation she passes into holy souls and makes them friends of God, and prophets; for God loves nothing so much as the person who lives with wisdom.

The typical figure of WisSol 2,10-24 is then recalled, where the righteous/wise man is one who claims to have a knowledge of God, and calls himself a child of God. The wicked condemn him to a shameful death on the contemptuous premise that if he is truly God's son then God will deliver him (cf. Ps 22,8f.). In the end, God does indeed vindicate him through the gift of immortality and eternal rest.[32] The same idea is thought to be at work in WisSol 10-11 where Israel's history is rehearsed and Wisdom's continual *protective* role is highlighted.[33]

The foregoing is certainly not an exhaustive catalogue of the features of the Wisdom myth, but those which are important will be brought up in the following discussion where they are appropriate. For now it suffices to have sketched in a few of the main outlines, and the groundwork has thus been adequately laid to advance to a discussion of the primary Matthean Wisdom texts. For its part, Mt 11,28-30 has nothing to do with pre-existence, creation, or rejected envoys. Here we are said to be dealing with a modified wisdom saying which on the one hand reinforces the impression of Matthew's interest in a Wisdom Christology, and on the other hand reminds us of the role of Wisdom *qua* Law, thus appearing to relate to that Matthean theme. Nonetheless, it is not likely that Matthew's approach to the Law

---

[31] M.D. Johnson, 44-64 (esp. 46-53), argues that when the most promising Wisdom texts are examined (Prov 9,3-6; Sir 24; 39,1-11; 44,3; 51; WisSol 7,27; 10-11; 1Bar 3,37; 1En 42; OdesSol 33,5-9) we are without evidence of Wisdom becoming "incarnate" or sending "envoys" who deliver her oracles (M.D. Johnson, 52, concedes that later thinkers may have read the notion of "envoys" into these texts, but maintains that it is not there in the texts themselves); likewise Gnilka, 2:300 n. 18; Meadors, 44; *contra* Bultmann 1967, 10-35; and Suggs, 38-44 and *passim*. Johnson's view has been seconded by Tuckett 1983, 164f., and Piper, 169, though they affirm Matthew's Wisdom Christology; their view is that the idea of Wisdom's rejected envoys was first conceived in the Q community. Mack 1971, is also more sympathetic with Suggs' overall thesis, though critical of Suggs' treatment of "Wisdom's envoys." Further texts discussed in this connection include WisSol 6,16; 39,1-11. Solomon is said to serve as an example in WisSol 6,1.4f.9.22, and Jesus ben Sirach as an example in Sir 24,30-34.

[32] WisSol 3,1ff.; 4,7. Cf. Sir 51,1-12, though the focus there is on *God* as the deliverer.

[33] It must be stressed that the tone of WisSol 10-11 is very different from the aspect of the myth it is usually called on to support. The human figures of WisSol 10-11 are not explicitly sent out by Wisdom, though she is said to guide them; Wisdom is sent out by God (9,10.17). More importantly, rather than focusing on the rejection of her "envoys," this passage focuses on the *preserving* role of Wisdom in Israel's history; this is a far cry from Mt 23,34-39.

owes much to wisdom conceptions.³⁴ Thus our attention will focus on the prior question of whether in using the Logion Matthew appears to have been interested primarily in Wisdom.

3. Matthew's Wisdom Christology?³⁵

3.1. Mt 11,19 (Q 7,35)

The Wisdom interpretation of this passage is founded on the twin editorial changes of Mt 11,2 and 11,19. Placing Mt 11,2 and Lk 7,18 side by side yields the following comparison:

Mt 11,2	Lk 7,18
Ὁ δὲ Ἰωάννης ἀκούσας ἐν τῷ δεσμωτηρίῳ **τὰ ἔργα τοῦ Χριστοῦ**	Καὶ ἀπήγγειλαν Ἰωάννῃ οἱ μαθηταὶ αὐτοῦ περὶ **πάντων τούτων**
When John heard in prison about **the deeds of the Messiah**...³⁶	The disciples of John reported **all these things** to him.

The phrase, τὰ ἔργα τοῦ Χριστοῦ, is generally understood as Matthew's editorial addition and a significant phrase referring to the totality of the messiah's deeds.³⁷ Following on from this there is a similar Matthean redaction in 11,19:

Mt 11,19	Q 7,35	Lk 7,35
καὶ ἐδικαιώθη ἡ σοφία ἀπὸ **τῶν ἔργων αὐτῆς**	καὶ ἐδικαιώθη ἡ σοφία ἀπὸ τῶν τέκνων αὐτῆς³⁸	καὶ ἐδικαιώθη ἡ σοφία ἀπὸ τῶν τέκνων αὐτῆς **πάντων**
wisdom is vindicated **by her deeds**	wisdom is vindicated by her children	wisdom is vindicated **by all her children**

Once again, Matthew's reading ("her works") is generally attributed to Matthew's hand.³⁹ The point is that if we read the two Matthean changes

---

³⁴ So Davies-Allison, 2:295.
³⁵ On Mt 8,20 cf. Kloppenborg 1987, 192; Piper, 165f.; Davies-Allison, 2:43. Discussions of other alleged Wisdom passages are summarized in Piper, 165f., 261 n. 31; cf. D.W. Smith, 79-101. We will confine ourselves to the passages where this aspect of Matthew's theology is usually thought to be most pronounced.
³⁶ Modified NRSV.
³⁷ Cf. Mt 11,4f.20-24. and Burnett, 89-91.
³⁸ "All" is generally considered Lukan; cf. Fitzmyer 1981, 679, 681; Carson 1994, 144; other views summarized in Piper, 168f. Cf. Jacobson, 89-91.
³⁹ E.g., Lührmann, 29-31; S. Schulz, 380 n. 18; Kloppenborg 1987, 110 n. 36. The text of Mt 11,19 is accepted as in NA²⁷.

together, Matthew narrows the referent of 11,19 to Jesus (as against the plural "all her children" of Luke), and thus suggests the interpretation, "Christ (Wisdom) is justified by his (her) deeds."[40]

There is, however, more to the argument than this. Beyond the mere fact of the twin editorial changes, v. 19b is taken as an addition to the parable which looks back to the entire section (vv. 2-19), functioning as an *inclusio* with v. 2.[41] The problems of the space between the two verses and the fact that ἔργα "is a common and colorless word"[42] are not felt; the assumption is that Matthew crafted the passage so that his readers would be alerted to the connection and thus identify the works in v. 19 restrictively as the "Christ's."

It is usually *assumed*[43] that the reference to σοφία is a reference to the cosmic, mythological figure, Wisdom, although the rhetorical device of personification might have been used in this saying simply because it was usual to do so with wisdom. There is no lead in or cue for the momentous appearance of *Wisdom* here,[44] and there is no *open* development of the Wisdom Christology in the subsequent context. She makes a rather startling entrance and just as suddenly withdraws. Neither the word σοφία nor σοφός occurs previous to 11,19, and thereafter they are descriptive of character traits or personal capacities.[45] The only real evidence that the referent of this

---

[40] E.g. Suggs, 56f.; Burnett, 91; Dunn 1989, 197; Christ, 75-77; Patte, 162, 202 n. 38; many others.

[41] Suggs, 34-38; Burnett, 85ff.; cf. Davies-Allison, 2:264.

[42] M. Smith, quoted from private correspondence in Suggs, 37 n. 13. Suggs' response exaggerates how unusual this language is and only assumes that the referent of the noun σοφία is lady Wisdom.

[43] This common assumption is rightly questioned by Winton, 20. D.W. Smith, 48f., does discuss the point.

[44] Piper, 165, 167, admits as much, though he affirms that this is a reference to Wisdom. Neither the Law in Matthew (Suggs, 99-127), nor the Matthean Son of Man (Suggs, 48-55; Gese, 38ff.) are clearly Wisdom themes, and lend scant supporting evidence; cf. Davies-Allison, 2:295; Guelich, 258. The Son of Man figure is nowhere identified with Wisdom in the Jewish writings (Deutsch 1987, 64f., 104f.; Piper, 163; Kloppenborg 1978, 141), and the relationship between Wisdom and the Son of Man is too easily exaggerated in the interests of setting in relief Matthew's Wisdom speculation. Yet the Matthean Wisdom Christology probably needs the Son of Man Christology more than the Matthean Son of Man needs Wisdom (cf. Piper, 186, 265 n. 78). Witherington, 357f., is more cogent when he shows the wisdom character of Jesus' teaching prior to ch. 11 and suggests that all of this is preparation for the announcement of 11,19. Yet I would maintain that if we did not begin reading the Gospel looking for Wisdom behind every pericope, as does Witherington, we would not think to find her in 11,19.

[45] Cf. Mt 12,42; 13,54; 11,25; 23,34. It is not merely that Matthew does not make an explicit connection between Jesus and Wisdom, but that he does not even use the figure of personification again in connection with the word σοφία. This is extraordinary in a writer who is alleged to have had such a developed interest in the idea of Jesus Sophia.

noun σοφία in v. 19b was understood to be the mythological figure -- aside from the question begging assumption that Matthew and his readers *would* have had her in mind -- is the reconstructed myth of Wisdom's envoys,[46] as Suggs explains with reference to the Q version (Q 7,35):

> Even though her [Wisdom's] characterizations in our diverse sources are fluid, certain traits are clear. Wisdom is a personified entity, with characteristics that are potentially fully mythological. She searches for men with a view to redeeming them. She sends her messengers (who may be individuals or the nation); she is found uniquely in the law. But, tragically, both she and her envoys are rejected by men.
> *When we set Matt. 11:2-19, Luke 7:18-35 in that context*, Q's saying about Wisdom's "children" (Luke 7:35) becomes transparent. Jesus and John are, as the logion implies, Sophia's representatives. They are, in fact, the eschatological emissaries who, like the emissaries before them, are rejected... "Yet Wisdom is justified by her children" -- that is, by Jesus and John in whose ministries her righteousness is demonstrated.[47]

Approaching Mt 11,19 from this angle involves some misrepresentation, however. There is no evidence that Matthew's readers possessed a triglot version of his Gospel -- the Gospel, Q, and the wisdom texts in parallel columns -- and what is almost always overlooked is that Matthew's version of the saying does not remind us of this story line in the least; Mt 11,19b does not so much as hint at *envoys*.[48] Grasping Matthew's meaning ultimately hinges, therefore, on an assumed familiarity with the wording of Q, and on being conversant in the wisdom speculation of the Q community in connection with the Q form of saying.[49] These are the essential

---

Clearly his reticence on this point cannot be due to general Christian traditions and conventions, as Q 11,49 makes plain.

[46] Cf. Stanton 1973, 36f., with reference to Q. Tuckett 1983, 164f., and Piper, 169, see no pre-Christian idea of Wisdom's envoys; they believe that the idea of Wisdom's envoys was itself conceived in the double tradition. Maybe it is idle to ask now whether the whole thesis of Matthew's Wisdom Christology would have even taken off if it had not been for the belief of Suggs and others that there *was* a pre-Christian idea of Wisdom's envoys.

[47] Suggs, 44, emphasis mine.

[48] M.D. Johnson, 57f., argues that the appropriate Wisdom background to Mt 11,19 would not be that of Wisdom's "envoys" but that of Wisdom's vindication in her "work" of creation (cf. Prov 8,22; 16,9.11; Sir 1,19; 18,1-4).

[49] One of the strengths of Suggs' work, it seems to me, is that it assumes that Matthew is not only heir to a saying (11,19), but to an *interpreted* saying; Matthew's redaction is not merely in relation to an accepted background (wisdom texts) but is in *dialogue* with an established and specific *Christian* strain of Wisdom speculation, one which had lodged Q 7,35 (Mt 11,19) in speculation about Wisdom's *envoys*. Matthew's Gospel was designed to be read primarily with respect to in-house, Christological disputes. Not all scholars who agree with Suggs' conclusions appear to follow through with his consideration of the interpretive context of the saying in the pre-Matthean Christian speculation, but neither do they provide -- as Suggs does -- a coherent historical framework within which the developing Wisdom speculation and its specific exegetical traditions make sense.

mechanisms of the Wisdom Christology in this passage, and not the *inclusio* or even the wisdom parallels.

This need of familiarity with Q is further impressed on us when we admit how naturally the saying reads like a general proverb. "A metaphorical personification of Wisdom in this context would seem to be an appropriate way of commending wise action, or ironically rebuking those whose actions were foolish."[50] This interpretation makes perfectly good sense in this context, and the ironic twist is consistent with the use of σοφός in Mt 11,25 which it may well anticipate.[51]

I am not arguing that the saying could not be taken as a statement about Jesus as Wisdom; given the right conditions it plainly could. The question is whether Matthew has done enough to alert any but the initiated[52] reader of what he is playing at...if indeed he is trying to identify Jesus with Wisdom at all. I myself find it unlikely that Matthew would have composed this passage so that its message could have been grasped only on the terms specified above. Yet questions such as whether Matthew's readers *would* have read him in the manner Suggs proposes, or whether Matthew could have expected them to, are at least premature. Given the level of ambiguity in the passage we may do better to continue on with our survey to see if there is better evidence elsewhere as to *Matthew's* interests. If it should emerge that Matthew is unconcerned to *express* the equation, Jesus = Wisdom, then we may with good reason eliminate that equation as the motive behind the redaction of 11,2-19.[53]

---

[50] Winton, 140; cf. T.W. Manson, 363; Meadors, 38; also the discussion in D.W. Smith, 48f. An additional ambiguity in this passage is that the "deeds" of 11,19 arguably include those of John and/or the disciples; cf. Mt 10,1.7-8; Held, 252; Davies-Allison, 2:240. In this case, "Wisdom's" deeds are not merely those of Jesus but also those of John and/or the disciples; M.D. Johnson, 57; Verseput 1987, 553 n. 51; most recently, Carson 1994, 133f.

[51] Others who steer away from a Wisdom Christology in 11,19 include Schmid, 195; Carson, 270f.; Mounce, 104; Hill, 202; Fenton, 182; Harrington, 158; Bruner, 423; Verseput 1986, 115f. (cf. Verseput 1986, 358 n. 209 for further literature; also 1987, 552 n. 43, 553 n. 51). Catchpole, 170, notes that Matthew's redaction draws Jesus and Wisdom closer together, but is unwilling to speak of a straight identification because of the use of αὐτῆς. D.W. Smith, 50-53, documents the wide range of proposed understandings of this verse.

[52] France, 183f., argues that Matthew consciously wrote for "different levels of comprehension" among his readers. Cf. in this connection Luz, 2:189: "Man darf sich diese Identifikation [of Jesus and Wisdom] m.E. nicht als einen bewußten theologischen Neuentwurf vorstellen. Matthäus identifiziert nie direkt Jesus mit der göttlichen Weisheit, sondern er setzt nur gerade ihre Identität voraus." Note, however, that Luz' suggestion contrasts with Suggs, Dunn, and others who stress emphatically that Matthew himself was responsible for the promotion of Jesus to the status of Wisdom.

[53] Cf. Verseput 1986, 116 (also, Verseput 1987, 553 n. 51).

3.2. Mt 11,25-27 (Q 10,21-22)

The context of this passage in Q appears to have been that of Lk 10,2-16.[54] This embraces the pronouncement of eschatological woes in Mt 11,20-24, but means that the context of Mt 11,2-19 is due to Matthean redaction. Vv. 28-30 were not in Q and their placement here is thus also due to Matthew's hand.

If we were to observe the strict concern of the present argument then we could justifiably pass over this passage with only brief comment for the following reason. The question of a Wisdom Christology in Mt 11,25-27 does not hinge in the first place on Matthean changes internal to 11,25-27,[55] but rather on the question of whether v. 27 represents a fully developed Wisdom Christology already in Q 10,22. If this is answered in the negative, then an appeal is made to the Matthean context, i.e. the placement of the saying in relation to Mt 11,19 and, more importantly, 11,28-30.[56] But many of those inclined to accept that Q 10,21f. effectively identified Jesus and Wisdom in the last stages of Q still see a clear enhancement of this Christology in Matthew's placement of the saying and the addition of 11,28-30.[57] Either way, then, it is the *context* which is the key to Matthew's Christological interests, and not so much the inclusion or editing of Mt 11,25-27.

As to the argument from the placement of the saying, even granting a full Wisdom Christology in v. 19, it is somewhat circuitous to say that "these things" which have been revealed to the "babes" (11,25) are the "eschatological signs mentioned in the woes against Galilean cities but these mighty works are interpreted...by the preceding section as the 'deeds of the Christ' which are nothing else than the 'deeds of incarnate Wisdom.'"[58] If there is no Wisdom Christology in the house it can be borrowed from the neighbor. In any case, we have already seen that the Wisdom Christology of v. 19 is not nearly so clear as it has been made out to be, and it scarcely provides sufficient momentum to carry vv. 25-27 along in its wake. By any account, a Wisdom Christology cannot be said to be the dominant theme of

---

[54] For details cf. Deutsch 1987, 21f.; Kloppenborg 1978, 133f.; Davies-Allison, 2:163f., 236f.

[55] For an attempt at reconstructing the Q form cf. Kloppenborg 1978, 132-135.

[56] E.g., Suggs, 95f.; Hamerton-Kelly 1973, 68-70; Schweizer 1972, 373 n. 278. Cf. Stanton 1973, 37. Most scholars have followed Suggs in denying that Jesus and Wisdom were identified in Q, and thus also in Q 10,22. The argument is that the saying teeters on the brink of a Wisdom Christology in Q 10,22, and Matthew's addition of vv. 28-20 pushes it over the edge. But if Mt 11,27 is identifying Jesus and Wisdom then why would the same not hold for Q 10,22? Cf. M.D. Johnson, 59f.

[57] E.g., Deutsch 1987, 103f., 111; 1990, 36; J.M. Robinson 1975, 8-10; Fiorenza, 17.

[58] Suggs, 95; cf. Gundry, 216.

the preceding sections, nor one item among the "things" which are "hidden" by the Father. It is much more natural to think of the messiahship and Sonship of Jesus as the significance latent in "these things,"[59] if not the presence of God's kingdom in Jesus.[60]

More promising would be the Matthean addition of vv. 28-30, commonly understood to be a declaration of Jesus Sophia, yet here also, as we will see, there are good reasons to doubt that Matthew's interest is primarily in portraying Jesus as Wisdom.

Having said all that, however, the intrinsic importance of 11,25-27 to the understanding of 11,28-30, not least due to their proximity, justifies a consideration of how we should view the use of wisdom motifs in them. Vv. 25f. and v. 27 are usually thought to have been originally separate, though they were joined in Q.[61] Moreover, the wisdom parallels adduced for v. 25-27 tend to cluster distinctively around 25f. and 27. Thus we will discuss them separately here.

3.2.1. Mt 11,25f.

Vv. 25f. are rightly considered to be heavily dependent on wisdom motifs and ideas.[62] Kloppenborg is nonetheless justified in stating that "in Mt 11,25f. a Wisdom Christology -- and indeed a Christology at all -- is excluded both on formal and material grounds."[63] One element of the saying stands out by way of contrast with the wisdom traditions, namely the denial of revelation to the "wise and understanding" and its bestowal on the "babes." It is not enough to cite received wisdom traditions which parallel this thought generally, *viz* traditions which deny wisdom to the "wise of this world" and which favor the "humble."[64] The fact is that "nowhere in wisdom literature is found a statement such as Mt 11,25 -- denying revelation to the 'wise' in favour of the simple."[65]

It seems evident enough that the σοφοί and συνετοί who are in view, whatever the pejorative connotations, are those who have heeded the call to go to the House of Learning (Sir 51,23) and to take up Wisdom's yoke; they are those who have applied themselves to the study of Torah, pre-eminently

---

[59] Gnilka, 1:435; Maier, 395.
[60] Mt 11,12; 12,25-28; Davies-Allison, 2:277.
[61] Cf. Davies-Allison, 2:279; Kloppenborg 1978, 135ff.; Deutsch 1987, 49.
[62] Dunn 1989, 198. For parallels see Christ, 82-91, and Deutsch 1987, 55-112.
[63] Kloppenborg 1978, 138f., 146 (he affirms the presence of wisdom motifs).
[64] E.g. Suggs, 83-87; Bertram 1967, 921f.; Davies-Allison, 2:274. For the idea of the "humble" as the recipients of wisdom, cf. e.g. Prov 26,12; WisSol 10,21; Sir 3,19; 1Bar 3,9ff.21-23; 1En 5,8; 1QS 11,6f.; 1QpHab 12,4; 1QH 2,8-10.
[65] Kloppenborg 1978, 139 n. 72; likewise, Hengel 1979, 153; Deutsch 1987, 110; Piper, 265 n. 84; cf. Lührmann, 65; Luz, 2:206f.; Gnilka, 1:435f.

Chapter Five: Matthew's Wisdom Christology

the scribes and Pharisees; they are the "wise" lauded by ben Sirach. The νήπιοι, on the other hand, are certainly the "humble" who traditionally receive wisdom, but in contrast to these σοφοί they are also the "uneducated."[66] The contrast with Sir 6 is sharp. There it is said (6,20) that Wisdom is very unpleasant to the unlearned (ἀπαιδεύτοις) and that the person that is without understanding (ἀκάρδιος) will not remain with her. Shortly thereafter (v. 34) the readers are told to stand in the multitude of the elders (πρεσβευτέρων) and to cleave to the one that is wise (σοφός); if they see someone of understanding (συνετὸν) they are to frequent that person's doorstep (v. 36). For Matthew "these things" are hidden from the σοφῶν καὶ συνετῶν and revealed to the νηπίοις. The invitation of vv. 28-30 is extended to those weary and burdened at least in part under the very Pharisaic Halakah which is assumed in Wisdom's yoke.[67]

The saying is scarcely parroting wisdom traditions though it certainly employs them,[68] and it is not in its basic thrust a statement of Christology any more than of theology proper. As it stands the saying is primarily a variation on well known OT *prophetic* denunciations of Israel's leadership generally, of human inability to grasp the purposes of God, and of the proud wisdom which God condemns.[69] Witherington has pointed out that much of Jesus' wisdom teaching should be described as "counter order" wisdom,[70] and he is probably right in viewing 11,25f. from this angle. Even so, this particular saying seems to me to be operating somewhere outside of a merely sapiential circle of ideas. In the case of this saying, at least, "prophetic"

---

[66] Cf. Davies-Allison, 2:275; Jeremias 1971, 111, 227 n. 2; Hengel 1981, 49f., 67f. There doesn't appear to be any good reason to deny the idea of relative ignorance, even after we allow for 13,51f. (cf. 23,34; Orton, 144, 155f.); *contra* Suggs, 84, and Deutsch 1987, 31f., 173 n. 210, whose attempt to reconcile this saying with a Wisdom Christology forces them to generalize the term νήπιοι to refer to nothing more than the "elect" and "disciples." The idea of relative ignorance is not only strongly implied by the contrast with the "wise and intelligent" but seems to have been an established component of Christian self-perception, usually with an ironic bent: 1Cor 1,26ff. (cf. 1Cor 1,26ff. with 2,6ff.); Acts 4,13; John 7,49. The description is not absolute in any sense, but only an observation about a *real* sociological trend with a view to God's judgment on the proud. On the relation of Mt 11,25f. to 1Cor 1-4, cf. Crossan, 193f.; Koester 1980, 247f.; Richardson, 91-111; Witherington, 308.

[67] Further, in Sir 22,13 the readers are warned away from a senseless (ἄφρονος) and unintelligent (ἀσύνετον) person; if they avoid such as this they will find rest (εὑρήσεις ἀνάπαυσιν).

[68] Witherington cites Dan 2,19-23 as the closest parallel to Mt 11,25f., noting both the similarities and the differences. Of course, wisdom and apocalyptic interpenetrate.

[69] Isa 29,14; 47,10; 26,5f.; 66,1f.; 57,15;Jer 8,9; 9,23; 31,34; Ezek 28,1ff.; 28,17; Zech 9,2f.; cf. Ps 8,2 (Mt 21,16). Cf. Davies-Allison, 2:277.

[70] Witherington, 359f., 161-183.

would seem to be "heuristically the most all-encompassing and satisfying term."[71]

3.2.2. Mt 11,27[72]

Elements of v. 27 do bear a resemblance to certain Wisdom texts or groups of texts, though the saying cannot be reduced to a simple expression of Wisdom ideas. In v. 27 it is not merely a matter of a close reciprocal relationship,[73] nor only of a father-son relationship,[74] but of the conferral of "all things" (v. 27a),[75] the uniqueness of the Son's knowledge, and the exclusivity of the revelatory prerogative.

The reciprocal knowledge of 11,27 is also characteristic of Wisdom.[76] Wisdom's dwelling place eludes people but is known to God;[77] on the other hand, she "is an initiate in the knowledge of God," one who possesses a unique knowledge of the transcendent, immaterial, ideal world,[78] and she reveals God and his secrets to people.[79] Furthermore, in this literature the

---

[71] Witherington applies this qualification to the label of "sage" since Jesus "usually sapientialized whatever he said, often expressing prophetic or apocalyptic ideas in some sort of Wisdom form of speech" (201). His concern is with a general description of Jesus, while I am attempting to describe only Mt 11.25f. Maybe I should add that my favoring of "prophetic" here does not ignore the way in which the later wisdom becomes increasingly prophetic in character (Sir 24,33; Witherington, 89f.). Yet neither should we forget the way in which prophecy often includes wisdom.

[72] On the textual questions of v. 27 cf. Suggs, 71-77. On the difficult question of the provenance of v. 27 see Suggs, 89ff.; Kloppenborg 1978, 140ff.; Davies-Allison, 2:282f.

[73] Cf. Tob 5,2 -- "he does not know me and I do not know him" (αὐτὸς οὐ γινώσκει με καὶ ἐγὼ οὐ γινώσκω αὐτόν). This appears to have been a Semitic way of speaking, which amounted to saying, "we (do not) know each other"; cf. Jeremias 1971, 58 n. 2; 1967c, 47. But again, there is more to the present saying than this; cf. Marshall 1978, 437f.

[74] See literature in previous note; Gnilka, 1:437-439. Luz, 2:208f., argues that the idea of "son" is not to be explained *religionsgeschichtlich*, but rhetorically, as the counterpart to the "father."

[75] The question is usually asked whether this is conferred "knowledge" or "authority." For the latter, cf. e.g. Kloppenborg 1978, 140f.; Sand, 252. Similarly, in Mt 28,18-20 a conferral of authority is followed by a commission to proclamation; cf. Dan 7,14. For restricting this to a conferral of "knowledge," cf. Hunter, 246; Gundry, 216; Luz, 2:210f.; Davies-Allison, 2:279f. "Knowledge" and "authority" are not, however, necessarily mutually exclusive alternatives; cf. Reicke, 895; Marshall 1978, 436; Carson, 277; Gnilka, 1:437.

[76] Cf. e.g. Christ, 86-91; Deutsch 1987, 55-112; Piper, 170-173.; Dunn 1989, 198.

[77] Job 28,12-28; Sir 1,1-9; 1Bar 3,15.20.23.31-36 (in Sir 24,28f. it is said that Wisdom was not known *fully* by either the first nor the last person; on the other hand, in Sir 6,27 it is said that if Wisdom is sought she will become known).

[78] WisSol 8,4.8; 9,13-18; cf. 7,25f.; Sir 24,4

[79] WisSol 9,13.16-18; cf. 7,21f.; 10,10; Sir 4,18; 11QPs[a] 18.

wise man is described as God's son.[80] Neither the wise man nor God's mysteries are understood by people.[81]

There is thus a general resemblance between Wisdom and the Son as profiled by Mt 11,27. With the possible exception of Moses, it would be difficult to find a closer peer from Israel's world. Still, it should be admitted that Wisdom's profile has been more than a little enhanced by this selective arrangement of texts. (1) In WisSol, it is not Wisdom but the *typical* wise man who is described as God's son. In 11,27, both the transcendent status of the Son and his unique knowledge of the Father set him off from the "wise son" of the Wisdom literature.[82] (2) What is known only to God about Wisdom is not Wisdom herself -- as with the Son -- but "the *source*, the locus of Wisdom..., which, for ben Sira and Baruch at least, is now sited in the Torah."[83] It is probably the case that for Matthew the saying is concerned with the Son's messianic status and role.[84] (3) The exclusive prerogative ($\hat{\omega}$ ἐὰν βούληται) to reveal (ἀποκαλύψαι) the Father is not well paralleled by the wisdom texts.[85] (4) Kloppenborg observes that,

> 11,27 lacks perhaps the two most distinctive features of the Jewish Sophia/Logos: pre-existence and the function of mediator of creation, while 27a implies the *transferral* of authority to Jesus -- which is...inconsequent [sic] with Wisdom traditions... [The] most distinctive attributes of Sophia do not appear in 11,27.[86]

(5) There is a gender conflict between Wisdom (feminine) and Jesus as Son.[87] Thus Philo struggles with the problem of Rebecca's father, Bethuel, being called both "father" (masculine) and "Wisdom" (feminine).[88] He finally overcomes the discrepancy by seeing in the feminine gender a deliberate attempt to express subordination to God the Maker. In contrast, the function of a Wisdom Christology would presumably be to *exalt* Jesus. One cannot exclude a Wisdom Christology on the basis of this consideration

---

[80] WisSol 2,13.18; Sir 4,11; 51,10; cf. JosAsen 6,2-6; 13,10; 21,3; TAb 12,5; TLevi 4,2; Kloppenborg 1978, 145; Dunn 1989, 199. In WisSol 7,21f. the wise son is a friend of God (7,27) who has learned both what is secret and what is manifest.

[81] WisSol 2,17-22; 4,10.13-15; 4,20-5,16.

[82] Luz, 2:209 n. 83; Kloppenborg 1978, 145f. Tuckett 1983, 151, observes further that "in the wisdom literature, Wisdom's 'sons' are always those who listen and respond to her call, rather than those who actually proclaim it."

[83] Dunn 1989, 199 (italics in original). Cf. Gundry, 217; Davies-Allison, 2:281

[84] Carson, 276; Bacchiocchi 1984, 294.

[85] Cf. Dunn 1989, 199. Christ, 90, cites only WisSol 7,28.

[86] Kloppenborg 1978, 147 (italics in original); in general see also Piper, 172.

[87] Cf. M.D. Johnson, 61f. Catchpole, 170 (cf. n. 21 in Catchpole) issues a caveat along these lines in relation to the use of αὐτῆς in Mt 11,19.

[88] *Fuga* 50-52. Cf. *Fuga* 109; *LegAll* II,49; *QuodDet* 54; *Cher* 49; *Sacr* 64; *Virt* 62; *QuaesGen* IV,97.

alone,[89] but it is reasonable to suppose that in such a milieu a writer would be sensitive to the issue: the reader is expected to recognize a feminine identity in imagery which is emphatically masculine.[90]

On balance then, the Wisdom texts probably offer parallels to separate components of the already existing saying (11,27) rather than a matrix out of which such a saying would arise. Coming from different quarters, the parallels to 11,27 cited by Jeremias[91] suggest a Semitic/proverbial way of speaking which does not exhaustively account for *this* saying, but which may help explain the form. Beginning from Jesus' unique awareness of God as his Father,[92] Jeremias' proposal is more promising as an explanation of the genesis of this saying than that the individual elements were gathered and pieced together like so many bricks out of Wisdom sources. I.H. Marshall rightly stresses that "the meaning of the saying is to be found in the two clauses taken together, and it is misleading to expound them separately... The meaning is, then, 'Only a father and a son know each other'";[93] in our saying this means, "only *the* Father and *the* Son know each other." The element of the transcendent which is strongly suggested may have been injected into the saying by association with the Son of Man traditions (11,27a).

Though the figure of Wisdom comes closer than most others to the Son in 11,27, there are other OT parallels which would give quite a different slant to the saying than the one proposed by Suggs and others, *viz* that Jesus appears in the saying "as the one who represents Israel in the last days, or represents the Israel of the last days."[94] One of the most convincing elements of 11,27 for those who see a Wisdom Christology in it is the

---

[89] Certainly the church would overcome this obstacle; cf. J.M. Robinson 1975, 11f. Along other lines, Jesus compares himself to a hen ($ὄρνις$) in Mt 23,37. But again, this is different from seeing the feminine imagery *implied* in a decisively masculine figure as in 11,27.

[90] Dunn 1989, 199; cf. Stanton 1992a, 370; Luz, 2:209. Witherington's discussion of this passage in Philo seems to ignore entirely *Fuga* 51 (Witherington, 293).

[91] 1971, 57f.; 1967c, 46-52.

[92] Cf. further Dunn 1989, 200, on the unique claims of Jesus about himself.

[93] 1978, 436. Cf. also Marshall 1967.

[94] Dunn 1989, 199; italicized in Dunn. In brief, the parallels (for the passages see Dunn) are Daniel's son of man (cf. Schweizer 1972, 72f.; Cerfaux, 147-149; de Kruijf, 65-76), Israel's claim to election which is often expressed in terms of being known by and knowing YHWH, the sonship imagery as expressive of Israel's election, and the expectation that in the last days the knowledge of God would fill the earth through Israel and the Servant. Dunn's stress is on the idea of "election," which runs through these parallels; against the use of "knowledge" in 11,27 in this sense, cf. Gundry, 217; Davies-Allison, 2:281; Luz, 2:211f. We might just the same allow these parallels as familiar and paradigmatic uses of the idea of reciprocal knowledge within the covenant relationship; in addition to the passages cited by Dunn cf. also 2Sam 7,20; 1Kgs 8,39; Ps 139,1; Isa 63,16; Jer 12,3.

exclusivity of the reciprocal knowledge and the revelatory role.[95] Yet one group of OT passages in particular -- *viz* Ex 33, Num 12, and Deut 34 -- relates to another towering figure of Judaism and in some respects foreshadows the language of 11,27-30. Ex 33,11-14 states:

> Thus the LORD used to speak to Moses *face to face*, as one speaks to a friend. Then he would return to the camp... Moses said to the LORD, "See, you have said to me, 'Bring up this people'; But you have not let me know whom you will send with me. Yet you have said, '*I know you by name*, and you have also found favor in my sight.' Now if I have found favor in your sight, show me your ways, so that *I may know you* and find favor in your sight. Consider too that this nation is your people." He said, "My presence will go with you, and *I will give you rest*."[96]

This dialogue leads to the well known revelation of God to Moses.[97] A passage closely related to this one is Num 12,3ff. The context is the opposition of Miriam and Aaron to Moses. "'Has the LORD spoken only through Moses? Has he not spoken through us also?'" The element of uniqueness, already evident in Ex 33, is thrust to the fore:

> Now the man Moses was very humble, more so than anyone else on the face of the earth... And he [the LORD] said, "Hear my words: When there are prophets among you, I the LORD make myself known to them in visions; I speak to them in dreams. Not so with my servant Moses; he is entrusted with all my house. With him I speak face to face -- clearly, not in riddles; and he beholds[98] the form of the LORD. Why then were you not afraid to speak against my servant Moses?"

As M. D'Angelo puts it, "the question seems to be: 'how does Moses know what he knows about God?' and the answer: 'More directly, and therefore more, than any other prophet.'"[99] Deut 34,5.10-12 seems to combine elements of the above passages. Moses, "the servant of the LORD" (v. 5) dies in Moab. After describing Joshua as "full of the spirit of wisdom, because Moses had laid hands on him" (v. 9), the books closes:

> Never since has there arisen a prophet in Israel like Moses, whom the LORD knew face to face. He was unequalled for all the signs and wonders that the LORD sent him to perform in the land of Egypt, against Pharaoh and all his servants and his entire land, and for all

---

[95] Cf. J.M. Robinson 1975, 9.

[96] Italics mine. The relevance of this passage to Mt 11,28-30 has been noted frequently, but most effectively by Allison 1988, 478-483; cf. Davies-Allison, 2:283-287. Much of what follows is indebted to the discussion of Ex 33,11ff. and the related passages by D'Angelo, 95-149. Allison expanded his case in 1993, 218-235, where he took up much of the same evidence as D'Angelo had.

[97] Ex 33,17-34,9.

[98] The LXX renders this with an aorist, $\epsilon\hat{\iota}\delta\epsilon\nu$, suggesting that it looks back to Ex 33,11ff.

[99] D'Angelo, 99.

the mighty deeds and all the terrifying displays of power that Moses performed in the sight of all Israel.[100]

One recalls the stress on Jesus' "deeds" in Mt 11. Sir 45,4f. represents an early midrash on these passages, combining Ex 33,11 with Num 12,7 and the theophany of Mt. Sinai:[101]

For his faithfulness and meekness he consecrated him, choosing him out of all humankind. He allowed him to hear his voice, and led him into the dark cloud, and gave him the commandments face to face, and the law of life and knowledge, so that he might teach Jacob the covenant, and Israel his decrees.

This passage also accentuates that the knowledge given Moses was knowledge which he mediated to Israel through the Law.[102] Nor is Sir 44 alone in early testimonies to Jewish reflection on these OT passages. Philo also combines Num 12,6.8 with Deut 34,10 and Ex 33,13,[103] and in the NT 1Cor 13,12 is often interpreted in connection with this complex of OT passages.[104] This complex may also have been in view when Num 12 was cited in Heb 3,1-6.[105]

Having considered these OT passages (Ex 33,11; Num 12,6-8; Deut 34,5.10) in the LXX, the Targumim, and the early Jewish and Christian passages just mentioned, D'Angelo concludes that the interpretations of Num 12,6-8 and its related texts "are normally concerned with establishing the uniqueness of Moses' prophecy in Israel"; moreover, "the uniquely direct character of Moses' revelation, i.e. the immediacy of God's communication with Moses, becomes the subject of speculation."[106] This she goes on to demonstrate further with other early Jewish midrashim, but for our purposes it is sufficient to have noticed that this OT focus on the uniqueness of Moses' relationship and his role in revelation -- which includes Ex 33,11ff. -- was not lost on early Jewish, and Christian,[107] interpreters.

---

[100] The LXX seems to connect this passage closer to Num 12,7f.; cf. D'Angelo, 101. Cf. also Deut 5,4f., where God speaks to *Israel* "face to face" though Moses is portrayed as a mediator between God and Israel. For further on Moses' unique status and role, cf. P.D. Miller 1987.

[101] Cf. D'Angelo, 104f.

[102] Allison 1988, 479.

[103] *Heres* 262; *LegAll* III,100-103.

[104] D'Angelo, 105f.; Allison 1988, 479f.; 1993, 226f.

[105] D'Angelo, 95-149.

[106] D'Angelo, 107.

[107] Allison 1988, 481, aptly comments on 1Cor 13,12 that "when ruminating upon the subject of knowing God and being known by him, Paul turned his thoughts to the lawgiver."

Beyond the uniqueness of Moses' relationship to God and his preeminent role in mediating revelation, Davies and Allison note further indications that Ex 33,11-14 *specifically* may have influenced Mt 11,27-30.[108] In both passages the context is that of a prayer; in both the statement of a unique experience of revelation is followed by a promise of rest (Ex 33,14: καταπαύσω σε); the ordering of the clauses in Ex 33, 12f. -- God knows Moses and Moses wants to know God -- corresponds to the ordering of the clauses in Mt 11,27 -- the Father knows the Son and the Son knows the Father;[109] and the description of Moses as "meek" (πραΰς)[110] in the related passage of Num 12 corresponds to the depiction of Jesus in Mt 11,29.

It is nonetheless difficult to accept that Ex 33 is the master key to Mt 11,27, not least because it lacks the Sonship motif which governs the latter.[111] It would be more promising to view the broader Moses traditions just reviewed as having had some role in the history of this *Jesuswort*, and *Matthew's* point as consisting precisely in the superiority of the *Son* over Moses.[112] In that case, however, the similarities of the Son to the uniqueness of Wisdom remain relevant.[113]

---

[108] Davies-Allison, 2:285f.; Allison 1988, 481-483. Allison added yet more arguments in 1993, 218-233.

[109] Hunter, 246, explains the ordering of the clauses with reference to the OT idea of *da'ath Elohim*; "in the prophet's view, if man is ever to know God, God must first 'know' (choose and care for) man"; cf. Schweizer, 270f.

[110] Num 12,3; cf. Sir 45,4; *1Clem* 17,1.5-6; cf. Hauck-Schulz 1968a, 648.

[111] But see EzekTrag 100 (II B.C.); Hengel 1976, 42 n. 85, 43f. n. 87; Allison 1993, 232 n. 224. Another element of 11,27 not as pronounced in Ex 33 par. is the Father's (God's) exclusive knowledge of the Son (Moses). Four things may be said: (1) We have already seen that the Wisdom parallels do not fare much better on this element. (2) In the same context that Stephen associates Deut 18,15 with Jesus (Acts 7,37; cf. Acts 3,22; Deut 34,10 par.) he stresses the failure of Israel to recognize Moses' divine appointment as ruler and judge (Acts 7,35). (3) Jeremias 1967c, 50, has suggested not only that 27b-c make up a unified thought, but that 27b is logically subordinate to 27c; thus the stress falls on the Son's knowledge of the Father as a prerequisite for his role in revelation. (4) The *historical fact* that so many failed to recognize Jesus' messiahship is the most obvious background against which 27b would have been understood; cf. Davies-Allison, 2:282; Morris, 294. This element of the saying is paralleled in certain ways by the Wisdom myth, but what is missing is any indication in this passage that Matthew has developed the historical fact of the rejection of Jesus as the messiah in the direction of that myth.

[112] Hengel 1976, 69, remarks on Deut 34,10, that Jesus corrects this verse in terms of himself in Mt 11,27. That Matthew has a general interest in a Moses typology is well established; see esp. Allison 1993, for a comprehensive review of the evidence (though Allison may not be as selective as some would like). We are on firm ground in supposing that Matthew would have understood 11,27 in this connection. This decision is confirmed by the prophetic stamp of 11,25f. and the New Exodus ideas underlying 11,28-30 (on which see below).

[113] Cf. Heb 3,1-6; Jn 1,17f.; it is interesting that in all three cases (cf. Mt 11,27) we are dealing with a Sonship Christology which bears traces of Wisdom speculation (cf. Heb

In the end none of the previously mentioned parallels fully accounts for the logion of Mt 11,27. None of them taken alone could be labelled the "mother" of this saying, though each of them makes a tolerably good parallel to this or that element of it.[114] Some elements of the saying are most closely equalled by statements about Wisdom, but those parallels neither expose the root of the saying nor account for the saying as it stands. It is more likely that what we have in Mt 11,27 is a glimpse of a Christology that makes it understandable that Jesus *could* be -- and may well have been[115] -- identified with Wisdom, than that the saying was composed and designed under the influence of Wisdom speculation or for the purpose of identifying Jesus and Wisdom. For his part, Matthew's main interests are probably elsewhere.

3.3. Mt 23,34-36 (Q 11,49-51)

Mt 23,34
διὰ τοῦτο ἰδοὺ ἐγὼ ἀποστέλλω κτλ.

Lk 11,49
διὰ τοῦτο καὶ ἡ σοφία τοῦ θεοῦ εἶπεν,
Ἀποστελῶ κτλ.

At its briefest, the argument is that Luke preserves Q, since Luke would not have changed an ἐγώ to a Wisdom saying. Thus, it is alleged, Matthew has clearly betrayed his Christology by substituting Jesus for Wisdom.[116] The fuller version includes the hypothesis that the saying (Lk 11,49b-51a) is a quote from a lost wisdom apocalypse[117] which Q had already applied to its contemporaries by the addition of the last statement (Lk 11,51b), and which Matthew has placed on the lips of Jesus Sophia.[118]

1,3f.). In Heb 3 and Jn 1 the comparison with Moses is explicit, and in Heb 3,1-6, D'Angelo (see previous notes) has detected the same Moses traditions we have just looked at. Moreover, if Mt 11,27 recalls 2Sam 7,14 par. (infra, 224f.) then these are the very passages cited in Heb 1 (immediately following the use of wisdom language) in reference to the Sonship of Jesus. See further below, 362-366; our findings there confirm that our proposal is correct.

[114] Kloppenborg 1978, 129f., 146f., prefers to label the process at work in 11,27 a "reflective mythology"; cf. Mack 1970; Conzelmann, 230-243; Fiorenza, 17-41. By this is meant that reflection on Jesus by the first Christians led to a creative use of familiar mythological language and imagery in accordance with their own theological interests to articulate his meaning, although without, in the present case, intending to identify him with Wisdom.

[115] See the next section (§ 3.3), and further below, 183-186, 234f. There is probably enough evidence to suggest that Matthew would have been aware of the connection.

[116] This assessment of Q and Matthew's redaction is very widely held. On Q, see Moreland-Robinson, 498; it is doubtful, according to the International Q Project, that τοῦ θεοῦ was included in Q, though some text may have been present there.

[117] Cf. Suggs, 15ff.; Haenchen 1951, 52f.; further on this in Garland, 173 n. 38. Marshall 1978, 503, grants this hypothesis tentative acceptance.

[118] See the summary of Marshall 1978, 503.

Chapter Five: Matthew's Wisdom Christology 181

The objection has been raised that "piling one hypothesis (the lost Jewish wisdom apocalypse) upon another hypothesis (Q)" is not a very convincing way to build a case.[119] Indeed it is not. Yet it is finally impossible to demonstrate that a lost wisdom apocalypse never existed[120] and for us the "lost" document is irrelevant since Matthew is drawing on Q.[121] Matthew's readers might have felt the presence of "wisdom language" in 23,34-36 due to its form and content,[122] though whether this would have by itself led them to identify Jesus as Wisdom is debatable. The argument that Luke has preserved the Q form of the saying's introduction is, however, more cogent and to the point; accordingly, it appears that Matthew has changed a saying of Wisdom[123] into an "I" saying.[124]

The significance of this change is variously assessed, however. M.D. Johnson, observing that the change removes the reference to Wisdom, sees in it a "*lessening* of Matthean interest in Wisdom speculation."[125] Gundry argues that "divine wisdom does not merge with Jesus, but with Christian 'sages.'"[126] Most are probably inclined, however, to expect that *Matthew* understood the Christological implications of his substitution, and this seems reasonable.

Yet would his *readers* have seen a Wisdom Christology here, given that there is no mention of Wisdom? If we assume that at least some of Matthew's readers had a special interest in this sort of speculation,[127] that they knew by heart Q 11,49, and that they would have been inclined to interpret editorial changes like good redaction critics, then they may well

---

[119] W.G. Thompson, 146.

[120] Its existence is possible but not probable; Dunn 1989, 201, is properly reserved. Cf. Gnilka, 2:306; Jacobson, 189. Suggs' preference, 20, for a hypothetical lost source over a hypothetical circumlocution in an existing saying is symptomatically unbalanced, especially when Suggs admits that a first century reader (Luke) took it as a circumlocution; cf. Meadors, 45.

[121] Correctly, Burnett, 40.

[122] Cf. Orton, 154; Marshall 1978, 502.

[123] It is likely that this use of $\sigma o \phi i a$ is a reference to the mythological figure of Wisdom; cf. Marshall 1978, 502f.; T.W. Manson, 394; Suggs, 19f.; Christ, 125f.; Wilckens 1971, 515.

[124] There is the matter of whether a saying had been included in Q which was attributed to Wisdom and *not* Jesus; cf. Bultmann 1972, 102. But if Jesus was assumed to be interchangeable with Wisdom in Q then Matthew's redaction would fix what was not broken, and arguably obscure the Wisdom connection; cf. M.D. Johnson, 55, 63.

[125] M.D. Johnson, 55; italics added. Tuckett 1983, 160, prefers to say that in Matthew Jesus is "almost" identified with Wisdom.

[126] Gundry, 469. Matthew's reference to "sages" in v. 34 is generally considered to be redactional.

[127] Cf. e.g. Burnett, 41f., who does not seem to appreciate the circularity in this assumption; also Dunn 1989, 202, 204; Stendahl, 27, 142. In line with his general argument, Meadors, 43-46, is sceptical about any strong Wisdom themes in Q 11,49-51.

have been alive to Matthew's meaning; Matthew might have assumed as much. Yet it is also necessary to appreciate fully that the saying, especially as it stands in Matthew, makes good sense without knowledge of the Wisdom parallels,[128] and it reminds us of a whole string of OT passages where it is *God* sending out messengers who are rejected: 2Chr 24,19-22; 2Kgs 17,13ff.; 2Chr 36,15f.; Ezra 9,11; Neh 9,26.[129] Indeed, this is such a strong OT theme that it would presumably take something very definite to point one's attention away from these passages and toward Wisdom specifically.[130] As the passage stands in Matthew, it is difficult to see what would have compelled his readers to look anywhere other than at these OT passages. Moreover, Jesus himself sends out messengers in Mt 10,1ff. and 28,18-20, so that Jesus' role in 23,34ff. fits naturally into Matthew's story; it does not seem necessary to appeal to a Wisdom myth to make sense of these verses. Matthew would surely need to be quite direct in saying that Jesus is Wisdom here. Such forthrightness is precisely what we do not find.

Allowing, then, that we do not know what Matthew could have assumed of his readers, it may nonetheless be doubted that Matthew's change is the application of a policy which is seeking to *express* the novel and daring[131] idea, Jesus = Wisdom.[132] At least his redaction would be a very clumsy way of pursuing such a policy.

---

[128] Here we are thinking of the idea of "Wisdom's envoys"; supra, 166.

[129] Cf. 1Kgs 18,4.13; 19,10.14; Jer 7,25f.; 15,15; 17,18; 20,11; 25,4-7; 26,4-6.20ff.; 29,18f.; 35,15; 44,4f.; M.D. Johnson, 55; Gundry, 469. Suggs, 59, admits that the role of sending envoys does not belong exclusively to Wisdom. Here it seems to be the ascription of the saying to Wisdom in Q which favors that subject over God, but that is what is missing in Matthew; we should recall how important that ascription has been for *our* recognition of this as a Wisdom saying. On the theme of the rejected prophets in general, cf. Steck; Knowles; Garland, 179ff., 209; and Mack 1971, 354. The parallel of Wisdom in WisSol 10-11 (cf. Dunn 1989, 201) speaks of how Wisdom *preserves* her own in the midst of their troubles, which is very different from Mt 23,34-36.

[130] The passage may well bear marks of Wisdom thought, which we would expect if the Q version was a saying of Wisdom. Yet by removing the reference to Wisdom in transferring the saying to Jesus, Matthew has in effect brought the saying closer to the OT passages just listed and reduced considerably the likelihood that his readers would have thought of Wisdom here.

[131] On the other hand, if the church already had a very "high" Christology then this would not necessarily be a "daring" development at all. In that case, however, Wisdom is not the "key" to the development of Christology which some apparently think she is; cf. in this regard the remarks with which Dunn introduces his discussion of the Wisdom Christology (1989, 163).

[132] Dunn 1989, 202, limits himself to the claim that Matthew evidences his own Christology in this passage and leaves the question open as to whether Matthew's readers would have recognized this alteration; cf. Davies-Allison, 2:295; M.D. Johnson, 55; France, 305. Those against reading a Wisdom Christology in 23,34-36 include Orton, 154; Gundry, 469; Verseput 1987, 552 n. 43.

This is an important observation, however, for if Matthew does not exhibit such a policy here then what are we to make of Mt 11,19? Q 11,49-51 is a veritable gift to anyone who is interested in articulating the equation, Jesus = Wisdom. More than in any of the other examples we here encounter a saying (1) known to be in Matthew's source, (2) explicitly ascribed to Wisdom, *and* (3) explicitly referring to the sending out of envoys.[133] If Matthew has let *this* passage go by without making his point, then *a fortiori* it is very unlikely indeed that the subtle editorial activity in 11,2-19 was driven by this concern.

On balance, Mt 23,34 may evidence Matthew's own Christology, but it does not indicate that making the identification with Wisdom belonged to his Christological *agenda*. This passage makes it *less* probable, not more, that he would have made the attempt specifically to identify Jesus and Wisdom elsewhere.[134] Where Matthew may have carried out an editorial change under the influence of a Wisdom Christology, he has done so in the course of developing other theological concerns which are of greater interest to him. His Wisdom Christology is resultantly so "quiescent" and the other themes are so dominant that the Wisdom Christology "can be entirely missed and altogether denied."[135]

3.4. Mt 23,37-39 (Q 13,34-35)

The wording is close, although the contexts are different. In Suggs' view, Matthew has probably retained Q's order which had this lament immediately following the oracle of doom in 23,34-36.[136] It is suggested that

---

[133] Burnett, 49, rightly observes that "Matthew 23,34-36 is the departure point not only for Suggs but for anyone who wishes to explore the possibility of a Sophia christology in Matthew. The logion is preserved in Q and there is no question that it is a saying from the Wisdom tradition."

[134] On the assumption that he is writing for a select group of initiates, Matthew can almost be accused of playing games: he shapes the identification of Jesus and Wisdom through meticulous editorial work, but just as meticulously conceals the identification from all save the initiates (the ambiguity of *both* 11,19 and 23,34 cannot be coincidental, esp. considering the fine editorial touches in 11,2-19 [supra, 167-170]). The simpler explanation is that Matthew does accept a Wisdom Christology, but he is not particularly concerned to advance it for its own sake. This Christology has something to do with his redaction of 23,34 (it makes it natural to substitute Jesus for Q's Wisdom), but little if anything to do with his redaction of 11,2-19 (where alternative interpretations appear preferable anyway). This explanation satisfies the data.

[135] Davies-Allison, 2:295.

[136] Suggs, 64-66; J.M. Robinson 1975, 13. The question of order is discussed at length by Garland, 187-197, with further literature. Garland decides against Matthew's ordering (23,34-36 and 23,37-39 were *not* together in Q), but at the expense of the supposed origin of vv. 37-39 as a saying of Wisdom. Others maintain that this is a Wisdom saying even

Jesus could not have said this,[137] since a trans-historical speaker seems to be assumed ("how often") and the image of a hen gathering her brood suggests a heavenly figure.[138] Assuming, therefore, that the speaker of the lament in Q was Wisdom,[139] and recalling the substitution which Matthew made in 23,34 (above), one can accordingly recognize that here also an utterance of Wisdom has been placed on the lips of Jesus. Because Jesus now stands in the place of the trans-historical Wisdom the final verse is altered by Matthew -- from ἕως ἥξει ὅτε in Q 13,35 to ἀπ' ἄρτι ἕως in Mt 23,39 -- both historicizing the saying and orienting it toward the Parousia.[140]

Suggs acknowledges, however, that, "considered purely from the point of view of content, the saying might also be attributed to God,"[141] and R.T. France aptly comments that, "if it had not been for the juxtaposition (in Matthew, not Luke) of these words with what is in Luke (not Matthew!) a saying of the 'Wisdom of God' there might have been less enthusiasm for identifying verses 37-39 as 'Wisdom language'."[142]

---

though Matthew's order is not that of Q; e.g. Stanton 1973, 37f.; Jacobson, 216-212; Tuckett 1983, 162, 221 n. 79.

[137] This is disputed by some, e.g. Garland, 196, 204 n. 129; Dunn 1989, 203f.; Schmid, 332; Gundry, 473. In this case the wisdom parallels suggest that Jesus spoke this as a *messenger* of Wisdom, rather than as Wisdom; cf. Marshall 1978, 574; D.W. Smith, 77f.

[138] Cf. Suggs, 66f.; Burnett, 65f.; Bacon, 248; the source of the saying could be either Jewish or Christian. Note the use of the same figure in 5Ezra 1,30 (ca. A.D. 200) where it is attributed to God; a heavenly subject seems to have been the natural choice there (though not Wisdom). The wings of the seraphim symbolized divine protection (e.g. Deut 32,11; Ruth 2,12; Pss 17,8; 36,7; 57,1; 61,4; 63,7; 91,4). Further, the idea of 'wings' and the Shekinah were associated, as well as (possibly) the Shekinah and Wisdom (Prov 8; Sir 24; 11QPs^a 18; John 1).

[139] Cf. Burnett, 64f.; Wilckens 1971, 516; Piper, 164f.; Christ, 138-145.

[140] Suggs, 70 n. 22; Burnett, 77f. Note that Matthew, different from Luke, has located this saying *after* Jesus' entrance into Jerusalem (ch. 21); thus the reference to the Parousia. Garland, 204-209, provides a cogent accounting of this redaction which is without recourse to the Wisdom myth.

[141] Suggs, 67 n. 14; likewise Deutsch 1990, 44f.; Garland, 195f.; cf. Burnett, 65; Dunn 1989, 203. Garland, 190 n. 90, 201 n. 121 (depending on Urbach, 64f.), argues that the association of the Shekinah and Wisdom may not be so strong as has often been suggested. The divine passive in Mt 23,38 (ἀφίεται) would admittedly be awkward if the saying were to be attributed *directly* to God (cf. Tuckett 1983, 162; Christ, 138), but in both Matthew and Luke Jesus is the *actual* speaker. For our purposes it is only a question of whether the content is generally fitting for God; cf. e.g. Hos 5-6 (esp. 5,6.9.15); Deut 1,45; 32,11; Ruth 2,12; Judg 10,12f.; 1Sam 28,15; Job 23,8f.; 35,12; Pss 17,8; 36,7; 57,1; 61,4; 63,7; 91,4; 118,26; Isa 31,5; Jer 12,7; 22,5; Ezek 8,18; Amos 8,12; 2Bar 41,4; *LevR* 25; Str-B, 1:927, 943. 5Ezra 1,30 puts the saying on God's lips. If the language of 23,37-39 is clearly that of Wisdom, it is instructive that Suggs, 67 (cf. S. Schulz, 352; Stanton 1973, 38), denies that this lament would have identified Jesus and Wisdom in Q; cf. Dunn 1989, 337 n. 179; M.D. Johnson, 58f.; Hamerton-Kelly 1973, 33. In general, see R.J. Miller, 235-237; also Meadors, 46f.

[142] France, 305.

Ultimately our judgment on this saying hangs on our assessment of the redaction of v. 34, since 23,34-39 is a continuous saying of Jesus in Matthew's Gospel. It does not seem likely that Matthew would have intended to introduce to his community a Wisdom Christology with the minor modification (v. 39) of an ambiguous Wisdom saying, when he has let pass the opportunity to do so in the major modification (v. 34) of an explicit Wisdom saying. Taken as a whole, 23,34-39 might be best construed as "reflective mythology."[143] Matthew's concern here is evidently not in the first instance to identify Jesus and Wisdom, though he applies directly to Jesus a passage which *he* knows is descriptive of Wisdom's activity. Given the extent to which the language of 23,34-39 recalls God's activity, the effect of Matthew's redaction is to depict Jesus in terms which ultimately belong to *God* and to God's redemptive-historical activities. Matthew was presumably cognizant of this (1,21-23).

3.5. Summary

Wisdom was an important contributor to the developing expressions of Christology in the primitive church,[144] and in the Matthean passages we considered above the presence of wisdom thought, specifically associated with Wisdom, is marked. Yet the evidence does not support the contention that Matthew had an interest in *formulating* the identification of Jesus and Wisdom.[145] This negative finding is most evident in 23,34-39, where the opportunity for expressing this idea appears to have been the greatest. A distinction must be drawn between Matthew's own Christology and the Christology of his Gospel; the former is almost certainly broader and more involved than the latter.

In some respects this distinction is not crucial. For instance, if Matthew knowingly substituted Jesus for Wisdom, then we are still confronted by a Christology which may go beyond some earlier or some other formulations, and we still need to recognize the possible contribution of Wisdom

---

[143] For the idea, cf. Mack 1970; Conzelmann, 230-243; Fiorenza, 17-41.

[144] Heb 1,1-3, which is probably earlier than A.D. 70, shows that this branch of Christological speculation was highly developed some time before Matthew's Gospel (A.D. 70 or later?), though Heb 1 employs different elements of the Wisdom myth. In general see the helpful and wide ranging study of Witherington which traces the development of Christology in terms of Wisdom; a more concise survey was already given by Hengel 1979.

[145] It is apropos that Matthew nowhere *openly* makes the identification of Jesus and Wisdom. It is usual to point out that the feminine figure of Wisdom would have discouraged a straightforward identification, but Matthew does not hesitate to have Jesus compare himself to a mother hen (23,37); we have no reason to doubt that a way would have been found with Wisdom if it had been desired. Interestingly, Grundmann 1978, 180, uses the gender argument in 23,37 against an attribution to the "son."

speculation to Matthew's Christology. In other respects, however, this distinction is important, for there is no indication in Matthew's editorial activity that the identification of Jesus and Wisdom was a *specific* concern of his, and thus also no indication that he was engaged in *polemic* against the "Q community" or anyone else over Jesus' status vis-à-vis Wisdom. Many will still want to believe that Wisdom speculation was developing along deviant lines in the Q community,[146] but Matthew's Gospel should not be used as evidence of it. The Q community has in that case gone its way and Matthew has gone his. Further, we should not think, as is so often done, that when we have isolated Wisdom parallels in connection with a Matthean text we have finished with our exegetical work and satisfactorily ascertained Matthew's interest and meaning.

In particular, the fallout from this conclusion is that it is much less likely that the subtle redaction of 11,2-19 was undertaken in order to identify Jesus and Wisdom. It is also somewhat less likely that Matthew employed 11,28-30 where he did specifically because it would present Jesus as speaking *in persona sapientiae*. That he in fact did not do so is firmly grounded on consideration of the Logion itself.[147]

4. Mt 11,28-30 and Wisdom

4.1. Introduction

The importance of Mt 11,28-30 to the argument for a Matthean Wisdom Christology is apparent in the attention given it in the discussions. This passage is the concern of the closing chapter of Suggs' book and is in fact the final word of the entire study.[148] Arvedson, Christ, and Deutsch devote large portions of their work to this Logion.[149] R.T. France calls Mt 11,25-30 the most important passage for Matthew's Wisdom Christology,[150] and as we have already seen the Wisdom Christology of this section hinges on vv. 28-30. Most recently, Witherington also refers to Mt,11-28-30 as "crucial" to his discussion of the NT's Wisdom Christology, and sums up his view of Matthew with this word.[151]

---

[146] But see below, 201 n. 225.
[147] In circular fashion, our conclusions on 11,28-30 will corroborate our analysis of the other passages.
[148] Suggs, 99-130.
[149] Arvedson, 158-228; Christ, 100-119; Deutsch 1987, 113-139.
[150] France, 303 n. 57.
[151] Witherington, 205, 368.

The Wisdom Christology of vv. 28-30 hinges, in turn, on the relation of this Logion to Sirach.[152] The argument in a nutshell is that there (esp. Sir 6 and 51) Wisdom's yoke brings rest, here (Mt 11,28-30) Jesus' yoke brings rest, therefore Jesus = Wisdom. Matthew's alleged reason for including the Logion is to portray Jesus as Wisdom incarnate by placing a saying of Wisdom in Jesus' mouth. Thus the semi-divine status and attributes of Wisdom are transferred to Jesus.

There are very good reasons, however, to doubt that this was Matthew's primary interest. Our examination will limit itself in this chapter to a critique of the Wisdom argument for the Logion. Essentially we will be comparing the Logion with Sir 51 (and 6), since it is this connection more than anything out of the Matthean context which governs the Wisdom interpretation. Before proceeding to that, however, we must take up the discussion of whether and how Matthew may have edited the Logion.

4.2. Matthean redaction of the Logion in 11,28-30[153]

Many sceptical eyebrows will be raised at the mere suggestion that we can speak in any productive way of Matthean redaction in a saying as brief as Mt 11,28-30 and without parallel in the NT. One understandably considers such an endeavor thoroughly speculative. Yet in defense of the following attempt to do just this the reader will be encouraged to bear in mind the somewhat firmer hypothesis that Matthew did alter a good many of the Markan and Q sayings he inherited.[154] We cannot assume he modified this saying too, but neither can we preclude the possibility.

If it is accepted with most that Q did not contain vv. 28-30,[155] there is the possibility that the Logion is entirely redactional.[156] Nonetheless, arguments

---

[152] Infra, 195. Although in discussing 11,28-30 Suggs, 99-127, attempts to link Matthew's theology of the Law to Wisdom speculation, his argument fails to convince; cf. Davies-Allison, 2:295; Guelich, 258.

[153] Probably the most important conclusion of this section is that the word "meek" is Matthean, and this conclusion is widely held to be true. Just the same, we will go over the ground with some care because of its intrinsic importance to this study and because the following has become an established component of the discussion of Mt 11,28-30, especially in relation to the later gnostic sayings.

[154] A very readable discussion of this matter is given by Stanton 1992a, 326-345, in a chapter entitled, "Matthew as a Creative Interpreter of the Sayings of Jesus." Stanton begins on the firmer ground of how Matthew worked with Mark, then proceeds on to Q, and finally suggests some samples of Matthew editing "M" (he includes 11,28-30 in the latter group).

[155] Supra, 4f. If Q did contain this Logion, either at Matthew's location or elsewhere, we would still have to undertake the sort of examination which we do in the following; we would only be released from doubt as to whether the saying was pre-Matthean.

[156] Thus Gundry, 218f. He does so due to what he sees as Matthean diction and because the stylistic parallelism strikes him as literary in origin. Also viewing vv. 28-30

for Matthean authorship have not been convincing[157] and there are external reasons to think that the saying may pre-date Matthew (below). This still leaves us with a number of proposals. It might be authentic or at least go back to an authentic saying,[158] it might be an ecclesiastical composition,[159] it might be a Wisdom saying placed in Jesus' mouth,[160] or it might be a mixture of these. G. Barth rightly points out that if we are to view it as a modified Wisdom saying then we are not released from the question of who modified it,[161] which could be the early Christian community, Matthew,[162] or even Jesus himself. We have already said that it is unlikely that Matthew is responsible for the saying,[163] but it is much more difficult, if not finally impossible, to conclusively establish whether the Logion is dominical or ecclesiastical in origin. For many the decisive argument against authenticity appears to be the implicit identification with Wisdom which is generally thought to be a later development,[164] but, apart from the strength of this

---

as a Matthean construction is Barth, 103 n. 1, who is depending on Hirsch, 285, and Bacon, 122f., 204, 208, 212. Cf. also Schrage, 172-174.

[157] Davies-Allison, 2:237f.; cf. Strecker 1962, 172; Hengel 1979, 162. That this is correct will emerge from the following discussion.

[158] For older scholars advocating authenticity, cf. Wilckens 1971, 516 n. 356; Bultmann 1972, 413 n. to page 160. Arguments for authenticity are in Hunter, 248f.; Bacchiocchi 1984, 311-316; Witherington, 205f.

[159] Many. The implied identification with Wisdom is widely thought to exclude authenticity. The saying has been attributed to a Christian prophet; cf. Beare 1962, 89 (cf. 1968, 156f.); Dunn 1975, 26-34 (cf. 1978, 178); Farmer, 66; but against this see Boring, 212 (the findings of Stanton 1992a, 345, are also relevant in this connection). Strecker 1962, 172, argues for a derivation from Matthew's own source (M; cf. Luz, 2:198), but Davies-Allison, 2:237, reject this. The latter, 1:121, appeal to a version of Q to which Luke did not have access (Q^{mt}) and assign our Logion to an editor of this version (2:238); the connection is thought to have been the background of Ex 33 which Mt 11,27 and 28-30 are thought to share. They leave the question open as to whether the editor was using a saying which was "ascribed to Jesus" or a wisdom source. It remains possible, however, that Matthew himself is joining the sayings according to the model of Ex 33, in which case we do not need Q^{mt}; the reference to Jesus' meekness -- which Davies-Allison consider to be one of the links with Ex 33 -- is assigned by them to *Matthew's* hand.

[160] Bultmann 1972, 159f.; cf. Bousset, 90; Dinkler, 117; Betz, 22; Klostermann, 102; Hirsch, 2:285; Schrage, 172f. Luz, 2:200, keeps this option open. The source could be either Sirach or a lost wisdom book.

[161] Barth, 103 n. 1. The hypothesis that this is a *direct* quote from a lost wisdom writing (Bultmann 1972, 160; cf. Wilckens 1971, 517 n. 362) is idle speculation; it is also some distance from the usual understanding of vv. 28-30 as some sort of allusion to Sir 51.

[162] Cf. Gnilka, 1:433.

[163] *GosThom* confirms the impression gained from non-Matthean vocabulary that the Logion pre-dated Matthew's Gospel; hints of a Semitic original further reinforce this. See further below.

[164] For Wisdom speculation as an ecclesiastical development, cf. Dinkler, 117; Davies-Allison, 2:293; W.D. Davies 1948, 155-158; Dunn 1989, 210; Beardslee, 238. If the

argument,¹⁶⁵ our own investigation is questioning the centrality of just this identification to the Logion. It appears most likely, in any case, that Matthew inherited the Logion, but without a parallel in the NT we are hard pressed to reconstruct its pre-Matthean form.

Among the post-apostolic writings, testimonies to the saying or to parts of the saying would include¹⁶⁶ the following:

You see, Beloved, what is the example which is given to us; for if the Lord was thus humble-minded [ἐταπεινοφρόνησεν], what shall we do, who through him have come under the yoke of his grace [ὑπὸ τὸν ζυγὸν τῆς χάριτος]? (*1Clem* 16,17)¹⁶⁷

...the promise of Christ is great and wonderful, and brings rest, in the kingdom which is to come and in everlasting life... For if we do the will of Christ we shall gain rest... (*2Clem* 5,5; 6,7)¹⁶⁸

Jesus said: Come to me, for my yoke is easy and my lordship is gentle, and you will find rest for yourselves. (*GosThom* 90)

Logion so obviously recalls Wisdom and implies that Jesus is speaking *in persona sapientiae* then when Hengel, for example, suggests (1979, 162) that the Logion may stem back to Jesus, he presumably means that it does so in a *very* different form. Betz, 22, reasons consistently with regard to the pre-Matthean meaning of the Logion that "we can only assume that here Jesus has taken the place of hypostasized Wisdom."

¹⁶⁵ Cf. Witherington, 201-208; also Christ, 100-119; P.W. Schmidt (cited in W.D. Davies 1948, 157); Balchin, 217f.; Carson, 484.

¹⁶⁶ The ubiquity of the rest motif in the gnostic literature means that the list of possible allusions to Mt 11,28-30 could be quite extended. E.g. Tuckett 1986, 39f., 63f., notes *GosTruth* 22,12; 33,5; *GosMary* 17,4f.; *TestimTruth* 37,22f. as possible vague and partial allusions to Mt 11,28-30. One might also note *Diogn* 7,3f., though it is more likely dependent on 2Cor 10,1 (διὰ τῆς πραΰτητος καὶ ἐπιεικείας τοῦ Χριστοῦ): "Yes, but did he send him, as a man might suppose, in sovereignty and fear and terror? Not so, but in gentleness [ἐν ἐπιεικείᾳ] and meekness [πραΰτητι], as a king sending his son, he sent him as King, he sent him as God, he sent him as Man to men, he was saving and persuading when he sent him, not compelling, for compulsion is not an attribute of God." 2Cor 10,1 is itself sometimes cited in connection with Mt 11,28-30, yet it will be difficult to establish that 2Cor 10,1 is anything more than a general statement about the totality of Christ's ministry. On the "chain saying" of the *GosHeb* par., see above, 138ff., 160ff. We should not overlook the possibility of an early echo in TDan 5-6 (cf. 5,12f.; 6,9), which may stem from Christian hands in the second half of II A.D. There is nothing particularly "Christian" about the reference to eschatological "rest" (TDan 5,12), but the references to "humility" may well have been added by a Christian redactor. If so this passage testifies to an early Christian understanding of Mt 11,28-30 (cf. Luz, 2:221 n. 148, 223) which combines the coming one from Judah with the OT rest tradition and the Sabbath rest. Lastly, 5Ezra, which is variously dated from the middle to the end of II A.D. (cf. Stanton 1992a, 256-272; Duensing and de Santos Otero, *NTApocr*², 2:641), and which draws heavily on Matthew (Stanton, *loc. cit.*) may have been influenced by Mt 11 at 2,24.34 (cf. 2,12; Stanton allows that 2,24.34 may evidence contact with gnostic thought, but this is not necessarily the case).

¹⁶⁷ Cf. Hagner 1973, 167f., regarding possible links with Mt 11,28-30.

¹⁶⁸ Supra, 138ff.; Davies-Allison, 1:131.

Matthew said, 'Why do we not rest at [on]ce?' The Lord said, 'When you lay down these burdens.' (*DialSav* 65f.)[169]

And he said to the crowds: '*He that hath ears to hear, let him hear.*' And: *Come unto me, all ye that labour and are heavy-laden, and I will give you rest!*'... But meekness has overcome death, bringing it under authority. Meekness has enslaved the enemy. Meekness is a good yoke. Meekness fears no man and does not offer <...> resistance. Meekness is peace and joy and exultation of rest. (*ActsThom* 82.86)

Because of this now I said to you once: 'Everyone who is weary and heavy-laden, come to me and I will give you rest. *For my burden is light and my yoke is compassionate.*' (*Pistis Sophia* 95)[170]

The case has been put that among these the versions of *GosThom*, *DialSav*, and *Pistis Sophia* are independent of Mt 11,28-30 and thus can be useful in reconstructing the pre-Matthean form of the Logion.[171] It seems, however, that the distinction between "independent of Matthew" and "earlier than Matthew" becomes too acute with *Pistis Sophia* 95 (III A.D.) to make this parallel very reliable in getting at the *pre*-Matthean "aphoristic core." *DialSav* 65f. (II A.D.), though earlier than *Pistis Sophia*, is fragmentary and transformed into the form of the dialogue which revolves around the "when" of the rest (cf. *DialSav* 1f. and 68); it may be no more than a very freely rendered allusion, and the degree of independence from Matthew is thus moot. Even if it is put in the dock it is probably more useful as a witness to what the pre-Matthean Logion included than what it did not include. Neither of these versions should be put on equal footing with Matthew as testimonies to the earlier form.[172]

J. Bauer has rendered the Coptic of *GosThom* 90 in Greek as follows:[173]

Λέγει Ἰησοῦς· δεῦτε πρός με, ὅτι χρηστός ἐστιν ὁ ζυγός μου καὶ ἡ κυριότης μου πραεῖά ἐστιν, καὶ εὑρήσετε ἀνάπαυσιν ὑμῖν.

The arguments that this version is not dependent on Mt 11 are convincing.[174] H. Montefiore points out that *GosThom* would most likely have utilized Mt 11,25-27 ("It is hard to think of a logion in the synoptic Gospels more appropriate to Thomas' collection than this") if he had been dependent on

---

[169] Also *DialSav* 1.2.68.
[170] All trans. of *Pistis Sophia* are from Schmidt-MacDermot.
[171] Esp. Koester 1980, 244-250; Crossan, 257-260; De Conick, 280-294; cf. also Bauer 1961, 103-106; Montefiore 1961, 245; D.W. Smith, 34; Strecker 1962, 172 n. 3; Betz, 19f.; Christ, 100-102; Sieber, 137-139.
[172] *Pace* Crossan, 257-260; and De Conick.
[173] 1961, 103; approved by Betz, 19.
[174] *Contra*, e.g., Schrage, 172-174; Wilson 1960, 57f., 82; Haenchen 1961, 73; apparently also, Grant-Freedman, 173f.; Davies-Allison, 2:292.

Chapter Five: Matthew's Wisdom Christology 191

Matthew,[175] and Bauer observes that *GosThom* has κυριότης in place of Matthew's φορτίον, though the latter is more common than the former; moreover, *GosThom* has a preference for the term κοπιάω, and it is unlikely that the compiler would have preferred a shorter version of the saying without that term if he knew of Mt 11,28, or that he would have deleted it if copying the latter.[176] It remains possible that Mt 11,28-30 had been lifted from its Matthean context, circulated independently, and modified in the rehearsing, but since we are without reason to think that Matthew authored the saying we are finally without grounds to exclude the *possibility* that *GosThom* may have drawn on an independent source.[177] Yet we have no way of knowing at present how corrupt or reliable *GosThom*'s source was, and how the compiler may have altered the saying as he found it.[178] Assuming for the moment that the saying is dominical, we cannot even know whether Jesus uttered this invitation on more than one occasion and, if so, whether its wording varied from setting to setting, thus giving rise to varient forms in the traditions. The latter is a possibility that is surprisingly ignored in discussions of the Logion. It may be better, therefore, to begin looking for the pre-Matthean form of the saying using other criteria, and draw in *GosThom* 90 where there is good reason to think its reading is vindicated.

One such criterion may be parallelism. It is possible to recognize parallelism in the saying as it stands in Matthew. For instance, Gundry finds such an involved parallelism in *all* the clauses of Matthew's version that he is inclined to view the Logion as literary rather than oral in origin.[179] Likewise, though she treats it as Matthew's revision of the more original form, A. De Conick suggests the following ABCB'A' structure for Matthew's version:[180]

A (28a) Δεῦτε πρός με (28b) πάντες οἱ κοπιῶντες καὶ πεφορτισμένοι,
B (28c) κἀγὼ ἀναπαύσω ὑμᾶς.
C (29a) ἄρατε τὸν ζυγόν μου ἐφ' ὑμᾶς (29b) καὶ μάθετε ἀπ' ἐμοῦ,
   (29c) ὅτι πραΰς εἰμι καὶ ταπεινὸς τῇ καρδίᾳ,
B' (29d) καὶ εὑρήσετε ἀνάπαυσιν ταῖς ψυχαῖς ὑμῶν·
A' (30a) ὁ γὰρ ζυγός μου χρηστὸς (30b) καὶ τὸ φορτίον μου ἐλαφρόν ἐστιν

---

[175] Montefiore 1961, 245; cf. Sieber, 134f.
[176] Bauer 1961, 105.
[177] So e.g. Sieber, 139; Bauer 1961, 106; Strecker 1962, 172 n. 3; Betz, 19f.; Koester 1980, 246; Crossan, 257-260; De Conick, 282-291; Grundmann, 319. Sieber adds that the ordering of sayings 78, 46, 61b, and 90 in *GosThom* betrays no knowledge of Matthew's ordering of Mt 11.
[178] Cf. Sieber, 263.
[179] Gundry, 218f.; but see Mounce, 107.
[180] De Conick, 289.

Alternatively, if a break is introduced between 29a-b and 29c, then there is an awkward but possible ABA'CB'C' structure.[181] In fact, none of these proposals produces a very smooth and convincing parallelism.

It is interesting, then, that if only v. 29b-c is taken out[182] we are left with four clauses which exhibit good parallelism, followed by a fifth as an undergirding reason:[183]

Δεῦτε πρός με πάντες οἱ κοπιῶντες καὶ **πεφορτισμένοι**,
  κἀγὼ **ἀναπαύσω** ὑμᾶς.
ἄρατε τὸν **ζυγόν** μου ἐφ' ὑμᾶς
  καὶ εὑρήσετε **ἀνάπαυσιν** ταῖς ψυχαῖς ὑμῶν·
ὁ γὰρ **ζυγός** μου χρηστὸς καὶ τὸ **φορτίον** μου ἐλαφρόν ἐστιν

The absence of 29b-c appears to be confirmed by the independent testimony of *GosThom* 90, which is also without those clauses. Moreover, Davies and Allison have pointed out that the clauses of 29b-c contain no words which link them to the others, in contrast to the rest of the saying (highlighted above),[184] although there might be reason to ask whether the word φορτίον was also a Matthean addition (below).

Analyses of parallelism in the Logion are admittedly a weak foundation on which to make a judgment of redaction,[185] but in addition to the symmetry of the saying in Mt 11 without the clauses of 29b-c, and their absence from the apparently independent version of *GosThom* 90, these clauses also show the clearest marks of Matthean vocabulary. In contrast to the rest of the

---

[181] Motte, 227, notes this but rightly rejects it as "unusual"; Motte's own proposal (transpose 29a-b and 29c) fails to convince, however, since it must appeal to textual corruption for which there is no evidence. Deutsch 1987, 40, is equally unconvincing (29a alone is the center of a "ring composition"; cf. Vivano, 190); hers is a transparent bid to accent the yoke image rather than that of "rest" (cf. Deutsch 1987, 46; Suggs, 100).

[182] It may be noted that this simple deletion eases somewhat the problem of the parallelism which Gundry finds too intricate to have originated in the spoken word. V. 30 still echoes themes from more than one of the preceding clauses but this is not incredible, especially if the saying was repeated often.

[183] For this proposal cf. Stanton 1992a, 340-342 (but see 370); Davies-Allison, 2:237f., 290. The result of Luz' analysis (2:198f.) is not very different from Stanton's, though he also considers "all," "heavy laden," and "light burden" to be Matthean. Stanton 1992a, 341 n. 1, alludes in this connection to the study of Filson. Cf. also Légasse, 129-137. In addition to 29b-c, De Conick, 284f., omits 29a and then transposes 29d and 30a-b as in *GosThom* 90. Her analysis takes too many liberties and rests far too heavily on the silence of the later gnostic parallels. Crossan, 257, considers *all* of v. 29 to be Matthean, but his argument assumes that vv. 28-30 followed Q 10,22 (Mt 11,27), and, again, gives too much weight to the silence of the gnostic parallels. Crossan considers the much later *Pistis Sophia* 95 to be an earlier form of the saying than Matthew's version!

[184] Davies-Allison, 2:290. Their observation is based on the Gk, but it seems reasonable to suppose that it would have applied to an Aramaic version if there was one.

[185] Note the variety of proposals in the preceding discussion and notes.

saying, which contains several words occurring nowhere else in Matthew,[186] 29b-c has more than one Matthean characteristic. Most noteworthy are the usages of τῇ καρδίᾳ,[187] and πραΰς,[188] but it is possible that μανθάνω[189] may be Matthean as well. The combined force of these arguments for considering 11,29c if not 29b redactional (parallelism, GosThom 90, Matthean vocabulary) is very strong.[190]

Thus far our analysis has been able to advance fairly smoothly. The description of Jesus as πραΰς, meek, belongs to Matthew's addition (29b-c). Yet reconstructions of a possible underlying Aramaic original have stressed that there is a word play (paronomasia) just between πραΰς (Aram: n^eyaḥ) and ἀνάπαυσις (Aram: 'anḥ).[191] Moreover, it is possible that GosThom 90 betrays an awareness of Jesus "meekness" in this saying as well (ἡ κυριότης μου **πραεια** [rmraš] ἐστιν).[192] Rather than argue that GosThom is here

---

[186] Cf. φορτίζω; ζυγός; χρηστός; and ἐλαφρός (but on the last, see below). It may also be noted that Matthew uses ἀνάπαυσις and ἀναπαύω only one more time each (12,43; 26,45) and both of these are drawn from his sources (Q 11,24; Mk 14,41). Ἀνάπαυσις does not occur elsewhere in the Synoptics; the only other occurrences of ἀναπαύω are in Mk 6,31, which Matthew leaves out of his parallel (Mt 14,13ff.), and Lk 12,19 (L). This observation about non-Matthean terminology is a telling one against Matthean authorship of the Logion; but see Gnilka, 1:433. Of the words within 29b-c, ταπεινός occurs nowhere else in Matthew; cf. ταπεινόω in 18,4; 23,12.

[187] Outside 11,29 this noun is used in the dative at 5,8.28; 9,4; 12,40; 13,15.19; 22,37; 24,48. Davies-Allison, 2:290 n. 244 note that Matthew follows (ἐν) τῇ καρδίᾳ with something other than a genitive personal pronoun five times, while Mark and Luke never do this. Gundry, 219, notes that Matthew inserts τῇ καρδίᾳ as a dative of respect (as in 11,29) at 5,8; cf. Strecker 1962, 174.

[188] This noun occurs among the Synoptics only in Matthew at 5,5; 21,5, and here (cf. 1Pet 3,4; πραΰτης occurs more often, but not in the Synoptics; cf. esp. 2Cor 10,1: διὰ τῆς πραΰτητος καὶ ἐπιεικείας τοῦ Χριστοῦ). Interestingly, both 5,5 and 21,5 are drawing on the OT (Ps 37,11; Zech 9,9). We will return to this idea of "meekness" below; cf. Stanton 1992a, 341f., 371f.

[189] The μαθ- stem is indeed prevalent in Matthew, but outside of 11,29 there is only the one passage where the verb μανθάνω has been inserted (9,13); the one other occurrence (Mt 24,32) is drawn from Matthew's source (Mk 13,28). It is not possible to make a sure judgment on this basis; see, however, Stanton 1992a, 341; Luz, 2:199.

[190] Stanton's argument (1992a, 340-342) appeared earlier in the collection of papers originally read at a 1982 Tübingen symposium which appeared in ET in 1991 (Stuhlmacher). P. Lampe and U. Luz, in their overview of the discussion, report that there was general acceptance of Stanton's proposal that 11,29c is Matthean; there was further support for the idea that 29b is also Matthean; cf. Lampe-Luz, 396f.

[191] Cf. Black, 183f.; Gundry 1967, 136; Bullinger, 322. A further indication of an Aramaic original is that the "prevailing sounds" of an Aramaic version "are all soft, smooth, and pleasant" (Black 183). It is to be noted that the older attempt to uncover Aramaic sources for the gospels has been called into question by more recent research (Wise; cf. further Rabin; Mussies). It is not yet apparent, however, that the attempt, particularly as regards our Logion, was entirely misguided or without foundation.

[192] Davies-Allison, 2:292, note this; cf. Witherington, 206.

relying on Mt 11,29b-c,[193] one might wonder whether the reference to Jesus' meekness wasn't contained, similar to *GosThom*, in Matthew's v. 30.

This is not without problems, since ἐλαφρός occurs only here in Matthew,[194] and the adjective πραΰς favors some noun other than φορτίον which is the sole linking word with 28a-b. It has been suggested that a rationale can be provided for the alternation of *GosThom*'s ἡ κυριότης and Matthew's τό φορτίον on the grounds of Hebrew and Aramaic usage of the ideas.[195] Moreover, the yoke image is often associated with that of "kingship,"[196] which is, in turn, conceptually close to the idea of "lordship." Thus it is at least possible that "lordship" might have been the more primitive reading.[197] If then, 30b was closer to the reading of *GosThom* 90 in Matthew's source, and if Matthew chose to highlight the idea of πραΰς by drawing it up into his 29c, then Matthew's use of φορτίον may easily have been suggested by πεφορτισμένοι in 28b.[198] Even so, it is difficult to explain why Matthew would have omitted the seemingly more suggestive ἡ κυριότης.[199]

A simple answer to this question does not readily suggest itself. For the present it may be best to suggest that the reference to Jesus' meekness may

---

[193] *Pace* Davies-Allison, 2:292. If, with Davies-Allison, the description of Jesus as "meek" should be considered Matthean, while a reconstructed Aramaic should be taken seriously (Davies-Allison, 2:238; though they do not refer specifically to the word play), then the reading of *GosThom* 90 suggests itself as a solution.

[194] Elsewhere in the NT it occurs only at 2Cor 4,17.

[195] Thus De Conick, 287f. De Conick is depending on a comparison of the MT and the Targumim of Isa 9,3; 10,27; and 14,25; she suggests that the ideas of "yoke," "burden," and "lordship" were interchangeable. Bauer 1961, 105, points out that the word "lordship" is rarer than "burden," and that the editor of *GosThom* would not likely have substituted the one for the other; cf. further Bauer 1961, 106 n. 28.

[196] Cf. esp. Büchler, 36-118; also Bauer 1961, 100-103; De Conick, 286; Stanton 1992a, 375; Bacchiocchi 1984, 302f.

[197] So De Conick, 287f.; Bauer 1961, 105.

[198] De Conick, 288, suggests that Matthew opted for φορτίον over κυριότης due to 23,4; such a thematic rationale is not to be excluded, but the use of πεφορτισμένοι in 11,28b is nearer and is a somewhat simpler explanation. Luz, 2:199, considers both φορτίζω and φορτίον to be Matthean; likewise, Bauer 1961, 105, who suggests that the whole of Matthew's 28b was Matthean and drew in its train the change of 30b, but this gives too much weight to the silence of *GosThom* 90. One must allow, after all, that *GosThom*'s source may have been defective. Neither φορτίζω nor κοπιάω (cf. 6,28 = Lk 12,27) are demonstrably Matthean additions. *GosThom*'s non-inclusion of Matthew's 11,28b may evidence *independence* from Matthew, but it does not have any special claim to being the more *original*; cf. De Conick, 282f.

[199] Favoring φορτίον as the more original are Koester 1980, 246; and Crossan, 257. Crossan notes that both *Pistis Sophia* and *DialSav* favor reading "burdens" over "lordship." De Conick, 288, leaves the question open as to whether Matthew or some pre-Matthean translator was responsible for the change from "lordship" to "burden." Bauer 1961, 106 n. 28, also considers whether δεσποτεία (rather than κυριότης) would not be a fitting equivalent of the Coptic.

well have been in Matthew's v. 30, without attempting a reconstruction. If this is correct, then Matthew has highlighted rather than inserted the idea of πραΰς through his editorial activity.

In sum, one can be reasonably confident that Matthew's 29c, if not also his 29b were his own additions. It is also possible that the reference to Jesus' meekness was contained in Matthew's v. 30, though this is less easy to demonstrate.

4.3. Comparison of Mt 11,28-30 and Sir 51

With justification the form of Mt 11,28-30 (invitation + promise) is itself termed "allgemein weisheitlich,"[200] and certainly the invitation to come and "learn" portrays Jesus as a teacher. Somewhat startling is the directness of Jesus' promise of rest in v. 28, which is most closely paralleled by *God's* provision of rest in the OT. Equally surprising and more often noted is the way that Jesus calls people to take *his* yoke. If this is to be taken as a unique manner of speaking among the Jews of that day,[201] then Jesus' claim is exactly on par with his authoritative, "but I say to you." This does not, however, amount to a *Wisdom* Christology. That depends on a *literary allusion* to Sir 6 and/or 51.[202] Of these two we will isolate Sir 51 for a detailed comparison, since this is far and away the most often cited parallel, and the one often thought to be the closest to Mt 11,28-30.[203] Many of the

---

[200] See Christ, 102, 113, and Deutsch 1987, 113-139, for parallels; cf. Hengel 1979, 161f.; Luz, 2:217. Yet Christ's claim, 103, that this alone identifies Jesus and Wisdom goes much too far. The personal appeal is typical of Jesus (Jeremias 1971, 159), and the form of invitation + promise is not restricted to wisdom thought (Mt 4,19; Jn 7,37f.; Isa 51,1-5). Gundry, 220, suggests that the invitation stems from Jesus' earlier call to discipleship (4,19; δεῦτε), and not Sir 51. One might note Ψ 33,2f.6.12.18f. [34,1f.5f.11.17f.]; Ψ 118,71.79 [119,71.79]; cf. Micah 4,1-5

[201] In her survey of Jewish literature Deutsch found nothing similar to Jesus' reference to *his* yoke (she does note that a "yoke" is implied in 1QH 6,19: "They who bore the yoke of my testimony"; 1987, 120; cf. Grundmann, 318), and she suggests that this is due to the association of the yoke image with submission to Torah, the covenant, and the Lord of the covenant; the sages avoided any hint that they stood in the place of those (1987, 133). On the other hand, Tyre, 117, states that "the yoke idea was readily employed in intertestamental and Tannaitic materials to depict the relationship between the teacher or his teachings and the disciples." For the image of a disciple bearing the "burden" of his teacher's teaching, cf. Berger-Colpe, 121. Cf. Gaechter, 385.

[202] The image of the yoke is used often enough of the Law, but it is used of *Wisdom* only in Sir 6 and 51; cf. Deutsch 1987, 113-139 (esp. 118); Christ, 108f. In addition to Sir 6 and 51 Christ refers only to OdesSol 42,7f., but there is no reference to Wisdom there. This combined with the other verbal links narrows the destination of an allusion down to Sirach, so long as we are speaking of a *Wisdom* Christology.

[203] Allen, 124, speaks of "undoubted dependence" on Sir 51; Gardner, 193, says that "nowhere is the parallel more striking...than in Sirach 51:23-27"; likewise, Klostermann, 103f.; Albright-Mann, 146; Schweizer, 272; Harrington, 169f.; Gnilka, 1:439;

following considerations apply to Sir 6, however, and especially the decisive consideration of Matthean redaction.

4.3.1. Mt 11,28-30 is not an allusion to Sir 51

When we turn to compare Mt 11,28-30 with Sir 51 we may note the following parallels.[204] I have printed the common words in bold type and underlined parallel ideas.

Sir 51,23-30
23 ἐγγίσατε **πρός** με, ἀπαίδευτοι, καὶ αὐλίσθητε ἐν οἴκῳ παιδείας. 24 τί ἔτι ὑστερεῖτε ἐν τούτοις καὶ αἱ **ψυχαὶ ὑμῶν** διψῶσιν σφόδρα; 25 ἤνοιξα τὸ στόμα μου καὶ ἐλάλησα Κτήσασθε ἑαυτοῖς ἄνευ ἀργυρίου. 26 τὸν τράχηλον ὑμῶν ὑπόθετε ὑπὸ **ζυγόν**, καὶ ἐπιδεξάσθω ἡ **ψυχὴ ὑμῶν** παιδείαν. ἐγγύς ἐστιν **εὑρεῖν** αὐτήν. 27 ἴδετε ἐν ὀφθαλμοῖς ὑμῶν ὅτι ὀλίγον **ἐκοπίασα** καὶ **εὗρον** ἐμαυτῷ πολλὴν **ἀνάπαυσιν**. 28 μετάσχετε παιδείας ἐν πολλῷ ἀριθμῷ ἀργυρίου καὶ πολὺν χρυσὸν κτήσασθε ἐν αὐτῇ. 29 εὐφρανθείη ἡ **ψυχὴ ὑμῶν** ἐν τῷ ἐλέει αὐτοῦ, καὶ μὴ αἰσχυνθείητε ἐν αἰνέσει αὐτοῦ. 30 ἐργάζεσθε τὸ ἔργον ὑμῶν πρὸ καιροῦ, καὶ δώσει τὸν μισθὸν ὑμῶν ἐν καιρῷ αὐτου.

Mt 11,28-30
28 Δεῦτε **πρός** με πάντες οἱ **κοπιῶντες** καὶ πεφορτισμένοι,

κἀγὼ **ἀναπαύσω** ὑμᾶς. 29 ἄρατε τὸν **ζυγόν** μου ἐφ' ὑμᾶς καὶ μάθετε ἀπ' ἐμοῦ, ὅτι πραΰς εἰμι καὶ ταπεινὸς τῇ καρδίᾳ, καὶ **εὑρήσετε ἀνάπαυσιν** ταῖς **ψυχαῖς ὑμῶν**· 30 ὁ γὰρ **ζυγός** μου χρηστὸς καὶ τὸ φορτίον μου ἐλαφρόν ἐστιν.

Firstly, the verbal links are not very strong.[205] The parallel wording is confined to "to me," "souls," "yoke," "labor," and "find rest." Yet "souls" is used so differently syntactically that it must be nothing more than coincidental,[206] and "to me" is generally unremarkable as a parallel.[207] The

---

Schnackenburg, 1:106. Both Suggs, 102, and Deutsch 1987, 118, cite Sir 51 as the closest parallel; likewise, Dunn 1989, 200f. France, 304 n. 51, refers to Deutsch and says that "the only true parallel [to Mt 11,28-30] is Ben Sira 51:23-30 (with the associated passage in chapter 6)." Others, e.g. D.W. Smith, 36f.; Davies-Allison, 2:293 n. 251; Witherington, 207, believe Sir 6 to be closer than Sir 51. Sir 24,19-22 is often cited as well.

[204] We will compare Matthew with the Greek Sirach primarily because this is the procedure most often encountered. Note, in addition, that the Hebrew of ch. 51 may have lacked the reference to rest (thus Skehan, 398; Skehan-Di Lella, 576, 579); but see above, 77 n. 1.

[205] Christ, 112f.

[206] Davies-Allison, 2:293, think that "souls," "find" and "rest" are all to be accounted for by the use of Jer 6,16; likewise, Gundry, 220; Carson, 278. Yet even if the phraseology of Jer 6,16 (MT; not LXX) has influenced our Logion (which is not easy to establish), it may have been mixed with Sir 6. This only highlights the independence of

syntactical difference in the way κοπιάω is used amounts to more than a slight change of meaning; it carries an altogether different idea. In Matthew the "laborers" are those offered rest, while in Sirach "laboring" (after Wisdom/wisdom) is what we are called to in order to attain rest in the end (cf. Sir 6,19; 24,34).[208]

A fact which is easily obscured by the tendency to arrange Mt 11 and Sir 51 in parallel columns is that the complex of "yoke," "labor," and "rest" is a "natural coalescence of themes" that scarcely needs a specific parallel to account for it.[209] C. Tyre, after a lengthy survey of the yoke image in the ancient Near East, the OT, intertestamental, and rabbinic literature, remarks:

The concept of yoke, with the widest variety of interpretations, was public domain during the New Testament times. The Matthew statement is akin to any number of statements concerning the yoke if one uses as the basis for judgment only similarity of language or ideas... [Mt 11,28-30], in all probability, arose quite naturally out of general, contemporary literary usage with no necessary specific relationship to any particular prior statement.[210]

Once we see Mt 11 and Sir 51 beside each other the parallel is indeed apparent, but the verbal pointers to Sirach, if indeed they are such, are hardly striking. Nor is it merely the fact that the complex is "natural" which makes the connection vague. It is also the very different usage of the separate ideas which weakens the case that this was an allusion (see further below). If we are to think that all these are deliberate reworkings of the saying on the part of Matthew, then we will need think that Matthew's interest in Sir 51 was substantial. It seems more likely, however, that these differences are not at all conscious and deliberate modifications of Sirach.

Mt 11,28-30 from any *single* source. I would judge it an independent and free formulation.

[207] This latter element of the saying is not paralleled in Sir 6. Elsewhere in Matthew, cf. 14,28; 19,14; 25,36.39.

[208] Cf. Hunter, 248f.; Gundry, 220; Carson, 278. Commenting on the use of the yoke image in the Apocrypha and Pseudepigrapha, Deutsch 1987, 116, observes that it "is an appropriate image for Wisdom and Torah for two reasons: (1) wisdom, particularly as reflected in the book of Sirach, is acquired through the hard work of study and requires total dedication; and (2) wisdom is a 'burden' because it is Torah, and therefore a correlative of covenant with all its social and religious responsibilities." It is true that in saying this Deutsch has one eye on the yoke image in Mt 11,28-30, and certainly it carries the idea of labor there as well. The point being made here, however, is that when the verb κοπιάω occurs in Sir 51 it falls in with this idea of "laboring" after Wisdom, and this is true in spite of the figure of speech ("labored *but little*").

[209] Davies-Allison, 2:293 n. 251; cf. Cerfaux, 154, 157. Note Lam 5,5, where yoke imagery is followed by the statement that κοπιάσαμεν, οὐκ ἀνεπαύθημεν. Likewise, Gen 49,15; Sir 33,25-30 (NRSV numbering); 40,1-7; 22,13; 1En 103,11-13; Ψ 65,11f. [66,11f.].

[210] Tyre, 110f.

Secondly, important elements of Mt 11,28-30 cannot really be accounted for by this parallel (all of these will be pursued further in the following chapter). The characterization of the invited as "weary and heavy laden" betrays a world of ideas which belongs to the Jesus of Matthew, and suggests neither a literary nor thematic link with Sirach and Wisdom.[211] It is remarkable, then, that one of the verbal parallels (κοπιάω) is embedded in this clause. The characterization of Jesus as "meek and lowly" will be taken up below; it is an enduring embarrassment to arguments for a Wisdom Christology. The "yoke" image in Mt 11 suggests the notion of discipleship, but this is scarcely the idea in the yoke imagery of Sir 6 and 51.[212] Even the idea of "rest" is not well accounted for. There is no parallel in Sirach for Jesus' direct offer of rest (28c),[213] and the closer literary parallel to 29c is probably Jer 6,16.[214] It is difficult to see how Sirach sheds any light on the "rest" as a *Heilsgut* beyond the observation that it is a fruit of wisdom. Indeed, the importance of the rest motif diminishes the more we stress the notion of a Wisdom Christology. It becomes increasingly less a matter of what Jesus says, and more a matter of the encoded Christology.

---

[211] Stanton 1992a, 369. *Contra* Luz, 2:217 n. 126, whose "parallels" do not fill the bill. Wisdom's call is more typically addressed to the "simple" (Prov 1,20ff.; 8,5; 9,4); alternatively, to those who are "worthy" of her (WisSol 6,16) and those who "desire" her (Sir 24,19). Christ, 119, observes that in 11,28-30, "Im Unterschied zur Weisheitstradition sind die Erwählten speziell Mühselige und Beladene." In Matthew these ideas are more typically explained with reference to the people of the land (הארץ עם), tax collectors and sinners, the lost sheep of the house of Israel, the harassed and helpless sheep without a shepherd, the poor; Mt 9,10-13.36; 10,6; 11,5; 15,24; 23,4 (12,11f.?); cf. Hengel 1979, 162; Christ, 111; Jeremias 1971, 109-113. Cf. Jer 31,25 [LXX 38,25]. See below, 239ff.

[212] Cf. Bacchiocchi 1984, 303. On the idea of being a "disciple" of Wisdom, cf. Deutsch 1987, 136, who cites Sir 4,11-19; 6,18-37; 14,20-15,10; 24,19-22; *Abot* 1,6.16; *BM* 2,11; *t.BM* 2,29. It is not at all clear, however, that the imagery of Sir 4,11-19; 14,20ff. and 24,19ff. should be read into the yoke image of Sir 6 and 51. The latter is more suggestive of the *labor* which is required if one is to acquire wisdom (cf. 6,25 [βάσταξον αὐτήν]; but who "carries" their rabbi, and is Jesus asking us to bear *him*?), and much less of any personal relationship which will be established between Wisdom and humans. Moreover, Sir 4,19 sounds very uncharacteristic of Jesus. Christ's claim (109) that Jesus *is* his yoke is baseless.

[213] There is a big difference between Jesus ben Sirach proclaiming how he has found rest for himself, and Jesus of Nazareth promising to give rest to others; Schmid, 204; Gundry, 220; cf. Philo, *QuaesGen* III,62. Wisdom does not make a promise of rest in either Sir 6 or 51, and neither Christ, 103 (the passages Christ cites on p. 105 are not real parallels), nor Deutsch 1987, 113-139, note a parallel to this elsewhere. The closest parallel to that idea in Sirach would in fact be 24,11 where God gives rest to Wisdom (there the verb is καταπαύω). Suggs, 100, states that the *sophos* promises that people will *find* rest, but only Wisdom can promise to *give* rest, but he does not ground the latter in evidence. Apparently it is an inference from Mt 11,28.

[214] Thus Christ, 103, 106; Cerfaux, 156; cf. Stendahl, 141f.; Gundry 1967, 136.

Chapter Five: Matthew's Wisdom Christology   199

Thirdly, when we assume an interpretive connection tensions ensue. The *invitation* in Sir 51,23 is not given by Wisdom but by ben Sirach the sage.[215] Again, although it would be over simplified and misleading to label 11,28-30 an anti-Halakah passage, it probably does contain a tacit polemic against many of the oral traditions which Sir 51 would have tacitly approved and, indeed, considered wisdom.[216] To that extent the invitation and promise of Jesus competes with rather than simply parallels Wisdom's; Jesus offers rest to those wearied by "Wisdom," or to those wearied in their pursuit of Wisdom.

On the basis of such a comparison it seems likely that if we suspend the effort to demonstrate a Matthean Wisdom Christology we will be somewhat less impressed with this parallel.[217] Although the Logion shares some formal and terminological similarities with Sirach, as it stands in Matthew the differences are so great as to suggest either a careful reworking or a free and largely disinterested use of similar wording. The Logion contains echoes[218] of the language and imagery of a familiar work (Sirach) but is so completely adapted to Jesus that the voice of Sirach has almost been lost. That *in Matthew* we should speak of an *allusion* to Sirach is unlikely.

---

[215] Noting this, Deutsch 1990, 37, argues that "we must conclude that Matthew is here casting Jesus not only as Wisdom, but as Sage." Cf. Deutsch 1987, 130; 1982, 400-409.

[216] Deutsch 1987, 115, admits that "wisdom" in Sirach may have included oral law as well.

[217] A similar reserve is expressed in different ways by Schlatter, 386; Gaechter, 383f.; Schmid, 204; Bonnard, 169; Hill, 207f. (clearly depending on Hunter, 248); Gundry, 220; Mounce, 107; Carson, 227f.; Davies-Allison, 2:292f. (they do see an identification with Wisdom, however; 289); Hoskyns, 76-78; T.W. Manson, 478; Bauer 1970, 749; Cerfaux, 153-159; de Kruijf, 69-71; Verseput 1986, 145; Stanton 1992a, 368ff. (Piper, 163, cites Stanton's argument favorably); and Bacchiocchi 1984, 311-313. Sand, 251-253, doubts whether this Logion gains its peculiar significance in relation to Sir 51. Lührmann, 67, 99, doubts whether one can speak of an identification of Jesus and Wisdom in 11,28-30. De Kruijf believes that Mt 11,28-30 may be a "spiritualized" version of Mk 6,31; similarly, Lampe-Luz, 397.

[218] As I use the term here, an "echo" may or may not be the result of a conscious choice, and the author may or may not intend for the reader to recognize the source; it is simply the presence of wording that is due to the influence of a familiar saying or passage and that has the potential of reminding the reader of that saying or passage. For instance, Jesus may have used Sirach's wording, consciously or not, without intending that his listeners understand him against that background, though some may have done just that; in the case of Jesus, we may speak of an echo. Yet those who might have taken up the saying, interpreted it in terms of Wisdom, and passed it on in that connection, would have come to regard the wording as an allusion (this is not to suggest that anyone did so use the saying). We will return to the question of the conscious use of Sirach, but for now it may be said that *in Matthew* we might allow for a secondary influence from (probably not an allusion to) Sirach, on which, see below, 205f., 234f. Nevertheless, Matthew's primary interests are elsewhere.

There is reason to think that this conclusion also holds for the earliest stage in the history of the Logion. We noted that many scholars have considered this Logion to be essentially a modified wisdom saying placed on the lips of Jesus by the church or Matthew. In favor of an ecclesiastical vs. a dominical origin, Davies and Allison have observed that Jesus nowhere else speaks of his yoke or promises rest, and further that the implied Wisdom Christology points to the church.[219] On the contrary, if the authenticity of the saying is to be questioned on the grounds that Jesus nowhere else speaks of his "yoke" or promises "rest," then it seems even more unlikely that the church would have fashioned a saying out of motifs which are simultaneously foreign to Jesus and incidental to the real point of the saying, which is (so it is thought) to suggest that Jesus speaks as Wisdom. Surely a more characteristic saying (of both Wisdom and Jesus) could have been utilized! It is more likely that even if the Logion is to be considered in some sense a modified wisdom saying, then it originally had no interest in a Wisdom Christology. The Logion originally found expression either by Jesus or the church as an invitation to salvation, not as a veiled hint at Jesus' identity vis-à-vis Wisdom.

Thus the more we look at the evidence -- at least as far as the Logion's earlier use and its use in Matthew -- the more likely it becomes that if Sirach is relevant to considerations of Mt 11,28-30 it is as a loose and informal influence on the phraseology, and the less likely it becomes that the interest was in a Wisdom Christology.

4.3.2. Two questions

The issues can be brought into sharper focus by posing two different questions. The one is whether there is any evidence that the language of this Logion was actually understood in relation to Sirach as suggesting that Jesus is speaking *in persona sapientiae*. The other is whether Matthew has *developed* this Logion in that direction, either in literary or in thematic terms.

As for the first question: arguing from silence, I am unaware of any external evidence in the first and second centuries that the connection with Sirach actually registered. In our eagerness to plot this saying on a trajectory from wisdom literature and Wisdom speculation to second century Gnosticism we have ignored the fact that the post-apostolic citations of this Logion do not evidence even a trace of Sirach, nor that Jesus speaks in the

---

[219] Davies-Allison, 2:293; similarly, Luz, 2:200.

saying as *Wisdom*.²²⁰ Such an observation is inherently inconclusive, but it does seem worth noting as often as the gnostic parallels are cited.

There is, however, some very tenuous internal evidence that at least the wisdom affinities of the saying had been appreciated, seen in that the Logion is connected to 11,25-27.²²¹ Since Matthew elsewhere evidences parallels with Sirach,²²² it is possible that he was alive to this *literary* parallel.²²³ Seemingly against this is the fact (see below) that Matthew himself develops the saying along lines which have no direct connection with Wisdom or Sirach. Nonetheless, it cannot be ruled out that the Logion had been associated with Wisdom speculation *prior* to Matthew,²²⁴ and that the present location of this saying reflects this.²²⁵ I cannot see the good in refusing to acknowledge this as a possibility, but it should remain only a possibility.

How then does Matthew himself *develop* this saying?²²⁶ We have said that Matthew probably added the clause of 29c, "because I am meek and

---

²²⁰ *Contra* Christ, 101f., who asserts without evidence that *GosThom* 90 "stellt sich als gnostische Interpretation von Sir 6 und 51...dar."

²²¹ Cf. Suggs, 99, though Suggs is of necessity more suggestive than specific on this point; likewise, Christ, 117f.

²²² E.g. cf. Mt 6,7 with Sir 5,2; 7,14, and Mt 6,14f. with Sir 28,1f. For further parallels between Matthew and Sirach, see Witherington, 143f. It is worth noting that Sirach was a popular and well known work (Witherington, 76f.).

²²³ Stendahl, 27, 142, argues that wisdom literature "had been studied in the school of Matthew and related to Jesus, equating Him with Wisdom..." In favor of some awareness of Sir 51 is the oft noted parallel of Sir 51,1 and Mt 11,25; Gundry, 220. But see also 4Bar 5,32 (I-II A.D.), which links a similar thanksgiving with an echo of Jer 6,16: "I will bless you, O God of heaven and of the earth, the rest of the souls of the righteous in every place" (on the echo, cf. Allison 1988, 483f., who argues that 4Bar is not dependent on Matthew). Similarly, cf. Isa 25,1-26,6 LXX, which bears more than one parallel with Mt 11,25-30: Κύριε ὁ θεός μου, δοξάσω σε, ὑμνήσω τὸ ὄνομά σου...εὐλογήσει σε ὁ λαὸς ὁ πτωχός... ἀνάπαυσιν δώσει ὁ θεὸς ἐπὶ τὸ ὄρος τοῦτο... καὶ πατήσουσιν αὐτοὺς [i.e., the proud] πόδες πραέων καὶ ταπεινῶν.

²²⁴ Thus, e.g., Betz, 22. The word "prior" is stressed because Matthew himself orients the Logion differently.

²²⁵ See further on the question of placement below, 205f. It can be noted at this point that Meadors, 47, has concluded on the basis of his examination of Q that "there exists no evidence that Q or the Q community ever interpreted Jesus along the lines of a 'wisdom myth' or proclaimed a wisdom christology which contrasted in some fashion with the general portrait of Jesus as proclaimed in the Synoptic Gospels"; see further, Meadors, 47 n. 57, 67. Meadors' own view is that "in Q Jesus is a wise teacher who acts authoritatively in pronouncing judgment" (68). However his results may be assessed by other Q scholars, his conclusion anticipates our own for *Matthew*.

²²⁶ It was noted that Matthew may have added the verb μανθάνω, and this is one of the conceptual parallels between the Logion and Sirach 51. Yet if the argument that this verb is Matthean depends on considerations of Matthean style (the μαθ- stem) and themes (teaching), then it will not do to forget or ignore *that* rationale and now suggest that he added this verb to enhance the parallel with Sirach. If the latter were the case we would have expected the use of παιδεία or one of its cognates, which are very common in Sirach, rather than μανθάνω, which is considerably rarer in the wisdom literature *and* in

lowly in heart." In *literary* terms this is certainly no enhancement of a connection with Sirach, and is completely unexplainable on the premise that Matthew was primarily concerned with that work.

In *thematic* terms, Stanton has pointed out that Wisdom is typically portrayed as boldly calling out on the street corner with pride and even arrogance (Sir 24,1f.; Prov 1,20ff.; 8,1ff.). He suggests then that this characterization of Jesus as meek and lowly stands in stark contrast to Wisdom.[227] It might be better, however, to put this point differently. One might prefer to ask whether this is the sort of characterization that one would use -- indeed, *add to the saying* -- if the intention was to make us think of Sirach and Wisdom. I would think that the answer to that would have to be negative. It is not enough to cite ways in which humility is associated with wisdom thought generally, for it is the characterization of *Wisdom* which is decisive here.[228] Moreover, the crucial considerations are that 11,29c is an *addition*, and that as such it almost certainly stands in line with *other* Matthean themes.[229] These we will explore further in the following chapter.

---

the Synoptics (cf. Rengstorf 1967, 406). When the "yoke" image probably stands for the whole relationship of discipleship, Matthew may have added μανθάνω partly because it is primarily in Jesus' teaching that the baptized community encounters the risen Lord; it is therein that the idea of discipleship continues to be meaningful; cf. 28,19f.

[227] Stanton 1992a, 369f.; likewise, De Conick, 283-285; Verseput 1986, 145; Schmid, 204.

[228] *Contra* Christ, 114-116; Deutsch 1987, 79f., 96-100, 130-133; Beardslee, 235. Christ faces the matter squarely: "Kommt hier vielleicht eine andere Christologie zur bisher festgestellten Weisheitschristologie hinzu? Schließt die Identifikation Jesu mit der Weisheit aus, daß Jesus gleichzeitig sanftmütig und demütig ist, oder gehört die Sanftmut und Demut als wesentlicher Bestandteil zur Weisheitschristologie?" He of course opts for the latter, based primarily on the "homelessness" of Wisdom, humility as a fruit of wisdom (cf. Jas 3,13), and the refreshment which wisdom brings. Nonetheless he admits that the lowliness motif in Mt 11,29 does not stem directly from wisdom backgrounds (he cites Zech 9,9), and is at best only compatible with Wisdom. Deutsch runs back and forth between the attributes of Wisdom and those of the sage, between wisdom motifs at Qumran and those in the Tannaitic literature, cutting and pasting together a picture which finally resembles Mt 11,28-30 (it is the humble sage from Qumran and the humble Hillel that provide the clearest parallels in this case). She has shown that a pure Wisdom reading of the passage is possible, but not that it is likely. Arvedson, 217, is less optimistic that Mt 11,29c can be applied directly to Wisdom (Christ, 115 n. 441 almost admits this), but like the others he finds a round about way. Hingle, 360, has pointed to the possible relevance of WisSol 1,6 -- "for wisdom is a kindly spirit [φιλάνθρωπον γὰρ πνεῦμα σοφία]" -- though this passage is not only isolated but conceptually (see the context) removed from Mt 11,28-30. It is because of these arguments, however, that I have not gone as far as Stanton in suggesting that the lowliness motif is *antithetical* to Wisdom; cf. Deutsch's criticisms (1987, 177f. n. 69) of Stanton. But these attempts to reconcile this element of the Logion to Wisdom do go against the grain and ignore a much simpler explanation.

[229] Most who argue for the Wisdom Christology in this saying give little if any attention to the question of Matthean redaction; e.g., Suggs, 99ff.; Christ, 114-116; Dunn

Where Stanton's point carries some more weight is actually in the following context of Mt 12,19. There Jesus is portrayed as one who does not quarrel or cry out and whose voice is not heard in the streets (Isa 42,1-4). On the other hand, according to Prov. 1,20f., Wisdom

> ...cries out in the street; in the squares she raises her voice. At the busiest corner she cries out; at the entrance of the city gates she speaks.

To be sure, Jesus is issuing an apparently public invitation in 11,28, but if the figure of Wisdom was at the forefront of Matthew's mind, then the characterization of 12,19 is somewhat surprising.

4.3.3. The "paradox" of yoke and rest

If all this is true, however, then what are we to make of the one significant parallel with Sir 6 and 51, that of the "paradoxical" juxtapositioning of "yoke" and "rest"?[230] Indeed, it is just there that the whole question of a Wisdom Christology resides, and it seems to have survived our critical analysis.

To begin with, the imagery is functioning so differently in the two passages that it is not clear that we should even speak of a parallel in the "paradox." The imagery in Sirach is fashioned after everyday agricultural life, so that the day's work is rewarded with the evening's rest, and the season's labor with the harvest's prosperity. This is assumed in Sir 51,27, and made explicit in 6,28: ἐπ' ἐσχάτων γὰρ εὑρήσεις τὴν ἀνάπαυσιν αὐτῆς.[231] There is nothing paradoxical in this.[232] The use of the word

---

1989, 198-201. In an early chapter of her study Deutsch 1987, 44f., does judge the noun πραΰς (not the clause of 29c) to be redactional and relates it to the servant motif of Mt 12, but she does not build on this or even raise the point again thereafter. Likewise Witherington.

[230] Deutsch 1987, 46, 117f., 134-137 (cf. 130), stresses this "paradox" in drawing the parallel with Sirach; cf. D.W. Smith, 34f. There is a hint of such a "paradox" in Gen 49,15.

[231] Cf. 6,19; 51,30. Cf. Schweizer, 273. In Sir 6,28ff. the yoke of Wisdom metamorphoses into royal garb to symbolize how perseverance in wisdom will be rewarded. It would be unjustified to read this into Mt 11,28-30, as does Arvedson, 180-185, 218-228.

[232] One can justifiably argue that the "labor" never goes out of the sage's life, but here it is a question of the imagery being used. What is being portrayed in Sirach is a movement from immaturity to maturity and from foolishness to wisdom; to this corresponds the movement from labor to rest: "Come to her like one who plows and sows, and *wait* for her good harvest. For when you cultivate her you will toil but little, and *soon* you will eat of her produce" (6,19; italics added). The fool does not keep at the task (6,20-22), but those who do persevere will find her rest "*at last*" (6,28). Deutsch 1987, 117, 123f., stresses that this "paradox" is missing elsewhere in the Pseudepigrapha

"labor" is synonymous with the taking up of the yoke, and the yoke is not one of discipleship or partnership but of bearing Wisdom herself (6,25).[233] Jesus' words, however, are somewhat different and do seem to imply the "paradox" which is so provocative and suggestive to interpreters. This is because the taking up of Jesus' yoke is not synonymous with the "laboring," but is somehow an *answer* to the laboring, even if it is a (light) burden; it is not one of carrying Jesus, but implies some sort of partnership; and its promise of rest is somehow contained in the very process of yoke bearing itself, even if it also holds forth the hope of the rest $\dot{\epsilon}\pi'$ $\dot{\epsilon}\sigma\chi\acute{\alpha}\tau\omega\nu$. The language of Mt 11,28-30 is by far the more innovative of the two passages, and its "paradox" has been too easily read *back into* Sirach.

To put things in perspective one should note the familiarity of the yoke image in the OT and Jewish literature generally[234] and its natural connection with the idea of rest from labor. We should also assume behind Jesus' offer the principle that life without *any* yoke is not a possibility.[235] When in the OT the Israelites would throw off YHWH's yoke it meant taking on the yoke of other nations.[236] Likewise,

A.R. Nehunya b. Haqqaneh says, "From whoever accepts upon himself the yoke of Torah do they remove the yoke of the state and the yoke of hard labor. And upon whoever removes from himself the yoke of Torah do they lay the yoke of the state and the yoke of hard labor."[237]

One might also recall the idea, expressed so forcefully by Paul in Rom 1, that God's judgment is seen precisely in his "giving over" of people to their sin. Thus his judgment consists in *releasing* them in some sense from his sovereignty. It is not a matter of yoke or no yoke, but of which and whose yoke. In spite of the negative implications of the yoke image,[238] it could often carry positive connotations,[239] and it is not without reason that J.G.

---

and in Philo, since outside of Sirach "rest" *follows* labor; I would suggest that this is the case in Sirach also.

[233] Cf. 6,21.

[234] Cf. esp. Tyre; also Büchler, 36-118; Str-B, 1:608-610; Bertram-Rengstorf, 896-901; Charette, 290-297; Deutsch 1987, 115f., 119f., 126-128, 133-135.

[235] Gaechter, 385; Robinson, 1928, 106; cf. 2En 34,1.

[236] Deut 28,47f.; Isa 14,3ff.; Jer 2,20; 5,5; 30,8f.; Lam 5,5; Ezek 34,15.27; Zeph 3,9-13.

[237] *Abot* 3,5.

[238] Acts 15,10; Gal 5,1-3; stressed by Morris, 296.

[239] My concern here is not with the question of how Christian and Jewish assessments of the yoke of the Law varied, but only with the fact that the imagery was used in a positive sense. In addition to the literature already cited, cf. Maher, 97-103. A noteworthy OT example of the yoke as a positive image is Zeph 3,9-13 (LXX) where the Lord promises to bring his people under one yoke; the Lord will take away Israel's pride and will leave $\dot{\epsilon}\nu$ $\sigma o\grave{\iota}$ $\lambda\alpha\grave{o}\nu$ $\pi\rho\alpha\ddot{\upsilon}\nu$ $\kappa\alpha\grave{\iota}$ $\tau\alpha\pi\epsilon\iota\nu\acute{o}\nu$. Tyre, 65f., 110, cites Hos 11,4 in

Janzen entitles his article about the covenant in Deuteronomy, "The Yoke that Gives Rest."[240] Viewed from that perspective, it is not the combination of *Jesus'* yoke and rest which is a paradox, but rather the *disjoining* of the two. Thus it is not really so incredible that a creative mind would make use of the same language as ben Sirach, and J. Bauer has in fact pointed to ancient Babylonian parallels which join a king's yoke to the enjoyment of rest.[241]

4.3.4. Once again, Matthean redaction

Our discussion of Matthew's redaction of this saying confined itself to the question of how he may have modified the wording of this Logion, leaving aside the question of placement. In the course of further discussion we allowed that the present location of the saying may evidence appreciation of the wisdom character of the saying. If we were less enthusiastic on this point than some, it is for good reasons.

Matthew appears to have no interest in formulating a Wisdom Christology, and his editorial changes in 11,28-30 confirm that his interests in using this saying lie elsewhere. Once we allow this we begin to notice rather obvious reasons for placing the saying at this point in the narrative which have nothing to do with Wisdom speculation. The saying falls at the tail end of a block of Q material and immediately before the resumption of Mark's outline;[242] there is a clear structural rational in Matthew's use of his sources for the Logion's placement. It also falls immediately before a discussion of the *Sabbath*, a thematic point which has not been lost on all commentators.[243] Again, this (1) invitation to (2) the weary and heavy laden is a very natural extension of 11,25d (revelation to the "babes") and 27d (the Son's prerogative to reveal), not to mention 11,5 (good news preached to the poor). Matthew's modifications in 11,29c anticipate 12,17-21. These observations are sufficient for now, though considerably more will be said in

---

connection with Mt 11,28-30: "Here, the one who bears the yoke of God is pictured as being guided by the lead rope of a loving Master. The yoke of service becomes light, for the Master loosens the harness. Under the yoke of the Master, the committed person finds purpose and provision for life. He finds a Sovereign who stoops in loving concern to be a service to His people."

[240] Janzen, 256-268; cf. also P.D. Miller 1984, 17-29. It might be recalled at this point that the LXX of Deut 5,33 (above, 82, 90f.) has an offer of rest which is sandwiched between the decalogue and the *Shema* (in which one takes on the yoke of the kingdom of heaven; cf. *Ber* 2,2), and which is conditional on obedience; cf. further Tyre, 118-123.

[241] 1961, 100-103; cf. 1970, 750. The quote is found in a Neo-Babylonian incantation addressed to Ishtar, and reads, "I have taken up thy yoke: give me rest (in return)" (trans. from Bauer 1970, 750). In general, note Philo, *QuaesGen* I,73; IV,218.236f.

[242] Cf. Strecker 1962, 172.

[243] Infra, 229f.

the following chapter to explain its presence here, even in connection with vv. 25-27.

It should only be stressed that wisdom themes are strong in Mt 11-12, and specifically in 11,25f. This is not to be ignored, and this is why we conceded that the connection with 11,25-27 may betray an awareness of the wisdom coloring of the saying. But we should not treat this faint hint of evidence as a firm basis for a Wisdom Christology, especially before considering other evidence and another hypothesis.[244]

4.4. Conclusions

Thus, none of this is to avoid the parallels with Sirach, which we have already accepted as a possible influence on our Logion. It is only to question the inevitability of the Christological deduction which is so fashionable at present. A mind steeped in the religious literature of that day may well have shaped an utterance under the influence of some familiar passage without making that text the primary source of content. Rather than assume that the use of parallel language can carry *only* the implied meaning, "Jesus speaks as Wisdom," and with that in mind deny the authenticity of the saying, we ought to consider whether Jesus might have used this "paradoxical" but evocative combination of metaphors for his own purposes, quite apart from the suggestion of a Wisdom Christology.[245]

When approaching the saying in Mt 11, it is apparent that our understanding of this text needs to be more nuanced. For the sake of making a point one might distinguish between meanings which are accidental, incidental, subsidiary, primary, and assumed. A meaning which is *accidental* is one which is unintended and unrecognized by the author though his or her wording might accommodate it. An *incidental* meaning is unintended but recognized by the author and allowed to remain. A meaning which is *subsidiary* is intended but secondary. An *assumed* meaning is inherent in the saying itself (for instance, in a saying borrowed from another, well known context) though the present speaker intends to make a further or even quite different point. In most cases an "assumed" meaning will be "incidental" or "subsidiary."

If we assume that 11,28-30 goes back to Jesus and if we are inclined to view a Wisdom Christology as an ecclesiastical development (which is not certain) then we would probably think that on his lips the implicit Wisdom

---

[244] We will return once more to this question below, 234f.

[245] Cf. W.D. Davies 1948, 158. I will not enter into the finally futile attempt to determine what the saying would have meant and implied on the lips of Jesus; we have no sure context. It should also be noted again that a case can be made for tracing a Wisdom Christology back to Jesus himself.

Christology was *accidental*. The vague evidence noted above *may* indicate that between Jesus and Matthew the saying had been taken up into wisdom currents, if not even Wisdom speculation.[246] This must remain purely hypothetical. For those very same reasons one should be slow to say that *Matthew* would have been completely unaware of the wisdom/Wisdom associations, though his addition of 29c makes it very unlikely that the connection with Wisdom was his *primary* concern. We might think that he could *assume* this association while he himself orients the saying in another direction.[247] We should then consider whether an identification of Jesus and Wisdom was a *subsidiary* meaning for Matthew, or merely *incidental*. But this will be best answered in the following chapter.

5. Conclusions

Not surprisingly, there have been three general response to Suggs' analysis of Matthew's Wisdom Christology. Some have accepted it virtually in *toto*. A few, very few, have rejected it outright. Most have been inclined to accept his conclusions on Q (Jesus remains an envoy of Wisdom), and in principle his conclusion on Matthew (Matthew *actively advances* the Wisdom Christology through his editorial activity), though they may differ on this or that Matthean passage.

The present examination has not entered directly into the question of Q's Christology, but our own conclusion on Matthew is that he is not actively advancing a Wisdom Christology. The evidence does not support the thesis that Matthew's concern has been to correct a gnosticizing tendency in Q, wherein Wisdom is supreme and Jesus is one of her envoys, by identifying Jesus and Wisdom. In 11,27, which is key in considerations of Q's Wisdom Christology, it is not Matthew's purpose to present the Son as Wisdom, but more likely to present the *Son* -- who is to some extent mirrored by Wisdom[248] -- as the final representative of Israel, probably also as the one greater even than Moses. Whatever was the case with the Q community, Matthew does not appear to be quarrelling with them over the matter of whether Jesus should be reckoned an envoy of Wisdom or Wisdom herself.

---

[246] Supra, 201.

[247] Cf. Luz, 2:218.

[248] It is precisely the concern of many to establish how the "Son" was construed in such an exalted way; hence the appeal to Wisdom. I confess that I do *not* work from the assumption that Jesus was himself incapable of innovating on a large scale, and I would favor the paradigm of an "unfolding" of Christology over that of an "evolution"; cf. Dunn 1994. In this light the Wisdom parallels are certainly important if relevant, but they are not necessarily the key; in other words, there is no reason to *limit* the Son in 11,27 to the status of Wisdom, or to the parallels associated with her.

The conclusion cannot but be that Matthew is not particularly interested to give Wisdom her own chair at the table of his Christology, though Wisdom speculation is one of the possible tributaries to his thought. Mt 11,28-30, which is often casually accepted as an utterance of Jesus Sophia, is actually a good example of just this. It does bear a formal resemblance to wisdom forms; taken as a whole, it is most closely paralleled by a saying about Wisdom; it has been placed cheek by jowl with other sayings which manifest the clearest marks of Wisdom speculation. Yet, the wording is so completely tailored to the Jesus of Matthew and at key points so much closer to non-sapiential OT language that the parallel with Sirach is almost completely obscured until we place the two sayings in parallel columns. More tellingly, precisely where Matthew's hand is most clearly detected we find a theme which is simultaneously distant from Wisdom and close to other, clearly central, Matthean interests. If the test of redactional tendency is trustworthy in exposing Matthew's participation in Wisdom currents, then it is also trustworthy here and should be given full weight.

Chapter Six

The Meek King and God's Promise of Rest

1. Introduction

If we are going to contend that Matthew's primary interest in his use of the Logion was not to put a saying of Wisdom onto the lips of Jesus, then we must provide a better alternative explanation. In doing so we shall find that the well worn path to Wisdom has not been entirely misdirected, but that it has been kept to overly stringently and followed too far. Our understanding of the Logion has been blocked off because we have come to see in it little more than the encoded equation, Jesus = Wisdom. Almost none of what follows receives so much as passing notice in studies like Suggs' and Deutsch's.

2. Explaining Matthew's redaction: the Servant

It has been stated repeatedly already that Matthew's addition to 11,28-30 consists of at least 29c if not 29b -- "learn from me; for[1] I am gentle and

---

[1] It is possible to translate ὅτι in 29c as "that" (explicative); cf. esp. Strecker 1962, 174, who is followed by Betz, 23f; Luz, 2:198, 221. Zahn, 443 n. 53, argues for this understanding based on an assumed Hebraism in 29a-b. Alternatively ὅτι can be translated in Mt 11,29 as "because" (causal; most scholars). Both options are grammatically allowable, and both make sense. If we opt for the former, then instead of just 29b, it will be 29b-c together which stand in parallel to 29a; the καί of 29d can then be taken as expressing either purpose or result. If ὅτι is causal, then the first two clauses (29a and 29b) are parallel to each other, with the last two (29c and 29d) giving the reason and the result, respectively. The causal sense of ὅτι is probably the primary one since, (1) 29c and 30a-b do seem to parallel each other (Gundry, 218); (2) the content of the "learning" is probably the revelation of 11,25-27 (Carson, 278; Davies-Allison, 2:291; for a parallel to μάθετε ἀπ' ἐμοῦ without specifying the content, cf. Col 1,7); and (3) although possible, it is slightly more obscure to say that rest is the result or intent of learning "that" he is meek (Betz, 23f., explains this with reference to Jesus' mysterious presence in "the least of these my brothers" [25,40]), than to say that it results from learning from the one who *is* meek and lowly; moreover, it seems very natural to coax

humble in heart" -- and that just this aspect of the saying fits least comfortably with both the literary parallel of Sirach and the mythological background of Wisdom. Matthew has provided an immediate context to just this element of the saying which can only be overlooked with some effort.

There are, of course, the often noted Sabbath debates of 12,1-14, which pit Jesus, the Lord of the Sabbath, against the life stifling Halakah of the Pharisees. One can easily think in terms of the easier yoke and lighter burden of a gentle Lord, even if a more nuanced understanding of what this means is necessary in order to avoid a clash with other Matthean statements about Jesus and the Law.

We will want to return to those pericopae below, but the following context of 12,15ff. shows that 12,1-14 was scarcely Matthew's definitive and final word on the Logion. When in 12,15f. Jesus is portrayed as withdrawing in the face of persecution, our minds naturally return to the almost immediately preceding wording of 11,29.

This connection is plainly deliberate. Though Matthew's narrative is following Mark's at this point, he has greatly abbreviated Mark's account of the withdrawal, healing, and command for silence down to what are for him the essentials. He has then relocated the selection of the twelve apostles (which Mark included at this point)[2] and inserted instead a quote from Isa 42,1-4 (Mt 12,17-21) which is unique to his Gospel, and which richly expands on the themes of vv. 15f.[3] These alterations are effective. The meek and lowly Jesus chooses the path which enables him to continue his ministry of compassion while avoiding open confrontation.

It is not merely the motifs of withdrawal and quietness which recall 11,28-30, but the description of those to whom the Servant ministers, the

---

people into taking up his yoke by assuring them that he is gentle. Still, it is Matthew's concern that we learn "that" Jesus is meek, and that in this role he brings salvation, i.e., rest.

[2] Cf. Mk 3,7-12.13-19.20-30. The selection of the twelve has already been given in Mt 10,1-4. In terms of Matthew's narrative, when many follow Jesus (12,15) and he heals them "all" ($\pi\acute{a}\nu\tau\alpha\varsigma$; probably Matthean; cf. Gundry, 228; Davies-Allison, 2:323), this comes as a response to the invitation of 11,28-30. That this is likely is seen in the adaptation of Isa 42 to the lowliness motif.

[3] On Matthew's use of Isa 42 in this context, see esp. Barth, 125-129; Hill 1980, 2-16; Stendahl, 107-115; Gundry 1967, 110-116. We are assuming that Matthew is himself responsible for the wording of at least some of his "formula quotations" (with Barth, Hill, Stanton [1992a, 346-363] and others who demonstrate this in detail; cf. also above, 162f.). Matthew's rendering of Isa 42,1-4 (cf. Hag 2,23; Isa 41,8f.; 44,2; Hab 1,4) evidences dependence on both Hebrew and Greek sources; for the details, see the scholars noted.

This OT passage is already suited to Matthew's purpose, but he modifies it at points in accordance with his contextual interests. In this regard the statements, $o\dot{v}\kappa\ \dot{\epsilon}\rho\acute{\iota}\sigma\epsilon\iota\ o\dot{v}\delta\grave{\epsilon}\ \kappa\rho\alpha\upsilon\gamma\acute{a}\sigma\epsilon\iota$ and $\dot{\epsilon}\nu\ \tau\alpha\hat{\iota}\varsigma\ \pi\lambda\alpha\tau\epsilon\acute{\iota}\alpha\iota\varsigma$ (both in 12,19) appear to be meaningful departures, and both times the change is best explained as an attempt to adapt the quotation to the humility and lowliness of Jesus (Barth, 127).

"bruised reed" and "smoldering wick." The modification of Isa 42,3c-4b which results in the clause, "until he leads justice to victory" (Mt 12,20c), suggests a more inclusive referent[4] for the "bruised" and "smoldering" ones than merely the sick of 12,15. These are the marginalized.[5] They are the same souls encountered elsewhere as the "harassed and helpless," the "poor," and the *"weary and heavy laden."*[6]

It is only with some effort that we can resist the flow of ideas from 11,28-30 to 12,15ff., and the Servant motif in the latter is a very natural extension and development of the lowliness motif in the former.[7] But in this case we are already on the way to saying that Matthew has employed this saying in 11,28-30 with a view to a theme which has little if anything to do with Wisdom. It is not merely that he located 11,28-30 and 12,15ff. in close proximity to each other, but that he edited 11,29 in anticipation of the following withdrawal and Servant motifs, and modified 12,15-21 in harmony with 11,28-30.

3. Explaining Matthew's redaction: the Son of David

3.1. Introduction

It is clear, therefore, that Mt 11,28-30 was shaped by Matthew along the lines of the Servant of the Lord theme in Isa 42. But why would Matthew edit *this* saying in this manner?[8] What was it that he saw latent in this Logion, this promise of rest, which he sought to draw out by his editorial changes? In other words, we must explain this editorial change not only on the side of Matthew's theology, but on the side of the saying itself as Matthew received it.

If we recall that in 8,16f. Matthew has already characterized Jesus' healing ministry along the lines of Isa 53,4, "He took our infirmities and bore ($ἐβάστασεν$) our diseases," then he may well have seen in the promise of rest to the "weary and heavy laden" the Servant's ministry to the afflicted

---

[4] So Barth, 127f.; Hill 1980, 12; Stanton 1992a, 373. The wording of Mt 12,20c omits Isa 42,4a, conflates 42,3c and 4b, and evidences possible influence from Hab 1,4 MT (Gundry 1967, 114f.).

[5] Davies-Allison, 2:326.

[6] Infra, 239ff.

[7] Esp. Stanton 1992a, 371ff. Also highlighting some or all of the Servant passages from Isaiah (Isa 42,1-4 [or, 1-7]; 49,1-9 [or, 1-6]; 50,4-11 [or, 4-9]; 52,13-53,12) as an influence on this saying are, among several, Cerfaux, 153-159, and de Kruijf, 69f.

[8] Though Mt 11,28-30 has often been associated with Isa 42 and the Servant theme, I do not believe that this particular question has been asked.

masses.⁹ G. Barth comments on 8,17 that Jesus' healings are "to be understood as a work of his obedience and his humiliation."¹⁰ It is possible, then, that the "weary and heavy laden" had already brought to mind the Servant of the Lord theme, and Matthew accordingly amplified this thematic association by characterizing Jesus as πραΰς and following up with a quote from Isa 42.¹¹

Thus by considering Matthew's interest in the Servant of the Lord theme, a rationale comes into focus for why he might have edited 11,28-30 as he did. However, we can go further, and posit a yet more likely rationale for Matthew's editorial activity if we consider another related Christological theme. From the quotation of Isa 42,1-4 Matthew merges his narrative immediately into another healing account (12,22),¹² and from there into the Beelzebul controversy. In the course of this transition, however, he *inserts* a Son of David reference (12,23), and it is this Christological claim which becomes the immediate catalyst for the ensuing Beelzebul controversy (cf. 12,24: ἀκούσαντες). This reference to the Son of David and the debate it inspires brings to resolution the dissonant chord which carried right through chs. 10-11 ever since it was struck toward the end of ch. 9.¹³

The movement from "Servant" to "Son of David" in ch. 12 is not the result of a rude joining of discrete Christologies, but indicates that *for Matthew* these roles had an inner affinity and considerable overlap. The Son of David is the lowly Servant of the Lord.¹⁴ It will be our contention that the

---

⁹ Matthew's quotation of Isa 53,4 is a translation of the Hebrew, apparently independent from the LXX (Gundry 1967, 109f.; Davies-Allison, 2:37f.). Jesus' activity is less a "bearing" of the sicknesses than a "removal" (healing), yet the ideas may overlap (cf. Davies-Allison, 2:38), and we may assume that Matthew was not ignorant of the sense of the Hebrew.

¹⁰ Barth, 128f.; cf. Hill 1980, 9.

¹¹ Note the use of ταπεινός in Isa 53,8; cf. Grundmann 1972, 11. The presence of χρηστός in the Logion may have given partial impetus to Matthew's alteration, though the ideas are not completely synonymous. Moreover, as we suggested when considering Matthean redaction (supra, 193f.) the reference to Jesus' meekness may have originally been in Matthew's 11,30. It still remains to explain why Matthew highlighted that motif.

¹² He omits Mk 3,20f.

¹³ Note 10,24f. On the connection between the Son of David and the rejection motif, see further below. In 9,34, when the Beelzebul accusation is first sounded (cf. 9,27 and below), Matthew's account breaks abruptly and gives way to Jesus' compassionate ministry (9,35-38; cf. Duling 1978, 403f.; note that when the story of 9,27-31 is repeated at 20,29-34, Matthew *inserts* a reference to Jesus' compassion [20,34]). It could not be more clear that these themes of the rejected Son of David *and his compassionate ministry* continue right through to ch. 12; thus immediately following the quotation of Isa 42 Matthew makes it a point to raise afresh at 12,23f. the direct link between the claim that Jesus is the Son of David and the accusation that he is in league with Beelzebul.

¹⁴ David is referred to often as "my servant"; e.g., 2Sam 7,5.8.19f.25-29 (supra, 25f.); Ezek 34,23f.; cf. Ps 89,20. In both 2Sam 7 and Ezek 34 the shepherd theme is employed, and F. Martin, esp. 271, points out that in Matthew's Gospel it is the "shepherd" theme

primary and *specific* thematic association of 11,28-30 consists in Matthew's Son of David Christology.

3.2. Matthew's Son of David Christology

Even the casual reader of the first Gospel cannot miss the importance of Matthew's Son of David Christology.[15] The Gospel opens with the words,

Βίβλος γενέσεως Ἰησοῦ Χριστοῦ υἱοῦ Δαυὶδ υἱοῦ Ἀβραάμ.

An account of the genealogy of Jesus the Messiah, the Son of David, the Son of Abraham.

The genealogy of Mt 1,1-17 is chiefly concerned to establish the Davidic lineage of Jesus, and the following account of 1,18ff. establishes that Joseph, son of David (v. 20), has officially adopted Jesus as his own.[16] The promise delivered to the house of David (Isa 7,13) that the "young woman is with child and shall bear a son, and shall name him Immanuel" (Isa 7,14) is applied to Jesus (Mt 1,23).[17] King Herod, alarmed by the mission of the Magi, is told that the messiah (ὁ Χριστός) was to be born in David's city, Bethlehem of Judea (Mic 5,2; Mt 2,6).[18] In fact, for Matthew the title, ὁ Χριστός, is clearly defined with reference to Jesus' Davidic ancestry.[19] For Matthew the Jews took it as axiomatic that the Christ would be the Son of

---

which unites the "Son of David" and "Servant." M. Strauss, 234f., 238-242, demonstrates that the "Servant" (e.g. Isa 42,1ff.) and "Son of David" (Isa 11,1ff.) themes overlapped in Isaiah (read as a unity), and that at least some Jewish traditions testify to their being associated (Strauss is duly reserved on the latter point; cf. HJP^2, 2:547-549). Strauss' concern is to show that Luke related these two themes as well. When it is said about the shoot of Jesse's reign that "with righteousness he shall judge the poor, and decide with equity for the meek of the earth" (Isa 11,4; cf. also Isa 9,6; Jer 23,5-6; 33,15; Ezek 21,27; PssSol 17,22.26.29.32.37.40; 4QpIsa[a] frg D 1-8; 1QSb 5,24-26; TJud 24,1.6; 1En 61,8f.; 62,1-12; M. Strauss, 232f.), we are in the same world of ideas which find expression in Mt 11,28-30. Cf. Christ, 115; Davies-Allison, 2:598f.

[15] For the wider OT and Jewish background of the Davidic messianic hope, cf. M. Strauss, 24-83, and literature therein; further: Nolan and Burger. On Matthew's Son of David Christology see esp. Gibbs 1964; Hummel, 116-122; R. Walker, 128-132; Suhl; Burger, 72-106; Sand 1974, 143-150; Kingsbury 1975, 96-103; 1976; Duling 1978; Nolan; Carson 1982a, 103-107; Loader 1982; Chilton; Verseput 1986; 1987, 532-556; France, 284-288; Mullins; Stanton 1992a, 169-191 (repr. in 1992b).

[16] Cf. *BB* 8,6.

[17] This formula quotation relies on the LXX (Gundry 1967, 89-91).

[18] On Bethlehem cf. Jn 7,42; 1Sam 16,1-13; 17,12.15.58; 20,6.28. On the source of this tradition of Jesus' birthplace (history or apologetics), cf. Brown 1977, 505-516. On the quotation, which depends on both the MT and LXX (cf. also 2Sam/2Kgdms 5,2; 1Chr/1Par 11,2), see Gundry 1967, 91-93; Stendahl, 99-101.

[19] Carson 1982a, 100, 105.

David,[20] and this appears to have been Matthew's own view. The birth narrative of Mt 1-2 ends with a statement about the lowly and despised[21] origins of Jesus (2,23), which is a probable allusion to (the Hebrew of) Isa 11,1:[22]

A shoot shall come out from the stump of Jesse, and a branch (נצר) shall grow out of his roots.

This Christological theme is thus decisively established right from the start, but it does not end there. Matthew's interest in Jesus as "Son of David" is evident from his editorial activity. Mark supplied Matthew with four passages where the lineage is explicitly referred to (Mk 10,47.48 = Mt 20,30.31;[23] Mk 12,35.37 = Mt 22,42.45[24]) and to these Matthew added six: 1,1; 9,27; 12,23; 15,22; 21,9.15.[25] In addition to the widely held view that this title appears to be Matthew's foremost title for the earthly as opposed to the exalted Jesus,[26] several observations have been made about these ten Matthean passages, a few of which we may highlight.

There is a recurring link between the use of the phrase, "Son of David," and Jesus' healing ministry.[27] Various explanations for this connection have

---

[20] Mt 22,42.

[21] Carson, 97; Nolan, 210-215; cf. Jn 1,45f.; Acts 24,5.

[22] B. Weiss, 57f.; Schlatter, 49; Schniewind, 20; Gundry, 40; Carson, 97; Davies-Allison, 277-279 (secondary allusion); Hagner, 1:40f.; cf. Stendahl, 103f.

[23] Lk 18,38f.

[24] Lk 20,41.44. Neither Mk 12,35 or 12,37 par. are actually using the title as such.

[25] 1,20, which states the lineage of Joseph as the "son of David," is also redactional. Chilton, 93-95, 96, refines the discussion of these passages by attempting to distinguish between titular and non-titular usages of the address.

[26] E.g. Bornkamm, 33; Strecker 1962, 118-120; Hummel, 121f.; R. Walker, 129-132; Suhl, 75f., 81; Burger, 82, 88f.; Sand 1974, 147, 150, 162-167; I owe these references to Kingsbury 1976, 591. The title, "Son of David," does not appear to have lent itself in any special way to descriptions of Jesus' future work, though this does not evidence any sort of demotion of the title (*contra* Kingsbury 1976, 592). Mt 23,39 converts Ps 118,26 into a reference to the Parousia, after Matthew has already identified the "one who comes" (Ps 118,26) as the "Son of David" (Mt 21,9).

[27] Mt 9,27 (R); 12,23 (R); 15,22 (R); 20,30.31; 21,15 (R; by implication also 21,9); see the relevant literature. These healings tend to be performed "in the midst of Israel" and are generally healings of individuals; Kingsbury 1976, 592, 598. Striking is the repeated exclamation, "Son of David, have mercy!" each time associated with the title, "Lord"; 9,27f.; 15,22; 20,30.31 (the presence of $κύριος$ suggests a confessional usage; cf. Verseput 1986, 27; *contra* Kingsbury 1975, 102; Brown 1977, 134). For the same address cf. TSol 20,1, which is probably dependent on the Synoptic tradition; Duling 1975, 243, 249; but cf. Chilton, 95f. The healing of blindness recurs; cf. esp. 9,27; 20,30f.; both 12,23 and 21,15 follow accounts which *include* a reference to blindness (12,22; 21,14; 12,22 is helped inasmuch as it clearly picks up from 9,27-34); less convincingly 15,22 (vv. 15.30); cf. Mullins, 117-126. Mullins' belief that the blindness motif is grounded in 2Kgdms 5,4-10 ($Τυφλοὶ καὶ χωλοὶ οὐκ εἰσελεύσονται εἰς οἶκον$

Chapter Six: The Meek King   215

been proposed,²⁸ but for our purposes we may simply make a few observations about Matthew's usage. Kingsbury has observed that the people whom Jesus engages and heals in Matthew *qua* Son of David and those who address him as such are typically the no-accounts and outcasts of Jewish society. Kingsbury is probably correct that Matthew is desiring to highlight by this the guilt of the official leadership in failing to recognize Jesus' messiahship.²⁹ "In Matthew's scheme, it is precisely such 'no-accounts' as these persons who are the ones in Israel who correctly perceive that Jesus is the Son of David."³⁰

G. Stanton has emphasized that as Son of David Jesus encounters resistance;³¹ in four places the acknowledgement of Jesus as Son of David provokes a response on the part of the Jewish leaders.³² Indeed, "no other major Christological theme in Matthew provokes such sustained opposition from the Jewish leaders."³³ Stanton has gone on from this to suggest that there may be in Matthew an early form of the two parousia schema, with Jesus as the Son of David corresponding to the first parousia: "Matthew contrasts the humility and meekness of the life of Jesus the Son of David with the glory of his future coming as Son of Man and judge."³⁴

κυρίου) is credible for Mt 21,14f. (Καὶ προσῆλθον αὐτῷ τυφλοὶ καὶ χωλοὶ ἐν τῷ ἱερῷ, καὶ ἐθεράπευσεν αὐτούς. ἰδόντες δὲ οἱ ἀρχιερεῖς καὶ οἱ γραμματεῖς τὰ θαυμάσια ἃ ἐποίησεν καὶ τοὺς παῖδας τοὺς κράζοντας ἐν τῷ ἱερῷ καὶ λέγοντας, Ὡσαννὰ τῷ υἱῷ Δαυίδ...); cf. Verseput 1987, 551 n. 26; France, 284 n. 10; Schweizer, 408 (if Carson, 442, is right that 21,14 implies that "something greater than the temple is here," then this passage may support our contention [infra, 231f.] that 12,6 is to be associated with Davidic ideas). For the remainder it is less convincing. More promising is the suggestion of intended irony as over against the "blind" leaders (15,15; cf. 13,13; 23,16.17.24); Gibbs 1964, 451-453.

²⁸ Cf. Loader 1982, 570-572; France, 285.

²⁹ Kingsbury 1976, 597-602. This favors the suggestion that the "blind" whom Jesus, Son of David, heals have symbolic import; their blindness is a spiritual counterpart to the blindness of the leaders. Loader 1982, 570-585, argues this interpretation of "blindness" at length.

³⁰ Kingsbury 1976, 599; cf. France, 286.

³¹ Cf. also Mullins, 119ff.

³² Stanton 1992a, 180-185; the four passages, each of which evidences Matthew's redactional activity, are 2,3; 9,27-34; 12,23 (note v. 24: οἱ δὲ Φαρισαῖοι **ἀκούσαντες** εἶπον); 21,9.15 (note v. 16: Ἀκούεις τί οὗτοι λέγουσιν;). The close connection in 12,23f. between the confession of Jesus as Son of David and the reaction of the Pharisees confirms that 9,34 is intended as a response to 9,27, even though 9,27-31 does not involve an exorcism; rather, for Matthew, the confession of Jesus as Son of David is intended to span the whole of 9,27-33.

³³ Stanton 1992a, 170; likewise, Verseput 1987, 536f.

³⁴ Stanton 1992a, 190; cf. 185-191, 381. The fact that the passages in question are redactional suggests for Stanton that the Davidic lineage of Jesus was a point of contention between Matthew's communities and their opponents (cf. also Verseput 1987, 548); the response of Matthew is to explain Jesus' earthly life as one of humility contrary

Finally here, D. Verseput has contributed to the discussion by working on the relationship of the Son of David and Son of God titles in Matthew.[35] In brief, Verseput argues that the Sonship of Jesus ("Son of God") was an idea familiar to Matthew's readers[36] and of little consequence in Christian-Jewish debates; it bespoke not only Jesus' divine status, but his obedience to his Father's plan and the Father's approval of him. The messianic status of Jesus as Son of David was, however, a bone of contention with Matthew's contemporaries because of its gentle and humble quality. Matthew brought these two forms of Sonship together to vindicate, as it were, the "humble appearance of the Davidic messiah" in the face of opposition and rejection.[37]

Verseput's treatment focuses on a number of passages, but especially on chs. 11-12,[38] which are of special interest to our own investigation. There are indeed good reasons to suspect a strong interest on the part of Matthew in Jesus' Davidic identity and role in chs. 11-12. We have already noticed the close nexus between the titles "Son of David" and "Christ," and it is significant that we have in Mt 11,2 the summary statement about the "deeds of the Christ."[39] This brief summary probably surveys the whole of Mt 5-10.[40] In addition, Jesus compares himself to David in 12,3f.,[41] he is effectively called the Son of David by the crowds at 12,23,[42] and he refers to himself as "something greater than Solomon" in 12,42. Matthew's Son of David Christology is of some importance to these two chapters.[43]

Structurally,[44] chs. 11-12 fall between the second (10,1-42) and third (13,1-52) discourses, and it is here that resistance to Jesus becomes burning

---

to *some* Jewish expectations of the Davidic messiah. For second century A.D. evidence of a more pronounced two-parousia schema along these same lines, cf. Stanton, *loc. cit.*

[35] Verseput 1987, 532-556 (cf. 1986, 29-35). Verseput resists the temptation to subordinate one title to the other (1987, 533, 544), whereas Kingsbury 1976, 591-602, had tried to establish that Matthew subordinated the Son of David to the Son of God idea, a thesis which has been justifiably criticized on more grounds than one; cf. Hill 1980, 2-16; also the methodological principles laid out by Keck. Verseput's approach to the relation of these two titles -- Son of David and Son of God -- is the more fruitful. Other attempts at relating these two titles in Matthew are summarized in Verseput 1986, 29.

[36] Thus its less prominent role in the early chapters of Matthew.

[37] Verseput 1987, esp. 542f., 548f.

[38] Verseput 1987, 542-544; Cf. also Verseput 1986, which is book length treatment of Mt 11-12.

[39] Cf. Verseput 1987, 535, 550 n. 16.

[40] Cf. Verseput 1986, 65, with discussion and literature.

[41] The choice of *David* for the analogy is probably Christologically motivated; cf. Davies-Allison, 2:308-312; Carson, 280f.; Chilton, 98.

[42] On the use of $\mu\acute{\eta}\tau\iota$ as expressing hesitation rather than the expectation of a negative answer, cf. Bauer-Aland, 1053; BDF § 427,2.3.

[43] See further below, 233ff.

[44] The question of the structure of Matthew's Gospel as a whole is too involved to be discussed here; Davies-Allison, 1:58-72, provide an extensive bibliography (1988) and a discussion of the issues; they conclude with Gundry, 10f., that Matthew's Gospel is

opposition.⁴⁵ Ch. 11 begins in v. 1 with the formula, καὶ ἐγένετο ὅτε ἐτέλεσεν ὁ Ἰησοῦς "instructing his twelve disciples,"⁴⁶ which refers back to the previous discourse. The remainder of these two chapters are analyzed by Verseput according to the repeated pattern of rejection and judgment, on the one hand, and validation of the humble messianic king, on the other.⁴⁷

Rejection/Judgment	Validation⁴⁸
11,2-24	11,25-12,21
12,22-45	12,46-50

Thus both 11,2-24 and 12,22-45 are launched with a reference to the Davidic messiah (11,2; 12,23f.), and both cycles end with a focus on the divine Sonship of Jesus.

Whether or not Verseput has rightly perceived the structural pattern of this portion of Matthew will not be settled by the present study.⁴⁹ What does

---

"structurally mixed," even if they are more hopeful that some sections (esp. the Matthean discourses and narrative sections through ch. 12) exhibit a highly structured format. Even so, Matthean themes are not usually confined to certain sections.

⁴⁵ Kingsbury 1975, 20, observes that "in 11:2-12:50, Matthew is predominantly concerned to portray the complete rejection of Jesus the Messiah of Israel."

⁴⁶ With different endings, but always in reference to teaching at the end of each of the five discourses: 7,28f.; 13,53; 19,1f.; 26,1f.

⁴⁷ Verseput 1986, 295-300 and *passim*; 1987, 542-544.

⁴⁸ "Validation" is my own label, since Verseput's designations vary. In the first of these (11,25-12,21) Jesus' humble ministry among the little ones is affirmed, and in the second (12,46-50) the disciples are declared to be the true family of God. Note that Matthew has inserted a reference to "my Father" at 12,50 and thus accentuated the divine Sonship motif; cf. Verseput 1987, 544. Gnilka, 1:470, notes that 11,25-30 and 12,46-50 seem to function in a parallel manner, as both follow words of warning and judgment with an invitation to join the new family of God.

⁴⁹ A cursory survey of proposed outlines of this passage will quickly show how differently it has been assessed, and also why it is difficult to outline. We may cite two more examples. Deutsch 1987, 21-25, insists that the context of 11,25-30 is that of 11,2-13,58 (not 12,50), and she highlights in this extended context the motifs of rejection, opposition, and unbelief, on the one hand, and those of revelation, concealment, and disclosure, on the other; she gives no indication that there is any structural pattern in the arrangement of these motifs. Few would disagree that these motifs are present here, although some will be convinced that there is in fact a pattern. Her emphatic insistence that ch. 13 should be included within the context of 11,25-30 may assume that the delineation of context establishes impenetrable barriers between sections, while that is not the case; it is not clear that this inclusion of ch. 13 is crucial to her case, and would probably not alter Verseput's (cf. 1986, 299). Neither does Deutsch consider the relationship of the rejection motif to Jesus' identity as Son of David. Davies-Allison, 1:67-69, 2:233f., break the whole passage of 11,2-12,50 into three triads, in which they view the two Sabbath pericopae of 12,1-14 as negative in tone (different from Verseput). Each of the triads then follows the pattern of (1) unmasking the false (11,2-19; 12,1-8; 12,22-37), (2) unmasking the false (11,20-24; 12,9-14; 12,38-45), (3) revealing the true

appear to be firmly established is the interplay of the Son of David and Son of God identities (sketched above) as these complement each other in Matthew's Gospel, and specifically in Mt 11-12. For Matthew, Jesus incites the greatest resistance and rejection as the Son of David, but his rejection and humble presence as the Davidic messiah are balanced and validated by his identity as the Son of God (cf. 11,25-30).

In short, Matthew's efforts at presenting Jesus as the Son of David are extensive, detailed, and extremely important to his Christology. Precisely as the Son of David Jesus is roundly rejected and Mt 11-12 highlight just this phenomenon of rejection, beginning in 11,2. As the rejected Son of David he is revealed to be the unique Son of God, and in that role he receives the Father's approval of his compassionate and gentle messianic ministry; indeed, Jesus himself affirms it. But has this specific Christological theme of Jesus as the Son of David shaped 11,28-30?

3.3. Two verbal pointers to Mt 21

Mt 11,25-30 has no explicit reference to Jesus as the Son of David, but there are definite indicators that this idea is in view. We have seen that the clause, ὅτι πραΰς εἰμι καὶ ταπεινὸς τῇ καρδίᾳ, bears the clearest marks of Matthew's hand. In general, it has been said that "the πραΰτης of the Messiah and his mercy towards the unprivileged...runs through the whole Gospel of Matthew, right down to the description of the judgment of the world (25.31ff.), in which the Son of man calls the unprivileged his brethren."[50] Likewise, G. Barth declares in his masterful if limited survey of the topic that "the lowliness of Jesus was in the forefront of Matthew's interest."[51] This is evident not least where we have already looked, in the quote from Isa 42 in Mt 12,18-21. Thus the addition of 29c to the Logion stands in line with one of Matthew's general Christological emphases. Yet it is possible to be more specific in view of two verbal parallels.

There is the use of the word πραΰς.[52] This word occurs only three times in Matthew, in dependence on the OT, and not at all in the other Gospels. It

---

(11,25-30; 12,15-21; 12,46-50). There is some justification, however, for Verseput's view that the whole of 12,1-14 is positive in its basic thrust.

[50] Bornkamm, 37.

[51] Barth, 129.

[52] Πραΰς occurs in the NT outside Matthew only in 1Pet 3,4. Πραΰτης occurs more often, but not in the Synoptics; cf. esp. 2Cor 10,1: διὰ τῆς πραΰτητος καὶ ἐπιεικείας τοῦ Χριστοῦ; Leivestad. Ταπεινός occurs only here in Matthew; elsewhere in the Synoptics only at Lk 1,52. For ταπεινόω, cf. Mt 18,4; 23,12 (2x). On πραΰς, cf. Hauck-Schulz 1968a, 645-651; Bauder, 256-259. On ταπεινός, cf. W. Grundmann 1972; Esser, 259-264. Cf. also Hauck-Schulz 1968b, 885-915; de Vaux, 1:72-74; von Rad, 1:400f.; Jeremias 1971, 109-113; Guelich, 67-72. In the LXX πραΰς generally translates עני or ענו; in usage it overlapped significantly with ταπεινός and esp. πτωχός (cf. Mt 5,3.5 in the

Chapter Six: The Meek King 219

occurs in Mt 5,5, which is dependent on Ps 37,11.[53] More importantly it occurs at 21,5 in a quote from Zech 9,9.[54] In 21,5 as in 11,29 it is descriptive of Jesus, thus its importance. Two things are noteworthy in this connection.

The first is that Matthew appears to have altered Zech 9,9 in such a way as to highlight just this idea of meekness:[55]

Zech 9,9	Isa 62,11
Rejoice greatly, O daughter Zion! Shout aloud, O daughter of Jerusalem! Lo, your king comes to you; triumphant [צדיק] and victorious [נושע] is he, humble [עני] and riding on a donkey, on a colt, the foal of a donkey.	Εἴπατε τῇ θυγατρὶ Σιων... אמרו לבת ציון

Zech 9,9	Mt 21,5
Χαῖρε σφόδρα, θύγατερ Σιων κήρυσσε, θύγατερ Ιερουσαλημ· ἰδοὺ ὁ βασιλεύς σου ἔρχεταί σοι, δίκαιος καὶ σῴζων αὐτός,[56] πραΰς καὶ ἐπιβεβηκὼς ἐπὶ ὑποζύγιον καὶ πῶλον νέον.	Εἴπατε τῇ θυγατρὶ Σιών,[57] Ἰδοὺ ὁ βασιλεύς σου ἔρχεταί σοι, πραΰς καὶ ἐπιβεβηκὼς ἐπὶ ὄνον, καὶ ἐπὶ πῶλον υἱὸν ὑποζυγίου.[58]

---

commentaries; on a conceptual level this overlap is true across Jewish literature). These terms had become standard terms of piety in the OT, signifying those who were desperately vulnerable among people (socio-economic dimension) and completely dependent on God who championed their cause (religious dimension). For πραΰς and ταπεινός (or cognates) occurring together, cf. Isa 26,6; Zeph 3,12; Sir 10,14f.; also, Ψ 146,6 [147,6]; Prov 16,19; Eph 4,2; and further Grundmann 1972, 10, 14, 20; Schlatter, 387; Luz, 2:221. Among these Isa 26,6 is of special interest, since it follows on a rest tradition passage in the LXX (cf. 25,10; supra, 82). Zech 9,9 stands out as a messianic passage (the rabbinic use of Zech 9,9 [supra, 124] in a messianic sense may be too late to have influenced Matthew [infra, n. 56]). Πραΰς is nowhere predicated of God, though the semantically related ἐπιεικής/ἐπιείκεια is so used in the LXX (1Kgdms 12,22; WisSol 12,18); the Lord is χρηστὸς καὶ ἐπιεικής (Ψ 85,5 [86,5]). Cf. Dan 3,87 LXX, ταπεινοὶ καρδίᾳ.

[53] Mt 5,5; Ψ 36,11; and Ps 37,11 MT all agree, except that the article with γῆν in Matthew corresponds to the Targum (Gundry 1967, 133). Cf. Isa 61,7 LXX, which also uses the article (κληρονομήσουσιν τὴν γῆν). Isa 61 is alluded to in 11,5 and Davies-Allison, 1:450f., count Isa 61,7 as a possible secondary allusion at 5,5.

[54] Cf. only Jn 12,15.

[55] Matthew's quotation of Zech 9,9 begins with Isa 62,11 (= LXX = MT); John begins with a different passage, yet also from Isaiah: Isa 40,9. The remainder of Matthew's quote from Zech 9,9 draws primarily on the MT (Gundry 1967, 120f.; Moo, 178-182). Matthew agrees with the OT Peshitta, the Targum, the LXX, and Aquila in understanding עני (humble) as ענו (meek; πραΰς); alternatively, Gundry, 409, suggests that the latter may have been the reading in Matthew's Hebrew text, since copyists often confused ׳ and ו.

[56] Noting that this clause should have been entirely suited to Matthew, Barth, 130, comments that "the only possible point in the omission is the emphasising of πραΰς." Stendahl, 119, suggests that the omission is due to the rabbinic interpretation of Zech 9,9

Matthew means for Jesus' πραΰτης to dominate the saying.⁵⁹ The second point is simply that this is a Son of David context. This is indicated not only by the reference to kingship in 21,5, but by the immediately following allusion to Ps 118,25f. into which Matthew has inserted a reference to Jesus as the Son of David.⁶⁰ Clearly when Matthew characterizes Jesus as πραΰς, he is thinking of him as the βασιλεὺς πραΰς, which means for him, the meek and lowly Son of David.⁶¹

(Str-B, 1:842-844; supra, 124) which laid the emphasis on the words "poor and riding on an ass" (Gaechter, 386 n. 66, claims that the rabbis are concerned more with the image of riding on an ass than the "lowliness" motif in Zech 9,9; note that the former is the element highlighted in Jn 12,15); yet Barth, 130, counts this as late evidence (Michel 1967, 285 n. 9, dates it as early as the early Tannaitic period). The options (Stendahl or Barth) are not mutually exclusive. We might also note that Matthew's version of Zech 9,9 sets Jesus' kingship and meekness in closest parallel, thereby highlighting the dissonance (Stanton 1992a, 371). This is similar to the juxtapositioning of Mt 11,27 (unique sonship) and 11,28 (lowliness).

⁵⁷ Gundry, 408, may be right in saying that this change converts Zech 9,9 into "an evangelistic challenge to unconverted Israel." Prabhu, 54 n. 41, suggests that the opening words of Zech 9,9 would be inappropriate in Matthew's context, where Jesus confronts his doom.

⁵⁸ On Matthew's translation of this clause, which differs from the LXX in favor of the MT (except for ἐπιβεβηκώς), see Gundry 1967, 120f.; Moo, 178-182. The best explanation of the reference to two animals is not that Matthew misunderstood the Hebrew parallelism (e.g., Barth, 129), but that he reshaped it to fit the historical circumstances of the event (Gundry, 409). Interestingly -- in view of the correspondence of thought which we are developing between Isa 11,1-10 and Mt 11,28-30 -- Carson, 438, suggests that the fact that Jesus was riding an unbroken animal through a noisy crowd demonstrated his rule over nature; "Thus the event points to the peace of the consummated kingdom (cf. Isa. 11:1-10)."

⁵⁹ Thus, Barth, 129-131; Stanton 1992a, 371; Gundry, 409.

⁶⁰ Cf. Mk 11,9f.; Lk 19,38. Matthew's version may downplay the potentially militaristic connotation of Mark's coming "kingdom," and link the allusion back to Mt 20,29-31. On the allusion to Ps 118, see Stendahl, 64-66; Gundry 1967, 40-43.

⁶¹ The fact that a vision of peace follows immediately on Zech 9,9 indirectly confirms that this passage may have influenced Mt 11,28-30 (cf. also Duling 1978, 404; Christ, 115f.; Arvedson, 217; Bonnard, 170). The use of πραΰς in 11,29 has been explained with reference to Moses (e.g., Hill 1980, 13; Grundmann, 318; Davies-Allison, 2:290). Moses' meekness was well known (beginning with Num 12,3), but Matthew himself applies the description directly to the king = Son of David (21,5.9), and lowliness is a theme of some prominence in Matthew's Gospel without, however, any direct connection to Moses. It is perhaps significant that Allison 1993, 233-235, finds it so difficult to connect Matthew's Servant theme to Moses. In general, πραΰτης "has a prominent place in depictions of rulers" among the Greeks (cf. Hauck-Schulz 1968a, 646; Bauder, 256f.). Yet this picture of David's lowliness also has roots in the Dtr history. All the time Saul is on the throne David is on the run, with all who are in distress or in debt or discontented gathering about him (1Sam 22,2). Once on his throne he announces, "And today, though I am anointed king, I am weak, and these sons of Zeruiah are too strong for me. May the LORD repay the evildoer according to his evil deeds!" (2Sam 3,39). Later he is forced to abdicate in the face of his own son's coup, fleeing in a state of abject humiliation. In

This impression that in Mt 11,29 the use of the word πραΰς bears *specific* conceptual links to Matthew's Son of David Christology is reinforced by another verbal link, this time the noun νήπιος in Mt 11,25. Apart from 11,25 and its parallel in Lk 10,21, the noun νήπιος occurs in the Synoptics only in Mt 21,16 in Jesus' response to the chief priests and scribes who, in turn, are *objecting to the children calling Jesus the Son of David* ('Ακούεις τί οὗτοι λέγουσιν;). Jesus declares:

Out of the mouths of infants (νηπίων) and nursing babies
you have ordained praise for yourself.[62]

Once again, no sooner has Jesus responded to the leaders' objection than he withdraws (21,17; cf. 12,15).

In ch. 21 both of these nouns, πραΰς and νήπιος, are attached directly to Jesus' identity as the Son of David. It is surely more than coincidence that these two nouns, otherwise rare in the Synoptics, occur *together* at these two points in Matthew, that the noun νήπιος in particular is used with very much the same connotations,[63] that Jesus makes strong statements about the temple in both contexts, and that in both instances Jesus withdraws in the face of opposition.[64]

---

reference to 2Kgdms 7,8 Josephus recalls how God raised David "from the humble station (ἐκ ταπεινοῦ) of a shepherd to so great a height of power and glory" and gave "liberty" (ἐλευθερίας) to the Hebrews (*Ant* 7,95; cf. 1Kgdms 18,23; Ψ 151,1; Ps-Philo 59,2). Later on he describes David as "having qualities which only the greatest kings are expected to have": he was "most apt in perceiving and understanding the course of future events and in dealing with the immediate situation, prudent, mild (ἐπιεικής), kind (χρηστός) to those in trouble, just and humane" (*Ant* 7,391; cf. also *Ant* 7,43.270). TJud 24,1-6, which depends in part on Isa 11,1-10, also refers to the future deliverer as "meek" or "gentle"; cf. M. Strauss, 62-64, who suggests that this reference to "meekness" stems from Ps 45,4 (the latter was interpreted messianically in *TgKet* Ps 45). Again, Ψ 131,1 [132,1] reads: Μνήσθητι, κύριε, τοῦ Δαυιδ καὶ πάσης τῆς **πραΰτητος** αὐτοῦ, which is in reference to David's ceaseless efforts to provide a "resting place" (ἀνάπαυσις/κατάπαυσις) for the ark; that done, God will provide bread for the "poor" (v. 15). This reference to David's meekness probably refers back to the events of 2Sam 6, and esp. vv. 16.20-22. In that passage David chastizes his wife with the word that the lowly maids will hold David in honor, in contrast to his wife, daughter of Saul. Clement of Rome also includes David in a list of OT exemplars of humility; *1Clem* 18 (immediately following a reference to Moses). Indeed a sharp distinction between the options of Moses and David may be artificial, since these two figure coalesced already in the OT; supra, 25f.; von Rad, 1:351.

[62] Ψ 8,3 [8,2]; on the quotation, which is drawn from the LXX, cf. Stendahl, 134f.; Gundry 1967, 121f. In 11,25 this noun was drawn from Matthew's source, but 21,16 still indicates how Matthew took it.

[63] Certainly νήπιος has a literal referent in Mt 21, but its metaphorical implications in view of the leaders' unbelief are not easy to miss; cf. Carson, 443.

[64] A further suggestion that Matthew related these contexts is seen in the way he foreshadowed the healing of 20,29-34 already in 9,27-31 (recalling how 9,27ff. is picked

3.4. Conceptual parallels

These two nouns are definite pointers to the world of ideas in which Matthew was almost certainly thinking in 11,25-30. It will have been noticed, moreover, that these verbal parallels to a specific Son of David context are of a fabric with the larger tendencies of Matthew's Son of David Christology as we outlined it above.

Thus, when Kingsbury comments,

> ...apologetically, Matthew utilizes the title Son of David in order to underline the guilt that devolves upon Israel for not receiving its Messiah. To this end Matthew calls attention to the 'no-accounts' of Jewish society -- the blind, a blind and dumb man, the children, and a Gentile woman -- in reproach of Israel: these perceive and confess what Israel does not (13:13; 15:14)...,[65]

our minds turn almost immediately to Mt 11,25-30:

> I thank you, Father, Lord of heaven and earth, because you have hidden these things from the wise and intelligent and have revealed them to infants... Come to me, all you who are weary and carrying heavy burdens...

Moreover, we have already highlighted more than once the degree to which Jesus' identity as Son of David provokes intense rejection on the part of the leaders. We should not think that the whole of Mt 11-12 is "Davidic" just because it has the motif of rejection. But 11,25-30 intensifies this motif by translating it into a reason for thanksgiving and throwing it back into the faces of the opponents.[66] It is precisely in his role as rejected messiah that Jesus brings salvation, and judgment. This expression of thanksgiving and the gracious offer of salvation stand out from the pronouncement of woes before, and the murderous opposition afterwards. In 11,25-30 Jesus seems to affirm his status and function as the rejected messiah.

In 11,25-30 Jesus is rejected by those who should have "seen," yet he exults in his repugnant lowliness and makes his appeal to the "no accounts" who do "see." Although he is not *called* Son of David in 11,25-30 he is certainly playing the part.[67]

---

up in ch. 12); most scholars consider 9,27-31 to be a Matthean duplication of 20,29-34, which was taken over from Mk 10,46-52. In both cases Matthew has a reference to the compassion of Jesus (9,35-38; 20,34). The result is the complex of Son of David, compassion, meekness, recognized by "babes" (but not the "wise"), a comment on the temple, withdrawal. *The narrative pattern of chs. 20-21 is foreshadowed in 9-12.*

[65] 1975, 103.

[66] Verseput 1987, 535, believes that the Davidic messiahship emerges in chs. 11-12 "as the christological category which absorbs the main force of Jewish opposition."

[67] See further below, 233ff.

3.5. The OT rest tradition

The theme of the Christ's lowliness is pervasive in Matthew's Gospel and not confined to his role as Son of David. Even the use of πραΰς does not of itself prove that Jesus stands in 11,28-30 as the meek Son of David. Yet the convergence of both nouns (πραΰς and νήπιος) which mirrors ch. 21, and the more general parallels with Matthew's Son of David Christology, make it probable that Jesus speaks in 11,28-30 as the lowly king, the Son of David.

This identification is clinched as soon as we recall the central place of the Davidic dynasty *in the OT rest tradition*.[68] In the Nathan oracle of 2Kgdms 7 David has been given victory over his enemies (7,1)[69] and decides to build a house for the ark. In the Lord's response through Nathan, Israel is promised that she will not be distressed anymore (οὐ μεριμνήσει οὐκέτι) and evildoers or sons of unrighteousness (υἱὸς ἀδικίας) will not humble her anymore (τοῦ ταπεινῶσαι αὐτόν). David is promised rest (ἀναπαύσω σε; v. 11) as well as a house, a son; ἐγὼ ἔσομαι αὐτῷ εἰς πατέρα, καὶ αὐτὸς ἔσται μοι εἰς υἱόν (v. 14). In 3Kgdms 5,17f. [5,3f.] this oracle is taken up by Solomon and the achievement of rest attached to his own reign. In 1Par 22,9f. Solomon is then described as a man of rest (ἀνὴρ ἀναπαύσεως) to whom the Lord will give rest (ἀναπαύσω αὐτόν) so that Israel will enjoy peace and quiet during his reign (εἰρήνην καὶ ἡσυχίαν δώσω ἐπὶ Ισραηλ ἐν ταῖς ἡμέραις αὐτοῦ). In this passage the statement of Solomon's sonship is repeated though this time with the clauses reversed:[70] οὗτος ἔσται μοι εἰς υἱὸν κἀγὼ αὐτῷ εἰς πατέρα. It is here also that David prays that the Lord will grant Solomon wisdom and understanding (ἀλλ' ἢ δῴη σοι σοφίαν καὶ σύνεσιν κύριος; v. 12)[71] in a passage reminiscent of Moses' commissioning of Joshua (cf. Josh 1,6-9; Deut 34,9).[72]

Matthew clearly saw in the Logion before him a reminiscence of a very familiar OT tradition, *God's promise of rest to his people*. He would have been well aware of its close tie to David, Solomon, and the Davidic dynasty. His own presentation (21,4ff.) of Jesus as the Son of David is, however, of the *humble* Davidic king. What is significant is that this picture of David meets the promise of rest in Mt 11,28-30. Allowing, then, that this Son of David was also David's Lord (22,41-46), and therefore that he is no longer the recipient but now the *giver* of rest, it is evident that such a connection of

---

[68] This paragraph will refer to the LXX; use of the MT would not alter our point.
[69] Cf. Mt 11,27a.
[70] This order corresponds to Mt 11,27.
[71] Cf. Witherington, 365. Note esp. 1Kgs 4-5.
[72] For the remainder the reader is reminded of the summaries already given in Chs. Two and Three; supra, 25ff., 58ff., 88ff., and *passim*. In particular, note Ezek 34 (supra, 83), where God's servant, David, will shepherd the scattered flocks of Israel when God gives them rest.

a Davidide and "rest" corresponds to the OT presentation of the rest tradition better than any other alternative. *That background thus exposes for us the rationale for Matthew's redaction.*[73]

4. Other indications that the OT rest tradition underlies

The foregoing considerations have established that in making use of 11,28-30, Matthew was working within the world of ideas associated with Davidic traditions. If there is any hesitance to say that this *is* a Son of David passage, it is not because the Davidic motifs are weak, but because there are good reasons to avoid an unbalanced emphasis on Christological titles.[74] Matthew's concern is not with Jesus' identity as Son of David so much as his *role* in that capacity. Our primary concern has been to show that in modifying and locating this saying in line with his Son of David Christology the conclusion begins to press in on us that Matthew is also thinking in terms of the OT rest tradition as the primary background; Matthew's recognition of the latter gave rise to the redaction.

Several further observations can now be advanced which show that this is very likely. Each of these will be handled briefly, as none of them are explicitly developed by Matthew, but cumulatively they suggest a context in which Matthew might well have been thinking. The likelihood that Matthew intends for 11,28-30 to signal the fulfilment of OT hopes that God would give his people rest is accordingly enhanced.

4.1. The rest tradition in Matthew's sources

The claim that Matthew would have edited 11,28-30 in line with the OT rest tradition assumes that he was aware of this tradition as such. We might well assume his acquaintance with it on the basis of the general prominence of the rest tradition in the OT and Jewish literature. Yet in addition to the temple saying of 12,6 (remembering that the temple is God's resting place and was erected by Solomon, the wise son of David, when God gave Israel rest [1Kgs 4-5]), specific passages of the rest tradition are contextually

---

[73] The influence probably stems primarily from the literature reviewed in Chs. Two-Three above, but our review of other Jewish and Christian literature in Ch. Four indicated that the rest tradition was a living one and Matthew would presumably have had contact with it in a variety of contexts and through more than one medium. Note also supra, 131 n. 146.

[74] In other words, we should listen carefully to arguments such as Keck; Hengel 1976, 57-59. The absence of the stress on *healing* which is typical of Matthew's use of the actual title also cautions against a simple labelling.

linked to OT texts which are either alluded to by Matthew or were arguably in his mind. All of the following are in the immediate context of 11,28-30.

Immediately preceding Mt 11,25-30, in the woe pronounced over Capernaum, there is an allusion to Isa 14,13.15:

And you, Capernaum, will you be exalted to heaven? No, you will be brought down to Hades.[75]

These words recall the taunt that "Jacob" and "Israel" were going to sing on the day that the Lord would break the "yoke" (MT: staff) of the wicked,[76] and give his people rest (ἀναπαύω) from their pain, turmoil, and hard service![77] With Isa 14,13.15 we are in close proximity to New Exodus language, and to a conceptual parallel to 11,28-30 out of the rest tradition.

A second instance comes with the Father-Son saying of Mt 11,27. There is no need to determine whether 2Kgdms 7 (2Sam 7) lies at or near the point of origin of either this saying or the Son of God Christology generally, and it can be readily conceded that Mt 11,27 goes far beyond 2Kgdms 7 and its parallels. All we need to show is how obvious the parallel is.

ἐγὼ ἔσομαι αὐτῷ εἰς πατέρα, καὶ αὐτὸς ἔσται μοι εἰς υἱόν (2Kgdms 7,14; 1Par 17,13)

καὶ οὗτος ἔσται μοι εἰς υἱὸν κἀγὼ αὐτῷ εἰς πατέρα (1Par 22,10)

κύριος εἶπεν πρός με Υἱός μου εἶ σύ, ἐγὼ σήμερον γεγέννηκά σε (Ψ 2,7)

αὐτὸς ἐπικαλέσεταί με Πατήρ μου εἶ σύ...κἀγὼ πρωτότοκον θήσομαι αὐτόν (Ψ 88,27f. [89,26f.])

That the Nathan oracle of 2Kgdms 7 par. with its Father-son imagery and the accompanying promise of rest (v. 11) would have been in Matthew's mind is a safe assumption when we consider not only the Scrolls,[78] and apostolic

---

[75] Mt 11,23. For the allusion, which does not definitely correspond to either the MT or LXX, see Gundry 1967, 81; Stendahl, 91.

[76] Isa 14,5: συνέτριψεν ὁ θεὸς τὸν ζυγὸν τῶν ἁμαρτωλῶν, τὸν ζυγὸν τῶν ἀρχόντων; cf. 14,25; Charette, 293.

[77] Isa 14,3: Καὶ ἔσται ἐν τῇ ἡμέρᾳ ἐκείνῃ ἀναπαύσει σε ὁ θεὸς ἐκ τῆς ὀδύνης καὶ τοῦ θυμοῦ σου καὶ τῆς δουλείας σου τῆς σκληρᾶς, ἧς ἐδούλευσας αὐτοῖς. Cf. 14,7 MT: "The whole earth is at rest and quiet." These verses were included in our discussion of Old Testament passages; supra, 49 (MT), 86f. (LXX); *note the proliferation of "rest" vocabulary in Isa 13,20-14,7 LXX (esp. 14,1.30)*.

[78] We have already noted the well known passage from Qumran, 4Q174 (4QFlor 10-14; supra, 111f.), wherein 2Sam 7,11 is interpreted to mean that the sons of light are promised "rest" from the children of Satan. The passage continues on to interpret 2Sam 7,14 -- I will be his father, and he shall be my son -- as a reference to the "Branch of David who will arise with the Interpreter of the Law [to rule] in Zion [at the end] of time." The reference to the "Branch" derives from Jer 23,5 and 33,15 (cf. also Zech 3,8;

traditions,[79] but how often 2Sam 7 crops up in modern commentary on this saying. 1Par 22,9f. (cf. 2Kgdms 7) demonstrates how tightly the Father-son and ἀνάπαυσις imagery cluster together in that background, and how both are bound up with the wise son of David and the temple.[80]

A third instance where the rest tradition may have been in Matthew's mind comes with Mt 12,21. We have already noted the natural connection between 11,29 and the quote from Isa 42,1-4 in Mt 12,18-21. The last line in Matthew reads καὶ [LXX ἐπὶ] τῷ ὀνόματι αὐτοῦ ἔθνη ἐλπιοῦσιν, which agrees in general with the LXX against the MT.[81] The parallel with Isa 11,10 is close: Καὶ ἔσται ἐν τῇ ἡμέρᾳ ἐκείνῃ ἡ ῥίζα τοῦ Ιεσσαι καὶ ὁ ἀνιστάμενος ἄρχειν ἐθνῶν, **ἐπ' αὐτῷ ἔθνη ἐλπιοῦσιν**, καὶ ἔσται ἡ ἀνάπαυσις αὐτοῦ τιμή.[82] When there is a probable allusion to Isa 11,1 back in Mt 2,23,[83] and when Isa 11,1-10 appears to have been a source of early Christian testimonia,[84] we can be reasonably confident that Matthew

---

6,12), but is also paralleled in Isa 11,1 (cf. also 4Q161 [4QpIsa^a] on Isa 11,1; 4QPBless; 4Q285 [Eisenman-Wise, 26, 29]). Here at least is a possible reference -- messianic or not -- via 2Sam 7,14 to an eschatological figure, a son of God, the Branch of David (Collins 1993, 78, does not hesitate to see here a reference to the Davidic messiah in view of 4QBless; cf. Brooke, 197-205; D. Guthrie 237 n. 38, 302f.). In the case of 4QFlor 10-14 the joining of the future son of God with eschatological rest is drawn from the biblical text (2Sam 7,11-14), but the same joining of motifs also occurs in 4Q246. It has been argued that the reference to the eschatological "Son of God" in the latter should also be taken as a reference to the future Davidic king (Collins 1993, 76-82; the reference to "rest" seems to favor Collins' view that this passage is Davidic; supra, 112 n. 50). Other proposals are that 4Q246 is a reference to a historical king, the Antichrist, Melchizedek, or the Jewish people collectively; these are reviewed with bibliography in Collins 1993, 67-69. 4Q246 is parallel to Lk 1,32.35 in more than one way; cf. Collins 1993, 66.

[79] Ψ 2,7 and 1Par 17,13 (cf. 2Kgdms 7,14) are joined in the discussion of Jesus' Sonship at Heb 1,5, and the use of Ps 2,7 in Acts 13,33 is part of a midrash on 2Sam 7 (cf. M. Strauss, 164-192 [esp. 169f.]). In the Scriptural collection of 4QFlor (4Q174), 2Sam 7,11ff. is followed by Ps 2,1f. The voice at Jesus' baptism (Mt 3,17) represents a conflation of Isa 42,1 and Ps 2,7 (Mt 3,17 has provoked much debate; discussion is in Davies-Allison, 1:336-339, who suggest that the earlier reading was closer to Isa 42,1 [Gk text like Mt 12,18 and not LXX], with Ps 2,7 worked in secondarily; cf. Carson, 109f.).

[80] Note 1Kgs 4,29--5,18; the wise son of David is given rest and is thus able to build the temple; here he lays a heavy yoke of forced labor on his people (cf. 12,4).

[81] MT: "and the coastlands wait for his teaching [וּלְתוֹרָתוֹ אִיִּים יְיַחֵלוּ]." Matthew and the LXX may be witnessing to a lost Hebrew text; cf. Gundry 1967, 115f.

[82] Cf. Carson, 287; Davies-Allison, 2:327. M. Strauss, 242, notes that the similar LXX version of Isa 42,4 and Isa 11,10 -- in both cases diverging from the MT -- "suggests a common tradition in some way linking the Servant of Isa 42 to the coming Davidic king of Isaiah 11."

[83] Supra, 214. Note that in 2,23 Isa 11,1 is used in such a manner that the lowly origins of the messiah are strongly implied. The parallel with 11,28-30 is strong.

[84] Cf. Rom 15,12; 1Pet 4,14; Rev 5,5; Dodd, 83; Davies-Allison, 1:277f. The "rest" promised in Isa 11 has to do with the Davidide's provision of justice for the "poor and meek" (11,4), which is also conceptually close to Isa 42,3.

would have been alive to this very important OT passage regarding the coming Davidide in connection with 11,28-30. Isaiah's statement about rest is not taken up by Matthew, but it was lurking in the passages which he was apparently studying.

Finally, when at 12:1ff. Matthew will renew themes from ch. 9[85] it is not reaching too far to recall the compassionate Shepherd imagery of 9,36, especially when Matthew inserts the sheep illustration into 12,9-14 (cf. Mk 3,1-6; Lk 6-11). This theme would have recalled Ezek 34, which combines a promise of rest (v. 34, LXX) with the hope of a future Davidide.[86]

In sum, more than one OT rest tradition passage lurked in Matthew's sources. It would be purely speculative to say without further justification that these were direct influences on his presentation, but they can be allowed to stand as corroborative evidence. Matthew was almost certainly aware of God's promise of rest to his people.

4.2. Verbal similarities to Ex 33,14 and Jer 6,16 in 11,28f.

If Matthew was alive to the OT rest tradition then it is likely that the wording of the Logion as he received it[87] would have had a familiar ring.

Both Ex 33,14 and Jer 6,16 are often cited as parallels to Mt 11,28f.[88]

Mt 11,28:   Δεῦτε πρός με...κἀγὼ ἀναπαύσω ὑμᾶς
Ex 33,14:   Αὐτὸς προπορεύσομαί σου καὶ καταπαύσω [נח] σε[89]

Mt 11,29d: καὶ εὑρήσετε ἀνάπαυσιν ταῖς ψυχαῖς ὑμῶν
Jer 6,16:   καὶ εὑρήσετε ἁγνισμὸν [מרגוע] ταῖς ψυχαῖς ὑμῶν[90]

In both cases we are closer to the wording of Mt 11,28-30 than we are in the case of the parallel in Sirach. Nevertheless, the fragmentary nature of these

---

[85] Cf. 9,12f. with 12,7; cf. 9,27ff. with 12,22f.; cf. 9,36 and 10,6 with 12,11f. (on the last, cf. F. Martin, 279f.).

[86] On Ezek 34, see above, 83; also immediately below. On the relevance of Ezek 34 to Mt 9, see F. Martin, 274-280; Davies-Allison, 2:147f.; most other commentators.

[87] Both clauses to be considered in this section (28c and 29d) are pre-Matthean.

[88] In both cases the parallel is closer in the Hebrew (cf. Stendahl, 141f.; Gundry 1967, 135f.; Cerfaux, 156; Strecker 1962, 173 n. 4; Zahn, 443 n. 52; Luz, 2:200 n. 19). Nevertheless, the use of καταπαύω in Ex 33,14 rather than the synonym ἀναπαύω (supra, 80f., 97f.) would not have obscured the parallel if Matthew was acquainted only with the LXX. It is also remains possible that Matthew knew of another Greek translation of Jer 6,16 which used ἀνάπαυσις or a synonym: Matthew "agrees with the LXX [of Jer 6,16] in the use of the future indicative verb against the imperative of the Hebrew and in the plural ταῖς ψυχαῖς for the collective singular of the Hebrew" (Gundry 1967, 136). In any event, Matthew did know the Hebrew OT.

[89] Supra, 32f., 78ff. Allison 1993, 222, mistakenly renders "*hymas*."

[90] Supra, 55f., 80.

parallels with Ex 33 and Jer 6 makes it difficult to establish whether these are intended to be allusions.[91] Moreover, 11,28 is in fact paralleled by other passages in addition to Ex 33,14. One can note further:[92]

Ezek 34,15, in which the Lord rejects Israel's "shepherds" and promises to become a Shepherd to his people who will feed his sheep καὶ ἐγὼ ἀναπαύσω αὐτά. The Lord will set his servant David over them.[93]

2Kgdms 7,11, in which the Lord promises that he will appoint a place for his people καὶ ἀναπαύσω σε ἀπὸ πάντων τῶν ἐχθρῶν σου. He will also build a house for David.[94]

Deut 5,33, in which Moses directs the people to pay attention to the Lord's words, ὅπως καταπαύσῃ σε.[95]

Jer 31,25: כי הרויתי נפש עיפה וכל־נפש דאבה מלאתי [96]

Rather than thinking that there is an "allusion" to one or more of these specific passages it seems better to think that the Logion in Mt 11,28-30 was originally an *independent formulation*, possibly influenced by Sirach, but freely mixing in OT phraseology from the world of ideas associated with

---

[91] The most substantial case for an allusion to Ex 33,14 is that of Allison 1988, 478-483 (1993, 218-233); Davies-Allison, 2:272f., 283-287. On Jer 6,16, see esp. Knowles, 214-217, who considers dependence "probable"; further Carson, 278; Arvedson, 203, 209; Christ, 106; Sand, 253; Allison 1988, 483-485; many others (cf. Knowles, 214 n. 1). The prominence of Jeremiah in Matthew's Gospel (Zucker; esp. Knowles) lends credence to the belief that there is an echo of Jer 6,16 here (or at least that Matthew would have recognized the parallel), though it need not be an allusion. Knowles' discussion of Jer 6,16 is flawed by his belief that there is "no hint of rejection" in 11,25-30, and in that he regards Sir 51 to be the primary parallel.

[92] The following parallels depend on the LXX in Deut 5 and Ezek 34, but not necessarily in 2Sam 7; the parallel idea in Jer 31 [LXX 38] is closer in the MT. In addition, note Isa 25,1-26,6 LXX: Κύριε ὁ θεός μου, δοξάσω σε, ὑμνήσω τὸ ὄνομά σου...εὐλογήσει σε ὁ λαὸς ὁ πτωχός, καὶ πόλεις ἀνθρώπων ἀδικουμένων εὐλογήσουσίν σε. ἐγένου γὰρ πάσῃ πόλει ταπεινῇ βοηθὸς καὶ τοῖς ἀθυμήσασιν διὰ ἔνδειαν σκέπη... ἀνάπαυσιν δώσει ὁ θεὸς ἐπὶ τὸ ὄρος τοῦτο... καὶ πατήσουσιν αὐτοὺς [i.e., the proud] πόδες πραέων καὶ ταπεινῶν. Also Lam 5,5: "With a yoke on our necks we are hard driven; we are weary, we are given no rest" (LXX: ...κοπιάσαμεν, οὐκ ἀνεπαύθημεν).

[93] Supra, 83. Note the reference to throwing off the foreign yoke in 34,27.

[94] Supra, 25ff., 78ff.

[95] Supra, 82, 90f. The *Shema*, which follows on in Deut 6, was associated with taking on the yoke of the kingdom of heaven (*Ber* 2,2).

[96] "I will satisfy the weary, and all who are faint I will replenish"; supra, 54 (note 31,2 in the MT). The LXX (38,25) reads, ὅτι ἐμέθυσα πᾶσαν ψυχὴν διψῶσαν καὶ πᾶσαν ψυχὴν πεινῶσαν ἐνέπλησα. Gundry 1967, 136, points out regarding this passage that the "Hebrew words in Jer denote one who is languishing and weary, especially through toil"; the phrasing in Mt 11,28 is thus closer to the MT than to the LXX. Yet Jer 31,25 is not the only parallel to this idea in the Logion; cf. above, 60.

God's promise of redemptive rest to his people.[97] Matthew's familiarity with passages like Isa 11; Isa 14; 2Sam 7; Ex 33; Ezek 34; and Jer 6, sensitized him to the echoes of this tradition in the Logion and encouraged him to interpret it in line with that OT rest tradition.

4.3. The idea of an eschatological Sabbath in Matthew

The foregoing considerations have been concerned with parallels between Matthew 11-12 and the OT rest tradition, but there is also a suggestion that Matthew saw in 11,28-30 a fulfilment of the OT Sabbath rest, thus providing us with a further indication of the world of ideas with which Matthew associated the Logion.

Mt 11,5 is certainly no simple equivalent of Lk 4,18f., but the statement πτωχοὶ εὐαγγελίζονται which receives the accent in the list of Mt 11,5,[98] derives from Isa 61,1,[99] which reads as follows (NRSV):

The spirit of the Lord GOD is upon me, because the LORD has anointed me; he has sent me to bring good news to the oppressed [LXX: εὐαγγελίσασθαι πτωχοῖς], to bind up the brokenhearted, to proclaim liberty to the captives, and release to the prisoners; to proclaim the year of the LORD's favor...[100]

But this passage was understood as a prophecy of the messiah's ministry in terms of the sabbatical year of jubilee.[101] If the language of Mt 11,28-30 foreshadows that of Isa 42,1-4 in Mt 12,18ff., then the language of Isa 61,1 in Mt 11,5 -- good news to the poor -- foreshadows Jesus' offer of rest to the weary and heavy laden. The connection is almost irresistible, consisting of a twofold similarity of an offer of salvation[102] and the characterization of those

---

[97] Matthew is probably not the author of the Logion, so that even if Matthew knows only the LXX (which we deny; supra, 162f.), Jer 6,16 (MT) would still be relevant to consideration of the *history* of the Logion.

[98] Verseput 1986, 71f.; Gnilka, 1:407; Davies-Allison, 2:243.

[99] Matthew's reading at 11,5 (cf. Lk 7,22f.) also draws on Isa 35,5f. (cf. Isa 26,19; 29,18; 42,7.18). For further on Matthew's allusions here, which are probably dependent on the LXX, see Stendahl, 91; Gundry 1967, 79f.

[100] Luke leaves off here in 4,18f., but the OT passages continues, "and the day of vengeance of our God; to comfort all who mourn."

[101] Cf. Lev 25,10f.; Jer 34,8-10; Ezek 46,17; esp. Sloan; Blosser; Lincoln 1982, 201f. It has been questioned, however, whether Luke appreciated the jubilary connections of Isa 61; cf. M. Strauss, 224 n. 68 (Strauss himself believes that Luke did appreciate the jubilary significance, though he allows that Sloan and others may have exaggerated the importance of this motif for Luke's Gospel). For further on Isa 61 in Jewish (esp. 11QMelch) and Christian traditions, cf. M.P. Miller; J.A. Sanders 1975; Hengel 1979, 180ff. On the relation of Isa 61 to Mt 5,3-11, cf. the discussion in Davies-Allison, 1:436-439.

[102] Compare 11,5, εὐαγγελίζονται, to the *Heilandsruf* of 11,28-30.

who receive that offer.¹⁰³ An explicit *offer of rest* follows up on an announcement -- couched in sabbatical imagery -- of good news preached to the poor.

There is to be combined with the hint of sabbatical imagery in Isa 61,1 (Mt 11,5) the fact that Jesus' promise of salvific rest abuts directly on Matthew's two Sabbath pericopae.¹⁰⁴ If the clear conceptual link should caution against the extreme of overlooking any purposeful association of "rest" and "Sabbath,"¹⁰⁵ then we should also avoid the other extreme of too closely identifying Jesus' rest with the Sabbath.¹⁰⁶ Whatever else might be said about these two Sabbath pericopae with regard to Matthew's theology and apologetic,¹⁰⁷ Carson is probably correct to say that by them Matthew was suggesting that "the gospel rest to which the Sabbath had always pointed was now dawning."¹⁰⁸

---

¹⁰³ Compare the πτωχοί to the "weary and heavy laden." Commenting on Isa 11,1-10, Watts 1985, 172, remarks, "Yahweh's commitment to justice for the *poor* is paramount. No regime that fails on this point can claim to be the work of Yahweh" (Watts' emphasis).

¹⁰⁴ Rightly stressed by Carson 1982b, 75; Bacchiocchi 1984, 300f.; Schweizer, 277; Gardner, 195; Patte, 167; Grundmann, 320; Beilner, 221; many others.

¹⁰⁵ It is typical, especially among those advocating a Wisdom reading of 11,28-30, to see in Mt 12,1-14 primarily (seemingly only) a debate over Halakah as an illustration of Jesus' easier yoke and lighter burden. But surely it is significant -- in view of 11,28-30 -- that these debates about Halakah occur on the *Sabbath*. Moreover, beyond the conceptual ("rest") and temporal ("at that time") links, the Sabbath debates are too Christologically slanted to be treated simply as illustrations of Jesus' gentler Halakah; Jesus suggestively compares himself to David (France, 169-171; Chilton, 98f.; Carson, 280-282; Fenton, 189; Gnilka, 1:444; Davies-Allison, 2:308, 311), declares that something greater than the temple is here (the "something" is probably Jesus himself), pronounces himself Lord of the Sabbath, and makes a veiled allusion to his saving role as Israel's Shepherd (F. Martin, 279f.), also suggesting that the Sabbath is the proper day for (real) healing; cf. Bacchiocchi 1984, 303-309.

¹⁰⁶ This is the mistake of Bacchiocchi 1977, 61f.; 1984, 299-301. Bacchiocchi regards the seventh day Sabbath as a continuing *Christian* festival which symbolizes salvation, and he interprets the Synoptic passages along these lines. In the case of Mt 11,28-12,14 he emphasizes (more than most) the chronological link (12,1: Ἐν ἐκείνῳ τῷ καιρῷ), and labels without reservation the ἀνάπαυσις of 11,28-30 the messianic Sabbath rest. For a good critique, cf. Carson 1982b, 75; in general, see also Hoskyns, 77.

¹⁰⁷ Discussion of the importance and observance of the Sabbath in Matthew's community would take us too far afield; cf. Stanton, 1989 (repr. in 1992a, 192-206); Wong; H. Weiss; Bacchiocchi 1984, 309f.

¹⁰⁸ Carson 1982b, 75; likewise, Lincoln 1982, 202; Hoskyns, 77; Rordorf, 109; Jenni, 39; G. Robinson 1975, 424f.; Christ, 118 n. 449; Riesenfeld, 118f.; Schlatter, 390; Schweizer, 277; Gardner, 193; Fenton, 187; Grundmann, 320 (the Sabbath rest [cf. Gen 2; Heb 3-4] is "das große Heilsgut... Jesus ist nach 11,28-30 der Spender dieses großen ewigen Heilsgutes..."); Davies-Allison, 2:288f. (the context of 11,28-30 "encourages one to think in terms of the sabbath and eschatology"). Possibly also Schnackenburg, 1:106 (he cites Heb 3-4 in relation to Mt 11,28-30).

Matthew does not take us beyond a good hint of this, but if the sabbatical typologies of (eschatological) redemption were as strong in the first century A.D. as they appear to be in the later Jewish literature, then a hint suffices. Immediately after Jesus offers salvation *qua* "rest" he proceeds to declare himself Lord of the *Sabbath* and to point out that his healing messianic work is appropriate to *that* day. Matthew does not actually walk us up this particular path, but he certainly points the way.

4.4. Something greater than the temple

In 12,6 Matthew inserts the statement: λέγω δὲ ὑμῖν ὅτι τοῦ ἱεροῦ μεῖζόν ἐστιν ὧδε; the "something (neuter) greater" is probably Jesus himself.[109] If the priests are excused from violation of the Sabbath by virtue of their temple duties, then know that "something" greater than the temple is here. The point, while it involves Halakah, carries us far beyond a simple dispute over Halakah to the announcement of a decisive shift in redemptive history.

The significance of the addition is thus apparent within the context of the debate, yet it is missing in Mk 2,23-28 and Lk 6,1-5 and it is a singularly remarkable claim within the Synoptics. Noting the immediately following quote from Hos 6,6[110] and with an eye on Mt 21-24, R.T. France even remarks that the Christian reader might have read here "already a pointer to the theology of the Letter to the Hebrews."[111] Yet if we recall the centrality of the temple in the OT rest tradition (cf. 2Sam 7) then this clustering of motifs is not completely surprising. Once again, however, the thought is only partially expressed, indicating a world of ideas which is in common with the OT. The "I" who promises rest is "greater than Solomon," "greater than the temple," and "Lord of the Sabbath."[112]

It might even be of benefit to reflect on this saying from the viewpoint of Isa 66,1ff. This OT passage is taken up by Stephen in his critique of the temple, and further on we will be considering the possibility that it played a part in the background of Heb 3-4. In other words, this is an OT passage

---

[109] So Gundry, 223; Carson, 281f.; Davies-Allison, 2:314; Stanton 1992a, 82f.; other views are that it is the kingdom of God, the community of believers, etc. Most of the major commentators are reticent when it comes to explicating this Christological claim, probably because it is not unpacked by Matthew. Schlatter, 396, and Schmid, 206, are less so, stressing the presence of God in Jesus.

[110] The quotation of Hos 6,6 in 9,13 and 12,7 is considered by Gundry 1967, 111, to be Matthew's own rendering of the Hebrew (LXX^{AQOr} is probably influenced by the NT). Stendahl, 128f., is noncommittal, considering the brevity of the quotation and the possibility that it is a free rendering of Jesus.

[111] France, 215.

[112] Cf. G. Robinson 1975, 424.

which had a place in Christian traditions. When we examined this passage above we said that it is not a rejection of the temple as such, but that it was attempting to shift attention away from a sacred building to the person of YHWH. Its point of view is close to Hos 6,6: "For I desire steadfast love and not sacrifice, the knowledge of God rather than burnt offerings."[113] The thought of Isa 66,1f., then, is that God's מנוחה, his κατάπαυσις is not the earthly temple, not even just creation, but "this is the one to whom I will look, to the humble and contrite in spirit, who trembles at my word."[114] In Mt 11,28-12,8 the one who is meek and lowly in heart views himself as uniquely God's מנוחה (12,6) and the one from whom God's promised rest emanates. Could it be that Isa 66 ties together the characterization of Jesus as meek and lowly in heart, the promise of rest, the declaration that something greater than the temple is here, the quotation from Hos 6,6, and the hint of an eschatological Sabbath (Isa 66,23)?[115]

4.5. Summary

Matthew has not explicitly developed any of the points reviewed above, so that we are finally without firm grounds to promote any one of them as the key to 11,28-30. Yet each testifies in its own manner to the likelihood that the idea of eschatological rest -- as foreshadowed in the OT -- was in Matthew's mind, and that he was influenced by this expectation.

Thus, soon after a clear allusion to Isa 61 Matthew includes an explicit promise of ἀνάπαυσις to the "poor," which is, in turn, immediately connected to the two Matthean Sabbath debates. No sooner has Jesus alluded to the taunt which would be sung on the day that the Lord would give his people "rest," than he himself makes just such an offer. The wording of the promise itself recalls specific phrases most closely paralleled in the OT rest tradition, and a reference to "something greater than the temple" is inserted at just this point. Some of these points may hold potential for further exploration, but we limit ourselves to our main concern. When Davidic motifs are at hand the conclusion is close by that in 11,28-30 we are intended to think of the fulfilment of the OT rest tradition, coupled with the fulfilment of the hope of salvation as a true Sabbath rest. That these two strains of eschatological rest would be so casually joined is not surprising in view of the Jewish[116] and Christian (Heb 3-4) parallels.

---

[113] Supra, 51f.

[114] The thought of Isa 66,1f. can be filled out by reference to 57,15: "I dwell in the high and holy place, and also with those who are contrite and humble in spirit..."

[115] Does the clear presence of Matthean redaction throughout 11,28-12,8 preclude all possibility of finding here a reminiscence of Jesus' own Christology? Might Jesus have viewed himself as uniquely God's מנוחה with an eye on Isa 66?

[116] Supra, 122f., 129.

5. The wisdom of the Son of David

Before remarking on the promise of rest itself, a few comments can be added at this point to the effect that our argument does not exclude the possibility that the wisdom associations of Mt 11,28-30 were appreciated by Matthew, a possibility which we have already considered more than once. But if Matthew has no general interest in drawing the equation, Jesus = Wisdom, and if 11,28-30 has been modified by Matthew in view of the OT rest tradition, then it is likely that any wisdom connections will play a *subsidiary* role here.[117] This becomes a very credible suggestion, however, in view of the way in which wisdom figures in the Davidic traditions.

David himself was considered a *wise man and a prophet*,[118] and the future Davidide of Isa 11,1-10 -- who would emerge from under the rubble, or, to use Isaiah's imagery, as a mere shoot out of a hacked down stump -- was to be one anointed with the Spirit of wisdom and understanding.[119] In fact the latter passage and theme played no small part in subsequent traditions of the Davidic messiah.[120] That the pre-eminent son of David -- Solomon -- was

---

[117] Here we pick up the thread we let drop in Ch. Five, supra, 205ff. Also for Luz, 2:218, an identification of Jesus and Wisdom is not here "die entscheidende matthäische Aussage, sondern nur ihre Voraussetzung." Kingsbury 1976, 592, points out that Matthew nowhere makes a direct connection between teaching and preaching and the Son of David; rather, as we have already seen, a strong connection exists with Jesus' *healing* ministry. Yet a few considerations mitigate against this point: (1) Not all the Son of David contexts are healing contexts (chs. 1-2; also 21,9; 22,42-45); cf. Chilton, 94f.; Loader 1982, 585; (2) The overlap between "Son of David" and "Christ" makes a precise assignment of roles problematic (cf. 23,10); (3) There is a fundamental connection between Jesus' preaching and healing ministry, as 11,2-5 makes evident.

[118] Cf. 11QPs^a 27,2-4; 2Sam 14,17.20 (David's wisdom is able to bring "rest"); Ψ 50,8 [51,6] (joined with David's humility; cf. *1Clem* 18). In 2Sam 23,1ff. David, "the favorite of the Strong One," utters an "oracle" that the Spirit of YHWH speaks through him and that YHWH's word is on his tongue; cf. 1Sam 16,1-13.14-23; 11QPs^a 27,10f.; Ps-Philo (*LAB*) 59f.; Josephus, *Ant* 6,166-168; 7,391; Acts 2,30; 1,16; 4,25; Mk 12,36; Fitzmyer 1972; M. de Jonge 1986, 334f.; 1991, 70-72. De Jonge's argument that this prophetic picture of the Son of David forms the *starting point* for Jesus' own and subsequent Christian reflection has not been universally accepted; cf. Meeks; H.J. de Jonge. It is not our concern at present, however, to discern the *origins* of Christology, but only to point out that here is *one well testified strand* of thought whose relevance may have been felt by Matthew, especially in view of Isa 11 and related passages.

[119] Watts 1985, 174, comments on Isa 11,2 that, "When a king rules by 'the Spirit of Yahweh,' in 'the fear of Yahweh,' and with the intent of spreading 'the knowledge of Yahweh,' the ethos of Davidic kingship is at work"; supra, 47f.; Meadors, 59-61.

[120] Cf. e.g., TLevi 18,2.4f.7.9; TJud 22,2f.; 24,1-4 (both include a vision of eschatological rest and peace); Hengel 1979, 167ff., esp. on the Spirit and wisdom. Also on Isa 11 in Davidic messianic hopes, cf. M. Strauss, 24-97, 241f., and *passim*. PssSol 17-18 are of special importance, on which see Hengel 1979, 170f., who rightly stresses the militaristic note which dominates the use of Isa 11,1-10 here and elsewhere in Jewish literature. On the Davidic messiah in PssSol, cf. M. Strauss, 44-50.

the wise person *par excellence* needs no demonstration.[121] In Solomon we find both a man of wisdom and a ἀνὴρ ἀναπαύσεως.[122] One aspect of the wisdom of both David and Solomon -- much studied of late[123] -- was its potency for exorcising demons. It is not necessary to discuss the evidence for this here,[124] but only to note that the NT *locus classicus* for discussions of this component of Davidic lore is right here in Mt 12.

In short, the foregoing gives us good reason to expect that wisdom would figure in Matthew's Son of David Christology as a *capacity* of the Son of David.[125] Matthew would probably have agreed that Jesus is not merely "something greater than Solomon," but that he is in some sense the full, eschatological embodiment of God's wisdom (23,34),[126] but it is unlikely that a straightforward identification with Wisdom was his intended point in 12,42.[127]

So also with Mt 11,28-30. This Logion features Jesus as a teacher summoning followers to himself, its wording might have been influenced by an important wisdom writing, and it is juxtaposed in Mt 11,25-30 with other sayings evidencing wisdom motifs. Yet time and again, upon examination the evidence points to the conclusion that Matthew saw in the saying *not* first of all a Wisdom Christology but *primarily* a reminiscence of YHWH's OT promise of rest, and that Matthew then proceeded to modify the saying in line with the person and ministry of the ultimate and true Son of David. In view of this we may think it most probable that Matthew was interested in this Logion not as a picture of Wisdom incarnate, but as a picture of Jesus, the βασιλεὺς πραΰς, the Son of David, the one greater than Solomon, who ushers in the endtime ἀνάπαυσις τῷ λαῷ τοῦ θεοῦ through his role as the Spirit anointed messianic teacher of wisdom.[128]

---

[121] Cf. 1Kgs 3,12.28; 4,29-34; 5,9ff.; *passim*. In the OT the phrase "son of David" refers to Solomon, with the exception of 2Sam 13,1 where it refers to Absalom.

[122] Cf. esp. 1Chr/1Par 22,9-12.

[123] Cf. e.g. Fisher; Lövestam; Berger 1973; 1974; Duling 1975; Chilton, 88-112; also Duling, in *OTP*, 1:945-951; Davies-Allison, 1:157.

[124] Cf. Josephus, *Ant* 8,45-49; also Ps-Philo (*LAB*) 60,3; WisSol 7,15-22; TSol 1,7; 20,1 and *passim*. For David as an exorcist, see 1Sam 16,14-23; Ps-Philo 60; Josephus, *Ant* 6,166-168; 11QPs[a] 27,2-11. In *Ant* 8 it is said that this power to exorcise demons was such that the demons were not able to return; cf. Mt 12,29.42-45.

[125] This is also Meador's judgment, 67f., on the use of wisdom ideas in Q and Mark.

[126] Cf. Gnilka, 1:467. It is far from clear, however, what *Matthew* would have meant by such a proposition.

[127] Cf. Grundmann, 334f.; Schmid, 214f.; Sand, 266f.; Schnackenburg, 1:114; Davies-Allison, 2:357-359; Marshall 1978, 486f.

[128] Cf. Jer 23,5f.; 33,15f. 2Bar 61 (early II A.D.) recalls the time of David and Solomon as a time when Zion was built, the sanctuary was dedicated, "rest and peace reigned...wisdom was heard in the assembly, and the richness of understanding was magnified in the congregations"; likewise Sir 47,12f.; cf. 4Ez 8,52. Brueggemann 1971, 325, emphasizes the necessity of wisdom in the king if there is to be "order" in his

Finally, we are now in a better position to remark on the relevance of Sirach to the question of the *location* of the saying in Matthew, especially in relation to vv. 25-27.[129] So long as we fully appreciate where Matthew's *primary* interests laid throughout the passage of vv. 25-30, and especially in relation to vv. 28-30, we can allow that the larger context of Sir 6 played some part in decisions as to placement, for here there is not only talk of a yoke, labor, and rest, but of the wise and understanding.[130] Yet as we already observed regarding Sir 6, there is no small amount of dissonance between that passage and Mt 11,25-30,[131] making it very unlikely that a Wisdom Christology is intended. What is found is a very loose parallel which provides no primary key to understanding our Logion, but one which does serve to set in relief the strong note of failure, judgment, condemnation, and, in a different vein, newness in Jesus' ministry. It was the *Son of David*, the one greater than Moses and Solomon, *indeed, the very Son of God*, who came and offered his people the long awaited rest, but the wise did not "see" him while the "babes" did. This was the historic mistake of "this generation" (11,16-19.25-27; 21,14-16; 22,41-46). Mt 11,25-30 is a resounding condemnation of conventional wisdom (cf. 1Cor 1-4) and the announcement of something quite new.

6. Jesus the sage

A last comment follows on from the foregoing and pertains to one of the recent books of Ben Witherington III, *Jesus the Sage*. Witherington's "third quest" study is a significant contribution to the discussion of Jesus and wisdom, and is worthy of separate mention. Indeed, though Witherington

---

domain. Moreover, this use of the idea of "meekness" as a character trait of the wise is more akin to the typical use of the idea in wisdom thought than is the contrived idea of "meekness" as a trait of Wisdom herself. On Jesus as the Spirit anointed messianic teacher of wisdom, see Hengel 1979.

[129] Supra, 201, 205f. Matthew is probably responsible for the present location of the Logion, as the observations above, 205f., indicate. The parallels with Hebrews that we will highlight in Ch. Eight cannot be coincidental (infra, 362-366), and should also be taken into account when considering Matthew's reasons for locating the Logion here.

[130] Noting that the parallels with Ex 33 and Jer 6 suggest dependence on the Hebrew Scriptures (supra, 227f.; Hunter, 248, for one, always assumed any dependence would be on the Heb Sirach.), we can observe that the original Hebrew of Sir 51 likely did not hold forth the promise of *rest* (so Skehan, 398; Skehan-Di Lella, 576, 579), and the Greek of Sir 6 did not use the word $\zeta\upsilon\gamma\delta\varsigma$ (Heb v. 30). Yet allowance must be made for the uncertainties of Sirach's textual history (supra, 77 n. 1), and also for the possibility that Matthew (or some earlier figure) knew both a Hebrew and Greek version of Sirach. Some have been convinced that Sir 6 is a stronger parallel than Sir 51 anyway (e.g., D.W. Smith, 36f.; Davies-Allison, 2:293 n. 251; Witherington, 207).

[131] Supra, 172f.

approaches Matthew from the viewpoint that we have been opposing, he arrives at conclusions remarkably similar to our own:

> In 2 Samuel 7 David is promised: (1) the establishment of his kingdom through (2) an offspring who will build God a house; (3) "I will be a father to him and he shall be a son to me." This promise is made in regard to Solomon. I would suggest that when one reads this text and couples with it the understanding of the importance of Solomon witnessed to in the sapiential literature one finds here all the major elements of Matthew's Christology.[132]

An important point for Witherington is that the identification of Jesus and Wisdom stems back to Jesus himself.[133] I would demur over his treatment of Mt 11,28-30 at this point (see below), and some of his other exegetical suggestions in this connection are less than compelling,[134] but his general case for the organic development from Jesus himself to the later Wisdom Christologies is well defended. However, there is no reason to evaluate that thesis in the present context. The view of the present study is not that there is no Wisdom Christology in evidence in Matthew's Gospel, but rather that there is such evidence but that this aspect of Matthew's Christology stayed in the background and did not form a part of Matthew's teaching or polemical agenda. A Wisdom Christology thus predates Matthew's Gospel and in theory could go back to Jesus. Yet the present study has focused on the meaning of the Logion in Matthew's Gospel, and the question of Jesus' own Christology is thus not a necessary concern.

My critique of Witherington is, first, that in his investigation of *Matthew's* Wisdom Christology he uses as a starting point the standard line of argument developed by Suggs.[135] This means that his many valuable comments and cogent arguments further down are plotted on a skewed line. Nothing needs to be added to what we have already said on that score. Witherington's own contribution to this exegetical tradition is merely to fill it out by demonstrating "how Matthew presents the story of Jesus in a sapiential fashion throughout much if not all of his work, and intends for his audience to read it that way."[136] There is much here that is of help, yet for

---

[132] Witherington, 365.

[133] Witherington, esp. 201-208. The same suggestion had been made before; cf., e.g., Christ, 100-119; Balchin, 217f.

[134] For example, his suggestion that the woman in the parable of Mt 13,33 par. is Wisdom (Witherington, 191). The basis of the argument is the fact that the figure is a woman. A more general critique of Witherington's overall investigation is that he seems never to have met a wisdom parallel that he did not like (a failing that Allison almost admits to in his pursuit of the new Moses theme).

[135] Witherington, 351, 359 n. 78. This is not to imply that he is in agreement with Suggs in all the details, esp. touching the genre of Q vis-à-vis *GosThom*. Yet he does view Matthew as actively forwarding Q's Wisdom Christology (228f.), and generally agrees with Suggs' assessments of Matthew's editorial changes of the key Q passages.

[136] Witherington, 351.

the most part the discussion only shows that Jesus was sage-like, and yet something more than an average sage; finally, it seems best to view him as Wisdom incarnate. There is nothing here beyond the "purple passages" (11,19.25-27.28-30; 23,34-36.37-39) to which Witherington makes repeated reference, however, that compels us to think that Matthew was attempting to draw the equation, Jesus = Wisdom. Rather, given our own treatment of the prooftexts, we are once again led to the view that this identification stood in the background, forcing itself on Matthew in the traditions themselves, informing Matthew's own presentation, but nowhere becoming a direct concern of his Gospel's Christology. I am convinced that the viewpoint of the present study does a better job of accounting for Matthew's presentation of Jesus, and certainly yields a more satisfying explanation of 11,28-30, especially in view of Witherington's own conclusion cited above.

The second concern relates to Witherington's use of Mt 11,28-30 in his investigation of Jesus' own Wisdom Christology. After making a case for authenticity, he proceeds to argue that the Logion would have implied an identification with Wisdom on Jesus' lips. The heart of his argument is that the Logion has its closest parallel in Sirach (esp. Sir 6), and that "if Jesus' audience had any memory of Sirach 6 they could have drawn the conclusion that when Jesus spoke the substance of what one finds in Mt 11:28-30, he was speaking as Wisdom."[137] This is a large assumption to make, however. We do not have the dominical context of this saying (Witherington takes the view that the Logion was originally independent of 11,25-27), and the context would have been crucial to how Jesus' audience understood him. Moreover, the parallel with Sirach 6 and 51 has been overplayed, as we have already demonstrated at length. Even if some in Jesus' audience had knowledge of Sirach, it is special pleading to assume that they would have connected the Logion with that work, and, further, drawn such a Christological conclusion. In any event, we have no evidence from the first or second centuries that anyone did understand the Logion primarily in terms of Sirach. As we have shown, both in literary and thematic terms Matthew points us in other directions. Even *Thomas* does not evidence any cognizance of the relevance of Sirach. One strongly suspects that Witherington has allowed his understanding of the Logion in Matthew's Gospel to determine his argument at the level of Jesus' Christology, in spite of maintaining a theoretical distinction between the two levels.

With these comments I do not wish to give the impression that I am in general disagreement with Witherington's perspective on the place of wisdom in the Jesus traditions and in the development of NT Christology. It is especially encouraging to see Witherington integrating the wisdom theme

---

[137] Witherington, 207.

into Matthew's Son of David Christology.[138] A thorough interaction with his study is beyond the scope of this one, but it is my view that the two should be generally compatible.[139]

7. The promise of rest

The question remains after all of the foregoing whether our researches have enabled us to bring into sharper focus the significance of the Logion. In spite of its universal appeal, key elements of the saying have been notoriously difficult to nail down. It is sometimes suggested that the ἀνάπαυσις is equivalent to the risen Jesus' *presence* with his disciples, an idea which is not a little suggestive in view of the fact that the parallel in Ex 33,14 connects rest to God's accompanying presence.[140] Yet however relevant the idea of Jesus' on-going presence is, it does not make matters much clearer to say that his presence *is* his rest. Rather, the point would appear to be that Jesus' on-going presence mediates that rest, or, to make the point on the basis of the English translation, that, "I will *give* you rest." Moreover, unless we are going to simply substitute a theological idea -- the presence of the risen Jesus -- for the actual wording of the saying -- "I am meek and lowly in heart" -- then we will need to say that it is his on-going presence *as the humble king* which mediates rest. This is a little surprising in view of the usual connection between Jesus' lowliness and his *earthly* ministry, but it does seem to be suggested by this saying.

It is also sometimes assumed that Jesus' ἀνάπαυσις can be understood as equivalent to the twin paradoxes: the "easy yoke" and "light burden."[141] Practically it may almost be true that the experience of rest *is* the enjoyment of the easy yoke, but logically the ἀνάπαυσις issues out of the latter. In any

---

[138] Summarized on pp. 352, 365f. in Witherington.

[139] Witherington is surprisingly dismissive of a new Moses theme in Matthew, however (esp. 350, 364). On this, see Allison 1993. In my view it does not have to be an either/or, either Wisdom or new Moses.

[140] Cf. Betz, 24; Deutsch 1987, 41f., 136f.; Luz, 2:222. This idea emerges especially when the parallels between 11,27-30 and 28,18-20 are highlighted; Gnilka, 1:440 n. 49, however, expresses scepticism on the relevance of the latter passage. We noted repeatedly in Ch. Two the way in which God's *presence* is connected to the promise of rest.

[141] E.g., for Betz, 23, the "'rest' is identical with the ζυγός of Jesus"; Hill, 208. These twin paradoxes have been a perennial problem for interpreters. There are, in fact, two levels to the paradox. The phrases (easy yoke; light burden) are themselves virtually oxymorons (level one). The question which has received more attention is how to reconcile them with Jesus' uncompromising ethic and view of discipleship (level two).

case, the ideas of the "easy yoke" and "light burden" have proved the most difficult to understand.[142]

Another difficulty is the apparent fact that life for Jesus' disciples is anything but restful! Jesus and Matthew both clearly expect that the lot of a disciple will be a difficult and painful one, involving not only a demanding ethic from within but persecution from without (10,16-23; 23,34-36). And yet, though it is tempting to take refuge in the wording of the saying ("rest *for your souls*") and understand here a purely inner rest, this does not appear to satisfy the implied scope of Jesus' promise, nor does the wording probably intend to limit the idea in this way.[143] The messiah's salvation -- which is effectively encapsulated in this promise -- appears to be somewhat more inclusive than an inner quietness in the midst of the world's turmoil, just as the promise of the *kingdom* is more inclusive.

It is probably best to acknowledge from the start that this saying does not permit of precision in understanding as the language is as non-specific as it is provocative. Surely this is why this invitation and promise have so often been found to be comforting words down through history and right across cultures and circumstances. It may be that Betz has overstated the matter in characterizing the saying as an empty vessel into which meaning can be poured, but he probably also errs on the other side in saying that "Matthew introduced the logion into a hermeneutical context in which it now takes on a definite meaning."[144] Even its Matthean context does not precisely delimit the meaning of the saying, seen in the absence of any scholarly consensus. Yet with these remarks as a caveat, we may advance to the following.

7.1. The weary and heavy laden

Rest is promised to the "weary and heavy laden." Who, then, are the weary[145] and heavy laden?[146] Several answers have been put forth. They

---

[142] For the range of interpretations of the "easy yoke," not all of will be mentioned here, cf. Betz, 23f.; Luz, 2:219f.; Davies-Allison, 2:291f. The latter list six opinions, but favor the suggestion that this "hangs in the air without explanation because it simply records the voice of experience." This is probably correct. In addition to those mentioned in these sources, see the more unique understandings of Schweizer, 272f., and Jeremias 1972, 194. Elsewhere in the NT it is written, αἱ ἐντολαὶ αὐτοῦ βαρεῖαι οὐκ εἰσίν, ὅτι πᾶν τὸ γεγεννημένον ἐκ τοῦ θεοῦ νικᾷ τὸν κόσμον (1Jn 5,3f.).

[143] *Contra*, e.g., Morris, 297; Gundry, 220. In both Jer 6,16 and Mt 11,28-30 the rest "for your souls" is a rest for the whole person, or, "for yourselves" (*GosThom* 90); supra, 55f.; cf. also Jacob, 620; Schweizer 1974, 639f.

[144] Betz, 10, 22.

[145] Κοπιάω (κοπιῶντες, cf. κόπος) is probably used here in the sense of "to weary" as the result of exertion (so Bauer-Aland, 901; Louw-Nida, 1:260; Morris, 295 n. 77), but it is often used in the sense of "toiling," or "working hard" (thus here for Fendrich, 307; Luz, 2:219). It is possible that both notions receive equal stress in the present case, thus:

might be those suffering under the weight of Pharisaic Halakah,[147] or under the weight of sin.[148] More generally, they might simply be all (cf. πάντες) who have not come to Jesus and who have therefore not tasted of rest.[149] Alternatively, if the invitation is addressed primarily to Jesus' own followers, they are those wearied by the demands of discipleship.[150]

By way of evaluation, the following may be said. A primary concern with "sin" in the sense of suffering under the burden of guilt would sound a discordant note in this context.[151] Yet if one is thinking more broadly of the effects of "evil" as the cause of weariness, then the idea is general enough to include most other options.[152] Moreover, when the saying has not only an immediate application but also a future orientation,[153] and when Jesus' unqualified promise stands in such stark contrast to his own characterizations of discipleship,[154] we should probably not exclude an application to Jesus' hard pressed disciples. The realization of the promise is hardly a once for all matter. Nevertheless, a *primary* reference to the

---

"exerting oneself to the point of weariness" (apparently Hauck, 828f.). The verb occurs in Mt 6,28 (Lk 12,27) and the noun in 26,10 (Mk 14,6). Cf. Jer 31,25 [LXX 38,25].

[146] Φορτίζω (cf. φορτίον) means "to load," or "burden" someone with something; the only other NT occurrence of the verb is Lk 11,46, "to cause to carry" (Louw-Nida, 1:207; on the double accusative, cf. BDF § 155). In Mt 11,28 the form is πεφορτισμένοι (perf. pass.) thus, "having been loaded/burdened." Carson, 278, calls this the "passive side of weariness, overloaded like beasts of burden." The verb occurs only once in the LXX (Ezek 16,33). For the noun, cf. Mt 11,30; 23,4 (Lk 11,46). Cf. K. Weiss 1974a, 86f.

[147] Many recent interpreters, esp. those stressing the Wisdom connection; cf. 23,4; Strecker 1962, 173. Variations on this understanding take it in the sense, e.g., of being "weary and heavy burdened in their struggle for redemption and union with God" (Maher, 103; Maier, 398), or as the result of works righteousness (Christ, 106).

[148] Davies-Allison, 2:288, assign this interpretation to most of the Fathers. Cf. e.g. Ψ 37,4 [38,4].

[149] E.g., K. Weiss 1974a, 86f.; Bruner, 437f.; Davies-Allison, 2:288.

[150] Stanton 1992a, 372-375.

[151] The programmatic statement of 1,21 and the atoning sacrifice of the crucifixion (26,28) make this meaning *relevant*.

[152] Sir 40,1-7 speaks of a ζυγὸς βαρὺς ἐπὶ υἱοὺς Αδαμ that weighs on them from birth to death and robs them of rest even in their sleep.

[153] Esp. Strecker 1962, 174. The eschatological orientation is not grounded in the tense of the verbs, but rather in the general tendency of Matthew's Gospel: "die Forderung Jesu allgemein durch den Blick auf die Vergeltung am Ende motiviert ist, wie ja umgekehrt Kennzeichen der pharisäischen Lehre ist, daß sie nicht in die Basileia führt." The immediate context of 11,5.20-24 reinforces the relevancy of this consideration; cf. also Mt 12,20. The eschatological orientation of this promise is emphasized by many, e.g. Schniewind, 154; Carson, 278; Grundmann, 317-320; Sand, 253; Gnilka, 1:439f.; Luz, 2:222; Davies-Allison, 2:289.

[154] Mt 10,16-39. The first Sabbath pericope of ch. 12 has to do with Jesus' disciples.

disciples is less likely.[155] This is essentially an evangelistic summons, a call to discipleship more than to disciples.

That πεφορτισμένοι in 11,28 has something to do with Pharisaic Halakah is suggested not only by the ensuing Sabbath debates (12,1-14) but by the verbal contrast of 11,30 (τὸ **φορτίον μου ἐλαφρόν** ἐστιν) and 23,4 (φορτία βαρέα).[156] Yet these two observations are only beginnings and not the answer itself. As has often been observed, Jesus can hardly be said to be offering an easier law to his disciples,[157] and thus a simple antinomian or anti-Halakah reading is to be excluded in 11,28-30. Moreover, the tendency to treat Halakah as a monolithic whole -- which is rejected *en bloc* by Jesus or Matthew -- is not justified.

We must ask in what sense the Pharisaic burdens are βαρύ.[158] The "heaviness" may have consisted in part in the sheer proliferation of rules, but this is never condemned directly, certainly not in chs. 11 or 23, nor does Matthew portray people struggling to fulfil such a code.[159] The more likely explanation is that the heaviness consisted in, or maybe better, resulted from the absence of mercy, justice, and faith as the controlling principles of Pharisaic religion (23,23). The people are thus "weary and heavy laden" along the lines of 23,4 because, according to Matthew, socially and religiously they feel the brunt of what Judaism had become. These are those who because of their profession, their education, or their physical state were pushed to the fringes and cut off from the healing waters. That this is right

---

[155] Stanton's interpretation takes its lead primarily from the belief that 11,25-27 is addressed specifically to the disciples. Yet the whole of 11,20-30 has a certain surreal quality to it. In 11,7-19 Jesus is addressing the crowds, and at no point through v. 30 is his address explicitly redirected. This is true even if the crowds recede somewhat in vv. 20-24 as Jesus pronounces woes from an almost transcendent perspective. The prayer of vv. 25f. has been fittingly compared by Dibelius, 281, to the prayer of Jn 11,41f.; it is a prayer in form, but it is clearly a public proclamation in actuality, and the same probably goes for Mt 11,27. Moreover, if the Isaianic Servant theme gave impetus to Matthew's addition of 11,29c (supra, 209ff.), then the recipients of the invitation are most likely to be the people in general since they are the objects of the Servant's ministry. Stanton is right to draw a parallel with Mt 9,36 which seems to picture as "harassed sheep" not only the crowds but also the disciples (cf. 10,16; 1992a, 374f.). If Stanton is nonetheless correct that the disciples are the primary recipients of this invitation in 11,28-30, then we should probably give more consideration to the possibility that Mk 6,31 is the source of this saying (de Kruijf, 69-71; Lampe-Luz, 397).

[156] The parallel with ch. 23 includes the reference to "humbling" oneself (23,12) and to the messiah as "instructor" (23,10). In Mt 11,28-30, however, it is the "yoke of discipleship" before it is a body of teaching; rightly, Stanton 1992a, 375.

[157] Cf. 5,19f.; 15,1-20; 19,16-29; 23,23; cf. Betz, 23; Stanton 1992a, 375.

[158] For discussion and literature on 23,2-4, cf. Garland, 49-55.

[159] In 23,23 Jesus would not have the Pharisees leaving off from their heroic efforts at tithing garden herbs. Yet for Schmid, 204f., Jesus' yoke is lighter inasmuch as it jettisons the 613 commands and prohibitions of Halakah and settles on the two-fold command of love for God and neighbor; cf. Grundmann, 317.

emerges clearly if we look at how Jesus actually differs in practice from the Pharisees in Matthew's Gospel.

If the Pharisees had had their way, Jesus would not have extended fellowship to the tax collectors and sinners (9,10-13). If they had had their way, Jesus' disciples would not have been able to satisfy their hunger in the way they did on that Sabbath (12,1-8). If they had had their way, the man with the withered hand would not have been healed that day (12,9-14). If they had had their way those possessed by demons would not have been brought to Jesus to be freed (12,22ff.). These are the leaders who had contrived "ethical" ways for children to abandon their parents to need (15,5). They had turned the temple into a shopping market while Jesus made it a place of healing (21,12-14). The effect of their leadership was to leave a people "harassed and helpless, like sheep without a shepherd" (9,36) and to leave the sick without a physician (9,12). The fruit of their labors was a people called the "poor," a people "bruised," whose life was only a "smoldering wick." Matthew probably sees it as symptomatic that Jesus is a teacher who has compassion on his listeners ($\sigma\pi\lambda\alpha\gamma\chi\nu i\zeta o\mu\alpha\iota$ $\dot{\epsilon}\pi\dot{\iota}$ $\tau\dot{o}\nu$ $\ddot{o}\chi\lambda o\nu$) and is even concerned that they not go away hungry lest they faint on the way (15,32ff.). His is a *much needed* announcement of good news to the poor (11,5).

The "heavy burdens" of 23,4 are best understood in connection with the (note the ironic reversal) "heavier matters"[160] of 23,23, justice, mercy, and faithfulness. In turn, 23,23 naturally recalls 9,10-13 where the Pharisees are similarly rebuked for having forgotten mercy (Hos 6,6), and where they are (in effect) "locking" people out of the kingdom (cf. 23,13). It is not only incidentally that Hos 6,6 is repeated in the Sabbath debate of Mt 12,7, immediately following 11,28-30.[161] Thus it is neither a matter of a simple accumulation of rules nor a more demanding interpretation which makes the Pharisaic burden heavy while Jesus' is light. It consists rather in *stacking the deck* against the very ones whom Jesus sees most in need by the neglect of justice, mercy, and faithfulness.[162] For the Pharisees the Law may have been a "hedge of lilies,"[163] but for the outcasts it had become a hedge of

---

[160] I.e., "more important," rather than "more difficult"; Gundry, 464.

[161] On the use of Hos 6,6, cf. Hill 1977. On the OT text, cf. above, 231 n. 110.

[162] Cf. K. Weiss 1974a, 85; Strecker 1962, 174; Deutsch 1987, 41. That something like this is the issue in 11,28-30 is suggested not only by the reassuring statement that Jesus himself is $\pi\rho\alpha\ddot{\upsilon}\varsigma$ and $\tau\alpha\pi\epsilon\iota\nu\dot{o}\varsigma$ -- in obviously deliberate contrast to the Pharisees (23,2-12) -- , but in that his "yoke" is described as $\chi\rho\eta\sigma\tau\dot{o}\varsigma$, and in that the related passage of 12,17-21 promises "justice" to the "bruised reed" and "smoldering wick."

[163] Cf. Maher, 100. "The obligation to obey" the numerous commandments of the written and oral law "was not seen by the Rabbis as imposing a heavy burden on observant Jews" (E.P. Sanders, 111).

thorns;[164] accordingly, the appeal of Jesus' invitation would have been felt by the "sick" but probably not by the "healthy."

We may conclude, therefore, that the weariness of 11,28 can be related to Pharisaic Halakah, but it is not a matter of merely exchanging one body of teaching for another -- Jesus' easier yoke for the heavier yoke of Halakah or of the Law. What is being condemned is not a body of teaching as such, and Jesus' "yoke" is not equivalent to a *nova lex*, as it were. The problem -- allowing for the differences in political and social circumstances -- is more analogous to the sort of thing the prophets condemned in Isa 28,12 and Mic 2,10.[165] According to Matthew, the situation in Jesus' day, as it was in the days of Isaiah and Micah, was one in which the "wise and understanding" -- *contra* Sir 6 -- had exploited their power base to put others at a disadvantage, to secure and enhance their own standing, to oppress and exploit the weak and vulnerable, and, ultimately, to make it difficult for many to find God. The leaders had imposed on the weaker members of their society the very conditions from which YHWH had delivered the nation, and Jesus' description of the people as the "weary and heavy laden" is thus an implied indictment. In this desperate situation Jesus signals God's desire to bring his promise of rest for his people to fulfilment. The language is that of a New Exodus.[166]

Finally, however, it must be said that the idea of being "weary and heavy laden" in 11,28 should not be limited to whatever corresponds to 23,4.[167] There is a large textual gap between these passages and the contexts are not identical. We have already focused on the correspondence between 11,29 and 12,20, and have cited a number of other characterizations of the "sick" whom Jesus came to heal. It is less likely that Matthew's understanding of the identity of the "weary" was precisely circumscribed and restricted, than

---

[164] Schmid, 204; Morris, 296.

[165] On these passages, cf. above, 49f., 57f.

[166] Cf. Charette, 294f.; Davies-Allison, 2:291 n. 247. Hauck, 828, says of κόπος that it is "a fixed term in OT piety," and "an important antonym of eschatological hope." One recalls the burdens placed on the children of Israel (though φορτίον is not used in that connection in the LXX); cf. e.g., Ex 1-3; 5,4f. (LXX); Ps 66,11f.; 81,6; Isa 14,3.5.7.25; Ezek 34,27. This is also the place to recall the use of the "weariness" motif in the rest tradition; supra, 60. Cf. Jer 31,25 [LXX 38,25] and Gundry 1967, 136. Allison 1993, 230, refers to private correspondence from W.D. Davies in which Davies suggests that our Logion contains exodus language; Allison himself doubts it, in spite of his comments at 1993, 222 n. 195.

[167] Deutsch 1987, 31f., 40f., is illustrative of too narrow an understanding, based on the parallel with 23,4. Her sharp distinction between the "babes" (v. 25) and the "weary and heavy laden" (v. 28) is overdone. True, the appellations apply to disciples and *prospective* disciples respectively, but Jesus does not say that people *become* "babes" as soon as they receive the gospel, nor by virtue of receiving it. Rather, the "babes" make up a general sociological group which *includes* those to whom the Father has revealed "these things" and it is to that same group that Jesus extends his appeal.

that it handily accommodated the multifaceted plight which Jesus' ministry addressed. Surely this evangelistic summons is intended to sound out through Matthew's readers, for whom the gospel goes forth to the "nations," and thus to people not directly affected by Pharisaic teaching. Yet this more general notion must remain true to Matthew's world which pits Jesus against Satan and the world and which posits a salvation which is far beyond longings for experiential tranquillity. The weariness most likely encompasses the more mundane -- and often very great! -- pressures of life because that is where people feel the burden, but almost certainly views those pressures as varied shoots from the root problem (Mt 1,21).

7.2. The easy yoke

The problem of the "easy yoke" is part and parcel of the larger problem of how Jesus can demand a greater righteousness and castigate the Pharisees for their moral laxity, while himself taking a more liberal approach to the Sabbath and accusing *them* of placing a heavy burden on the backs of the people. His promise of a light burden and rest appears to make this tension almost unbearable, and a resolution is by no means apparent.

Without pretending to offer a completely satisfying resolution the following points can be made: (1) The *common denominator* in the failure of the Pharisees appears to be their neglect of mercy, justice, and faithfulness. The opposite is true of Jesus. (2) Some of the tension is released if we cease thinking of the "yoke" narrowly as a body of teaching and think of it as the whole experience of discipleship.[168] If we are right in

---

[168] Cf. e.g., T.W. Manson, 478; Bauer 1970, 749 (cf. 1961, 101f.); Hunter, 248f.; Bacchiocchi 1984, 302f.; Stanton 1992a, 375; Jeremias 1972, 194; Hill, 208f.; *contra*, e.g., Deutsch 1987, 42. It seems to me that the tendency to understand the "easy yoke" narrowly as Jesus' teaching (or his law) contributes to the awkwardness of many explanations (e.g., Strecker 1962, 174, with his dialectical explanation), for then we are forced to reconcile it with Jesus' greater strictness. It is, however, the whole character of Jesus' ministry which is in view, which includes but is not restricted to his teaching. We should give as much attention to 12,17-21 as to 23,4. Thus Pauline ideas such as freedom from striving after righteousness are probably beyond the immediate concerns of this saying (*contra* Barth, 103 n. 1, 148 n. 2, 158f.). It is also difficult to accept Betz' suggestion that the yoke is "easy" because -- like the saints of 25,31ff. -- the disciples do not compute merit because of their certainty about the presence of the risen Lord (Betz, 24). This is ingenious, but puts too much weight on the theological notion of the "presence of the risen Christ," and not enough on the ministry of the earthly Jesus in which this saying is firmly embedded in Matthew's story. We must first attempt to understand it in the latter, and then assume that Matthew intends this to transfer to the risen Jesus' on-going ministry. Klostermann's interpretation, 104, puts too much stress on Jesus as teacher; there is something more than a method of teaching in view here. On the use of $\mu\alpha\nu\theta\acute{\alpha}\nu\omega$, cf. Rengstorf 1967, 406f.; Hengel 1981, 42ff. (esp. 51); B. Weiss, 228; Luz, 2:218f.

recognizing Son of David ideas in Matthew's version of 11,28-30, then even the notion of a king's yoke may not be too distant.[169] (3) It is likely that 11,29c indicates Matthew's own interpretation of the "easy yoke," since these clauses (29c and 30a-b) seem to function similarly.[170] In whatever manner we choose to finally resolve the larger tension, the stress for Matthew in 11,28-30 is on the Servant-like ministry of the βασιλεὺς πραΰς who "will not break a bruised reed or quench a smoldering wick until he brings justice to victory."

If it is objected that these points do not get to the theological nub -- which is how Matthew thought Jesus, even the risen Jesus, would successfully prosecute such a compassionate ministry with such uncompromising views of morality and discipleship -- then they do seem to represent what was foremost in Matthew's mind at this point (cf. 12,7.20). Jesus had emphasized the traits, mercy, justice, and faithfulness, in his own ministry. A direct result of this would be the *inclusion* of the outcasts and a compassionate ministry to those who needed it most "until he brings justice to victory." This is the ministry of the "Servant," with which Matthew has clearly associated the saying. That this would be a χρηστός[171] yoke leading to "rest" for spiritual orphans and outcasts may need to be experienced if it cannot be imagined.

---

[169] Josephus tells of how the people asked Rehoboam, Solomon's son, for a lighter yoke than the one Solomon had placed on them (according to Josephus, *Ant* 8,213, that he would be more lenient [χρηστότερον] than his father); cf. 1Kgs 12,1-16; 2Chr 10,1-16.

[170] Given that the description of 11,29c corresponds to the mark of the Davidic messiah (21,5), this clause probably *functions* to validate Jesus' ministry over against the proud Jewish leaders (23,2ff.; Deutsch 1987, 132; cf. Strecker 1962, 174) and to coax the people to trust him as one who will not be harsh and overbearing but rather like a gentle servant; it is not unlikely that Jesus is also expressing his solidarity with the "poor"; Gnilka, 1:440. Is the additional thought implied that Jesus is the *prototypical* "poor" one, and thus that if the "meek" will inherit the earth, then they will do so by virtue of their identification with *the* meek one? Both terms, πραΰς and ταπεινός/ταπεινόω, are used elsewhere by Matthew in terms of an ultimate reversal of fortunes. For ταπεινόω, cf. 18,4; 23,12. And if we are right to stress the connection of Jesus' word in 11,28-30 to the promise of God that he would give his people rest (in the land), then it has a deep running inner affinity with Mt 5,5 -- "blessed are the meek, *for they will inherit the earth*" (on which cf. esp. Hill, 111f.).

[171] Cf. K. Weiss 1974b, 483-492; Blomberg, 194; Morris, 297; Gaechter, 386. Χρηστός can mean "useful," or "serviceable," but when applied to persons (as it often is in the LXX) it usually has an ethical bent, "kind," or "mild." This term is often used of God in both the LXX (often joined with "mercy") and NT; e.g. Ψ 85,5 [86,5]; Ψ 68,16 [69,16]; Ψ 105,1 [106,1]; Lk 6,35; Rom 2,4. In Josephus, *Ant* 6,92, the people implore Samuel "as a gentle and kind father" (ὡς πατέρα χρηστὸν καὶ ἐπιεικῆ) to mediate God's grace to them. Though in 11,28-30 the idea is applied to an object (yoke), the personal relationship of Jesus with his disciples is only just under the surface.

7.3. Rest

So then, taking for granted what we have already argued -- that Matthew associated this ἀνάπαυσις with both the rest tradition and the Sabbath -- , assuming also that he saw in it both a present and future aspect, and assuming finally that the "rest" would be what the "weary and heavy laden" are not, we can ask whether the religious historical parallels which we reviewed in Chs. Two through Four above might shed light on this promise.

The pronounced apocalyptic vision of a resting place which "appears" at the end, e.g., 4Ezra 7 or 2Bar 73,1ff., is not apparent in Mt 11,28-30.[172] It is interesting, but not necessarily significant that two passages from Qumran link eschatological rest to a son of God.[173] Contact with the telltale mythology of Gnosticism and the metaphysical features of WisSol, Philo, and Clement of Alexandria is not in evidence, nor have we turned up any other indication that such works as these hold the key to understanding this saying. Those who have suggested otherwise -- bemused, perhaps, by the prominence of the rest motif in gnostic literature and by the presence of this Logion in *GosThom* 90 -- have been making this saying dance to the tune of their own religious historical hypotheses.

Wisdom literature has its own special emphasis on rest as the fruit of wisdom, and yet the ἀνάπαυσις spoken of in this literature cannot by itself do justice to this Logion. Of course the promise of ἀνάπαυσις in Mt 11,28-30 bears some similarities to wisdom literature. The form and wording of the Logion, the this-worldly application, the connection with "learning" from Jesus, and Matthew's general portrayal of Jesus as a messianic teacher

---

[172] Hill's comment (208) that the words, ἀναπαύω/ἀνάπαυσις, *belong to* Jewish apocalyptic (for which he cites Rev 6,11; 14,13; Mt 12,43) is poorly put, but possibly not misleading in this case. In addition to the general tradition of "the world which is wholly Sabbath" and the post-mortem/eschatological rest common in the Pseudepigrapha (Sand, 253, cites 2Bar 73,1 in connection with Mt 11,28 30), there might be a shade of apocalypticism here if the reign-rest complex is relevant (supra, 138ff., on the "chain saying" of seeking and finding) and if the contrast with Mt 12,43 is in any way meaningful. Mt 12,43 (Lk 11,24; cf. TSol 20,16) is the only other occurrence of ἀνάπαυσις in Matthew (cf. ἀναπαύω in 26,45; Mk 14,41), and the idea is one of "seeking" and (*not*) "finding" ἀνάπαυσις. We can note, then, that (1) it is usual in apocalyptic to contrast the "rest" of the elect with the "unrest" of the damned (cf. Rev 14,11.13; 4Ez 7,36ff.91ff.; 2Thes 1,6ff.; these are taken up below, 297ff.), and (2) the reference to the return of the demons in Mt 12,43-45 might stand in contrast to the traditions of Solomon's wisdom which had the power to cast out demons so that they would never return (*Ant* 8,45-49; supra, 233f.); if Jesus' wisdom as the Son of David is also in view in 11,28-30, then the Logion along with 23,43 could emerge from overlapping worlds of ideas. If all of this is not idle speculation then in both 11,28-30 and 12,43 the apocalyptic ἀνάπαυσις has been "historicized" in Matthew.

[173] Cf. 4QFlor 1 (drawn from 2Sam 7) and 4Q246 2; supra, 111f. But see below, 363ff.

of wisdom -- all these remind us of wisdom's rest. Yet every indication is that Matthew read this saying not primarily against the backdrop of Sir 6 or 51, but against the backdrop of hopes for an eschatological rest, especially in terms of repeated OT promises. As it stands in Matthew the saying is soteriologically, eschatologically, and messianically charged. If the Logion had in view the general notion that wisdom will lead to the good life, to peace and rest -- and well it might[174] -- then this has been transposed into another key to encompass the full scope of Jesus' work.[175] Jesus' ἀνάπαυσις is not simply the good life or "a more profitable way"[176] which is found in wisdom, but the realization of long harbored hopes in the Christ.

It seems reasonable to think that the *general* hope of the eschatological age as a time of rest and peace -- which was characteristic of Judaism and which was sourced in the OT rest tradition as well as the Sabbath -- had become a din in Matthew's ears, sounding out to him from the invitation and promise of 11,28-30.[177] The specific indications of Matthean redaction suggest that he understood it in this manner *and that he himself related it directly to the OT hopes surrounding the Davidic dynasty, rest, temple, and Sabbath.*[178] Characteristically, the militaristic, geographical, ethnic notes are muted,[179] and in their place stands the teaching and healing ministry of the

---

[174] Cf. above, 233ff.

[175] Cf. Bauernfeind 1964, 50; Luck, 49f. We must bear in mind the close nexus of 11,25-27 and 28-30. The ἀνάπαυσις is to be found in coming to the one to whom all things have been given, who alone knows the Father, and who alone has the prerogative of revealing the Father. *His* "rest" is certainly more than "the good life"! Yet Arvedson's suggestion (227f., 162ff.; cf. Christ, 118; Schniewind, 154; Gaechter, 384) that the ἀνάπαυσις issues from a share in the communion of the Father and Son owes more to later gnostic thought than the context of Mt 11,25-27.

[176] Bultmann 1972, 159.

[177] Cf. e.g. Bacchiocchi 1984, 289-316; Davies-Allison, 2:288f. TDan 5-6 -- which combines the rest tradition and the idea of an eschatological Sabbath with the coming one from Judah (supra, 104f.) -- shows traces of Christian redaction (later II A.D.) along the lines of Mt 11,28-30; cf. Luz, 2:221 n. 148, 223. This may be early evidence for how the Logion was understood by some Christians.

[178] After allowance is made for the ambiguities of the OT canon in I A.D., and the possibility that Matthew would have been influenced by other Jewish literature and traditions in his use of the Logion, the OT rest tradition parallels that we have noted remain the most promising alternative when taken as a group. These appear to have been basic to Matthew's understanding and use of the Logion.

[179] 4QFlor 1 interprets the promise of 2Sam7,11 eschatologically in terms of the enemies of the sectarians, yet here also the militaristic element is clear. That in Mt 11,28-30 it is not specifically a "rest from your enemies" is not a problem; cf. (where indicated, the point depends on the LXX) Ex 33,14; Isa 11,10; 14,1.30 [LXX]; 25,10 [LXX]; 28,12; 32,17 [LXX]; 57,20 [LXX]; 63,14; Jer 6,16; 31,2.25; Lam 1,3; 5,5; Ezek 34,14f. [LXX]; Micah 2,10; 4,4 [LXX] (all of these were addressed in Chs. Two-Three above). The range of the promise is wide even in the OT; supra, 60.

gentle king, in whose work, however, the long awaited kingdom of God is present.[180] It could not be otherwise.

If, however, the expected *means* have been disappointed, then the *end* is no less satisfying. The lowly Jesus announces the inauguration of the long awaited age of rest for God's harassed and suffering people. The lowly will be exalted, the oppressed will be given relief, the people will live securely,[181] the weak will no longer be afflicted, no enemy will menace, fear and sickness will be banished, the poor will receive the kingdom and the meek will inherit the earth, the weary will be refreshed, the sheep will lie down under the care of their Shepherd, each person will rest under a vine, God's people will live in a peaceful habitation, in secure dwellings, and in quiet resting places, the messiah will gather his people together like a hen gathers her chicks under her wings, the land will be full of righteousness, justice will be lead to victory, and they will neither harm nor destroy on all God's mountain. If such a vision was only partially realized in the humble earthly ministry of the messiah (Mt 11,5f.) there was no mistaking the promise of the full measure in good time.

In short, Jesus' offer of rest is best understood not by invoking this or that specific Jewish or Christian parallel, but rather by coming to grips with the nature of the total salvation which Matthew's Jesus claimed to usher in, and for Matthew that salvation was the fulfilment -- in the person and work of Jesus of Nazareth -- of what the OT had anticipated. If the ἀνάπαυσις has been understood fairly inclusively in the foregoing then this is in part because it had already become a very broad concept in the OT and also because it seems to be functioning as a sort of exemplary invitation and salvation promise here in Matthew.

What makes this saying effective, however, is the way in which it recalls specific and repeated promises made by God to his people, promises which looked toward an ultimate fulfilment in some future, cosmic, redemptive work. For Matthew, the saying is thus anchored in a definite historical and redemptive framework, and the way is then prepared to reflect on the implications and significance of Jesus' promise within that framework.

---

[180] Cf. Isa 11; *2Clem* 5-6. Is there a deliberate contrast intended with the earthly king, Herod Antipas, in Mt 11,29? The suggestion may be far fetched, but in its favor is the (possible) implied polemic of Mt 11,7f. wherein Herod Antipas might be the "reed shaken by the wind"; cf. Theißen 1992, 26-39; Jesus' humble reign is thus contrasted with that of the earthly king. Alternatively, the reference to royal clothing in 11,7f. has been taken to refer to popular Davidic-messianic expectations (cf. Davies-Allison, 2:247), once again suggesting a contrast with Jesus' own reign. Outside of Matthew's Gospel, a contrast exists between Jesus' offer and that of a "certain imposter" of a little later (ca. A.D. 59-62) who duped many by promising them salvation and a cessation of troubles (σωτηρίαν αὐτοῖς ἐπαγγελλομένου καὶ παῦλαν κακῶν) if they would follow him into the desert (cf. Josephus, *Ant* 20,188).

[181] Cf. Jer 23,5f.; 33,15f.

Moreover, if we have been keen to stress throughout that this saying is primarily concerned with soteriology, it is nonetheless axiomatic that soteriology and Christology advance in tandem. So also here, a "high" Christology is strongly implied when Jesus not only claims to bring to fulfilment the Sabbath rest and God's promise of rest, but takes to himself the authority hitherto reserved to YHWH, his Father. The way had been prepared for this in 11,27a, but it is a provocative claim nonetheless. In the midst of surging political and religious currents which threaten to both crush and drown the powerless among God's people, he draws on one of the characteristic expressions of Israel's experience of salvation in the OT...but with a difference. The man, Jesus of Nazareth, has the audacity to make the offer himself.

There are ecclesiological implications as well. Matthew and his readers viewed themselves as a "new people" in some sense over against Judaism, probably from the viewpoint of a community in the throes of recent separation from the synagogue.[182] In that context, and recalling the key OT role of the promise of rest in the history and identity of Israel, the Logion amounts to a repudiation of those from whom the kingdom will be taken, the "wise and learned" who have brought about such weariness, and the eschatological formation of a new community, those who will produce the fruit of the kingdom. The rest God promised his people Israel will be mediated only through the Son (11,27) and only (Jewish ancestry notwithstanding; cf. 3,9f.) to those and to *all* of those (including Gentiles) who "come to me." Those who do "come" have a part in Israel's promised salvation.

If, finally, we are going to theologize on this saying and extend its picture beyond Matthew's horizons, we might call on the idea of Heb 4,16 where the on-going ministry of the merciful and faithful High Priest (the "risen Christ") who is able to sympathize with our weaknesses leads to well timed and needed mercy and grace, and ultimately to God's κατάπαυσις where the people of God will enjoy a σαββατισμός. Moreover, just as the "rest" enjoyed by the OT Israelites was no time of tranquil passivity, but rather a time of unrestrained, full, and productive covenant life, such is the case also for the disciple who takes up Jesus' yoke. Again, we can say that Jesus' ἀνάπαυσις is the new creation in seminal form, available "in Christ." It is a "home," a "safe harbor"[183] in a menacing and too often cruel world. Yet if it

---

[182] As Stanton (1992a) has convincingly argued from a number of angles. Mt 21,43 is a key text here. I do not think that Matthew viewed those from whom the kingdom would be taken and those to whom the kingdom would be given simply as Israel and the Church respectively.

[183] Philo says that the temple is for the Jews "their port as a general haven and safe refuge from the bustle and great turmoil of life, and there they seek to find calm weather, and, released from the cares whose yoke has been heavy upon them...to enjoy a brief

is only a safe enclave "now," its walls will one day expand "as far as Damascus,"[184] indeed as far as the whole creation.

8. Conclusions

Mt 11,28-30 is not an allusion to Sirach. The dissimilarities of the passages should have suggested this, but when we examine Matthean redaction we are assured that Matthew's interest is elsewhere. Those scholars who have contended for a much less significant influence on 11,28-30 from Sirach have been thoroughly justified.

The promise of ἀνάπαυσις governs 11,28-30 and both of its offers of rest have closer verbal parallels in sayings out of the OT rest tradition than they do in Sirach. Matthew almost certainly knew of the OT rest tradition as such, and his addition of 29c suggests that he modified the saying in line with that background.[185] Moreover, his placement of the saying close after the allusion to Isa 61 and immediately before the two Sabbath pericopae suggests that the idea of the Sabbath rest was in his mind as well. Thus we have here a blending of the two primary OT traditions relating to rest, with both now connected to the present and (ultimately) future work of the messiah.

Mt 11,28-30 does not, of course, correspond exactly to some of the OT rest tradition passages, e.g., 2Sam 7,11 with its political and militaristic overtones. Yet even in the OT we saw that the promise of rest had a fairly extended range of application, depending on the circumstances in view, and that this sort of varied application continued into the intertestamental literature. In the present case the promise is shaped by the fact of the earthly ministry of the humble king, the Son of David.

---

breathing-space in scenes of genial cheerfulness"; *SpecLeg* I,69 (the word ζυγός does not occur here); from here we need only recall that Jesus refers to himself as "something greater than the temple."

[184] Recall here how the rabbis interpreted Zech 9,9 with reference to Ps 132; supra, 124.

[185] The relevance of Isa 42,1-4 and Zech 9,9 to Mt 11,29 has been noted repeatedly in commentaries and studies. What has not been hitherto argued is that the rationale for Matthew's redaction of 11,28-30 is best understood against the background of the OT rest tradition, where God's promise of rest is associated with the Davidic dynasty and with the temple. Thus the influence of the OT goes far beyond the snippets of Ex 33,14 and Jer 6,16. While some previous studies have tended to attribute too much importance to particular parallels, e.g. Sir 51, *GosThom* 90, or Ex 33,14, our recognition of the general OT background and the rationale behind Matthew's redaction has made it possible to appreciate the real relevance of these separate pieces of the puzzle, without giving undue weight to isolated elements.

The upshot is that for Matthew Jesus utters the Logion as the Son of David who himself claims to bring to fulfilment the oft repeated, OT promise of YHWH to his people, the promise of rest. The significance of this cannot be overplayed. This is another way of saying that the total salvation which God promised his covenant people, in its most far reaching and inclusive sense, is coming to realization through the person and work of Messiah Jesus. It is no longer circumscribed politically, ethnically,[186] or geographically, and its agent is not to be understood in militaristic, triumphant terms.[187] On the other hand, when its agent stands in the place exclusively reserved for YHWH in the OT, the Christological implications are significant indeed.

---

[186] Cf. 12,18.21; 28,19.
[187] Isa 11, 1-10, anticipates such a non-militaristic role of the Davidide in bringing about the eschatological ἀνάπαυσις; supra, 47f.

Chapter Seven

A Promise Remains

1. Introduction

1.1. Overview

In the survey of the discussion of Heb 3-4[1] we saw that much of that discussion has revolved around the question of religious historical derivation. We have now considered the relevant Jewish and Christian literature in some detail, but it remains to give our undivided attention to the letter to the Hebrews.

In contrast to Matthew, *Auctor* leaves no doubt that he is making use of the OT rest tradition and that he is connecting it with the hope of a future Sabbath Further, Hebrews' κατάπαυσις-idea has received considerable scholarly attention, while Christology, which is muted here, has received little.[2] Thus our approach to this passage will differ from the foregoing: we will begin with a discussion of the passage itself (§ 2), including a critique of some specific interpretations, and only then evaluate the proposals on the background of the passage (§ 3). In the interests of completing our wider survey we will incorporate into this discussion a few other first century Christian passages which also make use of the rest motif, namely, Acts 3; 7; 2Thes 1; and Rev 14, as well as Jn 5,17. These are not the direct concern of our investigation, but they may shed some light at particular points.

In the course of our investigation the following methodological considerations will be brought to bear on the evidence and the discussion:

(1) To the extent that the discussion of the κατάπαυσις-idea in Heb 3-4 has often revolved around the question of religious historical derivation, it has sometimes argued too circularly. We must make the attempt to pursue the logic and assumptions of this passage while suspending judgments on religious historical derivation, so far as that is possible.[3] (2) Related to (1) is the observation that *Auctor*'s treatment of Ψ 94 [95] is presented as an

---

[1] Supra, 10ff.
[2] Cf. only 3,14; on the Christology of this passage, cf. Zimmermann, 143.
[3] Rightly, Attridge 1980, 279f.

exegetical treatment of that passage in connection with Gen 2. Only after examining Heb 3-4 carefully in this light can we turn to ask after a religious historical "borrowing" which is only "secondarily" lodged in the OT. (3) The actual rest-speculation of the proposed backgrounds will be utilized as a reliable test of where their general "outlook" (e.g., "dualistic") would lead touching the notion of "rest." We *know* how a mainline Alexandrian like Philo or a Gnostic would think about and utilize the rest motif, and that information must not be marginalized. (4) Comparison of our exegetical results with religious historical parallels is an intrinsically helpful exercise. Leaving aside the question of derivation, and exercising restraint on reading intention or awareness into the "parallels," the similarities and differences with the parallels will help to bring into focus the conception of Heb 3-4. (5) The present study cannot undertake a full scale examination of the religious historical background of Hebrews as a whole,[4] though the answer to this question bears on our treatment of chs. 3-4. To that extent the conclusions we reach will be necessarily provisional.

1.2. Key terms

In addition to these methodological notes we should probably comment on the use of certain terms which have been crucial in previous discussions of this passage, and which will be used repeatedly in our own study, namely, "apocalyptic," "dualistic," "gnostic," and "Hellenistic."

The genre *apocalypse* has been defined as one

> ...of revelatory literature with a narrative framework, in which a revelation is mediated by an otherworldly being to a human recipient, disclosing a transcendent reality which is both temporal, insofar as it envisages eschatological salvation, and spatial, insofar as it involves another, supernatural world.[5]

It is important to note the stress on both temporal and spatial aspects.

Apocalypticism (apocalyptic) is described by M. Stone as a

> ...pattern of thought, primarily eschatological in character,[6] typifying some apocalypses and also a number of works belonging to other genres of literature of the period of the

---

[4] L.D. Hurst has provided a first-rate survey and critique of the main proposals for the background of Hebrews, including Philo, Qumran, Gnosticism, the Samaritans, Merkabah mysticism, Stephen (Acts 7), Pauline theology, and 1 Peter. The reader is referred to his work for the evidence, bibliography, and discussion; Hurst himself favors the Stephen traditions.

[5] Collins 1979, 9; cf. 1992, 283; Stone 1984, 393; Hanson 1992. A list of Jewish, Christian, and gnostic works which belong to this genre can be drawn up (for which see the literature just mentioned).

[6] Rowland, 23-48, denies that there is anything distinctive about the eschatology of the apocalypses, and also that eschatology should be included in definitions of "apocalypse"

Second Temple, such as some of the Qumran *pesharim*, *The Testament (Assumption) of Moses*, or *The Testament of the Twelve Patriarchs*.⁷

This "pattern of thought" includes the following features: the acute expectation of the fulfilment of divine promises; cosmic catastrophe; a relationship between the time of the end and preceding human and cosmic history; angelology and demonology; salvation beyond catastrophe; salvation proceeding from God; a future saviour figure with royal characteristics; a future state characterized by the catchword 'glory'.⁸ It is not necessary to find all of these characteristics in a single work. According to J.J. Collins,

> ...a movement might reasonably be called apocalyptic if it shared the conceptual framework of the genre, endorsing a world view in which supernatural revelation, the heavenly world, and eschatological judgment played essential parts... We should remember, however, that the argument depends on analogy with the apocalypses and the affinity is always a matter of degree.⁹

The book of Hebrews is plainly not an apocalypse, but the degree to which it exhibits apocalypticism, or to which apocalypticism is the

---

and "apocalypticism." Against this, see Collins 1984, 8f. According to Hanson, "apocalyptic eschatology" is distinguished from "prophetic eschatology" by its scepticism of human reform efforts and its "more rigidly dualistic view of divine deliverance, entailing destruction of this world and resurrection of the faithful to a blessed heavenly existence" (Hanson 1992, 281; cf. 1979, 11f.; Stone 1984, 384-388). Collins 1984, 9, distinguishes between different types of apocalyptic eschatology and claims that, while only some apocalypses refer to an end of history (e.g., Dan; 4Ez), *all* of them "involve a *transcendent* eschatology that looks for retribution beyond the bounds of history" (italics added). For instance, 3Bar and ApZeph speak of a judgment of individuals after death but without reference to the end of history.

⁷ Stone 1984, 394. Stone stresses that "apocalypticism" must be carefully distinguished from the *genre* apocalypse, since the former does not account for much of what is in many apocalypses, and since some literature that does not belong to the genre exhibits "apocalypticism." Collins 1984, 10f., prefers to preserve the implied link between the terms (apocalypse-apocalypticism), observing that "there may be many different types of apocalyptic movements, just as there are different types of apocalypses" (on the relationship between apocalypticism and social movements, see Hanson 1992, 281; Collins 1992, 284). Koch's list of features (immediately below in the text) corresponds to a certain type of apocalypse ("historical"; e.g., Dan; 4Ez), though there are other types (e.g., those inclining to mysticism and cosmic speculation) which would exhibit their own blend of features.

⁸ Condensed in Stone 1984, 393, from Koch, 28-33.

⁹ Collins 1984, 10. In 1992, 283f., Collins stresses that the "world view or 'symbolic universe'" typical of apocalypticism revolves around "the belief in a judgment beyond death and in the influence of angels and demons on human life"; there is thus a "heightened interest both in otherworldly regions and in supernatural beings" (see also Rowland, 9-72).

controlling framework of the thought of the book, is debated.[10] In most previous discussions, it has been the historical (horizontal temporal) and eschatological (successive ages, this age and the age to come[11]) aspects of Hebrews' thought that have been understood in terms of apocalypticism.[12] In any event, within the narrow limits of our present interests, we will attempt to use the terms "apocalypticism" and "apocalyptic" in line with what has been said here. Of course, we also have specific examples of usages of the rest motif in apocalyptic literature,[13] and these will be useful in the comparison of particulars.

The terms *dualism* and *dualistic* are frequently used in NT studies in a bewilderingly free and ambiguous manner, and without any consistent use of qualifiers if, indeed, a qualifier is used.[14] For our purposes we may bypass an attempt to delineate the full range of dualisms, and simply state how we will use these terms in the following discussion.

As we will see,[15] those exegetes who reject the notion that the κατάπαυσις-speculation of Heb 3-4 should be understood in terms of apocalypticism typically favor parallels with Jewish and Christian literature that is heavily influenced by Platonism. The basic outlook expressed in such literature seems to be crystallized for them in the term dualism.[16] "Was der Hebr letzlich dann aber doch von der Apokalyptik trennt, aber mit »Joseph und Aseneth« z.B. verbindet, ist sein »antikosmisch eschatologischer Dualismus«... [Das] Unheil der gegenwärtigen Welt liegt in ihrer

---

[10] Infra, 327ff.

[11] In Hebrews, as elsewhere in the NT, we encounter the idea that these ages "overlap" (6,5).

[12] E.g., Hurst, 7-11, and *passim*, who favors the phrase "linear apocalyptic," by which he means "those streams of thought *within* apocalyptic which seem to stress actions posited on a horizontal time line" (italics in original).

[13] Supra, 106-111, 134ff.; cf. 122-129, 138-141.

[14] NT studies which provide helpful discussions of various kinds of dualisms are Charlesworth 1972a (esp. 76 n. 1); Gammie; and Wright, 252-259. In addition to other standard works of reference, see Bianchi; Werblowsky (the idea does not, however, receive a separate discussion in *ABD* or *ISBE*). K. Rudolph 1984, 59-67, discusses the concept with reference to Gnosticism. Charlesworth, Gammie, and Wright, all settle on ten distinctive kinds of dualisms (leaving aside "modified" and "permissive" dualisms, which qualify the others [Bianchi, 508f., adds to these two dialectical and anticosmic]), though without complete agreement on either labels or definitions.

[15] Infra, 317ff., 338ff.

[16] Braun, 90-93, expresses this view most succinctly: "...kein Dualismus, in 4Esra 7,26-44 kein „himmlisch""; "Der Eintritt in die Ruhe meint dualistisch das Verlassen der Welt 13,13"; "Der Ruheort im Judentum und in der Apokalyptik, auch in 4Esra 7,26-44, liegt auf der erneuerten Erde. Der Dualismus des Hb verlegt den Ruheort in den Himmel; die Erde ist, wie in der Gnosis..., für den Hb ein Negativum"; "Die Ruhe des Hb trägt also, gerade was ihre dualistisch-himmlische Lokalisierung betrifft, nicht spätjüd, sondern gnostisches Gepräge." For support Braun cites as a group Philo, JosAsen, and gnostic texts, among others.

ontologischen Verfaßheit."[17] In this use of the term there is evidently a complex idea in view,[18] but what seems to be at or near the center is a Platonic cosmological and metaphysical[19] dualism, which we have already noted in our discussion of the rest motif in Philo, Gnosticism, and Clement

---

[17] Gräßer 1986, 175. Conversely, Runia 1993, 78, states that the antithesis ontological vs. eschatological dualism sums up much of the *difference* between Philo and Hebrews.

[18] E.g., in the same article from which I just quoted, Gräßer characterizes *Auctor's* dualism as "kosmische Dualismus" (173), and "ontologischen Dualismus" (166 n. 32). The anti-cosmic element mentioned in Gräßer's comment above is typical of Gnosticism, but not of the Platonic tradition, as K. Rudolph 1984, 60f., emphasizes with numerous statements from Plotinus (Bianchi, 509, however, doubts that either Plato or Plotinus is consistent on this). Gräßer 1986, 175, too, sees this *anti-cosmic* note in JosAsen, Hebrews, and Gnosticism, but not in Philo. So far as I know, however, neither Gräßer nor the others using the terminology in this connection have carefully defined the differing ways they are using the term.

[19] Our use of these labels does not seem to correspond to the definitions of Charlesworth 1972a, 76 n. 1. He defines *metaphysical* dualism as "the opposition between God and Satan," and does not elaborate further (cf. also Gammie, 358f.). *Cosmic* and *cosmological* dualism are related for him (cf. Gammie, 359), but since the latter is unnecessary for Charlesworth's discussion he opts simply for *cosmic*, which he defines as "the conception of two opposing celestial spirits or two distinct and present divisions of the universe." It is *physical* dualism which stands for "the absolute division between matter and spirit" (also Gammie, 358).

On the other hand, Wright, 253, describes *cosmological* dualism as follows: "The classic position of Plato: the world of material things is the secondary copy or shadow of the 'real' world of the Forms, which are perceived by the enlightened mind. In many different versions, this view filtered down as a mainline belief of the Greco-Roman (and the modern Western) world: that which can be observed in the physical world is secondary and shabby compared with that which can be experienced by the mind or spirit." *Cosmological* dualism "creates a context within which moves towards the normal Hellenistic dualism of material/spiritual become likely, linking the mainline Jewish duality of good and evil with the mainline Greek dualism of physical and non-physical; this is exemplified in the practice of extreme asceticism" (Wright, 257). Thus Isaacs, 56f., describes Platonic *cosmological* dualism as one "between the unstable inferior world of sense perception and the unshakeable, changeless, superior immaterial world of heaven," and relates this to *metaphysical* dualism (cf. Werblowsky, 242f.). Our usage conforms to that of Wright and Isaacs.

Both Gräßer and Runia (1993, 77f.) use the designation *ontological* dualism, but it is not clear how narrowly or broadly they define this. Charlesworth, *loc. cit.*, does not include *ontological* dualism in his list, and Wright, 253, defines it as "the postulation of heavenly beings other than the one god, even if these beings exist at his behest and to do his will." Possibly, Gräßer's concept of an *ontological* dualism is closer to what Wright, 253, calls *theological* dualism, "the differentiation between the creator god and the created order." This is illustrated when Jenny Morris, in HJP^2, 3/2:880f., characterizes Philo's monotheism in terms of a Hellenistically influenced dualism of God and the world: "God alone is good and perfect; the finite as such is imperfect." Here we recall *Cher* 87ff. (supra, 117) which posits a basic contrast between God and the world vis-à-vis God's rest. Plainly there is more than one type of dualism at work in Hebrews, but we will confine our use of the term to the concept (construed as a complex idea) of a cosmological and metaphysical dualism.

of Alexandria.[20] *The transcendent, immaterial world is one of stability, immutability, and immovability while the material world is one of instability, change, and motion.* The idea of rest (= stability) is thus defined *fundamentally* with reference to this metaphysical contrast. "Eine μετάθεσις der erschütterbaren Welt, damit die unerschütterbare bleibe (Hebr 12 27), das ist der deutlich gegebene Rahmen einer hellenistischen Jenseitserwartung. Die stete Bewegung und Unruhe der diesseitigen Welt kommt in der jenseitigen zur Ruhe."[21]

Therefore, without intending to obscure the fact that apocalyptic is itself dualistic,[22] we will conform our usage of the term *dualism* to the polemical usage of the exegetes just noted. That is, we will use the term in its unqualified form to express an essentially cosmological and metaphysical dualism as this controls the understanding and use of the rest motif in the ancient literature.[23]

We have already devoted an excursus to *Gnosticism* and have described at length the features of *gnostic* rest speculation.[24] Here we need only observe that there is a tendency in some discussions of the κατάπαυσις-idea in Heb 3-4 to work with a fairly broad concept of Gnosticism so that it seems to absorb, e.g., Philo's thinking.[25] Thus Gräßer refers loosely to "alexandrinisch-gnostischer Hebdomas-Spekulationen," which he illustrates with Philo, JosAsen, and various gnostic writings.[26] In what follows we will attempt to reserve the label *gnostic* for ideas (esp. the rest speculation) as they are encountered in the later gnostic literature, and use the term *dualistic* (above) for a feature of the rest speculation which is evidenced not only in the later gnostic literature but also in writings like Philo's. We will continue to group Philo and Gnosticism on occasion, since this is how the discussion has often handled the materials, but this should not be taken to imply an anachronistic view of Gnosticism as we have defined it, nor a rejection of our own determination that Philo is not gnostic.

---

[20] Supra, 113-122, 142-144, 149.

[21] Gräßer 1886, 165.

[22] E.g., Gammie discusses both spatial and ethical dualisms in apocalyptic. Apocalyptic, as we have described it above, plainly involves a temporal or eschatological dualism, and others could be identified.

[23] There will be a few exceptions to this, e.g., in order to make allowance for Hebrews' *spatial* dualism (cf., e.g., Sharp, 290-292).

[24] Supra, 145ff., 154ff. This is admittedly late evidence, but it is the only material we have to work with if we are going to speak intelligibly and credibly of "gnostic" rest speculation.

[25] E.g. Braun, 90-93; Gräßer, 1:209-211, 218-220, and *passim*.

[26] Gräßer, 1:219f. Likewise, Braun, 93, after judging that Heb 3-4 compares favorably with Philo, JosAsen, and Gnosticism, concludes, "Die Ruhe des Hb trägt also, gerade was ihre dualistisch-himmlische Lokalisierung betrifft, nicht spätjüd, sondern gnostisches Gepräge."

The term *Hellenistic* is another notoriously difficult one to use with precision.[27] In using it positively of *Auctor* we do *not* mean "non-Jewish" in outlook, nor *merely* "Greek speaking," though *Auctor* was evidently an accomplished speaker and writer of the Greek language, and, on the other hand, was apparently unable to read Hebrew.[28] *Auctor* expressed himself to a degree with the language of Greek philosophy, and his epistle betrays some training in Greek rhetoric.[29] There are enough parallels with Philo to suggest an overlapping "Alexandrian" heritage.[30] He evidences a number of parallels with the "Hellenists"[31] of Acts 6-7, suggesting the strong possibility of an historical and/or traditional link,[32] and he appears to have been conversant in traditions stemming from Judaism and Christianity often considered "Hellenistic."[33]

It is *possible*[34] that it would have been easier for *Auctor* to come to terms with, indeed positively embrace, the end to an earthly temple cultus than it

---

[27] I have assumed the view of Hengel-Markschies, 52, that this term "says too much, and precisely because of that says too little" (italicized in original), and have accordingly used it and its cognates as sparingly as possible throughout this study. In fact, this terminology is not used at all outside of the present chapter, except in quotations from other scholars. Yet in view of *Auctor*'s probable historical link to the "Hellenists" of Acts 6-7 (Hurst, 89-106; see immediately below) along with the other factors alluded to at this point in the text, it has seemed justified to use this terminology in the discussion of Hebrews. More generally, Betz 1992, 130, states that "the primary characteristic for Hellenism is the language; secondarily it is the way of life, education, and ethos mediated through that language." The matter of being "Hellenized" in the second sense is of course a relative one. For a recent and very helpful overview of the evidence and scholarly discussion concerning the Jews and Hellenization, see Grabbe, 1:147-170

[28] This is widely accepted on the evidence of *Auctor*'s use of the OT (Schröger, 262-265; Longenecker, 169f.; Ellingworth, 37; Lane, 1:cxviii) and is assumed throughout this study. Where we make reference to *Auctor*'s direct use of the OT, it may be assumed that the LXX is in view. In this connection, see above, 17 n. 1, 77 n. 1; below, n. 36.

[29] Spicq, 1:351-378; G. Guthrie, 29-33; Lane, 1:l-li, lxxv-lxxx; Isaacs, 56-61.

[30] R. Williamson 1970, 296; Ellingworth, 45-48; Isaacs, 49-51; Runia 1993, 78. It is not necessary to think that *Auctor* was from or had been to Alexandria. Runia posits the possibility of "some form of direct contact with Judaism as it had developed in Philo's Alexandria."

[31] We are adopting the consensus view that these are Greek-speaking Jews from the Diaspora who had returned to settle in Jerusalem and who are now Christians. Stephen's speech in Acts 7 "may at least provide the general contours of their views" (Betz 1992, 131; cf. T. Martin).

[32] Infra, 335-338; cf. Hurst, 89-106. Hurst is doubtful that the evidence supports literary dependence on a source also used by Luke, but maintains that it is likely that *Auctor* could have "been exposed to an independent form of the same use of OT traditions which also turn up in Acts 7." Likewise, Lane, 1:cxlix-cl, having considered similarities and dissimilarities, concludes that "Hebrews provides a developed and mature expression of the distinctive theology of the hellenistic Church" as articulated in Acts 7.

[33] E.g., the Wisdom Christology of 1,1-4. See Lane, 1:xlvii-lv.

[34] The word "possible" should be stressed. I am not sure that we can make judgments on *Auctor*'s psychological responses to the development of his theology. Some

would have been for some other Jewish Christians not sharing his broad participation in Greek culture, and it *may* have been more natural for him, by virtue of his cultural background, to construe Christ's work in terms of specifically *heavenly* realities. As for our immediate interests, it is reasonable to anticipate that in considering *Auctor*'s development of the κατάπαυσις-idea we might find parallels with Alexandrians like Philo and Clement, and it is altogether possible that we may find the most fruitful comparison is to be made with such "Hellenistic" writings as theirs. Nevertheless -- and this is crucial -- these results are not necessary or inevitable, and *Auctor* can still be considered "Hellenistic" in the sense just described if his development of the κατάπαυσις-idea is more like 4 Ezra's than like Philo's.

2. Exegetical questions

We shall gather our exegetical questions into three groups. The first group (§ 2.1) will aim at constructing an understanding of the passage; central to this section will be the exposition of 4,1-11. The second and third groups will respond to some specific interpretations (§§ 2.2-3). Clearly this list of questions is not exhaustive, but it should enable us to get at a well-founded understanding of the κατάπαυσις-idea.

2.1. General questions

2.1.1. Background?

The book of Hebrews is a fabric woven of OT passages, Christological exposition, and pastoral exhortation. *Auctor* is not only following a line of argument as he writes, but he is searching[35] the (Greek) Scriptures. Certain OT passages form a sort of literary sub-structure to everything he says in 3,7-4,11 and so before advancing to consideration of the context it will be helpful to consider the manner and extent of usage of the OT in this section.[36]

"Hellenists" appear to have returned to Jerusalem "with a sense of awe for their ancestral customs" and "had staunchly conservative attitudes toward the Law and Temple" (T. Martin, 135), though this is not to imply that *Auctor* was a "Hellenist" in the sense of Acts 6. Even Philo might have had difficulty in coming to terms with the destruction of the temple (Isaacs, 44f.).

[35] Acts 17,11; Ellingworth, 42.

[36] Important wider treatments of the OT in Hebrews include Caird; Kistemaker; Schröger; Ellingworth 1977; G. Hughes; further literature and discussion in Lane, 1:cxii-cxxiv. The difficulties of examining Hebrews' use of the OT are compounded by the

The passage begins with a quotation of Ψ 94,7-11 [95,7-11].³⁷ Portions of this passage are quoted again (Ψ 94,7f. in 3,15; 4,7; Ψ 94,11 in 4,3.5) or alluded to (Ψ 94,8 in 3,16; Ψ 94,10 in 3,17; Ψ 94,11 in 3,18.19; 4,1.3.6 [2x].10.11) and outside of these the wording of this psalm is woven into the remainder of the treatment: καρδία (3,12; cf. 4,12); ἡμέρα (3,13; 4,7.8); σήμερον (3,13; 4,8); σκληρύνω (3,13); ἐν τῇ ἐρήμῳ (3,17); καταπαύω (4,8); ἀκούω (4,2; cf. also ἀκοή).

With this glance at the use of the psalm, one can immediately observe that the rest motif does not come up for discussion until 3,19. Before that the exhortation focuses entirely on the warning value of the quotation, with the immediate contextual link being the need for perseverance (3,1-6). This is the essential concern of the whole section (cf. 4,1-3a.7.11), and the midrash on Ψ 94 [95] and Gen 2 in 4,3-10 is *subordinate* to this. In view of

---

textual uncertainties of the LXX itself and the question of what LXX text *Auctor* might have used (cf. Thomas; Ellingworth, 37f.). See further above, 77 n. 1, also 17 n. 1. Reference to "the" LXX is imprecise, but persists for lack of a good alternative. In the following we have attempted to take account of these complexities.

³⁷ A detailed discussion of Ps 95 in the MT, LXX, and Heb 3,7-11 along with textual problems is given in Ellingworth 1977, 1:102-117; cf. Schröger, 101-115; Kistemaker, 35-37, 108-116. Of the textual variants in Heb 3,7-11 only two need to be noted here. In v. 9, ἐν δοκιμασίᾳ is strongly supported by 𝔓¹³·⁴⁶ ℵ* A B C D* P 0243. 33. 81. 365. 1739. 1881 *pc*; this differs from the LXX (ἐδοκίμασαν; vg; ℵ² D² Ψ 0278 𝔐 all change in favor of the LXX). It has been suggested that this modification of the LXX serves to sharpen the note of accusation (Attridge, 115; cf. Hofius, 213 n. 797) or, alternatively, avoid the idea of human beings testing God (Ellingworth, 218). In 3,10, ἐκείνῃ (C D² Ψ 0278 𝔐) is likewise an assimilation to the LXX; *Auctor*'s use of ταύτῃ (𝔓¹³·⁴⁶ ℵ A B D* 0243. 6. 33. 1739. 1881 *pc*) probably anticipates the contemporization of the psalm. The most obvious change from the LXX is the insertion of διό in v. 10 which has the effect of attaching the "forty years" to the period of God's "works" rather than to the period of his "anger" as in the LXX. The change is all the more surprising in view of 3,17, which agrees with the LXX. In 3,9-10 the alteration achieves stylistic balance (it gives a tri-part structure to both 9a and 9b-10a; cf. Vanhoye 1963, 93f.), but the effect on meaning is too great to have gone unnoticed. The suggestion that in 3,9f. *Auctor* evidences a belief that there would be 40 years between Christ's first and second advents (so Bruce 1963, 220; Hughes, 144; P. Walker, 62f.; cf. Strobel, 40, 42f.; *Sanh* 99a) is possible but improbable; cf. Ellingworth, 32. Alternatively, we might take the "works" in v. 9 as works of judgment, although the use of διό then seems awkward (Attridge, 115 n. 28). A way forward is opened by the suggestion that the differences between 3,9f. and 3,17 may reflect different points of view; 3,9f. is speaking directly to the readers, while 3,17 is considering the situation of the wilderness generation (Ellingworth, 232; cf. Ellingworth 1977, 1:112f., 115f.). What the psalm, Heb 3,7-11, and 3,16-18 *all* have in common in terms of literary structure is that over against the historical events they have the oath at the *climax*, for rhetorical effect. What *Auctor* has done in 3,9f. is sharpen that effect in line with the situation of the readers (note also the change from ἐκείνῃ to ταύτῃ); their fitness to "enter" will be determined according to their response to their extended experience of God's works. In this case the "works" can retain their positive connotations (2,3f.; already in the OT there is a positive slant put on the 40 years; cf. Ex 16,35; Deut 2,7).

this, the suggestion that 3,7-4,11 is a piece of Alexandrian (esp. Philonic or gnostic) rest speculation only secondarily grounded in the OT is unlikely.[38]

In spite of its brevity, Gen 2,2 shares no less than three important words with Ψ 94 [95]: ἔργα (4,3.4.10), ἡμέρα (4,4; cf. 4,7), and κατάπαυσις (καταπαύω;[39] cf. 4,4.10). Gen 2 is first alluded to in 4,3c (τῶν ἔργων ἀπὸ καταβολῆς κόσμου γενηθέντων) and quoted in 4,4.[40] From here one notes the use of σαββατισμός in 4,9. The extent to which Ψ 94 [95] and Gen 2 have been brought together by *Auctor* is formally visible in 4,10 which is better described as a compound than a mixture (ὁ γὰρ εἰσελθὼν εἰς τὴν κατάπαυσιν αὐτοῦ καὶ αὐτὸς κατέπαυσεν ἀπὸ τῶν ἔργων αὐτοῦ ὥσπερ ἀπὸ τῶν ἰδίων ὁ θεός). Yet as we will see, this compound is the assumed idea behind the whole of 4,1-11. It is for this reason that the use of the word καταπαύω in 4,8 and ἡμέρα in 4,7f. cannot be assigned exclusively to one or the other passage, though both appear closer to Ψ 94 [95].

More generally, the Sabbath was just too much a part of the OT and the life of Jewish people to think that it did not exert a fairly wide and general influence on the thinking of this passage beyond the specific wording and idea of Gen 2,2. As for the rest tradition, we have already viewed at length its prominence in the OT, and when Joshua is explicitly referred to in 4,8 we may again assume a general acquaintance with this OT theme. Ψ 94,11

---

[38] Hofius, 29-33, points out -- against Käsemann, 73 -- that the gnostic literature is at a disadvantage on purely terminological grounds, since κατάπαυσις scarcely occurs there while ἀνάπαυσις is used widely; cf. Schröger, 305; Zimmermann, 138; Weiss, 271. This argument has impressed at least two specialists in Gnosticism; cf. Wilson, 76; Helderman 1984, 48f. J.W. Thompson, 101f., dismisses this linguistic point too casually; likewise Attridge 1980, 283f. n. 16. Hofius does not stop with mere word counts, however, but points out that the *intransitive* meaning of κατάπαυσις is wholly unique to the LXX and to works depending on it. Consideration of terminology does seem to indicate that *Auctor* is *taking his lead* from the OT, a suggestion which should never have been seriously doubted (Ellingworth, 37-42). Darnell, 309, goes further in contending that *Auctor* chose κατάπαυσις in conscious distinction from the gnostic-related ἀνάπαυσις; Ellingworth's observation, 8, 43-45, that there is a general dearth of gnostic terminology in Hebrews would lend credence to this hypothesis, assuming that Gnosticism was a vibrant force very early on. Yet without further evidence that 3,7-4,11 was shaped in deliberate contrast to gnostic thought Darnell's suggestion languishes. The noun κατάπαυσις stems directly from Ψ 94 [95], which had a value to *Auctor* beyond the mere occurrence of the rest motif. Judging from the use and non-use of this word in the LXX and elsewhere it is apparent that this term would have connoted some ideas and not others; infra, 326.

[39] The verbal parallel of "rest" would not have worked in the MT (שבת vs. מנוחה).

[40] The quotation of Gen 2,2 agrees with the LXX, except in the addition of ὁ θεὸς ἐν. Hexaplaric mss of the LXX likewise include this portion, though they may be influenced by Hebrews (Ellingworth, 248). In one place Philo (*Post* 64) also quotes Gen 2,2 with this portion, though he does not do so elsewhere; dependence on Philo is very unlikely; cf. Schröger, 109 n. 2; R. Williamson 1970, 539-543. If ὁ θεὸς ἐν is not merely an assimilation to Gen 2,2a, it may be sourced in a LXX text used by both Philo and *Auctor*.

[95,11] has a very natural connection with the OT tabernacle and temple traditions.

There is, beside these two, another OT passage which figures in 3,7-4,11 although it is nowhere quoted. Ψ 94 [95] recalls the events recorded in Ex 17,1-7 and Num 20,1-13, yet as Hofius has demonstrated at length it is apparent that *Auctor* has, like some of the rabbis, understood this psalm primarily against the backdrop of Num 14.[41] A careful study of the events of Kadesh in LXX Num 14 as well as the remainder of the OT and Jewish traditions brings to light a number of recurring and prominent features, several of which are plainly present in Heb 3-4: (1) God's command to take the land into possession was accompanied in that context by the promise that Israel *would* take the land into possession (e.g. Num 13,2; Deut 1,8.21). (2) The discouraging report of the spies is said to have "turned aside the *heart* of the children of Israel" (Num 32,9; καὶ ἀπέστησαν τὴν **καρδίαν** τῶν υἱῶν Ἰσραηλ).[42] (3) At Kadesh the people rebelled against God. Convinced that it could not enter the land the people murmured in their tents and refused to enter the place of promise. (4) The rebellious response of the people is described in different ways: (a) It is *disobedience* toward God (Num 14,43: ἀπεστράφητε **ἀπειθοῦντες** κυρίῳ).[43] (b) It is the refusal to *listen* to God or God's *voice* (Num 14,22: οὐκ **εἰσήκουσάν** μου τῆς **φωνῆς**).[44] (c) It is *unbelief* of God or his word (Num 14,11: οὐ **πιστεύουσίν** μοι).[45] (5) The unbelief and disobedience of the people is called a *turning away* from God (Num 14,9: ἀπὸ τοῦ κυρίου μὴ **ἀποστάται** γίνεσθε).[46] (6) That response is also called *sin* (Num 14,34: λήμψεσθε τὰς **ἁμαρτίας** ὑμῶν)[47] and a *repeated testing* of God (Num 14,22: **ἐπείρασάν** με τοῦτο δέκατον). The people are called an evil congregation (Num 14,27: τὴν συναγωγὴν τὴν **πονηρὰν** ταύτην).[48] (7) Their sin is a particularly weighty one because they had experienced repeatedly the miracles and signs of God's presence with them.[49] (8) God's *wrath* was therefore kindled against the faithless people (Num 14,34: γνώσεσθε τὸν θυμὸν τῆς **ὀργῆς μου**).[50] (9) God takes an *oath* that they will not enter the land[51] but will die in the desert.[52] (10) The

---

[41] Hofius, 117-153; on the connection of Num 14 and Ps 95, see above, 127f. The following points are taken from Hofius' summary, 124-127.
[42] Deut 1,28.
[43] Deut 1,26; 9,23.
[44] Deut 9,23; Ψ 105,25 [106,25].
[45] Deut 1,32; 9,23; Ψ 105,24 [106,24].
[46] Num 14,43 (ἀπεστράφητε ἀπειθοῦντες κυρίῳ); 32,9; Deut 1,28.
[47] Num 14,40; 32,14; Deut 1,41; Ψ 77,32 [78,32].
[48] Num 14,35.
[49] Num 14,11.22; Deut 1,30f.; Ψ 105,21f. [106,21f.]; Ψ 77,32 [78,32].
[50] Num 14,11.23; 32,10.13; Deut 1,34; 1Cor 10,5.10.
[51] Num 14,21ff.30; 32,11; Deut 1,35.
[52] Num 14,29.32ff.; 32,13; Ψ 105,26 [106,26]; cf. 1Cor 10,5.

generation of sinners must wander in the desert for 40 years.[53] (11) Only Joshua, Caleb, and the younger children will enter the land and take possession of it.[54] (12) The oath of God is irrevocable and the rebels cannot repent so as to change God's mind.[55]

In addition to the specific parallels between Num 14 and Ψ 94 [95], there will already have been evident several ideas which surface in Heb 3-4 but which are not expressed verbally in Ψ 94 [95]. The hardened hearts, the turning away from the living God,[56] the disobedience (ἀπειθέω; ἀπείθεια; cf. 3,18; 4,6.11), the exhortation to encourage one another,[57] the danger that the defection of "some" will lead to the downfall of the community,[58] and the conviction that once having set out there is no turning back[59] are all understandable against the events of Num 14. In 3,16 the stress on "all" and on "hearing" both find parallels in Num 14.[60] The reference to those ὧν τὰ κῶλα ἔπεσεν ἐν τῇ ἐρήμῳ in 3,17 is derived from Num 14,32: τὰ κῶλα ὑμῶν πεσεῖται ἐν τῇ ἐρήμῳ ταύτῃ.[61] These and other points[62] appear to

---

[53] Num 14,33f.; 32,13.
[54] Num 14,23; 14,30f.38; 32,12; Deut 1,36.38f.
[55] Num 14,39ff.; Deut 1,41ff.
[56] Hofius, 132, refers to Num 14,21.28 for parallels to the idea of the "living God."
[57] This stands in contrast to the discouraging influence of the wicked spies; cf. Deut 1,28; Num 14,36; 32,7.9.
[58] Cf. esp. 3,12f.; 4,1.11; cf. 12,15 and Hofius, 132f.
[59] Cf. Num 14,4 and Heb 3,14.16-19; 6,4-6; 10,26f.39; Hofius, 134f. The process of Israel's rebellion was just that, a process, an insidious slide into apostasy. Thus the urgent need to hold fast the beginning position (3,14) and the need to be on guard for each other against the deceitfulness of sin and its hardening effect on the heart.
[60] With the "all" in 3,16 cf. the repeated reference to the "whole community" in Num 14,1.2.5.7.10.22; 32,13. Along with this there is a repeated reference to the exodus out of Egypt in Num 14,2ff.13.19.22; 32,11; Deut 1,30. Neither Ex 17 nor Num 20 mention that the people "heard" God's "voice," but this is mentioned in Num 14,22; cf. 13,2; Hofius, 135f. Num 14,35 also mentions the rebellion of the people (Heb 3,16).
[61] Cf. 3,17 also with Num 14,34.
[62] Cf. further Hofius, 127-131, 136-139. In 4,1ff. note the references to "disobedience," to Joshua's leadership (cf. Num 14,23.30f.38), and the strong warning (4,1: "let us fear") which recalls the irrevocable judgment of God. In 4,11 the exhortation (σπουδάσωμεν...ἵνα μὴ ἐν τῷ αὐτῷ τις ὑποδείγματι **πέσῃ** τῆς ἀπειθείας) recalls again the literal "falling" of the corpses in the desert (3,17; Num 14,29.32; Weiss, 283 n. 113). Cf. Num 14,43 with the "sword" in Heb 4,12; Hofius, 138f. Yet Hofius' argument (cf. also Zimmermann, 136; Attridge, 115, 120; Lane, 1:88f.) that the difference between 3,9f. and 3,17 draws on the theme of just recompense (Num 14,22.34) is not convincing. The 40 years are seen from both negative (Num 14,33f.; 32,13) and positive (Ex 16,35; Deut 2,7) *perspectives* in the OT. The OT evidence is tenuous, however, that these are two *consecutive* periods of 40 years (Num 14,22; Deut 1,30f.; and Ψ 105,21f. [106,21f.] do not bear the weight of this; cf. Rissi, 17; Ellingworth, 232) and such an idea seems overly subtle in Heb 3. It is sufficient to take the changes in 3,9f. as an attempt to address the psalm more directly to the readers.

make the case very strong that *Auctor* composed this entire passage (3,7-4,11) with Num 14 open before him.

In short, the Scriptures are the matrix of Heb 3,7-4,11. The OT passages are exploited in such a manner that the present situation of the readers is seen to virtually merge with the situation of the "Fathers" at Kadesh. Whatever gap remains between then and now is all but completely closed with the use of Gen 2. The result is the revelation of a world prepared and promised long ago, a mirror in which the present situation is seen to correspond to an historical paradigm as recorded in God's word,[63] and thus a poignant warning against making the same mistake.

2.1.2. Context?[64]

Heb 3,7-4,11 is a warning against apostasy in a book which alternates sophisticated theological exposition with paraenesis. It is worth our while, therefore, to outline the character of the danger and the approach taken to confront it.

The dangers which threaten the recipients of this "word of exhortation" (13,22) are given expression in differing ways which can be described as passive, active, and external.[65] The passive aspect is depicted in such terms as "drifting" from what has been heard (2,1), "neglecting" the word of

---

[63] Hofius, 137, may not overstate the matter when he claims that $\beta\lambda\acute{\epsilon}\pi o\mu\epsilon\nu$ in 3,19 is meant in a quasi-literal sense, as if we are actually witnessing the events of Num 14.

[64] Questions of authorship (unknown), dating (A.D. 60-90; probably pre-70; cf. Ellingworth, 33 n. 105 for a broad sampling of opinion), and destination (Rome?) have not been found to significantly influence exegesis of 3,7-4,11 and will therefore be omitted here, though obviously the closer one gets to A.D. 100 the more likely it is that both Philo's writings and Gnosticism as we enounter it in the later writings could have had a direct impact (this is plainly not to deny that Philo, or a form of "proto-gnosticism," if there was such a thing, could have been an influence at an earlier date). In any case, the question of religious historical derivation is still answered by exegesis of the text.

We may describe *Auctor* generally as a well educated Christian male (cf. the masculine form at 11,32). Beyond his evident familiarity with important aspects of Greek culture (supra, 258f.), he was acquainted with a fairly broad array of traditional Jewish writings, traditions, and exegetical methods (for the last mentioned, cf. Schröger, 269-287, esp. 113-115; Lane, 1:cxix-cxxiv). He was very familiar with his Greek OT, and thought in cultic categories (Johnsson 1977; Lane, 1:l-li; Dunnill). In terms of his Christian background, *Auctor* was not himself an eyewitness of Jesus (2,3), he evidences a number of parallels with the Hellenists (cf. Hurst, 89-106), and he may have had contact with Pauline circles (13,23); there are, in addition, a remarkable number of parallels with 1 Peter (cf. Hurst, 125-130) and the Lukan writings generally (Jones). Just as with Jewish backgrounds, however, it is unlikely that *Auctor* can be simply grouped with Paul, 1 Peter, or the Hellenists. In general, there is an air of confidence and authority which breathes through his writing irrespective of what are traditional and what are new teachings in it.

[65] This paragraph is indebted to Ellingworth, 78-80.

salvation (2,3), or "failing to reach" the goal (4,1).[66] The active aspect is that of open rebellion which "turns away" from God (3,12), "disobedience" (4,11), "crucifying again the Son of God" and "holding him up to contempt" (6,6), or wilful persistence in sin (10,26).[67] Alongside these there are allusions to external threats, past and present/imminent pressures coming from without in the form of persecution.[68]

A general survey of these data and the subject matter of the book -- the extensive use of the OT and concern with the Jewish cultus -- gives the impression that this is a Christian group[69] of predominantly (Hellenistic) Jewish[70] derivation, some of whom are on various stages along the way to "apostasy" from Christianity, i.e., they are rejecting the messiahship and sacrifice of Jesus.[71] It is possible that a few had gone so far as to vocally deny Christ, though the strong affirmations (6,9-12; 10,32-39; 12,5-11) suggest that *Auctor* was far from despairing over the whole group.[72] There

---

[66] E.g. 4,14; 5,11.12-14; 6,7f.12; 10,19.23; 12,1.3.12f.; 13,9.

[67] Cf. also 10,29; 12,15.25.

[68] Cf. 2,18; 10,32f.; 12,4-11 (cf. 12,2f.). The subject matter of 11,32-38 is apropos, and this concern probably underlies 2,14; 5,7. In their early days the community had freely identified with those in prison and had joyfully endured public abuse, though their suffering had stopped short of martyrdom (12,4). This look back in time suggests that the suffering had eased for some reason (possibly their own withdrawal), though presumably those presently in prison (13,3) are there for the sake of the gospel. The letter can be understood as bracing the readers for a coming onslaught or simply as an encouragement to re-enter the fray.

[69] These are second generation Christians (2,3f.). They had received the gospel from those who had also been their original leaders, but who were now apparently dead (13,7). The exhortation to "obey your [present] leaders" (13,17) might suggest that this letter is targeting a group within a larger community.

[70] If the congregation is predominantly Gentile, it is nonetheless significantly "Jewish" in spirit and outlook. In any event, the word "predominantly" is used advisedly. In describing the readers as Hellenistic we are assuming enough shared background with the writer to make his message intelligible; supra, 258f. Cf. Lane, 1:liii-lv.

[71] "Messiahship" is used here in a very general sense for Jesus' revelatory and redemptive status. *Auctor* appears to conceive of Christianity within Judaism -- he makes no distinctions in these terms -- but it is not finally clear whether the recipients of his letter were returning to mainstream Judaism. If the book was written after A.D. 70 it could not have conceived of an actual return to the temple cultus. Just the same, the whole work is built on a deep reverence for the OT Scriptures and institutions; it is only argued that Jesus surpasses all this. If the readers do not share this reverence for the Scriptures, traditions, and institutions of mainstream Judaism then the argument loses its force. If they do share this reverence it is unlikely that they would have been abandoning both Christianity and traditional Judaism in one movement. Whether they would have done so *after* hearing *Auctor*'s Christ-or-nothing case (3,12) is another matter. In any event, there is no note of anti-Judaism.

[72] His intense sensitivity to what is real and what is possible may have impelled *Auctor* to speak at a high pitch at points. *Auctor* writes as one having an established relationship with his readers (13,19.23). He knows something of the origin (2,3f.; 13,7) and early life of the community (2,3f.; 5,11-14; 6,9-11; 10,32-34); he knew of their original leaders

were probably a number of factors in the apostatizing movement including the shock of the earlier sufferings, the decline of zeal due to the passing of a considerable period of time combined with the relative peace of the recent past, and looming storm clouds, as well as specific "theological" issues such as discouraging doubts as to the imminence of the Parousia,[73] lingering questions about the efficacy of Christ's sacrifice,[74] and possibly a belief that they could avoid persecution without forfeiting their hope by abandoning their distinctive Christian confession and social ties in favor of a more generally Jewish identity.[75] There was most importantly a failure to grasp the implications of the gospel which they had received and even what real faith has always entailed, though these would have been the least appreciated of the causes. Whatever the mix of factors in the individual case, *Auctor* senses that a disturbing apostatizing trend had begun.

The concern with apostasy is easy to see in the paraenetic sections, but it is also the driving concern of the doctrinal sections. Indeed, it is in the latter that we see *Auctor*'s own diagnosis of the root problem and his prescription for it. Supremacy and surety are two ideas which may capture a large portion of the theological exposition of the book, and these two ideas interpenetrate. The opening words of the book are a shot across the bow, a statement that the Son, the Great High Priest, is like no other -- in particular he is greater than the greatest of Judaism's figures and institutions -- and that in him the entire preceding history of creation, revelation, and salvation finds its only significance and goal. The implications are that there is no going back, there is no alternative, and there is no compromising with commitment. The Son *must* be heard. Yet the opening words are also a statement of that which is simultaneously the ground and the goal of faith,

---

(13,7) and appears to know their present ones (13,17.24). Any official status he himself might have is left undefined; it is not obvious that 13,17f. groups the writer with the leaders.

[73] Cf. 10,25.32-39; cf. 3,12-14; 9,28.

[74] Lindars 1991b, 4-15 (cf. 1989, 388, 394; 1991a, 410-433), argues that these believers were unsure of the efficacy of Christ's work for post-baptismal sins. Whatever the merits of this proposal, the ability of Christ's work to secure a clear conscience is stated emphatically (9,9f.14; 10,2f.22; cf. 13,18) along with a general emphasis on his continuing priestly work (e.g. 7,25) and the once-for-all character of his sacrifice (e.g. 9,25f.; 10,14).

[75] It is not my intention to exclude specific "heresies" (e.g., Bruce, 376f.; cf. McCullough), but this question does not materially affect our own discussion and so it will not distract us here. Some recent proposals on the situation of the epistle include Isaacs' argument that the events of A.D. 70 *precipitated* the crisis which *Auctor* must confront; P. Walker's argument that the epistle requires the readers to make a break with Judaism as an extension of their break with the *city* of Jerusalem (13,9-14), and all of this at least in part in the *expectation* of the events of A.D. 70; and Desilva's helpful emphasis on the values of shame and honor as these bring into focus the concerns of writer and readers.

and thus the source of unshakeable assurance. As *Auctor* develops these opening thoughts later in the book it is clear that an important aspect of the supremacy of this salvation is its ability to "perfect" the believer, thus to see the "sons" right through to the end.

For *Auctor* this salvation is a very real thing, not merely in the sense that he is sure of it, but in that it has to do with things and events which have real existence now in heaven.[76] Once again, this is not only a mark of its supremacy, but of its ability to perfect by providing a firm ground for faith and by drawing the believer into participation with the powers of that reality insofar as they can be experienced before the Parousia. Its heavenly and eternal character, the fact that it has to do with the actual "things" of God, makes it at once effectual and certain. The earthly copy always had purely derivative and therefore limited significance, and is now obsolete in view of historical changes brought about by the work of Christ. The "upper" has already begun to supplant the "lower."

The necessary response to the revelation ἐν υἱῷ of this salvation is portrayed through the exemplars of faith in ch. 11. However we are to translate the proposition of 11,1,[77] the OT and intertestamental figures mentioned in this chapter exhibit the capacity to conduct themselves in their present world-order and life-situation steadfastly in accordance with a heavenly or yet unseen reality simply because it is held forth to them in God's promise. They all (save Enoch) exhibit such faith to death, even violent death. Such a response receives God's approval and is (will be) rewarded with a share in the promised realities. For Christians such faith is no mere belief in "heaven," but in the whole soteriological reality which is described with so much care in the earlier doctrinal sections; it is the reality in which they must participate now to their own good (10,19-25), which determines the character of their behavior (10,26-34), and for which they wait expectantly (10,35-39). It is a reality which makes endurance in the face of suffering and possible death both necessary and possible. Without the vision of that unseen reality there can be no faith, but without faith the reality profits the person nothing, either now or in the future (4,2).

At the center of this entire world of thought is the writer's Christology. Christ is the object of the readers' confession (3,1), and his status and role is described with a rich variety of images, most prominently Sonship and priesthood. It is remarkable, then, that one of the outstanding features of

---

[76] The question of *Auctor*'s "dualism" will come up for discussion below, 327ff. For now we only allude to it in order to orient ourselves. The *spatial* dimension of Hebrews' soteriology has been highlighted recently by Isaacs.

[77] An influential treatment of faith in Hebrews is that of Gräßer 1965. For important criticisms of Gräßer's study, see G. Hughes, 137-142; also Lindars 1989, 386 n. 4, 401 n. 2; cf. further Attridge, 311-314.

3,7-4,11 is its dearth of explicit references to Christ (only 3,14). Instead, this passage nestles in between the announcement (2,17f.) and what appears to be the beginning of the discussion of Christ's priesthood (4,14ff.). This is not to say, however, that Christology does not contribute fundamentally to the thought of the passage; we may provisionally note four ways in which the passage is indebted to Christology.

Three need only to be mentioned. The idea that in these last days God has spoken definitively ἐν υἱῷ (1,1f.) gives way to the first warning in 2,1-4, that "we must pay greater attention to what we have *heard*" (τοῖς ἀκουσθεῖσιν). Moses himself was faithful "to testify to the things that would be spoken later"[78] (3,5), i.e., ἐν υἱῷ. Thus, having heard God's voice ἐν υἱῷ in these last days, "today," it is incumbent upon us to "listen" (4,2) lest our fate be like the former ones who did not listen.[79] The Son is not mentioned as the mediator of revelation in 3,7ff. but it is his assumed role which gives the whole passage its special urgency. Second, the notion of Christ as the pioneer and perfecter of faith (12,2: τὸν τῆς πίστεως ἀρχηγὸν καὶ τελειωτὴν Ἰησοῦν) probably also comes in here as the thought moves seamlessly from an exhortation to consider Jesus' faithfulness (3,1f.) to an exhortation to be faithful (3,6ff.).[80] Third, Jesus, the one worthy of more glory than Moses (3,3), will bring entrance into God's κατάπαυσις (3,14) where those who went out of Egypt with Moses rebelled and perished (3,15-19).

In addition to these ties to Christology, it is probable that Christ's *priestly* role was linked in *Auctor*'s mind directly to the warning of 3,7ff. such that the believer is called to work toward a distinctly future *Heilsgut* in the exhortation of 3,7-4,13, and is encouraged to do so fore and aft by the assisting priestly ministry of Jesus (2,17-3,6 and 4,14ff.). This concern with Jesus' priestly role, which is announced in 2,17f., probably does not drop out even in 3,2-6, although the reference to Jesus as the Apostle[81] and High

---

[78] The future passive participle τῶν λαληθησομένων is difficult (this is the only example in the NT; cf. BDF § 351,2), but it makes the most sense if we take it to refer to the final revelation of 1,1f.; cf. Attridge, 111; Lane, 1:78.

[79] Nonetheless, the *a fortiori* argument of 2,1-4 (cf. 3,3; 8,6; 9,13f.; 10,28f.; or 12,9.25) is not used in 3,7-4,11; *contra* J.W. Thompson, 97f., who reads into 3,7-4,11 the idea of a "metaphysically superior" revelation. In this instance the message is *in effect* (cf. Attridge 1988, 97f.) the same and the consequences are of equal weight.

[80] It is true that Jesus' and Moses' "faith" is here more a matter of being "trustworthy/reliable" (Ex 40,1; Mt 25,21; 23,1; 1Cor 4,1f.) than of their "trusting," but there remains a resemblance with 12,2; cf. Attridge, 95 nn. 189f.; Gräßer 1965, 21f. G. Guthrie, 136, 140, 143, argues that there is a structural relationship between 3,1-6 and 12,1-2.

[81] The single article (τὸν ἀπόστολον καὶ ἀρχιερέα) shows that the phrase constitutes a unity; cf. Rengstorf 1964a, 423. On the appellation, "Apostle" (unique in the NT, though the NT often speaks of Jesus as having been "sent", e.g. Gal 4,4; Mk 9,37; Mt

Priest of our confession[82] in 3,1 appears to give way entirely to a comparison of the Son with Moses in terms of faithfulness in/over God's house.

The programmatic statement of 2,17 -- "...merciful and faithful High Priest in the service of God" -- is developed first with respect to this High Priest's faithfulness (3,1-6) and then his mercy (4,14-16).[83] Although 3,2 is usually taken simply as an allusion to Num 12,7 in advance of 3,5, it is very probable that the reference to a "faithful priest" would have called to mind the important OT oracle of 1Kgdms 2,35, "I will raise up for myself a faithful priest... I will build for him a sure house" (ἀναστήσω[84] ἐμαυτῷ ἱερέα πιστόν...καὶ οἰκοδομήσω αὐτῷ οἶκον πιστόν[85]).[86] That this oracle is relevant to 3,2 is made more likely by the fact that 1Kgdms 2,35 was joined in Jewish traditions very closely to the Nathan oracle of 2Sam/2Kgdms 7; 1Chr/1Par 17; and related passages.[87] It is noteworthy,

---

15,24; Lk 4,43; Jn 3,17.34; 5,36; 6,29.57; 7,29; 8,42; 10,36; 11,42), see Michel, 171-175; Rengstorf 1964a, 419, 423f., 443f.; Ellingworth, 200.

[82] Ὁμολογία here is the content more than the act of confession; cf. 4,14; 10,23; also the verb in 11,13; 13,15. It is possible that traditional confessions used the titles of Apostle and High Priest (e.g. Käsemann, 169-171; Schierse, 158-204; Theißen 1969, 16; J.W. Thompson, 31; cf. Zimmermann, 47-52), though this is not necessary and it seems less likely when they are both entirely unique in the NT; cf. Lindars 1989, 392 n. 1. One could think that confession of Jesus in these terms was part of this particular community's liturgy (thus the relatively undeveloped idea of "Apostle"?), or that Auctor is appealing to a common confession but in his own language (for the latter, cf. Ellingworth, 199). Either way, it is likely that Auctor is carrying the idea forward through his own contribution, so that whatever was confessed in word would not have attained to what he gives in thought. As to specific placements of the confession in the liturgy, both a baptismal (10,23) and eucharistic (13,15) setting have been argued; for literature, cf. Attridge, 108 n. 43. Such theories stretch the evidence thin. The present point is that they should be reflecting on the one whom they have so long "confessed," for they have not yet grasped the implications (conceptual or practical) of that confession.

[83] Cf. Vanhoye 1963, 115-182; Vanhoye's breakdown is 3,1-4,14 and 4,14-5,10.

[84] Note the use of ἀναστήσω in the Nathan oracle traditions: 1Par 17,11; 2Kgdms 7,7-12; 23,1.

[85] In the Nathan oracle traditions, cf. 1Par 17,10 (οἶκον οἰκοδομήσει σοι κύριος); 3Kgdms 11,38 (οἰκοδομήσω σοι οἶκον πιστόν); cf. 2Kgdms 7,16.

[86] Evidence for taking 3,2 with 1Par 17 and 1Kgdms 2 is discussed at length by D'Angelo, 69ff. She is followed by Lane, 1:76f., and Ellingworth, 201 (partially), but not by Attridge, 109 n. 53, or Gräßer, 1:165 n. 59. D'Angelo takes her lead from Aalen; my discussion differs somewhat from theirs.

[87] D'Angelo, 78f., shows that in the Targumim the translations of 1Sam 2,35 and 1Chr 17,14 par. appear to have influenced each other, suggesting they were being understood together; the evidence from the LXX is less convincing. In the OT the oracle of 1Sam 2,35 was fulfilled first in Samuel (1Sam 3,20; Sir 46,25), but ultimately in Zadok (in connection with Nathan's oracle: 2Sam 8,17; 1Kgs 2,27-35; cf. Ezek 44,15) who was considered a descendent of Aaron (1Chr 6,50-53). Sirach 45,25 says, "Just as a covenant was established with David...that the king's heritage passes only from son to son, so the heritage of Aaron is for his descendants only." That 1Sam 2,35 and 1Chr 17,14 with their traditions were linked as "twin testimonies for the Davidic messiah and the messianic

then, that *Auctor* has already cited 1Par 17,13 back in 1,5 in connection with Jesus' Sonship,[88] and that the wording of 3,2 is reminiscent of 1Par 17,14 (πιστώσω αὐτὸν ἐν οἴκῳ μου).

That this idea of the "faithful priest" figures in 3,2-6 where the priesthood of Christ is nowhere explicitly invoked might also be indicated by some of the language used there. Thus the ideas of "appointment" and "glory/honor" (3,2f.) both bear strong associations with Christ's priestly role in Hebrews,[89] and the appellation "Christ" (3,6) itself may do so as well;[90] note that prior to ch. 13 this appellation is strongly associated with Jesus' *priestly* ministry. When several words or ideas of 3,1-6 cluster together in 5,4-6 we can assume that for *Auctor* the appellation Χριστός in 3,6 does bear a connection with Ψ 2,7 and 1Par 17,13 (cf. 1,5), and that it is simultaneously suggestive of Jesus' *priestly* ministry. Thus 10,21: ἱερέα μέγαν ἐπὶ τὸν οἶκον τοῦ θεοῦ.

Such a convergence of themes and passages (1Kgdms 2,35; 1Par 17,14; Num 12,7) in 3,2 is credible. The early chapters of Hebrews (1-4) are overshadowed by the notion that the God who spoke has now spoken definitively (1,1f.). In chs. 1-2 Jesus is compared primarily to angels, evidently with a view to their exalted status and function as mediators of the Law in Jewish traditions (2,2),[91] and from there *Auctor* reckons with the towering figure of Moses (3,2-6).[92] This discussion of the mediators of the

---

priest" (D'Angelo, 69) is evident from the Targumim, but it is not unlikely that someone such as *Auctor* who already combined the royal and priestly functions of the messiah would have read them together as testimonies to the promised royal priest; cf. Aalen, 233-237; D'Angelo, 83-91; Lane, 1:76; Ellingworth, 201. Cf. LXX Zech 6,11-13; D'Angelo, 82f.; Ellingworth, 210.

[88] On the use of 1Par 17,14 (vs. 2Kgdms 7,14) in 1,5 cf. Ellingworth, 114-116.

[89] The verb ποιέω is not used again in Hebrews for Christ's appointment, but see 5,4f.; 7,28; 8,3; cf. 1,2. For "glory and honor," see 5,4f. The use of the phrase δόξῃ καὶ τιμῇ in 2,9f. (taken from Ψ 8) may anticipate the discussion of Christ's priesthood; cf. Lane, 1:49.

[90] This is the first use of the latter appellation in Hebrews; it is used anarthrously in 9,11.24, and with the article in 3,14; 5,5; 6,1; 9,14.28; and 11,26; Ἰησοῦς Χριστός occurs in 10,10 and 13,8.21. There does not seem to be a firm distinction between the anarthrous and arthrous usages, and most of the occurrences appear not to be titular, though *Auctor* was capable of so using it (6,1; 11,26).

[91] Cf. Acts 7,38.53; Gal 3,19; Josephus, *Ant* 15,136; Dey, 36-38, 83-96, 127-154; Kittel, 80-82; Newsom, 251-253. It is possible that there is a deeper running issue, such as some sort of "angel Christology," but even so the chief concern seems to be expressed in 2,2.

[92] For the exalted status of Moses for Hellenistic Jews like Philo, see Dey, 63-68, 74, 157-161; D'Angelo, 95-149 (esp. for rabbinic literature); R. Williamson 1970, 449-456; further literature therein. In Philo note *VitaMos* I,158; *Somn* II,189. Cf. EzekTrag 68-82 (*OTP*, 2:811f.) and further evidence in Jeremias 1967a, 848-864. Jeremias notes (*art. cit.*, 852) that "in its desire to magnify Moses with supreme attributes Palestinian Judaism was not behind Hellenistic"; cf. Sir 44,22-45,5 esp. v. 2 Heb; also TMos 11,16. "Palestinian

Law/revelation is capped by the long warning of 3,7-4,13 to *listen* with a view to the right to participate in the Great Salvation which was anticipated from the beginning of time. Following 4,14-16[93] the argument advances to the *subject matter of the Law itself*, i.e., the priesthood and sacrificial cultus which were bound up with that Law. Yet even before the warning of 3,7ff. the subject matter of Christ's priesthood is announced in 2,17,[94] and then referred to explicitly again in 3,1. In other words, the subjects of Jesus' comparison to Moses, on the one hand, and Jesus' priesthood, on the other, run together like two currents in 3,1-6; to be precise, in 3,2 where the reminiscence of 1Kgdms 2,35/1Par 17,14 mixes with Num 12,7. There is thus a *structural* overlapping of the first and second movements of Hebrews' argument in 2,17-3,6. These movements also overlap *substantively* as (1) Jesus, the Great High Priest serving in the true temple in terms of a new Law/covenant of which he is the mediator over against (2) Moses, the human mediator of the first covenant, the one who had erected the first tent and inaugurated it through blood.[95] Both stylistically and rhetorically this is effective. Bearing in mind that 3,1-6 is still structurally located in the first movement,[96] it is understandable that Christ's role as mediator of revelation is stressed (3,5) and his priesthood is muted.[97]

Judaism" was influenced by the speculation of "Hellenistic Judaism," but tended to stay closer to the OT, to treat Moses as a fallible human (but see D'Angelo, 95-149, on rabbinic literature), and to place the stress on Moses' role as the mediator of revelation (Jeremias, *art. cit.*, 855f.). Whatever had called forth *Auctor*'s response, he himself does not treat Moses as anything more than human and the allusion to Num 12,7 in the context of Heb 1-3 suggests a primary interest in Moses' role as the unequalled mediator of the Law (3,5) but probably not without an interest in his role as the leader of the exodus (3,16); *pace* Gräßer 1984, 302.

[93] 4,14-16 has been notoriously difficult to fit neatly into outlines; cf. G. Guthrie, 23. It is best construed as transitional (*op. cit.*, 102-104), forming an *inclusio* with 10,19-25 (*op. cit.*, 79-82).

[94] The theme of angels is contained within the *inclusio* of 1,4.5-2,16; significantly, the reference to Christ's priesthood follows immediately thereafter in 2,17; cf. Ellingworth, 104.

[95] Moses is described as a priest only once in the OT (Ψ 98,6 [99,6]) but he was of the tribe of Levi (Ex 2,1-10), he had a unique access to God (Ex 33,12-34,35; Num 12,7-8), and he served at the altar (Ex 24,4-8; cf. Heb 9,19-21); cf. Sir 45,4. Philo openly calls Moses a high priest (*VitaMos* II,66-186; *Heres* 182; *Praem* 53.56); cf. Dey, 157-161.

[96] G. Guthrie, 65f., 128f., 144, categorizes 3,1-6 simply as exhortation and views as a single block, 3,1-4,13; he still considers this section (3,1-4,13) as a response to the first movement of 1,5-2,18 before the second main movement of 4,14-10,25. It may be, however, that there is a degree of *functional* overlap in 3,1-6, involving both exhortation and exposition.

[97] The context of Num 12,7 is clearly assumed by *Auctor*: "When there are prophets among you, I the LORD make myself known to them in visions; I speak to them in dreams. Not so with my servant Moses; he is entrusted with all my house. With him I speak face to face -- clearly, not in riddles; and he beholds the form of the LORD"; for the

We return then to the interest which launched our discussion of 3,1-6, namely the function of this passage with relation to 3,7-4,11. *Auctor* is not concerned merely with speculation about Christ's exalted status, but with the implications of this for a struggling group of believers. As he puts it more explicitly in 10,21-23 (cf. 4,16), "we have a *great priest* over the house of God"; *therefore*,

let us approach with a true heart in full assurance of faith... Let us hold fast to the confession of our hope without wavering, for he who promised is faithful.

Discussion of Christ's supremacy is in the service of surety: the very fact of Christ's supremacy which demands obedient faith (listening) is what -- by its very nature -- assures the believer of assistance in the journey of faith. Thus the long exhortation to "listen" (3,7-4,13) is framed by assurances of Christ's faithful, priestly ministry which can see us through to the end.[98] Alternatively -- to switch from Christology and soteriology to eschatology -- 3,7-4,13 is an exhortation geared to *future* eschatology which is itself supported by exhortations geared to *realized* eschatology. Heb 3,7-4,13, in spite of its dearth of explicit references to Christ, bears strong connections to *Auctor*'s Christology.

With this broad look at the context we can turn to consider the immediate transition to 3,7ff. By a deft twist of the metaphor in v. 6 the focus turns (or returns: v. 1) from the comparison of Christ and Moses to the covenantal responsibility of the believer.[99] The concern is not only with Jesus'

---

development of this Moses-tradition in the OT and Judaism cf. esp. D'Angelo, 95-149; some of her material was summarized above, 177ff. In Heb 3,1-6, the metaphor turns on the imagery of Sonship, which also accounts for the suppression of explicit references to Christ's priesthood.

[98] That both of these passages (2,17-3,6 and 4,14-16) serve as end-pieces to the exhortation in the middle is clear not only from the logical transitions on both ends, but the use of the hook-word, πειράζω in 2,18; 3,9; and 4,15 (cf. πειρασμός in 3,8). This is the only occurrence of πειρασμός in Hebrews; the verb πειράζω occurs elsewhere in Hebrews only at 11,17. Of course in 3,8f. it is human testing of God. 1Cor 10,1-13 is often cited in connection with Heb 3,7-19. In that vein it is worth noting that 1Cor 10,12f. gives a caution followed by a reassurance of divine assistance which is verbally reminiscent of Heb 4,11.14-16 (cf. 3,2.12; 4,1): ὥστε ὁ δοκῶν ἑστάναι βλεπέτω μὴ πέσῃ. πειρασμός ὑμᾶς οὐκ εἴληφεν εἰ μὴ ἀνθρώπινος· πιστὸς δὲ ὁ θεός, ὃς οὐκ ἐάσει ὑμᾶς πειρασθῆναι ὑπὲρ ὃ δύνασθε, ἀλλὰ ποιήσει σὺν τῷ πειρασμῷ καὶ τὴν ἔκβασιν τοῦ δύνασθαι ὑπενεγκεῖν.

[99] The imagery of a "house" was widespread and variously used; cf. Attridge, 108f. Against a pronounced Philonic or dualistic idea of the "house" in 3,6b, cf. Attridge, 111 n. 88; *contra* Dey, 174-177; Schierse, 108-112; J.W. Thompson, 92f. The notion of the "house" as God's people is naturally related to Num 12,7; cf. 1Kgdms 2,35; 1Par 17,14 par. In v. 6b-c the emphasis is on the conditional clause; the apodosis (οὗ οἶκός ἐσμεν ἡμεῖς) is an important proposition -- no doubt *Auctor* is accenting it through

relationship with Moses but with his relationship to his "brothers," and the other side of the coin is their relationship to him, *their* faithfulness. The stage has been set in view of the ultimacy of revelation in the recent word of the Son and the ultimacy of the salvation which he has ushered in[100] -- that for which they hope -- to exhort the readers to *listen* lest they forfeit that hope, namely, entrance into God's κατάπαυσις.

Our reason for reviewing the OT background prior to discussion of context can now be made clear. For *Auctor* there is an underlying drama being worked out, a paradigm of covenantal relations between God and his people which was brought to light in a normative fashion in the account of Num 12-14. From addressing Moses' unique revelatory role in Num 12 the account progresses naturally to Num 13-14, the events of Kadesh where the people refused to listen to God's voice. They not only forfeited salvation, but they were not able to win a reprieve through repentance.[101] For *Auctor* these events put into their true light the present situation of his readers, and he is keen to unfold the salient lessons from that history. His train of thought is being guided as much by the narrative of Num 12-14 as by his own developing argument, and once again we recognize the implausibility of the claim that the κατάπαυσις-idea of Heb 3-4 is an essentially pre-formed Alexandrian idea only *secondarily* grounded in the OT. From its very inception, *Auctor*'s use of the rest motif is grounded in the OT, and reflection on the κατάπαυσις-idea is subsidiary to the main paraenetic concern.

If we assume, with some justification,[102] that a connection between Num 14 and Ps 95 was a part of *Auctor*'s exegetical heritage then the use of Ψ 94 [95] *at this point* is fitting and natural. Ψ 94,7-11 [95,7-11] lends itself to

---

understatement -- but he will not be distracted from his immediate concerns and so leaves it unexplicated.

[100] This "great salvation" has been a constant theme already (cf. 1,2f.8f.13f.; 2,3-5.9-16.17f.), but it will be developed more directly from 4,14 on.

[101] Cf. Hofius, 137; Gräßer 1986, 167.

[102] The rabbis also related Num 14 and Ps 95; supra, 127f.; I am of course referring to a general association of the psalm and Num 14, rather than evidence for a linking of the LXX of these passages specifically. Hofius, 51-53, draws out parallels between Heb 3-4 and the use of Ps 95 by the rabbis. His suggestion that *Auctor consciously* agrees with those rabbis who saw the oath as final, excluding the desert generation from the world-to-come, is overly speculative; *Auctor* appears to take the oath at face value, and does not speculate further on the ultimate fate of either the OT wicked or the OT righteous. That the rabbis associated the מנוחה with the temple and Jerusalem specifically is only true with reference to *MidrPss* 95, and not so with the eschatological interpretation of the psalm. Yet the placement of an eschatological interpretation of this psalm against Num 14 is a strong parallel with the rabbis. Whether Ps 95 was a part of this particular tradition from its inception might be questioned in view of *Sanh* 10,3, but maybe Heb 3-4 is itself evidence of its currency.

the general interests of this work.¹⁰³ It is a poignantly expressed *contemporaneous* warning to *listen* to God's *word*. It testifies, as did LXX Jer 38 [31], to the "inadequacy of the old order."¹⁰⁴ Moreover, it is possible that Ψ 95,10 [96,10] had been in *Auctor*'s mind in writing about the "coming world" at 2,5,¹⁰⁵ thus bringing him into recent contact with Ψ 94 [95].

The word κατάπαυσις does not occur in Num 14, but as a theme it is wholly at home there, and it is equally at home in Hebrews.¹⁰⁶ Beyond the "heavenly land" and the "inheritance," *Auctor*'s concern with the tabernacle/temple would very naturally relate to the theme of Ψ 94,11 [95,11] and specifically to the word κατάπαυσις, as we have seen in the OT. More generally, by virtue of its development in the OT, the κατάπαυσις-idea was a powerful symbol of salvation consummated.

In sum, Heb 3,7-4,11 is an extended exhortation to *listen* before the argument turns a corner to the exposition of Christ's priestly ministry. It has several thematic ties to the immediate and general context and is embedded in the writer's Christology though it makes but one explicit reference to Christ. It follows the story line of Num 12-14 which in *Auctor*'s eyes is a normative paradigm for the present situation of the readers, and which Ψ 94 [95] had already converted into a powerful warning. The κατάπαυσις-idea rides in on the train of Ψ 94 [95], but its expression in Ψ 94,11 [95,11] is entirely amenable to *Auctor*'s interests and so warrants development.

2.1.3. Typology?

The comparison of the believing community with the "fathers" is an obvious piece of typological interpretation of the OT. Not infrequently one encounters the suggestion that *Auctor* is also presenting the heavenly/future κατάπαυσις as the (spiritual) anti-type of the earthly κατάπαυσις; in some sense the land was a "partial" fulfilment of the promise, but not the "true"

---

¹⁰³ In addition to what follows, Desilva, 452ff., argues that the theme of shame/honor, which he contends is of some importance throughout the epistle, is reflected in this psalm's reference to the wrath of God. His wrath "is an expression of God's understanding of being slighted, rather than simply being fed up with the Israelites."

¹⁰⁴ Caird, 47.

¹⁰⁵ Noted by Lane, 1:46. Heb 2,5 says, οὐ γὰρ ἀγγέλοις ὑπέταξεν τὴν οἰκουμένην τὴν μέλλουσαν. Ψ. 95,10 [96,10] (likewise Ψ 92,1 [93,1]) says, "Say among the nations, the Lord reigns, for he established the world [τὴν οἰκουμένην] which will not be shaken [ἥτις οὐ σαλευθήσεται]"; the use of σαλεύω in 12,27 suggests that Ψ 95 [96] may have been in *Auctor*'s mind at 2,5. Interestingly, the septuagintal title to Ψ 95 [96] -- which follows immediately on the heels of Ψ 94,11 [95,11] -- is, "when the house was built [ὅτε ὁ οἶκος ᾠκοδομεῖτο] after the captivity" (cf. 1Kgdms 2,35; 1Par 17,14).

¹⁰⁶ The κατάπαυσις-idea itself probably belonged to *Auctor*'s Christian background; infra, 335-338.

κατάπαυσις.¹⁰⁷ A more nuanced understanding comes with the argument that here as elsewhere the writer is actually presenting the heavenly κατάπαυσις as the anti-type of the earthly κατάπαυσις which is, in turn, the anti-type of a primordial archetype (Gen 2).¹⁰⁸

None of these suggestions take us very far, however, because in this passage the writer does not appear to be interested in the land of Canaan as such.¹⁰⁹ Rather than working with an earthly/past vs. heavenly/future κατάπαυσις, the writer's argument is concerned with entrance into the *one* κατάπαυσις which is encountered first in connection with Gen 2, then again in the offer to the "fathers," then again in Ψ 94 [95] "after all these days," and ultimately available in the same promise "today" for "us who believe"; the land itself is not even considered a partial fulfilment.¹¹⁰ This becomes clear as soon as we ask whether the "fathers" would have entered τὴν κατάπαυσίν μου in their time if they had been faithful and obedient at Kadesh. This is a hypothetical question which does not distract *Auctor* at all, but the statement about Joshua (4,8) suggests that it would have been answered negatively.¹¹¹

Our point is not that the land is unimportant to the passage, for the events surrounding the historical κατάπαυσις are obviously recalled and lend shape to the idea of the eschatological entrance into God's κατάπαυσις. Nevertheless, the passage betrays no interest in a *typology* between the "earthly/past" and "heavenly/future" land. The parallel (typology) which we do encounter is that between the two *situations* -- communities confronted by the one word/voice of God responding to the promise of the *one* great *Heilsgut*. In terms of both soteriology and ecclesiology,¹¹² far-reaching continuity is assumed in this passage.

---

¹⁰⁷ E.g., Rissi, 18; Westcott, 100; Bruce, 105, 109; many others.

¹⁰⁸ Attridge 1980, 284-287; followed by Lane, 1:101, 104. Attridge has insight in pointing to the importance for *Auctor* of primordial realities, but he goes too far in trying to excise the land-temple ideas from *Auctor*'s κατάπαυσις-idea. *Contra* Attridge, the κατάπαυσις is not redefined as a σαββατισμός, but rather the κατάπαυσις and the σαββατισμός are related to each other; see further below.

¹⁰⁹ Windisch, 34; Gräßer, 1:209; Weiss, 281; Ellingworth, 235, 254; Hofius, 56.

¹¹⁰ Cf. Braun, 109; Hofius, 178 n. 337, 179 n. 340, 180 n. 351. Different "rests" are often distinguished in this passage (e.g., Oberholtzer 1988, 185, 190; Toussaint, 71; for a list, cf. W.C. Kaiser 1985, 170), though at times pedantically.

¹¹¹ The figure mentioned in 4,8 is to be taken straightforwardly as Joshua; cf. Ellingworth, 252f. The antecedent to the pronoun αὐτούς in 4,8 is the unmentioned *second* generation; *contra* Rissi, 19f. (cf. Braun, 113).

¹¹² There is a formal (historical) distinction between the "fathers" and "us," but there is no indication that *Auctor* was concerned with a real distinction between "peoples" (e.g., Israel and the church; Jews and Gentiles; the "nearby" and the "far off"; even the "old" and the "new"). His overall understanding was clearly that the OT believers were to be united with "us" in salvation (11,39f.; 12,23), and nothing he says in chs. 3-4 suggests

2.1.4. Definition of terms

2.1.4.1. What is a σαββατισμός?

The assumption that the nouns κατάπαυσις and σαββατισμός are synonymous because of the apparent parallelism of 4,6 and v. 9 has often clouded interpretation.[113] This is reflected in translations of the latter term as "Sabbath rest," and the assumption that this is what *Auctor* meant by κατάπαυσις as well; it is essentially a rest from work, a quietistic ideal. On the other hand, when Käsemann construed the κατάπαυσις locally he assumed the same held for the σαββατισμός; it was understood as "aeon-like," as equivalent to the gnostic Hebdomad.[114] Both of these interpretations have been shown to be untenable.[115]

The word σαββατισμός occurs nowhere in Gk literature prior to Hebrews, prompting the suggestion that *Auctor* coined the term.[116] If so *Auctor* may have been thinking beyond Gen 2 of a wider sweep of OT passages where the verb σαββατίζω (from which the noun was formed) is used.[117] Against σαββατισμός having been coined by *Auctor*, however, is the fact that the noun occurs in the non-Christian writing of Plutarch.[118] It also occurs several times in later Christian literature independently of Hebrews.[119] The sense in those passages is not that of a "rest from works" narrowly conceived, nor does the word refer to the Sabbath *day* as such; the noun refers rather to the Sabbath *observance*, or Sabbath *celebration*. This accords both with Jewish conceptions of the Sabbath as a day not merely of cessation of activity but of *festive worship and praise*,[120] and with Hebrews' picture of the future πανήγυρις (12,22), "festive gathering," in the heavenly

---

another understanding; Ellingworth, 68f. Whether or not *Auctor* was allowing for the exceptions of Joshua and Caleb is not of great consequence (see discussions of 3,16).

[113] V. 9 is parallel with v. 6a but it is not *simply* parallel; taken together with v. 10, v. 9 says something more and something different than v. 6a.

[114] Käsemann, 68-75; cf. Gräßer 1965, 106f.

[115] Hofius, 102-115 (summarized in 1993, 19); Héring, 32 n. 8. Also on σαββατισμός, cf. Lohse, 34f.; Gräßer, 1:218-220; Ellingworth, 255.

[116] E.g. Spicq, 2:83; Moffatt, 53; Isaacs, 84.

[117] Ex 16,30; Lev 23,32; 26,34f. [3x]; 2Par 36,21 [= 1Es 1,58; 2x]; cf. also 2Mac 6,6 and on this view, Gräßer, 1:218 n. 133.

[118] Ca. A.D. 50-120; cf. *Superst* 3(166A) (cf. 8[196C]); Hofius, 106; Attridge, 131 n. 103; Lindars 1991b, 50 n. 35.

[119] Cf. Justin, *DialTrypho* 23,3; *AposCon* 2,36,2; Epiphanius, *Pan* 30,2,2; *MartPetPaul* 1; all discussed by Hofius, 103-106 (see additional references in 1993, 219). Attridge, 131, appears to correct his earlier dismissal of this evidence (1980, 283 n. 15).

[120] Cf. Ex 20,8-10; 2Mac 8,27; Jub 50,8f.; Ps-Philo 11,8; Lauterbach 1951, 438f., 444.

Jerusalem.¹²¹ The σαββατισμός is neither a quietistic ideal nor a locale, but a Sabbath celebration.

Gräßer attempts to resurrect Käsemann's interpretation by asserting that *both* Käsemann *and* Hofius can be right; it need not be either/or. He argues that the gnostic aeon-speculation is not far removed from the apocalyptic "world which is wholly Sabbath"; thus "σαββατισμός = höchster Äon im Sinne alexandrinisch-gnostischer Hebdomas-Spekulationen."¹²² This argument fails, however, partly because it assumes too broad a definition of Gnosticism,¹²³ but more fundamentally because it is simply not germane to ask how wide a gap separates (rabbinic) apocalyptic and gnostic concepts of the world-week¹²⁴ or the seven "aeons." The word σαββατισμός does not suggest that the κατάπαυσις is the "seventh aeon" (or even that it is "aeon-like"), whether that is construed gnostically *or* apocalyptically.¹²⁵ The noun merely tells us that life for the people of God in God's resting place will be an eternal, festive Sabbath celebration.

2.1.4.2. Κατάπαυσις: place and/or state?

A somewhat different judgment is to be rendered on the κατάπαυσις. As we have already seen¹²⁶ the question of whether or not the κατάπαυσις of Heb 3-4 is to be thought of essentially as a locale (vs. a state) is not crucial for the debate regarding background.¹²⁷ The local idea was emphasized by both Käsemann and Hofius although they came to very different conclusions regarding the religious historical background of the idea.¹²⁸ Be that as it

---

¹²¹ Cf. Losada, 126f.; Attridge, 375; Lane, 2:467; Ellingworth, 255. On πανήγυρις, see MM, 476; Philo, *Flacc* 118. Cf. also Lane, 1:101f.; Weiss, 282.
¹²² Gräßer, 1:218-220.
¹²³ Cf. Attridge, 127 n. 61, 128 n. 70.
¹²⁴ Supra, 103f.
¹²⁵ See also below, 320f.
¹²⁶ Supra, 11f.
¹²⁷ In addition to Käsemann and Hofius the local understanding is adopted (in some form or other) by Woschitz, 622-624; Lincoln 1982, 208f.; J.W. Thompson, 99f.; Rissi, 18f.; Scholer, 204 n. 1; Braun, 90f.; Weiss, 268f.; Gräßer, 1:209f., 218-220; Ellingworth, 235, *et al*.
¹²⁸ Theißen 1969, 121, 124, urges against Hofius that the κατάπαυσις is *both* a place and a state (likewise Braun, 90ff.; J.W. Thompson, 100; others), but the local element does not figure in his discussion; cf. Hofius, 255. In other words, in contrast to Käsemann there has been a decided softening of the local idea in the more recent arguments for a Philonic or gnostic conception. Attridge, 127 n. 55, 131, is emphatic that the κατάπαυσις should be understood as a *state* and that as such it is likely to be similar in conception to gnostic speculation (1980, 283f. n. 16; he seems to modify this somewhat in 1988, 97, where he allows that the κατάπαυσις might be a place; in his commentary, 127f., he is more sceptical of the gnostic parallels). On the other hand, Lane, who tends toward Hofius' interpretation overall, is ambiguous (cf., e.g., 1:98, 102)

may, our own interests take us beyond the question of religious historical derivation. In which case it is basic to grasp whether or not κατάπαυσις means "resting place" here.

We have already looked at the background of the term κατάπαυσις, as well as its Heb equivalent in Ps 95 (מנוחה). There is no lexical basis for insisting that κατάπαυσις *must* be understood in a local sense, though the local meaning is prominent in terms of usage in the LXX.[129] What is better founded is the argument that κατάπαυσις is essentially a local idea *in Ψ 94 [95]*, and that this is how the motif was understood in this psalm in Jewish traditions.[130] More generally, there is ample testimony in Judaism not only to the expectation of ultimate rest and peace but to the expectation of a heavenly and/or future resting *place* in some form or other;[131] it would be natural for *Auctor* to think in these terms. Moreover, the initial development of Ψ 94 [95] in Heb 3,16-19 clearly plays off the κατάπαυσις idea with Canaan, at which point the question of whether the term itself (κατάπαυσις) has the local component of meaning is largely academic. It is on this note that the pericope as a whole ends (4,11). It is certainly noteworthy that the term εἰσέρχομαι is used elsewhere in Hebrews exclusively of local realities,[132] and it cannot be denied that the κατάπαυσις, as the content of the

---

but appears to favor taking the κατάπαυσις as essentially a state here. Vanhoye 1971, 68, also questions the local idea; cf. Yeo, 10f. For further variations, cf. Hofius, 27f.

[129] Supra, 94ff.

[130] Cf. JosAsen 8,9; *MidrPss* 95; *ARN* 36 par.; supra, 124ff. See also the summary in Hofius, 51-53. We might add to these passages ApEl (I-IV A.D.) 2,53; 4,27. Although this work was heavily edited by Christians, O.S. Wintermute (in *OTP*, 1:744, 749) opines that the use of the rest motif in 2,53 and 4,27 is close to Ps 95,11 and that it "goes back to the early Jewish stratum within the text." It is given an eschatological interpretation, although it refers to the land of Egypt rather than Canaan. On ApEl 4,27 see also Hofius, 66f.

[131] Supra, 106ff.

[132] In our passage see εἰσέρχομαι in 3,11.18.19; 4,1.3 (2x).5.6 (2x).10.11. Cf. also 6,19.20 (the "inner shrine behind the curtain" of the heavenly temple); 9,12.24. (Holy Place of the heavenly temple); 9,25 (Holy Place of the earthly temple); 10,5 (the world); J.W. Thompson, 99; Ellingworth, 234. On the use of "entrance" language in the LXX and Hebrews, cf. Scholer, 150-184. In addition to passages in Hebrews using the verb εἰσέρχομαι, see also 9,6f. (εἴσειμι; assumed in v. 7); 10,19 (εἴσοδος; cf. Hofius, 53f., 176 n. 314). Finally, note εἰσάγω (1,6); εἰσφέρω (13,11); εἰς (esp. 2,10; 11,8f.). The force of this argument is partially mitigated by the observation that "rest" as a state is not infrequently objectivized, *viz* as some*thing* which one "gives" (e.g. 3Kgdms 8,56; LXX Isa 25,10), one "finds" (e.g. LXX Jer 51,33 [45,3]; Lam 1,3; Sir 6,28; 11,19; 22,13; 28,16; 51,27; LXX Hos 12,9 [12,8]), or "in" which one (or, something) exists (e.g. LXX Num 10,35 [10,36]; 1Par 6,16 [6,31]; Job 7,18; Ψ 65,12 [66,12]; Ψ 114,7 [116,7]; Sir 20,21; 34 (31),3.4; 38,23; 40,6). Among those in the last group one may note esp. Job 7,18 (καὶ εἰς ἀνάπαυσιν αὐτὸν κρινεῖς) and Ψ 114,7 [116,7] (ἐπίστρεψον, ἡ ψυχή μου, εἰς τὴν ἀνάπαυσίν σου), both of which are referring to a state, rather than a place of rest. The verb εἰσέρχομαι is utilized in Heb 3-4 because of its presence in the psalm

"promise" (4,1), stands in Hebrews alongside several other great eschatological, local realities which are likewise awaited: "the coming world" (2,5); the heavenly city (11,10.16; 12.22; 13,14); the heavenly fatherland (11,14); and the unshakeable kingdom (12,28).[133] The Odes of Solomon might provide an early Christian testimony for the idea of a resting place.[134]

In addition to these considerations Hofius argues that *Auctor* counted the resting place among the things created by God, and that Gen 2,2 was introduced in 4,3f. precisely to establish that the κατάπαυσις, God's resting place, had been in existence since creation. In fact, the idea of primordial creations which were hidden in the present but which would appear at the end was well known in Judaism.[135] To be sure, Gen 2,2 (Heb 4,3.4.10) does not speak of a resting place into which God entered, but it does speak of God having rested from *all* his works, so that we may assume, Hofius argues, that his resting place (κατάπαυσις) was in existence already at that time.[136] For its part, the word σαββατισμός (4,9) is not synonymous with κατάπαυσις but rather explains what takes place *in* the κατάπαυσις, i.e., a Sabbath celebration (cf. 12,22f.). Heb 4,10 then states how such a σαββατισμός will transpire: people will rest from their works upon entrance into the κατάπαυσις (the eschatological temple), just as was the case with God at creation when he entered his resting place. To Hofius' argument we can add the comment that if Isa 66,1 was in the background of Heb 3,7-4,11, as we will suggest below, then it can be noted that in that passage creation is in a

---

quote, and outside of Hebrews there are parallels to the idea of "entrance into" a state (e.g., Mt 25,21.23; Jn 4,38; cf. further Darnell, 226 n. 4); note the use of εἰς in 2,10.

[133] Cf. Käsemann, 33-37; Weiss, 269. The spatial dimension of salvation is uniquely important to *Auctor* within the NT; it is highlighted in particular by Isaacs, esp. 56, 61-66, 205-219. On the other hand, the hope can also be described more generally as salvation (1,14; 6,9), glory (2,10), and perfection (e.g., 6,1; 11,40).

[134] Supra, 132f.

[135] In the NT, cf. Mt 25,34; Jn 14,2f.; Gal 4,26; 1Pet 1,3f.; Rev 3,12; 21,2.10; in Hebrews cf. 11,16. Hofius, 178 n. 330, notes Acts 3,20 in this connection. For the Sabbath as a primordial creation, cf. *GenR* 10,2 (cf. Ginzberg, 5:111 n. 102); *MidrPss* 92 § 2; also the Samaritan commentary on the Pentateuch, *Memar Marqah* I § 9; II § 7 (MacDonald, 1:21, 37; 2:31, 56); Hofius, 97f. *MidrPss* 92 and *Memar Marqah* seem to construe the primordial Sabbath not only as itself a creation but as a locale.

[136] Hofius, 55, 96f.; Zimmermann, 138, 140. For Hofius and Zimmermann the κατάπαυσις is specifically the Most Holy Place of the heavenly temple; infra, 314f. Others also include the κατάπαυσις among the works mentioned in 4,3f., though without thinking of the heavenly temple, e.g. Schierse, 114; Woschitz, 622f.; Laub, 250; Gräßer, 1:209-211; Weiss, 269; Ellingworth, 244-247. Attridge, 129, allows this as possible. Alternatively, according to *GenR* 10,9 everything was created in six days except rest, which was created on the Sabbath; cf. Ginzberg, 5:111 n. 102; it is in this non-local sense that Montefiore, 83, takes 4,3.

sense God's καταπαυσις. It would seem possible to make sense of Heb 4,3 against that passage.

Hofius' interpretation is possible, but as we will suggest below vv. 3b-5 should probably not be made the basis of too much speculation on our parts. There are at least three points which tell against including the καταπαυσις among the "works" mentioned in 4,3f. (1) Such an idea is awkwardly expressed in 4,3-4, and seems to be outside the interests of 4,10 when the theme of "works" resumes. There is little here to make us think of anything other than the literary accounts to which *Auctor* alludes and the "works" mentioned there. On Hofius' interpretation, 4,4 would amount to, "God rested in the seventh day from making his resting place." V. 10 would say, "God entered his resting place to rest from making his resting place." Such a thought is possible, but poorly expressed if that is *Auctor*'s intended meaning. (2) The "entrance" is never applied directly to God.[137] This is probably not only due to *Auctor*'s desire to stay close to the wording of his texts, but is likely because the "entrance" -- taking the lead of the psalm -- is thought of as a secondary event, i.e., a subsequent and *soteriological* event for humans, and not a statement about what *God* once did. (3) It looks artificial to stress the "all" of 4,4b (Gen 2,2) so that it applies to the heavenly city, the καταπαυσις, etc.; that the "all" is missing in 4,3c should have cautioned against this.[138] *Auctor* betrays no further interest in speculation about how or when God created the heavenly world, nor whether God could only have rested with that work also finished.[139]

It is not proven, then, that *Auctor* counts the καταπαυσις among the "works" mentioned in 4,3f.[140] This is not, however, a sufficient cause to reject the local idea and understand καταπαυσις consistently as a state here. Yet in his case against a local meaning Attridge argues that,

...the author's argument, in his own estimation, hinges on the equation of *katapausis* and *sabbatismos*, that is, upon the redefinition of the first term by means of the second...

The most relevant factors for interpreting *katapausis* here are (1) the fact that it summarizes the implications of the *gezara shawa* argument of Heb 4:4-5, and (2) that it is in turn interpreted by the remark of v 10 "he who enters his rest himself has rested from

---

[137] That God "entered" his καταπαυσις is gathered from 4,10 by Schierse, 114; Hofius, 55, 177 n. 324.

[138] Rightly, Braun, 91, 109.

[139] There is an interesting example of such speculation in 2En 24,2b-5, where God claims that he did not find rest because "everything was not yet created"; thus God thinks up "the idea of establishing a foundation, to create a visible creation." The imagery is difficult, but it appears that here God is restless because he has not yet created, but it is the visible things which are yet to be created; the "invisible things" were already existent (cf. F.I. Andersen, in *OTP*, 1:142 nn. f-g; Rowland, 148f.). Andersen, *art. cit.*, 142 n. h, contrasts this primal restlessness of God with philosophical trends which allowed no change in God.

[140] Rightly, Lane, 1:99.

his work as God did from his"...To enter God's "rest" is not to take possession of the land of Israel, nor to enter a concrete eschatological temple. Rather, it is to have a share in God's eternal "sabbatical" repose.[141]

Of the two factors mentioned by Attridge, the second begs the question,[142] and the first assumes the equation of the two nouns, a mistake that Attridge himself later corrected in part.[143] Moreover, Attridge presents a false dichotomy by suggesting that if the κατάπαυσις is not the earthly land or the heavenly temple it must be a state, God's sabbatical repose. Might not the κατάπαυσις be more generally the world-to-come? In addition to casually dismissing the linguistic and contextual evidence noted above, Attridge gives too little weight to the prominence of the rest tradition in the OT and in Heb 3-4. The passage ends (4,11) by referring back once again to the exposition of 3,16-19, demonstrating that it was not lost in the meantime (cf. 4,8). It is artificial to pretend that we can simply ignore the local connotations which emerge against that background. Even most of those who render κατάπαυσις simply as "rest" are wont to speak of heaven or the world-to-come as the typological counterpart to the earthly Canaan, a tendency which can easily read too much typology into the passage but which instinctively recognizes the local imagery involved.

The common use of the word κατάπαυσις for a "resting place," its present usage and context, and the strong testimony in Jewish literature for an other worldly or future resting *place* cumulatively tilt the balance of probability in favor of taking it straightforwardly here as "resting place."[144] If we paraphrase the passage in those terms it gives an acceptable sense:[145]

---

[141] 1980, 282f. (cf. 283 n. 14).

[142] If we translate κατάπαυσις in v. 10 locally the sense is, "the one who enters God's resting *place* rests from his works as God did from his." The Sabbath celebration takes place in the resting place, and is made possible by resting from one's works. This is perfectly intelligible, and Attridge's objections (Attridge, 131 n. 108) are without force.

[143] Compare, Attridge, 131, with 1980, 283 n. 15.

[144] There is no question that a resting place embraces the state of rest, or that a state of rest in most cases assumes a place in which one rests. What is problematic is the contention that we can understand the κατάπαυσις in Heb 3-4 as now a place, now a state (coming-to-rest) or somehow as both, such as Theißen 1969, 92, 121, 124, seems to want to do; likewise, Braun, 90-93. Hofius, 255, is right to treat this understanding as suspect, pointing out that having embraced both meanings Theißen proceeds to speak of the κατάπαυσις only as a state; the local element drops out of his discussion just where it would have forced him to modify his interpretation (Theißen 1969, 128, barely alludes to it). The same criticism can be levelled at J.W. Thompson, 99f., who having just defined the κατάπαυσις as a *locale* (the transcendent, "stable" world) promptly disregards that definition in his interpretation of vv. 3-5.10a: "the eschatological κατάπαυσις of Ps 95:11 is identical to God's *rest* (κατάπαυσις) on the seventh day... The believer enters 'his *rest*.' The 'rest' of the believer is thus parallel to God's rest..., if not identical. Κατάπαυσις is, therefore, not only a place; it is also a status" (italics added); cf. likewise, Zimmermann, 141. If Thompson would have followed through with his own

For we believers will enter into God's resting place,[146] just as it has been said, "they will not enter into my resting place," although God has been done with his work since the time of creation. For you recall that in Gen 2 it is said, "God rested in the seventh day from all his works," and again here in Ψ 94, "they will not enter into my resting place." Since it is certain some will enter God's resting place and the former generation did not enter due to disobedience, he therefore appointed another day... There remains then a Sabbath celebration for the people of God, for those who enter God's resting place also rests from their works, just as God rested from his own works.

It is apparent that *Auctor* does associate God's creation Sabbath with a resting place, the resting place to which Ψ 94,11 [95,11] refers, God's resting place. Presumably, therefore, this locale existed "since the creation of the world." Nonetheless, it is *not* apparent that *Auctor* manipulates Gen 2 to establish that the resting place was itself a primordial creation into which God himself "entered." Moreover, in spite of the fact that this is a heavenly locale (*God's* resting place) as opposed to an earthly one -- and in spite of the fact that *Auctor* envisages the future salvation place as already existing in completed form in heaven -- this contrast between heaven and earth does not receive any separate emphasis here either.[147] So long as we appreciate that it is not Canaan which is in view it is not important to stress that it is *heavenly*

---

definition of κατάπαυσις he would have discovered that his conclusion doesn't follow (the believers enter God's resting *place* [κατάπαυσις], where they rest [καταπαύω] from their works as God did; it is thus not an entrance into God's *rest* but into God's resting *place*). It is a classic case of wanting to have one's cake and eat it too, of wanting to affirm the local meaning but ignore it in exegesis. Hofius, 259, is also correct over against Theißen that it is not the κατάπαυσις (noun) that is contrasted with the "work," but the rest (καταπαύω) of God from his works which is contrasted with his previous activity. We have only urged against Hofius that the κατάπαυσις is not included by *Auctor* among God's "works," and he probably did not envisage God as having "entered" his resting place at creation. Whatever inner harmony *Auctor* found in these two passages (Ψ 94 [95] and Gen 2) did not lead to a harmonizing treatment.

[145] In the following, liberty has plainly been taken in rendering the sense of the Greek, since this paraphrase is purely for the purpose of highlighting the local idea in the thought of the passage. While this paraphrase at points anticipates our discussion of particulars (e.g., the future rendering of εἰσερχόμεθα in 4,3 anticipates our discussion below, 305ff.; for the rendering of ἀπολείπεται in v. 6 as "it is certain," see below, 293f. n. 185), it is of only limited usefulness for understanding the passage.

[146] Attridge, 122, n. 6, picks up on the absence of τήν in v. 3 in $\mathfrak{P}^{13vid.46}$ B D* (it is present in A C D² [NA²⁷ = D¹] Ψ 0243. 0278. 33. 1739. 1881 𝔐) to suggest that this modification might anticipate the following exegesis of Gen 2: "What believers enter is 'a rest' different from 'the rest' of the land of Canaan." The article is probably secondary (cf. Braun, 108; Ellingworth, 244), but it is not clear that too much should be read into its absence here. The usage is parallel to the psalm quotation in 4,3b which possesses both the article and the local meaning; the absence of the article in 4,3a is primarily stylistic variation (cf. 4,6), though it might suggest that the κατάπαυσις is not only God's but ours (Ellingworth, 246).

[147] Cf. Ellingworth, 254.

in some specific metaphysical sense; what is of significance is that it is yet *future*.

Auctor is not interested in the existence of the κατάπαυσις, either its origin or its heavenly location as such, though both of these are assumed. The reference to Gen 2,2 serves rather to draw together protology and eschatology, to unite the purposes of God in creation and redemption, to account from the OT itself for what is plainly (for *Auctor*!) a transcendent and future *Heilsgut* which is in a special sense God's (*my* resting place), to give pregnant expression to the character of the eschatological event (σαββατισμός), and more (below).

The upshot of these remarks is that the local meaning is probably the right one for the noun κατάπαυσις throughout this passage, and *Auctor* does make a direct connection between the resting *place* mentioned in Ψ 94 [95] and God's Sabbath celebration; God's (my) resting place is where God enjoys his on-going σαββατισμός. It is entrance into this very place which is the one promise held out to the "fathers," and also to us "today" (4,1f.6). It is *in* this place that the people of God will ultimately rest from their works, just as God did from his, and thus join in the σαββατισμός (4,9-10).[148] This place is already in existence, but about its origin *qua* κατάπαυσις this passage says nothing explicit.[149]

2.1.5. *Exposition of 4,1-11*

2.1.5.1. Introduction

From 3,7 to 3,19 our passage focuses on the warning value of Ψ 94 [95], stressing in 3,16-19 the response to God's word which had led to the demise of the "fathers." With 4,1-11 the attention turns directly to our topic, the κατάπαυσις itself, and thus it is necessary to follow with some care the train of thought. Unfortunately, this is not a simple task. We find here a certain lack of clarity in the way Gen 2 and Ψ 94 [95] are juxtaposed in the

---

[148] To the extent that the κατάπαυσις and σαββατισμός are distinct as we have just described, there is a limit to the "unhistorisch allegorisierend" (Braun, 109; Gräßer, 1:211 n. 76) of *Auctor*. In other ways also the divine and human rests are linked but not simply unified; see further below. Yet it is true that it is with the one κατάπαυσις that *Auctor* concerns himself, and distinguishing between "rests" in this passage as is sometimes done quickly becomes pedantic (cf. W.C. Kaiser 1985, 170).

[149] Though believers have present access to the heavenly world it is not the heavenly world *qua* κατάπαυσις; infra, 309f. There is a murkiness about the origin and present existence or status of the resting place as such. There is also ambiguity as to the time when OT believers entered or will enter it. For Hofius' clarification of the latter point, cf. Hofius, 57, 181 n. 359. He argues that their spirits entered an intermediate state until the resurrection, which follows the judgment of the world and the revelation of the unshakeable kingdom. Cf. Bruce, 110.

argument; 4,3 in particular is opaque, and the following verses are equally difficult. Of 4,1ff. Westcott wrote that "this main thought is somewhat perplexed and finally incomplete."[150] Attridge likewise observes that "the thought of this midrash on Ps 95 does not progress in a simple linear fashion, but circularly."[151] It seems best to assume that *Auctor* is covering at least some familiar ground and that what he writes here is geared less to the needs of a discursive argument for a new idea than to the needs of an urgent and impassioned exhortation.

One could argue from Scripture itself (e.g. Num 14,24.30f.38; Josh 21-23; 2Kgdms 7; 3Kgdms 8; etc.) that God's promise of entrance into Canaan (κατάπαυσις) had not been rescinded with the rebellion of the "fathers"; thus the idea that a promise "remains"[152] might conceivably have been arrived at in some such inductive manner.[153] Yet *Auctor*'s treatment of Joshua's rest in 4,8 appears rather to disjoin the matter of the promise and entrance into God's resting place from the historical events surrounding the eventual conquest of Canaan, and his own expression of the continuance of the promise is more indebted to cosmological and eschatological pre-commitments stemming from his Christology. He finds in the wording of

---

[150] Westcott, 92.

[151] Attridge, 124; Ellingworth, 237, also alludes to the "typically cyclic nature of the argument," and Wilson, 80, labels the argument of vv. 3-5 as "tortuous and involved." For his part Calvin, 95, comments dryly that "the chief difficulty of this passage arises from this, that it is perverted by many."

[152] The idea that something "remains" is stated first in 4,1, repeated in v. 6, and then stated again in v. 9. It is also assumed when it is said ἐσμεν εὐηγγελισμένοι καθάπερ κἀκεῖνοι (4,2), which is alluded to again in v. 6, and it underlies v. 3a (cf. v. 11). Both καταλείπω (4,1; 11,27) and ἀπολείπω (4,6.9; cf. 10,26) can be rendered intelligibly in English as "remain." By way of distinguishing nuance, Westcott, 93, remarks that "ἀπολείπεσθαι is used from the point of sight of those who have gone away; καταλείπεσθαι of that which retains its original position"; similarly, Louw-Nida, 1:159, 164. The sense of καταλειπομένης in 4,1 is "to be yet outstanding [i.e., the promise]" (cf. Bauer-Aland, 840f.). Ἀπολείπεται in v. 6 has the sense of "it is certain [some will enter it]", and in v. 9, "it [the σαββατισμός] is yet coming" (Bauer-Aland, 189). It is important, moreover, to recognize that the statements of 4,1, v. 6, and v. 9 are functionally distinct; each statement must therefore be interpreted on its own and not simply taken synonymously. Finally, neither 4,1 nor 4,6 argue that an entrance remains *because of* the failure of the "fathers" to enter; rightly, Riggenbach, 103 n. 72; Delitzsch, 1:187; Hofius, 178 n. 329, 179 n. 340; it remains *in spite of*. This is also to reject the variation on this proposal which builds on the local idea by suggesting that the continuing availability is due to *room* having been left by virtue of the "fathers" absence (e.g. Braun, 111; Ellingworth, 74, 237, 244, 250). This is an unwarranted inference from the local idea, and it is difficult to see where such an argument is formulated. The order of the clauses in v. 6a-b tells against all such proposals, even if these clauses are not intended to be in strict logical order; cf. further Rissi, 19; Gräßer, 1:211 n. 81, and our own comments below.

[153] Lane, 1:97f.; cf. also Vanhoye 1968, 23.

the psalm testimony to the fact that the OT already anticipated this reality and event (4,7f.).[154]

2.1.5.2. Exposition of 4,1-11

Considered broadly, 4,1-11 falls into three main parts:[155] (1) vv. 1-2 (which can divided into v. 1; v. 2); (2) vv. 3-10 (which divides into v. 3a; vv. 3b-5; vv. 6-8; vv. 9-10); (3) v. 11.

Vv. 1-2 are transitional, summing up and driving home the argument of the foregoing verses, and raising indirectly the theme of the following division.[156] As a warning, they stand in parallel with v. 11. Structurally, vv. 1-2 follow a chiastic pattern, with v. 2c (beginning with ἀλλά) forming the complement to the warning of v. 1. In between is the premise, and the

---

[154] This is *Auctor*'s general approach to the OT, as is well put by Caird, 44-51.

[155] G. Guthrie, 67, 79, includes 4,1-2 as the concluding exhortation to 3,7-19. Nonetheless, his analyses of a "cohesion shift" at 4,2-3 and an *inclusio* in 4,3 and 11 are not very convincing; 4,1-2 and 11 form a more likely *inclusio* (Lane, 1:95). Elsewhere, 106 n. 27, 144, Guthrie categorizes 4,1-2 as transitional (he recognizes a "'median-level' cohesion shift" at 3,19-4,1), and this may be truer to the argument. Vanhoye 1963, 96f., marks inclusions at 4,1-5 and 4,6-11 (each with a quotation at the center) but the resulting impression of two discrete blocks of thought may be misleading.

[156] The genitive absolute καταλειπομένης ἐπαγγελίας should be taken as a motive for v. 1 which is grounded in the following rather than inferred from the fact that the "fathers" did not enter (rightly, Delitzsch, 1:187; Hofius, 179 n. 340); in view of 3,13 the syntax should probably be construed temporally ("*while* a promise remains..."; co-temporally with the "fearing"); less probably as a condition, "since" (cf. v. 6). The phrase, εἰσελθεῖν εἰς τὴν κατάπαυσιν αὐτοῦ, stands in apposition to "promise" (*pace* Wilckens 1972, 596 n. 19, who suggests taking it with ὑστερηκέναι); the promise is not the κατάπαυσις, but *entrance* into the κατάπαυσις. Ὑστερέω is used here in the sense of "to miss/be excluded" (Bauer-Aland, 1692; Hofius, 220 n. 904; *contra* Gräßer, 1:202; 1965, 107f.). Δοκέω should not be taken positively as "think," thus not as follows: "let us fear lest anyone should think he has come too late..."; the use of φοβηθῶμεν favors taking this as a warning rather than an encouragement (cf. Delitzsch, 1:185, and Braun, 101, who note that the phrasing does not favor taking this as an encouragement; *contra* Spicq, 2:80; Montefiore, 81f.). Δοκέω may rather be taken forensically as "be found/judged"; cf. Moffatt, 50; Michel, 191; Attridge, 124; Gräßer, 1:201f.; Weiss, 275. Alternatively, the sense may be the more common "seem," which can be taken either as a "stylistic softening" of the statement (so Ellingworth, 239f.; as in Bauer-Aland, 406) or, conversely, as an intensification, inasmuch as even "the mere appearance of failure...is a thing to be earnestly dreaded" (Westcott, 93); Delitzsch, 1:186, is probably correct in thinking that there is both a softening and intensification. Hofius, 217 n. 849, 138, understands δοκέω forensically and takes this as a reference to the final judgment, noting the perfect tense of ὑστερηκέναι. Nonetheless, the time frame suggested by the participle ("while") might favor taking δοκέω as "seems." This verse and v. 11 both contemplate a "fall" which can take place in the present but which has ultimate consequences (6,6). The use of the perfect ὑστερηκέναι is anticipatory; "...lest any of you should seem (now) to be those who will have missed it." *Pace* Darnell, 227f., v. 1 does not suggest that the believers should already have entered God's κατάπαυσις.

perfect passive participle in v. 2a (εὐηγγελισμένοι) no doubt seeks to express the similarity of the situations beyond the mere fact of having received the same[157] promise: we find ourselves, as they did, *living in the situation of having received* the promise. It is this thought that will be the primary focus in vv. 3-10, as the nature and content of this promise, and thus its eschatological orientation, is brought to light with the help of Gen 2,2. Historically, the scope of these verses is very broad: the promise remains for us, it was heard but not believed by the wilderness generation, and it was received in faith by those that preceded them.[158]

The ἀλλά clause of v. 2 expresses the thought, contrary to expectation,[159] that *hearing* God's promise does not guarantee benefiting from it, no matter the degree of involvement one has in the blessings worked by God on behalf of those who do believe (cf. 6,4f.; 3,16-19). Yet the thought is not expressed as theory. Rather, it is expressed in terms of historical communities and their relations: we stand in parallel with that ancient community, and they failed not merely because they did not believe but more exactly because they did not unite[160] in faith with those who listened (believingly[161]).[162] The

---

[157] The verb εὐαγγελίζομαι probably means "receive the promise" here (see below, § 2.1.5.3.2), yet we may doubt that *Auctor* was unaware of the technical use of this verb and its cognate in Christian preaching. He is probably doing all he can to stress that there is one promise that cuts across the generations.

[158] It would be possible to understand τοῖς ἀκούσασιν as a veiled allusion to Joshua and Caleb (e.g. Lane, 1:98; Ellingworth, 243), but there does not seem to be an interest in Joshua and Caleb as exceptions to the rebellion at any point in this passage (note πάντες in 3,16); Joshua is mentioned in 4,8 to emphasize that he did *not* "enter the κατάπαυσις." V. 3a (note the γάρ) combined with the assumption behind v. 8 (see below) suggests that τοῖς ἀκούσασιν are probably firstly the Patriarchs (ch. 11) but that this group also includes the new covenant believers (rightly, Attridge, 126). The fact that the participle is in the aorist tense is not a problem; *pace* Delitzsch, 1:190.

[159] I was formerly inclined to regard this as a simple contrast, with the assumed counterpart to the ἀλλά clause affirming that the word is profiting those who hear in faith. For the difference in categorization, see Beekman-Callow, 296, 305f. In this case, the statement of v. 2c is contrary to the expectation of some of *Auctor*'s readers.

[160] For this translation of συγκεράννυμι, cf. Spicq, 2:81; Attridge, 126 n. 45 (with examples).

[161] This use of ἀκούω in the deeper sense of "listen" is common enough (cf. Jn 5,24; 6,45.60; 8,43.47; 10,16; 1Tim 6,16; Acts 4,19), and its proximity to ἀκοή is not a difficulty.

[162] Textual and interpretational problems have fed off of each other to produce a myriad of possibilities for understanding 4,2c. The diverse and early testimonies to it favor the reading συγκεκερασμένους (with $\mathfrak{P}^{13vid.46}$ A B C D* Ψ 0243. 0278. 33. 81. 1739. 2464. *pc* a t v vg[st.ww] sy[h] sa[mss]; so Attridge, 125f.; Lane, 1:93 n. h; Weiss, 278 n. 88; Ellingworth, 242, with further references for and against; cf. B. Metzger, 665). The reading τοῖς ἀκούσασιν is generally considered original (cf. variants in NA[27]). The difficulty of the thought of this reading, in turn, best explains the other variants (B. Metzger, 665; Weiss, 278 n. 88), which have themselves called forth their own groups of

communal aspect of the author's argument is thus assumed, even as it cuts across history (cf. 11,39-12,1). It is not merely contemporaries who share a corporate interest in "watching" (3,12) and persevering together. As a community we stand (or fall) with those who went before.

Vv. 3-10 can be divided, as we have said, into four units. It is in this section that the path of *Auctor*'s argument is easily lost with its jumps and circles, yet it is apparent that there is indeed a line leading from v. 3 to vv. 9f. In anticipation of the following analysis we may suggest the following metaphorical outline of the passage: engagement (v. 3a); marriage (vv. 3b-5); consummation (vv. 6-8); child (vv. 9-10).

Engagement (3a). V. 3a states with surprising directness the hope that we who believe will[163] enter. This statement is also transitional. The author has already affirmed that the promise remains and that we have received the promise; he is now going to go on to develop the nature and content of the promise he has in mind. Yet once again he is not content to leave this in theoretical terms: for "we" will enter. Following a pattern not unlike 6,9 (cf. 10,39) the strong warning of vv. 1f. is now succeeded by an equally strong affirmation of hope, and the explanatory γάρ links "us" with "those who listened (believingly)." Further, the use of συγκεκερασμένους in v. 2, as we have seen, has introduced the idea of an essential link between the generations of believers in this matter of entering the κατάπαυσις. The assumed thought is thus that only together with us will the believing heroes of the past be entering God's resting place. The idea of the *promise* that cuts across generations and finds its fulfilment only in the Heir of all things, an idea that *Auctor* will develop further in the rest of the book, is making its presence felt here with the first use of the terminology.[164]

At the same time, the emphasis in 4,3a is not on the contrast with the wilderness generation, but on faith as the condition to entrance. The "we" is limited by the participle (οἱ πιστεύσαντες). In very pastoral fashion, 4,3a tactfully *warns* the readers -- having received the promise -- of the *condition of entrance* in the form of a positive affirmation.[165]

The effect of 4,3a is an even more emphatic affirmation than in the preceding verses that this is a matter that concerns the present community. The condition of faith remains in place, but entrance is no longer only potentially theirs in the promise. It is stated as if it were fact. As vividly and realistically as possible, *Auctor* intends to usher his readers into the

---

interpretational possibilities (cf. Hughes, 157 n. 62; Bruce, 103 n. 4; Attridge, 125f.; Ellingworth, 242f.) and so on.

[163] On the use of the present tense in v. 3a, see below, § 2.1.6.

[164] See below, esp. §§ 2.1.5.3.2-4.

[165] Cf. Hofius, 180 n. 353; Ellingworth, 246; Weiss, 255, 279f. Notice that the contrast of v. 2 is mirrored in v. 3a-b.

κατάπαυσις of which the promise speaks (cf. 12,22ff.). This may in part explain the economy of details in vv. 3-5. *Auctor* is after a *vision* and the impact of the image, and so he avoids a surplus of explanation. It may even be that he intends to surprise his readers in v. 3, seen in that he has not given any indication to this point that anything more than nationalistic hopes surrounding the land are in view.

Marriage (3b-5). The marriage of the two key OT passages is not so much justified in vv. 3b-5 as it is celebrated. They are joined, but we are left puzzling over the significance of the union. The formal symmetry of these verses is in contrast to the seeming incongruity of their statements. Looked at broadly there is an orderly chiastic pattern in the arrangement of the OT passages:

Ψ 94; oath prohibiting entrance (3b)
   Gen 2; connection to creation καταπαύω (3c)
   Gen 2; connection to creation καταπαύω (4)
Ψ 94; oath prohibiting entrance (5)

Thus 4,3b-5 functions as a bridge from 4,3a to 4,6. As a block it is connected to 4,3a by the introductory καθὼς εἴρηκεν announcing that herein is an elaboration on the proposition in 3a. This impression is reinforced by v. 6, which seems to begin in parallel with v. 3a. Yet, beyond the fact that these two OT passages make a surprising couple,[166] the *wording* of Ψ 94,11 [95,11] seems less appropriate when it is cited in v. 3b, and the allusion to Genesis in v. 3c uses but one word of Gen 2,2 ("works") while passing over the verbal link of κατάπαυσις-καταπαύω. The argument of v. 3 is not transparent. Vv. 4-5 are ostensibly an explanation, but do little more than set the OT passages in parallel.

It is best to admit from the start that in 3b-5 we encounter less of a strict logic than an allusive juxtapositioning of passages, and that the exposition begun in 4,3b does not end until the climax in 4,9f. It is methodologically unsound, therefore, to attempt to ferret *Auctor*'s meaning out of vv. 3-5 in isolation. Instead, we will make a few observations and then pass on to *Auctor*'s further development of thought in vv. 6ff.

Καίτοι in 4,3c tells us that the whole of 3b-c is a single thought.[167] Thus the *prima facie* sense of the quotation (4,3b) is no longer in view. This combined with the attachment back to 4,3a and the flow of thought from here to v. 11 tells us that Ψ 94,11 [95,11] is now of interest for its *positive* value. *Auctor* is no longer concerned to explain or otherwise dwell on *their*

---

[166] At this point we will simply deal with how Gen 2,2 is used, and reserve for later the attempt to account for the connection of these two passages; cf. below, 349ff.

[167] We follow the punctuation of UBS[4]; see the alternatives there and discussion in Ellingworth, 245

failure as in 3,16-19, but rather to draw out the possibility for *us* to which Ψ 94 [95] points.[168] Thus it is apparent that the argument of 4,3b-c is not that the "fathers" failed in spite of the fact that the κατάπαυσις already existed, or that the κατάπαυσις had to be in existence in heaven in order for it to have been a bonafide offer. The intent is more exactly to throw the wraps off the true subject matter with a view to the development in vv. 6ff. It is to show that "my resting place" is the one associated with God's primordial Sabbath. The oath of Ψ 94,11 [95,11] is turned inside out, so that its positive assumption is the main concern.

Τῶν ἔργων (4,3c; missing "all") and τῆς ἑβδόμης (4,4a; missing "day")[169] are *both* but fragmentary allusions to elements of the Genesis quotation, already suggesting their rhetorical function as transitions to the quote. The quote itself then begins with what is in reality the key verb, καταπαύω (4,4b). This brings to light a more intricate chiastic structure (4,3c-4) between the two citations of Ψ 94,11 [95,11] and places the key idea of God's creation rest at the very center:

A) κατάπαυσίν μου (3b)
  B) works (3c)
    C) seventh day (4a)
we will enter καθὼς εἴρηκεν   D) κατέπαυσεν ὁ θεός (4bα)   (for the idea, cf. 9-10)
    C') seventh day (4bβ)
  B') works (4bγ)
A') κατάπαυσίν μου (5)

The idea of "works" is taken up again in v. 10, but the idea of the number "seven" drops out entirely.[170] This is anticipated already in vv. 3-5. It was noted above that in 3b-5 the OT passages are arranged chiastically as follows: Ψ 94-Gen 2, Gen 2-Ψ 94. This broad chiastic structure hinges on the γάρ of 4,4a. Yet that same γάρ breaks the rhythm of the more intricate chiasmus (it intrudes between elements B and C immediately above). Thus, the γάρ tells us that 4,3b-c is a self-contained thought that is explained to some extent by vv. 4-5. Yet that explanation all but ignores the break suggested by the γάρ as it fairly glides in to the main theme -- rest -- and then back again to the catchword, "works," finally settling on the leading

---

[168] Ellingworth, 245; Lane, 1:99; Gräßer, 1:208. For this reason καίτοι should be understood in a positive sense, such as "and yet"; cf. BDF § 425,1; 450,3. This does not mean, however, that *Auctor* is not concerned to continue the warning through these verses.

[169] The omission of "day" in the expression is not exceptional; cf. Philo, *VitaMos* II,209.215.263; MHT, 3:17. This does not, however, exclude the relevance of our present observations.

[170] Cf. only 11,30, which refers to the fact that Jericho was encircled seven days (Josh 6). Our comments here apply to the idea of the number seven, and not to the idea of the "day."

quote (Ψ 94 [95]). Rather than beginning anew 4,4a simply extends the chiasmus which was begun in 4,3c. Thus, the idea of "works" is given some emphasis by virtue of its place in 4,3c, while the number seven has only a rhetorical function. This already cuts the ground from beneath suggestions that a more significant use of ἑβδόμη is intended here.

At first sight it is surprising that it is "work" rather than "rest" which is referred to in 4,3c. Yet the idea of "work" is not an entirely incidental element of the whole, as 4,10 shows. In typical manner this idea is quietly announced in advance, although in such a way that the immediate flow of thought is uninterrupted. Secondly, some sort of transition was needed for this dramatic movement from Ψ 94 [95] to Gen 2, and we have just seen the intricate chiastic pattern which leads into Gen 2 and then back out to Ψ 94 [95]; the wording of Gen 2,2 would suggest that the chiastic structure begins with "works." Moreover, the attempt to capture within a single and relatively smooth sentence (4,3b-c) the wording of Ψ 94,11 [95,11] with an enhanced meaning, is effectively accomplished through just such a subtle allusion as this. The way is then prepared for the explicit juxtapositioning of the two passages in full (4,4f.) without superfluous repetition. This is probably more a matter of reflex than deliberation, but carefully observing these things may help us to avoid misguided speculation.[171]

The phrase, ἀπὸ καταβολῆς κόσμου,[172] continues the transition to the citation by locating the "works" in literary terms, but also by rolling back the historical horizons well beyond Moses. This understanding of the κατάπαυσις was assumed in vv. 1-2, but here it very openly takes on trans-cosmic and trans-epochal scope. Auctor evidently desired to emphasize the temporal element, for just as here the time frame is extended from Moses back so in vv. 7f. it will be extended forward (μετὰ τοσοῦτον χρόνον; περὶ ἄλλης ἐλάλει μετὰ ταῦτα ἡμέρας). The psalm points us to God's Sabbath rest which began on the seventh day and continues even now, and thus to something which carried a significance beyond the immediate circumstances of the desert generation. From the lead-in (4,3a) the point is clearly that it will not remain unattained,[173] but this is left for us to infer at this point.

---

[171] Recognizing among the other points that the reference to "works" in 4,3c is in part in anticipation of 4,10 means that v. 10 tells us *how* the idea of "works" is important! It is not a reference to heavenly creations ("city," κατάπαυσις, etc.) but the character of the eschatological age, a rest from "works" which paves the way for a σαββατισμός.

[172] Here ἀπό has the temporal meaning, "since"; the phrase (9,26; Mt 13,35; Lk 11,50) refers to the conclusion of the work of creation; cf. Hofius 1991, 256. As we might have gathered from 4,4 in any case, the "rest" of God is not an attribute or his eternal state prior to creation.

[173] Gräßer, 1:208.

Consummation (6-8). Two general observations should help to orient our analysis of this unit. First, apart from the verb καταπαύω, which is used in direct connection with Joshua rather than the Sabbath, only the word ἡμέρα in Gen 2,2 finds a parallel in vv. 6-8. Yet the use of the pronoun in v. 6 (αὐτήν) points us back to the reality of vv. 3-5 for its antecedent and it is clear that this same *Heilsgut* is in mind throughout this unit, just as it had been in vv. 1-2. Glancing ahead to vv. 9f. it is evident that even the language of the two OT passages has merged in *Auctor*'s conception, and we should be prepared to find the same in vv. 6-8. Second, vv. 6-8 give the impression of a circular argument: it remains for some to enter, therefore he appointed another day (vv. 6f.); but, he appointed another day, therefore it remains for some to enter (v. 8). In fact, the author is not attempting to argue in linear fashion in these verses. Instead he uses two perspectives and exploits each paraenetically: first the perspective of David (vv. 6f.), then his own (v. 8). It is therefore not necessary to discuss the verses in order. Our approach to the understanding of this unit will be first to consider the use of the word ἡμέρα and then v. 8, as these shed light on the whole passage, before returning to vv. 6f.

As a one word appellation for the entire epoch between the advents of Jesus the idea of the ἡμέρα in v. 7 appears to derive from the contrast between τὴν ἡμέραν τοῦ πειρασμοῦ and σήμερον within Ψ 94 [95]. It is a variation on σήμερον which *Auctor* has already exploited in a different manner (cf. 3,13). Yet this word's link with Gen 2,2 may not be altogether broken; indeed, that link was probably assumed in the earlier usages. When reading 4,7 it is difficult not to recall the programmatic passage, ἐπ' ἐσχάτου τῶν **ἡμερῶν** τούτων ἐλάλησεν ἡμῖν ἐν υἱῷ, ὃν ἔθηκεν κληρονόμον πάντων, δι' οὗ καὶ ἐποίησεν τοὺς αἰῶνας (1,2).[174] The word of God, creation, the last days ("today"), and the inheritance (see below) are all common denominators. If the exact thought pattern is not clear, the clustering of ideas is unmistakable; a dim light is shed on the path which led from Ψ 94 [95] to Gen 2, and the key appears to be Christology.[175]

Interestingly, then, we read in 9,26 that if Jesus' sacrifice had been like the Levitical priests' it would have had to have been repeated ἀπὸ καταβολῆς κόσμου, but as it is he appeared once for all ἐπὶ συντελείᾳ τῶν

---

[174] The phrase, ἐν Δαυίδ, very likely recalls ἐν τοῖς προφήταις in 1,1; Attridge, 130; Weiss, 281 n. 100. The "day" seems to refer in this passage to the present epoch, which David anticipated. *Auctor* does not consider the application of the psalm to David and his contemporaries.

[175] In 7,3 Jesus is, like Melchizedek, without ἀρχὴν ἡμερῶν; note the contrast between beginning and end in 7,3. Again, ch. 11 begins with protology and ends with eschatology. Note that of the three words shared by Ψ 94 [95] and Gen 2,2 -- rest, works, and day -- the first two are accentuated by *Auctor*; it would not be surprising if "day" was also accented in this way.

αἰώνων and will appear a second time[176] unto salvation for those expecting him.[177] As in 4,1-11, protology and eschatology are joined. The use of the same phrase in 4,3 and 9,26 may therefore betray an interest of *Auctor*: the idea that the original order must be restored before the ultimate σαββατισμός can be celebrated by humankind.[178] What is manifest is that themes and thought patterns from elsewhere in this book are leaving their impress here.[179]

The other word from Gen 2,2 that is found in this section, the verb καταπαύω, occurs in v. 8 and an examination of this verse also sheds a broader light on the passage. The logic of v. 8 is more precisely: another day was later appointed, therefore Joshua did not give them rest.[180] This looks like a *non sequitur*. It might be reasonable to conclude that the setting of another day shows that the rest remains to be entered, but not necessarily that Joshua did not give them rest. The OT itself refutes such an idea. The statement rather assumes the meaning of κατάπαυσις brought to light in vv. 3-5, and thus it is that entrance into *this* κατάπαυσις has never been realized; it remains outstanding.[181] It is evident, then, that vv. 9f. follow

---

[176] In 10,25 the ἡμέρα is more narrowly the future "day" which is drawing near; this usage focuses on the theme of judgment and probably draws on an idea expressed in a number of OT passages; e.g. (all references to the ET) Amos 5,18-20; 8,9-14; Isa 2,12-22; 24,21-23; Zeph 1,14-18; Joel 1,15; 3,14; Zech 14,1; in the NT cf. 1Thes 5,4; 1Cor 3,13; Attridge, 291.

[177] Cf. also 12,24.

[178] Peterson 1992, 225 (Peterson makes no reference to this phrase as such); Westcott, 99.

[179] Cf. the similar contrast in 8,8-10 (10,16; LXX Jer 38,31ff. [31,31ff.]); there also new "days" are anticipated "after those days" which will not be like the earlier "day." There (8,13) the "new" covenant testifies to the obsolescence of the "first"; cf. 4,8.

[180] The pronoun, αὐτούς, refers to the *second* generation. It would seem possible to understand the logic of v. 8 either as protasis, therefore apodosis, or as apodosis, therefore protasis. The latter is most likely here, however, and this is how several other unreal conditions seem to function in Hebrews (cf. 7,11; 8,4.7; 9,26 [cf. Lane, 2:233 n. kk]; 10,2; 11,15; in general, BDF § 360; Westcott, 111-114). As to the meaning of καταπαύω in v. 8, it could be simply and concretely, "bring to a place of rest" (Bauer-Aland, 845; Hofius 1991a, 266; citing LXX Ex 33,14 as a parallel), but the verb could also be used as it is in v. 10 where we have the conflation of Ψ 94 [95] and Gen 2. The difference is not great, since the latter usage assumes that this rest from works takes place *in* the κατάπαυσις, and thus v. 8 amounts to a denial that Joshua brought them into God's resting place. The latter usage is probably to be favored.

[181] Even this does not necessarily follow, but we will return to that below, 302f. We may add that in a superficial sense a number of factors or a combination thereof could have given impetus to the claim of v. 8. For instance, awareness of the general historical fact that Joshua's campaign had resulted in "rest" required a response, indeed the specific statement of Num 14,31 could have been a direct cause. Again, the emphatic "today" of the psalm invited a comparison with earlier periods and the figure of Joshua was on the mid-point between Moses and David. It is not unlikely that such considerations played together to raise the issue of Joshua in the first place. Our concern, however, has been

naturally on from v. 8, both as a conclusion[182] and -- in the use of the word σαββατισμός -- as an expression of the assumption on which v. 8 was founded. Taken together vv. 8-10 explain at least part of what we were meant to infer from 4,3a-5. Whatever might be assumed with regard to the origin and heavenly existence of the κατάπαυσις, the thrust of the midrash in vv. 3-5 is toward establishing and depicting entrance into the κατάπαυσις as an *eschatological* event.

It is not clear that v. 8 attaches (γάρ) to one particular thought in the preceding context.[183] It may be best construed as an extension which answers a possible question about Joshua's entrance but which more importantly reinforces the notion that Ψ 94 [95] speaks of something altogether beyond the historical horizon of Joshua and David. It addresses a "promise" which remains unrealized as long as the psalm holds forth its "today." We can readily infer from v. 8 that even if the "fathers" had entered Canaan in obedience this would not have been an entrance (even partially) into "God's resting place." V. 8 also tends to corroborate (though this is not *Auctor*'s concern) that it was not the failure of the "fathers" at Kadesh to enter which is the reason that it "remains."[184] It is in this light that we should read v. 6.

V. 6 picks up where vv. 1-3a left off and yet gives a clear indication that the material in vv. 3b-5 was no side tracking excursus, but was making explicit what had been presupposed to that point. To be sure, the force of 3b-5 on its own is as emotive as it is logical, yet visual glimpses of the goal are just as important to the author's "word of exhortation" as is his argumentation (cf. 12,22ff., *passim*). Vv. 6ff. draw out the implications more clearly.

The οὖν in v. 6 is explained by the two conditional clauses. Adopting the perspective of David's day, the first conditional clause (6a) addresses itself to the reality formally introduced in vv. 3b-5 (αὐτήν = the very place where God's himself celebrates his Sabbath rest) and states that it is certain[185] that

---

with the substance of how Joshua's rest has been treated, and its actual role in the logic of the passage.

[182] The argument of v. 9 is accordingly not that the σαββατισμός remains because Joshua did not provide it, but that it remains because it was promised.

[183] The temporal indicator in v. 8 (μετὰ ταῦτα) recalls the subordinate clause of v. 7b (ἐν Δαυιδ λέγων μετὰ τοσοῦτον χρόνον), but v. 8 is hardly a reason or explanation of that clause alone.

[184] As Hofius, 178 n. 329, rightly comments with respect to v. 6. At present we are maintaining that for *Auctor* the entrance was *in principle* reserved for the future inasmuch as it was "promise."

[185] Thus is ἀπολείπεται to be understood here; cf. Bauer-Aland, 189 ("*es bleibt dabei, es ist sicher*"; BAGD, 94); Riggenbach, 103; Westcott, 96; Hofius, 55 (he explains this rendering as follows: "es steht mit Sicherheit zu erwarten"), 178 n. 327, with further references. Differently, Weiss, 280. In my judgment this rendering is justified by the

this same κατάπαυσις will be entered by people,[186] whatever the fate of the "fathers." The note of certainty that can be felt in 3a is thus resumed, though v. 6 is broader in scope. It was God's express intention that the κατάπαυσις where he holds his Sabbath celebration would be entered by humans and it can therefore be taken as certain that some will enter it. The basis of this claim is not firstly the eternal, heavenly character of the reality,[187] nor is it the failure of the wilderness generation to enter. It is the promise of God that had made this certain.[188]

Moreover, the "fathers," those who had received the *same* promise (πρότερον εὐαγγελισθέντες) at an earlier[189] time, did not enter through disobedience (v. 6b; cf. v. 2). Here is a direct response to the phrase, οἱ πιστεύσαντες, in v. 3a, and from there back to the warning in vv. 1f. But since this κατάπαυσις will be entered and yet *they* failed due to disobedience, God not only set another day (v. 7a) but in the same psalm added a strong warning against following their example (v. 7cβ; cf. vv. 1.11).[190]

That God would "again appoint a day" for entrance into the place of his Sabbath celebration was, on these premises, certain. It assumes a principle *Auctor* will state later, the inviolability of God's promise (6,17ff.), and probably also assumes the sort of thinking Paul uses in Rom 3,3f., namely,

---

insight that for *Auctor* the "entrance" ultimately depends on the inviolable promise of God (thus 6b makes a direct reference to the promise), and is therefore an eschatological event: participation in the Great Salvation, the unshakeable kingdom. Thus, "entrance" does not continue to be a possibility merely because of a failure of previous generations to get there first. See further below, 294f., 301-303.

[186] In v. 6a, τινάς has this general sense; rightly, Riggenbach, 103; Hofius, 178 n. 328. Certainly it is true that for *Auctor* only believers *will* enter (Braun, 111; Gräßer, 1:212 n. 90), but since this is made explicit in v. 6b it would be redundant in 6a. Michel, 195, sees in this use of τινάς a tactful suggestion that though the promise goes to the people of God, some of them are in question; cf. Weiss, 280. Zimmermann, 141, Braun, 111, and Gräßer, 1:212 n. 90, disagree with this distinction between individuals and the whole people here and interpret v. 6a simply as a statement that the promise has not yet found fulfilment.

[187] *Pace* Attridge, 130. At no point does *Auctor* base the continuance of the promise on the metaphysical character of the resting place (cf. e.g. v. 7).

[188] In vv. 6-8 the fact that he appoints another day is based on the fact and *demonstrates* that the promise continues; it is not the *basis* for the continuation of the promise.

[189] As viewed from David's time.

[190] The theme of "disobedience" did not drop out of vv. 3b-5; rather, it was so firmly established as the complement to the oath in 3,16-19 that it could be assumed in 4,3b and 5. The idea of "disobedience" should also be supplied in v. 7a-b; "in view of their disobedience he again set another day (and added to it a warning), just as was said before..." The logic of vv. 6b-7 is *not:* since the "fathers" did not enter, therefore it remains outstanding; rightly, Hofius, 178 n. 329. The order of the clauses in v. 6a-b tells against this, and it also misses that v. 6b functions as a response to 4,3a and is responded to in v. 7cβ.

that although we are unfaithful God is faithful.[191] It is not a new promise he gives, but a testimony to the fact that "a promise remains" (4,1),[192] and thus that those who believe are yet to enter (4,3a). It is a "day, 'today,'" which God appointed, an idea which *Auctor* has absorbed unapologetically into his eschatological framework, a "day" when God's φωνή has been heard and he has spoken ἐν υἱῷ, ὃν ἔθηκεν κληρονόμον πάντων, δι' οὗ καὶ ἐποίησεν τοὺς αἰῶνας (1,2). That it is appointed "after so much time"[193] is exploited to subtly suggest the point driven home in v. 8, i.e. that the psalm refers to a κατάπαυσις which has not yet been entered, a promise that continues in force and that has not yet been fulfilled.

Child (9-10). Taken together, Gen 2 and Ψ 94 [95] explicate for *Auctor* both the content of the promise and its continuing force, thus its eschatological orientation. The argument is summed up in both its logical and emotive senses in vv. 9f. A *Sabbath* celebration (σαββατισμός)[194] -- indeed, God's Sabbath celebration -- remains for the people of God. This celebratory *activity* will be possible inasmuch as those who enter God's resting place (Ψ 94 [95]) will rest from their works just as God rested from his own works (Gen 2). These verses testify to how absolutely fused Gen 2 and Ψ 94 [95] are, and they also show that *Auctor* is concerned not only with God's resting place, but with the character or quality of life within the κατάπαυσις.[195]

The phrase, τῷ λαῷ τοῦ θεοῦ, would appear to embrace God's people without distinction of "old" and "new." That the Sabbath celebration "remains" bespeaks an event to be realized by the whole people at a future time. This corporate element is interwoven through the whole argument, albeit in different ways.[196] Below we will note it again in relation to 4,2.8, and there it assumes that the OT believers would not "enter" before us. The

---

[191] Cf. also 10,23; 11,11; Rom 9,6.16; 11,29; Westcott, 92, 96; Hofius, 56. Weiss, 277, singles this out as a mark of apocalyptic; cf. 2Bar 21,25.

[192] Rightly, Hofius, 179 n. 340.

[193] This span of time is anticipated in the use of πρότερον and πάλιν (vv. 6f.). The reference to David, which doubtless assumes authorship, at this point serves to locate the psalm chronologically; it may also recall 1,1.

[194] Supra, 276f.

[195] In this sense, the repeated insistence by exegetes (usually against Hofius) that the "rest" is both a place and a state is justified. It must only be insisted *with* Hofius that this does not release us from consistently translating the noun κατάπαυσις as a local idea, including 4,10.

[196] Hofius, 132f., rightly stresses that with the emphasis on "some" (3,12f.; 4,1.11) *Auctor* expresses the belief that the apostasy of a few draws in its train the apostasy of the whole community as the events of Num 14 illustrated so poignantly. This idea recurs in 12,15, where the "bitter root" (LXX Deut 29,17) is seen to be a threat to the whole community. Käsemann, 21, and Gräßer, 1:202f., misrepresent the extent of the individualism here.

corporate element also surfaces in the obvious concern with mutual exhortation (3,12f.; 4,1.11). "Making every effort to enter that resting place" (v. 11) is not merely a matter of securing one's own salvation, but also of working to strengthen the community "so that no one may fall (as they did in the desert) through such disobedience as theirs."

V. 10 serves to show how this σαββατισμός will be possible,[197] and in so doing returns to the idea of "works" which had been foreshadowed in v. 3. "Rest" implies a "rest from something," and the question is therefore, "From what?"[198] Both "travelling"[199] and "enemy threats" (persecution) spring to mind, and their metaphorical senses probably merge in life. The statement of 4,10, however, models the rest after the Sabbath of Gen 2,2; it is a "rest from works" (αὐτὸς κατέπαυσεν[200] ἀπὸ τῶν ἔργων[201] αὐτοῦ ὥσπερ ἀπὸ τῶν ἰδίων ὁ θεός). The nature of the "works" themselves is not considered, but rather the parallel (ὥσπερ) with the divine rest is stressed and the whole is subordinate to v. 9,[202] so that a more general understanding of the "works" seems most likely. What is noteworthy in this connection is the emphatic ἴδιος which, as a modification of Gen 2,2, quietly distances God's rest from that of believers. *Auctor* has conflated but not confused Ψ 94 [95] and Gen 2. Believers will enjoy a Sabbath celebration not by means of a mystical union with God or by sharing in God's nature, which is rest, but by themselves (emphatic αὐτός) resting from their works, just as God rested from *his* works.[203]

The basic paradigm of God's "rest from works" does not demand that "works" be construed positively, yet to take the "works" in an outright negative sense -- i.e., in some sense as "dead works"[204] -- introduces more

---

[197] *Not* how it can be called a Sabbath *rest*; cf. Hofius, 106-110. The σαββατισμός is not a quietistic ideal.

[198] On God's own rest, see further below, 321ff.

[199] On this idea, see further below, 310ff.

[200] The aorist -- taken over from Gen 2,2 -- can be taken as "proleptic" (Lane, 1:94 n. u; Zerwick, § 257) or timeless (Weiss, 283 n. 108; Ellingworth, 256; BDF § 333); *contra* Hagner, 51. The aorist participle in the same verse (εἰσελθών) signifies coincident action (MHT, 3:79f.; Ellingworth, 256).

[201] Cf. also Heb 1,10; 3,9; 4,3f. The plural form does not appear to be significant; cf. Ellingworth, 257.

[202] Westcott, 99.

[203] *Contra* Zimmermann, 141, who claims that the rest into which humans enter is God's rest, and the works from which they rest are *God's* works.

[204] Cf. 6,1; 9,14; on these passages see Ellingworth, 314f., 458f. Heb 6,1 may be wider in scope than 9,14, but neither refers to rites of the OT cultus. Buchanan, 74, takes the "works" specifically as "grumbling." Others understand some form of works righteousness; e.g., Calvin, 98f.; Bacchiocchi 1977, 67f.; Lincoln 1982, 213. Sometimes included here are liturgical acts prescribed by the OT (Hagner, 52, allows this), but this seems unlikely in view of the pronoun (ἀπὸ τῶν ἔργων **αὐτοῦ**). In general, the idea of works righteousness is justifiably dismissed by Attridge as "a homiletic interpretation of

dissonance than seems warranted. When the description takes its lead from God's own "works," the most natural understanding would be a less pejorative one. Yet to choose between "good works"[205] and "toils" (which would amount to "endurance through persecution" here) is difficult; once again, they probably overlap in life.[206] The idea of "toils" recalls the paradigm of escape from oppression in Egypt[207] and the hardships which precede entrance into the κατάπαυσις. This is reflected in the Christians' endurance through persecution, but then "endurance" assumes perseverance in *good works*. Additionally, it is hard to suppress a note of "completion" in v. 10 which derives from the function of the seventh day in the biblical account; the Sabbath celebration of believers is assumed to be yet future.

At this point it is natural for a NT parallel in Rev 14,13 to spring to mind, a passage which also shares wording with Mt 11,28-30:

Mt 11,28-30[208]	Rev 14,13[209]	Heb 4,10
δεῦτε πρός με πάντες οἱ **κοπιῶντες** καὶ πεφορτισμένοι, κἀγὼ **ἀναπαύσω** ὑμᾶς...καὶ εὑρήσετε **ἀνάπαυσιν** ταῖς ψυχαῖς ὑμῶν...	μακάριοι οἱ νεκροὶ οἱ ἐν κυρίῳ ἀποθνῄσκοντες ἀπ' ἄρτι. ναί, λέγει τὸ πνεῦμα, ἵνα **ἀναπαήσονται** ἐκ τῶν **κόπων** αὐτῶν· τὰ γὰρ <u>ἔργα αὐτῶν</u> ἀκολουθεῖ μετ' αὐτῶν	ὁ γὰρ εἰσελθὼν εἰς τὴν κατάπαυσιν αὐτοῦ καὶ αὐτὸς κατέπαυσεν ἀπὸ <u>τῶν ἔργων αὐτοῦ</u> ὥσπερ ἀπὸ τῶν ἰδίων ὁ θεός

Obviously the motif of an eschatological rest from labors was common currency in the early church,[210] and it had apparently received no firm cast;

Pauline categories that are not in evidence"; Attridge, 131 n. 110; cf. Braun, 115; Hagner, 52; Ellingworth, 257. Hegermann, 102 (followed by Gräßer, 1:221), rightly rejects the notion that this is a rest from the burden of wrongdoing.

[205] Cf. 10,24; 13,21; 6,10; e.g. Rissi, 20, 128. On this basis Rissi insists that the rest is only in the future, since we do not rest from such works in this life.

[206] Cf. (if I rightly understand them) Barrett, 371f.; Oberholtzer 1988, 194; Michel, 196; Bruce, 109; Attridge, 131; apparently, Weiss, 282 n. 107 (Weiss probably reads in too much of a dualistic perspective at this point). Hegermann, 103, seems to combine good works and endurance in the idea of the completion of the fruit of salvation (cf. Heb 12,4-11; 13,20f.) in the lives of believers. Gräßer, 1:221, cites Hegermann favorably but only partially. Attridge, 131 n. 109, cites as parallels in Philo, *QuodDeus* 12; *Fuga* 173; *Migr* 27. As parallels to rest from persecution he cites 4Ezra 7,96 and Rev 14,13 (cf. Heb 10,32-36; 12,4-11).

[207] Cf. Ex 5,5, where Pharaoh says, μὴ οὖν καταπαύσωμεν αὐτοὺς ἀπὸ τῶν ἔργων.

[208] Cf. Mt 12,43 with Rev 14,11.

[209] NA[27] cites Heb 11,40 in connection with Rev 6,11.

[210] We may recall here OdesSol 37,3f.; supra, 132f. *Contra* Braun, 115, who states in the terse style of his commentary, "nur hier [Heb 4,10] im NT des Menschen καταπαύειν ἀπὸ τῶν ἔργων αὐτοῦ." That in Rev 14,13 the rest is promised to martyrs is ultimately inconsequential as it has a general application and in view of Heb 11 *Auctor* would hardly have excluded martyrs. That in Heb 4,10 the "rest from works" is combined with God's rest is distinctive.

in each case the expression is distinctive. Rev 14,13 is directly concerned with the intermediate state (as a foretaste of the final rest),[211] it makes no reference to an OT passage, sabbatical imagery is extraneous, and the accent is on their works of righteousness/endurance which carry over into their reward. In general this corresponds well to the usage of the resting-place-idea which we observed to be widespread.[212] 4Ez 7,88-94 is a close parallel to Rev 14,13 and is also speaking of the intermediate state:[213]

> Now this is the order of those who have kept the ways of the Most High, when they shall be separated from their mortal body. During the time that they lived in it, they laboriously served the Most High, and withstood danger every hour, that they might keep the Law of the Lawgiver perfectly. Therefore this is the teaching concerning them: First of all, they shall see with great joy the glory of him who receives them, for they shall have rest in seven orders... The third order, they see the witness which he who formed them bears concerning them, that while they were alive they kept the Law which was given them in trust...

In contrast to Heb 4, no Scriptural passage is cited in either Rev 14 or 4Ez 7 since the idea of a post-mortem and eschatological rest or resting place is stock apocalyptic imagery. The labors of obedient service, which take in endurance through persecution, faithfulness to Christ (in the NT), and righteous deeds,[214] are brought to a close as the faithful individual enjoys rest and the fruit of his/her labors while the wicked have unrest and torment.[215] Though 2Thes 1,7 does not make explicit reference to a rest *from labors* it can be cited here as well since the context -- which is colored apocalyptically and which reminds of Rev 14[216] -- suggests the same idea:

---

[211] With justification, 14,13 is generally considered to be a description of the final state; 6,11 is anticipatory; e.g., Charles, 1:369. On the other hand, Ladd, 198, states that the "rest" of 14,13 "is the same rest promised the martyrs in 6,11." It seems to me, however, that 6,11 (which is not a promise) is less a matter of a *Heilsgut* than a command to "be still" and wait for the Lord's judgment; it can be both compared and contrasted with 4Ez 2,24. Though 14,13 probably is written with a view to the final state it is directly associated with deaths which take place prior to the end (doubtless those in the present age as well as during the Great Tribulation). I will therefore consider it a reference to the intermediate state, though it is understood that it anticipates the ultimate state.

[212] Supra, 106ff.

[213] This passage was quoted at length above, 108.

[214] Cf. Rev 14,12: Ὧδε ἡ ὑπομονὴ τῶν ἁγίων ἐστίν, οἱ τηροῦντες τὰς ἐντολὰς τοῦ θεοῦ καὶ τὴν πίστιν Ἰησοῦ.; also 2,2.19.23; 3,2.15; 22,12. Cf. Heb 3,6.14; 10,36.

[215] Cf. Rev 14,11 with 4Ez 7,36-38.76-87.93.99.

[216] I am referring to the more superficial similarities between 2Thes 1 and Rev 14, namely the focus on faithfulness and endurance, the contrast of judgment and rest, and the angelic agency in the judgment scene. The following points may be added: (1) Aus argues that Rev 12 and 2Thes 1 are both utilizing Isa 66,7-9 in connection with the idea of the "Messianic woes" (Aus is followed by Wanamaker, 224-226). Since the promise of rest in Rev 14 is contextually related to ch. 12 it appears that in both 2Thes 1 and Rev

We must always give thanks to God for you, brothers and sisters, as is right, because your faith is growing abundantly, and the love of everyone of you for one another is increasing. Therefore we ourselves boast of you among the churches of God for your steadfastness and faith during all your persecutions and the afflictions that you are enduring. This is evidence of the righteous judgment of God... For it is indeed just of God to repay with affliction those who afflict you, and to give relief [ἄνεσιν] to the afflicted as well as to us, when the Lord Jesus is revealed from heaven with his mighty angels in flaming fire, inflicting vengeance on those who do not obey the gospel of our Lord Jesus. These will suffer the punishment of eternal destruction, separated from the presence of the Lord and from the glory of his might, when he comes to be glorified by his saints and to be marvelled at on that day among all who have believed, because our testimony to you was believed. (2Thes 1,3-10)

Although the idea of rest is muted here in comparison with Rev 14 and 4Ez 7,[217] once again faithfulness, righteousness, and endurance in the face of persecution merge with an apocalyptic scene of judgment and reward.

With the last mentioned passage we appear to be some distance from the thought of Heb 4,10, and we must, moreover, be careful of too casually drawing parallels. At least what these passages in Rev, 4Ez, and 2Thes tell us is that the notion of rest as an eschatological reward for endurance and faithfulness was in the air, and particularly in Christian apocalyptic traditions.[218] True, Heb 4,10 does not say that "their works will follow after

---

14 the rest motif is used in a typical apocalyptic manner and (if Aus is right) in connection with a similar exegetical tradition concerning Isa 66; note then that also in 4Ez 7,26ff. the revelation of the place of rest is explicitly connected to the description of the messianic woes (cf. 7,26; 6,20-24; Stone 1989, 100). Further on we will note the significance of Isa 66 for Heb 3-4, but the usage there does not make reference to the "Messianic woes." (2) One can cite a second century parallel to 2Thes 1 in *AscenIs* 4,15: upon his second coming, the Lord "will bring rest to the pious who shall be found alive in the body in this world" (*NTApocr*², 2:609). This passage falls in one of the Christian sections of *AscenIs* (3,13-4,22), the so-called *Testament of Hezekiah*, which is thought by some to date from early II or late I A.D. (Trafton, 508; M.A. Knibb, in *OTP*, 2:149). *AscenIs* 4,1-22 bears strong parallels to both 2Thes 1 and Rev 13, and follows contextually on the Jewish tradition of Isaiah's martyrdom which is also preserved in Heb 11,37 (cf. *LivPro* [I A.D.] 1). This may evidence a traditional association of ideas. (3) Cf. also above, 138ff., on the reign-rest complex.

[217] Marshall 1983, 175, remarks that ἄνεσις is used here not for inactivity or as a reward, but simply as absence of suffering. Bultmann 1964, 367, compares ἄνεσις here with the eschatological use of the idea in Acts 3,20 (ἀνάψυξις) and in *2Clem* 5-6 (ἀνάπαυσις. To this he adds the strange comment: "found in Gnosticism but not in the NT"). The word ἄνεσις probably is semantically closer to ἀνάψυξις in Acts 3,20 (cf. Louw-Nida, 1:246), but Mt 11,28-30 also has an eschatological orientation and Bultmann overlooked Rev 14,13 which has a more similar context. The accent in 2Thes 1,7 is on *relief* from suffering (cf. 2Cor 2,13; 7,7; 8,13), but I hesitate to say that it is not a reward for obedience in view of Rev 14, 4Ez 7 (esp. 7,95f.), and *2Clem* 5-6; cf. Wanamaker, 225.

[218] 1Pet 4,14 might also be mentioned here: "If you are reviled for the name of Christ, you are blessed, because the Spirit of glory, which is the Spirit of God, is resting on you [ὅτι τὸ τῆς δόξης καὶ τὸ τοῦ θεοῦ πνεῦμα ἐφ' ὑμᾶς ἀναπαύεται]"; cf. Hensel-Brown, 257f. The expression recalls Isa 11,2 (cf. Num 11,25-26) and Mt 5,11; the

them," but the idea is not foreign to *Auctor*'s thought: οὐ γὰρ ἄδικος ὁ θεὸς ἐπιλαθέσθαι τοῦ ἔργου ὑμῶν καὶ τῆς ἀγάπης ἧς ἐνεδείξασθε εἰς τὸ ὄνομα αὐτοῦ, διακονήσαντες τοῖς ἁγίοις καὶ διακονοῦντες.[219] On balance it seems very likely that this thought underlies 4,10, but we must hasten to add that it is decidedly subordinate to the main point, viz, that ἀπολείπεται σαββατισμὸς τῷ λαῷ τοῦ θεοῦ. It is characteristic of *Auctor*'s thought that obedience and endurance are not rewarded by being recognized as such, but by the inheritance of the promises.[220]

Thus, as *Auctor* interprets it with reference to Gen 2,2, Ψ 94 [95] testifies to the fact that a promise -- namely, of entrance into God's κατάπαυσις where the people of God will enjoy a σαββατισμός -- remains outstanding. In view of the fact that this was the same promise held forth to the "fathers," and in view of their disastrous failure, it is incumbent upon us to "make every effort" to enter as long as it is called "today," so that "no one may fall through such disobedience as theirs." The warning is then driven yet deeper by a brief, almost poetic meditation on the word of God, which recalls not only the reference to listening to God's voice (3,7), but even the opening of the book itself (1,1-3).[221]

Such is the thought of 4,1-11. There is, however, more than meets the eye in this passage, and since we have kept mainly to what is actually stated, we should pause to note a few less visible components of the passage. These are working assumptions which appear to drive the argument and its exegesis along the given course, but which do not receive any direct treatment in this passage.

---

passage blends realized and future eschatology. 1Pet 4,14 is probably the source of *Apocalypse of Peter* 16 (ca. A.D. 135): "And my Lord and God Jesus Christ said unto me, 'Hast thou seen the company of the fathers? As is their rest, so also is the honour and glory of those *who will be persecuted for righteousness' sake*" (*NTApocr*², 2:635; italics in original); cf. Mt 5,10. The thought is different, but the idea of rest which is given or enjoyed (vs. "resting on"), may not be missing from 1Pet 4 (cf. Isa 11,2 with 11,10).

[219] 6,10; cf. 10,35; Rev 2,19 (οἶδά σου τὰ ἔργα καὶ τὴν ἀγάπην καὶ τὴν πίστιν καὶ τὴν διακονίαν καὶ τὴν ὑπομονήν σου, καὶ τὰ ἔργα σου τὰ ἔσχατα πλείονα τῶν πρώτων); 2,2; 3,1.8.15. Indirect confirmation that this thought underlies 4,10 might derive from the apparent structural relationship of 4,3-11 (4,1-11) and 10,32-39; G. Guthrie, 136.

[220] Cf. 6,12; 10,36. It is likewise characteristic of this book that the fate of the persecutors is generally ignored; there is no interest in a "place of torment," or in the eternal unrest of the enemies; judgment is seen to fall on *apostates*.

[221] On the relation of 4,12-13 to the 3,7-4,11, see esp. Hofius, 138f. G. Guthrie, 81 n. 13, doubts that 4,12f. is structurally related to the opening of the book, but he might underestimate the affinities of these two distinctive passages.

2.1.5.3. Working assumptions

An exhaustive treatment of the assumptions of this passage would probably require a comprehensive study of the theology of Hebrews. Instead we will limit ourselves to a few themes found elsewhere in the book which seem not merely to surface here, but to exercise a control on what is said.[222] They do not appear to derive from *Auctor*'s exegesis of Ψ 94 [95] so much as to influence his discussion of that passage. One example of such an assumption would be the one proposed by Käsemann, "the wandering people of God," but as we will see the "travelling" motif does not seem to have exerted a controlling influence on the discussion of the κατάπαυσις, whatever the extent to which that motif is present or implied.

2.1.5.3.1. As the Holy Spirit says

The first such assumption to be noted is so obvious as to be easily overlooked. The opening words of our passage read, καθὼς λέγει τὸ πνεῦμα τὸ ἅγιον. The subject of the sentence is of less immediate interest than the tense of the verb. The contemporaneity of Ψ 94 [95] would have been understood from the idea of the "today," but it was antecedently a hermeneutical assumption of the writer in approaching the OT generally.[223] "The word of God is living and active," which in this context includes the word which was spoken and which continues to speak in Ψ 94 [95].

2.1.5.3.2. A promise remains

The occurrence of ἐπαγγελία in 4,1 is the first verbal appearance of this theme in Hebrews.[224] Though reference is made to OT people who have seen promises fulfilled,[225] there is a recurring use of this theme which reserves fulfilment for the future.[226] As touches the latter idea, this means that OT believers "died in faith without having received the promises...since

---

[222] Note also the use of the phrase ἀπὸ καταβολῆς κόσμου (4,3) which we have already discussed; supra, 290f.

[223] Cf. Ellingworth, 41f.; also Weiss, 276. The extent to which this psalm is seen to "speak" is evidenced in the changes of 3,9f. (esp. the insertion of διό and the change to ταύτῃ), which have the effect of addressing the warning more directly to the readers.

[224] For ἐπαγγελία see also 6,12.15.17; 7,6; 8,6; 9,15; 10,36; 11,9 (2x).13.17.33.39; for the verb, ἐπαγγέλλομαι, see 6,13; 10,23; 11,11; 12,26. The verb εὐαγγελίζομαι (only 4,2.6) should be taken in the sense, "to receive the promise"; cf. Strecker 1991, 69; Schniewind-Friedrich, 585 n. 67. For further discussion, see Käsemann, 26-37; Michel, 192f.; Gräßer, 1:200-203; Ellingworth, 238f.; esp. Rose 1989a-b; Peterson 1992, 225-228; cf. also Schniewind-Friedrich, 576-586; Hoffmann, 68-74; Sand 1991, 13-16.

[225] Cf. 6,13-15; 11,11.33. Cf. also γῆν τῆς ἐπαγγελίας in 11,9.

[226] Esp. 11,13.39; cf. also 6,12.17; 9,15; 10,23.36; 11,9; 12,26.

God had promised something better so that they would not, apart from us, be made perfect" (11,13.39f.). Thus *Auctor* speaks of a "promised eternal inheritance (τὴν ἐπαγγελίαν...τῆς αἰωνίου κληρονομίας)" which is realized in the new covenant of which Christ is the mediator (9,15).[227] Somewhat distinctively in the NT, the promise comes to NT believers also as *hope*.[228] Speaking of the promise made to Abraham,[229] it is said,

> ...when God desired to show even more clearly to the heirs of the promise [τοῖς κληρονόμοις τῆς ἐπαγγελίας] the unchangeable character of his purpose, he guaranteed it by an oath, so that through two unchangeable things, in which it is impossible that God would prove false, we who have taken refuge might be strongly encouraged to seize the hope set before us.[230]

Here we note the conception of the ἐπαγγελία which cuts across the covenants. Abraham, the recipient of the promise, looks beyond the land to which he travelled to the "city that has foundations, whose architect and builder is God" (11,10; cf. v. 16), to a "homeland" (11,14), a "better country, that is, a heavenly one" (11,16). Likewise believers, are to "hold fast to the confession of our hope without wavering, for he who promised is faithful" (10,23). It is said that "you need endurance, so that when you have done the will of God, you may receive what was promised" (10,36).

The discussion of the ἐπαγγελία to Abraham in 11,8-16 is plainly related to the theme of the κατάπαυσις, and we can be sure that in the promise-theme we have much of the explanation of how the continuing availability of the κατάπαυσις can be stated so emphatically as a positive ἐπαγγελία in 4,1ff. More, we can see a whole outlook which *Auctor brings to bear* on Ψ 94 [95], and which must have determined from the start the course of his thinking.[231] From the beginning he assumes that the κατάπαυσις is bound up in the ἐπαγγελία of an eternal inheritance, a promise which spanned the ages and which would come to fruition in the work of the Son.

2.1.5.3.3. Not without us

Having just mentioned 11,13.39f. we have touched another, related theme which has joined with the ἐπαγγελία-theme in influencing 4,1ff. *Auctor* is emphatic that OT believers did not, indeed could not receive the "promises"

---

[227] Cf. 1,14.

[228] It might be wondered whether 9,15 and 11,39f. do not suggest a note of fulfilment already; Rose 1989b, 186, however, categorizes these also as yet outstanding.

[229] At several points the notion of promise is associated specifically with the promise(s) made to Abraham; cf. 6,13.15.17; 7,6; 11,9.11.13.17; note also 6,12.

[230] Heb 6,17f.

[231] Rose 1989b, 191, goes so far as to insist that the theme of "promise and fulfilment" is the "Basismotiv des Hebräerbriefes." Cf. Weiss, 276f.

before the advent of the Son,[232] and thus "not without us."[233] This idea is too interwoven in the fabric of the book to think that it *derives* from the exegesis of Ψ 94 [95].

This idea appears to have influenced 4,8, "If Joshua had given them rest, God would not speak later about another day." For even if we allow for the definition of the κατάπαυσις supplied by Gen 2, it does not necessarily follow that an entrance with Joshua -- even into *that* κατάπαυσις -- would have precluded a continuing or later entrance; thus there is finally no need to deny Joshua's rest. It would be fair to say that one could reason as *Auctor* has in 4,8 without assuming the logic of 11,39f., but if we assume the latter then 4,8 becomes transparent. This understanding is confirmed by 4,2c, which is well translated in the NRSV as "they were not united by faith with those who listened." "Those who listened" most probably include "we who believe" in 4,3a.[234]

The whole idea of a "promise" which holds forth the same reality across the dispensations, which was to some extent symbolized by the earthly *Heilsgute* promised to and received by the OT believers but which actually beckoned for their attention beyond all that, which is realized finally in the Son and thus received eschatologically by the whole people of God *together* -- this whole conception appears to have formed a *presupposition* for the exegesis of Ψ 94 [95].[235]

2.1.5.3.4. Heir of all things

The theme of "inheritance"[236] is important in Hebrews, and is also bound up with the theme of "promise," as will already have become evident.[237] In

---

[232] Cf. e.g. 7,11; 8,7; 9,8f.15.25f.; 10,1-4.

[233] On 11,39f. cf. Peterson 1982, 156-159. Though the emphasis in 11,39f. is on the future, there is a present realization in view. We will stress below, 305ff., that the idea of a present realization is not primary in 3,7-4,11, and to that extent 3,7ff. differs from 11,39f. In his examination of perfection in Hebrews Scholer, 201ff., insisted that "perfection" and "rest" are two different things (against Attridge, 128); the former is realized, the latter is awaited. For my part, I am not ready to say how systematized *Auctor*'s soteriological imagery was, but I do not find it problematic to suggest that the logic of 11,39f. ("not without us") would find expression in 3,7-4,11 without necessarily demanding that the entrance into the κατάπαυσις be in some sense realized already.

[234] For this interpretation of 4,2, see our exposition above.

[235] Cf. Bruce, 110.

[236] Cf. κληρονόμος (1,2; 6,17; 11,7); συγκληρονόμος (11,9); κληρονομία (9,15; 11,8); κληρονομέω (1,4.14; 6,12; 12,17); Käsemann, 32-37; Foerster-Herrmann, 758-785; Ellingworth, 94f. Cf. Num 13,20; 14,24.31. For the basic connection of the themes of the inheritance and the κατάπαυσις, cf. Deut 12,9.

[237] Cf. 6,12 ("imitators of those who through faith and patience *inherit* the *promises*"); 6,17 ("God desired to show even more clearly to the *heirs* of the *promise* the unchangeable character of his purpose"); 9,15 ("the *promised* eternal *inheritance*"); 11,8f.

almost every case the idea of inheritance is associated with people who receive the promises, but it is joined in a fundamental fashion to Jesus in the programmatic statement of 1,2, "in these last days he has spoken to us by a Son, whom he appointed heir of all things ($\kappa\lambda\eta\rho o\nu\acute{o}\mu o\nu$ $\pi\acute{a}\nu\tau\omega\nu$), through whom he also created the worlds."[238] As D. Peterson remarks, "Christ is heir of everything which he, as God's agent, created."[239] Weiss comments, "As that one whom God has already appointed 'heir of all things, the 'Son' is also the guarantor for the obtaining of the promise of the 'inheritance' for Christians."[240] Indeed, we may add, he is the "mediator ($\mu\epsilon\sigma\acute{\iota}\tau\eta s$) of a new covenant, so that those who are called may receive the promised eternal inheritance" (9,15).[241] Not without and not before the advent of the Son could the "sons" enter into the inheritance.

The notion of the $\kappa a\tau\acute{a}\pi a\upsilon\sigma\iota s$ did not need to be inflated by association with Gen 2 to take on the cosmic proportions and transcendent status which it possesses, any more than the "land" or the "city" in 11,8-16. It was a great *Heilsgut* already in the OT, and was bound to be absorbed into and transformed by the promise theology (better: promise *Christ*ology) of this thinker as in fact it was.[242] As such it would from the start be considered among the "all things" of which the Son is (uniquely) heir. It was therefore reserved (eschatologically) for the advent and work of the Son who would mediate the "promised eternal inheritance." Thus we have the admonition to "exhort one another every day... For we have become partners of Christ, if we hold our first confidence firm to the end" (3,13f.). If this Christological note is sounded explicitly only once in the extended discussion of Ψ 94 [95], it is nonetheless a presupposition of the whole.

2.1.5.4. Summary

In *Auctor*'s hands, Ψ 94 [95] testifies to the fact that a promise of entrance into God's resting place where the people of God will enjoy a Sabbath celebration remains outstanding. In view of the fact that this was the same promise held forth to the "fathers," and taking to heart the lessons

---

("By faith Abraham obeyed when he was called to set out for a place that he was to receive as an *inheritance*... By faith he stayed for a time in the land he had been *promised*").

[238] The other passage which joins the inheritance idea to Jesus is 1,4, "the name he inherited."

[239] 1992, 221. Note the link between creation and inheritance which is reflected in 4,3f.

[240] Weiss, 142. Cf. Westcott, 92.

[241] Cf. 8,6; 12,24.

[242] JosAsen 8,9 construed the $\kappa a\tau\acute{a}\pi a\upsilon\sigma\iota s$ of Ψ 94 [95] as a heavenly locale (supra, 96f., 109f.; Hofius, 50); the rabbis construed the מנוחה of the oath as the world-to-come (supra, 127f.). Cf. ApEl 2,53; 4,27; O.S. Wintermute (in *OTP*, 1:744, 749); Hofius, 66f.

of their failure, it is necessary for us to "make every effort" to enter as long as it is called "today," so that "no one may fall through such disobedience as theirs."

Though 4,3-5 is somewhat opaque, the essential points are drawn out in vv. 6-10. The linking of Ψ 94 [95] with Gen 2 permits several inferences, namely: that the resting place is where God holds his own Sabbath celebration; that this resting place was always intended for human entrance; that this is the same resting place promised to the "fathers," it is the same promise; that it is certain that this promise will be realized; that the wilderness generation's failure to enter was due to its disobedience, and thus that entrance can only come with obedience; that this promise was not realized by Joshua, and is still unrealized; that entrance into this resting place will involve joining into the Sabbath celebration by resting from one's own works. We noted that several assumptions found elsewhere in the book appear to drive this exegesis, namely that the OT Scriptures speak directly to believers "today," that God's promise is unified and inviolable, that salvation could not be realized for God's people prior to the work of the Son at the end of the ages, and that the Son, the heir of all things, is also the one through whom God created all things; his work has a once-for-all quality which embraces the whole sweep of history.[243]

Further points were raised and discussed along the way, but since they will be taken up separately below we will leave them for now and take up a few specific questions.

2.1.6. Present and/or future?

Several factors play a part in answering the question of whether the entrance into the κατάπαυσις is reserved for the future or is already being realized. In favor of a present realization is the use of the present tense of εἰσέρχομαι in 4,3[244] coupled with an "already-not yet" eschatological pattern elsewhere in the book.[245]

---

[243] From time to time the hypothesis has been advanced that 3,7-4,11 had a separate history, possibly as a "Hellenistic synagogue sermon"; e.g., Michel, 28; Darnell, 12, 14, 54. This opinion is difficult to accept in view of the essential debt of this passage to Christological ideas expressed elsewhere in Hebrews; cf. also Attridge, 128; Ellingworth, 213f.; also Hofius, 54 (Hofius' arguments stem in part from his belief that the κατάπαυσις is the heavenly temple).

[244] Ellingworth, 246, points out that "the we-form makes it less natural to understand the clause as a general statement of principle."

[245] Fewer exegetes would argue for an exclusively present realization; cf. Darnell, 217f. Favoring some sort of already-not yet realization are among others Barrett, 363-393; Lincoln 1982, 210f.; J.W. Thompson, 99; Westcott, 95; Hagner, 49; Attridge, 126; Darnell, 218f., 288 with further references.

Yet there are not inconsequential considerations which tip the scales in favor of (at least) placing the accent on the future, corporate entrance of God's people.[246] (1) The present tense of εἰσέρχομαι in 4,3 is not necessarily used for action occurring in the present,[247] although a straightforward "progressive" present does seem to strike many exegetes as the more likely way of understanding the tense here.[248] In view of the following points a future reference is to be favored. (2) Our own analysis concluded that 4,3a functions more like paraenesis than like a theological proposition.[249] (3) The imagery of Ψ 94 [95] and the parallel with the wilderness generation suggest a *corporate* entrance, which would in this context imply that it is a future event. At least in the case of the "fathers" the "entrance" is not so much a process as the event which *follows* (or does not follow) the period of testing.[250] Thus the present call for mutual encouragement (3,12-14; 4,11) followed by the comparison of *communities* (the "fathers" and "us") and the assertion of a σαββατισμός "for the people of God" seem to betray a primary interest in persevering *as a group* toward the ultimate goal of entering God's κατάπαυσις.[251] (4) The "gospel" of the κατάπαυσις comes to us also as "promise" (4,1f.; cf. vv. 6.10), which suggests that it is an outstanding feature of the hope.[252] (5) The demand to "make every effort" to enter the rest (4,11) appears to place the reader before rather than in the act of entering, especially since the stress of the passage is on "listening" "today," upon which the entrance is contingent, and furthermore since the "effort" stands in tension with v. 10 ("rest from works"). One can conceive of the "entrance" itself as having a probationary character for the time being, in which case the "effort" is in sustaining the act of "entering," but this may make the "entrance" more of a process than is justified.[253] (6) To speak of a present enjoyment of rest favors understanding

---

[246] G. Guthrie, 136, argues that 4,3-11 is structurally related to 10,32-39, which, if correct, would tend to confirm that 3,7-4,11 is oriented to the consummation.

[247] Cf. Mt 11,3; Jn 8,14; BDF § 323; MHT, 3:63; the present tense is often used for future action with verbs of movement (underlined by recent discussions of verbal aspect). Many take it as "futuristic" here: e.g., Vulgate; Moffatt, 51; Michel, 194; Braun, 108; Weiss, 279; Ellingworth, 246; Hofius, 180 n. 352; Rissi, 18 n. 43; Scholer, 203 n. 2.

[248] E.g., Westcott, 95; Spicq, 2:81f.; Montefiore, 83; Hughes, 158; Hagner, 49; Wilson, 82; Attridge, 126; Lane, 1:99.

[249] Cf. also Weiss, 279.

[250] Scholer, 202 n. 2.

[251] Heb 4,10 is a general explanation of v. 9 and does not suggest an interest in individual eschatology. Note also the identification of the believing community as God's "house" immediately prior to the present exhortation (3,6).

[252] Ellingworth, 239, 246; Rissi, 18; Rose 1989a, 63f.; 1989b, 186-191. What believers have "today" is the *promise*, rather than the *entrance*; *pace* Rordorf, 112; Lincoln 1982, 212; Sharp, 294, and others.

the "works" of 4,10 in a negative sense as "self-justifying works" or "dead works" since Christians are not otherwise at rest from their labors.[254] But this is not likely, as we have seen. (7) The exhortation as a whole is keyed to the Parousia (3,14; μέχρι τέλους).[255]

It appears, then, that entrance into the κατάπαυσις is an eschatological event, and in this vein we may ourselves "enter into" a digression to consider yet another NT use of the rest idea, in addition to Rev 14 and 2Thes 1 which were discussed briefly above. Unlike Mt 11,28-30 which places the accent on realized eschatology, both Rev 14 and 2Thes 1 construed the rest as a future *Heilsgut*, Rev 14 associating it with death and the intermediate state (with a view to the end), and 2Thes 1 associating it with the Parousia (the "revelation") of Christ and the judgment. This is also the case with Acts 3,20,[256] which associates future[257] "seasons of refreshment [καιροὶ ἀναψύξεως]"[258] with the sending of the Christ and the "restoration" of all things.

What is noteworthy in Acts 3,20 is the way in which, on the one hand, the idea of "refreshment" is used as a summary of the eschatological state within Peter's presentation, and on the other, how it recalls the similar phraseology of Acts 1,6f. The latter passage has the disciples asking whether it is at "this time [ἐν τῷ χρόνῳ τούτῳ]" that the kingdom would be "restored [ἀποκαθιστάνεις]" to Israel. Jesus' reply is that it is not for them to know the "times [χρόνους]" and the "seasons [καιρούς]" which the Father appointed in his own authority. Thus also in 3,20f. the **καιροὶ ἀναψύξεως ἀπὸ προσώπου τοῦ κυρίου** are reserved **ἄχρι χρόνων ἀποκαταστάσεως**[259]

---

[253] *Pace* Delitzsch, 1:192f. Ellingworth, 246, assumes that if 4,3 is taken as present action it would suggest "a full and unconditional realisation of the Christian hope in the present" (he contrasts this with 3,6.14).

[254] Correctly, Rissi, 128; Scholer, 204 n. 1; cf. Michel, 196; Weiss, 282 n. 107.

[255] On 3,14 cf. Hofius, 57, 133f., 180 n. 356; Rose 1989a, 64 n. 27; Scholer, 202 n. 1; *contra* Gräßer 1965, 180 (cf. Gräßer, 1:191 n. 53). Possibly also 6,11, though in 6,8 and 7,3 τέλος refers to physical death. Hofius, *loc. cit.* (cf. also 142, 181 nn. 357, 359), argues that the author held to a near Parousia; this is probable (cf. 1,2; 9,26; 10,25.37; Rose 1989b, 188; Rissi, 126; *contra* Gräßer 1986, 176 n. 80; 1965, 171-184). The modifying clause, ἄχρις οὗ τὸ Σήμερον καλεῖται (3,13; cf. 4,7), seems a bit overdone if the concern is merely with personal eschatology; Ellingworth, 224. Nonetheless, it may be possible to overstate the importance of its "nearness" for the paraenesis; cf. Barrett, 391; Zimmermann, 136f.; Laub, 250-253.

[256] Cf. esp. Bayer, 245-248.

[257] I take the seasons of refreshment as yet future; cf. Bayer, 248; *pace*, e.g., Bock, 55-59.

[258] Ἀνάψυξις occurs only here in the NT; the verb ἀναψύχω occurs in 2Tim 1,16 for the refreshment granted to Paul by Onesiphorus.

[259] The doctrine of the *Apocatastasis* or "Return" (the restoration of the Pleroma) was to become an established feature of gnostic eschatology; cf. K. Rudolph 1984, 196-199, who attributes it to both Jewish-Christian and Stoic thought. In gnostic writings it is

πάντων which God foretold through all the prophets. The outlook is thus universalistic, but the nationalistic note sounded in the disciples' question (1,6) is mirrored not only in the particular audience to which Peter addresses his remarks, but the word "first" in 3,26.

There is no obvious link between this usage of the motif and any particular statement from the OT[260] or elsewhere.[261] The association of "refreshment" with the restoration of all things to the integrity of creation is somewhat natural, and may be only an *ad hoc* formulation which picks up on general expectations that God's decisive eschatological act would usher in an age of unprecedented peace and security.[262] On the other hand, the specific connection with the sending of the messiah (τὸν προκεχειρισμένον ὑμῖν Χριστόν), reminds us of the OT connection between the Davidic dynasty and rest.[263] The apocalyptic features might evidence an indebtedness to the sort of Jewish rest-speculation we saw to be

---

sometimes joined directly with the expectation of rest, as here; cf. *TreatRes* 44; Hofius, 87. If anything, the gnostic idea is dependent on apocalyptic traditions.

[260] The word ἀνάψυξις occurs in the LXX only at Ex 8,11 in reference to relief from the plague of frogs; this has nothing to do with Acts 3,20 (*contra* Haenchen 1971, 208 n. 8); cf. Aq Isa 28,12; Sym Isa 32,15. If we confine ourselves to this word and its cognates, possibly the closest OT parallel comes with the use of ἀναψυχή in Ψ 65,12 [66,12]. This "psalm of resurrection" (thus the LXX title) recounts the tribulations suffered by Israel and states that God led them εἰς ἀναψυχήν (probably a local idea: "into a place of refreshment"). The verb, ἀναψύχω, is used in Ex 23,12 for the refreshment gained on the Sabbath. The Heb of Ex 33,14 should also be noted here: my presence (face) will go with you and I will give you rest. Thus in Acts 3 the refreshment comes from the *face* of the Lord.

[261] Schweizer 1974, 664, cites 4Ez 11,46: after liberation from the eagle (cf. 4Ez 11,1ff. with Rev 13) the whole earth is refreshed and relieved, freed from violence.

[262] Lane 1962 (noted by Bayer, 246), argues that as in Sym Isa 32,15, the "refreshment" is linked to the outpouring of the Spirit. This is a legitimate parallel even if the noun ἀνάψυξις was not in the text known to Luke (or Peter); one can note also Isa 11,1-10; 63,14. It is only a short step from the association of rest with God's presence (e.g., Ex 33,14) to its association with his Spirit. If this is something Peter had in mind it may have included the present age in its idea, though his comment is oriented primarily to the future.

[263] Though the word ἀποκατάστασις (only here in the NT) does not occur in the LXX and is rare in Judaism generally (Oepke, 391), the verb ἀποκαθίστημι (Acts 1,6) was an established technical term for the restoration of Israel to its own land by God. "This was increasingly understood in a Messianic and eschatological sense" (Oepke, 388). In Acts 3,21 the term ἀποκατάστασις probably refers broadly to a restitution of the original order of creation (Oepke, 391; Haenchen 1971, 208), clearly in a messianic sense. A further indication that Luke was thinking along these lines comes with the expression, ἐλάλησεν ὁ θεὸς διὰ στόματος τῶν ἁγίων ἀπ' αἰῶνος αὐτοῦ προφητῶν, in 3,21. This is a verbally close parallel to Lk 1,70, where it is used with reference to the raising up of the "horn of salvation...in the house of his servant David...*that we should be saved from our enemies and from the hand of all who hate us*."

widespread.[264] The emphatically stated connection with the heavenly session of Christ during the interim period[265] reminds us in particular of Hebrews.[266]

Nonetheless we cannot speak of dependence or influence, but only of analogy. Just as in Hebrews, there is in Rev 14,13; 2Thes 1,7; and Acts 3,20 an expectation, couched apocalyptically, of an eschatological rest. If this is not a dominant NT idea, it was hardly foreign to apostolic traditions. Acts 3,20 testifies to the fact that it had a place right at the heart of the kerygma.[267]

Having said this, however, a caveat must be issued regarding Heb 3-4. The κατάπαυσις is ultimately an end-time *Heilsgut*, but the warning -- which is the main concern of this passage -- does not appear to hinge on the decision of a present and/or future realization. In view of 6,4f. and 12,22-24 I would be hesitant to insist that *Auctor* would have objected to the idea of

---

[264] See Schweizer 1974, 664; also Hofius, 178 n. 330. Cf. 2Bar 73,1ff. (early II A.D.): "And it will happen that after he has brought down everything which is in the world, and has sat down in eternal peace on the throne of the kingdom, then joy will be revealed and rest will apear..." The expression, ἀπὸ προσώπου τοῦ κυρίου, can be compared with 2Thes 1,9. Luke may also construe salvation in terms of jubilary-sabbatical imagery, though this is not certain (4,18f.; cf. Isa 61); supra, 229, esp. n. 101. See also the discussion of the "chain saying"; supra, 138ff.

[265] This is another parallel between Acts 3,20f. and 1,6-11.

[266] Cf. Bayer, 246f. The parallels between Acts 3,11-26 and Hebrews go beyond the heavenly session of Christ and the rest motif. The following may be noted as well: God's testimony to Jesus through signs (Acts 3,12f.; Heb 2,4); the firsthand testimony of the apostles (Acts 3,15; Heb 2,3); Jesus τόν ἀρχηγὸν τῆς ζωῆς (Acts 3,15; cf. 5,31; Heb 2,10; 12,2; the term ἀρχηγός occurs only in Hebrews and Acts; cf. *2Clem* 20,5; Haenchen 1971, 8, 206 n. 5, suggests that "we are dealing with an elastic figure of speech characteristic of sub-apostolic, Hellenistic edificatory language"; cf. Loader 1981, 20; Ellingworth, 160, is unsure); the mitigating consideration in Acts that the Jews had acted ignorantly compared with the stern warning in Hebrews against wilful sin (Acts 3,17; Heb 10,26); Peter's accusation that the Jews had killed Christ and *Auctor*'s warning against crucifying the Son of God again (Acts 3,13f.; Heb 6,6); the testimony of the prophets (Acts 3,18.21; Heb 1,1); the suffering of the Christ (Acts 3,18; Heb 2,9f.18; 5,8); the Christ as "sent" (Acts 3,20.26; Heb 3,1); the "prophet like Moses" to whom the people must "listen" or be cut off (Acts 3,22f.; Heb 3,1-6; 10,28f.); "these days" (Acts 3,24; Heb 1,2; 3,13; 4,7); the "seed of Abraham" (Acts 3,25 [probably Christ]; Heb 2,16). These things are not unique to these two passages, but the convergence of ideas suggests that *Auctor* had been schooled in such primitive preaching, if not standardized accounts thereof.

[267] Against the repeated claim that the rest motif is foreign to the NT we must insist that just as in textual criticism the evidence must be weighed and not merely counted. Mt 11,28-30; Acts 3,20; Heb 3-4; and Rev 14,13 all give the rest motif a place of importance. As to Rev 14,13, the command to "write" "emphasizes the importance of the message which follows" (Mounce 1977, 277); apart from 22,17 this is the only place in Revelation where the Spirit speaks directly; the promise of rest is contained in a beatitude, the second of seven in Revelation (cf. 1,3; 16,15; 19,9; 20,6; 22,7.14).

some sort of proleptic "entrance" of either the living or the dead[268] before the end, if such an idea was put to him. It does seem strange that elsewhere in the epistle he would think in such vivid terms of a present participation in the heavenly world, but think of entrance into the same place *qua* κατάπαυσις as only an eschatological-future event. That in practice he nevertheless does so results no doubt from the immediate concerns of this exhortation combined with the imagery and language of his main texts (Num 14; Ψ 94 [95]; Gen 2). The thrust of *this* passage points toward a future, corporate realization, but if the question of "when" had been central to the thought of the passage and to the definition of the κατάπαυσις-idea then presumably it would have been made clearer.[269]

2.1.7. "Wandering" and/or waiting?

By way of a preface to this discussion we may remark on one of the terms involved, *viz* "wandering," which we have used in our heading in deference to convention. This term derives from the title of Käsemann's classic study, *Das wandernde Gottesvolk*, which has become in the ET, *The Wandering People of God*. Most English discussions of the topic have used either this term "wandering" or else "pilgrimage." W.G. Johnsson has argued, however, that in spite of this tendency to use these English terms *interchangeably*, "wandering" and "pilgrimage" are not synonyms. From a phenomenological perspective he stresses that the idea of a "pilgrimage" entails specific features, namely, (1) a separation or departure from home; (2) a journey to a sacred place; (3) a fixed purpose for the journey; and (4) the involvement of hardship. Johnsson then finds all these features in Hebrews.[270] For our purposes, we may agree that the English word "wandering" somewhat misleadingly implies an *aimlessness*,[271] while Johnsson's case for the "pilgrimage" idea needs more scrutiny than we can give to it at present. We have therefore opted for the term "travelling" in this study.

---

[268] Loader 1981, 52f., argues that the κατάπαυσις is entered by the individual immediately upon death; likewise Bruce, 110. This is rejected by Rissi, 128. There are no good grounds to exclude this but we must insist that the *stress* appears to be on a corporate and ultimate entrance.

[269] Thus it is difficult to be as categorical on this point as Braun, 91 (who stresses that the κατάπαυσις is so completely restricted to heaven [i.e., construed dualistically] that it is not even experienced in anticipation), or as Scholer, 202-204. Cf. Lincoln 1982, 210f., though he overstates the matter.

[270] Johnsson 1978, esp. 244f. P. Walker, 54, makes the interesting suggestion that *Auctor*'s pilgrimage motif is in deliberate contrast to the pilgrimage to the *earthly* Jerusalem.

[271] In certain respects the idea of aimlessness might not be entirely inappropriate; 11,8.38.

Käsemann[272] had argued that the underlying motif of the entire book of Hebrews is that of the travelling people of God. Fundamental to his case was his argument that *Auctor*'s development of the κατάπαυσις-idea was like that of Philo, i.e., it was conceived of as the destination of the heavenly journey of the soul. Hofius rightly observed in response that even if the travelling motif is present in Hebrews, it would have no necessary resemblance or connection to the thought of Philo and Gnosticism.[273] In any event, Hofius[274] contended that in view of the heavy dependence on Num 14 in Heb 3-4, we should construe the idea here not as one of "travelling" but of "waiting." This is because in Num 14 the people are at the end of their journey, poised on the banks of the Jordan, ready to cross over. Only the response of faith is necessary to bring entrance. Correspondingly, the present people of God are poised and ready, they are on the verge of entering; they are *waiting* for the revelation of the κατάπαυσις which might come at any moment.[275]

Both of these interpretations -- as argued by Hofius and Käsemann -- have a direct connection to the respective religious historical hypotheses, for just as the idea of "waiting" is fitting for the apocalyptically conceived future revelation of the world which is now "hidden," so the idea of "travelling" is suited to the dualistically conceived movement from the created realm to the uncreated.[276] On this basis Gräßer argues that since Hebrews works with a pronounced overall dualistic outlook, "travelling" is the assumed form of existence.[277] Nonetheless, the religious historical distinction as posed by Hofius and Gräßer has not necessarily played a part in the decision of other scholars on the alternative of "waiting"[278] or "travelling."[279]

---

[272] Käsemann, 240, 68-96.

[273] Hofius, 116. Barrett, 377f., agrees with Käsemann that there is a journey motif here, but distinguishes it sharply from Philo.

[274] Hofius, 116-151.

[275] Hofius, 142, 181 n. 357, stresses that for *Auctor* the Parousia was imminent; this is probably correct (9,26-28; 10,25.37; 12,28; cf. 1,2; 3,12f.). Gräßer 1986, 167 n. 35, 176 n. 80 (cf. 1965, 171-184), argues, however, that this is not a determinative factor in Hebrews. Indeed, it does seem that although the Parousia is used as a motivation for faithfulness, the author does not place too much emphasis on it; cf. Zimmermann, 136f.; Laub, 250-253; Ellingworth, 77 n. 32.

[276] This distinction is drawn sharply by Hofius, 146, 150f., and Gräßer 1986, 164-167.

[277] Gräßer 1986, 167.

[278] Relatively few scholars have adopted this view. Cf., however, Schenke, esp. 432; Lincoln 1982, 211; Lane, 1:88, 90; also Laub, 248f. n. 199; cf. Strobel, 47f. Vanhoye 1968, 9-26 (cf. also 1971, 69), had independently arrived at a position similar to that of Hofius.

[279] Some but not all advocates of the "travelling" motif read into it a metaphysical dualism; cf. Barrett, 373-383; Spicq, 1:269-280; J.W. Thompson, 96ff.; Zimmermann, 138f., 144; Ellingworth, 74; Johnsson 1978; further references in Johnsson and Gräßer

The general subject of Hebrews' "dualism" will be considered further below, but here we will confine ourselves to 3,7-4,11. Looking just at this passage, Gräßer agrees with Hofius over against Käsemann that the "travelling" motif is not *determinative*,[280] but he stresses that alongside the conception of the κατάπαυσις as a *future* destination there is the imagery of Canaan as the destination of *journey*.[281] In general, the elements which probably sway most students are summed up in W.G. Johnsson's judgment that in 3,7-4,11,

we have no more than an *implied* pilgrimage motif: there is no actual reference to the people of Israel as wanderers, nor to the Christians in such terms. On the other hand, the *tone* of the entire passage is one of waiting, expectancy...
Thus, while not one specific term which directly bears on the idea of pilgrimage...is to be located in the passage, the setting and overall thrust of the passage (the implied wanderings of Israel, the goal set but not yet realized) support at least the idea of *movement toward a goal*.[282]

Among the elements in Num 14, the fact that at Kadesh the people were "waiting" is evidently not stressed by *Auctor*; thus the ambiguity of our passage. *This is because Auctor is not concerned to make* either *travelling*

1986, 160-179. Lindars 1991b, 126f., who doubts that the "pilgrim people of God" is really a leading theme in Hebrews as a whole, allows that it is used in Heb 3-4 (but see 1989, 393 n. 1). For Hofius' case against the travelling motif in the remainder of Hebrews, cf. Hofius, 146-151.

[280] Gräßer 1986, 167; cf. Braun, 91; also Johnsson's remarks (quoted below). The overarching concern, as far as both Gräßer and Hofius are concerned, was that there would be no second chance. Since Gräßer denies that the imminent Parousia was a factor he argues that the real danger was that of falling behind and thus "arriving late" (4,1); cf. Gräßer, 1:202; 1965, 107f.; likewise, J.W. Thompson, 98. Ὑστερέω (4,1; cf. 11,37 [pass.]; 12,15; Wilckens 1972, 592-596; Bauer-Aland, 1692) is often used in the sense of "to come after" or "to come too late" through one's own fault (cf. Philo, *Agr* 85; *Jos* 182); more emphatically, "to miss" (MM cites PSI IV.432,5, ἵνα μὴ ὑστερῶμεν τοῖς καιροῖς, "that we may not miss the season" with reference to seed-sowing operations), "not to attain," or abs. "to be excluded"; used passively (in 4,1 it is active) it can mean "to come short" (Rom 3,23; Sir 11,11). A passage from Philo, *Fragmenta*, is cited by Michel, 191 n. 5 (cf. Gräßer 1965, 108; Ellingworth, 240) which uses the form ὑστεριζεῖν in the sense of "stopping short" before the end of a journey. Context is evidently an important factor, and Hofius, 220 n. 904, cf. 138, rightly comments that Gräßer's translation of "lagging behind" (*Zurückhängen*) assumes a *prior* commitment to the journey motif. In view of the dramatic backdrop of Num 14 and the general disinterest in the journey motif in this context, the sense of "to miss" or "to be excluded" seems most fitting here; it is the result more than the process or cause which is contemplated (cf. 12,15). Another alternative is that the meaning which is common in the LXX, "to lack," "to have a deficiency," is used in 4,1 with a view to a lack of listening faith (cf. 4,2; Lane 1978, 954, hints at this; cf. Weiss, 275) or a lack of "rest" (so Darnell, 227).

[281] Gräßer 1986, 168f.

[282] Johnsson 1978, 240 (italics his); cf. MacLeod, 296-298.

or *waiting the structuring factor in the passage*. Or rather, *both* travelling *and* waiting are adequate descriptions of the believer's existence.[283]

Having said this, it must be added that the κατάπαυσις is not defined fundamentally with reference to "das Auf-dem-Weg-Sein." The series of statements in 3,16-19, though they bring to mind the whole period of Israel's exodus and travels, are shaped according to the structure of the psalm rather than the imagery of a journey.[284] We have just noted that the orientation to the future fulfilment of the promise suggests movement toward a goal, yet this goes completely undeveloped *qua* journey; the comparison between the Christians and the "fathers" hinges on both having "received the promise" (4,2), not the nature of existence as a "way."[285] The backdrop of Num 14 should have told us that *Auctor*'s own thinking was not being determined by a pronounced journey motif, however amenable his language might be to those inclined to find it there. If *Auctor* does not accent the idea of "waiting," neither does he replace it with "travelling." Moreover, when *Auctor* gets around to actually defining the nature of the rest involved it is a rest *from works* structured after God's rest following creation (4,10). No doubt in this context this image embraces "der Mühe und Unrast eines Weges,"[286] but in chs. 3-4 *Auctor* nowhere dwells on the hardships or dynamics of a journey as such.

---

[283] Rissi, 17.

[284] Heb 3,16-19 follows the structure of the psalm rather than chronology: (1) they rebelled, 3,8 = 3,16; (2) God was angry, 3,9f. = 3,17; (3) God swore, 3,11 = 3,18. Each answer corresponds to Num 14: (1) v. 16, Num 14,13.19.22; (2) v. 17, Num 14,10.29.32; (3) v. 18, Num 14,30.33.43. The logic of 3,16-18 is determined by 3,19 ("we see it was *unbelief*"; note that this is accented in 4,11 as well; Weiss, 283 n. 111): (1) they all went out, 3,16; (2) they all fell down, 3,17 (= they did not enter; cf. 4,11); (3) why? they disobeyed, 3,18 (cf. 4,6.11; note the placement of this idea at the end of v. 18 for emphasis). This theme of disobedience is highlighted in each of the three questions, stylistically varied: (1) παρεπίκραναν; (2) ἁμαρτήσασιν; (3) ἀπειθήσασιν. The whole passage revolves around this latter idea; *the travelling motif is not a concern*. As to the form of 3,16-18, Moffatt, 48, followed by Attridge, 120, considers this to be a diatribe; Lane, 1:84, describes it more precisely as *subiectio*, a recognized rhetorical method which is also displayed in the preaching of the Cynic Teles (III B.C.). Attridge notes a number of parallels in Philo: *Heres* 115.167.260f.277-279.285.288; *SpecLeg* III,25.78.116.165.174. In v. 16 some scholars adopt the variant τινές (indefinite; with K L P 0243. 0278.1739. 1881 *pm* latt) and thus render v. 16 as a statement rather than a question; most recently, Darnell, 204ff.; Ellingworth, 229f. Nonetheless, the parallelism suggests that τίνες is original, and the change may have resulted from the awkwardness of ἀλλ' οὐ (cf. BDF § 448,4; Darnell, 208-210) as well as a desire to qualify the "all" to take account of Joshua and Caleb (cf. also 1Cor 10). In fact, the use of "all" probably reflects the influence of Num 14 where it is repeatedly stated that the "whole community" rebelled (Num 14,1f.5.7.10.22; 32,13); cf. Hofius, 135.

[285] Hofius, 141, 143.

[286] Gräßer 1986, 168; supra, 296ff.

We should not be hesitant to speak of a journey here, but it is no mythologically conceived "motif of a highway leading through the cosmos to heaven, traversed by a people of God who sojourn on it."[287] It tells us nothing more of the religious historical derivation of the κατάπαυσις-idea than that it is drawn from stock OT imagery and set into the framework of an eschatological entrance into the world-to-come. It is the *futurity* of the goal which lends more substance to the travelling motif than the heavenly location.[288]

The fundamental concern of this passage is that the salvation -- already existing as to ontology but not yet "entered" *qua* κατάπαυσις -- is future and *until it arrives* (the Parousia) *the believers are on probation*. On the one hand, they are not yet entering (*travelling*). On the other hand, the entrance is about to "occur"[289] (*waiting*). It is a matter of perspective, but on either model they stand to lose out without a chance for a reprieve if they abandon their faith.

2.2. The temple and the Sabbath

2.2.1. The heavenly temple?

Hofius argues that in Hebrews the κατάπαυσις has as its referent nothing other than the Most Holy Place of the heavenly temple.[290] This is argued on

---

[287] Käsemann, 86.

[288] *Contra* Gräßer 1986, 168f., who tries to soft-pedal the temporal aspect in favor of the spatial.; G. Guthrie, 137 n. 49, notes that "movement" in the hortatory material tends to be horizontal rather than vertical. My point is not that the spatial element is not used nor that the κατάπαυσις is not "heavenly," but that the vertical-cosmological element does not figure in the travelling motif in 3,7ff.; the heavenly-earthly, upper-lower distinction plays no such role here (cf. Ellingworth, 254). The vertical element is, however, stressed in the two sections which frame 3,7-4,13; cf. 4,14 and 3,1. Thus in 3,1, the "heavenly calling" (κλήσεως ἐπουρανίου μέτοχοι) should be understood as "from" and "to" God (2,10, 6,20 *passim*; cf. Ellingworth, 198, for discussion), though the accent is probably on the divine origin and authority of the call (cf. 12,25; 2,1-4). In 3,1 and 4,14, unlike 3,7-4,13, the stress is on realized eschatology; the language is highly metaphorical in describing present patterns of worship and prayer (cf. Scholer, 201-207). It takes considerably more, however, to read in or behind any of these passages the doctrine of the *return* of the pneumatic to the *Urgrund* from which it emerged, a return which involves a renunciation of the world of matter and instability (13,13) and a drawing near to the transcendent world of stability and rest (e.g. cf. Braun, 92f.; J.W. Thompson [less gnostically], 99f.); see further below, 317ff.

[289] Cf. the parallel to 3,12f. in 10,25: "the day *drawing near* [ἐγγίζουσαν τὴν ἡμέραν]." In this image, we do not so much move toward the goal as the goal moves toward us.

[290] Hofius, 53f.; followed by Rose 1989a, 63; Zimmermann, 138. Hofius urges this against a number of exegetes who identify the κατάπαυσις with the heavenly world generally (for references see Hofius, 176 n. 318); cf. Gräßer, 1:211 n. 76.

the basis of both background and the immediate context. We have already examined the background in detail and have reached the following conclusions: the linguistic[291] and religious historical evidence is not compelling.[292] Neither JosAsen nor 4Ez -- both of which receive special emphasis in Hofius' presentation -- make a connection between the resting place and the temple.[293] *MidrPss* 95 makes the connection, but it is a solitary instance and considerably later than Hebrews.[294] Where Ps 95 is taken up in rabbinic discussions of eschatology the מנוחה is taken no more specifically than the "world-to-come."[295] Nonetheless -- and this deserves to be stressed -- anyone who takes the time to examine the LXX will come away convinced that so careful a student of those writings as *Auctor* could not but have associated the noun κατάπαυσις with the familiar OT temple traditions.[296] But did he identify the heavenly temple as the referent of the noun?

Hofius answers yes, on the basis of "entering in" language elsewhere in Hebrews, for in 6,20 and 10,19 the "entrance" of believers is into the Most Holy Place of the heavenly temple.[297] The assumption that *Auctor* would have made such a specific and important idea somewhat clearer than he has in 3,7-4,11 can itself predispose us against Hofius, but his remains a possible interpretation. Yet since κατάπαυσις is not a technical term for the temple, and since *Auctor* is apparently being more allusive than direct, we must ask how the κατάπαυσις is being *visualized* in this discussion as compared to the earthly vs. heavenly temple typologies elsewhere in the book. Firstly, it can be noticed, as several have urged, that entrance of believers into the heavenly temple appears to be a present privilege, while entrance into the

---

[291] Supra, 94ff.

[292] Hofius, 96f., admits that 4Ez does not identify the resting place with the temple. For the idea of entering into God's Most Holy Place he cites instead Ps-Philo 19,13 (cf. v. 10; 28,10; 49,6; cf. Hofius, 65), 1En 25,6 (εἰς τὸ ἅγιον εἰσελεύσονται; cf. Hofius, 203 n. 646), and Rev 7,9-17 along with the general OT aspiration to remain in the house of the Lord forever (e.g. Pss 23,6; 27,4f.; 36,8ff.; 52,10; 61,5; 63,3ff.; 65,5; 84,1ff.). However, none of these establish that *Auctor* identified the κατάπαυσις with the heavenly temple.

[293] Cf. Hofius, 30, 50, 52f., 67.

[294] Supra, 124ff. Lincoln's claim (1982, 209) that by the end of the first century A.D. Ps 95 had been linked by the rabbis with Ps 132,14 is not in evidence.

[295] Supra, 127f.

[296] Supra, 98.

[297] Hofius, 53f. "Entrance" language is used in connection with a temple (earthly or heavenly) in 6,19f.; 9,12.24f. (εἰσέρχομαι); 9,6f. (εἴσειμι); 10,19 (εἴσοδος); 13,11 (εἰσφέρω). Hofius' hypothesis gains some support from the suggestion of Scholer, 153 n. 3, that the use of the verb εἰσέρχομαι throughout Hebrews takes its lead from Ψ 94 [95]; Scholer himself, 204 n. 2, however, does not identify the κατάπαυσις and the temple. Hofius' argument from the parallel of entrance into the temple is mitigated by *Auctor*'s tendency to use diverse images without harmonizing them; cf. Isaacs, 206.

κατάπαυσις is primarily a future affair.[298] This consideration is inconclusive, however, since 3,7-4,11 might envision a more perfect and final entrance into the temple. Nonetheless, the impression gained from the chronological discrepancy is reinforced if we observe that elsewhere when *Auctor* speaks of entrance into a temple he is consistent in building a typology of priesthoods (Levitical vs. Jesus') and *their* entrances.[299] This pattern is broken, however, in 4,8, which recalls *Joshua*. If *Auctor* had been thinking in terms of the "entrance" theology of later passages (entrance into a temple) then the OT counterpart to Jesus would not have been Joshua but naturally the Levitical high priests.

As attractive as Hofius' reconstruction is, we cannot agree that in his discussion of the κατάπαυσις *Auctor* was visualizing entrance into the heavenly Most Holy Place specifically, but rather something more general. That said, he certainly visualized the heavenly land with Jerusalem and the temple at its center, and -- on terminological and thematic grounds -- could hardly have missed the relationships of these to the κατάπαυσις.[300]

2.2.2. A Christian Sabbath?

It has been suggested that Heb 3-4 is concerned with the weekly *Christian* celebration of the Sabbath in anticipation of the final Sabbath rest. This proposal for understanding the κατάπαυσις of Heb 3-4 has been championed in the main by Seventh-Day Adventist scholars. Thus G.H. Hasel writes in the *Anchor Bible Dictionary*,

> Physical sabbath-keeping on the part of the new-covenant believer as affirmed by "sabbath rest" epitomizes cessation from "works" (4:10) in commemoration of God's rest at creation (4:4 = Gen 2:2) and manifests faith in the salvation provided by Christ. Heb 4:3-11 affirms that physical "sabbath rest" (*sabbatismos*) is the weekly outward manifestation of the inner experience of spiritual rest (*katapausis*) in which the final eschatological rest is proleptically experienced already "today" (4:7).[301]

The argument that a reference to the Sabbath would have had a special significance for those in doubt on the general relationship of Judaism and Christianity is plausible. Yet if one is going to read between the lines about the assumed practices of Jewish Christians, then one might as well read there the idea that the weekly Sabbath has come to fulfilment in Christ's salvation

---

[298] Cf. Rissi, 18, 128; Braun, 91; Gräßer 1:218 n. 138; esp. Scholer, 201-207. Heb 6,19f. and 10,19 speak of the present entrance of believers; *contra* Hofius, 53f.

[299] Cf. 6,19f.; 9,6f.12.24f.; 10,19; 13,11.

[300] Cf. Lincoln 1982, 219 n. 37; Weiss, 269f.; Theißen 1969, 129.

[301] Hasel, 856; cf. Bacchiocchi 1977, 63-69; 1988, 164-170; Graham, 343-345.

and is of no binding significance for the Christian -- along with temple worship generally it is obsolete and fading.³⁰²

Nevertheless, though this would be an interesting contribution to the overall argument of this epistle, there is no evidence in Heb 3-4 that the writer is concerned with an on-going celebration of the Sabbath among the Christians beyond the general concern with things Jewish.³⁰³ The passage does not begin with the Sabbath, as one would expect if this was the primary concern, and after referring to Gen 2 the passage closes with a reference back to Ψ 94 [95].³⁰⁴ Though σαββατισμός is used elsewhere for the celebration of the *weekly* Sabbath festival, in the present context it has clearly been applied to the entirety of the future age of salvation. To say that a σαββατισμός "remains" is not to say that a "weekly Christian festival" remains, but it is rather to say that a final great salvation remains to be enjoyed, one which finds its roots and essence in God's own primordial Sabbath.³⁰⁵ This passage tells us nothing about Christian observance or non-observance of the Sabbath.

2.3. Questions arising from a dualistic interpretation

The following questions arise from attempts to closely align the thought of 3,7-4,11 with Philo or Gnosticism, or more broadly, Platonic traditions of thought. Some of the questions overlap, yet since they receive individual emphasis by certain scholars they should be touched on separately here.

2.3.1. Rest in God?

Theißen³⁰⁶ finds particularly significant for the question of religious historical derivation the point that the human and divine rests are joined

---

³⁰² So e.g. Calvin, 99. In general, see Lincoln's response, 1982, 213f., to Bacchiocchi.

³⁰³ We might try to uncover here also a key statement about the *land* (understood as the κατάπαυσις; e.g. Isaacs, 82; P. Walker, 50-52), which was no less an issue than the Sabbath to the Jews of that day (cf. W.D. Davies 1974 [also 1982]; Brueggemann 1977). Nevertheless, it is not apparent that *Auctor*'s treatment of the land theme is a corrective to "an enthusiastic attitude towards the contemporary Land" (P. Walker, 52), and 3,7-4,11 appears disinterested in the earthly-heavenly contrast as such. *Auctor* stresses similarities between the Patriarchs and the present believers vis-à-vis the land more than he does dissimilarities. It is not that the Patriarchs could look to the land while we in the New Covenant should not, but that we should look to the eschatological goal, just as they did.

³⁰⁴ Contrast this passage with *Barn* 15.

³⁰⁵ Darnell, 309, believes that the word σαββατισμός was chosen to distinguish the subject matter from the Jewish weekly Sabbath. It seems as likely that *Auctor* was not relating the discussion to the question of the weekly Sabbath at all.

³⁰⁶ Theißen 1969, 127-129. J.W. Thompson, 100, goes further in saying that, "The 'rest' of the believer is thus parallel to God's rest..., *if not identical..* The *identification* of

closely with each other in Heb 4,3f.10. He concedes that the two rests are not identical (ὥσπερ) and that the label "gnostic" cannot be justified, but insists that this idea -- that the future salvation of humans has its *Vorbild* in a pre-existent, divine coming-to-rest -- is not apocalyptic; he supposes that at least in Philo's "gnostic" strain[307] it has a very mystical sounding parallel.

This is not the place to decide whether such an idea is inherently "apocalyptic" or "gnostic," but we can seriously question whether Theißen's approach places background in the service of interpretation or the other way around. We may be helped by glancing at Theißen's "remarkable" parallel between Philo and Hebrews:

For Samuel who is appointed to God alone and holds no company with any other has his being ordered in accordance with the One and the Monad, the truly existent. But this condition of his implies the Seven, that is a soul which rests in God [ἀναπαυομένης ἐν θεῷ] and toils no more at any mortal task [θνητῶν ἔργων], and has thus left behind the Six, which God has assigned to those who could not win the first place, but must needs limit their claim to the second. (*QuodDeus* 11f.)

So then, a sabbath rest still remains for the people of God; for those who enter God's κατάπαυσις also cease from their labors as God did from his. (Heb 4,10)

Is there any question of *dependence* here, even of a shared proto-gnostic tradition? The most we can say is that only if we eviscerate Philo of everything essential to his thought there might remain a formal husk that might echo an antecedent tradition that might have seen some connection between salvation and God's rest following creation.[308] *Auctor*'s thought revolves around historical movements, the destinies of peoples and of creation itself. Philo's revolves around the inner life of the individual, the soul's mystical contemplation of and participation in the divine. Philo's number speculation is much more than window dressing, and undergirding the whole is his metaphysical contrast between the instable creation and the stable transcendent realm; neither of these contribute anything to *Auctor*'s conception (below). For *Auctor* the notion of "entering" God's κατάπαυσις derives directly from the language of the psalm and is so free of the Philonic conception that one could only think that he is either deliberately avoiding it or is simply unaware of any parallel. If we take note of the γάρ in v. 10, we can see that the upshot of the divine/human parallel is not a mystical concept

---

the believer's rest with God's rest has its closest parallels in Philo and Clement of Alexandria, those writers who are influenced by Platonic metaphysics" (italics added).

[307] I.e., what Theißen considers gnostic; cf. *QuodDeus* 10ff.; supra, 115ff.

[308] It is possible, after all, that Philo evidences the more general Jewish ideas to which we will refer shortly, although everything has been passed through the crucible of his own philosophy; cf. Weiss, 272f.

of the soul's union with God or its participation in his nature, but a corporate participation in a joyful (12,22), salvific, eschatological σαββατισμός!

We are intrigued by *Auctor*'s joining of Ψ 94 [95] and Gen 2, but the manner in which *Auctor* actually develops the connection must control our interpretation. He does not speak of an entrance into God's experience, or of sharing in God's nature or essence. Rather, he envisions some sort of participation in an anthropomorphically conceived divine festival, as if outsiders are invited to participate in someone else's celebration.[309] Humans will join in the σαββατισμός of God alluded to in the creation account, implying that they, like God before them, will "rest from their works." This will take place when they enter God's[310] κατάπαυσις -- his resting *place* [311]-- on the day of salvation. This is as far as *Auctor*'s language allows us to go.

Neither in their respective conceptions nor in how they argue for them is there any promising parallel between Philo and Hebrews. *Auctor* turns aside neither into the psychologizing, mystical, metaphysically based speculation of Philo, nor into the mythologically conceived return of the pneumatic to the heavenly *Urgrund* found in Gnosticism (below). If there is a parallel, it is in no meaningful way Philonic or gnostic.

It is worth observing, finally, that the Philonic and gnostic notion "daß die Erlösung des Menschen parallel zu einem innergöttlichen Geschehen vor sich geht,"[312] is by no means solitary in the Jewish tradition. Already in the OT the human Sabbath is grounded on the divine Sabbath, and the human coming-to-rest is paralleled with God's (Ex 20,11; 31,17). It is a far cry from Heb 4, but the basic connection is established. Again, God's rest in the temple and Israel's rest in the land are joined at the waist; there is no separating the end of the ark's journeys and Israel's, God's defeat of his enemies and Israel's, God's rest and Israel's blessings. Indeed, if we probe deeply there is reason to think that God's rest in the temple and his Sabbath rest following creation have deep running common roots, though any possible tie is not openly developed.[313] Moreover, looking broadly at Jewish traditions with their ideas of a "world-week," of a 7th world which is equated with the "world-to-come," of a "day which is wholly Sabbath and

---

[309] It is not only the use of ὥσπερ which separates the divine and human rests, but also ἴδιος; though ἴδιος is applied to God's *works*, it quietly distances the divine and the human coming-to-rests.

[310] The phrase, κατάπαυσιν αὐτοῦ, in v. 10 is "*God's* κατάπαυσις"; rightly, Hofius, 255; Ellingworth, 257; *contra* Theißen 1969, 127f.

[311] Here is where the attempt to construe κατάπαυσις as *both* a place *and* a state becomes convenient for those advocating a gnostic or Philonic sense; by first affirming and then deftly setting aside the local element in v. 10a the verse can be interpreted as an entrance into God's *rest*, i.e., into God's own experience; e.g., J.W. Thompson, 100.

[312] Theißen 1969, 129.

[313] Supra, 70ff.

rest,"[314] or of a rest associated with the future return to Paradise,[315] it is to be noticed that in each case there is a connection between *God's primordial rest* and a future *Heilsgut* for God's people.[316] Taken together, we can at least imagine that in such a milieu a reflective mind might have drawn a connection between God's coming-to-rest and the human coming-to-rest in the world-to-come.[317] The point is simply that Philo neither enables us to come to grips with what *Auctor* says about the κατάπαυσις nor does he represent the only possible source of the idea.

There are no grounds to move from the phenomenon of parallel divine and human rests to an enhancement of other features of Heb 3-4 in line with Philonic or gnostic ideas. The Alexandrians may often express the mystical goal of piety as "rest in God"[318] but *Auctor* does not, and interpretation of Heb 3,7-4,11 should not become the attempt to prove the contrary.

2.3.2. Speculation on the number 7?

Likewise, the view has been forwarded that the "seventh day" in 4,4 is itself understood as the eschatological Sabbath.[319] Or the "seventh day" and the σαββατισμός are referred to more suggestively as the ἕβδομος/Hebdomad and are said to compare favorably with Philonic and gnostic speculation about the seventh "aeon."[320] All this rests on the use of the words ἕβδομος and σαββατισμός.

To begin with, there is no question of the word σαββατισμός being used with reference to a locale, whether a seventh "world" or a seventh heaven. This word refers to the Sabbath celebration which takes place *in* the

---

[314] Supra, 103f., 122ff.

[315] Supra, 106; cf. e.g. 4Ez 7,36ff.; 2En 42,3; 8,3; 9,1; TDan 5,12; Hofius, 74.

[316] In *MidrPss* 92 § 2 the Sabbath was created by God on the seventh day, and *as such* was given to his people Israel; it is then said that God created seven worlds and chose for his own only the seventh, "and the seventh world, being all Sabbath and rest, will endure through eternity"; cf. *GenR* 10,9; LAE 51,2. Cf. Weiss, 272.

[317] Even a relatively non-speculative exegete could find in Gen 2,2 something not for God alone but a concern for the world, "almost as a third something that exists between God and the world. The way is being prepared, therefore, for an exalted, saving good" (von Rad 1972a, 62).

[318] Cf. ClemAlex, *Paed* 1,13,102; supra, 142-144.

[319] Gräßer, 1:210, though he admits (n. 67) that *Auctor* does not reflect on the number as such.

[320] E.g., J.W. Thompson, 101; Gräßer, 1:219. Thus in drawing parallels with Heb 3-4, Gräßer refers to "ἑβδομάς-κατάπαυσις-σαββατισμός-Spekulationen" (or "alexandrinisch-gnostischer Hebdomas-Spekulationen"; "Sabbat-Katapausis-Hebdomas-Äonenspekulation"); note Gräßer's significant substitution of κατάπαυσις for ἀνάπαυσις though the latter would be the more characteristic term for *Philo's* and for *gnostic* speculation.

κατάπαυσις.³²¹ That the idea implies the number seven goes without saying, but had *Auctor* wished to stress the number as such -- either cosmologically or eschatologically -- he would hardly have passed over so lightly the reference to the seventh day back in 4,4a. As we have already seen, short of deleting it altogether, *Auctor* could not have given it less emphasis; the word ἕβδομος has a purely stylistic and rhetorical function in 4,4a.

The importance of the number seven is evidenced in diverse Jewish traditions,³²² and it is impossible to be sure that *Auctor* would not have attributed some significance to it. Yet in the absence of any development of the ἕβδομος idea as such anywhere in this context or in Hebrews as a whole,³²³ the burden of proof is certainly on those who want to say or imply that it has anything more than a stylistic and rhetorical function in 4,4a. Indeed, we can ask whether it is credible to suppose that an Alexandrian indebted to Philonic or proto-gnostic rest-speculation could have passed so lightly over the idea of the ἕβδομος! Of course we might take just this as indirect evidence of contact with Alexandrian speculation, i.e., as deliberate suppression, but as Ellingworth has said, "there is not much that cannot be proved by the two prongs of such an argument."³²⁴

2.3.3. Is God's rest a state of inactivity?

Theißen maintains that one of the parallels between Heb 3-4 and the "gnostic" (so Theißen) strand of thought in Philo is that God's rest is conceived of as essentially an end to work rather than an on-going "effortless activity."³²⁵ Gräßer makes a litmus test out of the question of whether our passage contains the doctrine of the *creatio continua*. Barring the presence of the latter idea, a dualistic, and thus (for him) gnostic background is apparently to be assumed. In any event, he insists that *Auctor* conceives of God's rest as the *end* of work (12,27f.). "Anders," Gräßer continues, "würde er das Eingehen in die Ruhe nicht dualistisch das *Verlassen* der Welt sein lassen (13,13) und unser Ruhen von den Werken nicht das (negative) Abstandnehmen davon."³²⁶ Both of these scholars cite

---

[321] Supra, 276f.
[322] Rengstorf 1964b, 627-629.
[323] R. Williamson 1970, 542, 556; Ellingworth, 249.
[324] Ellingworth, 47, commenting on Spicq's case in general.
[325] Theißen 1969, 124, 127, 129.
[326] Gräßer, 1:218 (italics his); cf. Braun, 91; J.W. Thompson, 99f. In addition to Theißen, Gräßer cites in support Schierse, 112-115; and Rissi, 20. Braun, 92, -- while commenting on the κατάπαυσις idea of Heb 3-4 -- cites *GosPhil* 66 (Braun cites it as *GosPhil* 63) as a parallel to Heb 13,13: "While we are in this world it is fitting for us to acquire the resurrection, so that when we strip off the flesh we may be found in rest and not walk in the middle. For many go astray on the way. For it is good to come forth from the world before one has sinned." Although in general Braun may be grouped with

Barn 15 as an example of an apocalyptically conceived doctrine of the *creatio continua* wherein God's rest is not the end of his creative work but the creation of a new day, another world.[327] This is an idea which they place in sharpest contrast to Heb 3-4.

So far as I can see, the main point of Theißen and Gräßer is not that in Heb 4,1-10 God is completely inactive and still,[328] but that he is not engaged in continual creative activity; in particular, he will not create a new world as in *Barn* 15. The matter is confused, however, by a simple identification of the idea of a *creatio continua* with *Barn* 15, by using the latter as a typical apocalyptic expression of the "world which is wholly Sabbath," and by reading an anti-cosmic stance into Heb 4,1-10. Gräßer also freely mixes passages (4,10; 13,13; 12,27f.) without regard to their differing concerns.

In response it must be said, first, that the idea of a *creatio continua* has a more general application than the sort of apocalyptic, world-week idea in *Barn* 15, and must therefore be addressed on its own terms. If by *creatio continua* we mean that as in *Barn* 15 God's creative activity is extended over 6000 years, and that he will ultimately create a new world after the 6000 years, then such an idea is not expressed in Hebrews. Whether Hebrews leaves room for a new or renewed creation and the implications if he does *not* leave room for such are, however, separate matters (below). In any case, I cannot see that Heb 4,1-10 would suggest that God is *inactive*,[329] nor that it would exclude any idea of a *creatio continua*.[330] *Auctor* simply does not speculate on God's rest in these terms in this epistle. It seems very doubtful to me that 12,27f. is intended as a description of God's Sabbath rest as Gräßer suggests; the σαββατισμός for God's *people* is future.

Theißen and Gräßer, he appears to differ from them in arguing that "ruht auch in *gnostischen* Texten die Gottheit...nicht" (italics mine; Braun cites *ActsJohn* 112, as well as Philo, *LegAll* I,5.6.18; *Cher* 87; *Aet* 84) and points out that Hebrews differs from both Judaism and Gnosticism in not speculating explicitly on God's activity (115).

[327] My own understanding of *Barn* 15 is given in detail above, 134ff.

[328] This is confused somewhat by the fact that Theißen 1969, 126f. *contrasts* the idea of Heb 4,1-10 with Philo's thought in *Cher* 87 (*LegAll* I,5f.16-18) over against *QuodDeus* 11f. Theißen, at least, appears to want to intimate that for *Auctor* God is quite simply inactive. Contrast this with Braun, 92, 115. Even so, Theißen's primary contrast appears to be with *Barn* 15.

[329] Note τὰ ἔργα μου (3,9)! Clearly God remained active for *Auctor*; cf. 4,12f.; Ellingworth, 249; Hofius, 256f. Note that in *GenR* 11, Rabbi Joshua resolved the tension between God's Sabbath and his continued activity by saying, "If thou sayest also that on this day God rested from all his work, he certainly rested from his work on the world, but he did not rest from his work on the ungodly and his work on the righteous, but he still works with both"; cf. Bertram 1964, 640. This should warn us against making too much of *Auctor*'s words, since he does not enter into this discussion.

[330] Cf., e.g., the rabbinic idea that God renews the work of creation every morning; Foerster 1965, 1018. Is it really possible to say with certainty on the basis of 4,3f.10 that *Auctor* would not have affirmed some such idea in another context?

Chapter Seven: A Promise Remains

Secondly, it is artificial to present *Barn* 15 as a typical apocalyptic expression of the "world which is wholly Sabbath," since passages like *PRE* 18 and *ARN* 1 use the idea apart from the notions of the world-week, world-Sabbath, and *creatio continua*.[331] The logic of Gräßer and Theißen -- not *Barn* 15 therefore not apocalyptic therefore anti-cosmic, metaphysical dualistic -- is fallacious.

Thirdly, aside from coloring the "works" of 4,10 too negatively, the metaphysical understanding of 13,13 is unlikely.[332] Attridge's suggestion that the "camp" in 13,13 should be understood as the "realm of security and traditional holiness, however that is grounded or understood," is probably closer to the mark.[333] More fundamentally, that 13,13 should even be related to 4,10 in this manner is doubtful. There is no indication that the "rest from works" expresses or even assumes a negative valuation of creation.[334]

One may fittingly contrast Heb 4,1-10 with Jn 5,16-18 on the question of whether God is active or not. In that passage Jesus' opponents take issue with his being engaged in making people whole on the Sabbath. Jesus answers them by saying that, ὁ πατήρ μου ἕως ἄρτι ἐργάζεται, κἀγώ ἐργάζομαι. On account of this the Jews seek to kill him, not only because he is healing on the Sabbath but because he is making himself equal to God.

The belief that in spite of Gen 2,2f. God was continually active was certainly not confined to Philo; it finds expression in rabbinic Judaism as well.[335] In Jn 5,17 Jesus invokes this idea of God's continuing Sabbath

---

[331] Cf. Hofius, 112f. Hofius argues that the idea of the "world which is wholly Sabbath and rest" (in addition to *PRE* 18f. and *ARN* 1, cf. *Tam* 7,4; *RH* 31a; *MekShabbata* 1; *CantR* 4,4 § 6; *MidrPss* 92 § 2; *SER* 2; *FrgTg* to Ex 20,11) originally had nothing to do with the notion of the "world-week" and "world-Sabbath"; esp. Hofius, 208f. nn. 733, 739; also Volz, 385; *contra* Lohse, 20 n. 155; Gräßer 1965, 106 n. 241; Theißen 1969, 124. Yet *Barn* 15 -- the passage which Theißen and Gräßer cite for the idea -- did connect the "world which is wholly Sabbath" to the "world-week" (cf. *Sanh* 97a; *SER* 2), and thus to the doctrine of the *creatio continua*; cf. Windisch 1920, 382.

[332] *Contra* (in addition to Gräßer) Windisch, 119; Spicq, 2:427; Braun, 467; Schierse, 193; J.W. Thompson, 147-150.

[333] Attridge, 399. Heb 13,13 has provoked a multitude of interpretations; in addition to Attridge, the following treatments implicitly or explicitly reject the metaphysical (Philonic) line: Rissi, 23; Hagner, 228; Wilson, 244; Bruce, 381f.; Lane, 2:542-546; Weiss, 735f.; apparently also Ellingworth, 716f. Weiss and Ellingworth stress the *goal* of the "going out" which is "to him" (Jesus). Important fuller treatments of 13,13 include Thurén, 91-104, and Koester 1962.

[334] It is probably true that in most cases hope in an other- or future-worldly existence involves a rejection of the present world. Yet a metaphysical basis of such a rejection such as we find in the dualism of Philo or Gnosticism should not be imposed on 4,10.

[335] See Lohse, 27; Bertram 1964, 639f.; Str-B, 2:461f. In Philo see e.g. *Cher* 86-90; *LegAll* I,5f.18. Among the rabbis debate over this point seems to have been current at least in late I A.D.; cf. *ExodR* 30,9; *GenR* 11,10; *Taan* 2a; Jn 5,17, itself, probably evidences its currency. It is stressed by Cullmann, 90, and Lincoln 1982, 218 n. 14 (note Lincoln's critique of Bacchiocchi 1977, 42-44), that at least among the rabbis the idea

activity -- obviously a view he shares with "the Jews" -- to justify *his* activity on the Sabbath, and the audacity of it is not lost on his opponents. The points of contact with Mt 12,1-14 should not be lost on us, as Jesus, the Lord of the Sabbath, places himself in a position to rightly observe Sabbath precisely by making people "whole."[336] There may be a further point in Jn 5,17 if, with O. Cullmann, we take the phrase ἕως ἄρτι as a reference to the resurrection of Christ when the divine Sabbath would truly begin.[337] Yet even if this is right, it would be misleading to say that "John 5:17 presupposes an eschatological interpretation of Genesis 2:2-3, similar to that found in Hebrews 4."[338] That Jn 5,17 may -- along with Mt 11,28-12,14 and Heb 4,1-10 (if not also Col 2,16f.) -- testify to an expectation of an eschatological Sabbath in primitive Christianity can be accepted.[339] That its idea of God as continually active finds a parallel in Heb 4 is simply not in evidence. The contrast between Jn 5 and Heb 4 is not that for John God is continually active while for Hebrews he is not, but that John is interested in the point while *Auctor* evidently is not.

A comparison of Heb 4,1-10 to *Barn* 15 and its doctrine of the *creatio continua* suggests that *Auctor* does not give expression to the same idea. Yet no either/or -- either *creatio continua* or dualism -- is justified. The doctrines of the world-week, world-Sabbath, and *creatio continua* were

---

was not that of a *creatio continua* but of the continuing work of God in sustaining, giving life, and judging (cf. *GenR* 11). Whether or not the idea of a *creatio continua* should be entirely excluded from the rabbinic conception, John's expression seems to me to be open-ended though the stress would certainly be on soteriology.

[336] As noted by Brown, 1:217 (Brown attributes the insight to Ménard), *GosTruth* 32,18ff. combines Mt 12,11 and Jn 5,17.21. Brown cites this passage in *GosTruth* as confirmation of Cullmann's interpretation (below).

[337] Cullmann, 88-92; cf. likewise, Lincoln 1982, 202-205. In view of the emphasis in John on Jesus' "time" (7,6.8), on the "hour" (2,4; 4,21.23; 5,25.28f.; 7,30; 8,20; 12,23.27; 13,1; 16,25; 17,1), on "working" before the night comes (9,4; 11,9), and on Jesus' finishing his work (4,34; 17,4; 19,28.30) the temporal indicator in 5,17 may be more than just a way of saying that God is "still" working. It is therefore suggested by Cullmann *et al.* that the phrase ἕως ἄρτι anticipates the time when the divine work of revelation and salvation is completed, to wit, at the crucifixion and resurrection of Christ. "Then alone will there be the true Sabbath, the true rest of God" (Cullmann, 89; see further advocates in Lincoln 1982, 218 n. 21). This seems to me to be very subtle, but possible. To suggest, however, that according to Jn 5,17 God has not yet rested in any sense and that his Sabbath is yet future (cf. Rordorf, 98) is wrong; to this extent I can agree with Bacchiocchi 1977, 44.

[338] Lincoln 1982, 204.

[339] See also Carson 1991, 247-249. Carson makes no reference to the phrase ἕως ἄρτι, but stresses instead the point made by Jesus/John in 5,39 that the Scriptures testify to Jesus. Here it is the Sabbath festival that, like other festivals in John, pointed to Jesus and his work. Moreover, "if the Father's work continues without pause alongside his unbroken seventh-day rest, and if Jesus' work is of a piece with his Father's work, may it not also be that his rest is of a piece with his Father's rest?"

characteristic of some but not necessarily all of apocalyptic expressions of the "world which is wholly Sabbath," and the rest speculation of Heb 4,1-10 does not evidence the cosmological and metaphysical dualism which is fundamental to the Philonic and gnostic expressions of the divine and human rests. Neither does *Auctor* appear to be concerned with the question of God's continuing Sabbath activity, a point set in relief by comparison with Jn 5,17; on the whole he clearly envisages God as continually active.

2.3.4. Does rest = stability?

In the next section we will consider the matter of dualism as it relates to Heb 3,7-4,11. Related to that question but distinct from it insofar as exegesis of Heb 3-4 is concerned, is the question of whether the κατάπαυσις is to be construed as a participation in the stability of the transcendent, immaterial realm. We have already seen such an idea in Philo and Gnosticism, and J.W. Thompson argues that this is how *Auctor* conceives of the rest as well:

Κατάπαυσις, with its suggestion of immutability, is parallel in Hebrews to other terms suggesting the stability of the heavenly world. Just as Philo, Clement, and the Gnostics took the biblical category of ἀνάπαυσις and equated it with Platonic categories for the stability of the heavenly world, Hebrews equates κατάπαυσις with the abiding and unshakeable kingdom...
Just as the biblical words ἀνάπαυσις and ἑβδομάς in Philo and Clement were placed in the service of a Platonic metaphysic, κατάπαυσις in Hebrews is associated with the essential reality (i.e., ὑπόστασις) of the heavenly world... In addition, the use of the term κατάπαυσις in order to encourage the community to 'hold fast' indicates his agreement with Philo that proximity to a stable object confers stability.[340]

It is not necessary to dispute that within the context of Hebrews the κατάπαυσις would be associated with τὴν οἰκουμένην τὴν μέλλουσαν (2,5) -- as also the πατρίς and heavenly city -- and that this world is variously depicted along lines that can smack of Platonic metaphysics.[341] We can also ignore the suggestive reference to the word ἑβδομάς (see above). Yet Thompson's laconic claim to find in this passage Philo's dictum that "proximity to a stable object confers stability" is contrived even if the word ὑπόστασις is metaphysically impregnated, which is doubtful.[342]

---

[340] J.W. Thompson, 100f.

[341] E.g., 8,4f.; 9,8.11.23f.; 10,20.34; 11,1.10.14.16; 12,22.28; 13,14; cf. J.W. Thompson, 100 and *passim*, though Thompson certainly overstates the matter.

[342] The noun ὑπόστασις occurs elsewhere in Hebrews at 1,3 and 11,1; elsewhere in the NT at 2Cor 9,4; 11,17; 20x in the LXX for 12 Heb equivalents. Cf. Dörrie; Koester 1972, esp. 585-588; Hollander, 406f. The meaning of this word has been difficult to pin down. In spite of a long tradition continuing into the present of interpreting it as "confidence," "trust," there seem to be no known instances of this psychological

Moreover, that the "suggestion of immutability" is somehow *intrinsic* to the noun κατάπαυσις is not in evidence, either within or outwith Hebrews. If anything, the almost complete absence of κατάπαυσις in Philo and Gnosticism actually distances this word from such associations.[343] Missing, then, is any basis for the argument that Platonic metaphysical ideas of transcendent stability (possibly associated with the "unshakeable kingdom" [12,28] and "abiding possession" [10,34]) resonate in the use of κατάπαυσις; missing is any basis for thinking that this noun has a special affinity with such metaphysical notions, and thus a special affinity with those particular metaphors among the others in Hebrews.[344]

---

meaning. Koester argues that the word always refers to an underlying "reality." Thus, interpreting 3,14 in the light of 1,3, he claims that it refers "to the 'reality' of God which stands contrasted to the corruptible, shadowy, and merely prototypical character of the world but which is paradoxically present in Jesus and is the possession of the community of faith" (1972, 587f.); this is the line followed by J.W. Thompson, 94.

Ellingworth, 227f., however, properly assesses this understanding as speculative and artificially consistent; cf. Braun, 96f.; Weiss, 265. Dörrie, 39, suggests, "frame of mind," as described in 3,6; this is followed by BAGD, 847 (cf. Bauer-Aland, 1688). Ellingworth, 227f., also adopts this meaning, stressing that this is not to reduce faith to a virtue or quality; ὑπόστασις refers to the ground or basis for παρρησία. Similarly, Lane, 1:82 n. q, translates the word as "basic position," stressing that it is the antithesis of ἀποστῆναι in 3,12 (cf. Gräßer, 1:191-193; 1965, 18, 46-48; Hofius, 133; Weiss, 264f., who, along with many others give the sense as "firm stance"). Hollander, 406f., prefers "resolve" or "point of departure," and Attridge, 118 (cf. Westcott, 85), adduces evidence for "the underlying resolution with which a soldier or a martyr confronts a situation"; cf. Nardoni, 469 n. 27. All the same, appealing to *Auctor*'s delight in the "polyvalence of language" and the usage of 1,3, Attridge affirms Koester's interpretation equally enthusiastically: "What the addressees are told is above all to hold 'firm'...that heavenly reality in which they participate through Christ. The stability of what Christians have (12:28) serves as the ground for the firmness they are called to manifest."

Attridge is right that the latter sense cannot be excluded, and the idea of "that which is hoped for" is probably to be assumed, but the metaphysical connotations are simply surplus baggage in this context. Something more in the vicinity of "basic position," "frame of mind," or "undertaking" (cf. Hollander, 407) seems most fitting; cf. Ψ 38,7 [39,7]. Reflecting at length on passages which are closely related in function and terminology (in addition to 3,1.6 esp. 2,1-4; 4,14-16; 6,1-5.9-12.17-20; 10,19-25.32-39) seems to bring to light a whole idea of an essential frame of mind, a reality "tasted," and an ensuing lifestyle which, taken together, had been constitutional for the early days of the community (τὴν ἀρχὴν in 3,14 refers to the "beginning" rather than "first principles"; cf. Attridge, 118; Ellingworth, 227; 6,1 uses this word differently). This foundational situation was being set forth by *Auctor* as paradigmatic for the duration of the "last days" (μέχρι τέλους = Parousia; cf. 3,13; 6,11).

[343] Attridge, 127 n. 55, is also too dismissive of the distinction between ἀνάπαυσις and κατάπαυσις. True, the words overlap considerably in the LXX, but when κατάπαυσις is virtually unused in Philo and Gnosticism it can hardly be assumed to connote distinctive ideas of their literature.

[344] Thompson's work with this passage is certainly helpful in some important respects, but his general approach seems to be to isolate and amplify any word or idea which might be construed in terms of Platonic metaphysics and then to draw a direct line from each to

Existence in the κατάπαυσις is defined by *Auctor* as a "rest from works" which opens the way for a joyful (and active!) Sabbath celebration around God's throne. This involves joining in God's own transcendent and trans-epochal Sabbath, but there is not a hint -- insofar as the κατάπαυσις-idea is concerned -- that the believer is taking flight from the instability and turmoil of the corruptible material realm into the divine realm to "stand at rest" by sharing in God's nature, which is rest.[345]

2.3.5. A purely heavenly rest?

2.3.5.1. General response

Having answered the foregoing questions (§§ 2.3.1-4) we are ready to assess the matter of *Auctor*'s "dualism" and his discussion of the κατάπαυσις. The decisive consideration which for several scholars tips the scales in favor of the Philonic or gnostic materials as providing the closest parallels for Hebrews' κατάπαυσις-idea is the location of the κατάπαυσις in heaven *and not* on the renewed earth as in Jewish apocalyptic.[346] It is stressed in this connection that the rest involves a negative attitude to creation as something from which we must remove ourselves.[347] It is

---

the word κατάπαυσις. It seems that Thompson, 99, must construe the entrance into the κατάπαυσις as a realized event to sustain his claim that the believer somehow draws on the "stability" of God in order to continue in "stability." Unfortunately several of Thompson's propositions and parallels are too vague to be sure of their meaning, and it is not clear in what ways if any Thompson would *distinguish* Heb 3-4 and Philo. A more precise statement of how Philo's dictum regarding proximity to a stable object accounts for *Auctor*'s manner of expression might enhance Thompson's case.

[345] The "rest" of Heb 3-4 is not descriptive of an eternal attribute of God, but of his state following creation.

[346] Cf. Schierse, 114; Theißen 1969, 129; J.W. Thompson, 100; Gräßer, 1:209-211, 218-220 (cf. 1986, 164-167). Braun, 92, puts it succinctly: "Der Dualismus des Hb verlegt den Ruheort in den Himmel; die Erde ist, wie in Gnosis EvVer Nag Hammadi I2 24, 11-25..., für den Hb ein Negativum" (*GosTruth* 24,9-28 reads, "The Father reveals his bosom. -- Now his bosom is the Holy Spirit. -- He reveals what is hidden of him -- what is hidden of him is his Son -- so that through the mercies of the Father the aeons may know him and cease laboring in search of the Father, resting there in him, knowing that this is the rest. Having filled the deficiency, he abolished the form -- the form of it is the world, that in he served. -- For the place where there is envy and strife is deficient, but the place where (there is) Unity is perfect."). For Braun, 91, the dualism is so strictly maintained in Heb 3-4 that the κατάπαυσις is not experienced even in an anticipatory manner; he concludes (93), "Die Ruhe des Hb trägt also, gerade was ihre dualistisch-himmlische Lokalisierung betrifft, nicht spätjüd, sondern gnostisches Gepräge." Cf. also Laub, 249.

[347] Cf. in this connection the remarks of Gräßer, 1:218, on Heb 13,13; likewise, Braun, 92; J.W. Thompson, 99f. This interpretation of Heb 13,13 has already been rejected; supra, 323.

suggested that for *Auctor* believers had their origin in the heavenly world, from which they emerged; in other words there is an anthropological dualism.[348] To put the question in terms of the different tendencies in Judaism, it is a matter of whether Hebrews stands closer to the apocalyptically conceived 4 Ezra,[349] or alternatively to the more dualistically conceived Joseph and Aseneth.[350]

On the one hand, it is true that a reading of Hebrews leaves the student who comes to the passage and reads it in the light of the rest of the NT puzzled. One misses what would have been expected, especially at 12,27f., namely, a reference to a new or renewed creation.[351] Instead *Auctor* appears to envisage two parallel realities, the created (earth and heavens) and uncreated (heaven). The final state sees the removal of the created reality, that which can be shaken, so that only the heavenly reality, the unshakeable kingdom, remains. Thus one of the parallel lines dissolves into nothing while the other continues by itself and all of salvation with it.[352] *Auctor*'s language ("removed"; 12,27) precludes for most interpreters any suggestion of a *renewal* of the present creation. A *new* creation is seemingly superfluous, unless he would somehow merge it with the "unshakeable

---

[348] Cf. e.g. Käsemann, 94-96, 144; Braun, 91; Gräßer 1986, 176. The basis for this suggestion is the potential implication of πατρίς (11,14-16; cf. 2,11.14). Cf. also Theißen 1969, 121f., who contends that it is beyond dispute that in 2,11.14; 12,9; and 13,3 the pre-existence of the human "self" is assumed and along with it a dualistic anthropology. On this specific matter see the brief response below, 332f..

[349] On the eschatology of 4 Ezra see Stone 1989, *passim*. Of course, 4 Ezra is too late to serve as a literary source.

[350] On the eschatology of Joseph and Aseneth see Burchard, in *OTP*, 2:194; for our own discussion of 4Ez and JosAsen, cf. above, 106ff.; infra, 333f.; for the divide between scholarly proposals, cf. Gräßer 1986, 166.

[351] Cf. 2Pet 3; Rev 21,1.

[352] This sort of interpretation is widely advocated. Lane, 2:478-483 (cf. 443 n. ccc), however, argues that "heaven" in 12,26b refers to the new covenant revelation (12,22-24.25c), with the result that the passage refers not to the future destruction of the world but God's eschatological judgment. The created realm (πεποιημένων) is subject to God's scrutiny, but the essential difference between the shakeable and the unshakeable is in their relationship to God rather than in their status as created or uncreated (cf. also Attridge, 381 n. 45). What is "removed" is all that opposes God's rule, which would include the unfaithful portion of the community. By way of evaluation, it can be said that this interpretation not only pays close attention to the context and terminology, but gives sufficient attention to the OT background of key concepts. The modification of Hag 2,6 does place such a stress on "heaven" that it is probably natural to draw on the immediately preceding v. 25 (cf. e.g. 9,24 with 1,10; Ellingworth, 687). It also avoids the problem involved in a consistent Platonic interpretation of ὡς πεποιημένων (12,27a; cf. J.W. Thompson, 49; note the comments of Ellingworth, 689) which would have to either foresee the removal of believers also or appeal to their pre-existence in the heavenly realm. Lane, 2:481, is right that 12,27 is "suggestive and provocative rather than exegetical and exhaustive." Attridge, 380-382, also attempts to balance the Platonic and apocalyptic expressions, though he tends more toward the Platonic than Lane.

kingdom"; in any case, it goes unmentioned. In fact, for many, this passages makes sense only if we assume a substantial indebtedness to Platonic metaphysics, a judgment that is reinforced by the use of similar language elsewhere in the book.

On the other hand, the linear-historical dimension of Hebrews is inescapable for most interpreters, giving the appearance of stock Jewish eschatological and apocalyptic thought, and apocalyptic has always had a pronounced spatial and vertical dimension.[353] Thus it is not so much a mere "dualism" which divides the alternatives, but whether the dualism involves a pronounced Platonic metaphysic with its orientation away from material reality to the realm of pure idea. Our concern is whether it is a dualism in this particular Platonic sense that is present.

At the risk of over simplifying, it might be said that the debate is thus concerned with the respective roles of "vertical" and "horizontal" dimensions in the thought and argument of Hebrews. The way in which these dimensions relate to one another is not immediately obvious and attempts to reconcile them abound, stressing one at the expense of the other or seeking some middle ground.[354] For example, MacRae, in a helpful treatment, argues that "the realized, Alexandrian eschatology is...that of the author of Hebrews, and the futurist, apocalyptic eschatology that of the readers. The rationale for the presence of both lies in the literary genre of

---

[353] This spatial-vertical element in apocalyptic is emphasized by Lincoln 1981, 18-22, 169-195 (esp. p. 178); cf. Hengel 1974, 1:205, 253. See above, 253f.

[354] Of many possible discussions the following represent varying perspectives and touch on the main elements: Barrett, 363-393; Gräßer 1965, 171-184; MacRae; Ellingworth 1986; Cody, 35f.; Isaacs; for further on issues and bibliography, cf. Hurst, 7-42. The issue is a complex one, involving vertical and horizontal imagery of the cosmic or heavenly temple as well as the larger relationship of earthly-heavenly and past-present-future dimensions. A complicating factor has certainly been the inability of scholars to agree on what may be included in Gnosticism (cf. the critical remarks of Ellingworth, 43-45; Attridge, 128; Hengel 1976, 86 n. 147). For example, Braun and Gräßer mix passages from JosAsen, Philo, and the Nag Hammadi codices without distinction seemingly on the basis of a "dualistic" outlook alone (contrast this with Hofius, 17-21). The same can be said regarding the terms "dualistic," "eschatological," and "apocalyptic" (cf. Hurst, 11; supra, 253ff.). Additionally, there is so much cross-fertilization among the alternative backgrounds that simple distinctions become almost meaningless. Hurst, 21f., argues that contrary to much scholarship a "vertical" view of the universe was never an indication of a specifically "Greek" heritage of thought, and does not itself substantiate the thesis of direct and fundamental dependence on Platonically influenced traditions. The vertical view of the universe was already an ancient Jewish idea by the time of the NT; the sources include Babylonian thought and the OT as well as longstanding Hellenistic influences (Hurst, 11; cf. Eichrodt, 1:423f.). Hurst believes that it is in the Christian idea of the overlap of the ages that the vertical and horizontal frameworks merged. Comparison with Pauline thought (e.g. Col 3,1-4) is aided by the study of Lincoln 1981, who also discusses much of the relevant background material, esp. 18-22, 169-195.

homily. The preacher supports the audience's views with his own."³⁵⁵ Ellingworth concludes similarly that the author combines two pictures of the one universe which are distinct in origin, but adds that "the vertical language of 2:9; 4:14; 7:26 probably owes more to primitive Christian tradition, whereas the horizontal language of the heavenly and earthly tabernacles, though not without parallels elsewhere, is developed in a distinctive way to express the author's own typology."³⁵⁶

L.D. Hurst has helpfully distinguished four general approaches to this issue in the scholarly discussion:³⁵⁷ (1) there is no linear apocalyptic element in Hebrews; (2) there is an inconsistent juxtapositioning of the linear apocalyptic and Platonic perspectives; (3) there is an absorption of Platonic idealism into the idealist element of apocalyptic with the result that they become one; (4) the linear apocalyptic element satisfactorily explains the thought of this book.

Though one might yearn to explore the issues and evidence relating to this complex matter, this would take us beyond our brief. It will be sufficient to state that I believe the author to be working with a basically linear apocalyptic outlook which he tends to express in Platonic terms.³⁵⁸ It is not easy to determine, however, whether the author's probable Alexandrian background brought about a significant modification of the apocalyptic outlook in the direction of a more consistently Platonic world-view,³⁵⁹ causing him to abandon traditional apocalyptic ideas such as the new creation, or whether the "Alexandrian" influence only reinforced elements already present in the apocalyptic perspective (esp. its spatial dualism).³⁶⁰ For instance, Hofius might be justified in drawing a parallel between 12,26f. and the teaching of the "world destruction" (*Weltuntergang*) common to apocalyptic. He can then note that in apocalyptic this doctrine did not preclude the expectation of a world renewal or a new creation. Nonetheless, there is as much evidence that the resting place is associated

---

³⁵⁵ MacRae, 179.
³⁵⁶ Ellingworth 1986, 348-350.
³⁵⁷ Hurst, 10.
³⁵⁸ In terms of Hurst's four approaches, mine is probably closest to (3).
³⁵⁹ But how do we know that any "movement" in thought might not have been in the opposite direction for *Auctor*? Maybe a converted Alexandrian would modify his outlook in the direction of Jewish-Christian apocalyptic (Runia 1993, 78).
³⁶⁰ Lincoln 1982, 219 n. 42 (Lincoln is modifying MacRae's suggestion, mentioned above, that there is a mingling of two discrete thought worlds). This may have been *Auctor*'s way of expressing the difficult, and still somewhat new notion of the overlap of the ages, which had come about under the realization by Christians that the future resurrection and judgment had already occurred, in a sense, in the past. In Hebrews, the acute emphasis on the present aspect reinforces the obsolescence of the old, the help for the present, and the certainty of the future -- all of which have a clear pastoral and practical thrust.

Chapter Seven: A Promise Remains   331

with a renewed earth in 4 Ezra -- Hofius' favorite apocalyptic parallel -- as there is little in Hebrews.[361] Is this merely because of *Auctor*'s tendency to express himself Platonically? Is it because of certain strict interests and even the limits of this brief "word of exhortation"?[362] The author has at least exploited not only the language, but also the thought forms of Platonism to accomplish his paraenetic goals. The "vertical" appears to buttress the hope in the "horizontal" at more than one point.[363]

Yet even if we agree that *Auctor* may not have envisioned a new earth, we should not assume that his development of the κατάπαυσις-idea will correspond most closely to that of Philo or Gnosticism. The thought of Heb 3-4 involves no entry into God's experience, no speculation about the number 7, no suggestion that God's rest is inactivity, no equation of rest and the metaphysical stability of the immaterial world, no assumption that humans return to the κατάπαυσις from which they emerged, and no view of creation as unredeemable in its very ontological make-up.[364] The notion of a corporate (vs. individual) entrance into the κατάπαυσις at the Parousia (vs. in life or at death) in connection with a resurrection (vs. abandonment of the fleshly body)[365] and judgment removes this writer's thought at least as far

---

[361] Hofius, 257f.; Hofius refers to Volz, 333ff. On the doctrine of the world renewal in 4 Ezra, cf. Stone 1989, 70, 182, 77-79, 216ff. For the same doctrine in Hebrews Hofius refers only to 1,10-13 (cf. Ψ 101,26-28 [102,25-27]) where the Son is the renewer of creation (ἀλλαγήσονται). Yet this poetic imagery embedded in a quotation does not provide much support for the idea of a world renewal. Michel, 474, and Buchanan, 136, also advocate the idea of a world renewal in Hebrews (for others, cf. Attridge, 381 n. 41).

[362] There is no contemplation of the place of the damned, yet it would be precarious to infer from this that *Auctor* therefore believed in their annihilation. The resurrection also barely surfaces, though it does just (cf. 6,2; 11,19.35). We might ask why -- assuming that he accepted them -- *Auctor* might not have exploited such traditional symbols as the new creation, etc. (as opposed to why other apocalyptic works do exploit them) without reducing the matter to a simple rejection of such symbols in principle on the basis of silence. Cf. Hurst, 41; Stone 1989, 65, 71, 138, 145, 183, 216. Commenting on 4 Ezra, Stone observes that "in any given passage the omission of one or more elements of eschatology does not mean that the author of that passage did not believe in or accept that particular element" (65).

[363] MacRae, 195f.; Isaacs, 58.

[364] On the last point cf. Barrett, 388; Hofius, 257f.; *contra* Theißen 1969, 121; Gräßer 1986, 175. *Auctor* holds a positive view of creation as such; cf. 1,2f.10-12; 2,10; 3,4; 10,22; 11,3. In general, it is remarkable that it is the Sabbath of the *creation* account into which believers will ultimately enter. Cf. further Ellingworth, 42-45; Hurst, 73; Isaacs, 56f.

[365] References to the resurrection are few in number; cf. 6,2; 11,19.35. On possible allusions to Jesus' resurrection, cf. 5,7; Loader 1981, 52, 100; Attridge, 150; Weiss, 313; Ellingworth, 288; but see Lane, 1:120; cf. also 13,20 and Loader 1981, 49-54; Ellingworth, 728f. Neither of these (5,7; 13,20) amount to an unambiguous reference to Jesus' resurrection *specifically*, the latter being assumed in his exaltation. This dearth of references to the resurrection does not represent an unease toward the doctrine, but an *assumption* of it as common knowledge and elementary teaching (6,2). Observation of

from the dualistic JosAsen and Philo as Gräßer sees it removed from the apocalyptic 4 Ezra. Speculation about God's rest that assumes the same sort of cosmological and metaphysical dualism as we find in Philo and Gnosticism would presumably follow the course of Philo's and Clement's thought, thus expressing an interest directly and expressly in God's very essence as contrasted with the material realm which is subject to movement and change. Heb 3-4 contains just the subject matter to provoke such ideas from an Alexandrian after Philo's heart, but there is not a trace of it here.

Auctor's thought as expressed in this epistle is indeed dualistic in the broad sense that it involves certain types of dualisms (spatial, eschatological, etc.). Whether it is controlled at any point by a cosmological and metaphysical dualism, and, if so, in what sense, is debated. Unless we are willing to supply missing ideas, 12,26f. does stand in tension with much apocalyptic thought, including 4 Ezra, and the κατάπαυσις is correspondingly a heavenly reality. However, the κατάπαυσις-speculation of Heb 3-4 does not give any indication of an underlying cosmological and metaphysical dualism and it does not correspond in any meaningful way to rest-speculation like Philo's or Gnosticism's. To draw such a dualism out of 3,7-4,11 and enhance it until it looks and sounds like theirs is to produce something grotesque and out of keeping with what *Auctor* actually says.

2.3.5.2. Two specific sub-points

Two more points need be brought into focus because of their importance to some scholars. The one is the so-called *anthropological* dualism referred to above, and the other is the oft-mentioned comparison with JosAsen 8,9.[366]

2.3.5.2.1. Anthropological dualism

To take the word πατρίς in 11,14 as suggesting a prior existence of "pneumatics" in the heavenly world is possible, but an unlikely

---

this relative indifference to the doctrine of the resurrection should caution against a dogmatic stance relative to the writer's (non-)expectation of the "new creation," especially when belief in the resurrection sits uneasily with both an absolutely negative view of creation as such and an absolute exclusion of a "new creation" in any sense. Scholer's rather casual affirmation that the "'rest' is anticipated as the establishment of a renewed earth," (Scholer, 204; likewise Peterson 1992, 221) is too optimistic. But Ellingworth, 688f. (following J.W. Thompson, 48f.; cf. Gräßer 1986, 173), probably oversteps the evidence in saying that *Auctor*'s thought "has no place for a new heaven and new earth."

[366] Hofius, 30, 50, 67, stressed the relevance of JosAsen 8,9; 15,7; 22,13; these have been a part of the discussion ever since though with very different conclusions drawn; e.g. Braun, 90-93; Gräßer, 1:218-220; Attridge, 127.

understanding of the metaphor in this context.³⁶⁷ The image is invoked with reference to the Patriarchs' historical circumstances as emigrants rather than cosmogony. The point is that they had a place for which they *longed* like emigrants *long* for their homeland; the heavenly-future city had *in that sense* supplanted the place they left behind, the place from which they had actually emigrated. The "city" could also be called their πατρίς because it was their proper "place" in a sense which a normal use of language only assigns to one's homeland. Every metaphor has several components of meaning, some of which transfer from the image to the topic as the "point of similarity" and some of which do not; in the present case, the idea of "emigration" is a component of meaning which is most probably not included in the point of similarity. As for 2,11.14, though taken atomistically the language accommodates the notion of pre-existence, it is more likely that in this context ἐξ ἑνός refers to common human ancestry³⁶⁸ or to a common familial relationship to God.³⁶⁹ Finally, it must be underlined that the notion of the κατάπαυσις as the *Urgrund* of the believers -- or the eternal essence of God prior to creation -- is not even hinted at in 3,7-4,11. To drag it in is to immediately initiate a process of misunderstanding.

2.3.5.2.2. Joseph and Aseneth³⁷⁰

Not only is the language of Ψ 94,11 [95,11] taken up in JosAsen 8,9, but it is applied to a heavenly resting place which God has "prepared"³⁷¹ (cf. Heb 11,16) for the elect.³⁷² Further on we will consider the possibility that Isa 66,1 was in *Auctor*'s background,³⁷³ and in that light it is interesting that Ψ 94,11 [95,11] and Isa 66,1 alternate in JosAsen 8,9 and 22,13. Yet the differences between Heb 3-4 and JosAsen are very significant. In JosAsen, unlike Heb 3-4, the dualistic idea of the resting place is pronounced (15,7; 22,13);³⁷⁴ there is no future eschatological orientation or final cosmic

---

³⁶⁷ Cf. R. Williamson 1970, 326-328; Lane, 2:358; Ellingworth, 596. The same sorts of linguistic considerations given in this paragraph apply to 12,9 and 13,3. The notion of pre-existence is simply not present in these statements.

³⁶⁸ E.g. Ellingworth, 165.

³⁶⁹ Most ancient and modern commentators have favored the latter; cf. Attridge, 88f.; Lane, 1:58f.; cf. also the discussion of the issues and various proposals of this difficult passage in Weiss, 212-215; Ellingworth, 164f.

³⁷⁰ For a summary of the relevant passages, see above, 109f.

³⁷¹ On the reading of ἡτοίμασεν (aorist) in 15,7, cf. Burchard, 61, 67f. Hofius, 185 n. 401, notes that the future tense is also possible.

³⁷² For the comparison in general, see Hofius, 205 n. 659. Hofius and Weiss, 271f., both give separate emphasis to the fact that it is *God's* resting place in both Heb and JosAsen, yet this is simply to restate that the allusion is to Ψ 94,11 [95,11].

³⁷³ Infra, 335ff.

³⁷⁴ Note that in 22,13 the resting place is located in the seventh heaven.

cataclysm in view. The resting place is individualized (22,13),[375] and is the eternal abode of the righteous from the time of their deaths.[376] That the heavenly world is "prepared" is not unique, nor is it an explicit feature of the κατάπαυσις in Heb 3,7-4,11.[377] The use of Ψ 94,11 [95,11] in JosAsen 8,9 is fragmentary and incidental to the thought of an other worldly resting place which was common currency at the time. There is no exegesis involved of the sort found in Hebrews, and there is no interest in Gen 2.

JosAsen 8,9 is important inasmuch as it shows how the language of Ψ 94,11 [95,11] might have been taken up into speculation about the κατάπαυσις in the afterlife and how it could be construed dualistically, but it does not warrant wrenching a more consistently dualistic meaning, let alone a specifically Philonic or gnostic conception, out of Heb 3-4.

2.4. Summary

Heb 3,7-4,11 is a warning against apostasy which is steeped in the language and substance of Ψ 94 [95], Gen 2, and Num 14. The passage stands at a point of transition in the epistle between the opening concern with God's definitive word spoken through his Son and the character of the Son's work relative to OT institutions. It is a call to listen faithfully and obediently to God's voice, which has sounded out "today." As at Kadesh, the process of apostasy can begin with only a few individuals but rapidly spread to others. Just as at Kadesh it can strike as late as the very point of entrance. And just as at Kadesh apostasy, once it has run its course, is irreversible.

The κατάπαυσις is construed as a locale, as God's own resting place, where he celebrates his own Sabbath. Ψ 94 [95] testified to the promise that God's people would ultimately enter this place, but also recounted how and why the very same promise had not benefited the "fathers" when it had been extended to them. The promise had been renewed and the warning was forceful. Like people who in horror watch those ahead of them try and fail, in Num 14 *Auctor*'s readers had seen the "fathers" fall to their doom; now the same offer had been extended to them. Reassuringly, the warning is framed by the reminder of Christ's priestly ministry which promises to assist the believer in his struggle, to bring perfection.

The salvation thereby described comes to them also as a promise, the promise that they will enter into God's resting place. In one sense they are on a journey toward the goal of salvation, in another sense they are awaiting

---

[375] Cf. Hofius, 50, 67; at least there is an individualized eschatology; Burchard, in *OTP*, 2:194.

[376] Cf. Hofius, 52f.

[377] *Contra* Hofius, 55, 178 n. 325; Braun, 92, who stress this as a specific parallel.

the day which is drawing near. On either understanding they are on probation. The struggle to enter certainly involves the sort of faith which puts no stock in this world and this life, beyond exploiting it fully for works of righteousness and obedience. The *contrast* between the worlds is less prominent in 3,7-4,11, however, than is the concern that all the community members should remain firm in their faith -- with all that entails for behavior -- in the face of the threat that if they should turn away from God they stand to lose all. In other words, the present world is not viewed negatively as such, but only as a stage on which the drama of faith is enacted.

We are now able to consider directly the proposed backgrounds for *Auctor*'s discussion of the κατάπαυσις. The understanding already achieved -- along with the Jewish and Christian literature surveyed at length -- has given us a means of testing the hypotheses which have been forwarded to explain this passage.

3. Proposals on the background of the κατάπαυσις

Though it will involve some repetition, the main proposals for the background of this passage will be summarized here for the sake of clarity. Isa 66,1 (Acts 7,49f.), is not usually considered in this connection, though it is often cited in discussions of Heb 3-4. I think it is deserving of greater emphasis as regards the question of backgrounds.

3.1. Isa 66,1 in Acts 7

Isa 66,1 has already been mentioned because of its appearance in Stephen's speech and its several parallels in Heb 3,7-4,11. In the chart that follows it can be noted that the highest concentration of parallels is in line with Isa 66,1f. Yet in addition to the verbal and conceptual parallels between Stephen's speech and Hebrews generally (e.g., the tent; Ex 25,40; angels as mediators of the law; the narrative traditions of Joshua and God's "house"),[378] one notes that there are a number of parallels between Hebrews and the remainder of Isa 66, particularly involving the eschatological visions. Thus the three passages interweave at more than a merely verbal level.

---

[378] For a general comparison of Hebrews and the Stephen traditions, cf. Hurst, 89-106 (esp. 102f. on the κατάπαυσις-idea); Lane, 1:cxliv-cl. Hurst is largely interacting with W. Manson; for the following see also Ellingworth, 219f.

Chapter Seven: A Promise Remains

Acts 7,44-50	OT	Hebrews
Our ancestors had the tent of testimony in the wilderness [ἡ σκηνὴ τοῦ μαρτυρίου ἦν τοῖς πατράσιν ἡμῶν ἐν τῇ ἐρήμῳ], as God directed when he spoke to Moses, ordering him to make it according to the pattern he had seen [κατὰ τὸν τύπον ὃν ἑωράκει].		8,2; 9,1ff.; cf. 3,17
	Ex 25,40	8,5
Our ancestors in turn brought it in with Joshua when they disposed the nations that God drove out before our ancestors. And it was there until the time of David, who found favor with God and asked that he might find a dwelling place for the house of Jacob [τῷ οἴκῳ Ἰακώβ]. But it was Solomon who built a house for him [οἰκοδόμησεν αὐτῷ οἶκον]. Yet the Most High does not dwell in houses made with human hands [χειροποιήτοις]; as the prophet says, ὁ οὐρανός μοι θρόνος, ἡ δὲ γῆ ὑποπόδιον τῶν ποδῶν μου· ποῖον οἶκον οἰκοδομήσετέ μοι, λέγει κύριος, ἢ τίς τόπος τῆς καταπαύσεώς μου; οὐχὶ ἡ χείρ μου ἐποίησεν ταῦτα πάντα; You stiff necked people, uncircumcised in heart and ears, you are forever opposing the Holy Spirit, just as your ancestors used to do...		4,7f.
	Ψ 131,4f. (cf. v. 14 with Ps 95,11) 1Chr 22,6	3,2-6 (cf. 1Par 17,10-14; 1Kgdms 2,35)
	Isa 66,1f. ὁ οὐρανός μοι θρόνος, ἡ δὲ γῆ ὑποπόδιον τῶν ποδῶν μου· ποῖον οἶκον οἰκοδομήσετέ μοι; ἢ ποῖος τόπος τῆς καταπαύσεώς μου; πάντα γὰρ ταῦτα ἐποίησεν ἡ χείρ μου, καὶ ἔστιν ἐμὰ πάντα ταῦτα, λέγει κύριος· v. 2 But this is the one to whom I will look, to the humble and contrite in spirit, who trembles at my word... (cf. Isa 57,15 and Heb 3,6)	9,11.24 (χειροποίητος); 8,2; 9,1; heaven/ earth; God's throne; footstool; house (3,2-6) κατάπαυσις creator (3,4; 4,4) ...Holy Spirit says...; hard heart; evil heart; hear God's voice;
	v. 3 ...their own ways...	3,10 (my ways)
You are the ones that received the law as ordained by angels, and yet you have not kept it.		2,2
	v. 10 Rejoice with Jerusalem, and be glad [πανηγυρίσατε] for her, all you who love her; rejoice with her in joy... v. 22 For as the new heavens and the new earth, which I will make, shall remain before me [ἃ ἐγὼ ποιῶ, μένει ἐνώπιόν μου]... v. 23 From new moon to new moon, and from sabbath to sabbath, all flesh shall come to worship before me	12,22 (πανηγύρει) 12,27 (cf. NA[27]); cf. 2Pet 3,13 σαββατισμός; 12,22

The parallels are noteworthy and could likely stem back to some common, Hellenistic Jewish Christian tradition.[379] What is remarkable, then, is how very different Hebrews is from both Acts 7 and Isa 66.

---

[379] Note that Ψ 94,11 [95,11] and Isa 66,1 alternate in the conception of JosAsen (8,9; 22,13); here in Acts 7 an echo of Ψ 131 [132] is in close proximity to Isa 66,1. Further confirmation of a Christian tradition may stem from *Barn* 15-16. *Barn* 15, with its use of Gen 2,2, its concept of the world-week, and its characterization of the future world as a

Although *Auctor* works throughout with the earthly tabernacle he does not contrast it with the earthly temple as Stephen does; the earthly temple is simply ignored in Hebrews. Whereas for Stephen the mobile *tabernacle* derived status from being a copy of the divine "pattern," while the *temple* (the "house") was generally rejected as χειροποίητος because God had created his own place of rest (τόπος τῆς καταπαύσεώς μου), for *Auctor* -- who shows no interest in the earthly temple -- the *tabernacle*, while erected according to the divine "pattern" and valid in its own time, was generally inferior as χειροποίητος to the "true tent" erected in heaven. *Auctor* also does not seem to directly identify the κατάπαυσις and the heavenly temple as such, while Stephen does not explore how God's people relate to his cosmic place of rest, and *Auctor*'s eschatological orientation is missing from Acts 7,49. *Auctor* and Stephen are potentially reconcilable,[380] but their very different contexts/purposes and the fact that Stephen does not pursue his theme further make it very difficult if not impossible to confidently trace out the line of development from Stephen to *Auctor* touching the κατάπαυσις-idea.[381]

What may be significant is that Stephen rejects the earthly temple in favor of the notion that God's κατάπαυσις is not a house built with hands. Not only does this thought remind us of Hebrews' theology generally, but it highlights the nexus between the temple and the κατάπαυσις, in this case united in the OT passage.[382] If *Auctor* differs by not thinking narrowly of the temple as the κατάπαυσις, his thinking would likely have had Isa 66,1f. in

---

perfect Sabbath celebration, differs in fundamental ways from Heb 3-4 (cf. Hofius, 113-115; Theißen 1969, 124f.) but is close enough to call forth comment in studies of the latter passage. It may be noteworthy that only a few sentences later in *Barnabas* (16,2) Isa 66,1 is quoted, and in a text form which matches Acts 7,49; cf. Haenchen 1971, 285 n. 4. Haenchen wonders whether this points to the use of a "testimony book" on the parts of "Barnabas" and Luke. Interestingly, R.W. Thurston 1979 argues that Isa 66,1ff. was an important passage for *Auctor*, containing as it did several words which became "magnets" for other OT passages containing the same words; he mentions here "throne," "heaven," "earth," God's "hands," "footstool," "house," and "resting place." Based on the common use of Isa 66,1 and other passages by Stephen and *Auctor* Thurston argues that *Auctor* used a "book of testimonies." Thurston extended his argument in 1986. I am not ready to pronounce on the use of a "testimony book" by anyone, but there do appear to be indications that Isa 66,1ff. played some part in the genesis of *Auctor*'s thought and it may be possible to draw a line through Stephen, Hebrews, and *Barnabas* on this score.

[380] *Auctor* may simply have conflated the earthly tabernacle and temple, and extended the line of thought far beyond Stephen's expression; cf. also Hurst, 97.

[381] I have not determined precisely what role this particular Hellenistic tradition might have played in *Auctor*'s own development. I doubt that much of value can be said on that point. But we cannot ignore the remarkable parallels, which indicate that there is something more than merely a shared outlook.

[382] Note that Stephen's speech like Heb 3,1-6ff. moves from the "house" motif to the κατάπαυσις, yet on both scores the differences with Hebrews are apparent.

the background. Acts 7 tells us that there is a traditional element to Heb 3,7-4,11, but the differences are too great to use Acts 7 as a control on *Auctor*'s thought. Here, at least, is further evidence that first century Christians incorporated the OT rest tradition into their expressions of the new salvation. It is also evidence that *Auctor*'s thinking on the κατάπαυσις-idea *began with the OT* and was worked out at least partially in a mainstream Christian context. Beyond this, however, Stephen/Luke does not take us, and we can only guess at how Stephen would have construed the κατάπαυσις positively and how he might have developed the theme pastorally.[383]

3.2. Philonic and gnostic (dualistic)

3.2.1. Review of the case

There is no separating the proposals of a gnostic and Philonic understanding of rest as pertains to discussions of Heb 3-4. Käsemann had already linked the two, and his heirs have continued in this tradition as the survey of the discussion has already evidenced.[384] Therefore, although we separated Philo and the Gnostics when examining their literature, we will be forced to consider them together at this point.

The paths to this proposal are not, however, unified. Käsemann had argued that the notion of Heb 3,7-4,11 was that of a heavenly place of rest conceived according to a hebdomadal schema; such a place, the κατάπαυσις, formed the destination of the soul's heavenly journey. Such a notion had no home in the OT, but was strangely reminiscent of certain ideas of Philo. Yet the differences between Hebrews and Philo told against direct derivation. More likely, therefore, was the thesis of some sort of pre-Philonic Gnosticism which provided *Auctor* (and Philo) with a mythologically conceived way of talking about salvation. This mythological conception of salvation was taken over by *Auctor* without, however, a wholesale transfer of the gnostic world-view. A degree of transfer is to be expected, but not so much that it fundamentally altered the Christian gospel.

Following on from Käsemann, Theißen's strategy was to discern within Philo's treatment of the ἀνάπαυσις theme two strains of thought, one of which was more "gnostic" and the other more "Jewish." It was the gnostic strain which exhibited the closer affinities with Hebrews, particularly in *Auctor*'s (gnostic-like) dualism, his view of the divine rest as an end to

---

[383] Cf. Marshall 1980, 146.
[384] This is true even of J.W. Thompson. Thompson is primarily concerned to draw parallels with Philo, but his discussion belongs to the interpretive tradition associated with Käsemann, Theißen, Gräßer, and Braun. For the survey of the discussion, see Ch. One.

work, and his paralleling of the divine and human rests. Theißen's argument is thus similar to Käsemann's, albeit more nuanced in his treatment of Philo.

The approach of Braun and Gräßer has been more general. First of all, distinctions between Philo, JosAsen, and Gnosticism are minimized and at times done away with entirely. This enables them to draw up an extended list of ideas about rest which are found in all three domains, Judaism, Hebrews, and Gnosticism, and which therefore do not assist in narrowing down religious historical derivation.[385] A few other items point up differences in conception between Hebrews and Gnosticism, but again are not considered to be decisive in terms of derivation.[386] The question which decides the matter for them is whether the rest is located on the new or renewed earth, as in Jewish apocalyptic, or only in heaven, as in dualistic conceptions. Hebrews locates the κατάπαυσις in heaven, while the earth is assessed more negatively as that "which can be shaken," and that which will ultimately be removed. This invalidates 4Ez, among other apocalyptic parallels, as the key to Hebrews' κατάπαυσις-idea, since there also the rest is placed on the renewed earth. The closer parallels are to be found in literature such as JosAsen, Philo, and gnostic writings. From here other parallels with Gnosticism can be brought up for emphasis.

Finally,[387] J.W. Thompson's approach is to emphasize the metaphysical component of writings indebted to Platonic metaphysics, especially Philo and Gnosticism, and to draw out just such metaphysical features in Hebrews'

---

[385] Braun, 91f. This list of common denominators includes the following points (for the evidence see Braun): (1) the rest is both a place and a state; (2) it is attained following death (with Gnosticism it is also a present benefit); (3) the rest is something entered; (4) the rest is variably formulated as salvation; (5) the rest bears a sabbatical character; (6) rest is the cessation of troublesome activity; (7) God himself rests.

[386] Braun, 92f., mentions the following (these assume Braun's inclusive idea of what is "gnostic"). In Jewish and Christian (*Barn* 15) texts, as well as "gnostic" (only Philo), God's rest is not an end to activity as it appears to be in Hebrews. The gnostic texts place a strong emphasis on rest as a present experience (missing in Hebrews) and on the Redeemer as the giver of rest (weak in Jewish texts and in Hebrews). That God has created rest is evidenced in both Jewish and gnostic texts but is not formulated explicitly in Hebrews. Or again, Hebrews stands closer to Jewish texts in placing the rest motif in the context of the judgment and a warning against losing the rest, while gnostic texts tend to have a more inviting tone. Certain gnostic texts also have an erotic tone, missing in Hebrews.

[387] In addition to the scholars discussed in the text one can note also Dey, 77, 213f., 227-233, whose work is primarily concerned with issues outside the scope of this study, especially with larger patterns of perfection in Philo and Hebrews. Within this framework, Dey observes parallels with Philo's rest speculation exclusively. The idea of "entrance into God's κατάπαυσις" in Heb 3-4 thus appears to be exactly equivalent to Philo's thinking about rest for Dey. The same criticisms we are raising against Gräßer, Thompson, *et. al.* can therefore be applied to Dey. For a more general critique of Dey's study see Johnsson 1977; as regards Dey's treatment of perfection in Philo and Hebrews, see Peterson 1982, 30-33, and *passim*.

presentation. Thus Hebrews is seen to stand in the tradition of writings influenced by Platonic metaphysical speculation about the material and transcendent, immaterial worlds. Though differing in its details, Thompson's approach is broadly the same as the aforementioned inasmuch as it boils down to a question of a metaphysical dualism.[388]

3.2.2. Evaluation

The most important consideration in the post-Hofius discussion has been the apparent absence of a new or renewed earth in Hebrews, i.e., Auctor's supposed "dualism." It has been admitted by the advocates of this position that the full Philonic or gnostic understanding of the κατάπαυσις is not expressed in Hebrews, but it can be surprising how much is found.

As important as this consideration might be for other sections and ideas in Hebrews it is nonetheless somewhat less significant for a positive understanding of the κατάπαυσις-idea. An apparent assumption of Gräßer et al. is that the idea of a "heavenly" resting place (i.e., one not associated with a new creation) could only be derived directly from a source like JosAsen or Philo, but this is not so. Another apparent assumption is that a heavenly κατάπαυσις would necessarily involve Philo's and Gnosticism's speculative baggage; this is also erroneous.

True, associating the κατάπαυσις with heaven and *not* with the earth is formally closer to dualistic conceptions such as JosAsen 8,9, Philo, and Gnosticism, but (1) this is not a stated (or even necessarily implied) feature of the κατάπαυσις, and (2) the distinctive features of such dualistic rest speculation are simply not present in or behind Heb 3-4. What is distinctive for Philo's and Gnosticism's thought is not the fact of an already existent, heavenly resting place, nor yet the parallel of the divine and human coming-to-rests. What is distinctive is its metaphysical character and basis; the Philonic and gnostic rest-speculation is positively embedded in a metaphysical outlook which contrasts the earthly realm with the heavenly world of stability and immovability. What is distinctive is its essential debt to Pythagorean number speculation and its mythology of the cosmic journey of the soul out of the material realm into the heavenly realm. None of *this* sort of dualism is present in connection with the κατάπαυσις-idea in Heb 3-4. Indeed, the latter is remarkable for its lack of interest in vertical contrasts, heavenly vs. earthly. The whole passage is oriented to the future; movement, such as it is implied, is *horizontal*.

If it were not for the larger context of Hebrews we would probably not make as much of the *spatial* dualism in discussions of the κατάπαυσις in

---

[388] Cf. J.W. Thompson, 98-102, which utilizes the same argument as Gräßer and Braun above in relation to dualism.

Heb 3,7-4,11. This is not to say that there is no dualism at work here, and it is indeed the larger context which sets this in relief. It is only to make the point that if we isolate this unit of 3,7-4,11, i.e. the κατάπαυσις-idea, *Auctor*'s spatial dualism recedes considerably, suggesting that it was not of fundamental import to his development of this idea. When the attempt is made to align the κατάπαυσις-idea more closely with *Philonic and gnostic* rest-speculation with its underlying *cosmological and metaphysical* dualism the result is demonstrably forced, but since the main points were addressed in the exegetical section above we will leave the matter with those comments. To them may be added the detailed analyses and comparisons of Heb 3-4 and Philo and Gnosticism already supplied by Williamson and Hofius, whose remarks have enduring value and do not need to be repeated here.[389]

3.2.3. Conclusion

The method of Theißen, Gräßer *et al.* has been to work from the inside out, from a "dualistic" core out to various details of Philo's or Gnosticism's rest-speculation. Our approach has been rather to work from the outside in. We have sought first to show the alien character of the specific Philonic and gnostic features which have been advanced as extensions of the basic "dualism." But once we prune away all such overgrowth we are left with a "dualism" which does not -- *insofar as the κατάπαυσις-idea of 3,7-4,11 is concerned* -- help us to more sharply focus the matter of derivation beyond the label, "Jewish-Christian." There is nothing to finally separate it from the dualisms we encounter in apocalyptic.

If, on the strength of scattered parallels, someone wants to insist that *Auctor* might have been influenced by the rest-speculation of Philo or some sort of early "Gnosis,"[390] there is not much to protest against. But the evidence does not support the thesis that *Auctor* is being fundamentally guided by a specific strain of Alexandrian rest speculation which is essentially based in a cosmological and metaphysical dualism, and his statements should not be made to harmonize with Philo and Gnosticism.

What then has been the enduring contribution of this scholarly exegetical tradition to our understanding of the κατάπαυσις? For our interests it

---

[389] For comparisons of the rest idea in Philo and Hebrews, see R. Williamson 1970, 539-557; Hofius, 248-257 (a direct response to Theißen); cf. Barrett, 368-373; Schröger, 305f. For a detailed comparison of the rest idea in Hebrews and Gnosticism, cf. Hofius, esp. 98-101. The overall contrast stressed by these scholars is, I think, generally recognized. The opposing arguments which have persisted to the present were addressed in our examination.

[390] Theißen 1969, 128. Others would prefer to use the label "proto-gnostic."

reduces to this:³⁹¹ it has pointed up and placed in sharp focus the exaggerations of those who have argued one-sidedly for an "apocalyptic" concept of the κατάπαυσις.

3.3. Jewish Apocalyptic³⁹²

3.3.1. Review of the case

The view that the ideas that have influenced *Auctor*'s development of the κατάπαυσις-idea derive in the main from Jewish apocalyptic was not original with Hofius,³⁹³ but it does find its most precise and consistent advocate with him, and it is with his work that we will concern ourselves.

Hofius envisages the κατάπαυσις as follows.³⁹⁴ As the Most Holy Place of the heavenly temple, the κατάπαυσις is a locale prepared in heaven since creation for God's people.³⁹⁵ God himself entered his κατάπαυσις to rest following his work of creation, and it is there that he sits on his throne. The promise of entrance into this resting place was offered to the "fathers" in the wilderness (Deut 12 etc.) but they forfeited this *Heilsgut* through disobedience. The offer was renewed when David penned Ps 95 [Ψ 94], showing that no one had yet entered and suggesting that the promise

---

³⁹¹ More generally, there is a real value in highlighting the terminology and manner of expression used by *Auctor* with reference to Hellenistic Judaism such as we encounter it in Philo and elsewhere. At other points such comparisons will be more fruitful.

³⁹² For reasons of space we will by-pass the case which is put from time to time that Heb 3,7-4,11 anticipates a future life for God's people in Canaan (Buchanan, 61-79; cf. also 1975, 325-329), possibly during the millennium associated with the messiah's earthly reign (Delitzsch, 1:197f.; W.C. Kaiser 1985, 168-172, 174f.); cf. Darnell, 217 with further references. *Auctor* shows no interest in political affairs associated with Canaan, and there is no express interest or belief in a this-worldly, 1000 year reign of Christ. In general see the remarks of Ellingworth, 254. The Jewish literature never identifies the time of the messiah with a world-Sabbath as such; when in the rabbinic literature the messianic time is located in the schema of a world-week it is *separated* from the world-to-come by the 1000 year world-Sabbath (cf. Str-B, 4/2:989; Volz, 76; Hofius, 210 n. 754; Lincoln 1982, 217 n. 4; *contra* Rordorf, 50). Rev 20 speaks of a millennial reign of Christ on earth, but in post-apostolic literature the idea of a millennial reign is first connected with the "world-week" schema in Irenaeus; cf. Lohmann, 233 n. 83. Bauckham 1982b, 293 n. 112, makes the observation that in the post-apostolic literature "the metaphorical interpretation of the Sabbath commandment was rarely related to the concept of eschatological rest"; *Barn* 15 is exceptional; cf. also *EpApost* 19 (cf. *ARN* 1; *Ber* 17a). For all these reasons, one will need to be slow to assume that the rest-idea of Heb 3-4 can be simply connected with a millennium and "world-week."

³⁹³ E.g. Michel, 21-91, 184-186, others are reviewed in Hofius, 10-12, 24f.

³⁹⁴ Cf. esp. Hofius, 51-58, 91-101, 106-110, 115, 151, 255-259.

³⁹⁵ On exegetical grounds we found both of these ideas to be untenable, namely the κατάπαυσις as a primordial creation and its identification with the heavenly temple. That it is a local idea and is construed as prepared in heaven is to be accepted.

"remains." Jesus, the Great High Priest and "forerunner" has already entered on behalf of God's people, and Christians now wait expectantly (there is no ascent/journey through the cosmos) and faithfully for God's heavenly κατάπαυσις to "appear" from heaven, where it is now hidden. If they do not fall by following the pattern of disobedience set by the "fathers," they will ultimately enter that κατάπαυσις, i.e., the Most Holy Place of the heavenly temple, there to gather around God's throne in a joyful Sabbath celebration.

This whole idea Hofius considers to be thoroughly apocalyptic in outlook. He distinguishes it sharply from Gnosticism and from Philo, and compares it most closely with 4 Ezra, though the latter neither identifies the resting place with the heavenly temple nor connects it to the creation account.[396]

3.3.2. Evaluation

Hofius' evidence for a widespread belief in a heavenly and eschatological resting *place* reinforces the local conception in Hebrews (which is otherwise firmly based on lexical and contextual grounds), and it establishes that this idea was not unique to Philonic or gnostic conceptions.

Nonetheless, Hofius, like Gräßer and others, falls prey to the tendency to read elements into Heb 3-4 in the interest of enhancing the general religious historical parallel. For instance, he attempts to identify the κατάπαυσις with the heavenly temple. This interpretation not only has the effect of distinguishing the κατάπαυσις from the heavenly world in general -- *in contrast to Philo and Gnosticism* -- but of lodging it all the more deeply in traditional OT and apocalyptic images. It may not be surprising, then, that Theißen, Gräßer, and Braun all reject this understanding of the κατάπαυσις, but they are probably correct on this point over against Hofius. Just as the gnostic and Philonic parallels should never have been taken as a license to align Heb 3-4 with those usages of the motif more than the language allows, so the same is true of apocalyptic parallels.

In terms of the specific parallels which Hofius draws with 4 Ezra, most if not all of them could probably be explained by an appeal to the OT and other Jewish writings generally.[397] Yet rather than enter into a detailed debate over specific points we can make some general observations which favor the view that 4 Ezra is of only limited value in understanding Heb 3-4. It is to be

---

[396] Cf. Hofius, 91-98, 257f. The parallels with 4Ez are generally dismissed as overdone by Theißen 1969, 128; cf. likewise, Attridge, 128

[397] E.g., the fact that the resting place is a local idea, that it is "prepared," that sin would lead to exclusion, and that the idea of a resting place is joined with others such as the heavenly city.

noted that no direct dependence on 4 Ezra is assumed or implied, either on our part or Hofius'. Rather, 4 Ezra represents speculation that dates from a period very close to Hebrews, and which may testify to ideas that were current when *Auctor* wrote.

(1) Hebrews does not give any expression to a new or renewed earth as is typical of apocalyptic and particularly of 4 Ezra. I cannot see that *Auctor*'s language finally excludes such an expectation, but his present work has no interest in it. To this extent the objection of Theißen, Braun, and Gräßer holds, namely, that the overall conception of Hebrews does not correspond to typical apocalyptic expressions.

(2) Along with the idea that there would be a world renewal was the belief that the resting place would "appear" at the end. Unlike 4Ez 8,52, *Auctor* gives no expression to the notion that the resting place as such was "prepared" although it is implied in 4,1-10 and explicitly stated in connection with the "city" (11,16). Yet alongside this idea the motifs of "disclosure" and "appearance" -- movement out of "concealment" -- are emphatically expressed in 4 Ezra (7,26.36).[398] We have stressed throughout that *Auctor* has a future orientation and this is so. As Hofius points out, important expressions such as $\dot{\epsilon}\kappa\delta\dot{\epsilon}\chi o\mu\alpha\iota$ (11,10), $\dot{o}\rho\dot{\epsilon}\gamma o\mu\alpha\iota$ (11,16), and $\dot{\epsilon}\pi\iota\zeta\eta\tau\dot{\epsilon}\omega$ (13,14) jibe well with an apocalyptic outlook in which one "expects" and "awaits" the coming age, the day which "draws near" (10,25).[399] Yet, on the one hand, Hofius has probably exaggerated the "waiting" motif in 3,7-4,11, and on the other hand, neither the $\kappa\alpha\tau\dot{\alpha}\pi\alpha\upsilon\sigma\iota\varsigma$ nor any other reality[400] is envisioned as "appearing" or "coming down"[401] in conjunction with (or separate from) a new creation in Hebrews. Is this because *Auctor* carefully avoided such language, is it because he simply failed to use the language, or is it because it did not express his mental image of what would happen?

Specific features such as "appearing" (note the following points as well) can be dismissed as extraneous to *Auctor*'s immediate paraenetic and exegetical concerns, and one could find little basis for objection. Yet it seems as acceptable to me to say that if the conception expressed a little later in 4 Ezra was in *Auctor*'s background, so far from treating it as normative he allowed his idea of the eschatological resting place to be forged by the constraints of his OT texts and his homiletic concerns. With this, however,

---

[398] Cf. Stone 1989, 57f., 102f.; see also Rev 21,1f.

[399] Hofius, 92, 146-151. In all these cases Hofius is opposing any interpretation which construes these ideas along the lines of "travelling."

[400] In 9,26.28, however, there is reference made to Jesus' "appearance." Cf. 11,7, which is ambiguous, certainly not equal to the stress placed on the idea in 4 Ezra.

[401] Rev 3,12; 21,1f.10. This precise image of the heavenly city "coming down" is, however, almost unparalleled in Judaism; cf. Str-B, 3:796.

we begin to question the real value of the "parallel" in 4 Ezra for understanding *Auctor*'s idea of the κατάπαυσις.

(3) Unlike 4Ez 7,88-101 *Auctor* gives no expression to the idea of an intermediate resting place. Here too it must be said that there is no rule which says that *Auctor* must give expression to the entire idea of a given source, and in this case the idea of an intermediate resting place does not seem essential. By way of contrast, for instance, we could cite Philo's number speculation and his metaphysical conception of the rest; these are essential to his thought and therefore can be used as tests for dependence. Yet if we are going to say that there is such a thing as *an* "apocalyptic rest-idea," meaning the one expressed independently in the later work of 4 Ezra, and that *this* idea is the source of *Auctor*'s thought, then it is remarkable what *Auctor* does not say or even hint at. It is apparent that in more than one very significant way *Auctor* moves very independently of his source.

(4) Another example of the foregoing is in that *Auctor* does not construe the "resting place" as over against a "place of torment." This dual idea -- place of rest and place of torment -- is most emphatic in 4Ez 7, both in terms of the ultimate state (7,36-44) and the intermediate state (7,75-101).[402] This is no proof for or against an apocalyptic expression, but it does remove yet again the expression found in Heb 3-4 from that expressed in 4 Ezra.

(5) A third example is in that Hebrews does not explicitly envisage the heavenly "Paradise" which in 4Ez is bound up with the "resting place."[403] In general, references to Paradise are scant in the NT,[404] and this may be explained as a lack of interest in Paradise for its own sake in favor of an interest in "the restoration of the communion with God which was broken through Adam's fall."[405] Moreover, in Hebrews it may be that the idea of the heavenly Jerusalem with its temple amounts to the same thing as Paradise.[406] Nonetheless, once again, in addition to the intermediate rest and the place of torment, a gap is apparent between Hebrews and 4 Ezra. Prominent features of the latter are simply not expressed in Hebrews.

(6) On the other side we note that the references to rest and to a resting place in 4 Ezra are, as it were, anonymous; that is, they do not issue from any specific OT passage. We saw in our survey that much of the intertestamental use of the idea of rest does ultimately develop out of the OT, yet it is the case that the idea of a heavenly and future resting place was a stock feature of Jewish thought. This is how it appears in 4 Ezra, as well

---

[402] Cf. also 2,25.27f.; 8,50-54; also Rev 14,11.13; 2Thes 1,6-10; 1En 38,2; 39,4f.; 45,3.6; TAb 9,8 [Rec B].

[403] Cf. 4Ez 7,36.123; 8,52. Hofius, 93f., confronts this point.

[404] It is referred to directly only in Lk 23,43; 2Cor 12,4; and Rev 2,7.

[405] Jeremias 1967b, 772f. On this basis Jeremias considers the lack of references to Paradise as "hardly accidental" (1967b, 769).

[406] Hofius, 94; cf. Jeremias 1967b, 769, 772.

as in Rev 14,11.13. Very differently, *Auctor's* whole discussion is grounded in specific OT passages, especially Ψ 94 [95] and Gen 2. This *exegetical* interest shapes *Auctor's* thought and gives it its distinctive stamp.

Precision is a luxury which is not on offer, and in spite of the confidence with which opinions are sometimes put one can only give one's impression. Mine is that the parallel with apocalyptic -- in particular with 4 Ezra -- is generally satisfying, but that it is only a very loose parallel which gives no reliable guide to filling in the gaps nor a standard by which alternative parallels -- e.g. Philonic and gnostic -- can be excluded in principle.[407] As with apocalyptic, *Auctor* construes the resting place as a heavenly reality, prepared in advance for the elect and entered by them eschatologically; there, following the resurrection and judgment, they will rest from their labors of life, their good works and their endurance in the face of persecution, without which no one will enter. This rest will open the way for a joyful Sabbath celebration ("world which is wholly Sabbath and rest") around God's throne in the true tent, the heavenly Jerusalem, Mount Zion, the heavenly fatherland, the world-to-come. Yet unlike typical apocalyptic expressions, *Auctor* does not openly associate the resting place with a renewed earth; to that extent it remains for him essentially a heavenly reality. His thought is shaped largely by his own exegetical work.

3.3.3. Conclusion

It may be said in sum that the very strength of Hofius' interpretation -- the attempt to be precise and consistent -- is its weakness. As was the case with the aforementioned attempts to align this passage as consistently and precisely as possible with Philonic and gnostic conceptions, so Hofius' alignment with apocalyptic, especially 4 Ezra, fails to convince when it ends up having to force unlikely interpretations of specific ideas. The attempt to find in 4,3f. the idea that the κατάπαυσις is one of the "works" alluded to will always be subject to question because it sits very awkwardly with what is actually said. The identification of the κατάπαυσις and the heavenly temple will likewise be relegated to the footnotes. His insistence that the "travelling" motif has no place here will probably not be sustainable, largely because *neither* "travelling" nor "waiting" is crucial to the passage, or rather, *both* are assumed. His attempt to draw the κατάπαυσις idea into the closest possible relationship with 4 Ezra will continue to convince few scholars in view of the many differences. And finally, the matter of *Auctor's* Platonic manner of expression, especially in 12,27f., will continue to haunt any

---

[407] Cf. Theißen 1969, 129; Hofius, 259.

attempt to align 3,7-4,11 squarely with widespread Jewish expectations of a new or renewed earth.

The value of Hofius' work will, however, be enduring. He has isolated and highlighted a number of basic methodological issues. He has gathered, organized, and discussed a wealth of relevant linguistic and religious historical comparative materials. Through these he has refuted or neutralized the key arguments which Käsemann and Käsemann's disciples have used to build their case. He has demonstrated with patience and in detail the great differences between Heb 3-4 and the gnostic and Philonic concepts of rest. He has thereby placed in much sharper focus than was hitherto possible the location of Heb 3-4 in the surrounding literary and conceptual world. He has, in spite of his intended result, enabled us to see more clearly the *uniqueness* of Heb 3-4 in that world.

3.4. Independent Hellenistic Jewish Christian

3.4.1. General indications of independence

We may begin with some inter-related propositions which will set the framework for our discussion.

(1) *This treatment of the κατάπαυσις-idea probably received encouragement, if not its initial impetus from Christian traditions.* Along the way we have compared and contrasted *Auctor*'s development of the rest-idea with other usages of the motif in the NT, namely, Acts 3,20; Rev 14,13; 2Thes 1,7; Jn 5,17; and Acts 7,49. In the final chapter we will return to compare it more closely with Mt 11,28-30. For now, what can be said to emerge from these comparisons is that certain ideas -- namely, the expectation, expressed apocalyptically, of an eschatological rest both generally and specifically from the labors of righteousness and of endurance through persecution, as well as the idea of an eschatological Sabbath[408] -- were expressed elsewhere in first century Christianity, and are to that extent not unique to the writer of Hebrews. A noteworthy NT parallel is Acts 7,49, a passage which is at once distant from and remarkably similar to Heb 3-4. It is not necessary to determine how speculation on the rest motif developed from "Stephen" to *Auctor*, but only to observe that it is very likely that *Auctor* was working with a traditional, Christian idea in taking up the theme of the κατάπαυσις. The OT and Christian traditions become the most likely *starting point* for *Auctor*'s interest in this idea rather than speculation found elsewhere in Judaism.

---

[408] We also noted that the Odes of Solomon along with Jn 14 may testify to an early Christian parallel to the idea of a heavenly resting place; supra, 132f.

(2) *This passage is* fundamentally *indebted to the OT, not only in language but in substance.* This debt to the OT is palpable in the language of the passage, not only owing to Ψ 94,7-11 [95,7-11] and Gen 2,2, but very considerably to Num 14. The latter, possibly used under the influence of Jewish exegetical tradition, explains not only the transition from 3,1-6 to 3,7ff.,[409] but it forms a dramatic backdrop to the entire exhortation. The imagery of the κατάπαυσις thus brought in complements not only the ideas of the heavenly land and city which *Auctor* develops further, but the temple theme as well. The latter association in particular -- that with the temple -- is not pronounced in either the dualistic (esp. Philonic or gnostic) or the apocalyptic parallels, but is most strongly grounded in the OT.[410] Although *Auctor* did not directly identify the κατάπαυσις and the heavenly temple -- possibly in part because of the backdrop of Num 14 -- the association would almost certainly have been not only apparent but of interest to him.[411]

(3) *It is not the κατάπαυσις-idea which controls this passage, but Auctor's paraenetic concern, which is molded by the language and events of Ψ 94 [95] and Num 14.* The κατάπαυσις is important, but not the essential component of Ψ 94 [95]; there it was captured in a strongly worded warning against disobedience lest the eschatological salvation should be forfeited. For this reason the indebtedness to Ψ 94 [95] and Num 14 makes the OT of fundamental importance to grasping *Auctor*'s true concern. That concern is not to express a metaphysical contrast between heaven and earth and to call the readers to carry out a journey through the cosmos to the transcendent domain of stability where they will "stand at rest" or "rest in God," but rather to warn the readers against making the same mistake the "fathers" did, namely, spurning the *promise* and forfeiting participation in an eschatological, festive Sabbath celebration in God's resting place; the

---

[409] Cf. further above, 273f., on the transition to Ψ 94 [95] in this context.

[410] One finds it in the rabbinic literature when commenting on the OT; supra, 122ff. Hofius, 96f., is hard pressed to find a parallel for this in the apocalyptic literature.

[411] Several observations support this assumption: (1) *Auctor* was intimate with his OT; it is unlikely that he would have missed the relationship of the temple to the κατάπαυσις theme. (2) The term κατάπαυσις in particular had a very close connection with the temple in the LXX (supra, 98). (3) Heb 3,7-4,11 falls between the beginning and continuation of the exposition of Christ's priesthood; the thematic associations could hardly have dropped from *Auctor*'s mind in view of the two previous points. (4) In his examination of the term εἰσέρχομαι in Hebrews and the LXX, Scholer, 153 n. 3, concluded that *Auctor*'s use of this term throughout the epistle (thus its use in relation to entrance into the temple) derived from its occurrence in Ψ 94,11 [95,11]. (5) P. Walker, 55, points out that "the three concentric *realia* of Judaism are each dealt with in turn: the Land (chs. 3-4), the Temple (chs. 5-10), and finally the city (chs. 11-13)." The relationship of these realities is assumed. (6) In Acts 7,49, which we have argued had some place in *Auctor*'s exegetical tradition, the reference is explicitly to *God's* resting place (Isa 66,1), creation as God's temple. Moreover, this is brought into connection with Ψ 131 [132] (cf. Acts 7,46; noted in our diagram above).

warning is absolutely pressing in view of the normative paradigm of Num 14. The work with Gen 2,2 is part and parcel of this concern.

(4) *A number of assumptions -- expressed elsewhere in Hebrews, and essentially shaped by Auctor's Christology -- appear to drive this midrash along its given course.* Whatever dualistic or apocalyptic rest-speculation contributed to *Auctor's* thinking, he has his own agenda and Christian concerns which shape his κατάπαυσις-idea.

(5) *Auctor's development of the rest idea cannot be satisfactorily matched by any one religious historical parallel.*

(6) *The use to which Gen 2 is put in connection with Ψ 94 [95] is unique in the known Jewish literature.* Here is no speculation about God "causing to rest while he continues creating" or about attaining the metaphysical benefits of the number 7, no world-week or even merely a "world which is wholly Sabbath and rest." Here God's own primordial Sabbath becomes an eschatological salvation gift wherein God's people will rest from their works after the pattern of God's own rest. They will then participate in a σαββατισμός, God's own Sabbath celebration, which takes place in God's κατάπαυσις. Though this construct stems organically from the OT and is intelligible in relation to Jewish traditions, it is unprecedented in its bald statement and unique in conception.

3.4.2. The use of Gen 2,2

Having looked with some care at 4,1-11 it is apparent that Gen 2 belongs to the warp and woof of this passage. Not a statement is made which does not assume the fusion of the κατάπαυσις and God's rest from his work following creation. It may be surprising to find, then, that Gen 2 does not appear to be strictly necessary to the idea of a continuously available κατάπαυσις nor to the exhortation as such.[412] *Auctor* was perfectly capable of envisaging a heavenly and eschatological reality corresponding to the earthly land or city (11,8-16), and he might simply have done the same with the κατάπαυσις. The warning as such demanded only a typological correspondence between the "fathers" and Canaan, on the one hand, and believers and the heavenly/future κατάπαυσις, on the other. Moreover, turning from such considerations to the observation expressed from time to time, that "der Ruhegedanke des Psalms 95 hat mit diesem Sabbat-

---

[412] This is also observed by Attridge 1980, 281, though Attridge's claims that a straightforward typology is all there is to an interpretation which appeals to apocalyptic parallels (e.g. Hofius), and that "on this reading [Hofius'] the remarks of vv 3-5 are otiose, to say the least," are over simplified.

Ruhegedanken schlechthin nichts gemeinsam,"[413] we wonder what strange influence is at work here. Certainly there are several ways in which Gen 2,2 "fits" in this context but these only tell us *that* and *how Auctor* used this passage, without telling us on what basis Gen 2 was drawn into this exhortation in the first place.

From this perspective we note once again Käsemann's appeal to the speculation of Philo and the Gnostics, "according to which the highest aeon, the realm of the divine Spirit, the Sabbath, and the ἀνάπαυσις are identical." In Hebrews, too, "the κατάπαυσις is construed spatially, thus as aeon-like, as a heavenly sphere, and is linked to Sabbath speculation."[414] None of this derives from the OT, says Käsemann, but is rather linked to OT utterances secondarily. Theißen likewise remarks on the remarkable parallel between the divine and human coming-to-rest in Heb 4,10, a phenomenon which for him has a mystical sounding parallel in Philo.[415] Notwithstanding, reports of the irrelevance of the OT have been greatly exaggerated to the same extent that the "parallels" with Philo and Gnosticism have been overdone.

There are better, more fruitful, ways of coming to terms with this midrash. First, we may note two suggestions, neither of which is finally satisfying. (1) It is sometimes argued that Gen 2 and Ps 95 were joined already in the synagogue liturgies for the Sabbath,[416] but it is not well established that this stems back into the first century.[417] In any case, such an observation would provide only a formal rationale for joining the passages, whereas *Auctor*'s concern is with the substance of the two passages and their relationship.[418] (2) We may probably assume that the movement from Ψ 94 [95] to Gen 2 is owing in part to the application of the rabbinic *gezerah shawah* rule.[419] This is an argument from analogy, used when two Torah statements "make use of identical (and possibly unique) expressions."[420] Yet

---

[413] Schröger, 109. On the other hand, Weiss, 282, may underestimate the gap between these passages.

[414] Käsemann, 73.

[415] Theißen 1969, 129. Cf. also Gräßer, 1:219.

[416] Thus Lane, 1:100, who is depending on Elbogen, 107-115; likewise, Kistemaker, 36; for others, cf. Ellingworth, 247. Cf. Oesterley 1959, 420; Weinfeld, 511.

[417] The evidence is dated no earlier than the 16th century; cf. Hofius, 177 n. 323; Elbogen, 108, 113. Ellingworth, 248, also refers to a "similar association of Ps. 95 and Gn. 2" in *TgOnq* and *TgPs-J,* but it is not apparent to what he is referring.

[418] Rightly, Attridge, 129 n. 83.

[419] This is frequently mentioned; see esp. Hofius, 55. Cf. also Schröger, 109f.; Harder, 35f., 40 (Schröger and Harder do not make reference to the rule). This explanation is considered "one sided" by Kistemaker, 36. Longenecker, 181f., notes in addition to the use of the *gezerah shawah,* the use of the principle known as *dabar ha-lamed me-'inyanô;* the "argument from context" (Strack-Stemberger, 23).

[420] Strack-Stemberger, 21. In this case the connection would be based on the wording of the LXX.

the *gezerah shawah* rule demanded more than a mere verbal correspondence. It demanded also that,

> the expressions which form the basis of the analogy should not be required for the understanding of the statement; in this way it can be assumed that Scripture itself already used them with a view to the intended analogy (*Shab* 64a). What is more, *gezerah shawah* may only be used with great restraint and should be supported by tradition: "You should not apply *gezerah shawah* lightly" (*Ker* 5a); "No one argues from analogy on his own authority" (*p. Pes* 6.1, 33a).[421]

Interestingly, then, *Auctor* bypasses the OT passages which would have been the more likely candidates for the application of the *gezerah shawah* rule, e.g. Deut 12, Ψ 131 [132] (cf. *MidrPss* 95), Isa 66,1. In other words, this rule is once again a more formal than substantive explanation of *Auctor's* argument. It validates the exegesis but does not explain it, and in fact raises as many questions about the history of the tradition as it answers. It is more likely that *Auctor* had already associated the κατάπαυσις somehow with the Sabbath idea or with protology, than that recognition of the chance terminological correspondence set in motion an avalanche of speculation.

We may therefore advance some suggestions which already begin to make sense of this linking of Ψ 94 [95] and Gen 2. All of these take seriously *Auctor's exegetical* interests. In other words, we assume that he is not merely pretending to draw his thoughts out of the OT, nor is he self-deceived in doing so, but rather he is really drawing forth that which the text suggests to him.

(1) We may assume that *Auctor* took the κατάπαυσις as a *transcendent* resting place quite apart from the drawing in of Gen 2; we have just seen that this would have been all that was necessary to the warning as such. The rabbinic parallels wherein the מנוחה of Ps 95 was interpreted eschatologically,[422] JosAsen 8,9 which interpreted its κατάπαυσις transcendentally, and *Auctor's* own interest in heavenly realities as well as the specific reference to a transcendent land and city "prepared" by God in heaven -- not to mention the fact that the psalm itself to some extent loosens the κατάπαυσις from its historical moorings[423] -- all make it reasonably likely that *Auctor* would have construed the κατάπαυσις as a heavenly and

---

[421] Strack-Stemberger, 21. This rule was normally used in Halakah, but was sometimes used for Haggadah (Hofius, 42). We have no evidence of an exegetical tradition which related Gen 2 and Ps 95 specifically -- doubtless because the MT (Heb) would not have supported the link -- though the rest tradition and the Sabbath were broadly related.

[422] Cf. also ApEl (I-IV A.D.) 2,53; 4,27; O.S. Wintermute (in *OTP*, 1:744, 749); Hofius, 66f.

[423] Supra, 41ff.; Ellingworth, 248.

future *Heilsgut* right from the start.[424] Yet once this is done the mind readily contemplates the relatively few OT references to what might be called a "heavenly" *rest*, and not least among them would be Gen 2,2f.[425]

(2) We may also assume that *Auctor* took the personal pronoun -- *my* resting place -- not as an expression of the rest or resting place which God bestows, but of the rest and resting place which belongs to God himself. We have no reason to doubt that this way of construing the genitive construction was antecedent to the joining of the passages. Once again, the mind turns over relatively few OT candidates for such an idea.

(3) We can observe that Ψ 94 [95] and Gen 2 share not simply the καταπαυ- stem, as is always noted, but also the words "day" and "work," both of which have importance for *Auctor*. The overlap of the two passages is considerable from the perspective of *Auctor*'s interests.

(4) If we are right in thinking that Isa 66,1f. was somewhere in *Auctor*'s background (cf. Acts 7) then the earthly-heavenly contrast is already joined to the idea of God's own resting place and brought into direct connection with creation:

Heaven is my throne and the earth is my footstool; what is the house you would build for me, and what is my resting place? *All these things my hand has made*, and so all these things are mine.

The link between God's resting place and creation is sustained in Ψ 94 [95], which also refers to God's role as creator (vv. 5f.). What *Auctor* actually does with Gen 2,2 admittedly takes us some distance beyond this, but the link may have been formed further back in the traditions he inherited from Hellenistic Christianity.

Before proceeding further, however, it is necessary to adjust our perception of the relationship of Ps 95 and Gen 2 in the OT and Jewish

---

[424] Cf. also the assumptions discussed above, 301ff. In other words, a heavenly-earthly contrast did likely contribute to *Auctor*'s selection and use of Gen 2, but as far as the κατάπαυσις is concerned it is not a metaphysical contrast between stability and instability or an anti-cosmic dualism. It is no more than is expressed elsewhere in Hebrews, and no more than is commonplace in apocalyptic and apostolic Christianity, that the heavenly and future world was considered to be the primary and ultimate goal of hope. I cannot see any indication that Gen 2 was brought into the picture in order to transform the resting place into a specifically heavenly reality, since the midrash is geared to showing that the entrance is future; the heaven-earth contrast receives no emphasis. Rather, it seems more likely that Gen 2 was drawn in at least partly because it corresponded somewhat naturally to the pre-conception of the resting place as a heavenly reality.

[425] Beyond this one might think of the closely related passages Isa 57,20 (on the LXX cf. above, 87) and 66,1, the latter probably playing in *Auctor*'s background. Ψ 131 [132] and par. referred to God's rest in the *earthly* temple, and *Auctor* could well have avoided validating the latter by avoiding these passages.

Chapter Seven: A Promise Remains 353

traditions, for so long as we exaggerate the distance between these we confuse the matter needlessly. Having already looked broadly at the OT and Jewish traditions we will confine the following to summarizing remarks.

First, then, the OT. It is true that in the OT Israel's and God's rest in Canaan and the Sabbath are two broadly independent traditions. It is also true that in the OT there is no *clear* indication that humans participate or will participate in the Sabbath of Gen 2. But examination of these traditions in the OT brought to light a number of considerations which greatly reduce the impression of distance between them. (1) We noted there that alongside God's promise of rest and his own rest in the temple, *the Sabbath stands as the other great OT use of the rest motif*, and this in a framework of redemption.[426] (2) The OT already lays the groundwork for an *eschatological* understanding of the Sabbath, which stands alongside the eschatological application of the rest (מנוחה) tradition.[427] (3) In particular, the Sabbath of Gen 2 stands out as a unique and cosmically oriented use of the Sabbath traditions. If it is left largely unpacked in the OT and if there is no indication that this was something to be experienced by humans, it nonetheless cried out for reflection along redemptive lines.[428] (4) An examination of the OT already demonstrated the broad areas of overlap between the rest tradition (including Ps 95) and the Sabbath.[429] This may well stem back to common roots in mythology, though this is not developed openly or directly in the OT. What one encounters are rather broad areas of overlap and particular points where they come tantalizingly close.[430] *It is possible that the Sabbath and the rest tradition had never been completely separated either in the OT or subsequently.* Auctor's is just a variant expression of this underlying tradition, if he did not come to his position through his own study of the OT.

In this context we recall once again how Ps 95 itself had used the rest tradition in a unique and provocative manner, to some extent dislocating it from its original historical setting; in the same psalm there is a reference to God as creator. The LXX had reduced the distance between these traditions terminologically.[431]

---

[426] If a sober minded 20th century OT scholar such as G. Robinson 1975, 418-420, can round off his study of the Sabbath with a stress on the symbolic value of the Sabbath rest for redemption, then it seems rash to assume that this would have been lost on first century Jews.
[427] Supra, 65-67.
[428] Cf. von Rad 1972a, 62, on Gen 2,2f.
[429] Supra, 67ff.
[430] We noted the Sabbath rest for servants as a parallel to Israel's release from bondage; supra, 63, 68. Note also Isa 14 (supra, 49); LXX Deut 5,33 (supra, 82, 90f.).
[431] Supra, 89ff.

From here we move to other Jewish traditions, for these had certainly utilized the Sabbath idea in thinking about salvation,[432] and these would very naturally mix with other ideas of an eschatological rest or resting place. More than once the rest tradition and the Sabbath were rather casually joined in eschatological speculation, albeit in different ways.[433] It is also here that we can recall the later, more formal joining of Ps 95 and Gen 2 in the Sabbath liturgies which we referred to just above. If this is too late to serve as evidence of direct influence, it nonetheless warns against exaggerating the distance between these passages for ancient theologians. The fact that they would be linked is not so remarkable as we might tend to think.

What emerges from all this is that the OT gave expression to the basic traditions which were developed in a variety of ways in Judaism. Certain general ideas seem to have become almost commonplace, for instance the characterization of the eschatological age in terms of the Sabbath, sabbatical calculations of history itself, and the notion of heavenly and future resting places. There was a certain freedom in using these materials and conceptions, including the freedom to conflate ideas associated with the Sabbath and God's promise of rest. We are not dealing with fixed schools of thought, but with considerable freedom of expression.

3.4.3. Auctor: *A unique expression of the rest motif*

Heb 3-4 should be placed *alongside* the other intertestamental Jewish developments of the rest idea as an independent and creative use of the OT by a thinker with his own unique outlook and agenda.[434] Though he did not merely borrow ready-made speculation about heavenly and eschatological resting places *en bloc*, his interpretation of Ψ 94 [95] is plainly at home in a

---

[432] Cf. LAE 51,2 (*Vita*): "'Man of God, do not prolong mourning your dead more than six days, because the seventh day is a sign of the resurrection, the rest of the coming age, and on the seventh day the LORD rested from all his works'" (par. ApocMos 43,3). In general, cf. above, 122f.; Weiss, 272. Our work with Mt 11,28-30 is relevant here, for there we found that Jesus' offer of rest, also in an eschatological context, bespoke a fulfilment of the Sabbath rest; cf. Jn 5,17 (supra, 323f.). One might recall in this connection Col 2,16f. where the Sabbath is a σκια τῶν μελλόντων, τὸ δὲ σῶμα τοῦ Χριστοῦ.

[433] E.g., Isa 32,18 is brought into connection with the Sabbath as a day without armed conflict; *MidrPss* 92 § 5; *Shab* 6,4; supra, 122f.; also Mt 11,28-12,14. Cf. also above, 319f.

[434] Barrett, 373; Attridge, 126-128; Weiss, 268-273. Darnell, 10-53, argues in detail that the exegetical method employed in Hebrews differs markedly from both Qumranic (pp. 15-25) and Philonic (pp. 30-53) exegesis, leading Darnell to the conclusion that Heb 3,7-4,11 is an independent midrash on the OT. It may be appropriate to stress in this connection the way in which the use of the New Exodus motif reflects typical Christian thought; cf. Bruce, 96f.; Weiss, 256f. This does not explain the use of the rest motif here, but it highlights the traditional, Christian stamp of the passage.

world of such speculation, and he was doubtless familiar with at least some of the fairly widespread and varied characterization of the "world-to-come" (2,5) as "wholly Sabbath and rest."[435] After all, he was no mere spiritual and intellectual contemporary of David, and the OT was for him an interpreted document. Yet his own mix of ideas and exegesis in 3,7-4,11 is unique, and represents at its core a serious attempt at interpreting the OT from a (his) Christian standpoint.

Auctor is a writer manifestly interested in the theme of God as creator, and of the Christ, through whom God has spoken "in these last days," as "the heir of all things, through whom God made the worlds."[436] He presumes that if Christ had had to offer his sacrifice repeatedly, he would have had to have done so "since the foundation of the world"; instead he has appeared once for all at the completion of the ages. No sooner has the idea of God as creator been summoned up (3,4) than Ψ 94 [95] itself is quoted (3,7ff.), a psalm blending traditions of Israel's and God's rests only a few verses after mentioning God's role as creator.

This is a theologian whose fondest image of salvation is that of an entrance into God's very presence, an approach to God's throne, and, most eminently, a wondrously festive celebration in the city of the living God, the heavenly Jerusalem. He knows very well that the Sabbath celebration had a special relationship to the temple, and, as an accomplished student of the LXX, would have appreciated the broad overlap of the rest tradition, the temple, and the Sabbath in the OT.[437] To associate the ultimate Sabbath celebration -- based both on God's own rest and Israel's redemption out of Egypt -- with the temple, God's resting place, which could only be erected when God had brought his people to their resting place and given rest to them there, and to draw the whole construct into connection with the pristine state of the creation before the disastrous effects of disobedience...this all seems quite generally Jewish and Christian.

Here is a keen student of the LXX whose primary text (Ψ 94 [95]) contained not one but *three* words (day, works, rest) which came together in one tersely worded statement of far-reaching implications, Gen 2,2. Use of this passage would close the gap between then and now and fill in the

---

[435] Nonetheless, he is able to use Gen 2 without any reference to six or seven "aeons" or "worlds." His concern is only with the fact of God's rest from works, and the corresponding character of life in the κατάπαυσις for God's people.

[436] Cf. 1,2.10-12; 2,5.7.10; 3,4; 9,26; 11,3. In this vein, the reference to the "once for all" and "eternal" work (cf. 9;15; 10,12.14; 13,20) may be relevant.

[437] This connection was stressed in our study of the OT. One particular example may be noted here: In Isa 66 (cf. Acts 7,49) the τόπος τῆς καταπαύσεώς μου (v. 1), a joyful celebration (v. 10; πανηγυρίσατε; cf. Heb 12,22), and on-going, eschatological Sabbath observance (v. 23) are brought together in one vision.

content of the *one promise* which had spanned the epochs to be fulfilled in the Son.

Our awareness of the various Jewish ideas about rest has only made more stark the uniqueness of the exegetical course taken by *Auctor*. The gnostic and Philonic parallels should never have distorted our understanding of Heb 3-4 in the first place, and once we have worked through the passage we come up with an understanding which the apocalyptic parallels better only very marginally. *Auctor* is an independent and creative theologian who has set about interpreting the OT with his own agenda and in his own fashion. His use of Gen 2 must be understood in that light.

3.5. Conclusions on background

Certainly Heb 3-4 echoes a variety of intertestamental ideas about rest, and at points comes closer to them than to the OT. Doubtless this is because Hebrews participates in broad streams of Jewish and Christian thought about cosmology and eschatology and thus tends to treat basic components of thought in the same manner as others sharing the same outlook. Yet it is also probably because the OT traditions about rest had been taken up so prominently and pervasively into eschatological speculation right across the spectrum of Jewish literature. With *Auctor*'s share in more than one of the outlooks of his day, an allowance for commerce and cross-fertilization of rest-speculation among the different "Judaisms," and a few ideas belonging to the public domain we can allow that the thought of Heb 3-4 is a product of *Auctor*'s age without denying the fundamental importance of the OT to the form *and* substance of this passage.[438] The best explanation of this passage is the one which happens to give *Auctor* the benefit of a doubt. He is not pretending to exegete the OT, nor is he self deceived in doing so. Rather, he is a serious student of the OT who is drawing out of the text what he believes to be embedded in it.

What we have resisted, both in our exegesis of the passage and in our consideration of the background proposals, is the tendency to give short shrift to the OT, to *Auctor*'s own exegetical development, and to the uniquely Christian factors while simultaneously forcing the passage into the mold of one of the contemporary "Judaisms" and its specific use of the rest motif.

Granting that the thought of this passage is at home in first century Judaism, it is not Philonic, not gnostic, not simply apocalyptic. Its thought is uniquely *Auctor*'s, and more broadly a Christian interpretation of the OT. Once that is settled and insisted upon we can focus on the elements

---

[438] Ellingworth, 42; also 1988, 9.

evidencing parallels in specific domains of Judaism to which Christianity and *Auctor* were heirs without allowing our interpretation to be generally skewed by them.

4. Conclusions

In the context of an urgent warning against apostasy and an exhortation to listen to God's definitive proclamation, *Auctor* absorbs the κατάπαυσις of Ψ 94,11 [95,11] into his promise Christology. Without allowing himself to be distracted by the hypothetical question of what would have happened had the "fathers" entered Canaan, he reads in the language of Ψ 94 [95] a reference to a heavenly and eschatological *Heilsgut*. Behind the offer which had been made to the "fathers" and again in the implied offer of the psalm he finds the one promise of God which offers to his people the prerogative of entrance into his own resting place. Joshua had not led the second generation into *this* resting place because the entrance was reserved for the completion of the ages. Only then would the heir of all things mediate the new covenant so that the elect might receive the promised eternal inheritance.

Auctor knows well the backdrop of the κατάπαυσις in Israel's redemptive history, the repeated promise of rest to God's people which the OT had already transferred to the ultimate future. He recognizes, not least due to the terminology and phraseology of Ψ 94,11 [95,11], that this idea of Israel's rest and resting place was bound together with God's own rest and resting place, and that both together -- God's and Israel's rests -- could be traced from Israel's departure from Egypt to the erection of the temple under Solomon; in other words, he recognizes that the κατάπαυσις was a towering OT *Heilsgut*. He also knows that from beginning to end the reception of the promise was conditional on obedience.[439] It is possible that for *Auctor* these various elements had melded in Isa 66 which may have formed a part of his Hellenistic Jewish Christian exegetical heritage.

Under the influence of any number of a range of possible factors *Auctor* associated this future entrance into the resting place with God's own rest from his works at creation. The assumption that this place where God rests was a heavenly reality would have called to mind only a very few comparable statements in the OT, and as a part of a larger trend in the Gk translation of the OT, the terminological barrier between Ps 95,11 and Gen 2,2 had been removed. Doubtless the sweeping image resulting from the linkage of protology and eschatology appealed to *Auctor*. Popular

---

[439] Supra, 23-25, 26, 60f.

expectations of the world-to-come as a day which would be "wholly Sabbath and rest" would also naturally accrue to an expectation of eschatological rest, and the association of a great Sabbath celebration with an idea so closely related to both the exodus and temple traditions would have come natural. Thus when the people of God enter God's resting place they will finally be able to participate in a great Sabbath celebration around God's throne, for they will then rest from the labors of a faithful life in this world.

In view of the way in which the disastrous rebellion of a few had infected the whole community at Kadesh, and in view of the irreversible result of the rebellion of the "fathers" when they had been greeted with the very same promise, *Auctor* tells his readers to fear, to guard not only themselves but one another, and by this means to make every effort to enter God's resting place so that no one would fall as the "fathers" had fallen in disobedience. Lest his readers become discouraged by so powerful a warning and such a vivid illustration of failure, the entire exhortation is framed by firm assurances of Christ's compassionate, priestly assistance (2,17-3,6; 4,14-16). Both this assistance and the ultimate reward hinge on holding fast the confession until the Parousia, which was on the horizon. Of course his exhortation gains its special urgency from recognition that the advent of the Son has brought the historical unfolding of redemption to a head.

In terms of background the OT thus remains primary for understanding *Auctor*'s essential concerns and his thinking. More formally, he shares with apocalyptic the idea that the κατάπαυσις is prepared in heaven and entered eschatologically in conjunction with a resurrection and judgment, that the עולם הבא (world-to-come) will be a day which is "wholly Sabbath and rest," and that in that world God's people will rest from the labors of righteousness and endurance in this world. Yet *Auctor*'s general reticence on the subject of a new earth necessarily shapes his κατάπαυσις-idea and results in a noteworthy similarity with JosAsen 8,9.[440] Nonetheless, there is no hint of an interest in metaphysical speculation on the κατάπαυσις, and no anti-cosmic dualism; in that way among others the writings of Philo and Gnosticism stand in marked contrast to Heb 3-4. It is not unlikely that *Auctor* had come into contact with currents of Christian thought which, also under the influence of apocalyptic, had harbored expectations of an eschatological rest, if not of an eschatological Sabbath rest. In particular, it is possible that Isa 66,1 in the context of Hellenistic Christian preaching had been a starting point for *Auctor*, though his own thinking has long since developed in new directions. These Jewish and Christian precedents are not, however, merely cut and pasted. They are re-forged in the die of Ψ 94 [95] and Gen 2 to suit *Auctor*'s purposes.

---

[440] This does *not* entail direct influence.

Chapter Eight

Conclusion

This study has examined the background and significance of the rest motif in the NT with special reference to Mt 11,28-30 and Heb 3,7-4,11. It has done so in terms of (1) the OT and other Jewish and Christian literature, (2) the theological, practical, and literary interests of Matthew and *Auctor*, and also (3) the modern discussion of these two passages. All three of these factors were combined in the treatments of the NT passages, but (1) also received a lengthy and separate treatment as we sought to consider the usages of the motif by Jews and Christians within their respective frames of reference.

The rationale for examining the rest motif in these two passages was given in Ch. One. Mt 11,28-30 is usually construed as an allusion to Sir 51, and as a component of Matthew's Wisdom Christology. We have questioned both the relevance of Sir 51 and the importance of Matthew's Wisdom Christology. The κατάπαυσις-idea of Heb 3-4 has been construed alternatively along (cosmological and metaphysical) dualistic or apocalyptic lines. In spite of the impressive attempt of Hofius to refute Käsemann, who had interpreted Heb 3-4 in terms of Gnosticism, Gräßer *et al.* have successfully sustained Käsemann's basic thesis to the present.[1] A fresh appraisal of the evidence and arguments appeared necessary.

No attempt has been made either to harmonize these two NT passages with respect to the use of the rest motif or to establish contact or influence one way or the other; preliminary research already established that there would be no possibility of doing so, and there has arisen no compelling evidence which would warrant such an attempt.[2] A detailed examination

---

[1] E.g., though he leaves unclear whether he thinks Heb 3-4 is indebted to Gnosticism, Bruce 1987, 3510, assesses the debate between Gräßer and Hofius as follows: Hofius "does not succeed in refuting Erich Grässer's finding (1964) that Käsemann's thesis is confirmed by the prominence of the ἀνάπαυσις theme in the gnostic texts from Nag Hammadi (which, of course, were not known when Käsemann wrote in 1938)."

[2] If the question of contact or influence were to be pursued, the matters of authenticity in Mt 11,28-30 and of the dating of the two works would become of great importance. Influence would not at all need to be one way. If some form of Mt 11,28-30 was dominical or at least very early, then could not *Auctor* have known of it? And might it

which would look at each passage individually but also cast a glance at the NT more broadly would be a logical step beyond earlier treatments which had focused on only one or the other of the relevant passages.[3] Moreover, at least two factors suggested the appropriateness of discussing Mt 11 and Heb 3-4 together: (1) a tendency to associate both passages with Gnosticism; (2) parallel features of the passages themselves. We may take these up in turn.

(1) Both Mt 11,28-30 and Heb 3-4 have been interpreted in terms of the development of Gnosticism.[4] The relative dearth of references to the rest motif in the NT, compared to its ubiquity in the gnostic writings has moved more than one student to categorize it simply as "gnostic." Thus the Logion of Mt 11 is thought to be located on a line of development from wisdom thought to Gnosticism, from personified Wisdom through the Logos Christology to the gnostic Redeemer. In Hebrews, the development of the motif is thought to be fundamentally dependent on and to some extent expressive of conceptions of rest which are conceived in terms of a dualism such as we find in Philo and in the writings of second century and later Gnosticism.

It has *not* been the central concern of this study to refute these interpretations nor to suggest that they offer nothing of worth for the interpretation of Mt 11,28-30 or Heb 3,7-4,11, but it would be fair to say that we have found much to contend with in them. At more than one point we have detected a tendency to either import elements from the stream of thought stretching from wisdom and Philo to Gnosticism, or simply to exaggerate features of Mt 11 or Heb 3-4 with a view to enhancing the religious historical assignment. All of this was covered in detail and does not need to be reviewed here.[5]

---

not have already received an interpretive context of some sort, or at least an established function? Moreover, if we assign Hebrews a date just before A.D. 70 and, with the majority (cf. Davies-Allison, 1:127f.), locate Matthew somewhere after A.D. 80, then there is ample time for the thinking of Heb 3-4 to have been mediated to Matthew; alternatively, the antecedents to Heb 3-4 could have had a role in Matthew's background.

[3] Although the rest motif has not been the controlling interest of work on Mt 11,28-30, studies like Deutsch's on Mt 11,25-30 and Hofius' on Heb 3-4 have made redundant a similar, monograph length examination of one or the other passage alone. Lincoln 1982, Rordorf, and Bacchiocchi 1977 (1988) among others do consider Mt 11,28-30 and Heb 3-4 together in their investigations of the Sabbath and the Lord's Day.

[4] Vielhauer, 281, at least, points to the gnostic character of "rest" in *both* Matthew and Hebrews. Of course NT scholarship has for a long time had a strong interest in the origins and development of Gnosticism. Given the nature of academic research (combined with the obvious importance of the rest motif to Gnosticism), it should not seem remarkable that work on both Mt 11,28-30 and Heb 3-4 would be influenced by this scholarship.

[5] On Mt 11, see Ch. Five. On Heb 3-4, see above, 317ff., 338ff.

In the case of Hebrews this tendency toward distortion was not confined to the advocates of a "gnostic" interpretation, however. One of the chief issues to occupy students of Hebrews has been its location on the changing and developing religious historical map of the period; the chief rival of the gnostic (or more broadly dualistic) interpretation has been the Jewish apocalyptic. This larger discussion has subsumed Heb 3-4, and the κατάπαυσις-idea has been defined in terms of an on-going tug-of-war. Yet on the apocalyptic side, no less than the dualistic, the interpretation of the κατάπαυσις has owed too much to the favored religious historical background. Some of the alleged "apocalyptic" characteristics of the κατάπαυσις have been difficult to square with the actual statements of the passage and with Hebrews generally.[6] Thus the chief alternative interpretations of the κατάπαυσις-idea in Heb 3-4 have polarized, and the passage has been distended in one direction or the other.

While we have listened to the concerns and insights of these divergent theses we have not sought to subsume our examinations of Mt 11 or Heb 3-4 under the questions of the development of Christology or of NT theology generally. In Mt 11,28-30 our investigation in fact led us to associate the Logion more closely with Matthew's Son of David Christology than his Wisdom Christology;[7] indeed, we came to doubt the importance of the latter to Matthew's *Gospel*. Taken together with other evidence, it is likely that Matthew associated the Logion with God's OT promises of rest and with the idea of an eschatological Sabbath. The use of the Logion in post-first century gnostic writings tells us how the Gnostics valued and interpreted the saying, but it tells us nothing about how Mt 11,28-30 fits on any "trajectory," whether that is plotted from wisdom to Gnosticism, or from the OT, through apocalyptic, wisdom, and apostolic preaching to second century parallels like *2Clem* 5-6.[8]

Our investigation of Hebrews led us to question important features of both the dualistic and the apocalyptic interpretations. We found that Heb 4,1-11 is best described as an independent Christian midrash on Ψ 94,11 [95,11] and Gen 2,2. Though the thought of the midrash is generally closer to some apocalyptic ideas than to the dualistic conceptions we find in Philo and the Gnostics, its most distinctive features probably arose from the writer's own Christological and paraenetic concerns as these were brought to bear on the two OT passages.[9]

---

[6] Supra, 342ff.
[7] Above, Ch. Six.
[8] Supra, 160ff.
[9] Supra, 285ff., 347ff.

Thus our investigation has highlighted the distinctive concerns of the two writers and led us to doubt that they share a branch in the family tree of Gnosis.

(2) Not infrequently one encounters the claim that Mt 11,28-30 and Heb 3-4 are similar in conception or that they are somehow related.[10] Most often this claim alludes to the general fact that in both cases Christ is responsible for the ushering in of eschatological rest, even the eschatological Sabbath. Our own investigation has confirmed this initial impression, beginning with the observation that both Mt 11,28-30 and Heb 3-4 address the fulfilment of God's promise of rest to his people, a promise which had become an *essential* component of Israel's self-identity,[11] of her history of redemption and her eschatological hope. This hope was bound up with the *presence of God*, a union given pregnant expression in Ex 33,14 and acted out on a grand scale in the whole history of the tradition, joining as it did the rest of Israel with the rest of God in the temple.[12] Both Mt 11 and Heb 3-4 envision *the realization of this hope in the messiah, Jesus Christ*, and both see further that the Sabbath, which stood at the heart of the covenant and which summed up and symbolized the two great events of creation and redemption, reached its goal there. Both Matthew and *Auctor* associate this fulfilment of God's promise of rest with Christological interpretations of the temple. In both cases the rest is a rest for the laborers, and in both it is associated with Jesus' compassionate, assisting ministry during the great interim.[13] All of this, which we have already explored in Matthew and Hebrews separately, amounts to no insignificant parallel of substance. It is, however, difficult to more closely define the similarity of the passages along these lines, and it is

---

[10] Davies-Allison, 2:289, state emphatically "that Mt 11.28 is kindred to Heb 4.3." Likewise, Luck, 50 n. 50, while noting some of the differences between the two passages, remarks, "die Zusammenhänge nicht zu übersehen sind." See also Hoskyns, 78; Bacchiocchi 1977, 69; S. Gundry, 1456. The connection is hinted at by Grundmann, 320; Schnackenburg, 1:106; Fenton, 187; Gardner, 193.

[11] Supra, 56f.

[12] That this component of God's *presence* was appreciated by Matthew might be evidenced not only by the echo of Ex 33,14 but also by the correlation of 11,25-30 and 28,18-20; cf. Betz, 24; Davies-Allison, 2:289. It is in this light that we can appreciate the remarkable Christological claim of Mt 12,6: "I tell you, something greater than the temple is here!" Matthew's willingness to leave such a claim unexplained is astonishing. As for *Auctor*, his concern not only with the temple but with the "approach" to God captures the essence of the OT tradition; the participation in God's own Sabbath celebration is as strong an image of intimate fellowship with God as is contained in the NT. In this connection we can also recall Acts 3,20 which sought for "times of refreshing...from the presence of the Lord [$\kappa\alpha\iota\rho o\grave{\iota}\ \dot{\alpha}\nu\alpha\psi\acute{\nu}\xi\epsilon\omega\varsigma\ \dot{\alpha}\pi\grave{o}\ \pi\rho o\sigma\acute{\omega}\pi o\upsilon\ \tau o\hat{\upsilon}\ \kappa\upsilon\rho\acute{\iota}o\upsilon$]"; note also 2Thes 1, which contrasts the "relief" of the believers with the fact that the unbelievers are to be cut off from the presence of the Lord ($\dot{\alpha}\pi\grave{o}\ \pi\rho o\sigma\acute{\omega}\pi o\upsilon\ \tau o\hat{\upsilon}\ \kappa\upsilon\rho\acute{\iota}o\upsilon$).

[13] Cf. Mt 11,25-30 with 28,18-20; Heb 2,17-3,6; 4,14-16.

therefore not surprising that the general parallel, though often cited, is never much elaborated on.[14]

Yet in addition to these points there is another which takes its lead from the superficial parallel of the movement from Sonship (Mt 11,27; Heb 3,1-6) to "rest." It might have been gathered from 2Sam 7,1.11-14 (cf. 4QFlor) and 1Chr 22,9f. that there is significance in this configuration, and it seems to be confirmed by 4Q246 2[15] which, without apparent recourse to a specific OT passage, joins the son of God idea once again to "rest."[16] It is hard to resist the tendency to recall the Davidic traditions of 2Sam 7 and 1Chr 22 when reading Mt 11,27, and this same OT complex (Ψ 2,7; 1Par 17) probably underlies Heb 3,1-6 (cf. 1,5; 5,5).[17]

Probing further we find that there is a deeper commonality in the comparison of the *Son* to *Moses*, where the "Son" idea not only recalls Davidic traditions but also has been envisaged in terms reminiscent of Wisdom (Heb 1,2f.). This same sort of comparison seems to be reflected in Jn 1,17, although there it is the Logos which is determinative.[18] What is intriguing is that in the course of our investigation we were moved in the cases of both Matthew (11,27) and Hebrews (3,1-6) to recall a strand of speculation about Moses associated with a well-known complex of OT passages (Ex 33; Num 12; Deut 34), especially as these passages had been utilized in thinking about the revealer *par excellence*.[19]

This association of ideas -- Son (of David), Moses, rest -- is not, I think, a mere phantom, the result of a student's overly prolonged concentration on a single theme in two passages. In Acts 7 too, Stephen's thought progresses from the promise of Deut 18,15 -- "God will raise up a prophet for you from your own people as he raised me up" (Acts 7,37; cf. Deut 34,10) -- on to the subjects of David, Solomon, the tent and temple, and finally God's own κατάπαυσις; the "Sonship" idea is not expressed[20] but we might perceive a similar train of thought nonetheless. Similarly, Peter in Acts 3, having recalled the necessity of the Christ's suffering, issues a call for repentance,

...so that your sins may be wiped out, so that times of refreshing [καιροὶ ἀναψύξεως] may come from the presence of the Lord, and that he may send the Messiah appointed for you, that is, Jesus, who must remain in heaven until the time of universal restoration that

---

[14] The summary we have just given goes considerably beyond most allusions to the parallel.

[15] Supra, 111-113.

[16] Note also 4Ez 7,28ff., although in this case "son" is probably a modification of the original "servant"; cf. Stone 1989, 71-75.

[17] Supra, 225f., 269f.

[18] For the parallel, see Allison 1993, 223.

[19] Supra, 177ff., 269ff. (esp. 271 n. 97).

[20] We are ignoring the reference to the "Son of Man" in 7,57.

God announced long ago through his holy prophets. Moses said, 'The Lord your God will raise up for you from your own people a prophet like me. You must listen to whatever he tells you. And it will be that anyone who does not listen to that prophet will be utterly rooted out of the people.' (3,19-23; Deut 18,15-20)

In both Acts 3 and Heb 3-4 the warning against refusing to listen is issued to those *within* the community; the difference is an evangelistic (Acts 3) vs. ecclesiological (Heb 3-4) framework.

In any event, in both Mt 11 and Heb 3-4 the Christ, Son of David-Son of God, the "greater than Moses," is seen to usher in the fulfilment of God's promise of rest, the eternal Sabbath. At more than one point this train of thought draws from the same OT traditions, not least notably with respect to the promise of "rest."

Yet having now drawn out the similarities of Mt 11 and Heb 3-4, we must no less enthusiastically highlight the important *differences*. With regard to the *Moses traditions* (Ex 33; Num 12; Deut 34, etc.), Matthew makes only a sweeping gesture in the direction of the tradition as a whole[21] while *Auctor* makes a plain allusion to Num 12,7 specifically; Mt 11,27 focuses on mutual knowledge, while Heb 3,1-6 focuses on Moses' faithfulness *in* God's house. With respect to *Sonship*, the relevance of 2Sam 7,14 par. to Mt 11,27 is unclear and is frequently denied; what is evident is that Matthew edits 11,28-30 (which reminds us of 2Sam 7,11 and 1Chr 22,9) in line with his Son of David Christology. In contrast, *Auctor* develops his Sonship Christology with the direct citation of 1Par 17,13 and Ψ 2,7 (1,5; 5,5), but he gives no special emphasis to Jesus' Davidic lineage.[22] The relevance of *Wisdom* to Mt 11 is rather vague: after the exaggerated elements and forced parallels are removed from consideration, and after we appreciate that a direct comparison with Wisdom is probably not Matthew's main interest,[23] there remains a striking resemblance between the Son (esp. 11,27) and this exalted, almost divine figure. *Auctor*, on the other hand, transfers directly to the Son the sort of language typically used to describe Wisdom (1,2f.) and he does so immediately prior to the citation of 1Par 17,13 and Ψ 2,7. Mt 11,28-30 is again a generalized allusion to the *OT rest tradition* which probably does not point to any certain passage,[24] while *Auctor* develops a specific text, Ψ 94 [95], on the basis of Num 14 and alludes to Joshua's history. Matthew creates little more than an impression

---

[21] Allison 1988, 478-483 (1993, 218-233), would prefer to highlight Ex 33 in particular, though the parallel on its own does not bear the weight of this saying.

[22] Both 1,5 and 7,14 suggest that *Auctor* was *aware* of Jesus' Davidic descent, but he does not appear to be interested in it; cf. Ellingworth, 114-116.

[23] Matthew takes a "Wisdom Christology" for granted, though he is not interested in developing it.

[24] For specific parallels, cf. above, 227-229.

of an *eschatological Sabbath* by his redaction, while *Auctor* invokes Gen 2,2 and speaks unambiguously of a future σαββατισμός. Both writers leave the association with the temple only implicit.

Thus in more than one instance the difference stems partly from the fact that Matthew is not alluding to a particular OT passage, but more fundamentally there are diverging interests at work. In Mt 11, Jesus is concerned to mediate God's rest to the weary; his is an evangelistic summons to the harassed and helpless sheep of Israel. *Auctor* is concerned that his holy brothers and sisters remain faithful so that they might obtain the promise, *viz* entrance at Christ's Parousia into God's heavenly resting place. Matthew's interest is in the βασιλεὺς πραΰς, the Son of David who is also the Son of God. *Auctor*'s is in the Son, by whom God ultimately spoke, the heir of all things and mediator of creation, appointed by God as High Priest in the order of Melchizedek. Matthew's use of the Logion, while placed in the context of his eschatological and even apocalyptic outlook, largely retains the earthy feel of the Palestinian, messianic teacher of wisdom. In *Auctor*'s κατάπαυσις idea, on the other hand, protology and eschatology come together in a vision of a heavenly and future Sabbath celebration in the true tent around the throne of God.

Doubtless one could continue highlighting differences between the passages for some time, but we will stop with these observations. In spite of the similar configuration of ideas in Mt 11 and Heb 3-4, even a similar train of thought, I cannot see that it is possible to speak of influence either way. It is apparent that there is a common use of traditions, beginning with the OT where God's promise of rest is associated pre-eminently with Moses and with David's house. 4Q246 2 might indicate that there was in Judaism already a tendency to associate eschatological rest with a son of God figure; this idea had been suggested by 2Sam 7 and 1Chr 22. In Christian traditions,[25] at least in Matthew's and *Auctor*'s backgrounds, Christological reflection on this theme had assimilated Wisdom speculation as well as a belief that Jesus was the expected prophet like Moses, indeed, a Son who is

---

[25] See the summary of the other NT passages above, 347. Peter's address in Acts 3 makes evident that the hope of rest (refreshment) -- associated with the establishment of the Davidic messiah's kingdom -- was a living one. Rev 14,13 and 2Thes 1 evidence the currency of *apocalyptic* expressions of the hope; indeed, with the expectation of a rest from "labors" as a reward for endurance they manifest particular components of Heb 3-4. Some post-apostolic sayings, particularly *2Clem* 5 and the "chain saying" of the Gospel of Hebrews, *might* suggest that these NT passages (namely, 2Thes 1,7; Rev 14,13; Acts 3,20) shared some common features; certainly Rev 14 and 2Thes 1 are similar in conception. Jn 5,17 expresses the idea of an eschatological Sabbath rest in which the people of God might participate, and Jn 14,2f. -- viewed through the lens of the Odes of Solomon -- may even develop from ideas of heavenly-future resting places "prepared" for the elect. Stephen's use of Isa 66,1 in Acts 7 may well give us a glimpse at a particular Christian tradition which was developed in Heb 3-4.

"greater than Moses."[26] The linkage of the rest tradition and the Sabbath does not necessarily point to a common *Christian* tradition, but we cannot rule out some such early development.[27]

This, however, is probably as far as we can go. Both Matthew and *Auctor* are primarily interested in drawing on the OT promises and imagery of rest as a soteriological symbol in expressing the advent of the hoped for salvation. We are confronted with broadly similar interests in approaching and utilizing the OT idea of rest, a broad similarity which is helped along by shared exegetical traditions (e.g., the New Exodus; Moses) and the decisive consideration of the Messiah's advent. From there, however, Matthew and *Auctor* part company.

---

[26] If the particular Christian traditions represented by Acts 7 were in *Auctor*'s background then the precedent for his movement from the (prophet like) Moses theme to the κατάπαυσις is already visible there.

[27] In addition to Mt 11 and Heb 3-4, Jn 5,17 and possibly Col 2,16f. may evidence the currency of a Christological re-interpretation of the Sabbath in apostolic traditions. Neither of the latter associate the idea of an eschatological Sabbath with God's promise of rest, however.

Abbreviations and Bibliography

1. Abbreviations

For Biblical books, OT Pseudepigrapha, and OT Apocrypha see *OTP*. Rabbinic literature: Strack-Stemberger. Qumran scrolls: Vermes 1987. All other abbreviations correspond to D.N. Freedman, ed., *The Anchor Bible Dictionary*, (New York: Doubleday, 1992) (henceforth, *ABD*). These lists are supplemented by LSJM. The following are not included in these sources:

5Ez	5 Ezra
BEBT	J.B. Bauer, ed. *Bauer Encyclopedia of Biblical Theology*
ClemAlex	Clement of Alexandria
ClemRecogn	Pseudo-Clementine *Recognitions*
CorpHerm	*Corpus Hermeticum*
EBC	F. Gaebelein, ed. *The Expositor's Bible Commentary*
EDNT	H. Balz and G. Schneider, eds. *Exegetical Dictionary of the New Testament*
EpApost	*Epistula Apostolorum*
ExcTheod	(ClemAlex) *Excerpta ex Theodoto*
Haer	(Iren) *Adversus haereses*
Hipp	Hippolytus
HomClem	Pseudo-Clementine *Homilies*
Iren	Irenaeus of Lyons
Mand	(*ShepHerm*) *Mandates*
Paed	(ClemAlex) *Paedagogus*
Pan	(Epiphanius) *Panarion*
R	Redactional (= Matthean/Lukan/etc.)
Ref	(Hipp) *Refutation of all Heresies*
Sim	(*ShepHerm*) *Similitudes*
Strom	(ClemAlex) *Stromateis*
Superst	(Plutarch) *De superstitione*
TWOT	R. Laird Harris, Gleason L. Archer, Jr., and Bruce K. Waltke, eds. *Theological Wordbook of the Old Testament.*
Vis	(*ShepHerm*) *Visions*
WBE	Charles F. Pfeiffer, Howard F. Vos, and John Rea, eds. *Wycliffe Bible Encyclopedia.*

2. Bibliography

All works are alphabetized according to the abbreviations used in the body of this study. Reference works and primary sources listed here have been consulted, though not necessarily cited. Where dates are used in abbreviations they are of the edition consulted.

2.1. Reference Works

Bachmann-Slaby. Bachmann, H., and W.A. Slaby. *Computer-Konkordanz zum Novum Testamentum Graece*. Berlin: Walter De Gruyter, 1980.

BAGD. Bauer, Walter. *A Greek-English Lexicon of the New Testament*. Trans. and eds. W.F. Arndt, F.W. Gingrich, F.W. Danker. 2nd rev. ed. Chicago: University of Chicago Press, 1957.

Barthélemy-Rickenbacher. Barthélemy, D., and O. Rickenbacher. *Konkordanz zum hebräischen Sirach*. Göttingen: Vandenhoeck & Ruprecht, 1973.

Bauer-Aland. Aland, Kurt, and Barbara Aland, eds. *Griechisch-deutsches Wörterbuch zu den Schriften des Neuen Testaments und der frühchristlichen Literatur*. 6th ed. Berlin: Walter de Gruyter, 1988.

BDB. Brown, Francis, S.R. Driver and Charles A. Briggs. *The New Brown-Driver-Briggs-Gesenius Hebrew and English Lexicon*. Oxford: Clarendon, 1966.

BDF. Blass, F. and A. Debrunner. *A Greek Grammar of the New Testament and Other Early Christian Literature*. Trans. and ed. R. Funk. Chicago: University of Chicago Press, 1961.

Bullinger. Bullinger, E.W. *Figures of Speech Used in the Bible*. Grand Rapids: Baker, 1898.

Charlesworth-Mueller. Charlesworth, J.H, with J.R. Mueller. *The New Testament Apocrypha and Pseudepigrapha: A Guide to Publications, with Excursus on Apocalypses*. The American Theological Library Association Bibliography Series 17. Metuchen: Scarecrow Press, Inc., 1987.

Even-Shoshan. Even-Shoshan, Abraham. *A New Concordance of the Old Testament*. Jerusalem: "Kiryat Sefer" Pub. House, Ltd., 1985.

Fitzmyer 1990. Fitzmyer, J.A. *The Dead Sea Scrolls. Major Publications and Tools for Study*. Rev. ed. SBLRBS 20. Atlanta: Scholars Press, 1990.

HALAT. Koehler, Ludwig, and Walter Baumgartner. *Hebräisches*

	und Aramäisches Lexikon zum Alten Testament. 4 vols. Ed. W. Baumgartner and J.J. Stamm. 3rd ed. Leiden: Brill, 1967, 1974, 1983, 1990.
Hatch-Redpath.	Hatch, Edwin, and Henry A. Redpath. *A Concordance to the Septuagint and the Other Greek Versions of the Old Testament.* 2 vols. 1897; repr. Grand Rapids: Baker, 1983.
Holladay 1971.	Holladay, William. *A Concise Hebrew and Aramaic Lexicon of the Old Testament.* Leiden: Brill, 1971.
Jastrow.	Jastrow, Marcus. *A Dictionary of the Targumim, the Talmud Babli, Yerushalmi and Midrashic Literature.* New York: The Judaica Press, Inc., 1971.
H. Kraft.	Kraft, H. *Clavis patrum apostolicorum.* Munich: Kösel Verlag, 1963.
Lampe.	Lampe, G.W.H. *A Patristic Greek Lexicon.* Oxford: Clarendon, 1961.
Louw-Nida.	Louw, J.P. and E.A. Nida. *Greek-English Lexicon of the New Testament Based on Semantic Domains.* New York: United Bible Societies, 1988.
LSJM.	Liddell, Henry George, and Robert Scott. *A Greek-English Lexicon.* 2 vols. Eds. H.S. Jones and R. McKenzie. 9th ed. Oxford: Clarendon, 1968.
Mayer.	Mayer, Günter. *Index Philoneus.* Berlin: Walter De Gruyter, 1974.
MHT, 3.	Turner, Nigel. *Syntax.* Vol. 3 in *A Grammar of New Testament Greek.* James Hope Moulton. Edinburgh: T. & T. Clark, 1963.
MM.	Moulton, James Hope, and George Milligan. *The Vocabulary of the Greek Testament Illustrated from the Papyri and Other Non-Literary Sources.* Grand Rapids: Eerdmans, 1930.
Robertson.	Robertson, A.T. *A Grammar of the Greek New Testament in the Light of Historical Literature.* Nashville: Broadman, 1934.
W. Rudolph 1953.	Rudolph, Wilhelm. *Hebräisches Wörterbuch zu Jeremia.* 2nd ed. Einzelwörterbücher zum Alten Testament. Berlin: Töpelmann, 1953.
VOT.	Andersen, Francis I., and A. Dean Forbes. *The Vocabulary of the Old Testament.* Rome: Editrice Pontificio Istituto Biblico, 1989.

Zerwick.	Zerwick, M. *Biblical Greek*. Trans. J. Smith. *SPIB* 114. Rome: Pontifical Biblical Institute, 1963.

2.2. Primary Sources and Translations

ANCL 1/2/4/12.	Roberts, A., and J. Donaldson, eds. *Ante-Nicene Christian Library*. Edinburgh: T. & T. Clark, 1867, 1869.
ANET.	Pritchard, J.B. *Ancient Near Eastern Texts Relating to the Old Testament*. 3rd ed. with suppl. Princeton: Princeton University Press, 1969.
APOT.	Charles, R.H., ed. *The Apocrypha and Pseudepigrapha of the Old Testament in English*. 2 vols. Oxford: Clarendon, 1913.
Beyerlin.	Beyerlin, Walter, ed. *Near Eastern Religious Texts Relating to the Old Testament*. Trans. John Bowden. OTL. London: SCM, 1978.
BHS.	Elliger, K. and W. Rudolph, eds. *Biblia Hebraica Stuttgartensia*. Editio minor. Stuttgart: Deutsche Bibelgesellschaft, 1967/77, 1983.
Blackman.	Blackman, Philip. *Mishnayoth*. 7 vols. 2nd ed. Gateshead: Judaica Press, Ltd., 1964,1990.
Braude 1959, 1-2.	Braude, William G. *The Midrash on Psalms. Translated from the Hebrew and Aramaic*. 2 vols. YJS 13. New Haven: Yale University Press, 1959.
Braude 1968.	_____. *Pesikta Rabbati. Translated from the Hebrew*. 2 vols. YJS 18. New Haven: Yale University Press, 1968.
Butterworth.	Butterworth, G.W. *Clement of Alexandria; With an English Translation*. LCL. Cambridge: Harvard University Press, 1919.
Charlesworth 1973.	Charlesworth, J.H. *The Odes of Solomon. Edited with Translation and Notes*. Oxford: Clarendon, 1973.
Cohen 1965.	Cohen, A., ed. *The Minor Tractates of the Talmud. Translated into English with Notes, Glossary and Indices*. Vol. 1. London: Soncino, 1965.
Cohen 1984.	_____, ed. *Hebrew-English Edition of the Babylonian Talmud. Minor Tractates*. London: Soncino, 1984.
Colson *et al.*	Colson, F.H., G.H. Whitaker, J.W. Earp, and Ralph Marcus. *Philo; With an English Translation*. 10 vols and 2 suppl. vols. LCL. Cambridge: Harvard University Press, 1929-1962.

Drazin.	Drazin, Israel. *Targum Onkelos to Deuteronomy. An English Translation of the Text with Analysis and Commentary.* New York: Ktav, 1982.
Dupont-Sommer.	Dupont-Sommer, A. *The Essene Writings from Qumran.* Trans. G. Vermes. Gloucester: Peter Smith, 1973.
Eisenman-Wise.	Eisenman, Robert, and Michael Wise. *The Dead Sea Scrolls Uncovered.* Rockport: Element, Inc., 1992.
Epstein 1961a.	Epstein, I., ed. *The Babylonian Talmud. Translated into English with Notes, Glossary, and Indices.* 18 vol. ed. London: Soncino, 1961.
Epstein 1961b.	_____, ed. *Hebrew-English Edition of the Babylonian Talmud.* London: Soncino, 1961- .
Foerster, 1-2.	Foerster, W., ed. *Gnosis. A Selection of Gnostic Texts.* 2 vols. Trans. R. McL. Wilson. Oxford: Clarendon, 1972, 1974.
Freedman-Simon.	Freedman, H., and M. Simon, eds. *Midrash Rabbah. Translated into English with Notes, Glossary, and Indices.* 10 vols. London: Soncino, 1961.
Friedlander.	Friedlander, G. *Pirķê de Rabbi Eliezer. Translated and Annotated with Introduction and Indices.* London: Kegan Paul, Trench, Trubner & Co. Ltd., 1916.
Ginsburger.	Ginsburger, M. *Pseudo-Jonathan (Thargum Jonathan ben Usiël zum Pentateuch). Nach der Londoner Handschrift.* Berlin: S. Calvary & Co., 1903.
Goldschmidt.	Goldschmidt, L. *Der Babylonische Talmud.* Vol. 8. Leipzig: Otto Harrassowitz, 1909.
Grenfell-Hunt.	Grenfell B.P., and A.S. Hunt. *The Oxyrhynchus Papyr.* Part 4. London: Egyptian Exploration Fund, 1904.
Grossfeld.	Grossfeld, B. *The Targum Onqelos to Deuteronomy. Translated, with Apparatus, and Notes.* The Aramaic Bible 9. Edinburgh: T. & T. Clark, 1988.
Hammer.	Hammer, Reuven. *Sifre on Deuteronomy.* Yale Judaica Series 24. New Haven: Yale University Press, 1986.
Harris-Mingana.	Harris, R., and A. Mingana. *The Odes and Psalms of Solomon.* Vol. 2. London: Longmans, Green & Co., 1920.
Huck-Greeven.	Huck, Albert. *Synopse der drei ersten Evangelien mit Beigabe der johanneischen Parallelstellen.* 13th ed., rev. H. Greeven. Tübingen: Mohr, 1981.

Klein.	Klein, M.L. *The Fragment-Targums of the Pentateuch according to their Extant Sources*. 2 vols. AnBib 76. Rome: Biblical Institute Press, 1980.
Lake, 1-2.	Lake, Kirsopp. *The Apostolic Fathers; With an English Translation*. 2 vols. LCL. Cambridge: Harvard University Press, 1912/13.
Lake-Oulton, 1-2.	Lake, Kirsopp, and J.E.L. Oulton *Eusebius; With an English Translation*. 2 vols. LCL. Cambridge: Harvard University Press, 1926/32.
Lambert-Millard.	Lambert, W.G., and A.R. Millard. *Atra-Hasis. The Babylonian Story of the Flood*. Oxford: Clarendon, 1969.
Lauterbach 1933.	Lauterbach, J.Z. *Mekilta de-Rabbi Ishmael. A Critical Edition on the Basis of the Manuscripts and Early Editions with an English Translation, Introduction and Notes*. Vol. 1. Philadelphia: The Jewish Publication Society of America, 1933.
Lauterbach 1935.	_____. *Mekilta de-Rabbi Ishmael. A Critical Edition on the Basis of the Manuscripts and Early Editions with an English Translation, Introduction and Notes*. Vol. 3. Philadelphia: The Jewish Publication Society of America, 1935.
Layton.	Layton, Bentley. *The Gnostic Scriptures*. Garden City: Doubleday, 1987.
Lightfoot 1885.	Lightfoot, J.B. *The Apostolic Fathers*. Part 2. 2 vols. London: MacMillan and Co., 1885.
Lightfoot 1890.	_____. *The Apostolic Fathers*. Part 1. 2 vols. London: MacMillan and Co., 1890.
MacDonald.	MacDonald, J. *Memar Marqah. The Teaching of Marqah Edited and Translated*. 2 vols. BZAW 84. Berlin: Töpelmann, 1963.
Merino.	Merino, L.D. *Targum de Salmos. Edición Príncipe del Ms. Villa-Amil n. 5 de Alfonso de Zamora*. Bibliotheca Hispana Biblica 6. Biblia Poliglota Complutense IV,1. Madrid: Consejo Superior de Investigaciones Científicas Instituto "Francisco Suárez," 1982.
NA[27].	Aland, Kurt, Matthew Black, Carlo M. Martini, Bruce Metzger, Allen Wikgren, Barbara Aland, Johannes Karavidopoulos, eds. *Novum Testamentum Graece*. Stuttgart: Deutsche Bibelgesellschaft, 1993.
Nestle.	Nestle, E. *Psalterium Chaldaicum*. Tübingen: F.R. Fues, 1879.

Neusner 1979.	Neusner, J.B. *The Tosefta Translated from the Hebrew. Fifth Division: Qodoshim.* Vol. 5. New York: Ktav, 1979.
Neusner 1981.	_____. *The Tosefta Translated from the Hebrew. Fourth Division: Neziqin.* Vol. 4. New York: Ktav, 1981.
Neusner 1985.	_____. *Genesis Rabbah. The Judaic Commentary to the Book of Genesis. A New American Translation.* Vol. 2. BJS 105. Atlanta: Scholars Press, 1985.
Neusner 1987a.	_____. *Pesiqta deRab Kahana. An Analytical Translation.* Vol. 2. BJS 123. Atlanta: Scholars Press, 1987.
Neusner 1987b.	_____. *Sifre to Deuteronomy. An Analytical Translation.* Vol. 1. BJS 98. Atlanta: Scholars Press, 1987.
Neusner 1988a.	_____. *Mekhilta according to Rabbi Ishmael. An Analytical Translation.* Vol. 1. BJS 148. Atlanta: Scholars Press, 1988.
Neusner 1988b.	_____. *The Mishnah. A New Translation.* New Haven: Yale University Press, 1988.
NHL.	Robinson, James M. *The Nag Hammadi Library.* 3rd ed. San Francisco: Harper Collins Publisher, 1988.
NRSV.	New Revised Standard Version. New York: Oxford University Press, 1989.
NTApocr[1].	Hennecke, Edgar, ed. *New Testament Apocrypha.* Vol. 2. W. Schneemelcher. Trans. and ed. R. McL. Wilson. Philadelphia: Westminster Press, 1964-65.
NTApocr[2], 1-2.	Schneemelcher, Wilhelm, ed. *New Testament Apocrypha.* 2 vols. Trans. and ed. R. McL. Wilson. Rev. ed. Louisville: Westminster/John Knox Press, 1991, 1992.
Oldfather.	Oldfather, W.A., ed. *Epictetus. The Discourses as Reported by Arrian, the Manual and Fragments.* LCL Cambridge: Harvard University Press, 1967.
OTP.	Charlesworth, James H. *The Old Testament Pseudepigrapha.* 2 vols. Garden City: Doubleday, 1983, 1985.
Philonenko.	Philonenko, M. *Joseph et Aséneth. Introduction, Texte Critique, Traduction et Notes.* SPB 13. Leiden: Brill, 1968.
Rahlfs.	Rahlfs, A. *Septuaginta, id est Vetus Testamentum Graece iuxta LXX interpretes.* Stuttgart: Deutsche Bibelgesellschaft, n.d.

J.A. Sanders 1965.	Sanders, J.A. *The Psalms Scroll of Qumrân Cave 11.* DJD 4. Oxford: Clarendon, 1965.
Schmidt-MacDermot.	Schmidt, Carl, and Violet MacDermot. *Pistis Sophia.* The Coptic Gnostic Library. NHS 9. Leiden: Brill, 1978.
Septuaginta.	*Septuaginta, Vetus Testamentum Graecum.* Auctoritate Academiae Scientiarum Göttingensis editum. Göttingen: Vandenhoeck & Ruprecht, 1931- .
Sperber.	Sperber, A. *The Pentateuch according to Targum Onkelos Based on Old Manuscripts and Printed Texts.* Vol. 1 in *The Bible in Aramaic.* Leiden: Brill, 1959.
Stählin.	Stählin, O. *Clemens Alexandrinus.* Vol. 3. GCS. Leipzig: J.C. Hinrich'sche Buchhandlung, 1909.
Stählin-Früchtel.	Stählin, O., and L. Früchtel. *Clemens Alexandrinus.* Vol. 2. 3rd. ed. GCS. Berlin: Akademie Verlag, 1960.
Stählin-Treu.	Stählin, O, and U. Treu. *Clemens Alexandrinus.* Vol. 1. 3rd. ed. GCS. Berlin: Akademie Verlag, 1972.
Thackeray *et al.*	Thackeray, H. St. J., Ralph Marcus, Allen Wikgren, L.H. Feldman. *Josephus; With an English Translation.* 10 vols. LCL. Cambridge: Harvard University Press, 1926-1965.
Vattioni.	Vattioni, Francesco. *Ecclesiastico.* Naples: Istituto Orientale di Napoli, 1968.
Vermes 1987.	Vermes, Geza. *The Dead Sea Scrolls in English.* 3rd ed. Sheffield: JSOT, 1987.
H.G.E. White.	White, H.G.E. *The Sayings of Jesus from Oxyrhynchus, Edited with Introduction, Critical Apparatus and Commentary.* Cambridge: CUP, 1920.
Yadin.	Yadin, Yigael. *The Ben Sira Scroll from Masada.* Jerusalem: The Israel Exploration Society and the Shrine of the Book, 1965.
Ziegler.	_____, ed. *Sapientia Iesu Filii Sirach. Septuaginta, Vetus Testamentum Graecum.* Auctoritate Academiae Scientiarum Gottingensis editum 12/2. 2nd ed. Göttingen: Vandenhoeck & Ruprecht, 1980.

2.3. Secondary Literature

Commentaries on Matthew marked with one asterisk; commentaries on Hebrews with two.

Aalen.	Aalen, S. "'Reign' and 'House' in the Kingdom of God. Supplement: 'Kingdom' and 'House' in Pre-Christian Judaism." *NTS*, 8 (1961), 215-240.

Ackroyd.	Ackroyd, Peter R. *I and II Chronicles, Ezra, Nehemiah.* TBC. London: SCM, 1973.
Albrektson.	Albrektson, Bertil. *Studies in the Text and Theology of the Book of Lamentations.* Studia Theologica Lundensia 21. Lund: CWK Gleerup, 1963.
* Albright-Mann.	Albright, W.F. and C.S. Mann. *Matthew.* AB. Garden City: Doubleday, 1971.
L.C. Allen 1976.	Allen, Leslie C. *The Books of Joel, Obadiah, Jonah and Micah.* NICOT. Grand Rapids: Eerdmans, 1976.
L.C. Allen 1983.	_____. *Psalms 101-150.* WBC 21. Waco: Word Books, 1983.
* W. Allen.	Allen, Willoughby. *A Critical and Exegetical Commentary on the Gospel According to St. Matthew.* ICC. Edinburgh: T. & T. Clark, 1907.
Allison 1988.	Allison, Dale C. "Two Notes on a Key Text: Matthew 11:25-30." *JTS,* 39 (1988), 477-485.
Allison 1993.	_____. *The New Moses. A Matthean Typology.* Edinburgh: T. & T. Clark, 1993.
Althann.	Althann, R. *A Philological Analysis of Jeremiah 4-6 in the Light of Northwest Semitic.* Biblica et orientalia 38. Rome: Biblical Institute Press, 1983.
Anderson 1972.	Anderson, A.A. *The Book of Psalms.* 2 vols. NCBC. London: Marshall, Morgan and Scott, 1972.
Anderson 1989.	_____. *2 Samuel.* WBC 11. Dallas: Word Books, 1989.
Andreasen 1972.	Andreasen, Niels-Erik. *The Old Testament Sabbath. A Tradition-Historical Investigation.* SBLDS 7. Missoula: Scholars Press, 1972.
Andreasen 1974a.	_____. "Festival and Freedom. A Study of an Old Testament Theme." *Int,* 28 (1974), 281-297.
Andreasen 1974b.	_____. "Recent Studies of the Old Testament Sabbath, Some Observations." *ZAW,* 86, No. 4 (1974), 453-469.
Arvedson.	Arvedson, Tomas. *Das Mysterium Christi. Eine Studie zu Mt 11.25-30.* Arbeiten und Mitteilungen aus dem neutestamentlichen Seminar zu Uppsala 7. Uppsala: A.-B. Lundequistska Bokhandeln, 1937.
Attridge 1980.	Attridge, Harold W. "Let us Strive to Enter that Rest. The Logic of Hebrews 4,1-11." *HTR,* 73 (1980), 279-288.

Attridge 1988.	———. "New Covenant Christology in Early Christian Homily." *Quarterly Review*, 8 (1988), 89-108.
** Attridge.	———. *The Epistle to the Hebrews.* Hermeneia. Philadelphia: Fortress, 1989.
Aus.	Aus, R.D. "The Relevance of Isaiah 66,7 to Revelation 12 and 2 Thessalonians 1." *ZNW*, 67 (1976), 252-268.
Bacchiocchi 1977.	Bacchiocchi, S. *From Sabbath to Sunday. A Historical Investigation of the Rise of Sunday Observance in Early Christianity.* Biblical Perspectives 1. Rome: The Pontifical Gregorian University Press, 1977.
Bacchiocchi 1984.	———. "Matthew 11:28-30: Jesus' Rest and the Sabbath." *AUSS*, 22 (1984), 289-316.
Bacchiocchi 1986.	———. "Sabbatical Typologies of Messianic Redemption." *JSJ*, 17, No. 2 (1986), 153-176.
Bacchiocchi 1988.	———. *Divine Rest for Human Restlessness.* Biblical Perspectives 2. Berrien Springs: Biblical Perspectives, 1988.
Bacon.	Bacon, Benjamin W. *Studies in Matthew.* London: Constable and Co., Ltd., 1930.
Balchin.	Balchin, John F. "Paul, Wisdom and Christ." In *Christ the Lord. Studies in Christology Presented to Donald Guthrie.* Ed. H.H. Rowdon. Leicester: Inter-Varsity Press, 1982, 204-219.
Bammel.	Bammel, Ernst. "Rest and Rule." *VC*, 23 (1969), 88-90.
Barr 1960.	Barr, James. "Theophany and Anthropomorphism in the Old Testament." *VTSup*, 7 (1960), 31-38.
Barr 1994.	———. "Paul and the LXX: A Note on Some Recent Work." *JTS*, 45 (1994), 593-601.
Barrett.	Barrett, C.K. "The Eschatology of the Epistle to the Hebrews." In *The Background of the New Testament and its Eschatology.* Eds. W.D. Davies and D. Daube. London: CUP, 1956, 363-393.
Barth.	Barth, G. "Matthew's Understanding of the Law." In *Tradition and Interpretation in Matthew.* G. Bornkamm, G. Barth, and H.J. Held. Trans. P. Scott. London: SCM, 1963, 58-164.
Bartlet *et al.*	Bartlet, J.V., K. Lake, A.J. Carlyle, W.R. Inge, P.V.M. Benecke, and J. Drummond, eds. *The New Testament in the Apostolic Fathers.* Oxford: Clarendon, 1905.

Bauckham 1982a.	Bauckham, R.J. "The Lord's Day." In *From Sabbath to Lord's Day.* Ed. D.A. Carson. Grand Rapids: Zondervan, 1982, 221-250.
Bauckham 1982b.	_____. "Sabbath and Sunday in the Post-Apostolic Church." In *From Sabbath to Lord's Day.* Ed. D.A. Carson. Grand Rapids: Zondervan, 1982, 251-298.
Bauder.	Bauder, W. "Humility, Meekness." *NIDNTT*, 2:256-259.
Bauer 1961.	Bauer, J.B. "Das milde Joch und die Ruhe, Matth. 11,28-30." *TZ*, 17 (1961), 99-106.
Bauer 1970.	_____. "Rest." *BEBT*, 2:748-750.
Bauernfeind 1964.	Bauernfeind, O. "ἀναπαύω κτλ." *TDNT*, 1:350-351.
Bauernfeind 1965.	_____. "καταπαύω κτλ." *TDNT*, 3:627-628.
Bayer.	Bayer, H.F. "Christ-Centered Eschatology in Acts 3:17-26." In *Jesus of Nazareth: Lord and Christ. Essays on the Historical Jesus and New Testament Christology.* Eds. J.B. Green and M. Turner. Grand Rapids: Eerdmans, 1994, 236-250.
Beardslee.	Beardslee, W.A. "The Wisdom Tradition and the Synoptic Gospels." *JAAR*, 35 (1967), 231-240.
Beare 1962.	Beare, F.W. *The Earliest Records of Jesus.* Nashville: Abingdon Press, 1962.
Beare 1968.	_____. "The Sayings of Jesus in the Gospel according to St. Matthew." *Studia evangelica* 4. Berlin: Akademie, 1968, 146-157.
Beck-Brown.	Beck, H., and C. Brown. "Peace." *NIDNTT*, 2:776-783.
Becker.	Becker, Joachim. *1 Chronik.* Die Neue Echter Bibel Kommentar zum Alten Testament mit der Einheitsübersetzung 18. Würzburg: Echter Verlag, 1986.
Beckwith.	Beckwith, R. "Formation of the Hebrew Bible." In *Mikra.* Ed. M.J. Mulder. The Literature of the Jewish People in the Period of the Second Temple and the Talmud 1. CRINT 2. Philadelphia: Fortress, 1988, 39-87.
Beckwith-Stott.	Beckwith, R., and W. Stott. *This is the Day. The Biblical Doctrine of the Christian Sunday in its Jewish and Early Church Setting.* London: Marshall, Morgan and Scott, 1978.
Beekman-Callow.	Beekman, J., and J. Callow. *Translating the Word of God.* Grand Rapids: Zondervan, 1974.

Beilner.	Beilner, W. "σάββατον." *EDNT*, 3:219-222.
** Bénétreau.	Bénétreau, S. *L'Épître aux Hébreux*. Vol. 1. Commentaire Évangélique de la Bible 10. Vaux-sur-Seine: EDIFac, 1989.
Berger 1973.	Berger, K. "Die königlichen Messiastraditionen des Neuen Testaments." *NTS*, 20 (1973), 1-44.
Berger 1974.	_____. "Zum Problem der Messianität Jesu." *ZTK*, 71 (1974), 1-30.
Berger-Colpe.	Berger, Klaus, and Carsten Colpe. *Religionsgeschichtliches Textbuch zum Neuen Testament*. Texte zum Neuen Testament. NTD Textreihe 1. Göttingen: Vandenhoeck & Ruprecht, 1987.
Bernard.	Bernard, J.H. *The Odes of Solomon*. London: SPCK, 1913.
Berry.	Berry, George R. "The Hebrew Word נוח." *JBL*, 50 (1931), 207-210.
Bertram 1964.	Bertram, G. "ἔργον κτλ." *TDNT*, 2:635-655.
Bertram 1967.	_____. "νήπιος κτλ." *TDNT*, 4:912-923.
Bertram-Rengstorf.	Bertram, G., and K.H. Rengstorf. "ζυγός." *TDNT*, 2:896-901.
Betz.	Betz, H.D. "The Logion of the Easy Yoke and of Rest (Mt. 11,28-30)." *JBL*, 86 (1967), 10-24.
Betz 1992.	_____. "Hellenism." *ABD*, 3:127-135.
Bianchi.	Bianchi, U. "Dualism." *EncRel*, 4:506-512.
Biggs.	Biggs, Charles R. "Exposition and Adaptation of the Sabbath Commandment in the OT." *AusBR*, 23 (1975), 12-23.
Black.	Black, Matthew. *An Aramaic Approach to the Gospels*. 3rd ed. Oxford: Clarendon, 1967.
* Blomberg.	Blomberg, C.L. *Matthew*. The New American Commentary 22. Nashville: Broadman, 1992.
Blosser.	Blosser, D.W. "Jesus and the Jubilee, Lk. 4,16-30: The Year of Jubilee and its Significance in the Gospel of Luke." Diss. St. Andrews, 1979.
Bock.	Bock, Darrell L. "The Reign of the Lord Christ." In *Dispensationalism, Israel and the Church*. Eds. C.A.

Blaising and D.L. Bock. Grand Rapids: Zondervan, 1992, 37-67.

Boling-Wright.	Boling, Robert G., and G. Ernest Wright. *Joshua*. AB. Garden City: Doubleday, 1982.
* Bonnard.	Bonnard, P. *L'Évangile selon saint Matthieu*. CNT 1. Neuchâtel: Delachaux & Niestlé,1963.
Borgen.	Borgen, Peder. "Philo of Alexandria." In *Jewish Writings of the Second Temple Period. Apocrypha, Pseudepigrapha, Qumran Sectarian Writings, Philo, Josephus*. Ed. Michael E.Stone. The Literature of the Jewish People in the Period of the Second Temple and the Talmud 2. CRINT 2. Philadelphia: Fortress, 1984, 233-282.
Boring.	Boring, M.E. *Sayings of the Risen Jesus. Christian Prophecy in the Synoptic Tradition*. SNTSMS 46. Cambridge: CUP, 1982.
Bornkamm.	Bornkamm, Günther. " End-Expectation and Church in Matthew." In *Tradition and Interpretation in Matthew*. G. Bornkamm, G. Barth, and H.J. Held. Trans. P. Scott. London: SCM, 1963, 15-51.
Bousset.	Bousset, Wilhelm. *Kyrios Christos*. Trans. J.E. Steely. Nashville: Abingdon Press, 1970.
Braulik 1968.	Braulik, G. "Menuchah. Die Ruhe Gottes und des Volkes im Lande." *BK*, 23, (1968), 75-78.
Braulik 1988.	_____. "Zur deuteronomistischen Konzeption von Freiheit und Frieden." *Studien zur Theologie des Deuteronomiums*. Stuttgarter Biblische Aufsatzbände 2. Stuttgart: Katholisches Bibelwerk GmbH, 1988, 219-230.
** Braun.	Braun, Herbert. *An die Hebräer*. HNT 14. Tübingen: Mohr, 1984.
R. Braun 1976.	Braun, Roddy. "Solomon, the Chosen Temple Builder: The Significance of 1 Chronicles 22, 28, and 29 for the Theology of Chronicles." *JBL*, 95 (1976), 581-590.
R. Braun 1986.	_____. *1 Chronicles*. WBC 14. Waco: Word Books, 1986.
Briggs-Briggs, 1-2.	Briggs, C.A., and E.G. Briggs. *A Critical and Exegetical Commentary on the Book of the Psalms*. 2 vols. ICC. Edinburgh: T. & T. Clark, 1907.
Bright.	Bright, J. *Jeremiah*. AB. Garden City: Doubleday, 1965.
Brooke.	Brooke, G.J. *Exegesis at Qumran. 4QFlorilegium in its*

Jewish Context. JSOTSup 29. Sheffield: JSOT, 1985.

Brown, 1-2.	Brown, Raymond. *The Gospel According to John.* AB. Garden City: Doubleday, 1966, 1970.
Brown 1977.	_____. *The Birth of the Messiah.* Garden City: Doubleday, 1977.
Bruce 1963.	Bruce, F.F. "'To the Hebrews' or 'To the Essenes'?" *NTS,* 9 (1963), 217-232.
Bruce 1987.	_____. "'To the Hebrews': A Document of Roman Christianity?" In *ANRW* II.25.4 (1983), 3496-3521.
** Bruce.	_____. *The Epistle to the Hebrews.* Rev. ed. NICNT. Grand Rapids: Eerdmans, 1990.
Brueggemann 1968.	Brueggemann, Walter. "David and his Theologian" *CBQ,* 30 (1968), 156-181.
Brueggemann 1971.	_____. "Kingship and Chaos." *CBQ,* 33 (1971), 317-332.
Brueggemann 1972.	_____. "Weariness, Exile, and Chaos; A Motif in Royal Theology." *CBQ,* 34 (1972), 19-38.
Brueggemann 1977.	_____. *The Land: Place as Gift, Promise and Challenge in Biblical Faith.* Overtures to Biblical Theology. Philadelphia: Fortress, 1977.
Bruner.	Bruner, F.D. *The Christbook. A Historical/Theological Commentary. Matthew 1-12.* Waco: Word Books, 1987.
** Buchanan.	Buchanan, G.W. *To the Hebrews.* AB. Garden City: Doubleday, 1972.
Buchanan 1975.	_____. "The Present State of Scholarship in Hebrews." In Part One of *Christianity, Judaism and Other Greco-Roman Cults.* Ed. J. Neusner. SJLA 12. Leiden: Brill, 1975, 299-330.
Buchanan 1978.	_____. *Revelation and Redemption.* Dillsboro: North Carolina, 1978.
Büchler.	Büchler, A. *Studies in Sin and Atonement in the Rabbinic Literature of the First Century.* LBS. New York: Ktav, 1967.
Bultmann 1964.	Bultmann, R. "$ἀνίημι, ἄνεσις$." *TDNT,* 1:367.
Bultmann 1967.	_____. "Der religionsgeschichtliche Hintergrund des Prologs zum Johannes-Evangelium." *Exegetica.* Ed. E. Dinkler. Tübingen: Mohr, 1967, 10-35.

Bultmann 1972.	_____. *The History of the Synoptic Tradition.* Trans. from 2nd ed. with 1962 suppl. J. Marsh. Oxford: Blackwell, 1972.
Burchard.	Burchard, Christoph. *Untersuchungen zu Joseph und Asenath.* WUNT 8. Tübingen: Mohr, 1965.
Burger.	Burger, C. *Jesus als Davidssohn.* FRLANT 98. Göttingen: Vandenhoeck & Ruprecht, 1970.
Burnett.	Burnett, Fred W. *The Testament of Jesus-Sophia. A Redaction-Critical Study of the Eschatological Discourse in Matthew.* Washington, D.C.: University Press of America, 1981.
Butler.	Butler, Trent C. *Joshua.* WBC 7. Waco: Word Books, 1983.
Caird.	Caird, G.B. "The Exegetical Method of the Epistle to the Hebrews." *CJT*, 5 (1959), 44-51.
** Calvin.	Calvin, John. *Commentaries on the Epistle of Paul the Apostle to the Hebrews.* Trans. and ed. John Owen. Edinburgh: T. Constable, 1853.
Camp.	Camp, C.V. *Wisdom and the Feminine in the Book of Proverbs.* Bible and Literature Series 11. Sheffield: Almond, 1985.
Carlson.	Carlson, R.A. *David the Chosen King.* Stockholm: Almquest and Wiksell, 1964.
Carr.	Carr, G.L. "שָׁלֵם." *TWOT*, 2:930-931.
Carroll.	Carroll, Robert P. *Jeremiah.* OTL. London: SCM, 1986.
Carson 1982a.	Carson, D.A. "Christological Ambiguities in the Gospel of Matthew." In *Christ the Lord. Studies in Christology presented to Donald Guthrie.* Ed. H.H. Rowdon. Leicester: Inter-Varsity Press, 1982, 97-114.
Carson 1982b.	_____. "Jesus and the Sabbath in the Four Gospels." In *From Sabbath to Lord's Day.* Ed. D.A. Carson. Grand Rapids: Zondervan, 1982, 57-97.
* Carson.	_____. "Matthew." In vol. 8 of *EBC*. Grand Rapids: Zondervan, 1984.
Carson 1991.	_____. *The Gospel According to John.* Grand Rapids: Eerdmans, 1991.
Carson 1994.	_____. "Matthew 11:19b / Luke 7:35: A Test Case for the Bearing of Q Christology on the Synoptic Problem." In

	Jesus of Nazareth: Lord and Christ. Essays on the Historical Jesus and New Testament Christology. Eds. J.B. Green and M. Turner. Grand Rapids: Eerdmans, 1994, 128-146.
Catchpole.	Catchpole, D.R. "Tradition History." In *New Testament Interpretation.* Ed. I.H. Marshall. Grand Rapids: Eerdmans, 1977, 165-180.
Cerfaux.	Cerfaux, L. "Les sources scriptuaires de *Mt.*, XI, 25-30." *Recueil Lucien Cerfaux* III. BETL 28. Gembloux: Éditions J. Duculot, S.A., 1962, 139-159.
Charette.	Charette, Blaine. "'To Proclaim Liberty to the Captives': Matthew 11:28-30 in the Light of OT Prophetic Expectations." *NTS*, 38/2 (1992), 290-297.
Charles.	Charles, R.H. *A Critical and Exegetical Commentary on the Revelation of St. John.* 2 vols. ICC. Edinburgh: T. & T. Clark, 1920.
Charlesworth 1972a.	Charlesworth, J.H. "A Critical Comparison of the Dualism in 1QS 3:13-4:26 and the 'Dualism' Contained in the Gospel of John." In *John and Qumran.* Ed. J.H. Charlesworth. London: Geoffrey Chapman, 1972, 76-106.
Charlesworth 1972b.	_____. "Qumran, John and the Odes of Solomon." In *John and Qumran.* Ed. J.H. Charlesworth. London: Geoffrey Chapman, 1972, 107-136.
Charlesworth 1992.	_____. "Solomon, Odes of." *ABD*, 6:114-115.
Charlesworth-Culpepper.	Charlesworth, J.H., and R.A. Culpepper. "The Odes of Solomon and the Gospel of John." *CBQ*, 35 (1973), 298-322.
Chester.	Chester, A. "The Parting of the Ways: Eschatology and Messianic Hope." In *Jews and Christians. The Parting of the Ways A.D. 70 to 135.* Ed. J.D.G. Dunn. WUNT 66. Tübingen: Mohr, 1992, 239-313.
Chilton.	Chilton, B. "Jesus *ben David*: reflections on the *Davidssohnfrage.*" *JSNT*, 14 (1982), 88-112.
Christ.	Christ, Felix. *Jesus Sophia. Die Sophia-Christologie bei den Synoptikern.* ATANT 57. Zürich: Zwingli-Verlag, 1970.
Clark.	Clark, Kenneth W. "The Gentile Bias in Matthew." *JBL*, 66 (1947), 165-172.
Clements 1980.	Clements, R.E. *Isaiah 1-39.* NCBC. Grand Rapids: Eerdmans, 1980.

Clements 1988.	_____. *Jeremiah.* Interpretation. Atlanta: John Knox Press, 1988.
Cody.	Cody, A. *Heavenly Sanctuary and Liturgy in the Epistle to the Hebrews. The Achievement of Salvation in the Epistle's Perspectives.* St. Meinrad: Grail, 1960.
Collins 1979.	Collins, John J., ed. *Apocalypse. The Morphology of a Genre.* Semeia 14. Missoula: Scholars Press, 1979.
Collins 1983.	_____. *Between Athens and Jerusalem. Jewish Identity in the Hellenistic Diaspora.* New York: Crossroad, 1983.
Collins 1984.	_____. *The Apocalyptic Imagination.* New York: Crossroad, 1984.
Collins 1992.	_____. "Early Jewish Apocalypticism." *ABD*, 1:282-288.
Collins 1993.	_____. "The *Son of God* Text from Qumran." In *From Jesus to John. Essays on Jesus and New Testament Christology in Honour of Marinus de Jonge.* Ed. M.C. De Boer. JSNTSS 84. Sheffield: JSOT, 1993, 65-82.
Conzelmann.	Conzelmann, Hans. "The Mother of Wisdom." In *The Future of our Religious Past.* Ed. J.M. Robinson. Trans. C.E. Carlston and R.P. Scharlemann. New York: Harper and Row, Pub., 1971, 230-243.
Coppes.	Coppes, Leonard J. "גוה." *TWOT*, 2:562-563.
Craigie.	Craigie, Peter C. *Psalms 1-50.* WBC 19. Waco: Word Books, 1983.
Craigie-Kelley-Drinkard.	Craigie, Peter C., P.H. Kelley, and J.F. Drinkard, Jr. *Jeremiah 1-25.* WBC 26. Dallas: Word Books, 1991.
Cross.	Cross, Frank Moore. *Canaanite Myth and Hebrew Epic.* Cambridge: Harvard University Press, 1973.
Cross-Talmon.	Cross, F.M., S. Talmon, eds. *Qumran and the History of the Biblical Text.* Cambridge: Harvard University Press, 1975.
Crossan.	Crossan, D. *In Fragments: The Aphorisms of Jesus.* San Francisco: Harper and Row, Pub., 1983.
Crüsemann.	Crüsemann, Frank. *Bewahrung der Freiheit.* München: Chr. Kaiser Verlag, 1983.
Cullmann.	Cullmann, Oscar. *Early Christian Worship.* Trans. A.S. Todd and J.B. Torrance. Philadelphia: Westminster Press, 1953.

Curnock.	Curnock, G.N. "A Neglected Parallel (Matt. xi. 28 and Ex. xxxiii. 14)." *ExpTim*, 44 (1932-33), 141.
Dahood 1968.	Dahood, Mitchell. *Psalms II. 51-100*. AB. Garden City: Doubleday, 1968.
Dahood 1970.	_____. *Psalms III. 101-150*. AB. Garden City: Doubleday, 1970.
D'Angelo.	D'Angelo, Mary Rose. *Moses in the Letter to the Hebrews*. SBLDS 42. Missoula: Scholars Press, 1979.
Daniélou 1956.	Daniélou, J. *The Bible and the Liturgy*. London: Darton, Longman and Todd, 1956.
Daniélou 1964.	_____. *The Theology of Jewish Christianity*. Trans. J.A. Baker. The Development of Christian Doctrine Before the Council of Nicea 1. London: Darton, Longman and Todd, 1964.
Darnell.	Darnell, David. "Rebellion, Rest, and the Word of God." Diss. Durham (NC), 1973.
G.H. Davies.	Davies, G.H. "Psalm 95." *ZAW*, 85 (1973), 183-195.
W.D. Davies 1948.	Davies, W.D. *Paul and Rabbinic Judaism*. London: SPCK, 1948.
W.D. Davies 1962.	_____. "'Knowledge' in the Dead Sea Scrolls and Matthew 11,25-30." In *Christian Origins and Judaism*. London: Darton, Longman and Todd, 1962, 119-144.
W.D. Davies 1974.	_____. *The Gospel and the Land: Early Christianity and Jewish Territorial Doctrine*. Berkeley and Los Angeles: University of California Press, 1974.
W.D. Davies 1982.	_____. *The Territorial Dimension of Judaism*. Berkeley and Los Angeles: University of California Press, 1982.
* Davies-Allison, 1-2.	Davies, W.D., and D.C. Allison, Jr. *Matthew*. 2 vols. ICC. Edinburgh: T. & T. Clark, 1988, 1991.
De Conick.	De Conick, April D. "The Yoke Saying in the Gospel of Thomas 90." *VC*, 44 (1990), 280-294.
** Delitzsch.	Delitzsch, F. *Commentary on the Epistle to the Hebrews*. 2 vols. Trans. T.L. Kingsbury. Clark's Foreign Theological Library. Fourth series 20, 25. Edinburgh: T. & T. Clark, 1868, 1870.
Desilva.	Desilva, D.A. "Despising Shame: A Cultural-Anthropological Investigation of the Epistle to the Hebrews." *JBL*, 113 (1994), 439-461.

Deutsch 1982.	Deutsch, Celia. "The Sirach 51 Acrostic: Confession and Exhortation." *ZAW*, 94 (1982), 400-409.
Deutsch 1987.	_____. *Hidden Wisdom and the Easy Yoke. Wisdom, Torah and Discipleship in Matthew 11,25-30.* JSNTSS 18. Sheffield: JSOT, 1987.
Deutsch 1990.	_____. "Wisdom in Matthew: Transformation of a Symbol." *NovT*, 32 (1990), 12-47.
Dey.	Dey, Lala Kalyan Kumar. *The Intermediary World and Patterns of Perfection in Philo and Hebrews.* SBLDS 25. Missoula: Scholars Press, 1975.
Dibelius.	Dibelius, Martin. *From Tradition to Gospel.* Trans. from rev. 2nd ed. B.L. Woolf. London: Ivor Nicholson and Watson, Ltd., 1934.
Dillard 1980.	Dillard, Raymond B. "The Reign of Asa (2 Chr 14-16): An Example of the Chronicler's Theological Method." *JETS*, 23 (1980), 207-218.
Dillard 1984.	_____. "Reward and Punishment in Chronicles: The Theology of Immediate Retribution." *WTJ*, 46 (1984), 164-172
Dillard 1987.	_____. *2 Chronicles.* WBC 15. Waco: Word Books, 1987.
Dinkler.	Dinkler, E. "Jesu Wort vom Kreuztragen." *Neutestamentliche Studien für R. Bultmann.* BZNW 21. Berlin: Töpelmann, 1954, 115-117.
Dodd.	Dodd, C.H. *According to the Scriptures.* London: Nisbet & Co., Ltd., 1952.
Dörrie.	Dörrie, H. "Ὑπόστασις. Wort- und Bedeutungsgeschichte." *NAWG*, Phil.-hist. Kl. (1955), 35-92.
Doukhan.	Doukhan, Jacques B. *The Genesis Creation Story. Its Literary Structure.* Andrews University Seminary Doctoral Dissertation Series 5. Berrien Springs: Andrews University Press, 1978.
Dressler.	Dressler, H.H.P. "The Sabbath in the Old Testament." In *From Sabbath to Lord's Day.* Ed. D.A. Carson. Grand Rapids: Zondervan, 1982, 21-41.
Duhm.	Duhm, B. *Das Buch Jeremia.* KHC 11. Tübingen: Mohr, 1901.
Duling 1975.	Duling, D.C. "Solomon, Exorcism, and the Son of David."

	HTR, 68 (1975), 235-252.
Duling 1978.	_____. "The Therapautic Son of David: An Element in Matthew's Christological Apologetic." *NTS*, 24 (1978), 392-410.
Dumbrell.	Dumbrell, William J. "Creation, Covenant, and Work." *Crux*, 24 (1988), 14-24.
Dunham.	Dunham, D.A. "An Exegetical Examination of the Warnings in the Epistle to the Hebrews." Diss. Winona Lake, 1974.
Dunn 1975.	Dunn, J.D.G. *Jesus and the Spirit*. Philadelphia: Westminster Press, 1975.
Dunn 1978.	_____. "Prophetic 'I'-Sayings and the Jesus Tradition: The Importance of Testing Prophetic Utterances within Early Christianity." *NTS*, 24 (1978), 175-198.
Dunn 1989.	_____. *Christology in the Making*. 2nd ed. London: SCM, 1989.
Dunn 1994.	_____. "The Making of Christology -- Evolution or Unfolding?" In *Jesus of Nazareth: Lord and Christ. Essays on the Historical Jesus and New Testament Christology*. Eds. J.B. Green and M. Turner. Grand Rapids: Eerdmans, 1994, 437-452.
Dunnill.	Dunnill, J. *Covenant and sacrifice in the Letter to the Hebrews*. SNTSMS 75. Cambridge: CUP, 1992.
Durham.	Durham, John I. "שָׁלוֹם and the Presence of God." In *Proclamation and Presence. Old Testament Essays in Honour of Gwynne Henton Davies*. Eds. J.I. Durham and J.R. Porter. London: SCM, 1970, 272-293.
Ebach.	Ebach, Jürgen. "Zum Thema: Arbeit und Ruhe im Alten Testament." *ZEE*, 24 (1980), 7-21.
Eberharter.	Eberharter, Andreas. *Das Buch Jesus Sirach oder Ecclesiasticus*. HSAT 6/5. Bonn: Peter Hanstein, 1925.
Edwards.	Edwards, R.A. *A Theology of Q. Eschatology, Prophecy, and Wisdom*. Philadelphia: Fortress, 1976.
Eichrodt, 1-2.	Eichrodt, Walther. *Theology of the Old Testament*. 2 vols. Trans. J.A. Baker. Philadelphia: Westminster Press, 1961,1967.
Elbogen.	Elbogen, I. *Der jüdische Gottesdienst in seiner geschichtlichen Entwicklung*. 3rd. ed. 1931; repr. Hildesheim: Georg Olms Verlagsbuchhandlung, 1962.

Ellingworth 1977, 1-2.	Ellingworth, P. "The Old Testament in Hebrews." 2 vols. Diss. Aberdeen, 1977.
Ellingworth 1986.	_____. "Jesus and the Universe in Hebrews." *EvQ*, 58 (1986), 337-350.
Ellingworth 1988.	_____. "Hebrews and the anticipation of Completion." *Them*, 14 (1988), 6-11.
** Ellingworth.	_____. *The Epistle to the Hebrews*. NIGTC. Grand Rapids: Eerdmans, 1993.
Ellis.	Ellis, E.E. *The Old Testament in Early Christianity*. Grand Rapids: Baker, 1991.
Enslin-Zeitlin.	Enslin, Morton S., and Solomon Zeitlin. *The Book of Judith*. Jewish Apocryphal Literature 7. Leiden: Brill, 1972.
Esser.	Esser, H.-H. "Humility, Meekness." *NIDNTT*, 2:259-264.
Farmer.	Farmer, W.R. *Jesus and the Gospel*. Philadelphia: Fortress, 1982.
Feld.	Feld, Helmut. *Der Hebräerbrief*. ErFor 228. Darmstadt: Wissenschaftliche Buchgesellschaft, 1985.
Fendrich.	Fendrich, H. "κοπιάω." *EDNT*, 2:307.
* Fenton.	Fenton, J.C. *Saint Matthew*. Westminster Pelican Commentaries. Philadelphia: Westminster Press, 1963.
Ferguson.	Ferguson, Everett. *Backgrounds of Early Christianity*. Grand Rapids: Eerdmans, 1987.
Filson.	Filson, Floyd V. "Broken Patterns in the Gospel of Matthew." *JBL*, 75 (1956), 227-231.
Finkel.	Finkel, Asher. "Sabbath as the Way to Shalom in the Biblical Tradition." *JDharma*, 11, No. 2 (1986), 115-123.
Fiorenza.	Fiorenza, E.S. "Wisdom Mythology and the Christological Hymns of the New Testament." In *Aspects of Wisdom in Judaism and Early Christianity*. Ed. R.L. Wilkin. Notre Dame: University of Notre Dame Press, 1975, 17-42.
Fisher.	Fisher, L.R. "'Can this be the Son of David?'" In *Jesus and the Historian*. Ed. F.T. Trotter. Philadelphia: Westminster Press, 1968, 82-97.
Fitzmyer 1971.	Fitzmyer, J.A. *Essays on the Semitic Background of the New Testament*. London: Geoffrey Chapman, 1971.

Fitzmyer 1972.	_____. "David, 'Being Therefore a Prophet...' (Acts 2:30)." *CBQ*, 34 (1972), 332-339.
Fitzmyer 1981.	_____. *The Gospel According to Luke I-IX*. AB. New York: Doubleday, 1981.
Foerster 1965.	Foerster, W. "κτίζω κτλ." *TDNT*, 3:1000-1035.
Foerster-Herrmann.	Foerster, W., and J. Herrmann. "κλῆρος κτλ." *TDNT*, 3:758-785.
Ford.	Ford, J.M. "Millennium." *ABD*, 4:832-834.
France.	France, R.T. *Matthew. Evangelist and Teacher*. Grand Rapids: Zondervan, 1989.
Frankowski.	Frankowski, J. "Requies, Bonum promissum populi Dei in V.T. et in Judaismo." *VD*, 43 (1965), 124-149, 225-240.
Fridrichsen.	Fridrichsen, A. "Eine unbeachtete Parallele zum Heilandsruf." In *Synoptische Studien*. München: Karl Zink, 1953, 83-85.
Friedman.	Friedman, T. "The Sabbath: Anticipation of Redemption." *Judaism*, 16 (1967), 443-452.
* Gaechter.	Gaechter, Paul. *Das Matthäus Evangelium*. München: Tyrolia-Verlag, 1963.
Gammie.	Gammie, J.G. "Spatial and Ethical Dualism in Jewish Wisdom and Apocalyptic Literature." *JBL*, 93 (1974), 356-385.
* Gardner.	Gardner, R.B. *Matthew*. Believers Church Bible Commentary. Scottdale: Herald Press, 1991.
Garland.	Garland, David E. *The Intention of Matthew 23*. NovTSup 52. Leiden: Brill, 1979.
Gärtner.	Gärtner, Bertil. *The Theology of the Gospel of Thomas*. Trans. E.J. Sharpe. London: Collins, 1961.
Gerstenberger.	Gerstenberger, Erhard S. *Psalms, Part 1*. The Forms of Old Testament Literature 14. Grand Rapids: Eerdmans, 1988.
Gese.	Gese, H. "Wisdom, Son of Man, and the Origins of Christology: The Consistent Development of Biblical Theology." *HBT*, 3 (1981), 23-57.
Gibbs 1964.	Gibbs, J.M. "Purpose and Pattern in Matthew's use of the Title 'Son of David.'" *NTS*, 10 (1964), 446-464.

Gibbs 1968.	_____. "The Son of God as the Torah Incarnate in Matthew." SE 4/1. Berlin: Akademie, 1968, 38-46.
Gilbert.	Gilbert, M. "Wisdom Literature." In *Jewish Writings of the Second Temple Period*. Ed. M. Stone. The Literature of the Jewish People in the Period of the Second Temple and the Talmud 2. CRINT 2. Philadelphia: Fortress, 1984, 283-324.
Ginzberg, 5.	Ginzberg, Louis. *The Legends of the Jews*. Vol. 5. Philadelphia: The Jewish Publication Society of America, 1953.
* Gnilka, 1-2.	Gnilka, Joachim. *Das Matthäusevangelium*. HTKNT 1/1-2. Freiburg: Herder, 1986, 1988.
Goldsmith.	Goldsmith, D. "Acts 13:33-37, a Pesher on II Samuel 7." *JBL*, 7 (1968), 321-323.
Goppelt.	Goppelt, L. *Typos. The Theological Interpretation of the Old Testament in the New*. Trans. D.H. Madvig. Grand Rapids: Eerdmans, 1982.
Goulder 1971.	Goulder, M.D. "Review of *Wisdom Christology and Law in Matthew's Gospel*, by M. Jack Suggs." *JTS*, 22 (1971), 568-569.
Goulder 1974.	_____. *Midrash and Lection in Matthew*. London: SPCK, 1974.
Grabbe, 1-2.	Grabbe, L.L. *Judaism from Cyrus to Hadrian*. 2 vols. Minneapolis: Fortress, 1992.
Graham.	Graham, R.E. "A Note on Hebrews 4:4-9." In *The Sabbath in Scripture and History*. Ed. K.A. Strand. Washington, D.C.: Review and Herald Pub. Co., 1982, 343-345.
Grant.	Grant, R.M. *Gnosticism and Early Christianity*. New York: Columbia University Press, 1959.
Grant-Freedman.	Grant, R.M., and D.N. Freedman. *The Secret Sayings of Jesus*. London: Collins, 1960.
Grant-Graham.	Grant, R.M., and H.H. Graham. *First and Second Clement*. Vol. 2 in *The Apostolic Fathers*. Ed. R.M. Grant. New York: Thomas Nelson and Sons, 1965.
Gräßer 1965.	Gräßer, E. *Der Glaube im Hebräerbrief*. MTS 2. Marburg: N.G. Elwert, 1965.
Gräßer 1984.	_____. "Mose und Jesus. Zur Auslegung von Hebr 3 1-6." *ZNW*, 75 (1984), 2-23.

Gräßer 1986.	_____. "Das wandernde Gottesvolk. Zum Basismotiv des Hebräerbriefs." *ZNW*, 77 (1986), 160-179.
** Gräßer, 1.	_____. *An die Hebräer*. EKKNT 17/1. 1. Teilband. Heb 1-6. Zürich: Benziger Verlag GmbH, 1990.
G.B. Gray.	Gray, G.B. *A Critical and Exegetical Commentary on the Book of Isaiah I-XXXIX*. ICC. Edinburgh: T. & T. Clark, 1912.
J. Gray.	Gray, J. *I & II Kings*. OTL. London: SCM, 1964.
Groß.	Groß, Heinrich. *Klagelieder*. Die Neue Echter Bibel Altes Testament. Würzburg: Echter Verlag, 1986.
* Grundmann.	Grundmann, Walter. *Das Evangelium nach Matthäus*. THKNT 1. Berlin: Evangelische Verlagsanstalt, 1968.
Grundmann 1972.	_____. "ταπεινός κτλ." *TDNT*, 8:1-26.
Grundmann 1978.	_____. "Weisheit im Horizont des Reiches Gottes. Eine Studie zur Verkündigung Jesu nach der Spruchüberlieferung Q." In *Die Kirche des Anfangs: Festschrift für H. Schürmann*. Eds. R. Schnackenburg, J. Ernst, and J. Wanke. ErfThSt 38. Leipzig: St. Benno Verlag, 1978, 175-199.
Guelich.	Guelich, Robert A. *The Sermon on the Mount. A Foundation for Understanding*. Waco: Word Books, 1982.
Gundry 1967.	Gundry, Robert. *The Use of the Old Testament in St. Matthew's Gospel*. NovTSup 18. Leiden: Brill, 1967.
* Gundry.	_____. *Matthew. A Commentary on his Literary and Theological Art*. Grand Rapids: Eerdmans, 1982.
S. Gundry.	Gundry, Stanley. "Rest." *WBE*, 2:1975, 1455-1456.
Gunkel.	Gunkel, Hermann. *Die Psalmen*. 5th ed. Göttingen: Vandenhoeck & Ruprecht, 1968.
D. Guthrie.	Guthrie, D. *New Testament Theology*. Downers Grove: Inter-Varsity Press, 1981.
G. Guthrie.	Guthrie, G.H. *The Structure of Hebrews. A Text-Lingusitic Analysis*. NovTSup 73. Leiden: Brill, 1994.
Haenchen 1951.	Haenchen, Ernst. "Matthäus 23." *ZTK*, 48 (1951), 38-63.
Haenchen 1961.	_____. *Die Botschaft des Thomas-Evangeliums*. Theologische Bibliothek Töpelmann 6. Berlin: Töpelmann, 1961.

Haenchen 1971.	_____. *The Acts of the Apostles.* Trans. Bernard Noble and Gerald Shinn from 14th German ed. Philadelphia: Westminster Press, 1971.
Haering.	Haering, Th. "Matth. 11, 28-30." *Aus Schrift und Geschichte.* Eds. K. Bornhaüser *et al.* Stuttgart: Calwer, 1922, 3-15.
Hagner 1973.	Hagner, D.A. *The Use of the Old and New Testaments in Clement of Rome.* NovTSup 34. Leiden: Brill, 1973.
** Hagner.	_____. *Hebrews.* GNC. San Francisco: Harper and Row Pub., 1983.
* Hagner, 1.	_____. *Matthew 1-13.* WBC 33a. Dallas: Word Books, 1993.
Hamerton-Kelly 1971.	Hamerton-Kelly, R.G. "Review of *Jesus Sophia: Die Sophia-Christologie bei den Synoptikern*, by Felix Christ." *JBL*, 90 (1971), 239-240.
Hamerton-Kelly 1973.	_____. *Pre-Existence, Wisdom, and the Son of Man. A Study of the Idea of Pre-Existence in the New Testament.* Cambridge: CUP, 1973.
Hanson 1979.	Hanson, P.D. *The Dawn of Apocalyptic.* Rev. ed. Philadelphia: Fortress, 1979.
Hanson 1992.	_____. "The Genre" and "Introductory Overview." *ABD*, 1:279-282.
Harder.	Harder, G. "Die Septuagintazitate des Hebräerbriefs." In *Theologia Viatorum.* Ed. M. Albertz. Münich: Kaiser, 1939, 33-52.
* Harrington.	Harrington, D.J. *The Gospel of Matthew.* Sacra Pagina Series 1. Collegeville: The Liturgical Press, 1991.
Hasel.	Hasel, Gerhard F. "Sabbath." *ABD*, 5:849-856.
Hauck.	Hauck, F. "κόπος, κοπιάω." *TDNT*, 3:827-830.
Hauck-Schulz 1968a.	Hauck, F., and S. Schulz. "πραΰς, πραΰτης." *TDNT*, 6:645-651.
Hauck-Schulz 1968b.	Hauck, F., and S. Schulz. "πτωχός κτλ." *TDNT*, 6:885-915.
Hay.	Hay, David M. *Glory at the Right Hand: Psalm 110 in Early Christianity.* SBLMS 18. Nashville: Abingdon Press, 1973.
** Hegermann.	Hegermann, Harald. *Der Brief an die Hebräer.* THKNT

16. Berlin: Evangelische Verlagsanstalt, 1988.

Held. Held, H.J. "Matthew as Interpreter of the Miracle Stories." In *Tradition and Interpretation in Matthew*. G. Bornkamm, G. Barth, and H.J. Held. Trans. P. Scott. London: SCM, 1963, 165-299.

Helderman 1978. Helderman, Jan. "Anapausis in the Epistula Jacobi Apocrypha." In *Nag Hammadi and Gnosis*. Ed. R. McL. Wilson. NHS 14. Leiden: Brill, 1978, 34-43.

Helderman 1984. _____. *Die Anapausis im Evangelium Veritatis*. NHS 18. Leiden: Brill, 1984.

Hengel 1974, 1-2. Hengel, M. *Judaism and Hellenism*. 2 vols. Trans. J. Bowden. London: SCM, 1974.

Hengel 1976. _____. *The Son of God*. Trans. John Bowden. Philadelphia: Fortress, 1976.

Hengel 1979. _____. "Jesus als messianischer Lehrer der Weisheit und die Anfänge der Christologie." In E. Jacob ed. *Sagesse et Religion*. Paris: Presses Universitaires de France, 1979, 147-188.

Hengel 1981. _____. *The Charismatic Leader and his Followers*. Trans. J. Greig. Edinburgh: T. & T. Clark, 1981.

Hengel-Markschies. Hengel, M., and C. Markschies. *The 'Hellenization' of Judaea in the First Century after Christ*. Trans. J. Bowden. London: SCM, 1989.

Hensel-Brown. Hensel, R. and C. Brown. "Rest." *NIDNTT*, 3:254-258.

** Héring. Héring, Jean. *The Epistle to the Hebrews*. Trans. A.W. Heathcote and P.J. Allcock. London: Epworth Press, 1970.

Herkenne. Herkenne, H. *Das Buch der Psalmen*. HSAT 2. Bonn: Peter Hanstein Verlagsbuchhandlung, 1936.

Hermans. Hermans, A. "Le Pseudo-Barnabé est-il millénariste?" *ETL*, 35 (1959), 849-876.

Hertzberg. Hertzberg, Hans Wilhelm. *I and II Samuel*. Trans. from 2nd. rev. ed. J.S. Bowden. OTL. London: SCM, 1964.

Heschel. Heschel, Abraham J. *The Sabbath: Its Meaning for Modern Man*. New York: Noonday Press, 1951.

* Hill. Hill, David. *The Gospel of Matthew*. NCBC. London: Marshall, Morgan and Scott, 1972.

Hill 1977.	_____. "On the Use and Meaning of Hosea 6.6 in Matthew's Gospel." *NTS*, 24 (1977), 107-119.
Hill 1980.	_____. "Son and Servant: An Essay on Matthean Christology." *JSNT*, 6 (1980), 2-16.
Hillers.	Hillers, Delbert R. *Lamentations*. AB. Garden City: Doubleday, 1972.
Hingle.	Hingle, N.N. "Review of *A Gospel for a New People: Studies in Matthew*, by Graham N. Stanton." *EvQ*, 65 (1993), 358-360.
Hirsch.	Hirsch, E. *Frühgeschichte des Evangeliums*. Vol. 2. Tübingen: Mohr, 1941.
HJP²	Schürer, Emil. *The History of the Jewish People in the Age of Jesus Christ*. 3 vols. Rev. and ed. Geza Vermes, Fergus Millar, and Matthew Black. Edinburgh: T. & T. Clark, Ltd., 1973,1979,1986-87.
Hoffmann.	Hoffmann, E. "Promise." *NIDNTT*, 3:68-74.
Hofius.	Hofius, Otfried. *Katapausis. Die Vorstellung vom endzeitlichen Ruheort im Hebräerbrief*. WUNT 11. Tübingen: Mohr, 1970.
Hofius 1991.	_____. "καταβολή." *EDNT*, 2:255-256.
Hofius 1991a.	_____. "κατάπαυσις." *EDNT*, 2:265-266.
Hofius 1993.	_____. "σαββατισμός." *EDNT*, 3:219.
Holladay, 1-2.	Holladay, W.L. *Jeremiah*. 2 vols. Hermeneia. Minneapolis: Fortress, 1986, 1989.
Hollander.	Hollander, H.W. "ὑπόστασις." *EDNT*, 3:406-407.
Horbury.	Horbury, William. "The Aaronic Priesthood in the Epistle to the Hebrews." *JSNT*, 19 (1983), 43-71.
Hoskyns.	Hoskyns, E.C. "Jesus the Messiah." In *Mysterium Christi*. Eds. G.K.A. Bell and A. Deissmann. London: Longmans, Green & Co., 1930, 69-89.
Hossfeld.	Hossfeld, F.-L. *Der Dekalog*. Göttingen: Vandenhoeck & Ruprecht, 1982.
G. Hughes.	Hughes, Graham. *Hermeneutics and Hebrews*. SNTSMS 36. Cambridge: CUP, 1979.
** Hughes.	Hughes, P.E. *A Commentary on the Epistle to the Hebrews*. Grand Rapids: Eerdmans, 1977.

Hulst 1966.	Hulst, A.R. "Bemerkungen zum Sabbatgebot." In *Studia Biblica et Semitica*. Eds. W.C. van Unnik and A.S. van der Woude. Wageningen: A. Veeman & Zonen, 1966, 152-164.
Hulst 1970.	_____. "De betekenis van het woord *menûchā*." In *Schrift en Uitlig, Festschrift W.H. Gispen*. Kampen, 1970, 62-78.
Hummel.	Hummel, R. *Die Auseinandersetzung zwischen Kirche und Judentum im Matthäusevangelium*. 2nd ed. BEvT 33. München: Chr. Kaiser, 1966.
Hunter.	Hunter, A.M. "Crux Criticorum - Matt. XI. 25-30 - A Re-Appraisal." *NTS*, 8 (1962), 241-249.
Hurst.	Hurst, L.D. *The Epistle to the Hebrews. Its Background of Thought*. SNTSMS 65. Cambridge: CUP, 1990.
Hutton.	Hutton, W.R. "Hebrews iv. 11." *ExpTim*, 52 (1940-41), 316-317.
Isaacs.	Isaacs, Marie E. *Sacred Space. An Approach to the Theology of the Epistle to the Hebrews*. JSNTSS 73. Sheffield: JSOT, 1992.
Jacob.	Bertram, G., A. Dihle, E. Jacob, E. Lohse, E. Schweizer, and K.-W. Tröger. "ψυχή, κτλ." *TDNT*, 9:608-666.
Jacobson.	Jacobson, A.D. "Wisdom Christology in Q." Diss. Claremont, 1978.
Janzen.	Janzen, J. Gerald. "The Yoke that Gives Rest." *Int*, 41 (1987), 256-268.
Jellicoe 1968.	Jellicoe, S. *The Septuagint and Modern Study*. Oxford: Clarendon, 1968.
Jellicoe 1974.	_____, ed. *Studies in the Septuagint: Origins, Recensions, and Interpretations*. LBS. New York: Ktav, 1974.
Jenni.	Jenni, Ernst. *Die theologische Begründung des Sabbatgebotes im Alten Testament*. ThStud 46. Zürich: Evangelischer Verlag Ag. Zollikon, 1956.
Jeremias 1964.	Jeremias, J. "ᾅδης." *TDNT*, 1:146-149.
Jeremias 1967a.	_____. "Μωϋσῆς." *TDNT*, 4:848-873.
Jeremias 1967b.	_____. "παράδεισος." *TDNT*, 5:765-773.
Jeremias 1967c.	_____. *The Prayers of Jesus*. Trans. J. Bowden *et al*. Philadelphia: Fortress, 1964, 1967.

Jeremias 1972.	_____. *The Parables of Jesus*. Trans. of 8th German ed. based on S.H. Hooke's trans. of 6th German ed. New York: Charles Scribner's Sons, 1972.
Jeremias 1971.	_____. *New Testament Theology. The Proclamation of Jesus*. Trans. John Bowden. New York: Charles Scribner's Sons, 1971.
Jörg Jeremias.	Jeremias, Jörg. *Das Königtum Gottes in den Psalmen*. Göttingen: Vandenhoeck & Ruprecht, 1987.
A.R. Johnson.	Johnson, A.R. *The Cultic Prophet and Israel's Psalmody*. Cardiff: University of Wales Press, 1979.
M.D. Johnson.	Johnson, M.D. "Reflections on a Wisdom Approach to Matthew's Christology." *CBQ*, 36 (1974), 44-64.
Johnsson 1977.	Johnsson, W.G. "Issues in the Interpretation of Hebrews." *AUSS*, 15 (1977), 169-187.
Johnsson 1978.	_____. "The Pilgrimage Motif in the Book of Hebrews." *JBL*, 97 (1978), 239-251.
Jones.	Jones, C.P.M. "The Epistle to the Hebrews and the Lucan Writings." In *Studies in the Gospels. Essays in Memory of R.H. Lightfoot*. Ed. D.E. Nineham. Oxford: Blackwell, 1957, 113-143.
H.J. de Jonge.	de Jonge, H.J. "The Historical Jesus' View of Himself and of His Mission." In *From Jesus to John. Essays on Jesus and New Testament Christology in Honour of Marinus de Jonge*. Ed. M.C. De Boer. JSNTSS 84. Sheffield: JSOT, 1993, 21-37.
M. de Jonge 1986.	de Jonge, Marinus. "The Earliest Christian Use of *Christos*: Some Suggestions." *NTS*, 32 (1986), 321-343.
M. de Jonge 1988.	_____. *Christology in Context. The Earliest Christian Response to Jesus*. Philadelphia: Westminster Press, 1988.
M. de Jonge 1991.	_____. *Jesus, The Servant-Messiah*. London: Yale University Press, 1991.
O. Kaiser 1972.	Kaiser, Otto. *Isaiah 1-12*. Trans. R.A. Wilson. OTL. London: SCM, 1972.
O. Kaiser 1974.	_____. *Isaiah 13-39*. Trans. R.A. Wilson. OTL. London: SCM, 1974.
W.C. Kaiser 1973.	Kaiser, Walter C. "The Promise Theme and the Theology of Rest." *BSac*, 130 (1973), 135-150.
W.C. Kaiser 1985.	_____. *The Uses of the Old Testament in the New*.

	Chicago: Moody Press, 1985.
Käsemann.	Käsemann, Ernst. *The Wandering People of God*. Trans. R.A. Harrisville and I.L. Sandberg. Minneapolis: Augsburg, 1984.
Keck.	Keck, L.E. "Toward the Renewal of New Testament Theology." *NTS*, 32 (1986), 362-377.
Keller.	Keller, C.H. "Das quietistische Element in der Botschaft des Jesaja." *TZ*, 11 (1955), 81-97.
Kingsbury 1975.	Kingsbury, Jack Dean. *Matthew: Structure, Christology, Kingdom*. London: SPCK, 1975.
Kingsbury 1976.	_____. "The Title 'Son of David' in Matthew's Gospel." *JBL*, 95 (1976), 591-602.
Kistemaker.	Kistemaker, S. *The Psalm Citations in the Epistle to the Hebrews*. Amsterdam: Van Soest, 1961.
Kittel.	Kittel, G., G. von Rad, W. Grundmann. "$\ddot{\alpha}\gamma\gamma\epsilon\lambda o_S$ $\kappa\tau\lambda$." *TDNT*, 1:75-87.
Klijn.	Klijn, A.J.F. "Review of Jan Helderman, *Die Anapausis im Evangelium Veritatis*." *NovT*, 28 (1986), 93-94.
Kloppenborg 1978.	Kloppenborg, J.S. "Wisdom Christology in Q." *LavTP*, 34 (1978), 129-147.
Kloppenborg 1987.	_____. *The Formation of Q; Trajectories in Ancient Wisdom Collections*. Studies in Antiquity & Christianity. Philadelphia, Fortress, 1987.
* Klostermann.	Klostermann, Erich. *Das Matthäus Evangelium*. 2nd ed. HNT 4. Tübingen: Mohr, 1927.
Knowles.	Knowles, Michael. *Jeremiah in Matthew's Gospel. The Rejected-Prophet Motif in Matthaean Redaction*. JSNTSS 68. Sheffield: JSOT, 1993.
Koch.	Koch, K. *The Rediscovery of Apocalyptic*. SBT 2/22. Naperville: Allenson, 1972.
Koester 1962.	Koester, H. "'Outside the Camp': Hebrews 13.9-14." *HTR*, 55 (1962), 299-315.
Koester 1971.	_____. "One Jesus and Four Primitive Gospels." In *Trajectories through Early Christianity*. J.M. Robinson and H. Koester. Philadelphia: Fortress, 1971, 158-204.
Koester 1972.	_____. "$\dot{v}\pi\dot{o}\sigma\tau\alpha\sigma\iota_S$." *TDNT*, 8:572-589.

Koester 1980.	———. "Gnostic Writings as Witnesses for the Development of the Sayings Tradition." In *The School of Valentinus.* Ed. B. Layton. *The Rediscovery of Gnosticism.* SHR (Suppl. to *Numen*) 41/1. Leiden: Brill, 1980, 238-261.
Koester 1982, 1-2.	———. *Introduction to the New Testament.* 2 vols. Philadelphia: Fortress, 1982.
R.A. Kraft.	Kraft, R.A. *Barnabas and the Didache.* Vol. 3 in *The Apostolic Fathers. A New Translation and Commentary.* Ed. R.M. Grant. New York: Thomas Nelson and Sons, 1965.
Kraus 1960.	Kraus, Hans-Joachim. *Klagelieder (Threni).* 2nd ed. BK 20. Neukirchen: Neukirchener Verlag, 1960.
Kraus 1986.	———. *Theology of the Psalms.* Trans. Keith Crim. Minneapolis: Augsburg, 1986.
Kraus 1989.	———. *Psalms 60-150.* Trans. H.C. Oswald. Minneapolis: Augsburg, 1989.
Kronholm.	Kronholm, T. "רָגַע." *TWAT*, 7:347-350.
de Kruijf.	de Kruijf, Th. *Der Sohn des lebendigen Gottes.* AnBib 16. Rome: Biblical Institute Press, 1962.
Ladd.	Ladd, G.E. *A Commentary on the Revelation of John.* Grand Rapids: Eerdmans, 1972.
Lampe-Luz.	Lampe, P., and U. Luz. "Overview of the Discussion." In *The Gospel and the Gospels.* Ed. P. Stuhlmacher. Grand Rapids: Eerdmans, 1991, 387-404.
Lane 1962.	Lane, William L. "Times of Refreshment. A Study in Eschatological Periodization in Judaism and Christianity." Diss. Cambridge (MA), 1962.
Lane 1978.	———. "Want etc." *NIDNTT*, 3:952-956.
** Lane, 1-2.	———. *Hebrews.* WBC 47a-b. Waco: Word Books, 1991.
Lang.	Lang, B. *Wisdom and the Book of Proverbs: An Israelite Goddess Redefined.* New York: The Pilgrim Press, 1986.
Laub.	Laub, Franz. *Bekenntnis und Auslegung. Die paränetische Funktion der Christologie im Hebräerbrief.* BU 15. Regensburg: Friedrich Pustet, 1980.
Lauterbach 1951.	Lauterbach, J.Z. "The Sabbath in Jewish Ritual and Folklore." In *Rabbinical Essays.* Cincinnati: Hebrew

Union College, 1951, 437-470.

Légasse.	Légasse, S. *Jésus et L'Enfant.* EBib. Paris: Librairie Lecoffre, 1969.
Leivestad.	Leivestad, R. "'The Meekness and Gentleness of Christ' II Cor. x. 1." *NTS*, 12 (1965-66), 156-164.
Levenson.	Levenson, Jon D. "The Temple and the World." *JR*, 64 (1984), 275-298.
Lilla.	Lilla, S.R.C. *Clement of Alexandria. A Study in Christian Platonism and Gnosticism.* Oxford Theological Monographs. Oxford: Oxford University Press, 1971.
Lincoln 1981.	Lincoln, A.T. *Paradise Now and Not Yet. Studies in the Role of the Heavenly Dimension in Paul's Thought with Special Reference to his Eschatology.* SNTSMS 43. Cambridge: CUP, 1981.
Lincoln 1982.	_____. "Sabbath, Rest, and Eschatology in the New Testament." In *From Sabbath to Lord's Day.* Ed. D.A. Carson. Grand Rapids: Zondervan, 1982, 197-220.
Lindars 1989.	Lindars, Barnabas. "The Rhetorical Structure of Hebrews." *NTS*, 35 (1989), 382-406.
Lindars 1991a.	_____. "Hebrews and the Second Temple." In *Temple Amicitiae. Essays on the Second Temple presented to Ernst Bammel.* Ed. W. Horbury. JSNTSS 48. Sheffield: JSOT, 1991, 410-433.
Lindars 1991b.	_____. *The Theology of the Letter to the Hebrews.* New Testament Theology. Ed. J.D.G. Dunn. Cambridge: CUP, 1991.
Loader 1981.	Loader, W.R.G. *Sohn und Hoherpriester. Eine traditionsgeschichtliche Untersuchung zur Christologie des Hebräerbriefes.* WMANT 53. Neukirchen: Neukirchener Verlag, 1981.
Loader 1982.	_____. "Son of David, Blindness, Possession, and Duality in Matthew." *CBQ*, 44 (1982), 570-585.
Lohmann.	Lohmann, H. *Drohung und Verheißung. Exegetische Untersuchungen zur Eschatologie bei den Apostolischen Vätern.* BZNW 55. Berlin: Walter de Gruyter, 1989.
Lohse.	Lohse, E. "σάββατον, σαββατισμός, παρασκευή." *TDNT*, 7:1-35.
Lombard.	Lombard, H.A. "Katapausis in the Letter to the Hebrews." *Neot*, 5 (1971), 60-71.

Longenecker.	Longenecker, R. *Biblical Exegesis in the Apostolic Period*. Grand Rapids: Eerdmans, 1975.
Losada.	Losada, D.A. "La reconciliación como 'reposo'." *RevistB*, 36 (1974), 113-128.
Lövestam.	Lövestam, E. "Jésus Fils de David chez les Synoptiques." *ST*, 28 (1974), 97-109; trans. and repr. of "Davids-son-kristologin hos synoptikerna." *SEÅ*, 15 (1972), 198-210.
Luck.	Luck, Ulrich. "Weisheit und Christologie in Mt 11,25-30." *WuD*, 13 (1975), 35-51.
Lührmann.	Lührmann, D. *Die Redaktion der Logienquelle*. WMANT 33. Neukirchen: Neukirchener Verlag, 1969.
* Luz, 2.	Luz, Ulrich. *Das Evangelium nach Matthäus*. EKKNT 1/2. Zürich: Benziger Verlag, 1990.
Mack 1970.	Mack, B.L. "Wisdom Myth and Mytho-logy." *Int*, 24 (1970), 46-60.
Mack 1971.	_____. "Review of *Wisdom, Christology, and Law in Matthew's Gospel*, by M.J. Suggs." *JBL*, 90 (1971), 353-354.
Mack 1973.	_____. *Logos und Sophia. Untersuchungen zur Weisheitstheologie im hellenistischen Judentum*. SUNT 10. Göttingen: Vandenhoeck & Ruprecht, 1973.
MacLeod.	MacLeod, David J. "The Doctrinal Center of the Book of Hebrews." *BSac*, 146 (1989), 291-300.
Macrae.	Macrae, George Wesley. "Heavenly Temple and Eschatology in the Letter to the Hebrews." *Semeia*, 12 (1978), 179-199.
Maher.	Maher, M. "'Take my Yoke upon You' (Matt. XI. 29)." *NTS*, 22 (1975-76), 97-103.
* Maier.	Maier, Gerhard. *Matthäus-Evangelium*. Vol. 1. Bibel-Kommentar 1. Neuhausen (Stuttgart): Hänssler-Verlag, 1979.
T.W. Manson.	Manson, T.W. "The Sayings of Jesus." In *The Mission and Message of Jesus*. H.D.A. Major, T.W. Manson, and C.J. Wright. London: Ivor Nicholson and Watson Ltd., 1937, 301-639.
W. Manson.	Manson, W. *The Epistle to the Hebrews. An Historical and Theological Reconsideration*. London: Hodder and Stoughton Ltd., 1951.

Marcovich.	Marcovich, M. "Textual Criticism on the *Gospel of Thomas*." *JTS*, 20 (1969), 53-74.
Marshall 1967.	Marshall, I.H. "The Divine Sonship of Jesus." *Int*, 21 (1967), 87-103.
Marshall 1978.	_____. *The Gospel of Luke*. NIGTC. Grand Rapids: Eerdmans, 1978.
Marshall 1980.	_____. *The Acts of the Apostles*. TNTC 5. Grand Rapids: Eerdmans, 1980.
Marshall 1983.	_____. *1-2 Thessalonians*. NCBC. Grand Rapids: Eerdmans, 1983.
A.D. Martin.	Martin, A.D. "Σαββατισμός." *ExpTim*, 26 (1914-15), 563-565.
F. Martin.	Martin, F. "The Image of the Shepherd in the Gospel of Matthew." *ScEs*, 27 (1975), 261-301.
T. Martin.	Martin, T. "Hellenists." *ABD*, 3:135-136.
Mayes.	Mayes, A.D.H. *Deuteronomy*. NCBC. London: Marshall, Morgan and Scott, 1979.
Mays.	Mays, James L. *Micah*. OTL. London: SCM, 1976.
McCarter.	McCarter, P. Kyle, Jr. *II Samuel*. AB. Garden City: Doubleday, 1984.
McCarthy.	McCarthy, Dennis J. "II Samuel 7 and the Structure of the Deuteronomic History." *JBL*, 84 (1965), 131-138.
McCullough.	McCullough, J.C. "Some Recent Developments in Research on the Epistle to the Hebrews." *IBS*, 2 (1980), 141-165.
McKane.	McKane, William. *A Criticial and Exegetical Commentary on Jeremiah*. Vol. 1. ICC. Edinburgh: T. & T. Clark, Ltd., 1986.
J.L. McKenzie.	McKenzie, J.L. *Second Isaiah*. AB. Garden City: Doubleday, 1968.
S.L. McKenzie	McKenzie, S.L. "Deuteronomistic History." *ABD*, 2:160-168.
Meadors.	Meadors, Edward. "Jesus the Herald of Salvation: A Comparison of the Kingdom of God Sayings in Mark and Q." Diss. Aberdeen, 1993.
Meeks.	Meeks, W.A. "Asking Back to Jesus' Identity." In *From Jesus to John. Essays on Jesus and New Testament*

Christology in Honour of Marinus de Jonge. Ed. M.C. De Boer. JSNTSS 84. Sheffield: JSOT, 1993, 38-50.

Ménard.	Ménard, J.E. "Le Repos. Salut du Gnostique." *RevScRel*, 51 (1977), 71-88.
B. Metzger.	Metzger, Bruce M. *A Textual Commentary on the Greek New Testament.* New York: United Bible Societies, 1971.
M. Metzger.	Metzger, M. "Himmlische und irdische Wohnstatt Jahwes." *UF*, 2 (1970), 139-158.
E. Meyer.	Meyer, Eduard. *Ursprung und Anfänge des Christentums.* Vol. 1. 4th-5th ed. Stuttgart: J.G. Cotta'sche Buchhnadlung Nachfolger, 1924.
R. Meyer.	Meyer, R. "προφήτης κτλ." *TDNT*, 6:812-828.
Meyers.	Meyers, J.M. *II Chronicles.* AB. New York: Doubleday, 1965.
** Michel.	Michel, O. *Der Brief an die Hebräer.* 6th ed. Meyers Kommentar 13. Göttingen: Vandenhoeck & Ruprecht, 1966.
Michel 1967.	_____. "ὄνος κτλ." *TDNT*, 5:283-287.
M.P. Miller.	Miller, M.P. "The Function of Isa 61:1-2 in 11Q Melchizedek." *JBL*, 88 (1969), 467-469.
P.D. Miller 1984.	Miller, Patrick D. "The Most Important Word: The Yoke of the Kingdom." *Iliff Review*, 41 (1984), 17-29.
P.D. Miller 1985.	_____. "The Human Sabbath: A Study in Deuteronomic Theology." *PSB*, ns 6, No. 2 (1985), 81-97.
P.D. Miller 1987.	_____. "'Moses my Servant.' The Deuteronomic Portrait of Moses." *Int*, 41 (1987), 245-255.
R.J. Miller.	Miller, R.J. "The Rejection of the Prophets in Q." *JBL*, 107 (1988), 225-240.
** Moffatt.	Moffatt, James. *A Critical and Exegetical Commentary on the Epistle to the Hebrews.* ICC. Edinburgh: T. & T. Clark, 1924.
Montefiore 1961.	Montefiore, H. "A Comparison of the Parables of the Gospel According to Thomas and of the Synoptic Gospels." *NTS*, 7 (1961), 220-248.
** Montefiore.	Montefiore, H. *A Commentary on the Epistle to the Hebrews.* Black's New Testament. London: Adam and Charles Black, 1964.

Moo.	Moo, Douglas J. *The Old Testament in the Gospel Passion Narratives*. Sheffield: Almond, 1983.
Moore.	Moore, Carey A. *Judith*. AB. Garden City: Doubleday, 1985.
Moreland-Robinson.	Moreland, M.C., and J.M. Robinson. "The International Q Project Work Sessions 6-8 August, 18-19 November 1993." *JBL*, 113 (1994), 495-499.
* Morris.	Morris, L. *The Gospel according to Matthew*. Grand Rapids: Eerdmans, 1992.
Mosis.	Mosis, Rudolf. *Untersuchungen zur Theologie des chronistischen Geschichtswerkes*. FTS 29. Freiburg: Herder, 1973.
Motte.	Motte, A.R. "La Structure du Logion de Matthieu, XI,28-30." *RB*, 88 (1981), 226-233.
Mounce 1977.	Mounce, R. *The Book of Revelation*. The New London Commentary on the New Testament. London: Marshall, Morgan and Scott, 1977.
* Mounce.	_____. *Matthew*. GNC. San Francisco: Harper & Row, Pub., 1985.
Mugridge.	Mugridge, Alan. "'Warnings in the Epistle to the Hebrews,' An Exegetical and Theological Study." *RefTR*, 46 (1987), 74-82.
Mulder.	Mulder, M.J. "The Transmission of the Biblical Text." In *Mikra*. Ed. M.J. Mulder. The Literature of the Jewish People in the Period of the Second Temple and the Talmud 1. CRINT 2. Philadelphia: Fortress, 1988, 87-135.
Mullins.	Mullins, T.Y. "Jesus the Son of David." *AUSS*, 29/2 (1991), 117-126.
Murray.	Murray, D.F. "*MQWM* and the Future of Israel in 2 Samuel VII 10," *VT*, 40 (1990), 298-320.
Mussies.	Mussies, G. "Greek in Palestine and the Diaspora." In *The Jewish People in the First Century*. Eds. S. Safrai, M. Stern, D. Flusser, W.C. van Unnik. The Jewish People in the First Century 2. CRINT 1. Philadelphia: Fortress, 1976, 1040-1064.
Nardoni.	Nardoni, Enrique. "Partakers in Christ (Hebrews 3:14)." *NTS*, 37 (1991), 456-472.
Newsom.	Newsom, C.A. "Angels (Old Testament)." *ABD*, 1:248-253.

Nicholson.	Nicholson, E.W. *Jeremiah 26-52*. CBC. Cambridge: CUP, 1975.
Nickelsburg 1972.	Nickelsburg, G.W.E. *Resurrection, Immortality, and Eternal Life in Intertestamental Judaism*. HTS 26. Cambridge: Harvard University, 1972.
Nickelsburg 1992a.	_____. "Eschatology (Early Jewish)." *ABD*, 2:579-594.
Nickelsburg 1992b.	_____. "Resurrection (Early Judaism and Christianity)." *ABD*, 5:684-691.
Nolan.	Nolan, Brian M. *The Royal Son of God. The Christology of Matthew 1-2 in the Setting of the Gospel*. OBO 23. Göttingen: Vandenhoeck & Ruprecht, 1979.
Norden.	Norden, E. . *Agnostos Theos*. Darmstadt: Wissenschaftliche Buchgesellschaft, 1956.
Noth 1962.	Noth, Martin. *Exodus*. OTL. London: SCM, 1962.
Noth 1987.	_____. *The Chronicler's History*. Trans. H.G.M. Williamson. JSOTSS 50. Sheffield: JSOT, 1987.
Oberholtzer 1984.	Oberholtzer, Thomas Kem. "An Analysis and Exposition of the Eschatology of the Warning Passages in the Book of Hebrews." Diss. Dallas, 1984.
Oberholtzer 1988.	_____. "The Warning Passages in Hebrews Part 2 (of 5 parts): The Kingdom Rest in Hebrews 3:1-4:13." *BSac*, 145 (1988), 185-196.
Oepke.	Oepke, A. "ἀποκαθίστημι κτλ." *TDNT*, 1:387-393.
Oesterley 1912.	Oesterley, W.O.E. *The Wisdom of Jesus Ben Sirach or Ecclesiasticus*. CBSC. Cambridge: CUP, 1912.
Oesterley 1959.	_____. *The Psalms*. 2 vols. London: SPCK, 1939, 1959.
Orton.	Orton, David E. *The Understanding Scribe. Matthew and the Apocalyptic Ideal*. JSNTSS 25. Sheffield: JSOT, 1989.
* Patte.	Patte, Daniel. *The Gospel According to Matthew*. Philadelphia: Fortress, 1987.
Peters.	Peters, M.K.H. "Septuagint." *ABD*, 5:1093-1104.
Peterson 1982.	Peterson, David. *Hebrews and Perfection*. SNTSMS 47. Cambridge: CUP, 1982.
Peterson 1992.	_____. "Biblical Theology and the Argument of

	Hebrews." In *In the Fullness of Time. Biblical Studies in Honour of Archbishop Donald Robinson*. Eds. D. Peterson and John Pryor. Homebush West: Lancer, 1992, 219-235.
Pétrement.	Pétrement, Simone. *A Separate God. The Christian Origins of Gnosticism*. Trans. Carol Harrison. London: Darton, Longman and Todd, 1990.
Pettazzoni.	Pettazzoni, R. "Myths of Beginning and Creation-Myths." In *Essays on the History of Religions*. Trans. H.J. Rose. SHR (Suppl. to *Numen*) 1. Leiden: Brill, 1954, 24-36.
Piper.	Piper, Ronald A. *Wisdom in the Q-tradition. The Aphoristic Teaching of Jesus*. Cambridge: CUP, 1989.
Prabhu.	Prabhu, George M. Soares. *The Formula Quotations in the Infancy Narrative of Matthew*. AnBib 63. Rome: Biblical Institute Press, 1976.
Preuß.	Preuß, H.D. "נוּחַ." *TWAT*, 5:297-307.
Rabin.	Rabin, Ch. "Hebrew and Aramaic in the First Century." In *The Jewish People in the First Century*. Eds. S. Safrai, M. Stern, D. Flusser, W.C. van Unnik. The Jewish People in the First Century 2. CRINT 1. Philadelphia: Fortress, 1976, 1007-1039.
von Rad, 1-2.	von Rad, G. *Old Testament Theology*. 2 vols. Trans. D.M.G. Stalker. New York: Harper and Row, Pub., 1962,1965.
von Rad 1964.	_____. "שָׁלוֹם in the OT." *TDNT*, 2:402-406.
von Rad 1966a.	_____. "The Promised Land and Yahweh's Land in the Hexateuch." In *The Problem of the Hexateuch and Other Essays*. Trans. E.W. Trueman Dicken. London: SCM, 1966, 79-93.
von Rad 1966b.	_____. "There Remains Still a Rest for the People of God. An Investigation of a Biblical Conception." In *The Problem of the Hexateuch and Other Essays*. Trans. E.W. Trueman Dicken. London: SCM, 1966, 94-102.
von Rad 1972a.	_____. *Genesis*. Trans. J.H. Marks. Rev. ed. OTL. London: SCM, 1972.
von Rad 1972b.	_____. *Wisdom in Israel*. Trans. J.D. Martin. London: SCM, 1972.
Reicke.	Reicke, Bo, G. Bertram. "πᾶς, ἅπας." *TDNT*, 5:886-896.
Rengstorf 1964a.	Rengstorf, K.H. "ἀποστέλλω κτλ." *TDNT*, 1:398-447.

Rengstorf 1964b.	_____. "ἑπτά κτλ." *TDNT*, 2:627-635.
Rengstorf 1967.	_____. "μανθάνω κτλ." *TDNT*, 4:390-461.
Renner.	Renner, J.T.E. "The Rest of God in the Creation Account of Genesis." *LTJ*, 15 (1981), 18-22.
Richardson.	Richardson, P. "The Thunderbolt in Q and the Wise Man in Corinth." In *From Jesus to Paul*. Eds. P. Richardson and J.C. Hurd. Waterloo: Wilfred Laurier University Press, 1984, 91-111.
Riehm.	Riehm, E.K.A. *Der Lehrbegriff des Hebräerbriefes*. 2nd ed. Basel: Balmer and Riehm, 1867.
Riesenfeld.	Riesenfeld, H. "The Sabbath and Lord's Day in Judaism, the Preaching of Jesus and Early Christianity." In *The Gospel Tradition*. Oxford: Blackwell, 1970, 111-137.
** Riggenbach.	Riggenbach, E. *Der Brief an die Hebräer*. Zahn's Kommentar zum Neuen Testament 14. Leipzig: A. Deichert'sche Verlagsbuchhandlung Nachf., 1913.
Ringgren.	Ringgren, Helmer. *Word and Wisdom. Studies in the Hypostatization of Divine Qualities and Functions in the Ancient Near East*. Lund: Ohlssons, 1947.
Rissi.	Rissi, Mathias. *Die Theologie des Hebräerbriefs*. WUNT 41. Tübingen: Mohr, 1987.
Rist.	Rist, M. "Is Matt. 11:25-30 a Primitive Baptismal Hymn?" *JR*, 15 (1935), 63-67.
G. Robinson 1975.	Robinson, Gnana. "The Origin and Development of the Old Testament Sabbath. A Comprehensive Exegetical Approach." Diss. Hamburg, 1975.
G. Robinson 1980.	_____. "The Idea of Rest in the Old Testament and the Search for the Basic Character of the Sabbath." *ZAW*, 92 (1980), 32-42.
J. Robinson.	Robinson, J. *The First Book of Kings*. CBC. Cambridge: CUP, 1972.
J.M. Robinson 1962.	Robinson, J.M. "Basic Shifts in German Theology," *Int*, 16 (1962), 76-97.
J. M. Robinson 1971.	Robinson, J.M. "*LOGOI SOPHON*: on the *Gattung* of Q." In *The Future of our Religious Past*. Ed. J.M. Robinson. Trans. C.E. Carlston and R.P. Scharlemann. London: SCM, 1971, 84-130; also in J.M. Robinson and H. Koester. *Trajectories through Early Christianity*. Philadelphia: Fortress, 1971, 71-113.

J.M. Robinson 1975.	_____. "Jesus as Sophos and Sophia: Wisdom Tradition and the Gospels." In *Aspects of Wisdom in Judaism and Early Christianity*. Ed. R.L. Wilken. Notre Dame: University of Notre Dame Press, 1975, 1-16.
* T.H. Robinson.	Robinson, Theodore H. *The Gospel of Matthew*. MNTC. London: Hodder and Stoughton Ltd., 1928.
Rordorf.	Rordorf, Willy. *Sunday. The History of the Day of Rest and Worship in the Earliest Centuries of the Christian Church*. Trans. A.A.K. Graham. London: SCM, 1968.
Rose 1989a.	Rose, C. "Verheissung und Erfüllung. Zum Verständnis von ἐπαγγελία im Hebräerbrief." *BZ*, 33 (1989), 60-80.
Rose 1989b.	_____. "Verheissung und Erfüllung. Zum Verständnis von ἐπαγγελία im Hebräerbrief." *BZ*, 33 (1989), 178-191.
Roth.	Roth, Wolfgang. "The Deuteronomic Rest Theology: A Redaction Critical Study." *BR*, 21 (1976), 5-14.
Rowland.	Rowland, Christopher. *The Open Heaven. A Study of Apocalyptic in Judaism and Early Christianity*. New York: Crossroad, 1982.
K. Rudolph 1983.	Rudolph, Kurt. "'Gnosis' and 'Gnosticism' -- The Problems of their Definition and their Relation to the Writings of the New Testament." In *The New Testament and Gnosis. Essays in Honour of Robert McL. Wilson*. Eds. A.H.B. Logan and A.J.M. Wedderburn. Edinburgh: T. & T. Clark, 1983, 21-37.
K. Rudolph 1984.	_____. *Gnosis. The Nature and History of Gnosticism*. Trans. and ed. from 2nd German ed. R. McL. Wilson. San Francisco: Harper and Row, Pub., 1984.
W. Rudolph 1955.	Rudolph, Wilhelm. *Chronikbücher*. HAT 21. Tübingen: Mohr, 1955.
W. Rudolph 1968.	_____. *Jeremia*. HAT 12. 3rd. ed. Tübingen: Mohr, 1968.
W. Rudolph 1975.	_____. *Micha-Nahum-Habakuk-Zephanja*. KAT 13/3. Gütersloh: Gütersloher Verlagshaus Gerd Mohn, 1975.
Runia 1990.	Runia, David T. *Exegesis and Philosophy. Studies on Philo of Alexandria*. Hampshire: Variorum, 1990.
Runia 1993.	_____. *Philo in Early Christian Literature*. Jewish Traditions in Early Christian Literature 3. CRINT 3. Minneapolis: Fortress, 1993.
Sand 1974.	Sand, Alexander. *Das Gesetz und die Propheten*. BU 11.

	Regensburg: Friedrich Pustet, 1974.
* Sand.	_____. *Das Evangelium nach Matthäus.* RNT. Regensburg: Friedrich Pustet, 1986.
Sand 1991.	_____. "ἐπαγγελία κτλ." *EDNT*, 2:13-16.
E.P. Sanders.	Sanders, E.P. *Paul and Palestinian Judaism.* Philadelphia: Fortress, 1977.
J.A. Sanders 1975.	Sanders, J.A. "From Isaiah 61 to Luke 4." In Part One of *Christianity, Judaism and other Greco-Roman Cults.* Ed. J. Neusner. SJLA 12. Leiden: Brill, 1975, 75-106.
J.A. Sanders 1992.	_____. "Canon. Hebrew Bible." *ABD*, 1:837-852.
Schenke.	Schenke, H.-M. "Erwägungen zum Rätsel des Hebräerbriefes." In *Neues Testament und christliche Existenz.* Eds. H.D. Betz and L. Schottroff. Tübingen: Mohr, 1973, 421-437.
Schierse.	Schierse, F.J. *Verheißung und Heilsvollendung. Zur theologischen Grundfrage des Hebräerbriefes.* MTS 1/9. München: Karl Zink, 1955.
* Schlatter.	Schlatter, Adolf. *Der Evangelist Matthäus.* 5th ed. Stuttgart: Calwer Verlag, 1959.
* Schmid.	Schmid, Josef. *Das Evangelium nach Matthäus.* 5th ed. RNT. Regensburg: Friedrich Pustet, 1965.
Schnackenburg 1982, 1-3.	Schnackenburg, R. *The Gospel According to John.* 3 vols. Trans. K. Smyth, C. Hastings, *et al.* Tunbridge Wells: Burns & Oates, 1968-1982.
* Schnackenburg.	_____. *Matthäusevangelium 1,1-16,20.* Die Neue Echter Bibel Neues Testament 1/1. Würzburg: Echter Verlag, 1985.
Schneider.	Schneider, Carl. "Anapausis." *RAC*, 1:414-418.
* Schniewind.	Schniewind, Julius. *Das Evangelium nach Matthäus.* 8th ed. NTD 2. Göttingen: Vandenhoeck & Ruprecht, 1956.
Schniewind-Friedrich.	Schniewind, J., and G. Friedrich. "ἐπαγγέλλω κτλ." *TDNT*, 2:576-586.
Scholer.	Scholer, John M. *Proleptic Priests. Priesthood in the Epistle to the Hebrews.* JSNTSS 49. Sheffield: JSOT, 1991.
Schrage.	Schrage, Wolfgang. *Das Verhältnis des Thomasevangeliums zur synoptischen Tradition und zu den*

Koptischen Evangelienübersetzungen. BZNW 29. Berlin: Töpelmann, 1964.

Schröger.   Schröger, F. *Das Verfasser des Hebräerbriefes als Schriftausleger.* BU 4. Regensburg: Pustet, 1968.

S. Schulz.   Schulz, S. *Q. Die Spruchquelle der Evangelisten.* Zürich: Theologischer Verlag, 1972.

W. Schulz.   Schulz, Waltraut. "Stilkritische Untersuchungen zur deuteronomistischen Literatur." Diss. Tübingen, 1974.

Schweizer 1972.   Schweizer, E. "υἱός, υἱοθεσία." *TDNT*, 8:363-392.

Schweizer 1974.   Bertram, G., A. Dihle, E. Jacob, E. Lohse, E. Schweizer, and K.-W. Tröger. "ψυχή κτλ." *TDNT*, 9:608-666.

Segal.   Segal, Alan F. *Two Powers in Heaven: Early Rabbinic Reports about Christianity and Gnosticism.* SJLA 25. Leiden: Brill, 1977.

Sharp.   Sharp, J.R. "Philonism and the Eschatology of Hebrews: Another Look." *EAJT*, 2 (1984), 289-298.

Sieber.   Sieber, J.H. "A Redactional Analysis of the Synoptic Gospels with Regard to the Questions of the Sources of the Gospel According to Thomas." Diss. Claremont 1966.

Skehan.   Skehan, P.W. "The Acrostic Poem in Sirach 51:13-30." *HTR*, 64 (1971), 387-400.

Skehan-Di Lella.   Skehan, Patrick W., and Alexander A. Di Lella. *The Wisdom of Ben Sirach.* AB. Garden City: Doubleday, 1987.

Sloan.   Sloan, R.B. *The Favorable Year of the Lord. A Study of Jublilary Theology in the Gospel of Luke.* Austin: Schola Press, 1977.

Smend 1906a.   Smend, Rudolph. *Die Weisheit de Jesus Sirach. Erklärt,* Berlin: Georg Reimer, 1906.

Smend 1906b.   _____. *Die Weisheit des Jesu Sirach. Hebräisch und Deutsch.* Berlin: Georg Reimer, 1906.

D.W. Smith.   Smith, D.W. *Wisdom Christology in the Synoptic Gospels.* Rome: Pontifica Studiorum Universitas A S. Thoma Aq. in Urbe, 1970.

R.L. Smith.   Smith, Ralph L. *Micah-Malachi.* WBC 32. Waco: Word Books, 1984.

Smith-Ward-Bewer.   Smith, J.M.P., W.H. Ward, and J.A. Bewer. *A Critical*

	and Exegetical Commentary on Micah, Zephaniah, Nahum, Habakkuk, Obadiah and Joel. ICC. Edinburgh: T. & T. Clark, 1912.
Solzhenitsyn.	Solzhenitsyn, Alexander. *Rebuilding Russia*. Trans. Alexis Klimoff. London: Harvill, 1991.
** Spicq, 1-2.	Spicq, C. *L'Épître aux Hébreux*. EBib. 2 vols. Paris: J. Gabalda, 1952,1953.
Stanton 1973.	Stanton, G.N. "On the Christology of Q." In *Christ and the Spirit in the New Testament*. Eds. B. Lindars and S.S. Smalley. Cambridge: CUP, 1973, 27-42.
Stanton 1982.	_____. "Salvation Proclaimed, X. Matthew 11:28-30: Comfortable Words?" *ExpTim*, 94 (1982), 3-8.
Stanton 1989.	_____. "'Pray that your Flight May Not Be in Winter or on a Sabbath': Matthew 24.20." *JSNT*, 37 (1989), 17-30.
Stanton 1992a.	_____. *A Gospel for a New People. Studies in Matthew*. Edinburgh: T. & T. Clark, 1992.
Stanton 1992b.	_____. "Matthew's Christology and the Parting of the Ways." In *Jews and Christians. The Parting of the Ways A.D. 70 to 135*. Ed. J.D.G. Dunn. WUNT 66. Tübingen: Mohr, 1992, 99-116.
Steck.	Steck, O.H. *Israel und das gewaltsame Geschick der Propheten*. WMANT 23. Neukirchen: Neukirchener Verlag, 1967.
Stendahl.	Stendahl, K. *The School of St. Matthew and its Use of the Old Testament*. 2nd ed. Philadelphia: Fortress, 1968.
Stolz 1976a.	Stolz, F. "נוח." *THAT*, 2:43-46.
Stolz 1976b.	_____. "שבת." *THAT*, 2:863-869.
Stone 1984.	Stone, M.E. "Apocalyptic Literature." In *Jewish Writings of the Second Temple Period. Apocrypha, Pseudepigrapha, Qumran Sectarian Writings, Philo, Josephus*. Ed. Michael E.Stone. The Literature of the Jewish People in the Period of the Second Temple and the Talmud 2. CRINT 2. Philadelphia: Fortress, 1984, 383-441.
Stone 1989.	_____. *Features of the Eschatology of IV Ezra*. HSS 35. Atlanta: Scholars Press, 1989.
Stone 1990.	_____. *Fourth Ezra*. Hermeneia. Minneapolis: Fortress, 1990.
Strack-Stemberger.	Strack, H.L., and G. Stemberger. *Introduction to the*

	Talmud and Midrash. Trans. Markus Bockmuehl. Edinburgh: T. & T. Clark, 1991.
D.F. Strauss.	Strauss, D.F. "Jesu Weheruf über Jerusalem und die σοφια του θεου. Matth. 23,34-39, Luk. 11,49-51. 13,34f. Ein Beitrag zur johanneischen Frage." *ZWT*, 6 (1863), 84-93.
M. Strauss.	Strauss, Mark L. "The Davidic Messiah in Luke-Acts. The Promise and its Fulfillment in Lukan Christology." Diss. Aberdeen, 1992.
Str-B, 1-6.	Strack, Hermann L., and Paul Billerbeck. *Kommentar zum Neuen Testament aus Talmud und Midrasch.* 6 vols. München: C.H. Beck'sche Verlagsbuchhandlung, 1922-1961.
Strecker 1962.	Strecker, G. *Der Weg der Gerechtigkeit. Untersuchungen zur Theologie des Matthäus.* FRLANT 82. Göttingen: Vandenhoeck & Ruprecht, 1962.
Strecker 1991.	_____. "εὐαγγελίζω." *EDNT*, 2:69-70.
** Strobel.	Strobel, A. *Der Brief an die Hebräer.* 4th ed. NTD 9/2. Göttingen: Vandenhoeck & Ruprecht, 1991.
Stroker.	Stroker, William D. *Extracanonical Sayings of Jesus.* SBLRBS 18. Atlanta: Scholars Press, 1989.
Stuhlmacher.	Stuhlmacher, P., ed. *The Gospel and the Gospels.* Trans. J. Bowden. Grand Rapids: Eerdmans, 1991.
Suggs.	Suggs, M.J. *Wisdom, Christology, and Law in Matthew's Gospel.* Cambridge: Harvard University Press, 1970.
Suhl.	Suhl, A. "Der Davidssohn im Matthäus-Evangelium." *ZNW*, 59 (1968), 57-81.
Sun.	Sun, H.T.C. "Rest." *ISBE*, 4:142-144.
Swete.	Swete, H.B. "The New Oxyrhynchus Sayings." *ExpTim*, 15 (1903), 488-495.
Tate.	Tate, Marvin E. *Psalms 51-100.* WBC 20. Waco: Word Books, 1990.
Theißen 1969.	Theißen, Gerd. *Untersuchungen zum Hebräerbrief.* Gütersloh: Gütersloher Verlagshaus Gerd Mohn, 1969.
Theißen 1992.	_____. *The Gospel in Context: Social and Political History in the Synoptic Tradition.* Trans. Linda Maloney. Edinburgh: T. & T. Clark, 1992.
Thomas.	Thomas, K.J. "The Old Testament Citations in Hebrews."

	In *Studies in the Septuagint: Origins, Recensions, and Interpretations.* Ed. S. Jellicoe. LBS. New York: Ktav, 1974, 507-529; repr. of *NTS*, 11 (1965), 303-325.
J.A. Thompson.	Thompson, J.A. *The Book of Jeremiah.* NICOT. Grand Rapids: Eerdmans, 1980.
J.W. Thompson.	Thompson, James W. *The Beginnings of Christian Philosophy: The Epistle to the Hebrews.* CBQMS 13. Washington, D.C.: Catholic Biblical Association of America, 1982.
W.G. Thompson.	Thompson, W.G. "Review of M. Jack Suggs, *Wisdom, Christology, and Law in Matthew's Gospel*, 1970." *CBQ*, 33 (1971), 145-146.
Thurén.	Thurén, Jukka. *Das Lobopfer der Hebräer. Studien zum Aufbau und Anliegen von Hebräerbrief 13.* Acta Academiae Aboensis, Ser. A. Humaniora 47/1. Åbo: Åbo Akademi, 1973.
Thurston 1979.	Thurston, Robert W. "Midrash and 'Magnet' Words in the NT." *EvQ*, 51 (1979), 22-39.
Thurston 1986.	_____. "Philo and the Epistle to the Hebrews." *EvQ*, 58 (1986), 133-143.
Toussaint.	Toussaint, Stanley D. "The Eschatology of the Warning Passages in the Book of Hebrews." *GTJ*, 3 (1982), 71-80.
Tov.	Tov, E. "The Septuagint." In *Mikra.* Ed. J. Mulder. The Literature of the Jewish People in the Period of the Second Temple and the Talmud 1. CRINT 2. Philadelphia: Fortress, 1988, 161-188.
Trafton.	Trafton, Joseph L. "Isaiah, Martyrdom and Ascension." *ABD*, 3:507-509.
Tsevat.	Tsevat, M. "Basic Meaning of the Biblical Sabbath." *ZAW*, 84 (1972), 447-459.
Tuckett 1983.	Tuckett, C.M. *The Revival of the Griesbach Hypothesis.* SNTSMS 44. Cambridge: CUP, 1983.
Tuckett 1986.	_____. *Nag Hammadi and the Synoptic Tradition in the Nag Hammadi Library.* Studies of the New Testament and its World. Edinburgh: T. & T. Clark, 1986.
Tyre.	Tyre, Charles. "The Yoke in Ancient Near Eastern, Hebrew, and New Testament Materials." Diss. Nashville, 1963.
Übelacker.	Übelacker, Walter G. *Der Hebräerbrief als Appell.*

	ConBNT 21. Almqvist & Wiksell International, 1989.
Urbach.	Urbach, E.E. *The Sages. Their Concepts and Beliefs.* Trans. I. Abrahams. Jerusalem: Magnes Press, 1975.
Vanhoye 1963.	Vanhoye, A. *La Stucture Littéraire de l'Épître aux Hébreux.* StudNeot 1. Paris: Desclee de Brouwer, 1963.
Vanhoye 1968.	_____. "Longue marche ou accès tout proche? Le contexte biblique de Hébreux 3,7-4,11." *Bib*, 49 (1968), 9-26.
Vanhoye 1971.	_____. "Trois ouvrages récents sur l'épître aux Hébreux." *Bib*, 52 (1971), 62-71.
de Vaux, 1-2.	de Vaux, Roland. *Ancient Israel.* 2 vols. New York: McGraw-Hill Book Co., 1961.
Veijola.	Veijola, Timo. *Die Ewige Dynastie.* Helsinki: Suomalainen Tiedeakatemia, 1975.
Vermes 1961.	Vermes, G. *Scripture and Tradition in Judaism.* Leiden: Brill, 1961.
Verseput 1986.	Verseput, Donald J. *The Rejection of the Humble Messianic King. A Study of the Composition of Matthew 11-12.* European University Studies 23/291. New York: Peter Lang, 1986.
Verseput 1987.	_____. "The Role and Meaning of the 'Son of God' Title in Matthew's Gospel." *NTS*, 33 (1987), 532-556.
Vielhauer.	Vielhauer, Ph. "ΑΝΑΠΑΥCIC. Zum gnostischen Hintergrund des Thomasevangeliums." In *Apophoreta. Festschrift für Ernst Haenchen.* Beiheft zur Zeitschrift für die Neutestamentliche Wissenschaft und die Kunde der Älteren Kirche, 30. Berlin: Töpelmann, 1964, 281-299.
Vivano.	Vivano, B.T. *Study as Worship: Aboth and the New Testament.* SJLA 26. Leiden: Brill, 1978.
Volz.	Volz, P. *Die Eschatologie der jüdischen Gemeinde im neutestamentlichen Zeitalter.* Hildescheim: Georg Olms, 1966.
Wacholder 1975.	Wacholder, Ben Z. "Chronomessianism: The Timing of Messianic Movements and the Calendar of Sabbatical Cycles." *HUCA*, 46 (1975), 201-218.
Wacholder 1985.	_____. "The Date of the Eschaton in the Book of Jubilees: A Commentary on Jub. 49:22-50:5, CD 1:1-10 and 16:2-3." *HUCA*, 56 (1985), 87-101.
P. Walker.	Walker, Peter. "Jerusalem in Hebrews 13:9-14 and the

Dating of the Epistle." *TynBul*, 45 (1994), 39-71.

R. Walker.	Walker, R. *Die Heilsgeschichte im ersten Evangelium.* FRLANT 91. Göttingen: Vandenhoeck & Ruprecht, 1967.
Wallace.	Wallace, Howard N. "Genesis 2:1-3 -- Creation and Sabbath." *Pacifica*, 1 (1988), 235-250.
Waltke.	Waltke, Bruce K. "נֶפֶשׁ." *TWOT*, 2:587-591.
Wanamaker.	Wanamaker, Charles. *The Epistles to the Thessalonians.* NIGTC. Grand Rapids: Eerdmans, 1990.
Watts 1985.	Watts, John D.W. *Isaiah 1-33.* WBC 24. Waco: Word Books, 1985.
Watts 1987.	_____. *Isaiah 34-66.* WBC 25. Waco: Word Books, 1987.
Weinfeld.	Weinfeld, Moshe. "Sabbath, Temple, and the Enthronement of the Lord -- The Problem of the Sitz im Leben of Genesis 1:1-2:3." In *Mélanges bibliques et orientaux en l'honneur de M. Henri Cazelles.* Eds. A. Caquot and M. Delcor. Alter Orient und Altes Testament 212. Kevelaer: Butzon & Bercker; Neukirchen-Vluyn: Neukirchener Verlag, 1981, 501-512.
Weiser.	Weiser, Artur. *The Psalms.* London: SCM, 1962.
* B. Weiss.	Weiss, Bernhard. *Das Matthäus.* KEK. Göttingen: Vandenhoeck & Ruprecht, 1898.
** Weiss.	Weiss, H.-F. *Der Brief an die Hebräer.* KEK. Göttingen: Vandenhoeck & Ruprecht, 1991.
H. Weiss.	Weiss, Herold. "The Sabbath in the Synoptic Gospels." *JSNT*, 38 (1990), 13-27.
J. Weiss 1907.	Weiss, Johannes, ed. *Die Schriften des Neuen Testaments.* Vol. 1. Göttingen: Vandenhoeck & Ruprecht, 1907.
J. Weiss 1914.	_____. "Das Logion Mt 11.25-30." In *Neutestamentliche Studien für Georg Heinrici zum 70. Geburtstag.* Leipzig: J.C. Hinrich, 1914, 120-129.
K. Weiss 1974a.	Weiss, K. "$\phi\acute{\epsilon}\rho\omega$ $\kappa\tau\lambda$." *TDNT*, 9:56-87.
K. Weiss 1974b.	_____. "$\chi\rho\eta\sigma\tau\acute{o}\varsigma$ $\kappa\tau\lambda$." *TDNT*, 9:483-492.
* Wellhausen.	Wellhausen, J. *Das Evangelium Matthaei.* Berlin: Druck und Verlag von Georg Reimer, 1904.
Welten.	Welten, Peter. *Geschichte und Geschichtsdarstellung in den*

	Chronikbüchern. WMANT 42. Neukirchen: Neukirchener Verlag, 1973.
Wenham.	Wenham, Gordon J. *Genesis 1-15.* WBC 1. Waco: Word Books, 1987.
Werblowsky.	Werblowsky, R.J. Zwi. "Dualism." *EncJud,* 6:242-245.
** Westcott.	Westcott, Brooke Foss. *The Epistle to the Hebrews: The Greek Text with Notes and Essays.* 2nd ed. London: MacMillan and Co., 1892.
Westermann.	Westermann, Claus. *Isaiah 40-66.* Trans. D.M.G. Stalker. OTL. London: SCM, 1969.
W. White.	White, W. "רָגַע." *TWOT,* 2:832-833.
Whybray.	Whybray, R.N. *Isaiah 40-66.* NCBC. London: Marshall, Morgan and Scott, 1975
Wilckens 1971.	Wilckens, U. "σοφία κτλ." *TDNT,* 7:496-528.
Wilckens 1972.	_____. "ὕστερος κτλ." *TDNT,* 8:592-601.
Wildberger, 1-3.	Wildberger, Hans. *Jesaja.* BKAT 10/1-3. Neukirchen: Neukirchener Verlag, 1972, 1978, 1982.
Williams 1977.	Williams, Michael A. "The Nature and Origin of the Gnostic Concept of Stability." Diss. Cambridge (MA), 1977.
Williams 1981.	_____. "Stability as a Soteriological Theme in Gnosticism." In *The Rediscovery of Gnosticism.* Ed. B. Layton. Vol. 2. SHR (Suppl. to *Numen*) 41. Leiden: Brill, 1981, 819-829.
Williams 1985.	_____. *The Immovable Race. A Gnostic Designation and the Theme of Stability in Late Antiquity.* Ed. Frederik Wisse. NHS 29. Leiden: Brill, 1985.
R. Williamson 1970.	Williamson, R. *Philo and the Epistle to the Hebrews.* ALGHJ 4. Leiden: Brill, 1970.
R. Williamson 1989.	_____. *Jews in the Hellenistic World: Philo.* Cambridge Commentaries on Writings of the Jewish and Christian World 1/2. Cambridge: CUP, 1989.
Wilson 1960.	Wilson, R. McL. *Studies in the Gospel of Thomas.* London: A.R. Mowbray and Co., Ltd., 1960.
Wilson 1968.	_____. *Gnosis and the New Testament.* Oxford: Blackwell, 1968.
** Wilson.	_____. *Hebrews.* NCBC. Basingstoke: Marshall,

Morgan, Scott, 1987.

** Windisch.	Windisch, H. *Der Hebräerbrief.* Tübingen: Mohr, 1913.
Windisch 1920.	_____. *Der Barnabasbrief.* Vol. 3 of *Die Apostolischen Väter.* HNT. Tübingen: Mohr, 1920.
Winston.	Winston, David. *The Wisdom of Solomon.* AB. Garden City: Doubleday, 1979.
Winton.	Winton, A.P. *The Proverbs of Jesus. Issues of History and Rhetoric.* JSNTSS 35. Sheffield: JSOT, 1990.
Wise.	Wise, M.O. "Languages of Palestine." In *Dictionary of Jesus and the Gospels.* Eds. J.B. Green, S. McKnight, I.H. Marshall. Downers Grove: InterVarsity, 1992, 434-444.
Witherington.	Witherington, Ben III. *Jesus the Sage. The Pilgrimage of Wisdom.* Minneapolis: Fortress, 1994.
Wolff 1972.	Wolff, Hans Walter. "The Day of Rest in the Old Testament." *LTQ*, 7 (1972), 65-76; repr. *Concor*, 43 (1972), 498-506.
Wolff 1974.	_____. *Anthropology of the Old Testament.* Trans. by Margaret Kohl. Philadelphia: Fortress, 1974.
Wolff 1982.	_____. *Dodekapropheton 4. Micha.* BKAT 14/4. Neukirchen: Neukirchener Verlg, 1982.
Wolfson, 1-2.	Wolfson, H.A. *Philo. Foundations of Religious Philosophy in Judaism, Christianity, and Islam.* 2 vols. 2nd ed. Cambridge: Harvard University Press, 1948.
Wong.	Wong, Eric Kun-Chun. "The Matthaean Understanding of the Sabbath: A Response to G.N. Stanton." *JSNT*, 44 (1991), 3-18.
Woschitz.	Woschitz, K.M. *Elpis Hoffnung. Geschichte, Philosophie, Exegese, Theologie eines Schlüsselbegriffs.* Wien: Herder & Co., 1979.
Woudstra.	Woudstra, M.H. *The Book of Joshua.* NICOT. Grand Rapids: Eerdmans, 1981.
Wright.	Wright, N.T. *The New Testament and the People of God.* Vol. 1 of Christian Origins and the Question of God. Minneapolis: Fortress, 1992.
Würthwein.	Würthwein, Ernst. *Das Erste Buch der Könige.* ATD 11/1. Göttingen: Vandenhoeck & Ruprecht, 1977.

Yamauchi.	Yamauchi, E.M. *Pre-Christian Gnosticism. A Survey of the Proposed Evidences*. 2nd ed. Grand Rapids: Baker, 1983.
Yeo.	Yeo, Khiok-Khng. "The Meaning and Usage of the Theology of 'Rest' ($\kappa\alpha\tau\alpha\pi\alpha\upsilon\sigma\iota\varsigma$ and $\sigma\alpha\beta\beta\alpha\tau\iota\sigma\mu o\varsigma$) in Hebrews 3,7-4,13." *AJT*, 5/1 (1991), 2-33.
Young, 1-3.	Young, E.J. *The Book of Isaiah*. 3 vols. NICOT. Grand Rapids: Eerdmans, 1969, 1972.
Youngblood.	Youngblood, R.F. "Peace." *ISBE*, 3:731-733.
* Zahn.	Zahn, Theodor. *Das Evangelium des Matthäus*. Kommentar zum Neuen Testament 1. Leipzig: A. Deichert'sche Verlagbuchhandlg, 1903.
Zimmermann.	Zimmermann, Heinrich. *Das Bekenntnis der Hoffnung*. BBB 47. Köln: Peter Hanstein Verlag GMBH Köln-Bonn, 1977.
Zucker.	Zucker, D.J. "Jesus and Jeremiah in the Matthean Tradition." *JES*, 27 (1990), 288-305.

Index of Ancient Writings

1. Old Testament

Genesis		6,9	49, 60
	103	8,11	308
1-2	47, 64, 71, 72, 73	15	73
1,1-4	64	15,17	45, 125
1,1-2,3	69	16,23	90
2	18, 61, 64, 66, 116,	16,27ff.	66
	144, 230, 253, 260,	16,30	62, 276
	261, 264, 275, 276,	16,35	260, 263
	282, 283, 288, 289,	17	263
	290, 291, 292, 295,	17,1-7	41, 262
	296, 303, 304, 305,	17,11	20, 21
	310, 317, 319, 334,	20,8	134, 136
	346, 349, 350, 355,	20,8-10	276
	357, 358	20,8-11	69
2,1-3	64	20,10f.	63
2,2	10, 67, 90, 130, 131,	20,11	62, 64, 72, 73, 74,
	133, 134, 136, 138,		90, 122, 319, 323
	144, 261, 279, 280,	23,10-11	62
	283, 286, 288, 290,	23,12	49, 61, 62, 63, 90,
	291, 292, 296, 300,		97, 98, 308
	316, 320, 336, 348,	23,12 B	90
	349-354, 355, 356,	24,4-8	271
	361, 365	24,11	122
2,2a	261	24,16	116
2,2f.	62, 64, 65, 66, 73,	25,40	69, 335, 336
	113, 323, 352, 353	31,12-17	64
2,2-3	324	31,15	90
2,3	90, 119	31,17	61, 62, 64, 69, 73,
2,10-14	75		90, 319
5,29	119	32	32
8,9	79, 84, 95, 97	33	32-33, 177, 179,
49,15	22, 28, 79, 95, 97,		188, 235, 363, 364
	197, 203	33,1	32, 54
		33,7-11	32
Exodus		33,9	32
1-3	243	33,11	32, 178
1,14	49, 60	33,11ff.	177, 178
2,1-10	271	33,11-14	177, 179
3,8	47	33,12	32
5,4f. LXX	243	33,12f.	179
5,5	297	33,12-17	32, 54

33,12-34,35	271	12	177, 178, 179, 273, 363, 364
33,13	32, 178		
33,14	9, 21, 32, 33, 34, 36, 50, 54, 60, 61, 79, 179, 227-229, 238, 247, 250, 308, 362	12-14	273, 274
		12,3	179, 220
		12,3ff.	177
		12,6	178
33,14 LXX	292	12,6-8	178
33,16	33	12,7	178, 269, 270, 271, 272, 364
33,17ff.	32		
33,17-34,9	177	12,7f.	178
34,21	62, 90	12,7-8	271
34,21 B	81	12,8	178
35,2	81, 90, 97, 98	13-14	273
35,2 A	90	13,2	262, 263
39-40	73	13,20	303
39,1-40,33	69	14	13, 128, 262, 263, 264, 273, 274, 295, 310, 311, 312, 313, 334, 348, 349, 364
40,1	268		
Leviticus			
16,31	66, 90	14 LXX	262
18,24-28	58	14,1	263
23,3	68, 90	14,1f.	313
23,24	90	14,2	263
23,32	66, 276	14,2ff.	263
23,39	90	14,4	263
25,2	90	14,5	263, 313
25,4	90	14,7	263, 313
25,5	90	14,9	262
25,6	66	14,10	263, 313
25,8	66	14,11	262
25,8-55	68	14,13	263, 313
25,9	66	14,19	263, 313
25,10	66	14,21	263
25,10f.	229	14,21ff.	262
25,20f.	66	14,21-23	41
25,28 A B	81, 97, 100	14,22	262, 263, 313
25,42	57	14,23	262, 263
26,1-13	83	14,24	284, 303
26,6	47, 114	14,27	262
26,34f.	114, 276	14,28	263
26,43	114	14,29	262, 263, 313
36,34f.	62	14,30	41, 262, 313
		14,30f.	263, 284
Numbers		14,31	292, 303
10,33	28, 38, 79, 95, 97, 98, 125	14,32	263, 313
		14,32ff.	262
10,33ff.	39	14,33	313
10,35	32, 97, 98	14,33f.	263
10,35 LXX	79, 81, 97, 278	14,34	262, 263
10,35f.	39	14,35	127, 128, 262, 263
10,36	40	14,36	263
11,25f.	39	14,38	263, 284
11,25-26	299	14,39ff.	263

14,40	262	5,32f.	90, 91
14,43	262, 263, 313	5,33	82, 88, 89, 90, 91, 101
20	263		
20,1-13	41, 262	5,33 LXX	205, 228, 353
20,12	41	6	228
24,5f.	126	6,16	41
28,9-10	68	6,16-19	91
32,7	263	8,3	127
32,9	262, 263	9,22	41
32,10	262	9,23	262
32,11	262, 263	11,10-12	24
32,12	263	12	22, 25, 26, 27, 30, 44, 50, 89, 99, 124, 125, 126, 128, 342, 351
32,13	262, 263, 313		
32,14	262		
		12,5	25
Deuteronomy		12,8	30
	18, 205	12,9	20, 23, 28, 36, 41, 42, 56, 79, 81, 94, 95, 96, 97, 98, 99, 100, 124, 125, 126, 303
1,8	262		
1,21	262		
1,26	262		
1,28	262, 263		
1,30	263		
1,30f.	262, 263	12,9f.	23-25, 31, 32, 33, 41, 59, 61, 67, 125
1,32	262		
1,34	128, 262	12,9-10	19, 29, 31, 58
1,35	262	12,10	20, 21, 22, 23, 42, 79, 81
1,36	263		
1,38f.	263	12,11	25
1,41	262	12,14	25
1,41ff.	263	18,15	179, 363
1,45	184	18,15-20	364
2,7	260, 263	25	25, 29-31
3,2	20	25,17ff.	31
3,20	21, 22, 32, 49, 61, 79, 89	25,17-19	23
		25,18f.	50
4,6	84, 94	25,18-19	60
4,29-30	140	25,19	20, 21, 22, 24, 31, 34, 49, 79, 105
5	74		
5,1	90	26,6	49, 60
5,3	90	28	31-32, 56
5,4f.	178	28,47f.	204
5,6	90	28,65	20, 24, 47, 49, 53, 54, 56, 60, 79, 80, 95
5,12	90		
5,14	49, 62, 90, 101		
5,14f.	63	28,65f.	119
5,15	63, 68, 90	29,17 LXX	295
5,23	90	30,11-14	165
5,24	90	31,1-6	26
5,25	90	32,11	184
5,26	90	33,4	84
5,29	91	33,8	41
5,31	115, 119	33,12	81
5,32	90	34	177, 363, 364

34,5	177, 178	19,1	30
34,9	177, 223	20,43	20, 79, 95, 96
34,10	178, 179	20,43 A	81
34,10-12	177	21,25	30

Joshua

	18, 19	Ruth	
1,6-9	223	1,9	20, 28, 52, 53, 55, 58, 79, 95, 96, 97
1,11-15	25		
1,13	79	2,12	184
1,13-15	20, 21, 22	3,1	20, 52, 58, 79, 95, 97
1,15	79		
6	289	1 Samuel (1Kgdms)	
11,23	20, 30, 79, 80		19
12	25	2 LXX	269
12-17	30	2,5	115
13,1	30	2,35	269
14,9	30	2,35 LXX	269, 270, 271, 272, 274, 336
14,13	30		
14,15	20, 80	3,20	269
18,1	30	4,4	39
21	29-31	12	25
21-23	26, 284	12,11	20, 22
21,43-45	22, 28, 30	12,22 LXX	219
21,44	20, 21, 22, 23, 34, 79	15,2ff.	31
		15,22	51
22,1ff.	22	16,1-13	213, 233
22,4	20, 21, 22, 28, 30, 79	16,14-23	233, 234
		17,12	213
23	25, 29-31	17,15	213
23,1	20, 21, 22, 23, 24, 30, 31, 34, 79, 81	17,58	213
		18,23 LXX	221
23,2bff.	28	20,6	213
23,4-5	30	20,28	213
23,14	28	22,2	220
23,14f.	30	28,15	184
		30	31

Judges

	18, 37	2 Samuel (2Kgdms)	
2,11-23	25		19
2,14	20, 22	3,39	220
3,11	79, 86	4,4	52
3,11-30	20	5-7	72
3,30	79, 86	5,2 LXX	213
5,31	20, 79, 86	5,4-10 LXX	214
8,28	20, 79, 86	6-7	38, 39, 40, 165
8,34	20, 22	6,16	221
10,12f.	184	6,20-22	221
17,6	30	7	19, 24, 25-27, 28, 29, 30, 34, 35, 36, 38, 48, 67, 112, 212, 226, 228, 229, 231, 236, 246, 363, 365
18,1	30		
18,7	79, 86		
18,7-27	20, 21, 34		
18,27	79, 86		

Index of Ancient Writings: Old Testament

7 LXX	83, 89, 225, 226, 269, 284	4,25	20, 22
7,1	20, 21, 23, 27, 33, 363	4,29-34	234
		4,29-5,18	226
7,1 LXX	80, 223	5	19, 24, 25, 26, 27, 29
7,1ff.	25	5 LXX	80, 85
7,5	212	5,3	27
7,5 LXX	83	5,3f.	21, 26, 27
7,5f.	51	5,3-4	35
7,7-12 LXX	29	5,3-5	23
7,8	212	5,4	20, 27, 30, 33, 47, 87, 89, 106
7,8 LXX	221		
7,10	49, 112	5,9ff.	234
7,10f.	30, 47	5,17	27
7,10-11	31, 60, 63	5,17f. LXX	223
7,11	20, 21, 23, 27, 33, 111, 225, 247, 250, 364	5,18 LXX	21, 79, 81
		6	73
		8	19, 24, 25, 26, 27-29, 30, 33, 34, 73
7,11 LXX	79, 80, 81, 223, 225, 228		
		8 LXX	284
7,11ff.	226	8,27	51
7,11-14	226, 363	8,39	176
7,12-13	27	8,56	20, 22, 23, 28, 29, 34, 35, 40, 47, 73, 79, 81, 95, 96, 97, 98
7,12-14	112		
7,13	25		
7,14	180, 225, 226, 364		
7,14 LXX	225, 226, 270	8,56 LXX	278
7,16 LXX	269	8,56-61	28
7,19f.	212	11,11-13,32f.	86
7,20	176	11,38 LXX	269
7,24	212	11,43	92
7,25-29	212	12,1-16	245
8ff.	30	18,4	182
8,12	31	18,13	182
8,17	269	19,10	182
9,3	52	19,14	182
12,24-25	35		
13,1	234	2 Kings (4Kgdms)	
14,17	20, 96, 233		19
14,17 LXX	80, 95	2,15	39
14,20	233	6,41	97
17,11	32	11,4-12	68, 69
23,1 LXX	269	11,20	20, 21, 34
23,1ff.	233	11,20 LXX	79
		16,17f.	68
1 Kings (3Kgdms)		16,18	69, 70
	19	17	26
2,27-35	269	17,7-23	25
3,12	234	17,13ff.	182
3,28	234		
4-5	223, 224	1 Chronicles (1Par)	
4,24f.	27, 87, 89	2,52	34
4,24b-25	47	4,40	21, 34

4,40 LXX	79	10,1-16	245
6,16	98, 99	13-14	36, 37
6,16 LXX	79, 81, 94, 96, 97, 99, 278	13,15	37
		13,23 LXX	79
6,31	165	14,1	21, 34, 36
6,31	34, 35, 38, 95, 99	14,1-7	47
6,50-53	269	14,2-7	37, 140
8,2	34	14,4 LXX	79
11,2 LXX	213	14,5	21, 37, 79
17	35, 36, 38, 80	14,5 LXX	34, 79
17 LXX	269, 363	14,5f.	21
17,1	34	14,5ff.	36
17,10	34	14,6	21
17,10 LXX	269	14,6	34
17,10-14 LXX	336	14,7	34
17,11 LXX	269	14,12	37
17,13 LXX	225, 226, 270, 364	15,5-6	47
17,14	269	15,15	21, 34, 36, 37, 140
17,14 LXX	270, 271, 272, 274	15,15 LXX	79
22	38, 85, 363, 365	20,4	37, 140
22,6	336	20,20	37
22,6ff.	40	20,22	37
22,7ff.	35	20,30	21, 34, 36, 37, 140
22,9	21, 23, 34, 47, 96, 131, 364	20,30 LXX	79
		23,21	21, 34
22,9 LXX	79, 95, 99	23,21 LXX	79
22,9f.	363	24,19-22	182
22,9f. LXX	223, 226	26,5	37
22,9-12 LXX	234	26,7	37
22,10 LXX	225	31,21	37, 140
22,12 LXX	223	32,22	21, 34, 36, 37, 79, 140
22,18	21, 34, 35		
22,18 LXX	79	32,30	37
23,25	21, 34, 35, 38, 40, 42	36,15f.	182
		36,21	62, 114, 276
23,25 LXX	79		
28	165	Ezra	
28,2	34, 35, 38, 40, 96	9,11	182
28,2 LXX	79, 83, 84, 85, 95, 97, 98, 99		
		Nehemiah	
		9,26	182
2 Chronicles (2Par)		9,28	21, 79
2	35		
6	19, 40, 45, 72, 131, 165	Esther	
		9,16	79
6,41	19, 34, 38, 40, 42, 96	9,17	79
		9,18	79
6,41 LXX	79, 81, 94, 95, 98, 99, 100	9,22	79
		Job	
6,41b	40		78, 91, 92
6,41f.	64	2,9	92
7,11	37	3,13	92
10-36	37		

Index of Ancient Writings: Old Testament

3,17	49, 92	63,7	184
3,23	92	65,5	315
3,26	92	Ψ 65,11f.	104, 197
7,18	278	Ψ 65,12	278, 308
10,20	92	66,11f.	243
11,19	91, 92	Ψ 68,16	245
14,6	92	Ψ 75,9	79
21,13	92	76,2	69
23,8f.	184	76,8	21
28	164	Ψ 77,32	262
28,12-28	174	81	41, 44
28,25f.	164	81,6	243
35,12	184	81,7	41
		81,13-16	44
Psalms (Ψ)		84,1ff.	315
	75	Ψ 85,5	219, 245
2,1f.	226	Ψ 88,27f.	225
2,7	226	89	39
Ψ 2,7	225, 226, 270, 363, 364	89,20	212
		Ψ 89,4	134, 136
Ψ 8	270	90,4	103, 134
8,2	173	90,15	127
Ψ 8,3	221	91,4	184
11,4	51	92	122, 128
Ψ 14,1	143	Ψ 92,1	274
17,8	184	93	73
22,8f.	166	Ψ 94	12, 90, 95, 98, 101, 252, 260-263, 273, 274, 275, 278, 282, 283, 288-291, 292, 293, 295, 296, 300, 301-306, 310, 315, 317, 319, 334, 346, 348-352, 354, 355, 357, 358, 364
Ψ 22,2	79, 131		
23,2	41, 49, 95, 96		
23,6	315		
27,4f.	315		
27,5	69		
Ψ 33,2f.	195		
Ψ 33,6	195		
Ψ 33,12	195		
Ψ 33,18f.	195		
36,7	184	Ψ 94,5f.	352
36,8ff.	315	Ψ 94,7f.	260
Ψ 36,11	219	Ψ 94,7-11	260, 273, 348
37,11	193, 219	Ψ 94,8	260
Ψ 37,4	240	Ψ 94,10	260
Ψ 38,7	326	Ψ 94,11	12, 61, 79, 81, 89, 94, 96, 97, 98-100, 106, 109, 110, 127, 138, 153, 260, 261, 274, 282, 288-290, 333, 334, 336, 348, 357, 361
45,4	221		
50	41, 51, 128		
50,5	127, 128		
Ψ 50,8	233		
51,15f.	51		
51,16f.	51	95	12, 18, 19, 29, 41-45, 50, 52, 58, 60, 61, 124-129, 152, 260, 262, 273, 278, 284, 315, 342, 349-354
52,10	315		
57,1	184		
61,4	184		
61,5	315		
63,3ff.	315		

95,1-2	41	132,8-9	84
95,1-7a	41	132,8-10	40
95,4-6	41	132,10	39
95,6	41	132,11f.	39
95,7-11	10, 44	132,13f.	64, 125
95,7b-11	41, 43	132,13ff.	39
95,8	41	132,13-14	124
95,10	127	132,14	19, 28, 39, 41, 45, 65, 74, 84, 85, 95, 96, 123-125, 315
95,11	12, 28, 41, 42, 44, 45, 55, 59, 65, 67, 74, 95, 96, 106, 107, 123, 124-128, 278, 281, 336, 357	139,1	176
		Ψ 146,6	219
		Ψ 151,1	221
95,11b	125		
Ψ 95	274	Proverbs	
Ψ 95,10	274		
96	45	1	78, 91, 92
Ψ 98,6	271	1,20f.	164, 165
Ψ 101,26-28	331	1,20ff.	203
103,19	51	1,20-33	198, 202
Ψ 105,1	245	1,23-33	165
Ψ 105,21f.	262, 263	1,24	138
Ψ 105,24	262	1,28	165
Ψ 105,25	262	1,28-33	165
Ψ 105,26	262	1,33	140
113,5ff.	51	3,19f.	92, 93
Ψ 114,7	79, 131, 278	8	164
116,7	41, 42, 95	8,1ff.	164, 184
118	220	8,5	165, 202
118,25f.	220	8,18f.	198
118,26	184, 214	8,21	92
Ψ 118,71	195	8,22	92
Ψ 118,79	195	8,23-31	164, 169
120,7	47	8,25	164
Ψ 131	336, 348, 351, 352	8,27-30	164
Ψ 131,1	221	9	164
Ψ 131,4f.	336	9,1-6	164
Ψ 131,8	79, 97, 98	9,3-6	165
Ψ 131,8	84, 99, 100	9,4	166
Ψ 131,10	86	16,9	198
Ψ 131,14	79, 81, 97, 98, 336	16,11	169
Ψ 131,14	84, 89, 94, 99, 100	16,19	169
Ψ 131,14f.	88	21,16	219
Ψ 131,15	221	26,12	92
132	19, 24, 38-40, 42-45, 48, 58-60, 67, 72, 84, 89, 112, 123-126, 128, 165, 250	26,20	172
		29,17	91
			91
		Ecclesiastes	
132,1	40		78, 91, 92
132,7	51	4,6	92
132,8	19, 28, 39, 42, 84, 85, 95, 96	6,5	92
		10,20	128

Index of Ancient Writings: Old Testament

Isaiah		11,14	49
	19, 46-53, 75, 102	11,16	48
1,10-14	68	13	49
1,13	134	13,20f.	49, 87
1,18	136	13,20-14,6 LXX	46
2,1-4	46, 48	13,20-14,7 LXX	86, 225
2,2f.	124	13,21	86
2,2ff.	47	13,22b-14,7	49
2,12-22	292	14	49, 60, 88, 89, 229, 353
6,7	66		
7,2	46	14,1	46
7,4	46, 49, 50, 131	14,1 LXX	86-88, 225, 247
7,13	213	14,3	21, 45, 46, 47, 49, 52, 53, 58, 61, 63, 79, 86, 87, 89, 225, 243
7,14	213		
7,19	46		
8,17	50		
9,3	194	14,3ff.	204
9,6	213	14,4	86
9,6	46	14,5	225, 243
9,6f.	47	14,7	21, 46, 50, 52, 55, 79, 86, 87, 107, 225, 243
9,7	46, 47		
10,27	194		
10,33-34	48	14,13	225
10,33-11,9	47	14,15	225
10,34	49	14,25	194, 225, 243
11	47-48, 52, 53, 59, 60, 105, 141, 226, 229, 233, 248	14,28ff.	86
		14,30	49
		14,30 LXX	86-88, 225, 247
11,1	214, 226	14,32	86, 88
11,1ff.	47, 213	17,2	97
11,1-8	47	18,4	46
11,1-9	47	23,12	46, 49, 79, 97
11,1-10	220, 221, 226, 230, 233, 251, 308	24,21-23	292
		24,23	70
11,2	46, 165, 233, 299, 300	25,1	82
		25,1-26,6 LXX	201, 228
11,4	52, 213, 226	25,3	82, 88
11,5	219	25,10	46
11,6	66	25,10 LXX	82, 88, 89, 97, 219, 247, 278
11,6-9	114		
11,9	48	26,3	46, 49, 50
11,9-10	51	26,5f.	173
11,9-16	47	26,6	82, 88, 219
11,10	28, 42, 45, 46, 47, 48, 50, 52, 58, 60, 63, 79, 87, 88, 89, 95-98, 105, 226, 247, 300	26,12	46
		26,19	229
		26,19f.	104
		27,5	46
		28	49-50, 53, 59
11,10b	48	28,2	46
11,10ff.	47	28,12	21, 28, 46, 47, 49, 50, 52, 55, 56, 58, 60, 61, 63, 79, 80, 95, 96, 97, 243, 247
11,11	48		
11,11f.	85		
11,12	48		

28,12 Aq	308	45,7	47
29,14	173	46,7	46
29,18	229	47,10	173
30,15	46, 49, 50, 131	48,18	47
30,23	66	48,22	47
30,26	66	49,1-6	211
30,32	20, 46	49,1-9	211
31,5	184	49,6	85
32	52, 88	50,4	50
32,1	52	50,4-9	211
32,2	52	50,4-11	211
32,7	60	51,1-5	195
32,9	46	51,4	46
32,11	46	52,7	47
32,15	52	52,13-53,12	211
32,15 Sym	308	53,4	211, 212
32,16	52	53,5	47
32,17	46, 49, 52	53,8	212
32,17 LXX	82, 88, 89, 131, 247	54,10	47
32,17f.	47, 87	54,13	47
32,17-18	60	55,6ff.	140
32,18	45, 46, 47, 50, 52, 53, 58, 79, 82, 89, 95, 96, 123, 129, 354	55,12	47
		56,1-7	66, 73
		57,2	46, 47, 104
		57,13	87
33,7	47	57,15	51, 87, 88, 89, 138, 173, 232, 336
33,20	46		
34,14	46, 79, 95, 97	57,19	47
35,5f.	66, 229	57,20	46, 352
35,7	46	57,20 LXX	87, 88, 89, 247
37,28	97	57,20f.	104
37,29	46	57,21	47
38,10	46	58,13f.	67
38,17	47	59,8	47
39,8	47	60,17	47
40,9	219	61	66, 219, 229, 232, 250, 309
40,28-31	50		
41,3	47	61,1	229, 230
41,8f.	210	61,1-2	73
42	211, 212, 218, 226	61,7 LXX	219
42,1	226	62,1	46
42,1ff.	213	62,6	46
42,1-4	203, 210, 212, 226, 229, 250	62,7	46
		62,11	219
42,1-4	211	63	50-51, 60
42,1-7	211	63,9	50
42,3	226	63,10	50
42,3c-4b	211	63,11	50
42,4	226	63,11ff.	50
42,4a	211	63,14	33, 46, 47, 50, 61, 80, 247, 308
42,7	229		
42,18	229	63,16	176
44,2	210	65,10	46, 87, 97

65,15	46	12,12	53
65,25	66	13,19	53
66	51-52, 59, 74, 232, 299, 335-338, 355, 357	14,9	53
		14,13	53
		14,19	53
66,1	28, 42, 46, 47, 50, 51, 53, 59, 65, 74, 79, 81, 85, 94-99, 109, 138, 140, 142, 144, 279, 333, 335-338, 348, 351, 352, 355, 358, 365	15,5	53
		15,15	182
		16,5	53
		17,18	182
		20,10	53
		20,11	182
		22,5	184
66,1f.	51, 87, 89, 173, 232, 335-337, 352	23,5	225
		23,5f.	234, 248
66,1ff.	231, 337	23,5-6	213
66,1-2	51, 73	23,17	53
66,1-4	55	25,4-7	182
66,2	336	25,37	53
66,2b	51	26,4-6	182
66,3	336	26,20ff.	182
66,3ff.	51	26,27 LXX	79
66,7-9	298	27,11	53
66,10	336, 355	28,9	53
66,12	47	28,59 LXX	80
66,22	59, 336	29,7	53
66,23	65, 75, 114, 232, 336, 355	29,11	53
		29,13ff.	140
		29,18f.	182
Jeremiah		30,3	54
	19, 53, 75, 102, 228	30,5	53
2,20	204	30,8	54
4,10	53	30,8f.	204
5,5	204	30,9	54
6	55-56, 59, 235	30,10	21, 34, 53, 54
6,10	55	30,17	66
6,13	55	30,18	54, 123
6,14	53, 57	30,20	54
6,16	50, 53, 55, 56, 57, 61, 80, 163, 196, 198, 201, 227-229, 239, 247, 250	30,22	54
		31	54
		31,2	53, 54, 56, 58, 60, 61, 63, 228, 247
6,17	55	31,6	54
6,20	55	31,11	54
7,25f.	182	31,11 LXX	79
8,9	173	31,12	66
8,11	53	31,23	54
8,15	53	31,25	54, 60, 247
9,8	53	31,25	198, 228, 240, 243
9,23	173	31,31ff.	54
12,1	53	31,34	173
12,3	176	33,6	53, 66
12,5	53	33,9	53
12,7	184	33,15	213, 225

33,15f.	234, 248	20,33	70
34,5	53	21,17	20
34,8-10	229	21,22	21
35,15	182	21,27	213
38 LXX	274	22,8	68
38,2 LXX	80	22,26	68
38,3 LXX	85	23,38	68
38,4	53	24,13	20, 21
38,8 LXX	85	28,1ff.	173
38,22	53	28,17	173
38,25 LXX	131	34	88, 89, 212, 223, 227, 229
38,31ff. LXX	292		
43,6	53	34,4	83, 88
43,12	53	34,11	83
44,4f.	182	34,14	83
45,3	53, 55, 60, 95, 96	34,14f.	88, 89, 247
46,27	21, 34, 53	34,14ff.	88
48,11	53	34,15	83, 204, 228
49,23	53	34,16	83, 88
49,31	53	34,23	83, 88
50	54-55	34,23f.	212
50,6	53	34,26	88
50,33	55	34,27	204, 228, 243
50,34	53, 54, 56, 80	34,34 LXX	227
51,33 LXX	79, 97, 278	37,1	20
51,59	53, 95, 96	38,11	79
		40,2	20
Lamentations		41,7	123
	19, 56-57, 75	43,4	70
1	56-57	44,1-3	70
1,3	53, 55, 56, 57, 58, 60, 63, 79, 95, 97, 247, 278	44,15	269
		44,30	20
		45,17	68
1,4ff.	57	46,1-2a	70
1,14	57	46,4-5	68
2	68	46,17	229
2,6	68, 69, 70		
5	57	Daniel	
5,2	57		103, 254
5,5	56-58, 60, 63, 79, 197, 204, 228, 247	2,19-23	173
		3,87 LXX	219
5,16	57	7,14	174
5,18	56, 57	9	66
		9,24-27	103
Ezekiel		12,2	104
5,13	20, 21		
8,18	184	Hosea	
13,16	65, 70	2,18	66
13,20f.	65, 70	5-6	184
13,24	65, 70	5,6	140, 184
16,33 LXX	240	5,9	184
16,42	20, 21	5,15	184
20,12	65, 70	6,6	51, 231, 232, 242

11,4	204	9,2f.	173
12,9	278	9,9	124, 125, 128, 131, 193, 202, 219, 220, 250
Joel			
1,15	292	14,1	292
3,14	292	14,6f.	66
3,18	66		
		Tobit	
Amos		5,2	174
5,4	140		
5,18-20	292	Judith	
8,9-14	292	8,21	83
8,12	184	8,24	83
9,11	69	9,8	41, 81, 83-84, 85, 88, 89, 94, 96, 97, 98, 99
9,13f.	66		
Micah			
	19, 57-58, 75	Wisdom of Solomon	
2,2	57		91, 92, 93, 152, 153, 175, 246
2,6f.	57		
2,9	57	1,6	202
2,10	28, 50, 58, 60, 63, 79, 87, 89, 95, 96, 97, 98, 243, 247	1,6-7	165
		2,10-24	166
		2,13	175
2,11	57	2,17-22	175
4,1ff.	88	2,18	175
4,1-5	195	3	140
4,4	87, 88, 89	3,1ff.	166
4,4 LXX	247	3,3	140
5,2	213	3,8	140
		4,7	93, 104, 130, 140, 166
Habakkuk			
1,4	210	4,10	175
		4,13-15	175
Zephaniah		4,20-5,16	175
1,14-18	292	6,1	166
3,9-13 LXX	204	6,4	165
3,12	219	6,4f.	166
		6,9	165, 166
Haggai		6,12-11,1	164
2,6	328	6,13	165
2,23	210	6,16	165, 166, 198
		6,20	140
Zechariah		6,22	166
1,11	21, 57, 79, 86	7,15-22	234
3,8	225	7,21f.	174, 175
6,8	21, 57, 79	7,22	165
6,11-13 LXX	270	7,25f.	174
6,12	226	7,26	164
7,7	57	7,27	165, 166, 175
9-14	132	7,27f.	166
9,1	42, 57, 80, 95, 96, 123	7,28	175
		8,4	174

8,8	174	6,32-37	84, 94
8,16	93	6,34	173
8,16f.	130	6,36	173
9,9	164, 165	7,14	201
9,13	174	10,14f.	219
9,13-18	174	11,11	312
9,16-18	174	11,19	92, 278
9,17	165	12,3	85
10-11	166, 182	14,20ff.	198
10,1-11,8	165	14,20-15,10	198
10,10	174	18,1-4	169
10,21	172	18,16	91
12,18	219	19,20	84, 94
39,1-11	166	20,21	91, 278
		22,11	92
Sirach		22,13	91, 173, 197, 278
	4, 9, 17, 77, 78, 91, 93, 159, 160, 162, 187, 188, 195, 196, 197-204, 206, 208, 210, 227, 228, 235, 250	24	3, 163, 164, 165, 166, 184
		24,1f.	202
		24,1ff.	84, 165
		24,3-6	164
		24,3-7	84
1,1-9	174	24,4	174
1,4	164	24,7	84, 89, 97
1,19	169	24,7-11	84, 88, 89, 98, 165
1,25-27	84, 94	24,8	84, 85, 98, 164
3,6	91	24,8ff.	165
3,19	172	24,9	164
4,11	175	24,11	84, 85, 98, 198
4,11-19	198	24,19	198
4,18	174	24,19ff.	198
4,19	198	24,19-22	165, 196, 198
5,2	201	24,23	84, 94, 165
5,6	85	24,28f.	174
6	161, 164, 173, 187, 195, 196, 197, 198, 201, 203, 235, 237, 243, 247	24,30-34	166
		24,33	165, 174
		24,34	197
		28,1f.	201
6,3	85	28,16	91, 278
6,18-31	92	30,17	92
6,18-37	198	32,21	85
6,19	197, 203	33,25-30	197
6,20	173	34,3	85, 278
6,20-22	203	34,4	85, 278
6,21	204	34,21	85
6,25	198, 204	36,18	89
6,25ff.	93	36,18 [15]	41, 85, 88, 97, 98, 99
6,26-31	140		
6,27	174	36,29 [26]	91, 93
6,28	8, 55, 85, 92, 93, 94, 203, 278	38,7	85
		38,14	91
6,28ff.	203	38,23	92, 97, 278
6,30	235	39,1-11	166

39,11	92	51,26	165
39,28	85	51,26f.	93
39,32	85	51,27	85, 93, 94, 203, 278
40,1-6	92	51,27f.	92
40,1-7	197, 240	51,27-28	92
40,5	85, 92	51,30	203
40,6	92, 278		
43,26	164	(1)Baruch	
44	178	3,9	165
44,1ff.	85	3,9ff.	172
44,3	166	3,9-4,4	164
44,8	85	3,12	165
44,22-45,5	270	3,15	174
44,23	85	3,15-4,4	165
45,2	270	3,20	174
45,4	179, 271	3,21-23	172
45,4f.	178	3,23	174
45,25	269	3,31-36	174
46,19	85	3,36-4,4	165
46,25	269	3,37	166
47,7	86	4,1	165
47,12	86	4,12	165
47,12f.	234		
47,13	85-86, 88, 89	1 Maccabees	
47,14-17	86	1,3	86
47,18ff.	86	7,50	86
47,23	92	9,57	86
51	3, 4, 5, 6, 77, 93, 159, 160, 161, 162, 164, 166, 187, 188, 195-206, 228, 235, 237, 247, 250, 359	9,58	86
		11,38	86
		11,52	86
		14,4	86
51,1	201	2 Maccabees	
51,1-12	3, 166	6,6	276
51,1-27	3	8,27	276
51,10	175	12,2	86
51,13-19.30	4	15,1	81, 90, 97, 98
51,13-22	3		
51,23	172, 199	1 Esdras	
51,23ff.	5, 8	1,58	276
51,23-27	195	4,62	86
51,23-30	3, 196		

2. New Testament

Matthew		1,1-17	213
	78, 139, 159-208, 209-251, 360, 361	1,18ff.	213
		1,20	214
Q^{mt}	5, 188	1,21	240, 244
1-2	214, 233	1,21-23	185
1,1	214	1,23	213

2,3	215		189, 190, 191, 192, 197, 206, 217, 241, 360, 361, 362, 364, 365, 366
2,6	213		
2,23	214, 226		
3,9f.	249		
3,17	226	11-12	141, 206, 216, 218, 222, 229
4,19	195		
5-10	216	11,1	217
5,3	218	11,2	167, 168, 216, 217, 218
5,3-11	229		
5,5	193, 218, 219, 245	11,2-5	233
5,8	193	11,2-19	168, 169, 171, 183, 186, 217
5,10	300		
5,11	299	11,2-24	217
5,17	131	11,2-12,50	217
5,19f.	241	11,2-13,58	217
5,28	193	11,3	306
6,7	201	11,4f.	167
6,14f.	201	11,5	198, 205, 229, 230, 240, 242
6,28	194, 240		
7,7f.	140	11,5f.	248
7,28f.	217	11,7f.	248
8,16f.	211	11,7-19	241
8,17	212	11,12	172
8,20	167	11,16-19	235
9	212, 227	11,19	7, 159, 167-170, 171, 175, 183, 237
9-12	222		
9,4	193	11,20-24	167, 171, 217, 240
9,10-13	198, 242	11,20-30	241
9,12	242	11,23	225
9,12f.	227	11,25	168, 170, 171, 172, 201, 221, 243
9,13	193, 231		
9,27	212, 214, 215	11,25d	205
9,27f.	214	11,25f.	3, 172-174, 179, 206, 241
9,27ff.	227		
9,27-31	212, 215, 221, 222	11,25-27	3, 4, 6, 7, 159, 171-180, 190, 201, 206, 209, 235, 237, 241, 247
9,27-33	215		
9,27-34	214, 215		
9,34	212, 215		
9,35-38	212, 222	11,25-30	3, 4, 7, 82, 110, 186, 201, 217, 218, 222, 225, 228, 234, 235, 360, 362
9,36	198, 227, 241, 242		
10-11	212		
10,1	170		
10,1ff.	182	11,25-12,21	217
10,1-4	210	11,27	3, 171, 172, 174-180, 188, 192, 207, 220, 223, 225, 241, 249, 363, 364
10,1-42	216		
10,6	198, 227		
10,7-8	170		
10,16	241	11,27a	223, 249
10,16-23	239	11,27d	205
10,16-39	240	11,27-30	177, 179, 238
10,24f.	212	11,28	191, 195, 198, 203, 220, 240, 241, 243, 362
11	4, 18, 78, 102, 103, 151, 152, 168, 178,		

11,28a	191	12,18-21	218, 226
11,28a-b	194	12,19	203, 210
11,28b	194	12,20	240, 243, 245
11,28c	191, 198	12,20c	211
11,28f.	227-229	12,21	226, 251
11,28-30	1-9, 14-16, 31, 60, 61, 78, 88, 93, 112, 131, 133, 139, 140, 141, 159-208, 209-251, 297, 299, 307, 309, 347, 354, 359, 360, 361, 362, 364	12,22	212, 214
		12,22f.	227
		12,22ff.	242
		12,22-37	217
		12,22-45	217
		12,23	212, 214, 215, 216
		12,23f.	212, 215, 217
11,28-12,8	232	12,24	212, 215
11,28-12,14	230, 324, 354	12,25-28	172
11,29	55, 179, 192, 193, 202, 209, 210, 211, 219, 221, 226, 243, 248, 250	12,29	234
		12,38-45	217
		12,40	193
		12,42	168, 216, 234
11,29a	191	12,42-45	234
11,29a-b	192, 209	12,43	193, 246, 297
11,29b	193, 195, 209	12,43-45	246
11,29b-c	192-194, 209	12,46-50	217, 218
11,29c	191-195, 198, 201, 202, 203, 205, 207, 209, 218, 241, 245, 250	12,50	217
		13	217
		13,1-52	216
		13,13	215, 222
11,29d	191, 192, 209, 227	13,15	193
11,30	192, 194, 195, 212, 240, 241	13,16f.	4
		13,19	193
11,30a	191	13,33	236
11,30a-b	192, 209, 245	13,35	290
11,30b	194	13,44	140
12	131, 203, 212, 217, 222, 234, 240	13,51f.	173
		13,53	217
12,1ff.	227	13,54	168
12,1-8	217, 242	14,28	197
12,1-14	210, 217, 218, 230, 241, 324	15,1-20	241
		15,5	242
12,3f.	216	15,14	222
12,4	226	15,15	214, 215
12,6	215, 224, 231, 232, 362	15,22	214
		15,24	198, 269
12,7	227, 231, 242, 245	15,30	214
12,9-14	217, 227, 242	15,32ff.	242
12,11	324	18,4	193, 218, 245
12,11f.	198, 227	19,1f.	217
12,15	210, 211, 221	19,14	197
12,15f.	210	19,16-29	241
12,15ff.	210, 211	20-21	222
12,15-21	211, 218	20,29-31	220
12,17-21	205, 210, 242, 244	20,29-34	212, 221, 222
12,18	226, 251	20,30	214
12,18ff.	229	20,30f.	214

20,31	214	25,36	197
20,34	212, 222	25,39	197
21	184, 218-221, 223	25,40	209
21-24	231	25,45f.	139
21,4ff.	223	26,1f.	217
21,5	193, 219, 220, 245	26,10	240
21,9	214, 215, 233	26,28	240
21,12-14	242	26,45	193, 246
21,14	214, 215	28,18-20	174, 182, 238, 362
21,14f.	215	28,19	251
21,14-16	235	28,19f.	202
21,15	214, 215		
21,16	173, 215, 221	Mark	
21,17	221		187, 205, 234
21,25	218	2,23-28	231
21,31ff.	218	3,1-6	227
21,43	249	3,7-12	210
22,37	193	3,13-19	210
22,41-46	223, 235	3,20f.	212
22,42	214	3,20-30	210
22,42-45	233	6,31	193, 199, 241
22,45	214	9,37	268
23	241	10,24	140
23,1	268	10,46-52	222
23,2ff.	245	10,47	214
23,2-4	241	10,48	214
23,2-12	242	11,9f.	220
23,4	194, 198, 240, 241, 242, 243, 244	11,15-18	55
		12,35	214
23,10	233, 241	12,36	233
23,12	193, 218, 241, 245	12,37	214
23,13	242	13,28	193
23,16	215	14,6	240
23,17	215	14,13ff.	193
23,23	241, 242	14,33	140
23,24	215	14,41	193, 246
23,34	168, 173, 180, 181, 183-185, 234		
		Luke	
23,34ff.	182		184
23,34-36	7, 159, 180-183, 237, 239	1,32	226
		1,35	226
23,34-39	166, 185, 237	1,52	218
23,37	109, 176, 185	1,70	308
23,37-39	7, 159, 183-185	4,18f.	229, 309
23,38	184	4,18ff.	104
23,39	184, 185, 214	4,43	269
23,43	246	6-11	227
24,32	193	6,1-5	231
24,48	193	6,35	245
25,21	268, 279	7,18	167
25,23	279	7,18-35	169
25,31ff.	244	7,22f.	229
25,34	279	7,35	167

Index of Ancient Writings: New Testament

7,35 Q	7, 167-170	6,29	269
10,2-16	171	6,45	286
10,21	221	6,57	269
10,21f. Q	7, 171	6,60	286
10,21-22 Q	171-180	7	131
10,21-24	4	7,6	324
10,22	171	7,8	324
10,22 Q	192	7,29	269
11,9f.	140	7,30	324
11,24	246	7,37f.	131, 195
11,24 Q	193	7,42	213
11,46	240	7,49	173
11,49	180	8,14	306
11,49 Q	169, 181	8,20	324
11,49b-11,51a	180	8,42	269
11,49-51 Q	7, 180-183	8,43	286
11,50	290	8,47	286
11,51b	180	9,4	324
12,19 L	193	10,16	286
12,27	194, 240	10,36	269
13,34f. Q	7	11,9	324
13,34-35 Q	183-185	11,41f.	241
13,35 Q	184	11,42	269
18,38f.	214	12,15	219, 220
19,38	220	12,23	324
20,41	214	12,27	324
20,44	214	13,1	324
23,43	345	14	132, 347
		14,2	132
John		14,2f.	132, 279, 365
	131, 132, 133, 164, 165	16,25	324
1	180, 184	17,1	324
1,17	363	17,4	324
1,17f.	179	17,24	132
2,4	324	19,28	324
3,17	269	19,30	324
3,34	269		
4,21	324	Acts	
4,23	324		141
4,34	324	1,6	141, 308
4,38	279	1,6f.	307
5	324	1,6-11	309
5,1-15	131	1,16	233
5,16-18	323	2,30	233
5,17	252, 323, 324, 325, 347, 354, 365, 366	3	140, 141, 142, 252, 308, 363, 364, 365
		3,10	140
5,21	324	3,11-26	309
5,24	286	3,12f.	309
5,25	324	3,13f.	309
5,28f.	324	3,15	309
5,36	269	3,17	309
5,39	324	3,18	309

3,19-23	364	2 Corinthians	
3,20	279, 299, 307, 308, 309, 347, 362, 365	2,13	299
		4,17	194
3,20f.	141, 307, 309	7,7	299
3,21	308, 309	8,13	299
3,22	179	9,4	325
3,22f.	309	10,1	189, 193, 218
3,24	309	11,17	325
3,25	309	12,4	345
3,26	308, 309		
4,13	173	Galatians	
4,19	286	3,19	270
4,25	233	4,4	268
6	259	4,26	279
6-7	258	5,1-3	204
7	140, 252, 253, 258, 335-338, 352, 363, 365, 366	Ephesians	
		4,2	219
7,35	179		
7,37	179, 363	Colossians	
7,38	270		164, 165
7,44-50	336	1,7	209
7,46	348	1,15-20	164
7,49	74, 337, 347, 348, 355	2,16f.	324, 354, 366
		3,1-4	329
7,49f.	335		
7,53	270	1 Thessalonians	
7,57	363	5,4	292
13,33	226		
15,10	204	2 Thessalonians	
17,11	259		299
		1	140, 141, 142, 252, 298, 299, 307, 362, 365
Romans			
1	204		
2,4	245	1,3-10	299
3,3f.	294	1,5ff.	140
3,23	312	1,6ff.	246
9,6	295	1,6-10	345
9,16	295	1,7	141, 298, 299, 309, 347, 365
11,29	295		
15,12	226	1,9	309
1 Corinthians		1 Timothy	
1-4	173, 235	6,16	286
1,26ff.	173		
2,6ff.	173	2 Timothy	
3,13	292	1	133
4,1f.	268	1,16	133, 307
10	313		
10,1-13	272	Philemon	
10,12f.	272	7	133
13,12	178	20	133
16,18	133		

Index of Ancient Writings: New Testament

Hebrews	74, 78, 132, 153, 164, 165, 231, 252-358, 360, 361	3-4	1-2, 10-16, 18, 42, 43, 61, 67, 78, 94, 102, 103, 107, 111, 113, 115, 133, 138, 140, 144, 145, 151, 152, 230, 231, 232, 252-358, 359, 360, 361, 362, 364, 365, 366
1	180, 185		
1-2	270		
1-3	271		
1-4	270		
1,1	291, 295, 309		
1,1f.	268, 270	3,1	267, 269, 271, 272, 309, 314, 326
1,1-3	185, 300		
1,1-4	258	3,1f.	268
1,2	270, 291, 295, 303, 304, 307, 309, 311, 355	3,1-6	178, 179, 180, 260, 268, 269, 270, 271, 272, 309, 348, 363, 364
1,2f.	273, 331, 363, 364		
1,3	325, 326	3,1-6ff.	337
1,3f.	164, 180	3,1-4,13	271
1,4	271, 303, 304	3,1-4,14	269
1,5	226, 270, 363, 364	3,2	269, 270, 271, 272
1,5-2,16	271	3,2f.	270
1,5-2,18	271	3,2-6	268, 270, 336
1,6	278	3,3	268
1,8f.	273	3,4	331, 336, 355
1,10	296, 328	3,5	268, 269, 271
1,10-12	331, 355	3,6	270, 272, 298, 306, 307, 326, 336
1,10-13	331		
1,13f.	273	3,6b	272
1,14	279, 302, 303	3,6b-c	272
2,1	264	3,6ff.	45, 268
2,1-4	268, 314, 326	3,7	300
2,2	270, 336	3,7ff.	268, 271, 272, 303, 314, 348, 355
2,3	264, 265, 309		
2,3f.	260, 265	3,7-11	260
2,3-5	273	3,7-19	272, 283, 285
2,4	309	3,7-4,11	14, 259, 261, 262, 264, 268, 272, 274, 279, 300, 303, 305, 306, 312, 315, 316, 320, 325, 332-335, 338, 341, 342, 344, 347, 348, 354, 355, 359, 360
2,5	274, 279, 325, 355		
2,7	355		
2,9	330		
2,9f.	270, 309		
2,9-16	273		
2,10	278, 279, 309, 314, 331, 355		
2,11	328, 333	3,7-4,13	268, 271, 272, 314
2,14	265, 328, 333	3,8	272, 313
2,16	309	3,8f.	272
2,17	269, 271	3,9	260, 272, 296, 322
2,17f.	268, 273	3,9a	260
2,17-3,6	268, 271, 272, 358, 362	3,9b-10a	260
		3,9f.	260, 263, 301, 313
2,18	265, 272, 309	3,9-10	260
3	180, 263	3,10	260, 336
		3,11	278, 313

3,12	260, 265, 272, 287, 326	4,3a-5	293
		4,3b	282, 288, 289, 294
3,12f.	263, 295, 296, 311, 314	4,3b-c	288, 289, 290
		4,3b-5	280, 285, 287, 288, 289, 293, 294
3,12-14	266, 306		
3,13	260, 285, 291, 307, 309, 326	4,3c	261, 280, 288-290
		4,3c-4	289
3,13f.	304	4,3f.	279, 280, 296, 304, 318, 322, 346
3,14	252, 263, 268, 270, 298, 307, 326		
		4,3-4	280
3,15	260	4,3-5	281, 284, 288, 289, 291-293, 305, 349
3,15-19	268		
3,16	260, 263, 271, 276, 286, 313	4,3-10	260, 285-287
		4,3-11	300, 306, 316
3,16-18	260, 313	4,4	261, 279, 280, 288, 290, 316, 320, 336
3,16-19	263, 278, 281, 283, 286, 289, 294, 313		
		4,4a	289, 290, 321
3,17	260, 263, 313, 336	4,4b	280, 289
3,18	260, 263, 278, 313	4,4bα	289
3,19	260, 264, 278, 313	4,4bβ	289
3,19-4,1	285	4,4bγ	289
3,20	355	4,4f.	290
4	133, 146, 298, 319, 324	4,4-5	280, 288, 289
		4,5	260, 278, 288, 289, 294
4,1	260, 263, 265, 272, 278, 279, 284, 285, 294, 295, 296, 301, 312	4,6	260, 263, 276, 278, 282, 283, 284, 285, 288, 291, 293, 294, 301, 306, 313
4,1f.	283, 287, 294, 306		
4,1ff.	263, 284, 302	4,6a	276, 293, 294
4,1-2	285, 290, 291	4,6a-b	284, 294
4,1-3a	260, 293	4,6b	294
4,1-5	285	4,6b-7	294
4,1-10	322, 323, 324, 325, 344	4,6f.	291, 295
		4,6ff.	288, 289, 293
4,1-11	259, 261, 283-305, 349, 361	4,6-8	285, 287, 291, 294
		4,6-10	305
4,2	260, 267, 268, 284, 285, 286, 287, 294, 295, 301, 303, 312, 313	4,6-11	285
		4,7	260, 261, 291, 294, 307, 309, 316
		4,7a	294
4,2a	286	4,7a-b	294
4,2c	285, 286, 303	4,7b	293
4,2-3	285	4,7cβ	294
4,3	133, 260, 261, 278, 279, 280, 282, 284, 285, 287, 288, 292, 296, 301, 305, 306, 307, 362	4,7f.	261, 285, 290, 336
		4,8	260, 261, 275, 281, 284, 286, 291, 292, 293, 295, 303, 316
		4,8-10	293
4,3a	282, 284, 285, 286, 287, 288, 290, 294, 295, 303, 306	4,9	12, 261, 276, 279, 284, 293, 296, 306
		4,9f.	287, 288, 291, 292, 295
4,3a-b	287		

Index of Ancient Writings: New Testament

4,9-10	283, 285, 287, 289, 295	6,15	301, 302
		6,17	301, 302, 303
4,10	260, 261, 276, 278, 279, 280, 281, 289, 290, 292, 295, 296, 297, 299, 300, 306, 307, 313, 316, 318, 319, 322, 323, 350	6,17f.	302
		6,17ff.	294
		6,17-20	326
		6,19	278
		6,19f.	315, 316
		6,20	278, 314, 315
4,10a	281, 319	7,3	291, 307
4,10ff.	133	7,6	301, 302
4,11	260, 263, 265, 272, 278, 281, 284, 285, 288, 294, 296, 306, 313	7,11	292, 303
		7,14	364
		7,25	266
		7,26	330
4,12	260, 263, 300	7,28	270
4,12f.	322	8,2	336
4,12-13	300	8,3	270
4,14	265, 269, 273, 314, 330	8,4	292
		8,4f.	325
4,14ff.	268	8,5	336
4,14-16	269, 271, 272, 326, 358, 362	8,6	268, 301, 304
		8,7	292, 303
4,14-5,10	269	8,8-10	292
4,14-10,25	271	8,13	292
4,15	272	9,1	336
4,16	249, 272	9,1ff.	336
5-10	348	9,6f.	278, 315, 316
5,4f.	270	9,7	278
5,4-6	270	9,8	325
5,5	270, 363, 364	9,8f.	303
5,7	265, 331	9,9f.	266
5,8	309	9,11	270, 325, 336
5,11	265	9,11-10,18	55
5,11-14	265	9,12	278, 315, 316
5,12-14	265	9,13f.	268
6,1	270, 279, 296, 326	9,14	266, 270, 296
6,1-5	326	9,15	301, 302, 303, 304, 355
6,2	331		
6,4f.	286, 309	9,19-21	271
6,4-6	263	9,23f.	325
6,5	255	9,24	270, 278, 328, 336
6,6	265, 285, 309	9,24f.	315, 316
6,7f.	265	9,25	278
6,8	307	9,25f.	266, 303
6,9	279, 287	9,26	290, 291, 292, 307, 344, 355
6,9-11	265		
6,9-12	265, 326	9,26-28	311
6,10	297, 300	9,28	266, 270, 344
6,11	298, 307, 326	10,1-4	303
6,12	265, 300, 301, 302, 303	10,2	292
		10,2f.	266
6,13	301, 302	10,5	278
6,13-15	301	10,10	270

10,12	355	11,32-38	265
10,14	266, 355	11,33	301
10,16	292	11,35	331
10,19	265, 278, 315, 316	11,37	299, 312
10,19-25	267, 271, 326	11,38	310
10,20	325	11,39	301
10,21	270	11,39f.	275, 302, 303
10,21-23	272	11,39-12,1	287
10,22	266, 331	11,40	279, 297
10,23	265, 269, 295, 301, 302	12,1	265
		12,1-2	268
10,24	297	12,2	268, 309
10,25	266, 292, 307, 311, 314, 344	12,2f.	265
		12,3	265
10,26	265, 284, 309	12,4	265
10,26f.	263	12,4-11	265, 297
10,26-34	267	12,5-11	265
10,28f.	268, 309	12,9	268, 328, 333
10,29	265	12,12f.	265
10,32f.	265	12,15	263, 265, 295, 312
10,32-34	265	12,17	303
10,32-36	297	12,22	276, 279, 319, 325, 336, 355
10,32-39	265, 266, 300, 306, 326		
		12,22f.	279
10,34	325, 326	12,22ff.	288, 293
10,35	300	12,22-24	309, 328
10,35-39	267	12,23	275
10,36	298, 300, 301, 302	12,24	292, 304
10,37	307, 311	12,25	265, 268, 314, 328
10,39	263, 287	12,25c	328
11	267, 286, 291, 297	12,26	301
11-13	348	12,26b	328
11,1	267, 325	12,26f.	330, 332
11,3	331, 355	12,27	257, 274, 328, 336
11,7	303, 344	12,27a	328
11,8	303, 310	12,27f.	321, 322, 328, 346
11,8f.	278, 303	12,28	279, 311, 325, 326
11,8-16	302, 304, 349	13	270
11,9	301, 302, 303	13,3	265, 328, 333
11,10	279, 302, 325, 344	13,7	265, 266
11,11	295, 301, 302	13,8	270
11,13	269, 301, 302	13,9	265
11,14	279, 302, 325, 332	13,9-14	266
11,14-16	328	13,11	278, 315, 316
11,15	292	13,13	314, 321, 322, 323, 327
11,16	279, 302, 325, 333, 344		
		13,14	279, 325, 344
11,17	272, 301, 302	13,15	269
11,19	331	13,17	265, 266
11,26	270	13,17f.	266
11,27	284	13,18	266
11,30	289	13,19	265
11,32	2, 264	13,20	331

13,20f.	297	3,1	300
13,21	270, 297	3,2	298
13,22	264	3,8	300
13,23	264, 265	3,12	279, 344
13,24	266	3,15	298, 300
		5,5	226
James		6,11	246, 297
3,13	202	7,9-17	315
		12	298
1 Peter		13	299, 308
	264	14	140, 141, 252, 298, 299, 307, 365
1,3f.	279		
3,4	193, 218	14,10f.	141, 142
4	300	14,11	246, 297, 298, 345, 346
4,14	226, 299, 300		
		14,12	298
2 Peter		14,13	133, 141, 246, 297, 298, 299, 309, 345, 346, 347, 365
3	328		
3,8	134		
3,8ff.	104	16,15	141, 309
3,13	336	19,9	141, 309
		20	104
1 John		20,6	141, 309
5,3f.	239	21,1	328
		21,1f.	344
Revelation		21,2	279
	299	21,10	279, 344
1,3	141, 309	22,7	141, 309
2,2	298, 300	22,12	298
2,7	345	22,14	141, 309
2,19	298, 300	22,17	309
2,23	298		

3. OT Pseudepigrapha

Apocalypse of Elijah		38,4	165
2,53	104, 106, 278, 304, 351	41,4	184
		51,3f.	165
4,27	106, 109, 278, 304, 351	51,7	165
		61	89, 234
		61,3	105
Apocalypse of Sedrach		72,2-6	105
16,3	110	73,1	109, 246
		73,1ff.	141, 246, 309
Apocalypse of Zephaniah		73,1-2	105
	254	73,6-7	105
2b	84	85,9	104
		85,11	109
2 Baruch		85,12	104
4,2-4	107		
21,25	295		

3 Baruch

	254

4 Baruch

	201
5,32	110, 201
5,34f.	111

1 Enoch

	104
5,8	172
25,6	315
37-71	164
38f.	105
38,2	109, 345
38,2-39,4	105
39,4	132
39,4f.	109, 345
39,7	109
42	164, 165, 166
42,1f.	84
42,2	164
45,3	105, 132
49,3	165
53,7	104
61,8f.	213
62,1-12	213
62,14	104, 109
91,11ff.	103
93,1ff.	103
93,8	165
96,3	104
103,11-13	197

2 Enoch

	132
8,3	106, 110, 320
9,1	106, 110, 320
24,2b-5	280
33	135
33,1f.	104
33,1-2	135
34,1	204
42,3	104, 106, 110, 320
61,2f.	132
65,9	106
70,3	104

Ezekiel the Tragedian

68-82	270
100	179

4 Ezra

	104, 106, 107, 108, 109, 111, 254, 259, 299, 315, 328, 331, 332, 339, 343-346
2,24	298
2,25	345
2,27f.	345
4,41	110
5,9f.	165
6,20-24	299
7	105, 107, 246, 298, 299, 345
7,26	107, 299, 344
7,26ff.	299
7,26-44	107, 255
7,27-31	135
7,28	107
7,28ff.	363
7,32	110
7,36	107, 108, 344, 345
7,36ff.	105, 106, 110, 246, 320
7,36-38	298
7,36-44	345
7,38	107, 108
7,75	108
7,75-101	345
7,76-87	298
7,80	110
7,85	108
7,88-94	298
7,88-98	108, 110
7,88-101	345
7,91ff.	246
7,93	298
7,95	110
7,95f.	299
7,96	297
7,99	298
7,121	108
7,123	108, 345
8,47	107
8,48-52	107
8,50-54	345
8,52	234, 344, 345
10,24	106
11,1ff.	308
11,46	308

Greek Apocalypse of Ezra

1,12	104, 111

Joseph and Aseneth

	109, 111, 131, 153, 255, 256, 257, 315, 328, 329, 332-334, 339, 340
6,2-6	175
8,9	97, 99, 109, 127, 131, 278, 304, 332-334, 336, 340, 351, 358
8,11	106
11,1f.	135
13,10	175
15,5	135
15,7	97, 98, 109, 110, 332, 333
15,7f.	109
21,3	175
22,9	106
22,13	97, 98, 109, 332, 333, 334, 336

Jubilees

	103
1,26	103
1,29	103
2,17ff.	103
4,30	103
23,29	106
25,19	91
36,15	91
50,1-5	103
50,8f.	276

Life of Adam and Eve (LAE)

43,3 ApMos	106, 354
51,2	106, 320, 354

Lives of the Prophets

1	299

Odes of Solomon

	129-133, 142, 144, 279, 347, 365
3,5	129, 132, 133
4,8	131
6,11	130
8,18	131
9	5
11	132
11,6f.	131
11,12	129, 130, 131, 132, 133
11,23	132
16,12	130, 131, 133
20,8	130
23,2f.	131
25,12	129, 133
25,12 Cop.	133
26,3	129, 130
26,12f.	130, 131
28,3	130, 131, 133
30,1-7	131
30,2f.	130, 131
30,7	130, 131
33	3
33,5-9	166
35,6	130, 131
36,1	130, 131, 133
37	131
37,3f.	133, 297
37,4	130, 131
38,4	130
42,7f.	195

Psalms of Solomon

	233
17-18	233
17,22	213
17,26	213
17,29	213
17,32	213
17,37	213
17,40	213

Pseudo-Philo, Liber Antiquitatum Biblicarum (LAB)

	110
3,10	110
11,8	276
19	109
19,10	315
19,13	315
20,5	104
25,1	105
28,6ff.	103, 110, 135
28,10	109, 315
28,20	110
33,6	105
48,4	105
49,6	106, 109, 315
55,10	105
59,2	221
59f.	233
60	234
60,3	234

Sibylline Oracles			Levi	
2,308	104		4,2	175
3,311-318	106		6,4	106
7,140	135		13	165
			16-18	103
Syriac Menander			18	141
I,34ff.	104		18,1ff.	105
II,104	104		18,2	233
II,126-130	104		18,4f.	233
II,371-376	104		18,7	233
II,470ff.	104, 110		18,9	140, 233
			18,12	140
Testament of Job				
14,5	81		Judah	
			22,2f.	233
Testament of Moses			24,1	213
254			24,1-4	233
11,16	270		24,1-6	221
			24,6	213
Testament of Solomon				
1,7	234		Zebulon	
20,1	214, 234		10,4	104
20,16	246		13,20	126
			14,6	126
Testament of the Three Patriarchs			14,8	126
Abraham			119a	126
	110		119b	126
7,16	110			
7,16f.	103, 135		Dan	
9,8	105, 110			109
9,8 Rec B	345		5-6	189, 247
12,5	175		5,7-13	109
			5,10-13	104, 152
Isaac			5,12	106, 189, 320
2,13	108, 111		5,12f.	140, 141, 189
2,15	108, 111		5,13	105
			6,9	189
Jacob				
2,26	111		Gad	
5,6	111		7,3	91, 106
Testament of the Twelve Patriarchs			Asher	
	103, 105, 254		6,3	91
Simeon				
6,4-7	140			

4. Qumran

1QH		4Q285	
2,8-10	172		226
6,19	195		
8	112	4Q504	
18	113	3 ii	112
		4	112
1QSb			
5,24-26	213	4QPBless	
			226
1QS			
11,6f.	172	11Q Melch	
			103, 229
1QpHab			
12,4	172	11Q Ps^a	
			4
4Q161 = 4QpIsa^a		18	174, 184
	226	21,11-17	4
frg D 1-8	213	22,1	4
		27,2-4	233
4Q174 = 4QFlor		27,2-11	234
	111, 112, 226, 363	27,10f.	233
1	112, 140, 246, 247		
10-14	225, 226	11QT = 11Q19	
		29	112
4Q246			
	226		
2	112, 140, 246, 363, 365		

5. Philo

De Abrahamo		De Migratione Abrahami	
27	113, 119	27	297
28	113, 114	28ff.	114
30	113		
		De Cherubim	
De Aeternitate Mundi		49	175
84	118, 119, 322	77	120
		83ff.	120
De Agricultura		86	120
85	312	86-90	323
		87	113, 118, 322
De Confusione Linguarum		87ff.	116, 117, 118, 120, 122, 256
30f.	118, 119		
		90	118
De Ebrietate		108ff.	120
30f.	164		

De Congressu quaerendae
Eruditionis gratia
45	119
48	119
130	120

De Decalogo
86	119, 120
96ff.	114
97f.	114
102-104	135
142	119
143ff.	119
162f.	114
164	114

De Fuga et Inventione
50f.	113
50-52	175
51	176
109	164, 175
112	164
166ff.	119
170ff.	114
173	113, 114, 297
174	113

De Gigantibus
49	118, 119
51	113n

De Iosepho
182	312

De Legatione ad Gaium
156	114

De Mutatione Nominum
239f.	119
256	164

De Opificio Mundi
7	118
100	117, 118

De Plantatione
8f.	164
18	164

De Posteritate Caini
22ff.	120
23	118
23ff.	119
28	118
28f.	118
64	261
183	113

De Praemiis et Poenis
53	271
56	271
85-93	114
116	119
121	119
153	114
153ff.	114
154ff.	114
157	114
157f.	114

De Providentia
I,6	118, 119

De Sacrificiis Abelis et Caini
54	120
64	175

De Sobrietate
34ff.	119
44ff.	119

De Somniis
I,174	113, 119
I,241	164
II,189	270
II,223ff.	118, 119
II,228	118
II,229	119
II,230ff.	120
II,233	121
II,238ff.	120

De Specialibus Legibus
I,69	113, 250
I,170	114
II,39	114
II,44	113
II,60	114
II,60ff.	114
II,64	114
II,89	114
II,89ff.	114
II,96f.	114
II,156f.	114
III,25	313
III,78	313

III,116	313		II,46	116
III,165	313		II,118	164
III,174	313			
IV,79ff.	119		Quaestiones et Solutiones in Genesin	
			I,42	120
De Virtutibus			I,73	205
62	164, 175		I,87	119
			III,39	114
De Vita Mosis			III,62	198
I,158	270		IV,1	116, 120
II,21f.	114		IV,97	164, 175
II,66-186	271		IV,218	205
II,209	114, 289		IV,236f.	205
II,211f.	114			
II,215	289		Quis Rerum Divinarum Heres	
II,219f.	114		36	164
II,263	289		115	313
			167	313
Fragmenta			182	271
	312		188	164
			199	164
In Flaccum			260f.	313
118	277		262	178
			277-279	313
Legum Allegoriae			285	313
I	113		288	313
I,5	322			
I,5f.	113, 118, 323		Quod Deterius Potiori insidiari solet	
I,5ff.	117		54	164, 175
I,6	119, 322		121f.	119
I,16	113, 119			
I,16-18	116, 117, 118		Quod Deus immutabilis sit	
I,18	113, 322, 323		7ff.	116
I,43	164		10ff.	115, 116, 117, 118, 119, 120, 122, 318
II,49	175			
II,100-103	178		11	114
III,77	116, 119		11f.	318, 322
III,114ff.	119		12	297
III,128ff.	119		23	116, 120
III,160	119		23ff.	119
III,169	113			

Quaestiones et Solutiones in Exodum
II,29   116
II,40   116

6. Josephus

Jewish Antiquities			6,166-168	233, 234
3,14	81		7,43	221
6,92	245		7,95	221

7,270	221	8,213	245
7,391	221, 233	15,136	270
8	234	20,188	248
8,45-49	234, 246		

7. Targums, Rabbinic, Other Later Jewish and Samaritan Literature

Abot de Rabbi Nathan (ARN)
           122
1   122, 132, 142, 323, 342
1,6   198
1,16   198
3,5   204
36   127, 128, 278

Aquila
      219

Babylonian Talmud
  Berakhot (Ber)
    17a   132, 142, 342
    57b   123

  Hagigah (Hag)
    10a   127, 128

  Keritot (Ker)
    5a   351

  Ketubot (Ket)
    104a 111, 124

  Rosh Hashshanah (RH)
    31a   103, 122, 135, 323

  Sanhedrin (Sanh)
    97a   103, 135, 323
    97b   103
    99a   127
    110b 127, 128

  Shabbat (Shab)
    64a   351
    152b 111, 124

Ecclesiastes Rabbah
  10,20 § 1 127, 128

Exodus Rabbah
  30,8 125
  30,9 323

Fragmentary Targum (FrgTg)
      122, 323

Genesis Rabbah
  10,2   279
  10,9   279, 320
  11   322, 324
  11,10 323
  17,5   123
  44,17 123
  56,2   41, 124, 128

Leviticus Rabbah
  25   184
  32   128
  32,2 127, 128

Mekhilta de R. Ishmael
  Pisha
    1   125

  Shabbeta
    1   122, 123, 323

Memar Marqah
       279
  I § 9 279
  II § 7 279

Midrash Pesiqta
  186a 84

Midrash on Psalms
       123
  1-118 124
  5 § 1 126
  92   279
  92 § 2 122, 279, 320, 323
  92 § 5 123, 129, 354

95	128, 273, 278, 315, 351
95 § 3	124, 126, 127
95 § 5.2.1	124
95 § 5.2.2	124
132 § 2	126
132 § 3	125

Midrash Rabbah
    123

Midrash Taanaim
  2a   323

Mishnah
    122
  Baba Batra (BB)
    8,6   213

  Berakhot (Ber)
    2,2   205, 228

  Baba Mesia (BM)
    2,11   198

  Kelim (Kel)
    1,6-9   125

  Sanhedrin (Sanh)
    10,1-4   127
    10,3   273

  Shabbat (Shab)
    6,4   123, 129, 354

  Tamid (Tam)
    7,4   65, 122, 135, 323

Numbers Rabbah
  14,19   127, 128

Palestinian Talmud
  Hagigah (Hag)
    1,76c,48ff.   127

Pesahim (Pes)
  6,1,33a   351

Sanhedrin (Sanh)
  10,29c,5   127, 128

Pesiqta de Rab Kahana (PRK)
  20   123, 125

Pirqe de Rabbi Eliezer (PRE)
  18   122, 323
  18f.   323
  19   122

Seder Eliahu Rabbah (SER)
  2   103, 122, 135, 323

Sifre Deuteronomy
    125
  § 1   41, 123, 124, 125
  § 2   125
  § 66   126

Song of Songs Rabbah (CantR)
  4,4 § 6   122, 323
  7,5 § 3   123, 125

Targum of the Writings (TgKet)
  Ps 45   221

Targum Onqelos (TgOnq)
    126, 350

Targum Pseudo-Jonathan
    126, 350

Tosefta
  Baba Mesia (BM)
    2,29   198

  Sanhedrin (Sanh)
    13,10   127, 128

8. Nag Hammadi

Allogenes
(XI,3)
65	155

Apocalypse of Peter
(VII,3)
16	300

Authoritative Teaching
(VI,3)
35,8ff.	148

The (First) Apocalypse of James
(V,3)
3,24-34	157

The Apocryphon of James
(I,2)
24,11-25	327

The Apocryphon of John
(II,1, II,1, IV,1, and BG 8502,2)
BG 40,20-41,1	147
BG 65,12-16	147

The Dialogue of the Savior
(III,5)
	190, 194
1	190
1f.	190
2	190
65f.	190
68	190

The Gospel of Mary
(BG 8502,1)
17,4f.	189
17,4-7	156

The Gospel of Philip
(II,3)
	145
63	321
66	321
66,16-20	148
66,16-21	156, 157
72,22-23	157
79,3-13	157

The Gospel of Thomas
(II,2)
	6, 139, 160, 161, 162, 188, 190, 191, 193, 194, 237
2	144, 161
2 Cop.	140
46	191
61b	191
78	191
90	4, 5, 8, 160, 161, 162, 189, 191, 192, 193, 194, 201, 239, 246, 250
90 Cop.	190
92	161
94	161
174	139

The Gospel of Truth
(I,3 and XII,2)
	121, 146, 147, 148, 157, 158, 324
22,9	148
22,9-12	156
22,12	148, 189
23,25-30	155
24,9-28	327
24,14-20	154
24,16-20	155
28,29-30,4	148
32,18ff.	324
33,3-5	156
33,5	189
36,35-39	155
37,19-21	155
38,25-32	155
40,23-43,24	147
41,3-16	155
41,28f.	155
42,17-33	157
42,21-23	154
42,21-25	147
43,1-3	155

The Paraphrase of Shem
(VII,1)
	145

Index of Ancient Writings: Nag Hammadi 451

The Prayer of the Apostle Paul
(I, *1*)
  A,3-10   157

The Testimony of Truth
(IX, *3*)
  35,25-36,3   156
  37,22f.   189

The Treatise on the Resurrection
(I, *4*)
  44   141, 308

The Tripartite Tractate
(I, *5*)
  53,16-20   155
  55,13-19   155

  70,14-19   155
  70,15ff.   155
  71,20-21   155
  72,14-16   154
  85,7-9   147
  90,20-21   154
  91,3-5   154
  92,4-9   155
  101,25-28   157
  102,16-26   156
  121,25-28   156
  122,23f.   154
  128,15-19   154
  131,20-21   156
  132,12-14   156

9. Other Christian Literature

Acts of John
  112   322

Acts of Thomas
  82   190
  86   190

Ascension of Isaiah
  3,13-4,22   299
  4,1-22   299
  4,15   138, 299

Apostolic Constitutions
  2,36,2   276

Athenagorus
  Supplicatio
    9,2   142

Barnabas
  15   104, 134, 135, 138,
                          139, 144, 145, 317,
                          322, 323, 324, 336,
                          339, 342
  15-16   336
  15,3   134
  15,3-5   136
  15,3-7   135
  15,3-9   136
  15,5   136
  15,5a   136, 137
  15,5b   136, 137
  15,5-7   135, 137
  15,6-7   136
  15,7   136, 137
  15,8   136, 137
  15,8f.   135, 137
  15,8-9   136
  16   136, 144
  16,2   138, 142, 337

1 Clement
  16,17   189
  17,1   179
  17,5-6   179
  18   221, 233
  57,3-7   140
  57,7   138
  59,3   138

2 Clement
                      138-141, 142, 144
  5   141, 365
  5-6   141, 142, 144, 248,
                      299, 361
  5,1   139
  5,2-5   138
  5,5   138, 139, 140, 142,
                      189
  5,6   139
  6,3-7   139
  6,5   138

6,7	139, 140, 142, 189	Fifth and Sixth Ezra	
20,5	309		189
		1,30	184
Clement of Alexandria		2,12	189
Excerpta ex Theodoto		2,24	189
63,1	156, 157	2,34	189
65,2	157		
		Gospel of the Hebrews	
Paedagogus			138-141, 144, 160,
1,6,29	143		161, 189, 365
1,13,102	144, 320		
		Hippolytus	
Stromateis		*Refutation of All Heresies*	
2,9,45	139	VI 32,8	145
5,14,96	139	VIII 14,1	145
6,14,108	143		
6,16,137f.	143	Ignatius	
7,9,57	143	*Ephesians*	
7,11,68	143	2,1	133, 142
Epistle to Diognetus		*Magnesians*	
7,3f.	189	15,1	133
Epiphanius		*Trallians*	
Panarion		12,1	133
30,2,2	276	12,2	133
Epistula Apostolorum		*Romans*	
	145	10,2	133
12 Cop.	142		
18	135	*Smyrnaeans*	
19	142, 342	9,2	133, 142
19 Cop.	132	10,1	133
22	142	12,1	133
26	142		
26 Eth.	142	Irenaeus	
26 Cop.	142	*Adversus haereses*	
27	142	1,7,1	157
28	142	1,7,5	157
28 Cop.	142	1,4,1	147
44 Cop.	138, 141, 142	4,16,1	141
		5,28,3	141
Eusebius		5,30,4	141
Historia ecclesiastica		5,33,2	141
3,28,2	138		
3,39,11ff.	138	Justin Martyr	
		Dialogue with Trypho	
Praeparatio evangelica			142
13,12	164	8,2	142
13,12,9-16	142	23,3	276
13,12,10	164	80,5	141
		121,3	141

Martyrdom of Peter and Paul
  1   276

Oxyrhynchus Papyri (POx)
  654   139, 161

Pistis Sophia
                   160, 190, 194
  95   5, 160, 190, 192

Pseudo-Justin
  Oratio ad Graecos
    5   5

Shepherd of Hermas
  Similitudes
    9,1   134
    9,5   133
    9,27   134

10. Other Ancient Literature

Arrian's Discourses of Epictetus
  IV,8,28   5

Corpus Hermeticum
                   3, 5, 139
  4,2   139
  9,10   139
  13,20   139

Enuma Elish
  ANET, 60   71
  ANET, 61   71
  ANET, 68   71

Instruction for King Merikare
  ANET, 417   71

Plato
  Timaeus
    19b   119

Plutarch
  De superstitione
    3 (166A)   276
    8 (196C)   276

The Theology of Memphis
  ANET, 5   71

Theophrastus
  de Ventis
    18   81, 146

Index of Names and Subjects

Aaron, 177, 269
Abimelech, 110
Abraham, 1, 302, 304, 309
Absalom, 234
Adam and Eve, 345
affliction, 52, 53, 57, 60, 106
Ahaz, 86
allusion. *See* echo
apocalyptic
— apocalypticism and, 253-255, 299, 308, 317-334, 341, 342-347, 348
— conception of rest in, 12, 14, 132, 255, 298, 299, 339, 342-347, 348, 356, 358, 359, 361, 365
— Hebrews as, 253-255, 257, 277, 295, 298, 299, 308, 317-334, 339, 341, 342-347, 348
— literary genre of, 44, 141, 173, 174, 180, 181, 257, 277, 295, 349
Apsu, 71
Aristobulus, 93, 117, 142, 164
ark of the covenant, 1, 27, 30, 32, 34-36, 38, 39, 40, 43, 72, 95, 96, 97, 98, 165, 221, 223, 319
Asa, 36, 37
Aseneth, 95, 109
Augustine, 142

Barnabas, 134-138
Baruch, 175
Beliar, 105
Ben Sira, 77, 166, 173, 175, 198, 199, 205
Bethuel, 175
bondage, 53, 63, 66, 68, 76, 83, 123, 353

Caleb, 263, 276, 286, 313
Canaanites, 58
Cerinthus, 138
Clement of Alexandria, 129, 135, 139, 142-144, 145, 152, 153, 246, 256, 259, 325, 332

Clement of Rome, 221
cynic Teles, 313

Daniel, 176
David
— as wise man and prophet, 224, 230, 233, 234, 291
— dynasty of, 18, 19, 23, 26, 28-31, 34, 38, 39, 41, 48, 56, 59-60, 67, 69-70, 76, 78, 88, 105, 112, 140, 209-251, 269, 308
— meekness of, 220-221
— rest tradition and, 19, 25, 26, 27, 31, 33, 35-36, 37, 39, 40, 54, 59, 74, 80, 83, 85, 86, 89, 111, 143, 228, 236, 293, 342, 355
"day which is wholly Sabbath and rest," 65, 67, 122, 123, 128, 135, 152, 319, 322, 323, 325, 346, 349, 355, 358
death, 92, 93, 94, 104-111, 124, 128, 148, 156, 166, 190, 254, 298, 307, 331, 334, 339
dualism
— Clement of Alexandria's, 256, 318
— definition of, 255, 256, 257, 317-334
— Gnosticism and, 4, 14, 130, 150-151, 153, 253, 255, 256, 257, 317-334, 338-342, 348, 358, 360
— Hebrews and, 153, 253, 255, 267, 272, 297, 311, 312, 317-334, 338-342, 348, 358, 359, 360, 361
— Philo and, 253, 255-257, 272, 317-334, 338-342, 348, 358, 360

Ea, 71
echo
— allusion and, 195, 199, 228, 229, 265, 271, 362, 364, 365
Elisha, 39
Enoch, 267
exile, 32
Ezra, 106, 107

gift, 24
gnostic Redeemer, 3, 6, 148, 150, 157, 339, 360
gnostic Revealer. *See* gnostic Redeemer
Gnosticism
— date of, 8, 150-151, 200
— definition, of 4, 115, 122, 135, 150-151, 161, 163, 277, 329
— dualistic concept of rest in, 130, 150-151, 153, 253, 255, 256, 257, 317-334, 348, 358, 360
— Philo and, 11, 12, 78, 92, 93, 94, 95, 102, 115, 117, 120, 121, 122, 140, 144, 145, 149, 152, 153, 156, 246, 253, 255, 256, 257, 261, 264, 277, 311, 317-334, 338-342, 347, 348, 356, 358, 360
— rest motif and mythology of, 4, 5, 6, 8, 10, 12, 14, 78, 93, 94, 95, 102, 115, 117, 120, 121, 122, 129, 130, 133, 139, 140, 141, 142, 143, 145-149, 153, 154-158, 159, 161, 162, 163, 189, 192, 200, 201, 207, 246, 247, 257, 277, 299, 307, 338-342, 347, 356, 358, 359, 360, 361
Gospel of Thomas
— dating of, 139
— gnostic character of, 4-6, 8, 139, 140
— Q and, 6, 8

Hadrach, 123
Hannah, 115
hebdomas, 12, 135, 144, 276, 320, 321, 325, 338
hellenism
— definition of, 258, 259
— Hebrews and, 253, 258, 259, 264, 265, 305, 309, 329, 337, 342, 347-356, 358
— Hellenists and, 258, 264, 347-356
Herod, 213
Herod Antipas, 248
Hezekiah, 37
humility, 52, 53, 105, 107, 113, 172, 173, 177, 189, 202, 210

Ignatius, 133-134, 142
inheritance
— rest and, 23, 28, 30, 57, 58, 80, 81, 82, 84, 85, 87, 124, 126, 274, 291, 302, 303-304, 355
Irenaeus, 138, 141, 142, 150
Isaiah, 299

Ishtar, 205
Issachar, 95

Jacob, 112, 126
Jehoshaphat, 36, 37
Jerome, 140
Jesus, 3, 4, 6-9, 12, 55, 131, 159-208, 209-251, 265, 268, 269, 270, 271, 291, 304, 307, 309, 316, 323, 324, 331, 343, 354, 363
Job, 92
John, 324
John (the Baptizer), 167, 169, 170
Joseph, 95, 109, 213, 214
Josephus, 221, 245
Joshua, 25, 26, 30, 36, 177, 223, 261, 263, 275, 276, 284, 286, 291-293, 303, 305, 313, 316, 335, 336, 357, 364
Josiah, 38
Judah, 105
Judith, 83
Justin, 141, 142

Kenaz, 110
kingship, 209-251

labor. *See* work
land, 9, 18, 22, 24, 26, 28, 33, 34, 41-45, 48-50, 56, 58, 59, 63, 65, 67-68, 73-76, 78, 82, 83, 85, 87, 88, 95, 98, 114, 124, 125-128, 198, 245, 262, 263, 274, 275, 281, 302, 304, 308, 316, 317, 319, 348, 349, 351
law. *See* Torah
Levi, 105, 109
local idea of rest
— Hebrews and the, 10-12, 277, 278, 280, 281, 282, 283, 308, 334, 342, 343
— Jewish literature and the, 103, 111, 125
— LXX and the, 94-97, 99, 100, 278, 308
— NT and the, 10-12, 277, 278, 280, 281, 282, 283, 308, 334
— OT and the, 1, 10, 12, 23, 24, 28, 42, 94, 278, 281, 282, 283, 308, 334
logoi sophon. *See* sayings of the wise
logos christology, 3, 5, 8, 148, 155, 159-208, 359-361, 363, 364
Luke, 168, 180, 181, 188, 193, 213, 229, 258, 308, 309, 337, 338

magi, 213
Marduk, 64, 71, 73
Mark, 193
Matthew
— christology of, 2, 7, 131, 159-208, 359, 360, 361
— redaction of Q by, 3-5, 7, 8, 161, 162, 166, 167-186, 187-195, 205-208, 214, 232, 236, 247, 250, 365
— OT in, 2, 14, 15, 17, 18, 77, 78, 163, 179, 208, 210, 211, 212, 218, 219, 220, 223-231, 233, 234, 238, 242, 243, 247, 250, 361, 364
meekness
— David and, 220-221
— Jesus and, 179, 188, 189, 193-195, 198, 202, 209-251
— Matthew's idea of, 179, 187, 188, 190, 193-195, 198, 201, 202, 209-251
— Wisdom and, 179, 235
Melchizedek, 291,365
millennium, 45, 138, 140, 342
Miriam, 177
Moses
— angels and, 270
— David and, 25, 26, 220, 221, 292, 336, 363, 365
— Jewish thought regarding, 117, 126, 175, 177-179, 180, 207, 223, 270
— Matthew's Gospel and, 159, 175, 178, 179, 180, 207, 220, 235, 238
— prophet like, 32, 33, 82, 177-179, 180, 268, 271, 309, 363-366
— revelatory role of, 178, 179, 180, 268, 270-273, 363

Nahor, 115
Nathan, 35, 223, 225, 269
new exodus, 9, 18, 48, 53, 54, 56, 85, 90, 179, 225, 243, 354, 358, 366
Noah, 115, 119

ogdoad, 135, 144, 156, 158
Old Testament
— Hebrews' use of the, 12, 14, 15, 17, 18, 77, 78, 252-358
— Matthew's use of the, 2, 14, 15, 17, 18, 77, 78, 163, 179, 208, 210, 211, 212, 218-220, 223-231, 233, 234, 238, 242, 243, 247, 250, 361, 364
— typological use of the, 42-45, 66, 69, 179, 231, 274-275, 281, 316, 349

Onesiphorus, 307
Origen, 142
otiositas, divine, 64, 65, 70-73, 74, 76

Papias, 138
paradox of rest and yoke, 9, 203-206
Paul, 178, 204, 294, 307
peace, 25, 43, 46, 47, 53, 63, 66, 85-87, 105, 112, 113, 114, 121, 123, 140, 141, 190, 220, 223, 233, 234, 248, 308
Peter, 307, 308, 309, 363
Pharaoh, 177, 297
Pharisees, 210, 215, 241-244
Philo
— Gnosticism and, 5, 11, 12, 78, 92, 93, 94, 95, 102, 115, 117, 120-122, 140, 144, 145, 149, 152, 153, 156, 246, 253, 255, 256, 257, 261, 264, 277, 311, 317-334, 338-342, 347, 348, 350, 356, 358, 360
— Moses and, 270, 271, 272
— rest motif and, 12, 78, 91, 93, 94, 95, 102, 113-122, 140, 142, 149, 153, 204, 246, 249, 258, 259, 261, 338-342, 345, 347, 348, 350, 356, 358, 360
— wisdom and, 175, 176, 178
pilgrimage. *See* travelling; wandering
Plato and platonism, 93, 94, 119, 121, 122, 139, 142, 143, 144, 145, 149, 153, 156, 255, 256, 317-334, 340, 346
Plotinus, 149, 256
Plutarch, 276
presence of God, 32, 33, 36, 40, 50, 52, 59, 60, 69, 122, 172, 177, 231, 238, 262, 308, 355, 362
Ptah, 71

Q
— Gospel of Thomas and, 6, 236
— Matthew's redaction of, 3-5, 7, 8, 161, 162, 166, 167-186, 187-195, 205-208, 214, 232, 236, 247, 250, 365
— Mt 11:28-30 and, 3-8, 16, 166, 187-195, 205-208, 236
— as sayings of the wise, 6

R. Aqiba, 127, 128
R. Eliezer ben Hyrcanus, 127, 128
R. Hillel, 202

Index of Names and Subjects

R. Joshua, 322
R. Tachlipha, 127
R. Yehoshua ben Hananyah, 127, 128
R. Yehudah, 125, 126
R. Yose, 125
Raba, 127
Rebecca, 175
redeemed Redeemer. *See* gnostic Redeemer
Rehoboam, 245
rest of God, 1, 12, 19, 33, 34, 38-40, 42-45, 46, 51, 59, 62, 64, 65, 72-76, 84, 85, 88, 89, 95, 108, 109, 110, 112, 116-121, 123, 124, 125, 127, 128, 136, 153, 158, 259, 262, 277, 281, 319, 337, 352, 353, 358
Ruth, 96

Sabbath
— Christianity and the, 111, 134-138, 210, 231, 323
— eschatological, 14, 65-67, 75, 91, 104, 106, 108, 122, 123, 128, 129, 134-137, 144, 152, 229-231, 247, 252, 297, 316-317, 320, 324, 343, 347-349, 353-355, 358, 361, 362, 364-366
— Gnosticism and the, 134-138, 143, 146, 317-326, 346, 351
— OT on, 1, 41, 117, 134, 246, 308
— primordial, 1, 279, 282, 289, 290, 296, 305, 317, 319, 320, 331, 349, 353, 354
— rest and the, 1, 18, 41, 49, 61-65, 67-75, 76, 78, 88, 89-91, 98, 102, 103, 111, 113, 114, 121, 129, 189, 205, 247, 250, 261, 276-277, 279, 281-283, 291, 293-295, 304, 316-317, 327, 350, 351, 366
— structure of history and the, 103, 122, 135, 136, 246, 281, 282, 292, 319, 322-324, 336, 342
Samuel, 115, 245, 269, 318
Saul, 220, 221
sayings of the wise, 6
servant of YHWH, 25, 66, 105, 176, 177, 203, 209-211, 212, 213, 220, 223, 226, 228, 241, 245, 308, 363
seven, the number
— Gnosticism and, 134-138, 143
— Hebrews and, 281, 282, 289, 290, 318, 331, 349, 354, 355
— Judaism and, 122, 349, 354

— OT tradition and, 106, 281, 282, 349, 355
— Philo and, 113-116, 117, 121, 318, 354
Sheol, 93, 104, 110

shepherd, 26, 41, 83, 86, 112, 198, 212, 223, 227, 228, 230, 242, 248
Simeon, 140
Sirach, 85
Solomon
— as builder of the temple, 19, 27, 29, 33, 35, 36, 38, 40, 80, 86, 89, 357, 363
— rest tradition and, 26, 34, 35-38, 59, 74, 85, 86, 89, 131, 223, 231, 235, 245, 363
— as son of David, 26, 27, 35, 40, 216, 223, 224, 226, 233, 236
— wisdom of 166, 224, 234, 246
Son of David
— servant and, 211-218
— shepherd and, 112
— Matthew's idea of the, 131, 141, 211-218, 220, 221-224, 226, 233-235, 238, 245, 246, 250, 251, 361, 363-365
— Psalms of Solomon and the, 213
— *See also* Solomon; sonship
Son of God
— Matthew and the, 166, 175, 216, 226, 364, 365
— Hebrews and the, 304, 309, 364, 365
— *See also* sonship
sonship
— Matthew's and Hebrews' shared idea of, 363, 365
— Matthew's idea of, 168, 172, 176, 207, 216, 217, 226, 363, 365
— Moses and, 180, 235, 269, 270, 272, 273, 363-365
— rest and, 205, 207, 225, 235, 363
— Wisdom and, 168, 174-176, 179, 180, 185, 207
— *See also* Son of God; Son of David
Sophia, 6, 155, 158, 159, 168, 169, 172, 175, 180, 181, 185, 208, 236. *See also* Wisdom
Stephen, 179, 231, 253, 258, 335, 337, 338, 363
suffering, 53, 92, 93, 108, 143, 265, 266, 267, 299, 308

tabernacle
— Hebrews and the, 12, 262, 274, 330, 337, 363
— Judaism and the, 83, 84
— Stephen's sermon and the, 337, 363
— OT and the, 30, 31, 32, 69, 73, 75, 126, 262, 274, 363
temple
— God's resting place and the, 12, 19, 38, 40, 42, 44, 45, 51, 64, 72-75, 95, 108, 112, 123, 124, 127, 224, 259, 262, 281, 319, 352, 353, 362
— heavenly, 12, 94, 279, 281, 305, 314-316, 329, 342, 343, 345, 346, 348
— rest tradition and the, 9, 18, 23, 24, 26, 28, 30, 31, 34, 35, 37, 43, 51, 53, 56, 59, 67, 68-69, 76, 78, 84-86, 88, 89, 94-96, 98-101, 106, 107, 108, 125-127, 165, 215, 226, 231-232, 247, 262, 274, 337, 348, 355, 358, 363, 365
— Most Holy Place and the, 12, 94, 127, 278, 279, 314-316, 342, 343
— *See also* throne, God's
Tertullian, 142
throne, God's
— David's throne and, 39-41, 60, 220
— resting place and, 39, 59, 72, 327, 337, 343, 346, 352, 355, 358, 365
— OT rest tradition and, 12, 85
Tiamat, 71
toil. *See* work
Torah, 9, 94, 108, 159, 165, 166, 168, 172, 175, 178, 195, 197, 204, 210, 241-243, 259, 270, 271, 335, 350
trajectories, 5, 8, 200, 361
travelling
— dualism and, 148, 310-314
— Hebrews and, 12, 296, 302, 310-314, 344, 346
— OT and, 19, 20, 27, 31, 39, 48, 50, 53, 57, 63, 125, 127, 296, 302, 310-314
— waiting vs., 12, 310-314, 344, 346
— *See also* wandering
typology, 13, 42-45, 66, 69, 179, 231, 274-275, 281, 316, 349

Uzziah, 37

waiting. *See* travelling
wandering
— pilgrimage and, 10, 310-314

— travelling and, 10, 27, 31, 57, 301, 310-314
— basic motif of Hebrews, 10, 263, 301, 310-314
— *See also* travelling
water, 131, 165
weariness
— early Christian literature on, 143, 156
— Matthew on, 173, 198, 199, 205, 212, 229, 230, 249, 365
— OT rest tradition and, 31, 32, 50, 53, 54, 56, 57, 60, 76, 83, 88, 106, 112, 211, 228, 230
wilderness, 91, 95, 127, 128, 260, 286, 287, 294, 305, 306, 336
wisdom (quality), 107, 140, 141, 147, 153, 159, 165, 169, 172, 185, 195, 197, 198-201, 202, 203, 205, 206, 208, 222, 223, 235, 360, 361, 365. *See also* Wisdom
Wisdom (personified)
— envoys of, 6-8, 166, 169, 182, 183, 184, 207
— feminine identity of, 170, 175-176, 185
— homelessness of, 84, 98, 163, 165, 174
— journey of, 163, 165, 169
— law and, 84, 94, 159, 165, 166, 172, 195, 197
— OT rest tradition and, 48, 78, 84, 89, 91-94, 104, 113, 114
— personification of, 3, 6-9, 84, 89, 93, 94, 98, 114, 121, 163-167, 209-211, 233-235, 236, 237, 238, 240, 258, 359, 360, 363-365
— Shekinah and, 184
— *See also* Matthew, Sophia, wisdom
work, 21, 57, 60-63, 67, 70, 73, 76, 92, 93, 106, 108, 114, 116-119, 133, 146, 148, 154, 196, 197, 198, 203, 204, 239, 280, 282, 289, 290, 291, 292, 295-297, 305, 307, 321-325, 327, 346, 352, 355, 357, 362

yoke
— connotations of, 204
— discipleship and, 189, 190, 194, 195, 198, 202, 203-205, 210, 241, 242, 243, 244-245, 249
— image of, 194, 195, 196, 197, 204, 205
— paradox of, 9, 203-205, 206, 238

— rest tradition and, 1, 9, 56, 57, 83, 87, 93, 94, 141, 159, 187, 192, 195-198, 200, 202, 225, 226, 228, 230, 235, 239, 242, 243, 244-245
— Wisdom's, 9, 93, 94, 153, 172, 173, 187, 195, 203-205

Zadok, 269

www.ingramcontent.com/pod-product-compliance
Lightning Source LLC
Chambersburg PA
CBHW071433300426
44114CB00013B/1411